ARCHITECTING SOFTWARE INTENSIVE SYSTEMS

INTENSIVE SYSTEMS

A Practitioner's Guide

ARCHITECTING SOFTWARE INTENSIVE SYSTEMS
A Practitioner's Guide

Anthony J. Lattanze

CRC Press
Taylor & Francis Group
Boca Raton London New York

CRC Press is an imprint of the
Taylor & Francis Group, an informa business

Auerbach Publications
Taylor & Francis Group
6000 Broken Sound Parkway NW, Suite 300
Boca Raton, FL 33487-2742

Library of Congress Cataloging-in-Publication Data

Lattanze, Anthony J.
   Architecting software intensive systems : a practitioner's guide / Anthony J. Lattanze.
      p. cm.
   Includes bibliographical references and index.
   ISBN 978-1-4200-4569-7 (hardcover : alk. paper)
   1. Software engineering. 2. Systems engineering. 3. Software architecture. I. Title.

QA76.758.L3285 2009
005.1'2--dc22
                                                      2008039859

Visit the Taylor & Francis Web site at
http://www.taylorandfrancis.com

and the Auerbach Web site at
http://www.auerbach-publications.com

Dedication

To God and my family

Dedication

Contents

Preface

Today our civilization is highly dependent upon software-intensive systems. Software-intensive systems are those systems that are highly dependent upon computing infrastructure and software for the basic functionality they provide and the properties they possess. Architecture design of software-intensive systems as a separate and distinct discipline within software engineering is about 15 years old, depending upon who you ask and how they define architecture design. System design dates back to around 1945 and formally emerged from the RAND laboratories building large government weapons and data systems. Much of this early work in systems design and engineering was funded by the U.S. Department of Defense. The design of large complex systems in those early years tended to focus on partitioning the system into electromechanical elements, and integrating the elements into a system. At that time data automation hardware was very large and expensive to buy and maintain. Software applications were relatively small and still insignificant in terms of complexity and cost compared to hardware. Early systems engineering approaches and techniques emerged from this domain and were deeply influenced by government, military, and large business organizations. The systems engineering community still retains much of the spirit of this domain to this day. As systems requirements became more demanding, and computer hardware became cheaper and smaller, the demand for software in these complex systems grew exponentially. Software applications grew in complexity, and the cost of software quickly rose exponentially. In many ways, traditional systems engineering approaches and methods did not, and arguably still do not, address systemic software design. Because of the role and importance of software in modern systems and the dramatic impact if poorly designed, a system must be designed holistically. Traditional systems engineering approaches emerged from the design of electromechanical systems, and systemic software design was left behind for many years by this community. What experience has shown is that the computer hardware, peripherals, software, and other electromechanical parts of the system cannot be designed and built in isolation without first designing the overall architecture of the system. This is true for embedded or IT-oriented software-intensive systems.

Today's marketplace is vastly different than it was in the earlier years of system design. The largest consumer of software is no longer government organizations, but rather the broader consumer marketplace. Data automation is not in the hands of an elite few. Nearly all businesses and government organizations require software and hardware regardless of size or domain. Because the software industry is no longer dominated by government and military applications, these domains no longer drive marketplace or innovation leading to development standards, languages, operating systems, computer hardware, and so forth. Remember the Ada language and POSIX operating system mandates of the 1980s? These kinds of sweeping mandates would be difficult for government organizations to make today. Today, innovation is driven by a very broad marketplace and no longer takes place exclusively in government and university laboratories. New products and innovation are routinely introduced by small and large companies, as well as individual entrepreneurs—literally anyone with an idea and a computer has the ability to change and influence the world with software. Another stark difference between early and modern software-intensive systems is that today's systems routinely utilize millions, or tens of millions, of lines of code. In most products and organizations software is not optional—it is at the heart of product functionality. Today cars will not start and planes will not fly without software. Modern information systems are not just big database systems, stuck in some big government building, bank, or insurance processing center—these systems are in our homes, cars, airplanes, desktops, literally everywhere! Today's appliances, automobiles, cars, information systems, and other products are more capable, smarter, safer, and more efficient than ever before. Ubiquitous data automation has influenced and changed society—in many ways it has redefined human existence. It is possible for humans to communicate, conduct business, and play in ways never dreamed possible only 20 years ago.

All of this capability comes at the cost of complexity. Despite ever more sophisticated integrated circuitry and single-chip processors, hardware is not usually the source of systemic complexity and cost. The cost of software surpassed the cost of hardware long ago. Often it is the software that is the source of design and development problems—it is often costly to design, construct, and maintain in a timely and cost-effective way. Systems engineering approaches and techniques have their origins in traditional hardware design methods and tend to abstract away systemic software design. Because software cuts across many of the elements of a system, software deserves as much design attention as any other electromechanical element of the system to address broad systemic complexities. Although software design techniques have emerged, they tend to abstract away system design concerns and focus on function, procedure, or method level of design. This is far too detailed and narrow for addressing systemic software design.

Certainly hardware is complex, but hardware design is relatively well understood. The elements of hardware systems are commodities that are literally traded like beans, rice, and corn on the open marketplace. It is a different story with software. Software is the soul of these complex machines—and like a human soul, we cannot hold software, it weighs nothing, it cannot be observed, yet its presence is undeniable and defines the character and behavior of the machine. Software is multidimensional. What we see in terms of static structures like code is different from what we see when the code is compiled and is executing. This ethereal nature of software is why it is so difficult to design and construct software-intensive systems. My late grandfather illustrated this problem of comprehending software perfectly. My grandfather was an extremely practical man of modest means, yet possessed an abundance of practical knowledge and common sense that came from years of working as a chef and gentleman farmer. He could understand and appreciate an airplane flying in the air and the role that wings played in the physics of flight, but it was impossible for him to comprehend the software control systems. The invisibility and multidimensional nature of software violated his understanding of the world. Because of the lack of physical evidence for software, he was always somewhat skeptical of my choice of vocation as a software engineer and found my explanations of software impossible to comprehend until the day he died. In his practical mind he could not comprehend why people would pay a good salary to his grandson to design and build something that could not be seen, weighed, or held in his hand. Although he was happy I made decent money, he could not help thinking that I had a gimmick going on! And although he never said so much, I am convinced that he feared at some level his grandson had become a charlatan.

To a large extent, this is the problem we face as designers of software-intensive systems. Engineers and architects are constantly striving to find techniques, methods, and abstractions to design and analyze complex software-intensive systems—this includes the systemic software that enables the system to do what it is specified to do. Software design emerged in parallel with systems engineering, but focused on detailed code design concerns. It started with abstract data types in the late 1960s and continues today with component-based construction. In many ways systems engineering and software design communities have merged to some extent. Traditional systems engineering approaches are viewed by many as inadequate for designing modern IT systems. As such, an enterprise architecture community has emerged over the last 10 years or so to specifically address the design of IT systems. Enterprise architecture merges many of the traditional systems engineering concepts with software design and engineering concepts. However, enterprise architectures tend to focus on business process engineering. It has been about 13 years since the first textbooks on architecture design of software-intensive systems started to emerge. In many ways the art and science of designing software-intensive systems has taken some strides forward. However, a great deal of frustration remains for practicing architects, and there is still a long way to go.

- The very term *architecture* is still ill-defined, and the role of an architect in an organizational context is still open to debate. We have few definitive, formalized, and widely agreed upon first principles and best practices that architects can call upon to guide their design decisions.
- Although difficult to believe, many organizations around the world do not regard software engineering as a first-class engineering concern or discipline. These same organizations largely ignore basic disciplined software engineering practices and architectural design, and their products and systems are often plagued by software problems.
- There are very few tools to document the designs of software-intensive systems. Architects often use a combination of tools, methods, and processes that are cobbled together in an ad hoc way. This makes it hard to capture design choices and communicate them to implementers.

I should be very clear that this book is not exclusively about embedded software engineering, systems engineering, or software engineering, but about building software-intensive systems, which includes IT systems, simulators, or embedded systems. The primary goal of this text is to present architecture design principles that are applicable to any organization or domain building software-intensive systems. Many university computer science curricula today are biased toward the IT domain, so many of the assumptions made by trained computer scientists may not be valid in other domains, such as embedded systems. Language assumptions, available resources, environmental conditions, performance, security, availability, and other kinds of requirements are very different in IT and embedded domains. A key goal of this text is to provide principles that will serve an architect building a software-intensive system for either of these extremes and any of those in between. With a principled understanding of design, architects can temper their visceral instinct to react and are better prepared to address a broader range of design problems regardless of business context or their domain experience. Satisfying broad systemic concerns such as performance, security, availability, and so forth is impossible without an overall architectural design that sets the framework for subsequent detailed design and implementation!

Acknowledgments

This work represents seven years of research, industrial practice, and writing that have depended upon many people and organizations who have supported this work through their efforts, patience, feedback, ideas, and a multitude of other contributions. In particular I thank Bob Gazda of Interdigital LLC, who was an early champion of the Architecture Centric Design Method described in Section III. Bob was an early reviewer of the Architecture Centric Design Method, and his critique provided valuable information for improving it. I thank Sony Corporation for the many opportunities they provided me to interact with their world-class engineers and for so diligently using many of the methods described in this text. In particular, I thank Minori (Micha) Endo, who embodies the organizational champion who works tirelessly to improve how Sony engineers design and build software-intensive systems. Also at Sony, I thank Toshiya (Toshi) Hasegawa; he is a talented architect and reviewed this manuscript.

I want to thank the engineers at LG in Osan, Korea, who also contributed by utilizing the methods described within this text and provided valuable feedback. Matthew Bass of Siemens Corporate Research also played a pivotal role in the development of this text by providing numerous opportunities to interact with Siemens engineers around the world and who also introduced me to my publisher, John Wyzalek at Taylor & Francis. John has been a wonderful and patient man to work with in the often stressful process of writing a book—I highly recommend John as well as Taylor & Francis for any aspiring authors out there.

This book would have been impossible without the many students of the Master's of Software Engineering (MSE) program at Carnegie Mellon University (CMU) over the last ten years and our partner universities in South Korea, Portugal, and India. Multitudes of MSE students from all over the world contributed mightily during that time by trying out the various methods and techniques described in this book and providing valuable feedback before industry trials began. I thank Eunjeong Choi, Jihyun Lee, Hye Eun You, Taeho Kim, and Woo-Seok Choi from Information and Communications University (ICU), our partner university in South Korea. These individuals' contributions helped shape Chapter 18.

I thank my colleagues at CMU for their support and encouragement and tolerance while I hid and wrote much of this book in the summer of 2007: David Garlan, Mel Rosso-Llopart, Gil Taran, Dave Root, Jane Miller, Ellen Saxon, and Linda Smith. It has been a privilege and an honor to work with David Garlan and to teach software architecture with him in the MSE program at CMU—what a wonderful place for an architect to be! Many of my colleagues at the Software Engineering Institute (SEI) have also helped shape my thinking as an architect and have influenced the methods and techniques described in this text. In particular, I thank Mark Klein, Scott Hissam, Felix Bachmann, and Len Bass of the SEI, who as project mentors have provided valuable feedback on the Architecture Centric Design Method. Also at CMU, I thank John Kang, Jiyeong

Yoon, John Grasso, and the executive education staff: Ann Papuga, Beverly Flaherty, and Cathy Baek. These folks have provided me with valuable opportunities to work with organizations and engineers around the world. These opportunities have proven to be an extremely valuable education and have opened my eyes to how systems are designed and built beyond the shores of the United States. This has had a deep and profound influence on me as an engineer, architect, and teacher, and upon the methods and techniques described in this text.

Finally, but most importantly, I must thank my family, Karen, Anthony, and Nathaniel Lattanze, for tolerating the long hours I spent away from them traveling, developing, and testing these concepts, and the long difficult hours spent writing them down in this book.

Reader's Guide

The intent of this book is to focus on architectural design, independent of domain, language paradigm, tool, or other similar kinds of bias. The hope is to establish principles that will enable an engineer designing a software-intensive system to approach design in an independent and unbiased way; understand what concerns should influence design decisions; know what design options are available at any point in time; quantitatively weigh trade-offs and better judge between the various design options; and create more optimal system designs. While this book could certainly be used in a graduate course on architecture design, the original intent was to put practical architecture design principles into the hands of the practitioner. This book is divided into three major sections:

- Section I (Chapters 1–6): The focus of Section I is to define architecture and present basic concepts of architectural design for software-intensive systems. This includes the topics of architectural drivers, architectural structures, and fundamental guidance for architectural design.
- Section II (Chapters 7–15): In this section, the Architecture Centric Design Method is presented. This is an industry-tested framework for designing the architecture of software-intensive systems. Each stage of the method is described along with all of the supporting templates, checklists, and guidance.
- Section III (Chapters 16–18): This section is dedicated to the practical matters of adopting disciplined architecture design practices and using the Architecture Centric Design Method with existing organizational development processes.

The reader is advised to read each section in the order presented. Section I establishes the key concepts and vocabulary utilized throughout Sections II and III. Because the Architecture Centric Design Method has well-defined stages, each stage should be read in the order presented in Section II. Once the key architecture design principles and the Architecture Centric Design Method are understood, various ways of transitioning and utilizing these methods are explored in Section III.

SECTION I

Chapter 1

Introduction

It is beginning to be hinted that we are a nation of amateurs.

Archibald Philip Primrose, Earl of Rosebery (1847–1929)

The very word *architecture* conjures up a great many images in the minds of software engineers today. Unfortunately, there is rarely a common understanding of exactly what is meant by the term *architecture*, and the exact meaning is often dependent upon the context in which it is used. As such, the word *architecture* becomes an empty vessel into which meaning is poured by the best intentions of the engineer, manager, marketer, or other stakeholder—often on the spur of the moment. The term *architecture* is used by hardware engineers to describe IC chip designs, mechanical structures, circuits, and electromechanical parts and pieces of a system. In terms of software design artifact, *architecture* is typically used to refer to coarse-grained designs that describe gross partitioning of a system into some collection of elements that can be code-oriented, runtime, or physical structures. Descriptions of software systems usually include informal box-and-line drawings and prose that are often taken as the architecture of the system. Although there is a great deal of intuitive appeal, these descriptions usually lack any formality, precision, or basic consistency, leaving the interpretation of the design to the whim of the reader. Unfortunately, different readers interpret these artifacts differently, undermining the design as an effective means for communicating what will be built and resulting in a multitude of construction problems. Defining terms is the basic function of language that permits human beings to communicate complex concepts using words that have an agreed to meaning. Because the term *architecture* is grossly overused and overloaded, there is often a great deal of confusion when different engineers attempt to describe the architectural design of the system they are building—even if it is the same system. Various engineering communities, domains, and even organizations ascribe different meanings to the term *architecture*. The very title of this book, *Architecting Software-Intensive Systems*, could be interpreted in many ways. Our first job will be to sort out basic concepts and terminology and to try to put some bounds upon what kind of architecture we will address in this book; but first, let us look at the title a bit closer. The intent of the term *architecting* is a verb meaning to design the architecture of a system. As the title indicates, the focus of this text will be the architecture of *software-intensive systems*, but what does this mean?

Software-intensive systems are any systems that intimately depend upon software, the associated computational hardware, operating systems, data, and so forth to render service to stakeholders. Although many authors in the software engineering community address the design concerns of Web-, Internet-, and information technology (IT)–centric systems and applications, this text will focus more broadly on the architectural design of these and other software-intensive systems that are integrated into products such as airplanes, automobiles, refrigerators, environmental control systems, and any other similar systems dependent upon software to render service to the user. Software is at the soul of these systems and is responsible in many cases for the most basic services these systems provide. Obviously, we will not discuss the specific architectural design of all these systems, but systems from various domains will be used as examples to illustrate general architectural design concepts applicable in any software engineering domain. Software-intensive system design principles are not domain specific. Design principles that apply to a three-tier customer-relationship management system also apply to an embedded automotive engine controller. For this reason, design principles and the process of design will be the primary focus of the text. Without principles to guide the intuition of a designer, all of his or her designs and solutions will look the same regardless of the design forces imposed upon them. Pure intuition can serve us well when the design forces remain constant; however, advancing technology, shifting business models, organizational structures, market demands, and so forth constantly alter the design forces at work on the architect. What may have been good intuition for the last product, market, organization, and so forth may not serve as well on the next product. Hence the need for guiding design principles and disciplined processes. The focus of this text is not just software design in isolation. It is almost impossible for an architect designing a software-intensive system to design software without considering the broader systemic infrastructure (hardware, peripherals, etc.), operating systems, legacy elements (hardware and software), and a multitude of other factors. In practice, the design of a software-intensive system is rarely one-dimensional, but is often hierarchical, where one designer constrains another downstream designer, who constrains another designer or implementer, and so on. Sometimes hardware and operating systems are specified as constraints, often by other architects, before the software architects even think about design. Software cannot execute in thin air yet, and thus, architects building software systems are often in a position to select physical elements of systems, like computers, sensors, network infrastructure, and peripheral devices. In either case, whether a constraint or a design choice, hardware is an important part of a software-intensive system. Hardware and operating system choices or constraints deeply impact the software architecture design and must be part of the architectural design of the system or systems. Although important, the focus of this text is not about the detailed design of hardware elements, but rather the impact these elements impose on architects designing software-intensive systems.

The natural question on the minds of most engineers at this point is, How does detailed design differ from architectural design? The quick answer is that not all design concerns are architectural in nature. Architecture design is the place where engineers turn the corner from the requirements space to the design space. Software architectural designs should serve as a springboard for detailed design or implementation activities and should define clear boundaries for downstream designers and implementers. Software-intensive systems built without deliberately designed software architectures will possess emergent properties that will not be well understood because they were not designed into the system. Properties such as performance, availability, modifiability, security, and so forth must be designed into the system to meet the needs of the stakeholders who will utilize, buy, and maintain the system. If not designed into the system, understanding and fixing systemic shortcomings in these properties is often problematic, and in some cases impossible to remedy. In systems of any consequence, properties such as these cannot be achieved through detailed-level design because they require broad coordination across most or all system elements. In cases where detailed code structures (e.g., objects, classes, functions, etc.) are designed first, the resulting system structure is large and flat, with numerous dependencies between parts of the system that are not well understood. The overall systemic properties that emerge as a result of numerous software engineers designing small pieces of the system without the framework of structure provided by an architecture design will not be well understood until the system is implemented. Architecture provides a means to partition the system into elements that can later be designed in detail. The architecture can be scrutinized and studied to expose weakness before detailed element design and implementation. Finally, the architecture can be used to guide overall construction by serving as a prescription for how the elements can be assembled, resulting in a system with predictable properties and behavior. Architectural design differs from detailed software design in terms of concerns addressed, such as:

■ Architectural designs address the partitioning of the system into parts or elements and interaction among the elements, where as detailed designs address the implementation details of the parts. Architects focus on the external properties of elements, the ensemble of elements, and system structure, whereas detailed designers focus on the internals of elements, data structures, and algorithms utilized within an element. In fact, external interactions may be hidden from the detailed designer. Architecture does not replace detail design but rather complements it by framing the work of downstream designers and implementers and guiding the integration of the elements into a system.

■ Architectural design addresses the overall properties of a system such as performance, modifiability, security, and others in addition to general functionality. Detailed designs are concerned with specific computational properties and functionality provided by individual elements.

■ Architectural design is declarative. Architects partition, design, and document system elements based largely on intuition and experience because an all-encompassing, standardized, formal architecture specification language is still an aspiration rather than a reality. Indeed, a primary goal of this text is to temper and guide the hard-earned intuition of architects with design principles. Given the current state of the practice, there are no "architecture compilers" to check the syntax and semantics of architecture designs. Detailed designs are operational in nature in that they are meant to be translated directly into code, while architectural designs are meant to frame the work of detailed designers.

Architecture design is required to address the problem of scale and is therefore fundamentally different from software class diagrams and structure charts. It is intellectually difficult to build large systems directly by focusing on detailed structures without an architectural design to provide a roadmap for detailed designers and implementers. While it might be very easy to build small stand-alone applications with a few stakeholders and business concerns with no architecture and very little detailed design, this approach does not scale very well.

Building large complex software-intensive systems with many competing stakeholders and business concerns is a very different proposition requiring layers of coordinated design abstraction to guide implementation. It is very difficult to reason about and satisfy broad systemic properties in systems with many developers, many customers, many users, and other stakeholders without architectural designs to bridge the gap between system requirements and detailed software designs. Software architectures can help engineers identify, define, and systematically analyze requirements for large systems before detailed design and construction of system elements commence.

The Architectural Life Cycle

The term *software process* is used to describe the ritualization of software development in organizations. An organization's software process describes the preconditions, postconditions, activities, artifacts, roles, and so forth that are used by the people in an organization to develop software. What we find in practice is that an organization's software process is really comprised of many smaller processes that address key organizational functions such as configuration management, requirements, testing, quality assurance, estimation, project tracking, and so forth. Unfortunately in practice, design is the most underserved member of this set of processes. The process improvement communities address the less technical concerns of how software is designed in terms of gathering requirements, analysis, configuration management, testing, and quality assurance. While organizational process definitions include the artifacts required from the design process, the process of design is usually not given the same level of attention as other organizational processes. Architectural design is usually treated as a milestone measured by the presence of an artifact. Design is a unique technical process that requires as much attention as any of these activities, but rarely receives it. A central theme of this book is that design is a process, not just an artifact or milestone (Figure 1.1). Design is a technical process that needs to be established and defined, just like any other process in an organization.

Figure 1.2 describes the natural life cycle of architectural design around which organizations should think about establishing their design processes (we will introduce a specific architectural design process later). The architectural life cycle fundamentally begins with business context and system stakeholders. The marketplace, organizational structures, budgets, schedules, available technology, and so forth form the business context in which systems are built. The term *stakeholders* is used here (and throughout the text) to refer to a much broader community than *users*. As Figure 1.2 illustrates, stakeholders provide unstructured sets of wants and needs within a business context that must be organized into architectural drivers. Because architectural drivers are the critical requirements for shaping the design of the architecture, broad stakeholder involvement is necessary in their identification and quantification. It is critical that architects are part of the process of identifying and structuring the architectural drivers. As we will see, architectural drivers are the coarse-grained functional requirements, constraints, and quality attribute requirements. Architectural drivers are not all the requirements for a system, but those that will influence the structures that an architect selects as he or she designs architectures. Once established, the architectural driv-

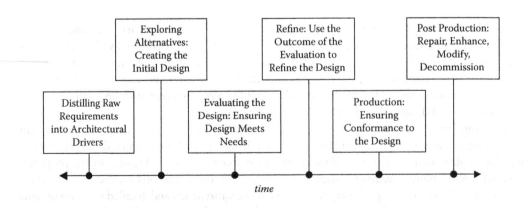

Figure 1.1   Key activities of the design process.

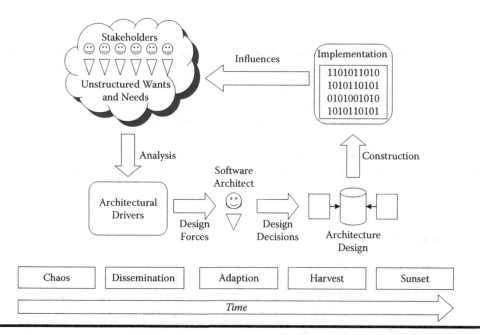

Figure 1.2   The architectural life cycle.

ers will impose design forces upon architects that influence their selection of structures. In response to design forces, architects select and design ensembles of structures to satisfy them.

While the topic of this text is architecture and design, do not let anyone fool you: *in the end, implementations matter!* Customers buy products, not architectures, processes, manufacturing, and so forth. Customers evaluate and select products based upon the features and properties they possess or do not possess. Customers place value on products based on cost, quality, function, and perceived value of the product. However, code is not enough. Whether deliberately designed or not, all software-intensive systems have architectures, and products distribute architectures, whether we intend them to or not, with all their strengths and weaknesses. Although not directly visible to customers, the quality of a product's architecture deeply impacts the deliverable features, properties, perceived quality, and value of a product today and tomorrow. If a product fails to meet the expectations of a stakeholder because of a design flaw, he or she may not use your product or service as a result. So while the vast majority of stakeholders do not directly care about architecture, architecture design is critically important in meeting their needs today and tomorrow. This means that you should care about architecture design, even if the customer, user, or other similar stakeholders do not care about it.

Architects play a vital role in the entire product life cycle, not just in the initial architectural design. Once the architecture has been designed by the architect, the system can be implemented. At this point, architects must guide downstream designers and developers during construction to ensure that the implementation matches the architectural design. This is one of the most crucial roles that architects play in system development. If the implementation structures do not match the design structures, then any promises made vis-à-vis the architecture design may not be fulfilled by the implementation. Once implemented and deployed the architectural life cycle generally follows a path of chaos, dissemination, adoption, harvest, and sunset. Architects play a critical role in this life cycle.

Chaos

During the period of chaos, various vendors compete for the same market space. Those best equipped to exploit architecture have a natural advantage over competitors. First is not always best, and history is replete with examples, such as Minitab, Wordstar, DB, Novel, Mac GUI OS, and others. An introductory product with a bad architecture can leave an organization in a weak position where it must significantly refactor for the next release. This is usually a losing proposition unless you are well funded—consider Microsoft and Windows 95. The transition was painful and costly, but left them in a better position to maintain their hold on the operating system market. Better architectures usually win in the long run. From the chaos leaders emerge and some competitors die or divest themselves from the competition.

Dissemination

Once a leader does emerge, others follow because they see profit in the leader's architecture. Early adopters will embrace the product and the underlying architecture. Open architectures that are market driven usually enjoy the widest diffusion rather than those formulated through the compromise and mandates of standards bodies. Some products that seemed to be leaders are overtaken and never realize wide dissemination and die at this point.

Adoption

At this point there is a clear leader in the marketplace. It firmly establishes control of a market through a critical mass of stakeholders creating an architectural ecosystem. Adoption is firmly established when other players in the domain look to the leader for architectural changes.

Harvest

During harvest, the leaders become the "owners" of the architecture and are recognized as the experts and leaders. What they say and do regarding the architectural paradigm is the definitive word and action. At this point leaders enjoy high profitability from multiple revenue streams. Products and the underlying architecture are maintained and extended to meet ever-increasing demands from a growing stakeholder community.

Sunset

During the sunset period, architectural structures erode to the point that it is more cost-effective to redesign a replacement. In general, better architectures live longer, but the life spans of a product and the underlying architecture are greatly influenced by the volatility of the market and technology more than anything else. If you are building products using rapidly evolving technology for markets that move rapidly, expect relatively shorter life cycles for products and their underlying architectures. In these markets, a better designed architecture may last longer, but will also take more time, possibly impacting your ability to hit an anticipated market window. This is a financial, marketing, and engineering trade-off that will require participants from each of these communities to optimize the amount of time that can and should be spent designing the architecture.

During the sunset period, leaders are on to the next thing and the early adopters follow their lead. If leaders fail to move on, they risk losing their leadership position. IBM nearly suffered this fate in the 1980s when it failed to recognize the change in market forces from the mainframe to the desktop computer. Fortunately its cash reserve allowed it to reinvent its business model and live on. Other companies, such as Digital Equipment Corporation (DEC), Control Data Corporation (CDC), and Sperry UNIVAC, were not so fortunate. During the sunset period, scavengers emerge in the marketplace to maintain the legacy and can become a lucrative business venture given the right balance of supply (scavengers that support legacy) and demand (users of legacy).

Having an architect or architectural team that is in tune with the architectural life cycle and the business needs and goals of the organization is critical to the competitiveness of an organization. This is primarily true because progression through the architectural life cycle always means the original architectural design must evolve, and architects play a pivotal role in design systems that can evolve and in managing evolution of products through the architecture.

As Figure 1.2 illustrates, once implemented and deployed, the system will begin influencing the very stakeholders that influenced the system's original design in the first place. More broadly, architectures are influenced by a variety of external forces. It is common to hear the lament of architects and engineers regarding requirements change; however, we can be more proactive rather than reactive to requirements change. The architecture design and the architectural life cycle can provide crucial insight into those factors that may lead to changes in requirements. Figure 1.3 illustrates the key factors influencing the business context and hence the architectural drivers. Once deployed, architecture designs are impacted by changes in stakeholders, business models, marketplace, technology, and organizational structures.

Stakeholders

During the architectural life cycle stakeholders may come and go. Often we become victims of our system's successes. New stakeholders with slightly different need than the original stakeholders may adapt our products. When stakeholders leave, some architectural drivers may no longer be valid and new stakeholders bring new expectations into the design space. Architects need to pay attention to the ebb and flow of stakeholders in the system context and evaluate the impact their presence or absence has on the architectural drivers.

Business Models

Business models are those financial and business operations in which a system is designed and built. Examples of business models might include:

- Financial models for the marketing, selling, and distributing of the system
- Business processes and operations implemented by the system
- Business and financial arrangements made with suppliers and providers

Business models can be internal or external to an organization. After systems are deployed, business models evolve, and those business models that motivated original design decisions may no longer be valid. When internal or external business models evolve, you can anticipate changes to the architectural drivers.

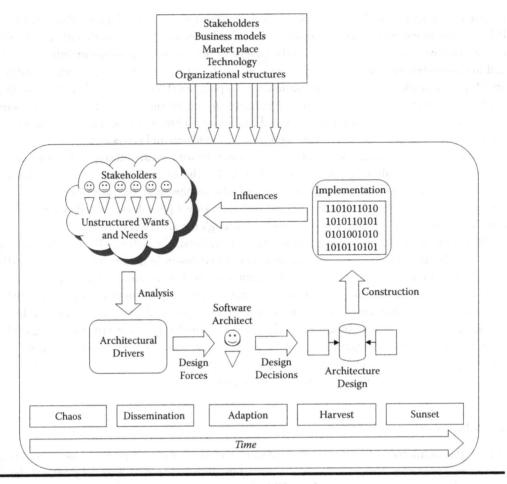

Figure 1.3   External influences on the architectural life cycle.

Marketplace

The marketplace is where products provide value and begin to provide return for investment dollars. The marketplace is ever changing and evolving, and it is essential that we not only react to changes in the marketplace but also proactively identify changes and potential opportunities for our products. Some markets are more volatile than others, and this volatility will be reflected in our designs. In an extreme example, the cell phone market is highly volatile, and the organization that is first to market with the newest features wins the day. After initial product delivery, prices for cell phones drop dramatically over a short 18-month window. This results in an architectural life cycle that is short and furious. In another example, consider n-tier Internet applications such as a point-of-sale system, customer relations management, and so forth. The market for these systems is relatively stable and the general operational model has been well established for many years now. In most cases, once deployed, the core structure of these systems remains relatively unchanged even though features and functions may be added and changed over the architectural life cycle. Often these systems must scale in various ways to meet growing market demand. When markets evolve and change, expect changes to the architectural drivers.

Technological Environment

Fundamentally, software-intensive systems depend upon technology, so it is surprising that architects are not more proactive about looking ahead at the evolving technological landscape to identify emerging technology that cause requirements change. In some system contexts, it makes sense to embrace riskier leading-edge technology to be more competitive. In other cases, this can be disastrous—newer is not always better. For example, in the consumer electronics marketplace the demand for novel features often drives product developers to assume the risk of developing or adapting the newest and latest technology available. However, in the avionics control system domain risky new technology is not a good idea for the commercial aviation sector. These systems have to be extraordinarily reliable, so proven technologies and methodologies are the order of the day. Technological evolution in the avionics (or similar) domain is necessarily slower and more deliberate than that of the consumer electronics market. However, in both cases technological change is inevitable. Aside from the pace of adoption, new technology lies at the heart of doing it better, faster, and cheaper. Architects need to pay attention to emerging technology to evaluate its impact on their systems, design, and eventually the architectural drivers.

Organizational Structure

Systems are built in human organizations. Once a system is designed, organizations spring up around the structures of the system. In a very real sense technical designs beget organizations for better or worse. Because of this fact, changes in organizational structures can often cause changes to architectural drivers. Eliminating or adding organizations that support systems or elements of systems can have very real impact to the structure of a system that is built or in the process of being built. Similarly, if we attempt to change architectural structures in radical ways, this could impact existing organizational structures. Organizational structures can be internal or external to the producing organizations. Changes in a supplier's organizational structure can impact a system's structure as deeply as a change in an internal organizational structure. Consider the example in Figure 1.4.

This example comes from an actual experience where a system was built at time point A. The system consisted of three key elements: input processor, display process, and history processor. Each of these was a minicomputer with a set of applications. These systems were connected by a high-speed shared memory bus. A workforce sprang up around this design to support each of these elements. The largest workforce was needed to support the complex display processor and its suite of data visualization and analysis applications. However, after five years or so of successful use the system was to be redesigned and replaced with a more capable new-generation system. Because of technological advancements, it was possible to build the new system with only an input processor and history processor. These were significantly smaller, cheaper, and more powerful computers. In the new system design, the display processor was replaced with workstations and the shared memory was replaced with a high-speed network. Figure 1.5 illustrates this new-generation system.

This system was a vast improvement over the old system in many ways. It was faster, cheaper to build, more reliable, and able to process more data. Sounds like a great idea, except that with the second-generation system design the legacy workforce did not align with proposed architecture. Only a fraction of the original display group was needed to support the new system. The team that supported the shared memory access and applications was no longer needed at all, and fewer personnel were needed to maintain the history and acquisition processor. This presented a great deal of consternation among the legacy workforce and the new design, while technologically

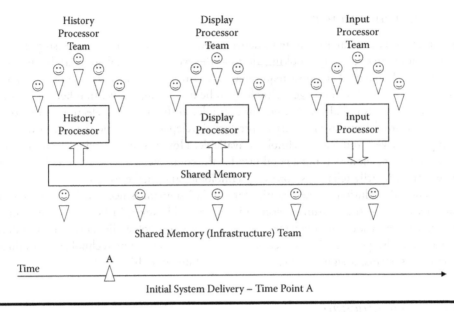

Figure 1.4 Initial system design and its relationship to organizational structure.

better, was a challenge for the organization to adapt and transition to. Similarly, if organizational changes occurred, they could impact the ability to support, maintain, or evolve the system over time. Architects should pay close attention to organizational structures and their relationship to the design structures—changes in either could deeply impact the business drivers.

The architectural life cycle can and should be analyzed as part of an organizational technology management strategy. Changes to the system must be evaluated by the architect to determine the impact on existing systemic properties and to determine how best to implement and integrate the changes to the system. The architectural life cycle continues until the architecture erodes to the point where it is no longer able to accommodate changes or is not cost-effective to maintain. Sometimes the architectural life cycle is relatively short (one to three years) and sometimes relatively long (decades). In either case, organizations should understand the business context they must operate in, devise an appropriate architectural strategy, and proactively manage the architectural life cycle.

Theme, Purpose, and Organization

The key theme underlying this text is that first and foremost, architectural design is a technical endeavor that requires intuition and principle. Second, design activities must be organized and defined by an organization to reduce the cost of design and the time it takes to design, and increase the predictability and value of the design process. The purpose of this book is to provide practicing engineers that are responsible for designing software-intensive systems with:

■ A background in architectural design principles
■ Guidance for how to design architectures for software-intensive systems design

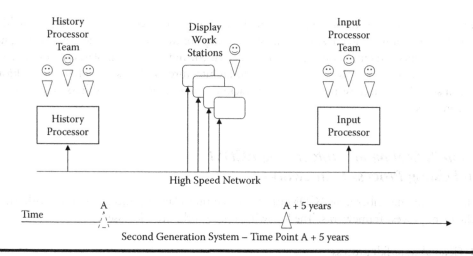

Figure 1.5   Second-generation system design and its impact to the organizational structure.

- An Architecture Centric Design Method that can help organizations more easily integrate disciplined and repeatable architectural design processes into organizational software development processes
- Practical guidance for transitioning to more disciplined architectural design practices

To these ends this book is organized into three general sections, as follows.

Section 1: Architectural Principles

This section introduces concepts of basic architectural principles that are essential for the remaining topics presented in the text. This section includes the following topics:

- The term *architecture* is defined more clearly, and in particular, *software architecture design* is clearly defined. System, enterprise, and software architectural design concerns are distinguished, and terms used throughout the text are defined.
- Those requirements that drive architectural designs are explored, and methods for capturing and analyzing them are presented.
- The structures of software-intensive systems and their effects on system properties are discussed in detail.
- Using the architectural principles outlined thus far, guidance for the design activity is presented and reinforced through examples.
- Strategies for documenting software architectures are discussed.

Section 2: The Architecture Design Process

In this section, the principles of Section 1 are put into practice within a methodological design framework that can be used to instantiate a design process in an organization. The theme of Section 2 is that the architectural design of software-intensive systems is a technical process, not an event or milestone measured only by the presence or absence of an artifact. The Architecture Centric Design Method (ACDM) is introduced, which is a strategy for gathering architectural requirements, organizing and analyzing them, designing the architecture, evaluating the architecture, and refining it in an iterative way. The specific steps of the method are described throughout the section. Inputs and outputs at each stage are described, and various templates and examples are provided. This section also discusses ways that the architecture can be used to align the workforce, provide insight for project estimation, help in tracking and oversight, and address other programmatic concerns.

Section 3: Scaling and Integrating ACDM with Existing Process Frameworks

The final section describes how ACDM can be scaled up to larger projects and used with various development process frameworks. The following frameworks are addressed:

- General waterfall process
- Team Software Process˚ (Registered Trademark of the Software Engineering Institute, Pittsburgh, Pennsylvania)
- Rational Unified Process˚ (Registered Trademark of International Business Machine, Inc.)
- Scrum (Schwaber and Beedle, 2004)
- Extreme Programming (Beck, 2000)
- Capability Maturity Model Integrated˚ (Registered Trademark of the Software Engineering Institute, Pittsburgh, Pennsylvania)

For each of these process frameworks, the basic framework will be described and how it addresses architectural design. Recommendations will be provided that describe how to weave ACDM and general architectural design practices into the framework to more effectively address architectural concerns. In addition to these process frameworks, this section will also discuss what process areas of the Capability Maturity Model Integrated can be addressed by using ACDM.

Chapter 2

Architecture Defined

Architecture is frozen music.

John Bartlett (1820–1905)

The idea that systems are not composed of individual machines but of distributed ensembles of elements with complex relationships underlies most modern engineering theory and practice today. For the past 50 years the role of software in modern systems has been growing in importance. As a system element, software enables designers to build more flexible, capable, and intelligent systems. Today software is pervasive in modern systems and can be found in cameras and watches, air- and spacecraft, automobiles, medical systems, and a universe of IT systems essential to the operation of virtual business, global enterprises, and governments. However, while software has enabled the creation of more flexible and capable systems, it has further complicated the construction, deployment, maintenance, and operation of modern software-intensive systems. Various design, documentation, and notation methods have been developed over the years to describe the design of software-intensive systems and help engineers analyze the properties of these systems. The terms *system architectures, enterprise architectures*, and *software architectures* are often used today to describe the coarse-grained designs and underlying structures of complex ensembles of elements comprising systems, enterprises, and large complex software applications. However, in recent years the term *architecture* has become grossly overloaded. Unfortunately, there are no standard, widely accepted definitions of systems, enterprise, and software architectures, although many of the concepts that underlie these terms are closely related.

Architecture as a design concept has been around at least since ancient Egypt, with the design and construction of the pyramids. The use of the term *architecture* to describe the designs of human dwellings appears at least as early as the first century BC, when prominent Roman architect Vitruvius used the term to describe the basic principles of architecture design. The thesis of his work was predicated upon three key qualities that formed the basis of design principles. Vitruvius (1914, Book I, Chapter 2, page 13) wrote "Architecture depends on order, arrangement, eurythony, symmetry, propriety, and economy." He argued that architectures and the resulting structures must satisfy their intended uses, must be physically sound, and must convey aesthetic meaning. He also indicated that the best architectural designs will result in buildings that outlast their original use—a very important goal today in the design of software-intensive systems. His treatise marks the first time that architectural design principles were documented in an attempt to codify principles for architects. Since the term first appeared in Roman literature, architectural design concepts have been broadly applied to many domains. The term *landscape architecture* was used in a book published by Gilbert Laing Meason in 1828 and may be the first use of *architecture* to refer to the design of something other than buildings. Today the *Oxford English Dictionary* has a very broad definition of architecture that includes much more than the traditional design of building structures, for example:

■ Actions: The act or process of building
■ Artifacts: Design, structure, building
■ Conceptual: The conceptual structure and overall logical organization of a computer or computer-based system from the point of view of its use or design

Today the term *architecture* is often used to refer to design of technological devices. In this context, architecture is fundamentally about the design of coarse-grained structures or parts that comprise a product, device, system, and so forth. Architects decompose the system, enterprise, or software into elements in a declarative way guided largely by intuition and experience. Architectural design is declarative in the sense that architects declare what the parts or elements of a system are, their properties and interfaces, and how the elements relate to one another. When designed, developed, and integrated, those parts create an ensemble that works together to provide some service greater than any single part by itself. Because architecture design is declarative, it is deceptively easy to do. However, it is difficult to get it right, difficult to do well, and dreadfully easy to make mistakes. The early choices an architect makes have a deep, long-lasting impact on the product and the organization. If the wrong choices are made early, then it may be impossible to undo them later. While architecture is design, not all design is architectural in nature. Architectural designs omit the detailed internal designs of the elements of decomposition. The detailed design of these elements is deferred to downstream designers who focus on the details of how the elements provide the services the architect declares that they shall provide.

A common misperception is that architectures are just pictures—pictures are not architectures. Architectural representations are mere pictures of structures that exist or those that will be built. However, software-intensive systems have real structures formed by elements and relationships between them—and this is the real architecture. Long before construction and the real structures are built, design representations serve as a basis to support the analysis of the larger ensemble of elements. The ultimate goal of analyzing architectural designs is to ensure that the implemented system delivers the required services and possesses the required properties. Software-intensive systems are multidimensional in that system structures visible statically are not the same structures that are visible at runtime, and there are still more physical structures visible as well. Because software-intensive systems are multidimensional, architects have to think in three dimensions, and architectural design representations must be multidimensional to represent the many structures of the thing being built. For example, to adequately represent a modern residential house we would need a representation that describes the building's structure, another that describes the heating and air conditioning ductwork, another for the electrical system, and still another for the plumbing. Each of these structures is quite real, and taken together they compose an ensemble of elements that is the house. We can use these various views to reason about the properties the dwelling will possess when built: Is it big enough? Will it be bright enough? Is it energy efficient?

Can people easily get from room to room along expected flow patterns? Can I change or add to the dwelling? Can I repair it? The same is true for software-intensive systems. Architectural design representations are pictures of the structures that will be, or are, present in the implementation. Like the house example above, software-intensive systems require many representations from various perspectives to describe the system. Taken together, these representations allow stakeholders to communicate about the system, reason the properties it will and will not possess, and guide detailed design and construction.

Architectural designs can provide essential insight for engineers when designing software-intensive systems. Just as in the previous building architecture example, these architectural designs identify the parts of the system, enterprise, or software, and how they will interact to render a service. Design representations can be used to analyze the overall behavioral and nonbehavioral properties of systems, enterprises, or software. Behavioral properties include the essential functional requirements, whereas nonbehavioral properties include performance, modifiability, interoperability, and security, among others. In this text, these nonbehavioral properties will be referred to as *quality attributes* (Bass et al., 2002). Designers of systems, enterprises, and software must continually make trade-offs between behavioral and quality attribute requirements to achieve a balance acceptable to the stakeholder community. For example, some architectural design decisions might promote data throughput (performance) but undermine the ability to change the system (modifiability). Architectures allow designers to identify and reason about these trade-offs early in the development so these properties can be designed into the system, rather than fixing, tuning, or refactoring after development.

Although the terms *system, enterprise*, and *software architecture* are part of engineers' vocabulary today, these communities rarely agree on precise definitions for these concepts. Furthermore, the responsibility for who creates them, what they are used for, and how they are written down is rarely well defined in organizations today. Frequently the differences between system, enterprise, and software architectures are the topic of heated debates among engineers. Organizations and engineers in these communities have an intellectual commitment and monetary investments in their system, enterprise, and software architectural designs. Unfortunately, there are no authoritative sources for defining systems, enterprise, and software architectures where all three are in agreement and work together symbiotically in principle and in practice. As a result, many misconceptions, prejudices, and unrealistic expectations have developed in these communities. To clarify these terms, we will present and discuss the commonly used definitions of architectures from the system, enterprise, and software engineering communities. For systems, enterprise, and software architectures, it is helpful to understand the history, the state of the practice, and what each addresses and does not address.

The History of Modern Systems Concepts

The use of the term *system* to refer to technological devices is a relatively new practice that has emerged during the 20th century. This term evolved over more than a century, as engineers grappled with designing increasingly complex interacting machinery as well as coordinating its construction and operation over broad geographical areas. A historical perspective on systems thinking provides essential background for understanding how and why designers began to use terms like *system architecture, enterprise architecture*, and *software architecture* to describe the designs and structures of large, distributed, technological entities. Before the 19th century the word *system* was not associated with technology at all. The term was used to describe physiological systems, such as the nervous or circulatory systems in the body; philosophical systems representing coherent sets of ideas, such as those found in legal, political, or religious belief systems; and natural dynamic systems, such as those used to describe ecological systems or planetary systems.

Systems thinking as we know it today had its origins with the intercontinental railroad being built in the United States early in the 19th century (circa 1830). The emerging maze of railways was comprised of many complex technological devices, diverse workflows, and timing and resource allocation problems. To describe the railroad as a mere machine poorly captured the grandeur and scope of a much larger collection of interoperating machines, processes, and people. The railroad system included the rails, the trains, watering and coal stations, maintenance facilities, switching junctions, and so forth. During this age, the body of knowledge that comprised the traditional mechanical arts proved increasingly inadequate to address the design complexities emerging in the national railroad system. Emerging problems included designing standardized and compatible parts, scheduling and timing of trains, coordination of various diverse workforces, and a host of other problems well beyond the body of engineering knowledge available at the time. The limits of the traditional mechanical/electrical arts were pressed further in the 19th century with the development of the electric power (circa 1880) and telephone (circa 1877) industries. These systems emerged from small parts often designed in isolation, where incompatibility was commonplace. In the early years, the overall designs of these systems emerged in an ad hoc fashion rather than by deliberate design—an accidental ensemble of sorts. As the difficulty, cost, and complexity of connecting geographically distributed, dissimilar parts into a larger whole became evident, engineers began to realize the importance of high-level systemic design and interface standardization for the parts of the system. By 1920, AT&T engineers referred to their national telephonic network as "the system," had job titles for system engineers, and had a systems development department (Hughes, 1989) in an attempt to inject formality and discipline into the design of the system.

As complex systems emerged, engineers realized that creating parts in isolation, then attempting to connect them together to serve a larger purpose, resulted in systems that were convoluted, brittle, and costly to build and maintain, scaled poorly, and behaved unpredictably. This proved to be an inadequate approach for specifying, building, and operating the new generation of systems that would be needed in the 20th century. A new systems design philosophy emerged that espoused the idea of designing the larger system first, then identifying and designing the parts, and finally assembling the system from the parts. This was a radical departure from the detailed design and construction of the parts, connecting the parts together in an ad hoc fashion, and allowing systems to emerge from happenstance rather than by design. This new approach to system design gave rise to more powerful abstractions and methods that enabled engineers to reason about the behavior and properties of complex systems prior to designing the parts and assembling the system. During and after World War II, system complexity grew dramatically with technological advances—the vanguard of this advance was the U.S. military industrial complex. As a result, a formalized system engineering discipline began to emerge around 1950 when researchers from the RAND Corporation, under a newly formed U.S. Air Force, developed systems analysis and design techniques and methodologies. RAND experimented with a variety of novel approaches for managing design complexity and organizing the human capital required to construct, operate, and maintain large complex systems. This was a time when system complexity was increasing at a dizzying pace with global communications, command, and control systems to support rapid global surface, air, and space warfare. Systems like the Trident submarine, modern aircraft carriers, intercontinental ballistic missile systems, and space and satellite systems were difficult enough, but connecting them as a contiguous system proved to be a daunting task. This period of systems engineering is best characterized by Rear Admiral Grace Hopper, who is often quoted as saying, "Life was simple before World War II, after that we had systems."

Systems engineering has evolved into a design and management discipline useful for building large, complex, interdisciplinary, and geographically distributed systems. Systems engineering approaches flourished during the Cold War years, and many of these techniques are still with us today. Modern system engineering methods evolved from the design and development of large U.S. government weapon systems like the Nike surface-to-air missile system, the SAGE missile defense system, and the Atlas intercontinental ballistic missile programs from 1940 through the 1960s. Virtually all major weapons systems acquired by the U.S. military since the 1950s have used some form of disciplined system engineering techniques. Global systems of systems are the norm today not only in complex military and government domains, but also throughout commercial industry to support inventory management, customer relations, logistics, and so forth. For example, the 747 aircraft with over six million parts made in 33 different countries presented unique and daunting engineering challenges for the Boeing Corporation. Although there are many definitions for what a system is, for our purposes we will define a system as "a set of physical, electromechanical elements so connected or related as to perform a unique function not performable by the elements alone." This is similar to the definition given by Maier and Rechtin (2000).

System Architectures

Eberhardt Rectin is viewed by many as the father of modern systems engineering and system architecture following his classic textbook *Systems Architecting: Creating and Building Complex Systems* (Rechtin, 1991). Rectin defined and formalized the roles and responsibilities of the system architect. He defined and prescribed specific knowledge and skills sets that should be part of a system architect's intellectual repertoire, and also introduced a number of design heuristics and analytical techniques that could be used by system architects to develop architectures for systems. Until Rechtin's work, it was not clear to many practitioners that systems engineering could rise to the level of an engineering discipline, or that designing and constructing massive complex systems could be a predictable, repeatable endeavor. Various systems engineering philosophies and methodologies have been developed and established over the years, and today there are many system architecture and engineering textbooks that define formal theories and scientific principles on which to base system engineering discipline (Thome, 1993). Many top-notch universities around the world now offer advanced degrees in system engineering, and system architecture design is an essential part of system engineering education.

Although there are many specific systems engineering approaches for translating a customer's need arising from a specific mission or business objective into an architectural design, in general modern systems engineering espouses a top-down hierarchical philosophy, where the first design artifact created is the system architecture. According to the International Council on System Engineering (INCOSE), system design is "the process of defining the architecture, components, interfaces, and other characteristics of a system or component of a system." In this definition, the term *component* is used to refer to a physical part or element that is a member of the system. The term *interface* refers to the boundary of a component and the point of connection between components. In systems engineering, interfaces can be mechanical, electrical, or electromechanical. "Other characteristics of a system or component of a system" refers to the functional behavior of the system as well as the broad systemic properties it possesses, such as performance, modifiability, availability, and so forth. Designing the system's architecture is a critical first step in system construction because the architecture is used to ensure that the overall system objectives are being met. The system architecture frames the detailed design and construction of the parts that will make up the system and can help identify potential functional and quality attribute issues. Through the architecture design, these issues can be addressed early in the development process, minimizing downstream production cost and maximizing overall product quality.

Given that modern systems are often large, distributed, and require the talent of multiple engineering and scientific disciplines, it is usually impractical for a systems architect to be concerned with every minute detail of design. Systems architects are concerned with partitioning the system into components and identifying their responsibilities and rules for interaction to ensure that functional and quality attribute requirements are met. However, they do not concern themselves with the internal design details of the components that comprise the system. In architectural design, components are treated as *black boxes*, where the details of how input is transformed into output are abstracted away—these details are deferred until later in the design process. Most modern system architecture design methodologies prescribe designing a complex system using hierarchical decomposition by first decomposing the system into components. These methods generally focus on functionality and use functional requirements to guide the decomposition. This process is recursively repeated on each component until off-the-shelf or easily designed and constructed components are all that remain. Once the elementary components of a system are defined, the detailed interfaces for each component can be defined and the appropriate engineer (or organization) for each component can proceed with the detailed design, implementation, and test of the functional element. In principle, constructing the system then is accomplished by integrating the lowest-level components one level of abstraction at a time. Each level of decomposition becomes a level of construction and integration where the results of the previous level are verified and validated. Therefore, a key tenant of system engineering is that bottom-up integration is only possible with sound top-down design that begins with a robust system architecture. This divide-and-conquer approach allows engineers to build very large systems, with a distributed workforce, uncover defects, and address them before they are deeply buried in the system.

Systems engineering and architecture continues to flourish and evolve in a variety of domains. However, the most visible and explicit use of systems engineering methodologies tends to be in large government systems built by many hundreds or even thousands of geographically distributed contractors. After all, this is the community from whence system engineering emerged. Program managers of these large projects often rely on the basic tenants of system engineering to manage the complexity of system design, construction, oversight, and management. System engineering concepts are even embedded in government procurement laws and guidelines. Although these engineering approaches seem to serve in the construction of ships, air- and spacecraft, and other systems with significant physical presence, different approaches are being used to address the specific needs of very large information technology (IT)–centric systems. The term *enterprise architecture* is used today to describe designs of large IT-centric systems, and various design strategies and methods are emerging to address the needs of this domain. In the early 1990s the term "system of systems" became popularized in the systems engineering community, and in many ways gave birth to the enterprise architecture community so prominent in IT-centric communities today. Stepping back from this emerging picture, it is clear that the design of large and complex systems is hierarchical. The larger the system, the more layers there are to the hierarchy.

Enterprise Architecture

The term *enterprise* has been broadly used since antiquity to refer to large distributed business ventures, the military, or other grand human endeavors. The 1828 *Webster's Dictionary* defines enterprise as:

> That which is undertaken, or attempted to be performed; a project attempted; particularly, a bold, arduous or hazardous undertaking, either physical or moral; e.g. "The attack on Stoney-Point was a bold, but successful enterprise."

Today the term *enterprise* is used to refer to organizations engaged in a grand business or mission, referring to the entity doing the undertaking, not the undertaking itself.

In many ways, enterprise architecture concepts evolved from the systems engineering community but specialized to address the specific design concerns of very large, highly distributed IT systems and organizations dependent upon them. Enterprise architects, like system architects, design large systems of systems to serve the needs of widely distributed organizations comprised of stakeholders, infrastructure, and other resources. Enterprise architecture frameworks are essentially design methodologies focusing on business modeling, business processes, and the technological infrastructure that supports the enterprise. One of the chief difficulties is identifying the enterprise and its boundaries. Enterprise systems, software, and infrastructure are sometimes referred to as net-centric computing (Goodyear et al., 2000) to highlight the highly distributed and IT nature of enterprise structures. Many of the concepts embraced by the enterprise architecture community emerged from the commercial information systems development that was taking place at IBM in the 1970s for large, distributed, business-oriented applications. These roots have given enterprise architectures a decidedly business and IT-centric flavor. John Zachman, an employee of IBM, was a key contributor to IBM's information planning methodology: business systems planning. In Zachman's early work, he observed how building architecture, construction, engineering, and manufacturing industries evolved over hundreds of years to handle the construction of complex products (Zachman, 1987). Later he applied these concepts to the design and construction of business enterprises and the computer systems that empowered them. Zachman coined the term *enterprise architecture* and created the *Zachman Framework* for defining enterprise architectures (Sowa and Zachman, 1992).

Enterprise architecture is no longer based only on John Zachman's work and the Zachman Framework, although this is a commonly cited example of a method for defining an enterprise architecture. Today there are many different enterprise architecture frameworks (EAFs) for designing and constructing enterprise architectures. At the writing of this text there were 14 EAF standards mandated by the U.S. government and hundreds available that were proprietary or domain specific. Some examples include:

- The Zachman Enterprise Architecture Framework
- Federal Enterprise Architecture Framework (FEAF)
- Treasury Enterprise Architecture Framework (TEAF)
- Popkin Enterprise Architecture Framework
- Extended Enterprise Architecture
- The Open Group Architecture Framework (TOGAF)
- Department of Defense Architecture Framework (DoDAF)

The term *framework* is used to describe a prescribed set of steps and artifacts that are created as a course of designing an enterprise system or system of systems. EAFs embody design strategies and provide step-by-step guidance, and even templates, for designing and documenting the enterprise. EAFs prescribe a set of artifacts for specific enterprise stakeholders. Using the EAF, the enterprise architect creates various artifacts intended to be views of the system from the perspective of the enterprise stakeholders. Most enterprise architecture frameworks identify a number of concerns that will guide the design of enterprises, such as:*

- Business requirements: The business needs of the organization.
- Business processes: A series of activities leading to the achievement of a measurable business result.
- Environment: Those conditions in which the enterprise must operate.
- Data: High-level data designs that describe the structure of an enterprise's data needs in terms of entities and relationships between entities.
- Infrastructure: The enterprise's general IT assets, such as networks, hardware, computing systems, routers, and so forth.
- Software: The standard software suite that is closely coupled to the infrastructure, such as operating systems, drivers, database systems, and so forth.
- Stakeholders: Those who will interact with the enterprise in some way.

These concerns are common themes addressed in many enterprise architecture frameworks, although the terminology, processes, and methods used to derive and document them differ widely. However, a concept common in the enterprise architecture community is the notion of the *business process*. A business process is a description of the dynamic interaction of stakeholders and the flow of information between the various entities comprised by the enterprise. Business processes drive the analysis and design of the enterprise architecture and are used to identify organizations, pertinent stakeholders, systems, data, and other entities relevant to the enterprise. In most enterprise methodologies, business processes may or may not be directly implemented or supported by IT infrastructures and systems, but most often they are.

EAFs are intended to be more than a means for designing computer networks, servers, web pages, databases, and so forth. They are a means for identifying, documenting, and analyzing complex networks of human interactions with organizations and the IT systems they use to provide services, communicate, and generally conduct business operations. Contrary to common perception, IT infrastructure is an element of the enterprise; it does not define it. For example, assume that an organization's business model is to sell products to other businesses via the Web, track inventory and shipping, manage customer relations, and so forth. This business model could be distilled into various business processes that describe the activities of the organization. Business processes might describe the dynamic aspects of how a customer's order is processed, how the product is manufactured, how the inventory is updated, how quickly the product is delivered to the customer, and so forth. The enterprise might be composed of customer service, inventory, shipping, and production organizations. These are some of the business structures that may make up this enterprise. Business processes define how these entities interact, and identifying the enterprise business processes is the chief aim of most EAFs. Some EAFs may a go little further into technical design, usually in an area of enterprise infrastructure design required to support the

---

* These concerns and their definitions come from a broad distillation of ten different enterprise architecture frameworks.

business processes. Key objectives are to model the enterprise networks, databases, middleware, security, fault handling, and transaction processing, and connectivity to the Internet so customers can access services. The purpose of an EAF is to help enterprise architects manage the complexity of highly distributed systems of systems by providing techniques and methods to identify key stakeholders and their role in the enterprise, discover relationships between various entities of the enterprise, and in some cases map business process to IT infrastructure. Most EAFs provide comprehensive documentation guidelines, templates, and frameworks for documenting the enterprise architecture.

Although there is no definitive claim made by the enterprise architecture community that EAFs address more coarse-grained abstractions than system or software architectures, much of the literature and experience of the authors seems to indicate that this is the case. Consider a quote from Zachman when he describes enterprise architectures (Zachman, 1987):

> It is not hard to speculate about, if not realize, very large, very complex systems implementations, extending in scope and complexity to encompass an entire enterprise. One can readily delineate the merits of the large, complex, enterprise-oriented approaches…. However, there also is merit in the more traditional, smaller, suboptimal systems design approach. Such systems are relatively economical, quickly implemented, and easier to design and manage.

Certainly the families of EAFs in use today seem to address very coarse-grained, system-of-system concerns for IT-centric organizations, and this might be the best differentiation between systems and enterprise architectures. EAFs do not provide detailed prescriptions for how the architectures of individual systems or software architecture designs should be carried out, documented, analyzed, evaluated and so forth. For example, while an embedded system might be part of a larger enterprise, designers of embedded systems rarely rely on EAFs to guide the architectural designs of their embedded systems and software. After an enterprise architecture is defined, it is usually the case that significant architectural design work remains for the systems and software that will be an essential part of the enterprise.

A Brief History of Modern Software

The first electronic computers began to appear between 1939 and 1942. The Atanasoff-Berry Computer, Colossus, and Electrical Numerical Integrator and Calculator (ENIAC) are considered by historians to be among the first electronic computers on earth. In these early years computers were utilized in very few domains. One of the early uses of computers and software was for ballistics calculations for the U.S. Army. At this time, computers were expensive exotic tools of researchers usually developed in cooperation with governments, large corporations, and universities. Software was constructed by system scientists who would manually enter programs through switches on the front consoles of computer systems. Applications were small, monolithic in organization, and written in machine code. The cost and complexity of software applications was trivial in comparison to the cost and complexity of the computer hardware. Because there were very few computers in the world, the demand for software was pretty low.

By the middle of the 1960s, commercial organizations were producing new computers every year or two. Many of these computers were custom built, special-purpose computers. Although rapid advancement was welcomed, the pace of innovation quickly rendered existing computer hardware, operating systems, and applications obsolete fairly quickly. At this time, the idea of a general-purpose, relatively inexpensive, accessible computer became the goal of leading computer companies. The IBM 3XX family of computers was a good example of this new paradigm of commodity-based computer hardware. These general-purpose computer systems effectively combined scientific and business applications onto one machine, promoting broader use than the special-purpose computers of former generations. These systems were widely available on the market, reliable, usable, and affordable by modest-sized organizations. This broad accessibility created an insatiable demand for not only the computer, but also software applications and people to write them. High-order languages like FORTRAN, COBOL, and ALGOL were developed to address software complexity and allow developers to more easily create applications and also allow applications to be more portable as platform hardware and operating systems changed. In theory, as platforms and operating systems changed, source code would only have to be recompiled on the new platform. At this time the concepts of modular programming, data abstraction, information hiding, and the process of software development became important research topics driven by the increasing complexity of software applications. Structured programming and design was introduced in the early 1970s (Parnas, 1972) to address the increasing difficulty of designing large software applications. Embedded computer systems technology also made great advances during this time and were used on the Apollo lunar lander that took men to the moon. It became clear that software was not a fad and that humans were becoming increasingly dependent upon software at an alarming rate, far outstripping our ability to create it. At this time, another trend emerged. While it is deceptively simple to write small software applications, building big, complex software-intensive systems is often fraught with problems due to inherit difficulty in developing large complex software applications. In October 1968, software received international attention when the NATO Science Committee sponsored a conference to examine the issue of software development. During this conference, delegates discussed the world's growing dependence on software, especially for infrastructure critical to society and human survival. They also discussed the cost and problematic nature of developing software-intensive systems. It was during this conference that the term *software engineering* was coined—more as an aspiration than a description of the state of the practice of building software (Broy and Denert, 2002).

Since this 1968 NATO conference, the price of computing and data storage has continued to drop dramatically, making ubiquitous computing the norm. Low-cost, powerful, desktop computers are common in homes around the world, and the World Wide Web has driven the demand for computing systems, applications, and computing infrastructure. Because of the availability of small, inexpensive, and capable processors, computers and software applications have found their way into everything from automobiles, aircraft, and missiles to bread machines and cameras. Software is an enabler of complex systems and enterprises. Software provides features and capabilities in IT systems and products desired by users and consumers, and better software often provides significant competitive advantage. Today the marketplace demands software that is not only functional, but also safe, available, secure, and possessing many similar system properties. Although we have learned much about writing software applications, building software-intensive systems is still a complex and problematic undertaking. Computer science and software engineering are part of collegiate curriculums around the world. Despite these advancements, the demand for software still exceeds human capacity to produce it, and the cost of software production far outstrips the cost of the hardware on which it runs. Software can be counted among humankind's most complex creations, and modern society is completely dependent upon software-intensive systems to manage our critical infrastructure, control our airplanes and airspace, control our automobile engines, defend our countries, manage the money in our banks, monitor and protect the banks, entertain us, and so much more.

Toward Architecting Software-Intensive Systems

Software development is inherently manual labor-intensive, and the history of software development has been a quest for more powerful design abstractions to help engineers design and build more and more complex systems. Over the years, various approaches have emerged that have helped engineers design software, such as Jackson System Development (Jackson, 1983), Yourdon Structured Analysis (Yourdon, 1989a), Structured Analysis and Design Technique (Marca and McGowan, 1988), and myriad of object-oriented techniques. These techniques have helped greatly in the design of software to maintain separation of concerns, aid in the analysis of functionality, and generally provide structure to code. However, as software continues to grow in size and complexity, these methods tend to break down in a number of ways. These methods tend to focus inwardly on code structure and on functionality, not on the broader properties required of systems. These properties must be designed into the system, before detailed design of systemic elements can be undertaken. However, in the development of software-intensive systems, software engineers tend to focus on detailed design concerns too early, overlooking the design of system structures that have broader influence on systemic properties. When applied to large system development, these methods often result in many small structures (classes or functions), and large, flat system structures with many interdependencies that are not well understood, duplication of code structures, and generally complex systemic structures. In short, we are back where we were at the beginning of the chapter, with discussion of the development of system engineering principles with the railroad, power distribution, and telephony systems. Large systemic structures will emerge even when they are not designed intentionally. When small, fined-grained elements are built and assembled into a system, it can be difficult or impossible to predict systemic properties. How modifiable is the system? How well will it perform? Is it possible to tune the system for optimal performance? Is the system secure? And so forth. Another issue is that these methods largely focus on structures that maximize encapsulation to optimize fine-grained reuse, modifiability, and conceptual integrity. However, these qualities come at a cost and are not always the most important design considerations in the development of software-intensive systems. At the level of abstraction addressed by these detailed design methods, it is nearly impossible to address broader systemic concerns. The structures that support broader systemic properties such as performance, modifiability, security, and so forth often become tangled and scattered across many fine-grained, detailed design elements if they are not addressed by the architecture before detailed design is undertaken. Architectural design is required to frame the detailed design. Many broad systemic properties such as these cannot be retrofitted into the system after implementation because they are broad, crosscutting concerns—these properties must be designed into the system from the very beginning. This becomes especially problematic in larger, complex systems with distributed workforces. Today systems of this type are the norm rather than the exception, and software-intensive systems built today need more coarse-grained abstractions than are generally available with these methods. Software architecture design can help designers establish the initial partitioning of software-intensive systems to address broad crosscutting concerns in a deliberate way. Architectural design does not preclude the need for detailed designs or design methods, but rather complements the detail by defining coarse-grained structures in which detailed design can proceed such that broader systemic properties are satisfied by the detailed software designs and resulting implementation. As the complexity of software-intensive systems increases, more powerful design abstractions are required to help engineers reason about the behavior and properties of the system, as well as guide the construction effort. This need has given rise to the emerging discipline of *software architecture* that is used to complement system or enterprise design as well as detailed software design.

The Software Engineering Institute (SEI) uses the following definition of software architecture:

> The structure or structures of the system, which comprise software elements, the externally visible properties of those elements, and the relationships among them. (Bass et al., 2002)

This definition requires parsing.

"Software elements" are those parts of the architecture such as code units, data stores, classes, objects, processes, threads, tasks, and so forth. The elements that are visible depend upon the perspective of the observer—a topic that will be discussed later.

"Externally visible properties" are those responsibilities assigned to elements and their partitioning. This includes functional responsibilities such as services and data provided to other elements, services and data expected from other elements, and quality attribute properties of the software, such as performance, reliability, availability, security, and so forth. Satisfaction of functional responsibilities is often assigned to a specific element or elements, but often quality attribute requirements are satisfied by the partitioning itself.

The "relationships among" the elements refer to the interactions that occur between elements. Relationships between elements might include data or control flow, uses, events, allocated to, depends-on, and so forth. Again, the relationships that are visible depend upon the perspective of the observer—a topic that will be discussed in greater depth later.

Software architects define software elements, assign responsibilities to the elements, and define how the elements relate to each other. Like systems and enterprise architectures, software architecture is multidimensional. Software architectures comprise more than one structure, and no one structure can be *the* architecture. Software architectures are not just drawings. Representations are used to communicate the architecture design to other stakeholders, but software architectures are real structures that are present in the implementation. Structures and relationships may include processes, threads, objects, events, data flow, control flow, classes, modules, packages, application programming interfaces, libraries, and so forth. Software architecture design is multifaceted, and many of the structures that architects design, document, and analyze are intangible. This greatly complicates the task of documenting and communicating software architectural designs. Accurate representations of these structures are difficult, but are essential to ensure that downstream designers and implementers understand the boundaries of the elements for which they are responsible. The documented architectural design is a prescription for construction. If the architectural element boundaries are not clearly established and documented, they will be violated during detailed design and implementation, and promises made based on the software architecture may not be fulfilled in the implementation.

The Design Hierarchy

> Always design a thing by considering it in its next larger context—a chair in a room, a room in a house, a house in an environment, an environment in a city plan.
>
> **Gottlieb Eliel Saarinen (1873–1950)**

It is difficult to establish precise relationships among system, enterprise, and software architectures. What granularity of abstraction you and your organization needs will depend upon factors such as domain, scope, responsibilities, design and construction roles, and so forth. Each of these communities focuses on different design concerns, as illustrated in Figure 2.1.

Although nice, neat partitioning is shown here, in practice it is impossible to establish a general model for all organizations that defines clear and precise relationships among system, enterprise, and software architecture design concerns. Establishing these relationships is not the subject of this book, but providing principles to guide and temper the architect's intuition and experience is. The best that any architect can do today is identify the architects or organizations whose upstream design defines their design context and what architect, organization, or implementer they will in turn constrain with their design. This is the design hierarchy.

Figure 2.2 shows increasingly more detailed abstractions that focus inwardly based on a frame of reference established by a higher abstraction. Each architect in this example constrains the downstream architect, and although not shown here, detailed designers and implementers would finally be constrained at the finest granularity of abstraction.

The purpose of Figure 2.3 is not to definitively establish the relationships among enterprise, system, and software architectures and architects. The intent is to demonstrate the design hierarchy in an ideal kind of way to provide the reader with a benchmark of sorts. Reality is never so kind— the best organizations are chaotic, leaving architects and managers to their own judgment as they operate within organizational and technical constraints to design, build, and deliver systems.

Abstraction Granularity:	Key Design Concerns:
Enterprise Architecture	• Business Processes and Models • Business Data • Organizational Structure and Relationships • Enterprise Stakeholders • IT Infrastructure
System Architecture	• Identification of System Context • Partitioning (hardware/infrastructure focus) • Identification of Software Requirements • Overall Systemic Functional Requirements • Systemic Integration and Testing
Software Architecture	• Identification of Crosscutting Design Concerns (quality attributes) • Software Functional Requirements • Partitioning of Software Application(s) • Software and Systemic Integration and Testing
Detailed Software Design	• Language Features • Algorithmic Efficiencies • Data Structure Design • Software Application Testing • Implementation of Functionality

Figure 2.1   Design concerns.

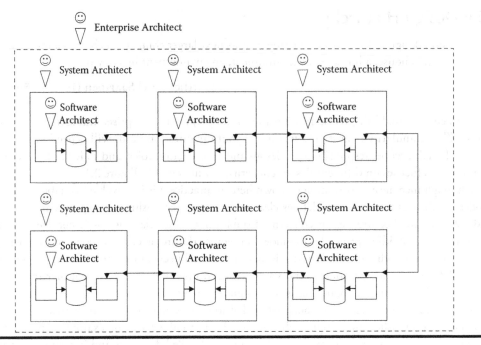

Figure 2.2 Example design hierarchy.

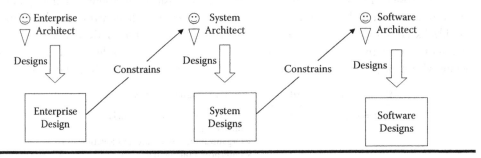

Figure 2.3 Constraining downstream designers.

In most development contexts the design hierarchy is not deliberately established with explicitly defined responsibilities. In practice, ad hoc design hierarchies emerge without well-established boundaries. This is often the source of conflict and inertia in large system development. Although this particular example may suggest an information technology (IT) domain, the reader should not conclude that design hierarchy is only present in these domains. Any time many organizations (internal, external, or both) are engaged in the design of a system or product, a design hierarchy will emerge.

The design hierarchy can be difficult to establish or even discover in many situations. However, it is helpful to understand the granularity of abstraction that each of these architectures addresses to better understand how each can be helpful in building complex systems. What is common among system, enterprise, and software architectures is that they are abstractions that show the elements of a greater whole. While the terms *system, enterprise, software architecture*, and others such as *Model-Driven Architecture* and *Service-Oriented Architecture* are part of the industry jargon today, practitioners find it difficult to agree upon what these terms really mean. How do these concepts really help designers and implementers build real systems? Most find it difficult to understand what value they provide, how to use them, and so on once they get past the initial set of buzzwords. System, software, and enterprise architectural paradigms differ in the terminology to describe them, the level of abstraction addressed by them, the prescribed artifacts, and the methods used to create the architectural designs. Despite these huge differences, they share the same spirit at their core, which becomes more apparent if we use the definition of software architecture given earlier as a basis to compare enterprise, system, and software architectures. We can see that the definition, with little generalization, seems to fit for all.

> The <enterprise|system|software> architecture of <an enterprise|a system|software> is the structure or structures, which comprise <enterprise|system|software> elements, the externally visible properties of the elements, and the relationships among them.

Structures

Enterprise, system, and software architectures all comprise a variety of structures. No one structure can comprise the entire architecture of the enterprise, system, and software architecture. Structures are the implemented parts of the system, and views are used to represent the underlying structures.

Elements

The notion of element is similar across enterprise, system, and software architectures—each partitions the largest entity (enterprise, system, software) into small manageable parts or elements to manage complexity.

Externally Visible Properties of the Elements

Elements of enterprise, system, and software architectures have *provides* and *requires* assumptions. Requires assumptions include an element's expected inputs, physical connections, or services required from other elements or stakeholders. The provides assumptions include an element's expected outputs, physical connections, and services that will be provided to other elements or stakeholders.

Relationships among the Elements

Relationships exist among enterprise, system, and software elements. The kinds of relationships that exist depend upon the enterprise, system, and software elements that are being represented and the type of structures being represented in any particular view.

These abstractions can help designers to incrementally address complexity and are necessary in complex systems to provide a means for reasoning about functionality and, more importantly, broad systemic properties of the system during detailed design. Although rarely done in practice, a deliberate definition of the roles and responsibilities of enterprise, systems, and software architects can greatly aid in the design of large systems. This requires judgment and authority. Judgment in terms of technical insight is required to correctly identify the need for various architectural abstractions. Authority is required to create the organizational structures to complement the use of architectures and to define and staff the necessary roles for carrying out the architecture design tasks. Once established, system, enterprise, and software architectures constrain downstream designers and builders of the elements. Each architecture design constrains the next downstream architect, who incrementally adds details to the design. In doing so, the architect (or architecture team) is able to predict and achieve the overall system functional and quality attribute properties in the implementation of large, complex systems. In practice, efficiently and effectively designing and using architectures is an exercise too often left to the architect, managers, and organization. But which architect—the architect of the enterprise, system, or software? In the landmark book *The Mythical Man-Month*, Fred Brooks (1995) provides a convincing argument that conceptual integrity is the key to sound system design. Conceptual integrity, while difficult to measure, means that any system should feature a small number of simple interaction patterns. That is, the system should do the same things in the same way throughout. This aids in understanding, reduces development time, increases reliability, and enhances modifiability (Bass et al., 2002). This builds a strong argument for the need of a single *lead architect* to be in charge of the architecture design effort. This is not to imply that there should not be other architects. An architecture team might include enterprise, system, and software architects as well as other domain experts in data engineering, hardware, and many others. However, the architecture team must be led by one architect who is responsible for the overall design of the enterprise, system, or software being built. In large systems development, the lead architect must work with his or her team to:

- Establish the context of the thing being built and define the boundaries of the enterprise, system, and software architecture
- Establish the roles and responsibilities of the architecture team
- Define the architectural design artifacts that must be created
- Coordinate the efforts of the architecture team with management

Architects are often faced with decisions that broadly affect the elements of the enterprise, system, or software, and the potential impact of those decisions is not understood or considered. When design decisions are being made, architects need to think about the whole system or enterprise, not just hardware, software, or stakeholder wants and needs. Seemingly small, innocuous architectural design decisions at any level of abstraction can ripple across an entire system or enterprise. For example, it is not unusual for system and enterprisewide decisions to be deferred to software architects. A software architect may select the hardware that will be used locally within the boundaries of his or her responsibilities, but these choices can more broadly impact the larger system or enterprise. Local decisions might be good with respect to the immediate local needs, but may not be a good decision in the larger system or enterprise context. These kinds of problems can be avoided with the development of suitable involvement of a broader stakeholder community and architectural abstractions to balance global and local needs. Local and global concerns of architects need to be balanced and coordinated by a chief architect.

To illustrate the hierarchical nature of system design, imagine the design of a large commercial aircraft. Designers decompose such a system into components that might include subsystems such as the airframe, propulsion, navigation, hydraulics, flight control, entertainment, software, and so forth. In addition to partitioning the system into these components, the system architecture must address the interconnection of these components, the overall behavior and quality attributes of the system, how the components will be integrated and tested, and so forth. However, it should be kept in mind that each of these parts is a complex system (or subsystem) whose design would be deferred to experts in the individual component domain. Because the components of modern systems are often large, distributed, and interdisciplinary systems themselves, it is common to hear the term *system of systems*. Each of these complex components possesses a system architecture unto itself requiring further decomposition and detailed design work involving the expertise of specific engineering disciplines provided by mechanical, electrical, or software engineers. It should be obvious that it is impossible for a single architect to address all the details of each component of the system. But what might not be obvious is that such a system will not possess the critical systemwide qualities that are essential to the success of the product. Obviously, the system must fly— this is a basic functional requirement. However, in addition to this functionality there are other quality attribute requirements, such as fuel efficiency requirements, the number of passengers the aircraft will carry, payload requirements, aesthetics of the passenger compartment, and business models that the aircraft targets. This last point is critical—architects must be aware of the business context they are designing within. At the writing of this text, there is a battle between Boeing and Airbus regarding the future of air travel. Boeing is building the smaller B787, and Airbus is building the super jumbo A380. Ironically, this battle is not about architecture, aircraft design, or any other technology, but about market and business goals. Airbus is betting the big interhub market will be larger and thus designed the huge A380 to meet that market, and Boeing is betting that the regional markets will yield greater profits. This is less a battle of technology—each of the combatants could build the other's product. However, this is a battle for market share, where architectural design is a sword and a shield against competitors—this is often the case with software-intensive systems design and development. In this battle for market share, architectural design embodies more than just technological choices; it embodies business goals and market strategy. Although it is certain that both planes will fly, at the writing of this text it is not clear which approach will win in the battle for market share. Being a great technologist is a prerequisite for being an architect, but it is not enough. The ability to map market and business strategy to the architectural design space is critically important to an organization's survival—and a skill that must be developed in aspiring architects. The design of a product extends well beyond mere technological and functional concerns. The properties these systems possess are supremely dependent upon the early design choices of the architects. These early choices will permit or preclude their ability to compete in the target marketplace and will establish the framework for the choices that all other subsequent downstream designers and implementers make. The purpose of the system architecture is to constrain the downstream subsystems and component designers to ensure that the functional and quality attribute requirements are achieved in the implemented system. While engineers responsible for the detailed designs of the components are often experts in the specific component domain, if the downstream designers of the system's elements do not adhere to the constraints established by the architect, then the overall functionality and quality attribute properties of the system may not be achieved. Regardless of the size of the design team or the scope of the project, all members of the architecture team should be engaged early in the design process to ensure that systemwide properties can be addressed throughout design and implementation.

Clearly not all systems are large enough to warrant enterprise, systems, and software architects. Regardless of the size of the system or enterprise, software is a critical element in systems and enterprises. Because software cuts across systemic and enterprise elements, it too has an architecture that requires first-class engineering attention. Software must be designed to meet the broader needs of multiple elements in system and enterprise architecture designs.

Abstraction Granularity:	Key Design Concerns:
Enterprise Architecture	• Business Processes and Models • Business Data • Organizational Structure and Relationships • Enterprise Stakeholders • IT Infrastructure
System Architecture	• Identification of System Context • Partitioning (hardware/infrastructure focus) • Identification of Software Requirements • Overall Systemic Functional Requirements • Systemic Integration and Testing
Software Architecture	• Identification of Crosscutting Design Concerns (quality attributes) • Software Functional Requirements • Partitioning of Software Application(s) • Software and Systemic Integration and Testing
Detailed Software Design	• Language Features • Algorithmic Efficiencies • Data Structure Design • Software Application Testing • Implementation of Functionality

Figure 2.4   Focus of this text shown in gray.

Because software has such a deep impact on the ability of systems and enterprises to achieve their broader business goals, we will focus on the software architectural design concerns throughout the text, as shown in Figure 2.4.

However, our study of software architecture will not be done vacuous of systemic or enterprise concerns. Further, we will not ignore the role of hardware elements in the design of software. This text outlines an approach for architecting software-intensive systems, not just designing software, hardware, or IT infrastructure. Software architecture design can provide a great leverage in achieving short- and long-term goals in small software-intensive systems or in large, global enterprise systems.

Chapter 3

Architectural Drivers

> The hardest part of the software task is arriving at a complete and consistent specification, and much of the essence of building a program is in fact the debugging of the specification.
>
> **Frederick P. Brooks (1931–)**

While engineers generally enjoy their chosen vocation, organizations rarely build software-intensive systems for the fun of it. Software-intensive systems are built to achieve specific business goals and meet the needs and expectations of customers, users, and various other stakeholders. Too often in the development of software-intensive systems, engineers focus only on the wants and needs of end users, but users are only one of many stakeholders that influence the design of a system. If we consider the user stakeholder community alone, we find out that any given system may have many kinds of users, such as:

- Those who use the system to enter or retrieve data
- Those who configure the system, add users, and set up security
- Those who install the system
- Those who have sophisticated wants, needs, and expectations
- Those who are unsophisticated and will need help using the system

This is not intended to be a complete list of potential end users, but exemplifies the diversity of concerns in only one of the potential stakeholders. Focusing on users as the only stakeholder can cause an overemphasis upon functionality as a prime driver of system structure—this is not such a good idea in systemic development. In the construction of software-intensive systems there are many different kinds of stakeholders whose wants, needs, and expectations of the system will influence the design of the architecture. In addition to users, other stakeholders include coders, managers, marketers, maintainers, sales persons, and so forth. Each of these stakeholders often has different goals, expectations, and visions of the system based upon the way that he or she will interact with the system, use it, manage its construction, sell it, maintain it, market it, and so forth.

The requirements for a system are in the minds of the stakeholders, but unfortunately it is often difficult for them to articulate what they want or even know what is possible in many cases. This makes setting the exact requirements for a system problematic for the architect. A common fallacy is that all of the requirements must be set and fixed before architecture design can begin; this is not only impractical, but is most often impossible. The first principle of architecture design and the central theme of this book is that architecture design is a process, not an event or milestone. During the process of designing the architecture, requirements will be discovered and refined, and problem areas discovered. To begin designing the architecture of a software-intensive system, architects need the key requirements that are most likely to affect the fundamental structure of the implementation. These key requirements will determine the structure of the system; they are the *architectural drivers*. Architectural drivers are the design forces that will influence the early design decisions the architect makes. The term *architectural drivers* was introduced by the Software Engineering Institute (Bass et al., 2003) but is not precisely defined by these authors. A more precise and complete description of architectural drivers is provided here and will be a key theme throughout this text. Architectural drivers are not all of the requirements for a system, but they are an early attempt to identify and capture those requirements that are most influential to the architect making early design decisions. Uncovering the architectural drivers as early as possible is critical because these early architectural decisions are binding for the lifetime of a system.

Architectural Drivers Defined

Architectural drivers consist of coarse-grained or high-level functional requirements, technical constraints, business constraints, and quality attribute requirements. Each of these exerts forces on the architect and influences the early design decisions that the architect makes. However, the impact of each on the design can be radically different, and they are often in tension with one another. *High-level functionality* is an obvious architectural driver and refers to those general requirements for what the system must do. *Technical and business constraints* are fixed premade decisions that are in place before design begins. *Quality attribute requirements* are properties that the system must possess, such as availability, security, high performance, and so forth. Although it may seem counterintuitive, functional requirements have the least influence on design. Of the architectural drivers, constraints and quality attribute requirements will have the most influence over the design. Any number of structures can deliver specified functionality, but only a few can deliver the specified functionality, meet the constraints, and also satisfy the quality attribute requirements. We design systems to adhere to technical constraints, meet schedules, be scaleable, modifiable, fast, secure, and other requirements. The architectural drivers come from the minds of a system's stakeholder community. The architectural drivers will form design forces that will influence the architectural design decisions that the architect makes. The resulting architecture design will be used to frame downstream design and implementation. Each of the architectural drivers will be explained in detail, but their influence on the design process is shown in Figure 3.1.

Although Figure 3.1 looks very much like a waterfall development model, it is not necessary that architectural design is undertaken as a one-pass activity. In fact, a major theme of this text, as we will see in Section 2, is that architectures should be designed iteratively. Understanding the architectural drivers and their effect upon the design space is critical and helps an architect to ask the right questions of the stakeholders. Analyzing and establishing the architectural drivers can help architects pay attention to the right details at the right time. Because of the impact architectural drivers have on designs, architects must be involved early in the life cycle to participate in

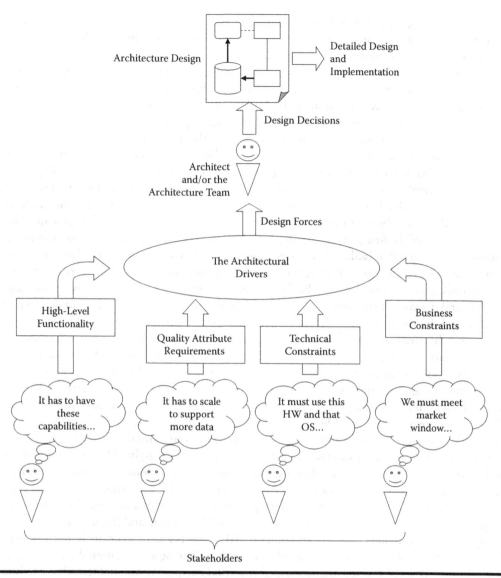

Figure 3.1   The architectural drivers and their influence on system design.

the process of eliciting the architectural drivers directly from stakeholders. In many cases, architects are disconnected and isolated from stakeholders throughout the development process. For
example, consider a common situation where a marketing/sales team bids for work and architects
are expected to fulfill the promise made by sales and marketing staffs. The flow of requirements
is one way—from stakeholders to marketing/sales, from marketing/sales to architecture design
team. The marketing/sales force of an organization is critical to the success of the organization,
but may not be equipped to negotiate technical requirements that balance the interests of the customers and the developing organization. This is often a recipe for frustration, disaster, and disappointment for all stakeholders involved. Architecture design teams must be empowered, have the
opportunity and the will to identify and engage key stakeholders early to better define and understand the architectural drivers. The architectural drivers will be the basis by which the earliest,

most binding design decisions will be made. If they have the responsibility to build the product, they must have commensurate power and authority to directly participate in the elicitation and negotiate of the architectural drivers.

Sometimes we can clearly identify stakeholders, and projects often begin with informal dialog between likely stakeholders and engineers. Sometimes there are documents that describe what stakeholders want and need in a system. Typically these documents are imprecise, but are often good starting positions. In other cases, where products are targeted for an anticipated marketplace, designers must guess (via market/product research) who the potential stakeholders are and what they expect in a product. If stakeholders are not available, surrogates can be used in their stead. This is better than relying exclusively on the personal experiences of the designers, or using similar products as exemplars, or just guessing at what stakeholders might want. The output of the initial requirements elicitation is a list of raw requirements. These are unstructured wants and needs that are the result of pure brainstorming with stakeholders, surrogates, and the design team. Once established, one of the first tasks of the architect is to analyze and organize this raw information and put it into a form that facilitates the design process. The raw statement of need has to be refined into a concise set of architectural drivers as a result of negotiating with stakeholders. As the project proceeds, more stakeholders may be discovered, new ones may emerge, and as a result, some architectural drivers will change and new ones will be discovered. The best way to understand the architectural drivers is to iteratively explore the architectural design and refine the architectural drivers in a deliberate, disciplined way based on what is learned through design exploration. Initial forays into the design space will uncover potential technical problems and the need for more requirements elicitation and refinement. This information can be used to refine the design before production. Design, requirements elicitation, and refinement are intimately intertwined. This is why architectural design is a process, not a one-time event. Again, architectural drivers are not all of the requirements; they are those requirements that will influence the architect as he or she initially decomposes the system and selects the fundamental structures that will form it. These are easy choices for the architect to make, but they are difficult to get right. Although initial design choices are relatively easy to make, they are binding decisions and come with long-term impact. Selecting the correct structures is a critical first step in establishing systemic designs that satisfy functionality and the broader quality attribute properties required of a system. The architectural design forms the scaffolding for the downstream detailed designers and implementers. Without clearly defining the architectural drivers before initial design begins, it is nearly impossible to get the architectural design right. Below we will discuss the following architectural drivers in greater detail: high-level functional requirements, quality attribute requirements, and technical and business constraints.

High-Level Functional Requirements

High-level functional requirements describe in general terms what a system must do. The term *high-level* is used here to mean general descriptions of functionality, not the details of what is needed. Consider an air traffic control system. For architectural design, it is important that the system tracks air traffic, records flight plans, and prevents collisions, but the kinds of widgets, the colors of the entities on the displays, and other details are not important for architectural design. Although these are important requirements, they typically have little impact on systemic design choices, and they will be developed in detail as the project progresses. To illustrate high-level functionality, consider a system called the SmartMarquee.

The SmartMarquee is a product that features a bundled flat-panel display, processor, and software that enables it to be configured to display advertisement information and graphics in a variety of ways, including scrolling displays, static pictures, text, and video. The target market for the SmartMarquee is a variety of environments, such as restaurants, hotel lobbies, store fronts, and so forth, where advertisement information can be displayed. The SmartMarquee must support various configurations, such as wall-mounted units, free-standing floor units, and ruggedized units for outdoor applications. The device housing and applications must be customizable to meet the exact aesthetic and functional desires of the user. The software for the system has to flexible and portable to support the various hardware configurations. The software must also support dynamic local and remote configurations of the advertisement space. Given this example, an exemplar listing of the high-level requirements for the SmartMarquee includes:

1. The system shall provide the capability to display text and graphical advertisement information to include:
   - A panel with scrolling banner (graphical) advertisements
   - A panel that will display advertisements comprised of mixed text and graphics that will display each advertisement for a period, then page to the next advertisement
   - A panel that will display video advertisements
   - A system that will support sound and no sound options
2. The system shall be configurable as a wall-mountable or free-standing floor unit.
3. The system shall support any size LCD device.
4. The system shall provide the capability to configure and reconfigure advertisements at runtime.
5. The system shall support scripted, automatic advertisement reconfiguration based upon time of day.
6. The system shall provide the capability to accept, process, and display continuous data-streaming stock market quotes (in the Market Data Definition Language (MDDL)) in a scrolling banner panel consistent with requirement 1's definition of a scrolling banner panel.
7. The system shall support local and remote configurations via USB jump drives, wireless/wired networks, or dial-in capabilities, depending upon availability.
8. The SmartMarquee shall include an interactive tool that will allow an administrator to define and configure advertisements. The support tool shall allow administrators to export configurations to a deployed SmartMarquee locally or remotely.

These requirements are stated in traditional "shall" statement form, and it is easy to see that while one may have a general notion of what the SmartMarquee system is, there are many ambiguities in these requirements. Such raw requirements statements serve only as a starting point and may be enough to begin the architectural design process. Some of these requirements are functional requirements, others are constraints and quality attribute requirements, and still others mix functionality with constraints and quality attribute requirements. Initial requirement statements like these must be identified and organized as functional requirements, quality attribute requirements, and technical or business constraints—an exercise undertaken in Section 2. Once the raw requirements are organized, the architectural drivers can be identified, refined, and their significance to the architectural design assessed.

We will begin with the high-level functional requirements. High-level functional requirements are best described with *use cases* (Jacobson et al., 1992). Use cases are developed from raw requirements statements as a starting point. Use cases are an informal and imprecise modeling technique for articulating functional requirements. In the development of use cases it is natural to ask lots of clarifying questions of stakeholders. Therefore, use cases facilitate discussion and analysis of early, ill-formed requirements statements from the stakeholders' operational point of view. Although too cumbersome for modeling detailed requirements, use cases are excellent for discovering, analyzing, and documenting functional requirements necessary for designing the architecture. Traditional use cases describe functional requirements in terms of actors, and their interactions with the system. Each use case defines a set of interactions between actors and the system we intend to design. Use cases model system interaction with actors at a coarse-grained level of abstraction. This can help in establishing the scope of the project and in guiding architects through the critical initial decomposition and structuring of the system. Because use cases were popularized by object-oriented analysis and design methods (specifically Unified Modeling Language (UML)), they are thought to be relevant only when using object-oriented methods and languages. However, use cases are not inherently an object-oriented modeling technique. Therefore, projects using structured methodologies or languages should not preclude the use of use cases to model requirements. Use case modeling did originate with the object-oriented community and was developed to address finer-grained design and analysis concerns than those of broader software-intensive system architectural design. The idea of describing system requirements as they are in use cases is not really new. A similar technique called concept of operation (CONOP) has been used by the U.S. military for many years to describe how systems will be used once deployed. CONOPs were originally verbal or graphic statements of a military commander's assumptions or intent with regard to a military operation or series of operations. The CONOP is designed to give an overall picture of the operation and how it will play out to clarify the purpose, goals, and intermediate objectives of the operation. Today CONOPs are often used by U.S. Department of Defense scientists, engineers, and procurement specialists to describe system requirements for contractors who will build systems. In fact, IEEE Standard 1362-1998 is a guide for developing CONOPs and is frequently used in these communities to create concepts of operation to describe system requirements. In practice, CONOPs are remarkably similar to use cases, but typically address more coarse-grained systemic operations, whereas traditional use case modeling tends to address software application usage.

In traditional use case modeling, use cases are user interaction-centric, where actors are strictly viewed to be users. This perspective originated in part with researchers and practitioners whose backgrounds were in domains where systems were user or IT-centric. Because of this, use cases are often shunned in embedded, special-purpose applications or larger systemic development. However, use cases can be effective if a more general view of the interaction is modeled. For example, when designing architectures it can be helpful to view actors more broadly as entities that are strictly biological or technological in nature. Practically speaking, many systems have aspects of both user interactions and interactions with the environment vis-à-vis sensors, actuators, peripherals, other systems, and so forth. In particular, the interaction of both embedded and user-centric requirements may have relationships and interactions that can (and should) be modeled. Use cases can be used to model these interactions as well.

Clearly the SmartMarquee system described by the requirements above has user-centric and embedded system requirements. For example, to create advertisement panes and configure the system, intensive user interaction will be required. Perhaps a separate tool will be needed because the SmartMarquee must be configured remotely. However, the display of advertisements and support for uploading advertisement display configurations remotely are embedded within the SmartMarquee device and embedded software, where no human will interact directly with the system. Both aspects must be modeled to clarify the architect's understanding of the functional requirements. For this reason, it is helpful to generalize the role of an "actor" in modeling high-level functional requirements. We will use the term *entities* rather than *actors* to imply a broader inclusion of things that might interact with the system in addition to human users. This may seem trivial or even picky, but change starts with a different mental picture. If the definition of *actor* is broadened in this way, then use cases can be applied in any domain and can more effectively model all important systemic interactions whether user-centric or otherwise. It is also important that use cases are consistent in the level of detail that they address. Strict definitions for all situations are impossible to provide. In general, architectural use cases should focus on systemic interactions with entities rather than focusing only on software application interactions as in traditional use case modeling. As design proceeds, the use cases can be refined to the level of interelement interaction, but the detailed modeling of the internals of each element should be deferred to downstream designers or implementers.

Use cases are not models for functional decomposition, nor should designers use them to describe how the system provides services. Use case models describe what is needed in a system in terms of functional responses to given stimuli. A use case is initiated by an entity, and then goes on to describe a sequence of interactions between the entity (or entities) and the system that, when taken together, model systemic functional requirements. Use cases may also include variants of the normal operation that describe error occurrences, detection, handling and recovery, failure modes, or other alternative behaviors. Initially in use cases, the system is treated as a black box and the use case describes the requirement—what is needed—not how the system delivers the services. Use cases can also help establish system context or scope, that is, what is inside the design space and what is outside of the design space. While functionality has less influence on structure, establishing a clear context is an essential first step in design. Unclear or poorly defined context can lead to severe design problems. This may be difficult or impossible to rectify after implementation. Certainly, use cases can be refined as part of design or to aid in design. The body of use case models may be refined by adding information to existing use cases, and adding new use cases as the architectural design is refined into finer-grained designs. Use cases can and should be used throughout the entire system's life cycle. Use cases are generally written in narrative language that can be understood by all stakeholders. For example, Table 3.1 provides a description of how the SmartMarquee is configured with a new advertisement.

This is not the refined use case, but rather the raw operational description from the user that will be used to create a use case model. Note that there are some assumptions made in this description that sound like partitioning and design decisions. For example, the description in the table implies that there is a workstation where the advertisements are created and staged, and that there is a network connection from the workstation to the SmartMarquee where the advertisements

Table 3.1   Example of Use Case Information Gathered from a User Describing How It Would Like to Configure the SmartMarquee

Use case title	SmartMarquee configuration
Stakeholder	User responsible for uploading a configuration to a SmartMarquee
Description	After the configuration has been developed, the user would like to select the SmartMarquee to send the configuration to. Once the appropriate SmartMarquee is selected, the user will be prompted to select the configuration to send. After confirming his or her choice, the selected configuration will be sent to the selected SmartMarquee.

are displayed. Another assumption is that the workstation can have many configuration files and that it can connect to many SmartMarquees. Although it is important that use cases state what is needed and not how the system works, how it is partitioned, or how it is designed, assumptions such as these should not be dismissed, but explored. There is a requirement that the SmartMarquee can be remotely configured—so this does imply that the system follows some kind of client/server model. There are numerous things left out of this description as well. For example, shouldn't there be some kind of authentication before sending data to a remote SmartMarquee? The fine line between what is a valid system need and what is a premature design decision is always a difficult issue when trying to capture architectural drivers. Sometimes users may specify that particular software components, protocols, hardware, operating systems, and so forth be used, and they really mean it—these are technical or business constraints. In other cases, users are just describing system features and operational interaction with the system in terms of what they have experienced in other system designs. For this reason, it is a bit too Draconian to dismiss out of hand any discussion with stakeholders where assumptions like those in Table 3.1 are made and may be a bit premature. However, the architectural drivers should be analyzed and explicitly distinguish constraint from functional requirement from quality attribute requirement.

UML use case diagrams are often created as part of this analysis to describe functional requirements, but they can be more confusing than enlightening because architects often do not include any supporting prose to describe what the drawings mean. Use case diagrams (or any diagrams for that matter) cannot stand alone. Pictures are worth 1,000 words, but we want all readers to get the same 1,000 words—drawings by themselves are interpreted differently by different readers. Pictures with prose communicate a more complete and consistent idea in the minds of the reader. Because of their simplicity, use cases can be used to explain requirements and requirements analysis in plain language to all stakeholders—not just the engineers. Use case models serve as a communication vehicle and encourage dialog between technical and nontechnical stakeholders. This is a barrier to communication that is often difficult to overcome and one that undermines the discovery and analysis of requirements. In many cases all you get in a requirements specification is the functional requirements. This is only part of the design forces acting on the architect, and the influence of the functional requirements on systemic design is usually far less than the influence of the constraints and the quality attribute requirements. Gathering, identifying, documenting, and refining raw functional requirements into well-crafted use case models and using them to support architecture design will be discussed in Section 2.

Quality Attribute Requirements

Use cases do not explicitly capture what is traditionally called nonfunctional requirements. The term *nonfunctional requirement* is often used as a place holder for every other property a system must possess, like modifiability, performance, and so forth, in addition to functionality. This introduces a nice, neat, but totally fallacious partitioning between functional requirements and other requirements. In practice, quality attribute requirements and functionality are usually intimately intertwined. As such, it is impossible and meaningless to say a system "shall have high performance." Without associating the nonfunctional requirement of performance to some specific behavior in the system, architects cannot hope to design a system to satisfy this need. The term *nonfunctional requirement* will be avoided in this text in favor of the term *quality attribute requirement* (Barbacci et al., 2003). A typical description of a quality attribute requirement might be "the system shall have high performance." This kind of requirement is nondescriptive and puts forth only general notions that are impossible for architects to design into a system or measure in the system once implemented. What kind of performance does this refer to? Does performance mean response time, throughput, or something else? For architects to fully understand what is needed in terms of quality attributes that are required of the system, more detailed descriptions in terms of stimuli and quality attribute responses are required. While functional requirements describe *what* the system must do, quality attribute requirements describe *how* the system must do it; however, both parts are required for a full understanding of the quality attribute requirement. We can think of any given quality attribute requirement and associate it with any number of operational elements. Together it provides a fuller understanding of the requirement in terms of what must be done functionally and how it must be done in terms of a quality attribute response. This is illustrated in Table 3.2.

To guide design choices and measure the fitness of the design, quality attribute requirements must be described with respect to some operational context. To do this we will use quality attribute scenarios (Barbacci et al., 2003) to more completely define the quality attribute properties a system must possess. Quality attribute scenarios describe some quality attribute requirement in terms of stimulus, source of stimulus, environmental condition, architectural element, response, and response measure. This is a basis for the six-part quality attribute scenario framework for recording, negotiating, and analyzing quality attribute requirements. Each element of this framework is discussed below:

- Stimulus: The stimulus is the condition affecting the architecture. This can be an event, a user request for data, the initiation of service, or a proposed change to the system.
- Source(s) of the stimulus: This is the entity (human, organizational, or technological) that is the source of the stimulus described above. There can be one or more sources.
- Relevant environmental conditions: These are the conditions present in the system's operational environment during the receipt of the stimulus. Relevant environmental conditions can be diverse and will depend upon the stimulus, but examples might include "during runtime execution," "during initial development," "after deployment," "during peak load," "while seven hundred users are logged in," and so forth.
- Architectural element(s): This is the element or elements of the architecture that are directly or indirectly affected by the stimulus. In early requirements gathering, when quality attribute requirements are initially developed, the artifact is probably not known. However, after architectural design has commenced and is successively refined, the architectural element information should be added to the quality attribute requirements information.

Table 3.2 Quality Attribute Requirements and Associated Operational Elements

Example Raw Quality Attribute Concern	Example Operational Contexts of Concern
Modifiability	Functionality gained or lost in modifying the system Capacity gained or lost in modifying the system
Performance	Service(s) that must be rendered within a specified deadline Volume of data transferred under various conditions
Security	Data and services that must not be compromised Intrusion detection and allowable responses to intrusion
Safety	Services that are sensitive to system safety Error conditions that can compromise safety and fail-safe system responses

■ System response: A description of how the systems stakeholders would like the architecture/system to respond to the stimuli.

■ Response measure: A measure of how the system responds. The kind of response measure listed will depend upon the stimuli. For change/modification stimuli, we might have response measures that measure the cost of change in terms of time, manpower, cost, and so forth. For a performance stimulus, we might have response measures in terms of throughput, response time, and so forth.

We can think of quality attribute scenarios as a short story or description of how a system responds to a given stimulus in terms of a quality attribute property that a system must possess. Quality attribute scenarios differ from use case scenarios in that quality attribute scenarios focus on the quality attribute response, whereas use cases focus on functional responses to stimuli. In most requirement specifications, all the architect gets is one word, such as *security, performance, availability,* and so forth. To better understand raw quality attribute requirements like these directly from stakeholders, they must be cast into quality attribute scenarios that better clarify the need to guide the design choices of the architect. This reinforces the assertion that architects need to be part of the requirements process to ensure that the information needed for design is captured as completely as possible.

To illustrate these points, let us consider the SmartMarquee's raw requirements again as presented in the previous section. The prose description of the SmartMarquee included the following requirement:

> Because the SmartMarquee and applications must be customizable to meet the exact aesthetic and functional desires of the customer, the system software has to be flexible and portable to support the various hardware configurations.

Clearly there are requirements for flexibility and portability, but there is not enough information in this description for the architect to design these features into the system. Each of these requirements may refer to the same aspect of the system's ability to deploy the software on any kind of SmartMarquee device hardware configuration. This is still not enough information. After all, its software! Given enough time, it could be modified to operate on any hardware. The issue is not whether it can be changed, but rather the cost of change. A key aspect of this requirement that is missing is that we do not understand what portable and flexible mean in this context. A flexible and portable system in this context means that the SmartMarquee software can be installed on any SmartMarquee device hardware configuration with little effort, which translates into reduced cost and schedule (cost). What is not known is how much stakeholders are willing to pay for portability/flexibility and when they want to pay for it. For example, will stakeholders assume higher design costs versus reduced development and deployment costs, or is it more crucial to get some out fast and pay more in development and deployment costs when we have to accommodate new platforms? The architect's job now is to press the stakeholders for a specific story that describes flexibility and portability, but how should this interaction be structured?

The architect can use the six-part quality attribute scenario framework to guide the discussion with stakeholders to develop a quality attribute scenario to describe the requirement. What is needed is a specific instance of stimuli that occurs under specific environmental conditions, and then describes how the system should respond to the stimuli under those conditions. Although difficult, the architect should press stakeholders to be as specific as possible in defining responses to the stimuli. For example, see the six-part scenario in Table 3.3.

Once captured, the quality attribute scenario could be rephrased in paragraph form, if desired, as follows:

> A customer orders a special SmartMarquee device that meets his or her aesthetic and operational needs. After the device platform is assembled the SmartMarquee application can be loaded on the hardware platform in less than 30 minutes without custom software development or recompilation, using a standard, common configuration with all of the inherit application functionality and properties available.

Although a much clearer description of the flexibility/portability requirement, this scenario can be further analyzed, leading to more questions that might not have been asked and left unstated until code was being written and hardware designed. A few immediate questions might include: What does the term *platform* really mean? Does it refer to the processor or just the housing? Does this mean that different platforms can use different-size display devices? What do technicians know? Are they trained computer technicians or less qualified?

As the quality attribute requirements are developed, they will lead to more questions that will result in acquiring more information about the quality attribute properties the system must possess. As design progresses, the quality attribute requirements may need to be revisited and refined. As we will see later, the collection of quality attribute scenarios will be refined throughout the design process to answer questions like these as they emerge. The six-part scenario framework fosters deeper thinking about what the quality attribute requirements really mean and forces stakeholders to think about how they want their system to respond to specific stimuli. A quality attribute requirement may have many aspects. For example, performance may refer to fast response time, throughput, schedulability, deterministic response, or something else. One or more scenarios may be required to adequately capture the quality attribute requirement of performance. Taken as a group, they would describe the particular quality attribute requirement for a system. All of the quality attribute scenarios describe the quality attribute properties the system must possess. Once fully developed, the words we began with in the SmartMarquee example, *flexibility* and

Table 3.3 Example of Six-Part Quality Attribute Scenario for SmartMarquee

Raw quality attribute	SmartMarquee flexibility and portability
Stimulus	Install the SmartMarquee application on a new custom device hardware platform
Source(s) of the stimulus	Customer
Relevant environmental conditions	SmartMarquee hardware platform has been developed and is being prepared for deployment at the customer location.
Architectural elements	SmartMarquee application and SmartMarquee hardware
System response	Smart Marquee application is loaded on the custom device hardware platform by a technician.
Response measure(s)	Application installation should take less than 30 minutes without custom software development or recompilation, using a standard, common configuration and installation procedures. All of the application functionality and properties are present on the custom platform.

portability, are described through quality attribute scenarios in a way that will actually facilitate design. We will also see how these scenarios can be used to evaluate the architecture design and even test the system once implemented. The quality attribute scenarios describe ambiguous system properties that a system must possess in more quantifiable terms. Often these ambiguities exist in the minds of the stakeholder, and the architect must work with the stakeholders to identify and resolve the ambiguities. Using the six-part quality attribute scenario framework helps architects ask the right questions to negotiate and define the quality attribute requirements and clarify their meaning for all stakeholders.

Quality attributes are not restricted to a particular software domain and can be used in any software-intensive system domain, from small, tightly embedded applications to large, global IT systems. In an information technology example, system stakeholders indicate that the system must be reliable. Pressing the stakeholders further to discover the meaning of *reliability* in the system context, we discover that the order processing feature must be online and available 24/7, and not lose customer order transactions. The word *reliability* does not capture the real depth of this requirement, so it would be impossible to ensure that the system can adequately be designed with these properties. Using the six-part framework, we can easily spot missing information in this requirement and ask the right questions to create a more useful quality attribute scenario (Table 3.4).

In this situation, we can see that a specific kind of hardware failure is explored and the desired response of the system in the face of this failure is described, and that other scenarios might be required to fully describe the reliability properties required of the system. Note that in this scenario the response measure is described in terms of availability ("no transactions are lost") but also in terms of performance ("processing is resumed in less than 30 seconds"). This illustrates how quality attribute requirements are often intertwined and multidimensional. Here system availability is dependent upon no lost transactions and the amount of time it takes to recover from a fault. The architecture design is critical to balancing these kinds of quality attribute concerns before detailed design, implementation, or investing in upgrades to a software-intensive system. This reinforces the point that a mere word, such as *availability*, *performance*, or *security*, is inadequate for describing complex and ambiguous quality attribute requirements.

Another example of how quality attribute requirements become twisted together is common in usability requirements. Usability is frequently an important quality attribute in IT systems, and in many cases systemic design problems are labeled as usability problems. Often systemic problems

Table 3.4 Example of Six-Part Quality Attribute Scenario for an Order Processing Server

Raw quality attribute	Server availability
Stimulus	The primary order processing system experiences a catastrophic hardware failure
Source(s) of the stimulus	The order processing systems server processor hardware
Relevant environmental conditions	During peak usage load
Architectural elements	Transaction processing software; server software
System response	The hardware fault is detected, processing is switched from a primary server to a secondary server, and processing is resumed
Response measure(s)	Processing is resumed in less than 30 seconds and no transactions are lost

are labeled as usability problems because end users often perceive systemic problems as difficulty in using a system. The usability of a system can suffer when various other quality properties are not satisfied within a system. For example, if a system is slow, this will impact the perceived usability of the system; however, the real underlying issue is performance. Another common example is the situation where a system requires that you enter passwords many times to gain access to and use a system. Again, one could argue this is a usability problem. However, the real underlying problem is probably a weak security model. One could even argue that if it is easy to add functionality, then the system will be more usable, but this usability is achieved by designing a system that will easily accommodate certain kinds of change. This is why it is so important to carefully describe quality attribute requirements using quality attribute scenarios.

Usability is a very important property for many systems, and user interfaces deserve first-class design attention. However, the design of user interfaces can often be separated and isolated from the overall architectural design. The user interface becomes an element in the overall design. Because the architecture of a system is exposed to the end users of a system, usability is very sensitive to the other quality attribute properties of the system. However, problems with usability are often a symptom of something deeper that is wrong with the design of the system. This can be compared to a person who has a fever. A person may get a fever because of the flu. However, a person with malaria, the black plague, or hundreds of other diseases may also have a fever. The fever is the symptom of a systemic problem and should serve only as a starting position for deeper analysis of other system properties. Although the symptom is the same in each case, the underlying cause and treatment are very different.

The ability of a system to meet all quality attribute requirements is supremely dependent upon the ensemble of architectural structures selected by the architect. If the architect has an inaccurate understanding of the architectural drivers, then he or she may create an inaccurate design.

After the business and technical constraints, the quality attribute requirements will profoundly influence the design of the architecture. Perfect designs are usually not practical, but perfect compromises are. Compromise is made in terms of balancing systemic quality attribute properties in design. However, it is impossible to strike the optimal design balance if the quality attributes are poorly articulated, poorly understood, or remain unstated. If architects are not aware of the exact quality attribute requirements, they will rely on intuition, experience, or simply guess when making architectural choices to promote or inhibit various quality attributes in the system.

Technical Constraints

Technical constraints are direct, premade design decisions that become like load-bearing walls in the design space that can have dramatic impact on the permissible design choices that the architect can make when designing a system. They are mandatory technical conditions placed upon an architect before he or she makes a single design decision. Technical constraints are firmly established design decisions that are already made for the architect before he or she begins the process of design. It is often the case that architects must incorporate various kinds of hardware, software products, operating systems, legacy elements, and systems in their architectural designs and the resulting implementations. Technical constraints can be within the system context or exert force upon the architect from outside the system context.

Technical constraints are often confused with quality attribute requirements; the most common misunderstanding is in area performance. We may have a requirement that specifies: "The system shall process 70 widgets per minute." Often this is misconstrued as a technical constraint, but it is not a technical constraint; it is a performance or capacity requirement of the system. This describes what is needed from the system; this requirement does not specify what technology must be used or how to build or design the system. This requirement describes a desired response of the system—there are no premade design decisions levied by this requirement. Technical constraints take the form of premade design solutions, design directives, technological choices, or limitations to which the architect must adhere. Assume the requirement reads: "The system shall use product XYZ in order to process 70 widgets per minute." This would still be a quality attribute requirement in terms of performance or capacity of the system. However, there is a condition placed on how to satisfy this requirement—the architect must use product XYZ, and this defines a constraint.

In practice, technical constraints are often more subtle and may direct the use of commercial products, design methods, algorithms, specific design structures, hardware, operating systems, tools, languages, and so forth. Sometimes technical constraints are implied. Often secondary technical constraints are imposed by direct implicit constraints in terms of available memory, capacity, connectivity, throughput, performance, and so forth. For example, assume that a technical constraint is that a particular processor must be used for an embedded product. This implies secondary constraints in terms of the OS that is used, the amount of memory available for applications, the available processing bandwidth, and so forth. Each constraint levied on an architect will affect the quality attribute responses of the system and may limit the flexibility (sometimes in dramatic ways) that an architect has in designing a system.

One of the worst positions to be in as an architect is when you are constrained to the point that it is impossible to meet the functional or quality attribute requirements for a system. For this reason, it is imperative that any technical constraints are explicitly identified early in the design process, the reason for them, and any flexibility there may be in meeting them. A flexible constraint starts to look more like a requirement than a hard and fast constraint. For example, a stakeholder may specify that a particular product is used because it is compliant with a communication standard the stakeholder wants to adhere to. The architect should explore this constraint further to determine if the product is the constraint, or if adhering to the communication standard is the constraint. In the latter case, the constraint is significantly relaxed and the architect may have far more flexibility than he or she would if forced to use a particular product. If adhering to a communication standard is the real constraint, then the architect has flexibility in selecting a product (or developing from scratch) to best balance the overall design of the system. If the constraint really is to use a particular product, then the architect is often forced to design around the strengths, weaknesses, and capabilities that exist in the product. In many cases technical constraints can often create irreconcilable tensions between the architectural drivers. For example, imagine a constraint that mandates the use of a specific distributed relational database product. In addition to this technical constraint imagine a functional requirement to store medical information for 1 million patients and a performance quality attribute requirement to access any one patient record in 1 second. Clearly there is tension between the constraint and the functional and quality attribute requirements that will need to be reconciled before design can commence. This may seem obvious here because these two pieces of information are presented in the same paragraph.

In many requirements specifications, this tension is often less obvious because the information can be spread across the sections of a big document. Identifying and exploring the technical constraints and any flexibility that might exist in them can be helpful if negotiations with stakeholders are required to resolve these kinds of conflicts as they arise. Often constraints are established in a less than precise ways and are too inflexible or invalid in their assumptions and should be explored to expose the underlying reasons for the constraint.

Another situation that arises is that architects often select their own technical constraints and they are unaware that they are doing so. If we consider the requirement "Store 1 million patient records," it obvious that this is a functional requirement that could be satisfied by using an off-the-shelf commercial database or writing our own. It would be insanity in most cases to consider developing a relational database from scratch today, so as an architect we simply buy a database and move on. However, in selecting and buying a database we have just made a design decision, but we have also selected our own technical constraint. First, it is a design decision (it may be an obvious choice in this example), but often these choices are far more subtle. Second, this design decision will become a constraint now and for this system in the future. This decision will become a constraint as the system changes and evolves and for other systems that may need to interact with this system. These kinds of decisions are self-imposed constraints that architects bind themselves and their organizations to—often for the lifetime of a system or systems. It is wise to recognize these situations and choose wisely.

Business Constraints

Business constraints are indirect, premade design decisions with dramatic impact to the design and can severely limit the permissible design choices available to the architect. They are indirect in the sense that business constraints generally do not specify particular technical approaches, solutions, or products, but imply the use of specific technical approaches, solutions, or products. For example, consider the case of a business constraint that states, "In order to reduce development cost, system Z shall maximize reuse of system Y's software." It is unclear in this case what "maximize" or "reuse" means, but there is a clear business goal articulated in this constraint that says to reduce cost, we will amortize development costs. Because such mandates usually come from lofty levels of management, architects are often compelled to closely adhere to such constraints. This business constraint will deeply impact the structures that the architect selects and the overall design of the system to achieve this goal.

Just as with technical constraints, it is imperative that we try to identify the source and reason for such business constraints, especially because business constraints often seem to be less well formed than technical constraints. In the previous example constraint, we saw that there is an implied assumption that reuse would lead to savings. This constraint requires further study as to whether system Y's software is reusable and what the real cost of reuse might be, and then determining if reuse of the software yields savings. Unfortunately, assumptions such as these are often left unexplored, unchallenged, and are not validated. This can result in mismatched expectations and disappointment. The architect is obligated to explore such constraints and try to quantify the real costs and savings and report his or her findings. Not doing so is tantamount to professional malpractice. Although the architect might still be forced to reuse, even if he or she discovers and reports that it is not cost-effective to do so, he or she has still applied due diligence. Just as with technical constraints, the architect has to try to understand the real underlying constraint.

At face value in this example, reusing code seems to be the constraint, but maybe funding is the real issue. If this is the case, maybe the architect can offer other ways to save money that make sense if his or her analysis shows that reuse is problematic in this context. Again, if cost is the real constraint, then the architect should know so that he or she can identify what is truly important and find ways to cut cost that are acceptable to all of the system's stakeholders. For both business and technical constraints, architects must press stakeholders to discover what the real constraining issue is and not except constraints at face value. Constraints are often reasonable and obvious, but without analysis it is impossible to know for sure, and it is impossible to identify any flexibility in the constraints that might be needed later.

Summary

- Architectural drivers are not all of the requirements for a system, but they are the requirements that have architectural impact and significance.
- The architectural drivers include the high-level functional requirements, quality attribute requirements, and technical and business constraints.
- To accurately capture the architectural drivers, architects or architectural design teams need to be involved with the process of discovery, analysis, and refinement of the architectural drivers.
- High-level functional requirements for architecture design are best articulated as use case scenarios.
- Quality attribute requirements must include more than words like *performance, modifiability, security, availability*, and so forth. The meaning of these terms depends upon the system context in which they are used. Quality attribute scenarios should be used to describe these kinds of systemic properties required by the stakeholders.
- Technical constraints have direct influence on the design because they specify that a particular product, tool, language, OS, platform, network, protocol, algorithm, and so forth must be used in the system. They are design decisions that are made before the system design commences.
- Business constraints have indirect influence on the design, although the impact can be as deep as any technical constraint. Business constraints can include schedule, cost, and procedural demands that will impact how the system is designed or implemented or influence the design decisions that an architect makes.

Chapter 4

Architectural Structures

> A structure becomes architectural, and not sculptural, when its elements no longer have their justification in nature.

> **Guillaume Apollinaire (1880–1918)**

Architects are great artists! Roman architect Vitruvius stated that, in regards to the education of architects, "he must have a knowledge of drawing so that he can readily make sketches to show the appearance of the work which he proposes" (Vitruvius, 1914, Book I, page 6). In practice, architects designing software-intensive systems draw a multitude of pictures that they call the architecture of the system. It is tempting, but dangerous to think that pictures are *the* architecture of a software-intensive system. Pictures are not architectures; pictures are abstractions or representations of real structures that comprise a system that will be built, or the structures of an as-built system. Software-intensive systems have many structures that must be deliberately selected, each must be designed, and the overall ensemble of structures must be designed to meet the anticipated needs of a community of stakeholders. The ensemble of structures that comprise an architecture must be described to communicate the design of a system or product for evaluation, analysis, construction, repair, modification, and so forth. Box-and-line drawings are informal yet common ways for architects to illustrate the structures of a system and the relationships among them to communicate their design decisions to other stakeholders. As Figure 4.1 illustrates, the boxes, circles, and other polygons used by architects depict the elements of the system, whereas the various lines show the relationships among the elements.

Each of these drawings attempts to convey a design intuition regarding the partitioning of the system, but it is unclear what the exact nature of the elements are and what the relationships among them mean. Often the documented structures and relationships depicted are inconsistent and fail to accurately communicate the design. Elements and relationships taken together form system structures. The kinds of structures and relationships that are visible depend upon the perspective of the observer of the structure or structures. Any software intensive system should be designed and can be analyzed from three perspectives: the static, the dynamic, and the physical. Inconsistent design representations start when architects are inconsistent in the perspective they take as they design the architecture. Perspective is an intellectual construct—if the architect

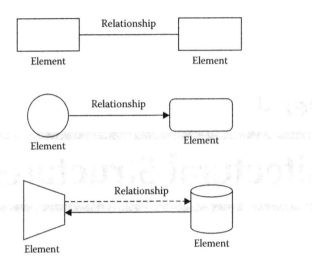

Figure 4.1   Typical examples of box-and-line representations.

cannot keep perspective consistent intellectually, it will never be right in the representation. If the representation is inconsistent, then the architectural designs will not be effectively communicated. If the design is not effectively communicated, we cannot expect the right structures to be selected in the implementation.

Structure and Perspective

Before discussing structure, it is important to discuss the relationship between structures and the perspectives they are associated with. The concept of perspective should not be confused with documentation. A perspective is an intellectual construct; it is a mindset that we take when we think about designing systems, selecting structures, or analyzing an existing structure or system. It is impossible to precisely and consistently identify and reason about architectural structures without deliberately and clearly considering perspective. Maintaining a consistent perspective is vitally important for supporting analysis and creating effective architectural documentation. During system design, analysis, and/or design evaluation, architects will necessarily have to consider a system from many perspectives to precisely describe or analyze a design. Unfortunately in practice, architects are not often conscience of, or deliberate with, the perspectives they are taking as they design, document, or analyze system structures. Imprecision with regards to perspective results in design representations that mix structures from various perspectives in nonsensical ways.

The dangers of not being deliberate and consistent with perspective are numerous, but chief among them is that inconsistent perspective results in poorly communicated designs. Efforts to use the architecture to guide detailed design and construction will be difficult or impossible. This makes it difficult for downstream designers and implementers to adhere to the architecture and fulfill the promises made in the design. The notion of perspective is a fundamental concept to design that should be second nature to seasoned architects, but also seems to be one of the most difficult to convey to aspiring architects. Engineers new to architectural design tend to lean on whatever experiences and formal training they may have to design software-intensive system

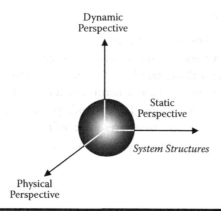

Figure 4.2   Dimensions of perspective in software-intensive systems.

architectures. Software engineers tend to focus on code oriented software structures. Electrical and mechanical engineers will focus on electromechanical elements and other similar hardware-centric concerns. Neither is incorrect, however, either approach alone provides an incomplete picture of the system design and focuses on one aspect of the systemic design.

Architects must consider all perspectives at all times. The good news is that there are only three fundamental perspectives. As Figure 4.2 shows, this is a deceptively simple concept, but seems to be something that many architects have a weak grasp of in theory and in practice. Each of these perspectives is further elaborated upon in the following sections.

The Static Perspective

In the static perspective structures, that are apparent include code-oriented structures like modules, classes, database table structures, file and data structures, layers, and so forth. Relationships among structures may include uses, inherits, extends, and other similar static structures. Although it is tempting to think of code structures as a single class, procedure, or function, it is more common in architectural design to group such structures into more coarse-grained structures that offer a suite of related services. It is often useful for architects to bundle fine-grained structures such as classes and functions to provide a larger abstraction that represents a large architectural element and structure to achieve some broader design goal. Architects define coarse-grained structures and assign those services and data that will be exposed and those that will remain hidden within the structure. What is hidden and exposed often differs in detailed code designs and the architectural designs of software-intensive systems. Architects define the external properties that structures must possess and the relationships among the structures, but they defer the internal detailed design and construction concerns to downstream designers. The static perspective is critical for reasoning about construction-oriented concerns and the cost of code-oriented change most often associated with quality attributes such as modifiability, extensibility, scalability, reuse, portability, and so forth. Note that achieving modifiability in the static perspective does not imply that the design (and resulting system) will accommodate all kinds of change. For example, if a system must support modifiability at runtime, studying static code structures alone will not suffice. Once code structures are compiled, their structure gives way to a whole new set of structures visible at runtime. To achieve runtime modifiability, the system must be designed and analyzed from the dynamic perspective as well.

The Dynamic Perspective

The dynamic perspective reveals those structures that are apparent at runtime and tend to be the loci of computation such as processes, threads, objects, data repositories (usually represented as a "hockey puck," omitting the underlying tabular structures and relationships), and similar runtime structures. Relationships among dynamic structures include data flow, control flow, events, call-return, and similar runtime relationships. The dynamic perspective is critical for analyzing runtime operational concerns such as concurrency, resource utilization, loading, and quality attributes such as performance, availability, fault detection and recovery, and other similar systemic properties.

The Physical Perspective

In the physical perspective we will often see the "real stuff" of the system, such as computers, networks, routers, mechanical systems, sensors, wiring/cabling, and so forth. The physical perspective is essential for procuring, designing, and build the essential system infrastructure or enterprise; integration, testing, and deployment. The physical perspective is critical for supporting system and mapping software structures to physical hardware structures. In some systems the structures of the physical perspective are established through purchase of plug-and-play elements. This is commonly the case in IT-oriented systems. However, in other situations, the physical perspective can be the subject of complex design of electromechanical systems, circuit boards, and even micro-chips.

Earlier, architectures were described as ensembles of elements and the various relationships between them. However, the term *element* is only useful for talking about architectural structures in a general way without regard to perspective. An element is a general reference to some structure of the architecture from some perspective. A relationship defines some interaction between elements from some perspective. When we bind an element to a perspective it yields something specific such as a process (dynamic perspective), a module (static perspective), or a computer (physical perspective). When we bind a relationship to a perspective it yields something specific such as data flow (dynamic perspective), uses (static perspective), or a network cable (physical perspective). As architects reason about and design the properties of a system, it is necessary that they identify specific structures—this means that they must be specific with regards to perspective. Architects must discipline themselves to design and analyze systemic structures with specific perspectives in mind. When perspective is taken into account, specific elements and relationships (structures) emerge. When architects analyze a system, they must first decide what perspective best supports the analysis. For example, in a dynamic perspective the kinds of elements that are visible include processes, threads, objects, and data stores. The kinds of relationships among these elements include events, call-return, control flow, data flow, and so forth. This perspective is essential for analyzing systemic properties such as performance, concurrency, deployment, and installation, among other runtime concerns. During design or analysis of the architecture, it is left to the architect to ensure perspective consistency. There is no "architectural compiler" that prevents architects from mixing perspectives in their designs. Consistent architecture designs start with a consistent perspective—again, perspective must be an intellectual construct before it becomes a picture or view of system structure. Architectural designs with elements and relationships from mixed perspectives often reflect muddy thinking. If perspective is not clear in the mind, it will never be clear on paper. If the design is not clear on paper, the implementation will not follow the design. Any promises made vis-à-vis the design may not be kept by the implementation.

Abstraction granularity plays a role in revealing structure as well—not the type of structures, but rather the detail of the structures. While the type of structures exposed depends upon the perspective, the granularity of detail that an architect may be concerned with for the purposes of design, analysis, or construction will depend upon his or her position and role in the design hierarchy, described and discussed in Chapter 2. If possible, organizations should strive to understand and preferably define this hierarchy and the roles and responsibilities of engineers in a deliberate and explicit way. Often this is idealistic because organizational structures are the most difficult thing to change in the universe. In many cases, the best that can be done is to understand and cope with existing organizational structures and relationships. However, these often form business constraints that can deeply impact systemic design.

To illustrate this concept, imagine an architect who partitions a system or enterprise into a set of elements and relationships among them that describe the design of the infrastructure. Infrastructure designs typically include computers, networks, devices, and so forth, and are therefore from the physical perspective. Sometimes at this level of coarse grained design dynamic representations are used to show general software applications, their interactions, and how they satisfy the business processes. Although an important step in design, this is not the end of design. The next step may be to design and build each element of the system or enterprise. These elements may be complex systems requiring architectural design (hence the term system-of-systems). The overall system or enterprise architectural design frames the detailed design of the downstream designers. Ideally, downstream engineers use the representations from the system or enterprise architect and complete the detailed design of the elements of the infrastructure design. In many cases the elements of the larger system or enterprise can be developed in isolation. These elements will be integrated together to compose the overall system. This emphasizes the role the overall system or enterprise architecture design plays in defining the boundaries of the elements for downstream designers or implementers. Without an overall structure, element designers would be left to coordinate how the system or enterprise elements would interact and provide services. This is a path to chaos. Each downstream architect focuses inwardly on the detailed design of the elements, but his or her designs may be further refined by more downstream designers. Each architect in the hierarchy adds details to the design and partitions the system into more elements, but defers internal element design decisions to the next designer. At each level of decomposition, designers must remain faithful to the upstream architect's designs. Doing so will make it possible to assemble the elements into a cohesive, functioning ensemble, possessing the broader required systemic properties designed into the system.

This example should illustrate two key points. First, if the design hierarchy is not well understood, then it is difficult to know how much detail is appropriate at any given point in the hierarchy. Second, this example illustrates the importance of representations of architecture designs that consider all of the relevant perspectives of the design space. Each perspective reveals various structures that are not visible from the other perspectives and are necessary for adequately communicating the architecture to downstream designers and implementers. Any software-intensive system possesses structures from all of these perspectives, as shown by the sphere at the intersection of the three axes shown in Figure 4.2.

The intent here is not to fix the granularity of architectures, specifically enterprise, system, and software architecture. Indeed, there may be various levels of abstraction within each of these design concerns. The point here is to indicate by example that to clearly identify structure, architects must explicitly consider perspective and granularity to communicate the design, assign work

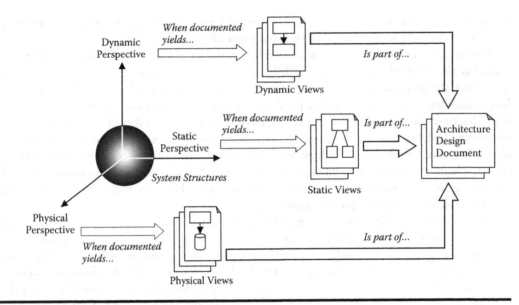

Figure 4.3   Views of a software-intensive system from various perspectives.

to organizations, and ensure implementations adhere to the architecture design. In practice, architects often are imprecise with respect to perspective, and the design hierarchy is not well understood or established. The combination is often problematic, and structures and relations become mixed and the designs quickly become muddied and do not communicate essential design decisions to downstream designers an implementers. This is a key principle for designing and documenting architecture design, but also for guiding the analysis of the designs.

The bad news is that although there are only three perspectives to consider, there are many ways to represent the various system structures within each perspective. Documentation from a particular perspective is called a view. Views from the various perspectives are used in part to document the system structures, as shown in Figure 4.3.

It is often necessary to show how structures from one perspective map to structures of another perspective; however, this should only be done with great care and deliberation. This will be discussed later in the text (Chapter 6). In general, it is usually not a good idea to try to show all of the structures from multiple perspectives in a single picture, as it is confusing to the reader, and it is not clear what kind of reasoning is supported by combining perspectives. Again, it is easier to avoid unintentional mixing or to combine structures in a meaningful way if the architect pays close attention to perspectives in the first place. It is generally impossible for a single view to accurately represent an entire system from all perspectives. In the best case, such a drawing is cluttered and usually results in representations that do not make any sense. For example, to reason about a system's runtime properties (e.g., performance, concurrency, and so forth), we need to analyze the system from a dynamic perspective. Through the course of analysis and design we would model the system's runtime structures, such as processes, threads, data flow, sequencing, and so forth. Conceivably, it may take several artifacts to accurately model all of the relevant runtime structures and their associated relationships. However, to communicate construction concerns to downstream designers, this dynamic perspective alone may not be enough. So we would need another set of views from the static perspective to consider the construction of the runtime elements from the static perspective. This perspective is critical for construction of the system. Although we may need to show a relationship between the runtime and static elements of the system, it would not be a good idea to model and document structures from these two perspectives in the same view. This may be confusing, cluttered, and could be an inaccurate representation of the system's structures and relationships, and would not support the analysis of the runtime concerns or enable construction of the system. Consider the architectural representations in Figure 4.4a, b, c, and d. Figure 4.4a shows a dynamic view of a software application with a set of elements that incrementally processes data. Each element is a separate process. Data is initially read from a repository. Once the data is read and processed, it is passed to the next element until it reaches the last element, where it is written to another repository. Data is sent to the next element in a bytewise, serial fashion.

From the dynamic perspective as shown in Figure 4.4a, we can reason about systemic performance, throughput, and identify potential bottlenecks. However, assume that we want the filters to be portable and that we want the communication services to be common for all of the processes, allowing reconfiguration without recompilation. It is impossible to ascertain if the design will possess this property and accommodate this requirement from the dynamic perspective. We need to switch to the static perspective as shown in Figure 4.4b to consider the code-oriented structures to design or determine if the architecture possesses these properties. Although Figure 4.4b can support reasoning about how well the design supports code level changes, we know nothing about how these software structures map to physical devices. Figure 4.4c shows the system from the physical perspective and shows the physical structures of the system. Although Figure 4.4c shows the physical structures of the system, we know very little about how the operational software elements map to the hardware elements. Again, if we mix perspectives, we should do so with great care and deliberation. Whenever we must show how applications, processes, threads, and so forth map to hardware, this is usually a good situation for showing how elements from the dynamic perspective (Figure 4.4a) map to processors in the physical perspective (Figure 4.4c). This type of mapping between physical and dynamic perspectives is common and effective if done with care. This mapping is shown in Figure 4.4d.

This very simple example illustrates the principle of perspective and the role that it plays in designing architecture and how the various perspectives support the analysis of systemic properties. From here, downstream designers could design the details of the software, select the appropriate hardware, implement and test the element, integrate the elements, and test the system. Again, architecture design does not preclude the need for detailed design. However, the reader should note that architectural design tends to be language paradigm neutral—the elements in the static view (Figure 4.4b) could be designed using structured or object-oriented analysis and design methods. However, the decoupling between architectural design and language is not total. For example, if inheritance is utilized in the architectural design (static perspective), yet the implementation language will not support inheritance, then this design mechanism may not be a good choice. This is a situation where the design will be constrained by language technology.

At this point, it should be obvious that documentation is an important part of architectural design. Documenting the architecture for a software-intensive system is a process of considering the system from various perspectives, documenting the structures apparent from those perspectives, relating the structures from the various perspectives, and capturing relevant design information. The collection of views becomes an orderly mosaic that is the architecture design representation. When the representation is faithfully followed we realize the structures and relationships in the implementation, and it will possess the functionality and properties promised in the architectural design. If the architectural documentation cannot be understood, it will not be communicated to implementers and the consequences are obvious. Guidelines for documenting architectures will be discussed later (Chapter 6); however, understanding the relationships among

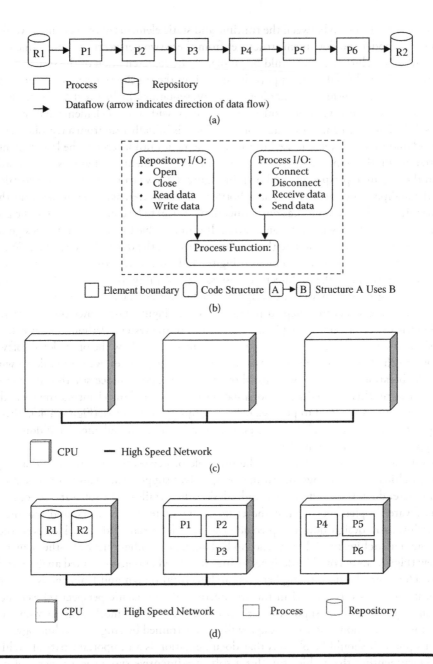

Figure 4.4 **Example of system structures. (a) Dynamic perspective. (b) Static perspective of a process from (a). (c) Physical perspective. (d) Physical perspective, mapping elements from the dynamic perspective (a) to physical elements (c).**

perspective, granularity, structure, and views is fundamental to good architectural design and essential to architectural documentation. It is essential that when architects design they are mindful of perspective, granularity, and structure first. If they are mindful of these issues, then the chore of documenting the architecture design is far easier. Deliberately considering these facets of design can help architects focus on the key systemic structures and their broader impact to the architectural drivers with much higher accuracy.

Structures and Systemic Properties

At this point it should be obvious that functionality has little influence upon the structures we select. Properties such as performance, modifiability, security, and other quality attribute requirements have deep influence on the architectural design; we partition systems to make them modifiable, secure, and so forth as well as provide the expected functionality. The architectural design choices that an architect makes early in the development life cycle will deeply influence these properties in the implementation today and throughout the lifetime of the system, enterprise, application, or product. Every structure the architect selects promotes certain quality attributes and inhibits others. The structures that the architect selects to be part of the system or product ensemble will cumulatively promote and inhibit overall system quality attribute properties. Without a clear understanding of the architectural drivers (particularly the quality attribute requirements), any set of structures will suffice. However, for a system or product to possess the desired quality attribute characteristics in a predictable way, the architect must constantly weigh every structural choice he or she makes in terms of the quality attributes promoted and inhibited during systemic design. If these properties are not addressed until engineers write code, it will be impossible to achieve these properties systemically. At all times there is a virtual scale before every architect whose equilibrium is determined by the quality attribute requirements and structures. Every structural choice is heaped upon the scale and weighed against those systemic properties expected by the stakeholders—the architect must strike the balance with the structures he or she selects. Most discussions of patterns, styles, or other structures are generally silent regarding their effects on broader systemic properties; however, this is the one most important aspect of architectural design. What we would like, as architects designing software-intensive systems, is a few key principles upon which to base our analysis or design decisions.

In 1909, Alfred Hamlin was an American architect who wrote, "All architecture is based on one or more of four fundamental structural principles; that of the lintel, of the arch or vault, of the truss, and of cohesive construction" (Hamlin, 1909). Hamlin, in a few paragraphs, explained the principles of each and their relationship to architectural design choices. Now, almost a hundred years later, we are searching for a similar set of principles for designing software-intensive systems. When we examine the structures of software-intensive systems, there are a few general design techniques that influence a few key quality attributes that have broader impact on other quality attributes. Although certainly not the definitive word on the topic, a few structural principles worth noting include decoupling, coupling, cohesion, consolidating resources, scattering resources, and redundancy. These concepts have been understood for a time with respect to static code structures, but architects can broadly apply these fundamental principles to the design of software-intensive systems.

Decoupling

Architectural decoupling is a design technique of partitioning a system into independent, self-sufficient elements or structures. Highly decoupled elements are not dependent upon other elements or information sources to render service. The relationships that highly decoupled elements have with one another are easily established or broken, usually with runtime binding but not necessarily so. Highly decoupled elements that are bound at runtime usually result in common, but dynamic topographies of communicating concurrent or sequential processes. Code-oriented decoupling is achieved with few types of interfaces, simple relationships, and repeated consistently throughout the architecture. Architectural decoupling promotes various kinds of modifiability (scale, extensibility, flexibility, maintainability, and so forth) and reuse. To achieve architectural decoupling, a minimal number of simplified relationships between elements is necessary. However, although these kinds of relationships promote decoupling, this approach generally inhibits performance in terms of throughput, latency, response time, and so forth. Decoupling is visible in all perspectives. From a static perspective, classes, procedures, and other code-oriented structures can decouple to encapsulate related concerns, and separate different concerns and relate them only as necessary. From a dynamic perspective, processes, threads, and other runtime structures can be decoupled with simple interaction mechanisms. These elements can work together synchronously or asynchronously to provide systemic services. Physical structures can also be decoupled or distributed. However, decoupling in one perspective does not mean that the decoupling will be present in another perspective. For example, highly decoupled static structures, when compiled, may result in a tightly coupled dynamic structure. Decoupling in each perspective can affect modifiability differently. A highly decoupled static structure may support code changes, whereas a highly decoupled dynamic structure may support certain runtime modifications or additions (such as plug-and-play). There may be dependencies among the decoupling strategies used in each perspective as well. For example, consider a system with a high degree of decoupling, designed into the system's dynamic structuring to support a future distributed processing requirement. If the physical structures are not similarly decoupled, then it is unlikely that the distributed processing requirement will be easily realized. In this case, both physical and dynamic structures must be designed to work hand in hand to achieve the example distributed processing requirement.

Coupling

Architectural coupling is the opposite of decoupling, where architects partition a system into a few elements with a high degree of interdependence among the elements. Again, perspective plays a similar role as that described earlier. To a software engineer used to detailed-level design, the idea of intentionally coupling elements in this way may be nauseating (especially object-oriented purists). However, architecturally there could be sound reasons for creating a tightly coupled system. Obviously coupling will inhibit many forms of modifiability promoted by decoupling, and may also result in a system that has a more complex arrangement of relationships and interdependencies. This can inhibit long-term maintainability. However, other quality attributes are promoted by coupling—key among them is performance. Coupling can often result in systems with a much smaller executable memory footprint as well. Although these properties may not be important to IT-centric applications, they are important qualities in the embedded domain—and why many embedded applications tend to be closely coupled architecturally.

Cohesion

Cohesion has been studied in detailed software design for many years, but can be trickier to achieve architecturally and has benefits and costs associated with it. Architecturally, an element is highly cohesive when it does a single, precise task, or offers a collection of related services and data. The more an element (and its subordinate elements) is focused on a single goal, the more cohesive it tends to be. As we will see, when architects design systems, they should explicitly assign responsibilities to elements. To achieve cohesion, architects should try to assign closely related responsibilities to a single architectural element. However, if the element is further decomposed by downstream designers and implementers, cohesion may be compromised by their decomposition. The principle of cohesion in design can result in systems that are more maintainable. In highly cohesive designs, elements provide related services, making it easier to find defects and isolate elements for modification and extension. However, cohesion may result in higher element counts, more relationships among elements, and more abstractions, which can impact performance and lead to larger executable memory footprints. Again, this can be a decisive issue in some application domains for not designing architectures with high cohesion. Architectures designed with low cohesion tend to have services and data scattered throughout the system, inhibiting maintenance and various kinds of modifiability; however, in many cases performance can be better and the executable footprint is often smaller. Still, in systems with low cohesion, it is nearly impossible to predict how systemic properties (e.g., performance) will be affected with changes in the system. The principle of cohesion can be applied in each perspective as described earlier.

Consolidating Resources

Consolidating is a technique where systemic resources such as data, memory, peripherals, processing bandwidth, and so forth are pooled together and managed for many consumers of the resources. Systemic resources are abstracted by architectural elements restricting visibility and direct access to these resources through a single or few ports, interfaces, middleware, or other access mechanisms. Consolidating resources promotes modifiability in terms of scale or extensibility; pooling resources also can allow more elements to be added in a uniform way, easing access to resources that these elements may require. It can be easier to scale or extend resources and update or change data provided the structure of data or access protocols do not change. If protocol or structural changes are anticipated, other mechanisms may be required to easily accommodate these changes. However, consolidating resources can create bottlenecks around centralized or pooled resources, thereby inhibiting performance. When consolidating resources, the resources and elements or structures housing them also become a point of sensitivity in the system. If the access protocol, data format, or data structure changes, all of the system elements accessing the resources can be affected, or an intermediary structure will have to be introduced to preserve the old protocol, data format, or data structure. Obviously, this can inhibit the ability to modify the structure of a resource or the access protocol, and the introduction of an intermediary will further inhibit performance and introduce new complexity. Another potential issue with consolidating resources is increased complexity. If multiple concurrent elements require access to shared, pooled resources, then mutual guaranteed exclusion, consistency, scheduling, fairness, priority, and so forth can complicate design concerns. Designing and implementing mechanisms to handle these concerns can be complex, potentially inhibiting maintainability and performance, and can make the system difficult to test and ensure correct operation. Pooled consolidated resources are often visible from the dynamic and physical perspectives as elements representing logical data stores or storage devices with data flow connectors into and out of the elements. While static structures will have to be designed to achieve resource consolidation, the actual consolidation is not visible from the static perspectives.

Resource Scattering

Scattering resources is the counterpoint to consolidating resources. We say that resources are scattered when one or more elements access two or more logically or physically separated resources, possibly using different protocols, or different data structure. Scattered resources may include data repositories, processing bandwidth, peripherals, memory, and other similar system assets. Resources may be scattered for numerous reasons. First, scattering resources promotes performance and may resolve issues and complexities associated with multiple element access to a single resource. However, scattering must be carefully managed, or it can result in spaghetti dependencies between consumers of resources and the resources—scattering should be done with caution and careful design. What should be done with the greatest care is providing two or more identical data resources for two or more different elements. Maintaining data consistency across the scattered identical resources can be problematic, requiring complex mechanisms. However, this is a common redundancy technique for achieving availability. Often scattering evolves in systems over time as features and resources are added to the system. A common way this can happen is when designers strive to build flexible systems and use a variety of small configurations. If not designed or managed, numerous unrelated files emerge here and there, and before long, there can be hundreds of configuration files. Along with these configuration files various resources are often added to support the system configuration. While deliberate, designed, and managed scattering can be a useful design technique (for availability and performance), ad hoc scattering such as that described here should be avoided because it can inhibit modifiability and maintenance, performance can be unpredictable, and it can significantly increase system complexity. Just as consolidated resources and the structures that support them are typically visible from the dynamic and physical perspectives, so it is with scattering strategies.

Redundancy

Redundancy can occur in elements, communication paths, messages, computer hardware and devices, processes, threads, and any other system elements. In general, redundancy can promote availability or improve performance. The concerns of reliability and performance as addressed by redundancy are mutually exclusive. That is, redundancy techniques used to address availability may not improve performance, and redundancy techniques used to address performance by enabling more concurrent processing may not promote availability. These are separate design concerns that can be addressed by using redundancies. While redundancy can promote availability and performance, it can also result in systems that are more complex, potentially making it more difficult and costly to maintain and modify. Redundant elements and relationships are almost always visible from dynamic and physical elements as processes, threads, and physical devices, and the connections among them.

Certainly this is not all of the possible quality attributes that can be affected by the application of the principles outlined here and the potential side-effects of applying these strategies will depend upon the context and the exact structures that the architecture utilizes. For example, assume that we have a requirement to build a system with reusable elements. Reuse is a business strategy and the structures the architect selects will affect the degree to which elements can be reused. Based upon the previous principles discussed, a broad strategy of decoupling elements would promote reuse. While reuse and even modifiability are promoted, performance will be inhibited. But sometimes these influences are more subtle and the exact nature of the tradeoffs often requires a more detailed examination of the architectural design choices and structural ensembles. In this example, the principles of decoupling and high cohesion are paired (as they often are) to achieve a high degree of separation of concerns, allowing elements to be isolated and reused in other similar systems. Ideally, the number of relationships among elements should be limited to the greatest extent possible (according to principles of cohesion). However, this separation of concerns is usually only reflected in the static perspectives. Depending upon the nature of reuse, a separation of concerns may also be necessary in the dynamic perspective (and even the physical perspective) to achieve reuse. Excessive dynamic interelement relationships could not only compromise reuse, but also affect other quality attributes, such as security and longterm systemic maintenance and the ability to efficiently test the system. The strategies of decoupling and cohesion (as an example) may also affect availability if operation depends upon precisely coordinated loosely coupled elements. This simple example illustrates how the basic structural properties of architectural designs can be reasoned about using the principles outlined here to guide design and analysis.

Structures, Styles, and Patterns

Enterprises and systems are usually not comprised of a single structure, but rather structures of structures—ensembles that work together to do something that no single element or structure of the system could do by itself. As engineers solve similar problems again and again, patterns of structures emerge in the systems they build. Researchers over the years have recognized these repetitious structures and have attempted to identify and codify them. This kind of problem-solution pairing is common in many fields of engineering, and identifying repeating structures can yield valuable information for designers about what structures to use and when to use them. These repeating structures are called many things in the software engineering community, such as patterns, architectural patterns, design patterns, idioms, styles, and so on. For our purposes we will think of patterns as structures. Software-intensive systems are collections of structures and the associated relationships between them, from a particular perspective. Often these structures are consistently repeated in different systems, revealing common patterns repeating.

Part of the difficulty facing the architectural design community is a lack of common consistent terminology, which makes it difficult to communicate key concepts. A prime example of this is when terms such as *style* and *pattern* are used to describe architectural structures. Many authors over the years have attempted to define terminology for describing and communicating systemic structures. It can be helpful to look at some of the significant work done in the area for historical context.

Garlan and Shaw (1996) introduced the term *style* in their work of the mid-1990s and defined an architectural style as "a vocabulary of components and connector types, and a set of constraints on how they can be combined." They also indicate that they use the term *style* interchangeably with the term *architectural pattern*. In their groundbreaking work, Shaw and Garlan focus on very coarse-grained software structures, such as pipes and filters, client/server, repositories, and other similar repeating structures. Bushmann et al. (1996) is another very important text that attempts to define and codify software architectural structures that are repeatedly found in practice. Bushmann et al. define a pattern: "A pattern addresses a recurring design problem that arises in specific design situations, and presents a solution to it." Again, this text provides a great deal of analysis of specific patterns and the various structures comprising them. Another popularly sited work on software structures is the so-called gang of four's (GOF) work on patterns (Gamma et al., 1995).

These authors define a pattern as "descriptions of communicating objects and classes that are customized to solve a general design problem in a particular context."

To their credit, these authors attempt to identify problem-solution pairings that can be helpful in the training of software designers. . Each identifies structures from what he or she perceives as a relevant point of view and analyzes the use of these structures in more or less realistic contexts and engineers can apply the knowledge found in these books in various design situations and business contexts. However, in a general critique of these works, consider the following issues (please keep in mind that this critique is made with the greatest humility, as these researchers represent some of the best and brightest in the design world):

■ Each of these works analyzes various structures and the resulting patterns from varying and inconsistent levels of abstraction. In most cases, the granularity of the patterns is not explicit and varies widely from architectural design patterns to more fine-grained detailed design patterns to those patterns found in data structure and code abstractions. Sorting out the granularity of abstraction is left to the reader.

■ Most of these works are silent regarding the perspective of the structures and resulting patterns analyzed. Some focus on code-oriented structures, while others focus on runtime structures. In some cases, the authors are not explicit in regards to perspective, and some clearly mix perspectives when presenting various structures in ways that can be confusing. Sorting out perspective is an exercise left to the reader.

■ Some of these authors describe structures that are necessarily object oriented in nature and are inextricably woven into the object-oriented paradigm. Object-oriented analysis and design are technologies for designing object-oriented software, not necessarily all software-intensive systems. This is particularly the case in Gamma et al. In fact, all of the examples in this text are in C++ and Smalltalk, and the design granularity is fine grained, focused on the class and object. The Gamma et al. text states, "A design pattern names, abstracts, and identifies the key aspects of a common design structure that make it useful for creating a reusable object oriented design." There is an implicit assumption in this statement (and in object-oriented analysis and design in general) that reusability is the first and foremost quality attribute of importance in design patterns and therefore in all systemic design. Certainly, we would like to preserve conceptual integrity in our designs and reuse whenever possible, but reuse is only one of many quality attributes of interest in the development of a software-intensive system. However, reuse may or may not be of primary importance to the stakeholder community. We will discover that it is usually the case that those structures that promote reuse often inhibit performance and other quality attributes that we might care about more than reuse. A considerable number of systems are still built without the use of object-oriented languages and the object-oriented paradigm—this is common in the embedded systems domain. Often other qualities matter more than reuse, such as performance or making the executable fit within bandwidth and memory constraints. Again, this is often the norm in the embedded systems domain.

■ There is no general framework or guidance for cataloging or analyzing structures that practitioners might stumble upon in practice. There is not a lot of guidance about how practitioners can use the information provided in these texts in practice. There is little guidance on how to analyze structures and the resulting patterns, and what analysis is provided focuses on general functionality, not upon the broader quality attributes affected by the structures of the pattern.

Certainly there are many other works on the subject of patterns. However, these are the key works that have been important historical stepping stones in identifying structures (especially repeating structures) in software-intensive systems. This family of authors introduced to the world repeating structures (patterns and styles) found in software-intensive systems, and their work is the result of careful observation and analysis of what practitioners do when they design and build real systems. While these works provide a great deal of insight into system structure, they seem to lack practical guidance for practicing architects, who often want to know:

- How can I use this information to design and build better systems?
- Is it OK if a system has more than one pattern or style?
- What happens when you connect lots of styles and patterns together?
- How can I rectify the different bodies of information in patterns, styles, and so forth in practice?

These are a few of the many questions that resonate in the minds of practitioners when trying to wade through all the information available today about patterns and attempt to put these concepts into practice.

In a great act of cowardice (given the critique above), this text will not attempt to redefine the terms *pattern*, *style*, or other similar terms. Although cowardly, this should come as a welcomed relief to the reader because new meaning will not be poured into these words. For our purposes, patterns and styles will be treated as structures that can be used in architectural design. Each of these structures brings to the design space various properties, and when connected to one another, we get structures of structures or ensembles that are the architecture of the system. Structures are made of elements and relationships between them. The structures and relationships that comprise an identifiable structure depend upon granularity and perspective. Unfortunately, granularity, perspective, and the language used to describe them can vary so greatly in the existing body of work, it can be difficult for practicing architects to distill and utilize this information in a useful way. However, consistent structural information can be extremely useful for designing architectures, analyzing architectural designs, and training architects.

What is needed by practitioners is a general framework to guide the identification and analysis of structures and patterns. So rather than analyze and catalog, or reanalyze and recatalog specific occurrences of patterns or styles, we will introduce a framework to guide architects in the identification, cataloging, and analysis of structures. This is the difference between giving someone a fish and teaching someone how to fish. In one case you feed them for a day; in the latter you feed them for a lifetime.

Using Structures

If savvy, practicing architects will recognize and deliberately try to identify structures occurring (especially reoccurring) in their own domains—by the way, these will not appear in any textbook. Architects are interested in generalized structures for a variety of reasons. Generalized structural properties can establish vocabularies that designers can use to communicate among themselves and with various stakeholders about systemic design and the properties the implementation will possess. Structures can serve as templates to guide architects as they make design decisions. Codified structures facilitate knowledge reuse by providing insight into the properties of a structure without having to know all of the underlying details of how a structure works. Knowing something about individual structures can provide valuable insight into ensembles of structures and in overall systemic properties.

These are all compelling reasons for developing a deep understanding of patterns and using them in practice; however, an all-encompassing structure, pattern, or style catalog is simply not available at this point in time. Such a catalog will not be available anytime soon—if ever. Furthermore, what about all of those proprietary structures found in existing organizations? These will not be in a textbook, nor do we want them to be, because they may be the key to an organization's strategic plans and at the heart of an organization's competitive advantage. The next best thing to an all-encompassing structure or pattern book would be an analysis framework that could help architects identify, reason about, and codify structures. Most importantly, such a framework can help architects reason about structures that do not appear in the books and papers currently available.

A Structural Reasoning Framework

Rather than depend upon a community of researchers to identify patterns, styles, or any other similar structures, what follows is an analysis framework for discovering and recording information about systemic structures and their use. The framework presented here is intended to be a simple structural analysis framework that can be used by architects to reason about structures. The framework can be used to analyze structures encountered in real systems or to further analyze structures (like patterns, styles, and so forth) described in textbooks. The intent is to create a comprehensive but simple framework that can be internalized by architects over time and become part of the way they think about the structures of software-intensive systems. This framework can be used by architects for:

- Providing a starting point for design
- Helping architects to select structures that address specific quality attribute requirements
- Codifying and analyzing existing structures and ensembles of structures
- Facilitating knowledge reuse and leveraging from the experience of other designers—not only generally, but also specifically within organizations and highly specialized domains
- Providing a common vocabulary for designers to describe structures and designs, and discuss and analyze their properties, merits, and shortfalls in a given context
- Promoting broad systemic, strategic reuse.

This framework categorizes structures according to the dimensions of perspective, topology, semantics, quality attributes promoted and inhibited, contextual usage, and structural variants. A summary of this framework is presented in Table 4.1. What follows is a detailed discussion of each of these dimensions.

Perspective

Before we can analyze or reason about any structure, we must first ask the question: From what perspective is this structure apparent to the architect? Perspective is the first step in analyzing existing structures. For example, if we want to understand something about how a system is constructed (in particular, the software), we often refer to static structures. If we want to understand performance characteristics, we need to study runtime structures. If we want to understand

Table 4.1 Structural Framework

1. Structure name or reference	Provide a name or reference nomenclature for the structure of interest.
2. Related system(s)	The system or systems, products, and so forth that the structure appears in within the organization (optional).
3. Perspective	List the perspective from which this structure is visible. There are three perspectives: static, dynamic, and physical.
4. Elements and relationships	Describe the elements and relationships of the structure. For each element, list the functional responsibilities; describe the relationships and their responsibilities.
5. Topology	This describes the graphical arrangement of elements and the relationships among them. Typically a graphic will suffice. Ensure that the elements that appear in this section are consistent with the element and relationship descriptions that appear in row 4.
6. Semantics	Describe any restrictions or rules on usage of the structure. Rationale for restrictions and rules should be provided.
7. Quality attribute effects	
Quality attributes promoted	**Quality attributes inhibited**
List the quality attributes that the structure promotes and reasons why these qualities are promoted.	List the quality attributes that the structure inhibits and reasons why these qualities are inhibited.
8. Usage context	Describe common uses of the structure and domains in which the structures might appear. Describe the granularity. If applicable, describe any associated paradigm (e.g., object oriented, structured, so forth).
9. Structural variants	If applicable, describe variants of the structures. Describe the variants in terms of the elements and relationships, topology, semantics, and so forth. A key point is to describe what effect the variants have on the quality attributes.

deployment issues, we generally need to see physical structures. Determining the perspective is a critical first step in design. Some architects instinctively design from a particular perspective and will omit other perspectives. Sometimes architects create designs without explicit attention to perspective. Because structural perspectives are not deliberately considered, the structures that appear in designs are often combined in ad hoc ways that do not clarify the intent of the architect. Process and thread elements appear with code elements in the same diagram as hardware elements and so forth. If not done very carefully and with great deliberation, these combined perspectives confuse more than they communicate. When examining structures, architects must deliberately separate perspectives and only combine them with great caution and care.

Elements and Relationships

Recall that structures are composed of elements and relations between them. Depending upon the position in the design hierarchy, an element could be coarse grained (a system), fined grained (a single code structure), or some granularity in between. The elements of the structure depend upon the perspective. Relationships are the ways in which the elements of a structure interact, and are also dependent upon the perspective taken when analyzing the structure. This is why it is critically important that before design begins, before specific elements and relationships are identified, the perspective must be clearly established in the mind of the architect. A good way to think about documenting elements and relationships is to use an element-relationship. The element-relationship catalog, along with meaningful legends, can help ensure that the representations are consistent.

Topology

Often structures are represented with a canonical abstraction or representation that shows a topological arrangement of elements and their relationships to one another. These representations are often idiosyncratic and imprecise, but communicate essential information about systemic structures. It is often necessary to tease apart such drawings and analyze the elements and relationships in isolation to better understand perspective and granularity and ensure consistency. Once elements and relationships are clearly understood from the proper perspectives, topology naturally flows from them. For example, consider the simple client/server pattern as shown in Figure 4.5. As shown in Figure 4.5, the very term client-server conjures up an image of two boxes (elements) and a simple line connecting them (relationship). The role of the box on one end is a client, the role of the other box is that of a server, and data flow is the relationship between them. However simple this may seem, such a topological arrangement is a first indication of such a structure—it is like the structure's calling card.

Although topology is important for identifying structure, it is not the end of design, but only the beginning. After identifying such structures we can begin a more thorough analysis. Unfortunately, these kinds of imprecise drawings are often all you get, and there is a great deal of confusion with this kind of imprecision. For example, does this show client and server hardware or software? Both are commonly mixed together in the same representation. What does the line mean between client and server? Another problem with this type of representation is that the granularity is not explicitly stated, making it difficult to determine what the elements and relationships are and what kind of stakeholders can use this information. There are two boxes, one labeled client, the other server, with a line between them. Combined with the ambiguity of perspective such a representation is almost useless—pictures are simply not enough. The purpose of this framework is to guide architects to identify this kind of imprecision. This can provide an opportunity to apply some

Figure 4.5   A simple client server pattern.

rigor to ensure that the elements, relationships, and topological arrangement are consistent with the stated perspective and granularity, and that designs properly communicate the intent of the architect.

Semantics

The semantics of a structure are the rules for using it. For example, consider the semantics of layered pattern: any given layer can only call on layer directly below it for services and only provides services to the layer directly above it. Semantics are established for structures as a baseline. If the semantics are followed, then we know that the quality attribute properties inherent in the structure will be realized in the implementation. If the semantics are violated, the structure police will not show up at your house in the middle of the night and haul you off to prison. However, the properties promised in the structure may not be realized in the implementation and the inherent properties of the system may be unpredictable. Sometimes semantics are clearly identified for some structures, but implied in other cases and should always be explicitly defined by architects. Semantics must also be consistent with perspective. Again, there is no standard, consistent way to document repeating structures, so the nomenclature and semantics vary widely.

Quality Attribute Effects

As discussed earlier, the structures that architects select deeply influence the properties of a system. Each structure will promote certain quality attributes and inhibit others. Structures are often selected on the basis of the qualities they promote. For example, we might select layering because this structure promotes certain kinds of modifiability. However, this comes at the cost of performance and the size of the executable. These are trade-offs inherently part of the structure. If the architect adheres to the semantics of layers (stated above), then he or she can be relatively certain of achieving certain kinds of modifiability in the implementation. If he or she violates the semantics (say, introduces layer bridging), then modifiability will be adversely affected. Although determining the quality attribute properties of a structure is one of the most important parts of this framework, unfortunately, it is one of the least discussed aspects of structure in much of the existing documentation.

Usage Context

Usage context is a description of common uses of the structure. In domain-specific applications, the use context description could be quite unique or specific to systems that a particular organization builds. In other cases, the use context could be quite broad. Use context is handy in terms of alerting architects to situations, applications, and systems where the structure might be especially applicable.

Structural Variants

Often variations of major structures are used and the variants begin to be repeated. It can be useful to note variants of a structure that an architect might find and describe variations in elements, relations, topology, semantics, and use contexts, and most importantly, the impact variations have on the baseline structure's quality attribute properties.

The usefulness of this framework is more apparent if you consider the fact that:

- Known patterns and styles proliferate, but they are poorly and inconsistently documented.
- Architectural structures are often documented at varying levels of abstraction—often the granularity of abstraction goes unstated.
- Not all structures used in practice are documented (consider those structures regularly used in your own domain or organization that do not appear in textbooks). You need to analyze these too, not just the structures that appear in textbooks!
- Most importantly, real systems consist of many structures that coexist simultaneously. No system of any consequence is composed of one pattern, style, or any other structure for that matter. Real systems are ensembles of structures.

This framework can serve as guide for analyzing and writing down salient information regarding structures. Missing information can easily be identified, and the completed framework can aid architects analyzing structures that they may find in their specific domains, or in documents and textbooks. Identifying repeating structures in systems and products that organizations build can be a significant source of competitive advantage, promoting reuse and product line construction and helping architects identify strengths and chronically weak structures in the systems they build.

Example Framework Applications

To illustrate the use of the framework to aid in understanding and reasoning about structures, we will use an example from a very important textbook on architectures: *Software Architecture: Perspectives on an Emerging Discipline* (Garlan and Shaw, 1996).

In our first example, Garlan and Shaw (1996, pp. 21, 22) describe the pipe-and-filter style as follows:

> In a pipe-and-filter style each component has a set of inputs and outputs. A component reads streams of data on its inputs and produces streams of data on its outputs. This is usually accomplished by applying a local transformation to the input streams and computing incrementally, so that output begins before input is consumed. Hence components are termed filters. The connectors of this style serve as conduits for the streams, transmitting outputs of one filter to inputs of another. Hence the connectors are termed pipes. Among the important invariants of the style is the condition that filters must be independent entities: in particular, they should not share state with other filters. Another important invariant is that filters do not know the identity of their upstream and downstream filters. Their specifications might restrict what appears on the input pipes or make guarantees about what appears on the output pipes, but they may not identify the components at the ends of those pipes. Furthermore, the correctness of the output of a pipe-and-filter network should not depend on the order in which the filters perform their incremental processing—although fair scheduling can be assumed.

Table 4.2   Example Using Structural Framework Table

1. Structures Name or Reference:	*Pipe and Filter per Shaw and Garlan*
2. Related System(s):	*Not Applicable*
3. Perspective:	***Can't Be Determined From Text***
4. Elements and Relationships:	*Elements are filters than transform the input stream into and out put stream. In terms of implementation, filters could be processes or threads, but typically memory space is not shared.* *General relationship between elements is that of data flow in the form of data-streams, transmitting outputs of one filter to inputs of another.*
5. Topology:	*Boxes are the filters.* *Lines indicate the pipes.* *Arrows show the direction of data flow through the network.*
6. Semantics:	*Filters must* • *be independent entities that do not share state with other filters* • *not know the identity of their upstream and downstream filters* *Filters may specify what appears on pipes, but they may not identify the elements at the ends of those pipes.* *The correctness of the output of a pipe-and-filter network should not depend on the order in which the filters are connected.*

7. Quality Attribute Effects

Quality Attributes Promoted:	Quality Attributes Inhibited:
Can't Be Determined From Text	***Can't Be Determined From Text***

8. Use Context:	***Can't Be Determined From Text***
9. Structural Variants:	***Can't Be Determined From Text***

Certainly there is a great deal of information provided by this discussion of pipe-and-filter structures; however, it is difficult to distill the key information in the prose format in which it is presented. We can summarize what information is provided by this description by using the framework outlined in Table 4.2—this information is shown in Table 4.3. This table shows us what we know and, maybe more importantly, what we do not know.

The description of pipes and filters is pretty clear in terms of describing the elements and relationships, general topology, and semantics of the structure. The second item of the framework (related systems) is probably not applicable because this item pertains to a domain or organizational specific use of this structure. However, in terms of perspective, the text only implies that the relevant perspective is dynamic. We can reason that the perspective may be dynamic because

Table 4.3   Example Availability Tactics

Quality Attribute	Quality Concern	Specific Tactics
Availability	Fault detection	Ping/echo
		Heartbeat
		Exception
	Recovery, preparation, and repair	Voting
		Active redundancy
		Passive redundancy
		Spare
	Recovery, reintroduction	Shadow
		State resynchronization
		Rollback
	Prevention	Removal from service
		Transactions
		Process monitor

the elements (processes) and relationships (data flow) of the structure are apparent at runtime. This description does offer some general descriptions of the advantages and disadvantages of using this structure; and, that information can be consolidated in the table. Clearly this structure will promote reuse of filters, and pipe-and-filter networks generally support runtime reconfiguration. However, to ensure these runtime properties hold in the pipes and filters, we have to consider the system from the static perspective. The dynamic perspective does not allow us to reason about the code-oriented structures that will permit or preclude easy configuration of pipe-and-filter networks and the ability to reuse filters. This illustrates the importance of considering structures from many perspectives and the dangers of limiting oneself to a single perspective.

Another point that Shaw and Garlan make is that pipe-and-filter networks are conceptually simple, but there are some conditions that may undermine their simplicity. Should circular dependencies be permitted? If not, how would they be detected? How should pipe-and-filter networks be configured and by whom? This could drive the need for a supporting infrastructure to configure and operate pipe-and-filter networks depending upon the application—this will lead to additional complexity. There is typically an exception to the pipe-and-filter paradigm in terms of the data source and sink. Often the mechanisms used to read data from the source and write to the sink are not the same as the typical pipe mechanism—sometimes it does not follow the same semantic rules. Again, this very practical exception can undermine the conceptual simplicity promised by a naive description of the structure. A quality attribute property of the system that is inhibited is performance in terms of throughput and determinism. Certainly throughput is impacted because data flow through a pipe-and-filter network is stream oriented and processing is incremental. Although the filters of a pipe-and-filter network could operate concurrently with the presence of data on the input side of a filter, the performance of the network is bound by the slowest filter in the network. Determinism is also impacted because pipes and filters can be arranged in any fashion to form a network, and the processing time of any given network configuration may be impossible to guarantee or determine. Another property that is inhibited by the pipe-and-filter structure is error detection and recovery. Because of the filter semantics of isolation, it is very difficult to detect errors within a filter. Once an error does occur, filters can hang and data can be corrupted. Because error detection within a filter is so difficult with this style, recovery is also difficult. Therefore availability is impacted. Even if an error could be detected, because of the semantics of incremental processing, recovery from an error is nearly impossible. Finally, the text offers little description in terms of use context and structural variants: How is this structure typically used? What level of granularity does it address? What are some common variants of this structure? In terms of use context, this description of pipes and filters is decidedly software architectural abstraction. There is no mapping to hardware elements—a network could operate on one processor or be distributed across many. Applications that might use pipes and filters are those that need runtime reconfigurable processing and do not need to maximize performance in terms of throughput and deterministic behavior that could be inhibited by this structure.

Structural variants of pipes and filters are numerous; some typical variations include:

■ Buffering filters: In this variation, filters will buffer some amount of data before actually processing it. An example might be a case where some frame of data is ordered before being sent to the next filter. The effect of this variant is that performance in terms of throughput and determinism will be further inhibited. Another problem is that buffering information can consume large amounts of system memory. If memory becomes unavailable, the buffering filter will fail. Buffering data to disk is not generally a good idea. This creates a dependency that violates the semantics of the structure and could undermine the reuse and reconfigurable properties promoted by using the structure. Besides the problem of creating a dependency that violates the semantics, buffering to disk will be ponderously slow, further inhibiting performance.

■ Concurrent networks: It is possible that a processing task could be satisfied by dividing the processing among two or more concurrent pipe-and-filter structures. Concurrent pipe-and-filter networks make it possible to increase the overall performance of a single pipe-and-filter network. It is highly desirable that the concurrent networks remain completely separate to maintain the highest performance possible. If at some points the data flow is merged into a single filter, performance will become constrained at that filter and any potential performance gains could be lost.

■ Broadcasting filters: Because it can be difficult to detect errors in pipes and filters, this variation modifies filters to include an event-casting mechanism that allows it to broadcast events or messages under certain conditions. One classic condition where event casting is useful is when a filter has a problem of some kind. Obviously this introduces a dependency that could undermine the semantics of the structure. However, it is typically the case that event or message broadcasting loosely couples elements. In the ideal case, event broadcasting filters are not aware of what outside elements (or if any outside elements) receive events or messages from the filters. In this case, the semantics of the structure can be maintained while improving its ability to accommodate error detection in a pipe-and-filter network. Various mechanisms exist that can provide filters with this kind of loose coupling that can promote error detection and still maintain the semantics of filters. Examples include signals, observer-observable, and aspect-oriented language mechanisms, among others. The challenge with broadcasting filters is to ensure that the detailed designs and implementation maintain the loose coupling to achieve error detection without introducing dependencies, and also maintain the semantics of pipes and filters. Again, deviating from the semantics of any structure is only important in that what we know about the structure in terms of the properties it promotes and inhibits will be undermined. Deviation from structural semantics is not necessarily a bad thing, but if we do deviate from them, what we knew about the structure (when we adhered to the semantics) may no longer be true. Essentially, we enter the unknown and must analyze the structure anew.

Often authors are not as generous as Shaw and Garlan in describing systemic structures such as these. More importantly, the structures that architects are faced with are not usually documented in textbooks—this situation is the norm rather than the exception for practicing architects in industry today. However, the framework introduced here is designed to help architects in their work as they identify, document, and analyze structures found in practice.

Tactics

It is often the case that patterns or styles are among the first choices that architects make when they design systems. These structures promote some quality attribute properties and inhibit others. What is needed is some way to compensate for those quality attributes that are inhibited by specific structures without compromising the original structure (pattern or style). The Software Engineering Institute (SEI) calls these architectural design choices *tactics* (Bass et al., 2003), which is an important emergent concept worth mentioning here. The SEI has developed tactics for the quality attributes of availability, performance, modifiability, security, usability, and testability. An example from this work is shown in Table 4.3.

Table 4.3 shows three columns, where the first column lists the quality attribute of interests, the second lists the quality concern, and the third lists the specific tactic that will promote the quality concern of interest. Although tactics are not structural in nature, they can be broadly applied to a variety of systemic structures. For example, ping-echo could be applied to client/server structures or to communicating processes co-located on a single process. Obviously these tactics are not new design options, as the authors indicate, but viewing them in terms of the influence they have on quality attribute properties is a novel and powerful concept. The current state of the work should not be viewed as a complete representation of all possible tactics either. An interesting aspect of tactics is that they do not depend upon specific structures, that is, they do not depend upon specific elements, relationships, topologies, and so forth. Tactics can be broadly applied to existing structures to promote various quality attribute responses. One can think of tactics as "dials" that can be used to fine-tune a design's inherent quality attribute properties.

However, while tactics can promote some quality attributes, it can have a broad impact on others, depending upon how they are designed into the system and implemented. Let us consider an example. Assume that availability is an important property for a system to have as described via quality attribute scenarios. To meet this quality attribute requirement, the architect may select any number of structures. In addition to these structures, assume that the architect selects ping-echo as a tactic to further promote availability. In this case, while the ping-echo tactic may promote availability (in terms of fault detection), this tactic comes with a cost. To practically implement the ping-echo tactic, messages will have to be sent between decoupled elements over some medium, such as a network or another similar communication mechanism. The additional traffic over the medium to support the ping-echo tactic could potentially inhibit performance. To further illustrate the relationship between structures and tactics, consider the example in Figure 4.6a. In this case, the architect has selected an overall structure of concurrent processes

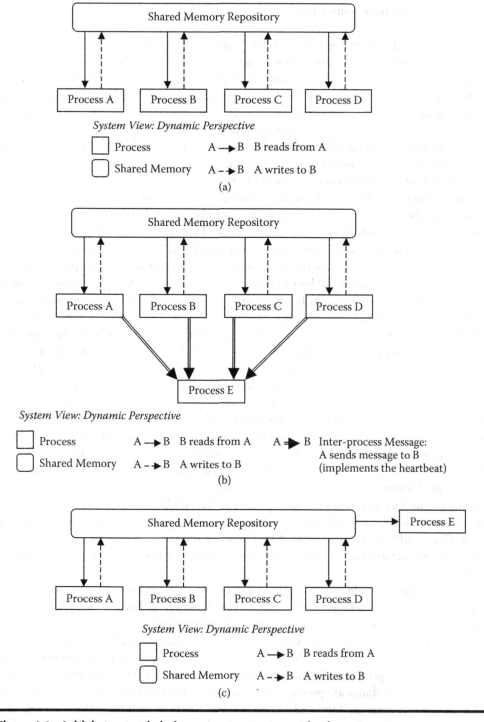

Figure 4.6   Initial structural choice: concurrent communicating processes.

utilizing a shared memory common repository. Note that no specific tactics have been applied as of yet.

In the example above, the need for availability suggests a tighter coupling between elements and redundancy; however, to maximize performance, concurrency is also desired. It may be difficult in this case to detect when one or more of the critical processes (processes A, B, C, and D) have critical errors or abort. Assuming that both performance and availability are required properties, it should be clear that these qualities are in tension with one another in the structure selected. In this case, the architect can apply one or more tactics to compensate for the quality attribute properties inhibited by the initial structural choices. To complement the initial structural choice, we could select a tactic that would promote availability in terms of fault detection. Assume that we implement heartbeat in the system as shown in Figure 4.6b.

In this example, the heartbeat tactic was selected to make it possible to detect when a process has failed. Note that the choice of this tactic affects overall structure: a new element and relationship is added to facilitate the heartbeat tactic. However, the additions do not corrupt the overall communicating concurrent processes pattern. To facilitate heartbeat, another process is added to the system that receives messages from the other processes via interprocess message passing. Downstream designers will have to ensure that processes A to D send heartbeat messages to process E within some time limit. If a message is not received by process E from processes A to D within the established time limit, then an error is reported or recorded in some way and an alternative course of actions and operation can begin. This choice of heartbeat implementation comes with advantages and disadvantages. The advantage is that now there is a way to ensure that if processes A through D have errors and abort, there is a mechanism to detect them. However, this design introduces a new weakness in the system. If process E has a problem or aborts, then it can be impossible to detect failure. Another trade-off is that interprocess communication traffic between processes A and D and process E will be increased—this could impact performance. This choice also introduces new relationships into the system and more complexity that must be managed and may adversely impact the ability to scale or otherwise change the system.

Note that this is only one way that the tactic of heartbeat could have been designed into existing structures. Another option is shown in Figure 4.6c.

In this alternative implementation, each process A through D writes a heartbeat message into memory that process E will read. The key advantage of this approach is that existing structures are used. One disadvantage is that more shared memory is consumed. Another potential issue is that its effect on performance is unclear and may require experimentation to be discovered and verified.

The point of this example is to show that tactics can be used to control the quality attribute responses in a system. Generally, tactics have no specific structure but can be applied to many kinds of structures to fine-tune systemic quality attribute responses.

However, in a critique of this work, it is often not clear how to apply the various tactics to architectural structures in practice. The text (Bass et al., 2003) provides few examples of how to design with and apply tactics in practice. Another issue is that while the authors are clear about what quality attributes are promoted by the application of tactics, there is no discussion of what quality attributes are inhibited by tactics. An important skill for architects to develop is to be able to recognize, discern, and catalog tactics that they might be familiar with or those that they may find in practice. To these ends Table 4.4 can be used to help document and reason about tactics that architects may discover or be familiar with that are not documented in Bass et al. (2003).

Table 4.4 Tactic Descriptions

Tactic name	List the name or reference of the tactic here.
Description of tactic's key technical approaches and mechanisms	Describe the general technical design details of the tactic here. Make sure that the tactic is structure independent. Include enough details so that the tactic can be designed and eventually implemented.
Specific quality attributes promoted by the tactic	Describe the general quality attributes promoted by employing the tactic, but also include any specific quality attribute concerns addressed by the tactic. For example, if the tactic promotes availability, describe the availability concern the tactic addresses (see Table 4.1).
Description of why the tactic promotes these qualities	It can be helpful to clearly describe why the tactic promotes the quality attributes described above; otherwise, the reader will have to extrapolate why. Over time, the reasons for why a tactic promotes the qualities may be lost, especially if the tactic is a unique, domain-specific approach.
Specific quality attributes inhibited by the tactic	Describe the general quality attributes that will be inhibited by using the tactic. Think more broadly to include cost, complexity, implementation difficulty, and so forth.
Description of why the tactic inhibits these qualities	Describe why the tactic inhibits the quality attributes described above; otherwise, the reader will have to rediscover what is already known. Over time, this information can be lost.
Design and implementation guidance	Provide any design or implementation guidance for architects, downstream designers, or implementers to consider as they refine the design or build the tactic into the system.

Summary

- Architectural structures go by many names, such as design patterns, styles, architectural patterns, and so forth.
- There have been many attempts to document architectural structures over the years, although there is no complete comprehensive, commonly agreed to description of architectural structures or their properties.
- This chapter presented a framework for analyzing structures and capturing useful information about structures in a clear and concise way, whether the structure appears in a textbook or is one that uniquely appears in a real system.
- Tactics do not suggest a particular structure, but are specific design choices that can be applied to a variety of structures to fine-tune systemic quality attribute responses.

Chapter 5

The Work of an Architect

> A good scientist is a person with original ideas. A good engineer is a person who makes a design that works with as few original ideas as possible. There are no prima donnas in engineering.

Freeman Dyson (1923–)

If you look at the selection of courses at any school of architecture in the world, there is no single course or course series named "How to Design an Architecture 101." Design is taught through mentored practice in a studio setting where design and structural concepts are put into practice by students. The work of students is critiqued by experts. Students then reflect upon what they did, the critique of their work, and what they might do differently in a similar situation next time. Designing building architecture is part science, part engineering, part art form, and part economics. This makes it impossible to develop a recipe for architectural design that fits all situations and business contexts. What students of building architecture must learn is a few principles and how to apply intuition and judgment. So it is for software-intensive systems architectural design. In this section the most important word is *guidance*. The reader should not look for or expect a simple, easy-to-follow formula that will yield a design—architectural design simply does not work that way. Recall that architectural design is a process, not an event. Sitting at a desk, partitioning a system into elements, and designing structures are parts of the larger design process. This is the fun stuff that architects long to do. The purpose of this chapter is to provide practicing architects with some ideas to guide them in undertaking the fun part of the design process.

What Does an Architect Do?

A common question is: What does an architect do? A common variant of this question is: What do architects do after they design the architecture and draw the pictures? Organizations often do not know what to do with architectural designs or the architects once the designs have been created. In this spirit, it might be helpful to look at the specific things architects should be doing within an organization creating software-intensive systems.

Requirements Engineering

Architects should be among the first engineers brought onto a new project, and their first task must be to work with stakeholders to identify system requirements. Architects are not generally responsible for coordinating and documenting all of the requirements, but they must be a close participant in the requirements engineering activities. Their technical insight will play a crucial role in setting realistic expectations for stakeholders early in the development life cycle. Ideally teams establishing system or product requirements should include marketing, management, and architectural talent. Such a teaming can develop more realistic and better articulated requirements. Architects who have no role in requirements engineering are often faced with unrealistic and poorly articulated requirements, and little understanding of stakeholder expectations. This often puts engineers into situations where it is impossible to build the specified system (or systems) possessing the required functional features and quality attribute properties with the resources and schedule available to them. This usually results in a lose-lose-lose situation. The customer is not happy because his or her expectations were unrealistic, the engineers are demoralized because they have been given an impossible task, and more broadly, the organization suffers by not delivering on its promises. Involving the architect early can help set realistic expectations for products and systems rather than saying yes to all stakeholders for all requirements. Saying "no, we can't do that" to a customer is never an easy thing to do. However, it is better to say no early rather than say yes early and lie later by not delivering what was promised. This may not have been the intent, but this is the perception.

Participating on the Management Team

It is essential that organizations involve architects in the business of creating systems, enterprises, products, and so forth. Too often architects focus on technical details, and while some fault lies with the individual architect, it is usually the case that there is not a place at the table for architects on management teams. How can we expect architects to design systems and products that meet broad strategic business and organizational goals if they are not given access to them? In many cases, it may even make sense to involve the architect as a full partner on the management team responsible for defining, establishing, and articulating these goals. Often what they design and build (or fail to design and build) will achieve (or undermine) these goals.

Designing the Architecture

This is the fun stuff! Design is what all architects want to do, but usually have precious little opportunity to do it. Many young engineers who aspire to be architects think that design is all that architects do—being an architect is much more than finding a quiet place and thinking deep thoughts. Designing the architecture also means writing it down for all stakeholders, and it means maintaining it over time. This is probably enough said for now about designing the architecture because much of this chapter, indeed the entire text, is devoted to this.

Evaluating the Architecture

Once the architecture is designed, the architect must participate in an objective evaluation of the design to ensure that it is fit for purpose. It is critical that the architect participates in this evaluation, but it is very helpful to engage stakeholders in this evaluation. There are various methods, techniques, and philosophies with regards to architecture evaluation. In addition to the mechanics of evaluation, there is the question of when the architecture should be evaluated. Architecture can be evaluated once, usually after design, it can be evaluated more than once, or it can be evaluated continuously. Evaluation will be discussed at some length later; suffice it to say here that it is critical that the architect participates in this effort. Evaluating the architecture is usually difficult for architects, especially when outsiders are part of the evaluation process. The architecture design is like the offspring of the architect—and no one likes to hear that their baby is less than perfect. It is essential that the architect take an objective view when his or her design is being evaluated. It is hard to do, but architects must stow their egos and use evaluations as an opportunity to learn how to improve their designs.

Guiding Implementation

One answer to the question "What do architects do after they draw the pictures?" is that they help turn them into real systems and products. One of the most difficult problems in the construction of software-intensive systems is ensuring that the detailed designs and implementation adhere to the architectural design. Ensuring that the implementation conforms to the architecture is currently a manual process that should be led by the architect. This starts with documented architectural representations that clearly describe the architectural design in such a way that detailed designers and implementers know what to build. The architectural representations must be instructive in that they explain what the element boundaries are, the nature of the relationships, and other important restrictions imposed on the detailed designers by the architectural design. Specific guidance for architectural conformance is provided later, but typically architectural conformance is achieved through the use of a disciplined review process that uses the architecture to guide the reviews. The detailed design of each element is compared to the architecture to ensure that they adhere to the architecture. Similarly, implementers must adhere to the detailed designs. If this pedigree is not adhered to, the implementation will not deliver the promises made based on the architectural design. Some tools are available to help with conformance; however, often this level of conformance is accomplished with the use of inspections.

Managing Product/System Evolution

Once a system is deployed, stakeholders will want to change it, add functionality, fix it, make it bigger, make it smaller, make it faster or more secure, and contort it in other ways. Organizations always seem to have time to change code, but not maintain the architectural documentation. This is because there is no perceived value in the architecture design once the system is built and deployed. However, up-to-date architecture designs can help organizations predict the cost and impact of systemic changes and manage evolution. In the most basic case, changes to a system can be divided into local, nonlocal, or gross structural changes with respect to the architecture. Changes confined to a single element are local changes and are typically less expensive in terms of time and money to accommodate. Changes that ripple outside of a single element are nonlocal changes and could impact many elements. Obviously, nonlocal changes have the potential to be significantly more expensive in terms of time and money to accommodate. Gross structural changes generally mean that the architecture of the system will need to be redesigned to accommodate the change. Gross structural changes are often the most expensive and intrusive changes that can be made. However, this basic analysis is impossible if the organization does not have architectural representations that match the as-built system. Architects are in the best position to maintain these critical documents that are necessary for providing key technical insight to manage change and long-term systemic evolution.

Designing Decommissioning and Transition Strategies

Rarely is it the case that organizations "turn off" the old system and "turn on" the new system at a single instant in time. Although this can happen, it is difficult, and usually there is a period of transition from old to new systems and technology. Decommissioning and transition from old technology to new technology is usually a challenging project in itself and can be the source of significant technical and business constraints for designing new systems. New systems can be designed to provide new services to replace old services in an incremental way. Organizations can use the architecture of both the legacy and new systems to strategically decommission the old system and transition to new technology in the most cost-effective way. Again, the architect can play a key role in managing this difficult process.

Providing Organizational Technical Leadership

The technical expertise of an architect is generally unique. A good architect is technically savvy, but also understands systemic design, and the economics of engineering as well. The expertise of good architects should be exploited within an organization, and they should be engaged in mentoring, coaching, and advising younger engineers and teams. They should play an active role in maintaining good stakeholder relations, by briefing them on progress, informing them of technical issues, and helping to resolve issues they may have. Architects also play an important technical leadership role by surveying the technical landscape and looking for opportunities to exploit new and emerging technologies. Again, to do this effectively, they must understand the financial implications of embracing new technologies—not just jumping on the latest technological bandwagon.

This is a full plate of responsibilities by any measure, and often this is too much to be done by a single architect. Many organizations have architectural teams; however, it is essential that architecture teams are lead by a single chief architect who is able to accept input and critique from other engineers and lead them in design efforts. Design by committee generally does not work; it is difficult or impossible to reach consensus on many design issues, and there must be a chief architect to arbiter and decide where consensus cannot be reached. Being an architect is challenging in that it requires that one person has many diverse talents that bridge a few key domains. The following sections list a few key qualities that aspiring engineers should strive for as aspiring architects.

Technical Background

It should go without saying that the architect must first and foremost be the consummate engineer and technologist. However, it is not enough that architects merely understand the current state of technology; they must also possess an understanding of emerging technologies. Additionally, a good understanding of the history of technology can be helpful in terms of understanding future directions because history often repeats itself, even in the technical word. Architects need not know all the intimate technological details of every system at every line of code or circuit, but they need to at least know the architectural impact technology can have on architectural design. An important technical skill an aspiring architect needs to develop is a sense for the relationships between structures and quality attribute properties that are promoted and inhibited in a system.

Experience

We often hear that the best teacher is experience. Architects start their careers with a bag full of luck and an empty bag of experience. The goal of aspiring architects is to fill their bag of experience before they empty their bag of luck. Unfortunately, experience without thoughtful reflection can lead to simple reflex actions. If you put your hand on something hot, your body will issue a reflex action to yank your hand away from the hot surface. This is a characteristic built into the human body to protect it from being hurt, but it is not the best way to design systems. Architects must cultivate mindsets where they view their own work critically and where they are open-minded enough to seek out and accept constructive criticism of their design. Rather than react by instinct only, architects should strive to turn painful experiences into knowledge rather than view them as something to viscerally avoid forever and always. Objectively reflecting upon design experiences—good or bad—is a cultivated discipline that can help engineers grow as architects. It is common to hear that domain experience is critically important for an architect, but it is best brought to bear when tempered with principled self-analysis. Design experience is a must, and understanding of basic design principles is a must, but experience in a particular domain is not always necessary. Although domain experience is certainly an asset, it is not the most important characteristic an architect possesses. Principles of structure and their quality attribute properties, perspective, design documentation, and others are true for all software systems, not just one particular domain. Architects with domain experience can sometimes better understand the needs of various stakeholders, but this can also be a liability as well as an asset in some situations. If architects become too entrenched in their design approaches with respect to a particular domain, it can be difficult to innovate. Innovation is not always important, but if it is, entrenchment in a given approach does not always lend itself to new approaches and techniques. Again, architects can avoid this by looking at each design experience as a unique opportunity to reflect, learn, and grow, rather than as an opportunity to become entrenched in thinking and developing reactionary approaches and rote recipes for design.

Business Savvy

Architects must have a clear understanding of their organization and the broader stakeholder community's near- and long-term business and mission goals. Chief architects must be afforded the opportunity to participate in management teams, even if it is only to keep them abreast of corporate strategy. Architecture design is strategic, but the architecture can only embody and promote the strategy if the person designing the architecture is aware of the strategy. Architects often need to understand the economics of system construction, sales models, downstream maintenance costs, and other business-oriented concerns, in addition to understanding the market space the system is to fill. These facts often have a profound impact on the design and how the process of design unfolds. In developing this insight, the architect will be better equipped to understand the relationships between the design choices they make and their relative benefits and costs. This is important because the best technical solution is not always the best business solution (cost-effective, timely, and so forth). Having insight into the business of architecture can help architects analyze alternative design choices and optimize between the best technical solution and one that is most optimized in terms of broader business concerns.

Communication Skills

Architects must be expert communicators. The designs of software-intensive systems are often cerebral and abstract. If not effectively communicated, there is no way that the implementation will achieve the intended goals the architect designed the architecture for. As such, architects must be able to clearly communicate designs and design concepts to other architects, detailed designers, and implementers. Verbal and written communications skills are critically important. Architects must create documents for particular stakeholder communities that describe their designs. However, architects must be comfortable with creating presentations and public speaking, as they are frequently called upon to describe their designs to various stakeholder audiences, from users to managers. Architects must learn how to communicate more than technical details for a technical audience. They must learn how to describe how the resources and technology at hand can be brought together to design and build a system that meets the expectations of the stakeholder community. Architects must also learn how to communicate technical and design concepts to nontechnical stakeholders.

Managerial and Leadership Skills

Hand in hand with communications skills, architects will often play an implicit part as a manager, and directly as a leader (to varying degrees), depending upon the organization. Architects will frequently be called upon to interact with senior management, clients, suppliers, and so forth to inform them of progress, address issues, and solve problems. Architects must develop the ability to actively listen to and negotiate between the competing interests of multiple stakeholders. At times, this can be very challenging and contentious; however, architects must learn to foster and maintain an open and collaborative environment for design and construction. Because architects often occupy senior technical positions in most organizations, architects will be looked to as someone who can work to resolve conflict, provide direction, help plan and track projects, develop contingency plans, and so forth. All of these require technical insight to provide better management and leadership to an organization.

In wolf packs, leadership comes from the dominant male, who is the strongest, fastest, toughest, and the best hunter and fighter. Unfortunately, in technical organizations, the dominant engineer is usually the one who possesses the best technical skills. However, the dominant engineer does not possess the best managerial and leadership skills. These are separate skill sets—the best architects possess both. Good leaders possess all of the qualities mentioned above as well as personality traits that compel others to follow them. Being a good leader does not mean being a good manager— these too are mutually exclusive skills. Good leaders are able to point and say, "Let's take that hill from the enemy," and those around them feel compelled to do so. Good managers are able to plan the attack and measure progress toward the summit. Of course, one person could do both, but the point here is that they are different skill sets. Organizations often do not involve the technical community in the managerial decisions and leadership of the organization. This is partially because architects are not equipped to assist management and provide leadership, and also because technical people often shun these duties. However, these are essential skills of a good architect. Chief architects are often leaders and managers, whether their role as leader and manager is formally defined or not. As the chief architect, when the project succeeds, it is the team's success; when the project fails, it is your fault. Leadership skills are learned through experience and maturity. We mellow a bit as we get older, and the egos we had as young hot-shot engineers subside. Experience can only be gained by doing—leadership is best learned by leading. Although many engineers desire the coveted architecture title, unfortunately they avoid leadership roles. This is usually an indication that they view the architect role as being solely a technical endeavor and do not understand the full scope of what architects really do within an organization. If you want to be an architect and you lack leadership qualities, cultivate them by looking for opportunities to lead.

When Do We Architect?

If you view architecture design as an event, then you may have never really thought about when architecture design occurs. Often organizations focus on the artifacts that magically materialize on the ascribed due date. However, architecture design is a process—it takes time and resources that must be invested early before the design artifacts materialize. When we begin the design of the architecture, how much time we invest in design depends largely upon business context, the organization, the architect's place in the design hierarchy, and the development life cycle. Each of these factors will influence how and when the architect designs to varying degrees, and some of these factors are closely related to one another.

Business Context

The business context determines what products will be produced, when they must be delivered, and the general expectations of stakeholders. In some cases a business context will favor delivering a product without elaborate architecture design in order to meet a market window. In other cases, the architectural design of a product or family of products might be essential to the competitiveness of the product in the marketplace. These are two extremes that deeply impact when and how much architectural design is necessarily possible. In the first case, schedule demands will make it difficult for a lot of time to be spent on architectural design. The effect of this priority is that the product may fulfill the short-term functional needs and properties required to meet the immediate market window. However, other properties requiring more design attention may be compromised. Often such a short-term focus compromises long-term needs and opportunities, such as modifiability that might accommodate scaling the system, or missed opportunities creating reusable structures that enable an organization to amortize development costs. In the second case an organization may make an extensive investment in architecture design. This will come at a high cost in terms of money, talent, and schedule. Such an approach may be taken to guarantee various properties in the implementation to ensure a high degree of quality in the implemented product. However, if the length of time spent in design results in missed market windows or other opportunities, the time spent designing the architecture would have been for naught. To find the right balance between time spent in design and meeting schedule demands, architects need to be engaged with the management and marketing stakeholders early in the requirements gathering and analysis process. Architects can bring technical insight into a situation that might otherwise be driven entirely by short-term economic concerns of managers and marketing stakeholders. Similarly, management and marketing stakeholders can inject a bit of economic reality into veins of architects who may be focusing on the perfect architecture design without regard to cost and schedule.

Organization

Architectures are deeply influenced by organizational structure as described earlier in this text, and from this standpoint, how and when we architect can be impacted by organizational structure. Besides the influences of internal organizational structures, other factors might include organizational processes, partner organizational structures, and distributed organizational structures. In terms of processes, some organizations must follow very strict development processes that prescribe various deliverables at certain times. Rigid, inflexible processes are not always good or bad, but definitely influence how and when the architecture is designed. Some organizational processes are imposed externally. For example, government organizations around the world buying systems and software from suppliers must follow detailed procurement laws. These mandates can preclude organizations from adopting various practices that conflict with the prescribed processes that must be adhered to. Again, this can deeply affect how and when the architecture is designed. Some organizations are highly dependent upon various suppliers, or utilize highly distributed development teams and organizations. These can be very challenging situations for the technical work if there is not a chief architect to coordinate these efforts. The effect of multiple suppliers or highly distributed organizations will make coordinating the architecture design challenging at best.

Place in the Design Hierarchy

The design of complex, software-intensive systems is often hierarchical in nature. One architect's design space can be an element in another architect's design. Sufficiently large systems may necessitate the use of multiple levels of architectural abstractions that address enterprise, system, and software architecture design concerns. Sometimes the designs can be developed concurrently, but more often, they are sequential because they address dependent hierarchal design concerns. Upstream architects constrain downstream architects—this necessitates some level of dependency. This can affect when architecture design at any level of abstraction can proceed.

Development Life Cycle

First and foremost, architectural design concepts and techniques can be used in any kind of life cycle or software process framework. A common thing to hear is: "We cannot design the architecture because we are doing iterative development." This is entirely untrue. In fact, architecture complements iterative development in a couple of ways. First, the entire system can be designed and each iteration and integration cycle can be planned. This helps to ensure that the implemented system can accommodate changes and additions to the system at each iteration by anticipating and designing the architecture to accommodate change and the additions. This can help forestall the need for and the cost associated with redesigning the architecture (*refactoring* is the politically correct word that we use for this today). If product design space is being explored through iteratively developing the product, then it can be difficult to anticipate what will be added to the system. In this case, the architecture should be baselined, documented, and analyzed at each iteration to understand the strengths and weaknesses of the architecture as it evolves over time. As the system grows, functionality is usually enhanced, but over time some properties can erode, such as performance, security, modifiability, and many others as well. Without benchmarking the architecture design at each iteration, it is difficult to see the effects that changes have on systemic structures and properties. Over time, the architecture will erode and be lost if it is not recorded—all of the good will be lost with all of the bad. At each iteration the existing architecture can be studied to better understand the impact of change and to evaluate various options for adding new features.

Using architecture in a waterfall or big-bang process may seem straightforward. You gather the requirements, analyze them, design the system, build it, test it, and move on to the next project, right? Wrong. The idea of a pure waterfall process like this is a bit naive. Unknown requirements and technologies need to be explored through prototypes—this is true for implementations as well as for architectural designs. Architects cannot pay attention to every systemic detail, nor are there infinite resources to do so. The question facing most architects is: What details are important and where should investments be made? Using the architecture design as a basis, architects can uncover risk and point out where investments in prototypes can be made. It is foolhardy to design something if you are not sure it can be implemented. The purest application of waterfall assumes that each step of the development process can be completed and will never have to be revisited again. Architectural concepts should be explored just as implementation concepts are often explored. This means that architecture designs should be grown over time—it is difficult to create them perfectly the first time. Throughout the development life cycle, there are requirements changes affecting the architectural drivers, issues will be discovered as design unfolds, and problems can be found during implementation that can impact the design. These things can affect the architectural design and necessitate revisiting the architecture design repeatedly. Although it may be reasonable to "baseline" the architecture for a period of time for detailed design and construction, the architecture should be revisited often throughout the life cycle of the system. Unfortunately, there always seems to be time to modify code, but not keep the architecture artifacts up to date. Over time, the documented architecture becomes out of sync with the actual architecture. At this point, control over the architecture will have been lost. The architecture should be the first artifact that is examined when a system is to be changed, not the last place where we change a few pictures to match the new implementation if we have the time. By analyzing the architecture first, it is possible to:

- More effectively identify the cost changes
- Analyze the effect changes will have on structures and systemic properties
- Plan how to implement changes
- Communicate changes to various stakeholders

Maintaining the architecture is often viewed as a time-consuming chore, but it is only a chore if the architecture is not used to guide development and ongoing maintenance throughout the life cycle.

Guidance for Architectural Design

Before we begin to take the first steps in designing the architecture, it is essential that the initial set of architectural drivers have been established. In Chapter 3, the concept of sorting architectural drivers according to their type was presented, as well as specific techniques for writing down the architectural drivers. The assumption made here is that an initial draft of the architectural drivers is organized and documented according to these principles. If this is the input to initial architectural design, then the output is the notional architectural design that includes system context, decomposition of the system into elements and relations, assignment of responsibilities, and the initial architectural representations. A constant theme throughout the text thus far has been that architectural design is a process, not an event. Keeping this theme in mind, the reader should be aware that the guidance provided here is for creating the initial design, and that it will be refined throughout the process. Recall that so far the case has been made that architectural design is most often hierarchical in nature, and here we will start at the top of the heap. The purpose of this chapter is to present principles to guide the architectural design activity in isolation. Other critical aspects of the design process will be presented, discussed, and woven together with the design activity in Section 2 of the text.

Establishing System Context

The purpose of establishing system context is to clearly define the boundaries of the thing we are designing (system, enterprise, element, and so forth). While seemingly simple, establishing a clear context is a commonly overlooked step in architectural design that leads to misunderstandings and incorrect assumptions about who is responsible for what parts of system design and construction. This often translates into poorly established responsibilities. If this first step in architectural design is a misstep, then the results can be painful, long lasting, and costly. Establishing system context starts with a clear perspective in the mind of the architect. System context can be established from any or all of the three perspectives that have been introduced thus far: static, dynamic, or physical. Sometimes system context needs to be established from multiple perspectives; however, it is common in practice for system context to be described from the dynamic and physical perspectives (certainly this is not a rule). A dynamic perspective is often used initially because it can be easier for architects to describe the end, operational state of the system as an application, set of applications, or interoperating processes or threads. Often the dynamic structures that appear in the context diagram are very coarse grained and even naive in their simplicity and will require considerable decomposition before the architecture design is complete. Once context is established, the key system elements are rendered. This simple drawing becomes the system. Around the system we draw a boundary. This boundary is very important and establishes what entities are outside of the system boundary or design context. As architects we may have little or no influence over those things outside the design context, which are often the source of technical constraints imposed upon the design. Often those entities outside of the boundary of such fixed relationships as processes, signals, events, human interaction, and so on become constraints on the design space. In many cases these can be found in the list of architectural drivers that form the technical and business constraints. Those entities inside the boundary are within the design context and usually (but not always) what the architect will be responsible for designing. However, it is fair to note that constraints can still be levied within the design context as well. So while an architect will usually have greater latitude to design within the context boundary, he or she will still face specific constraints limiting his or her design choices. However, those entities and connections that reach outside the boundary of the system are most often fixed as constraints imposed on the design.

Architectural Decomposition

Before partitioning begins, the architectural drivers for the system must be established per the descriptions in Chapter 3. This includes the functional and quality attribute requirements and the technical and business constraints. It is also important for the stakeholders of the system to prioritize the quality attribute requirements in terms of their relative importance. The functional and quality attribute requirements will become responsibilities for the architecture to satisfy.

Functional requirements are typically satisfied by elements, whereas quality attributes are often satisfied by the very partitioning of elements. For example, consider a system that has a functional requirement to read a continual stream of input data, process the data by adding a correction coefficient and unit conversion, and display and store the processed data. Figure 5.1 shows one way to decompose such a system.

Note that this decomposition is from the dynamic perspective. The functional responsibilities for the elements would be assigned as follows:

■ Stream source: This is the source for the input raw data stream. In this case, assume that this element is external to the system context and that the data format and data rates are a technical constraint upon the system.
■ Stream reader: This element's responsibility is to connect to the stream source and read the input data and pass the data on to the next element.
■ Correction constant: This element's responsibility is to apply a numeric constant to each data item as it arrives and pass the corrected data on to the next element.
■ Units conversion: This element will convert the incoming data item from the raw data units to a predetermined unit type (e.g., meters per second, pounds per square inch) and pass the data on to the next element.
■ Display: This element will display each value on a continuous graph over time and pass the data on to the next element.
■ Stream recorder: This element will write each incoming data item to permanent data storage.
■ Data repository: This is the sink for the output data stream. In this case, assume that this element is external to the system context and that the data format, data rates, and storage capacity are a technical constraint upon the system.

The initial partitioning and the assignment of functional responsibility may seem simple enough, but what is more subtle is the effect the partitioning has upon the quality attributes the system possesses. This decomposition certainly satisfies the functional requirements; however, it also permits new elements to be added relatively easily under certain conditions (described by quality attribute scenarios). Assume that we need to apply another correction constant or otherwise manipulate the incoming data stream. Given this decomposition it would be easy enough to insert such an element somewhere between the stream reader and the display ele-

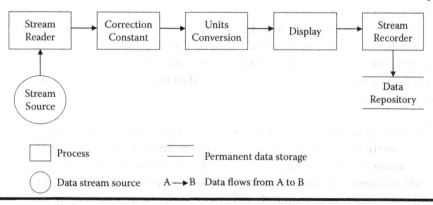

Figure 5.1   Example of system decomposition optimized for modifiability.

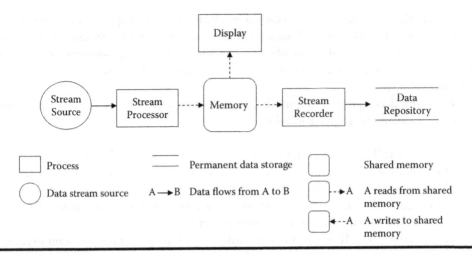

Figure 5.2   Example of system decomposition optimized for performance.

ments. However, although this kind of modification is relatively easy, this same decomposition will inhibit performance in terms of throughput because the processing of data is sequential. Figure 5.2 shows a very different decomposition.

In this design, responsibility is assigned as follows:

■ Stream source: This is the source for the input raw data stream. In this case, assume that this element is external to the system context and that the data format and data rates are a technical constraint upon the system.
■ Stream processor: The stream processor's responsibilities are to:
 1. Read the raw data stream from the stream source
 2. Apply a numeric constant to each data item as it arrives
 3. Convert the incoming data item from the raw data units to a predetermined unit type (e.g., meters per second, pounds per square inch)
 4. Write the data into shared memory
■ Shared memory: The shared memory element is a repository for the constant-corrected and unit-converted data.
■ Display: The display process reads the constant-corrected and unit-converted data from shared memory and displays it.
■ Stream recorder: The stream recorder process reads the constant-corrected and unit-converted data from shared memory and writes the data to the data repository.
■ Data repository: The data repository element provides permanent storage for data. It is external to the system context, and the data format, data rates, and storage capacity are technical constraints upon the system.

In this second partitioning, the stream processor, display, and stream recorder processes all operate concurrently, thereby improving system performance (in terms of throughput) over that of the previous design (Figure 5.1). However, notice that the abundance of responsibilities assigned to the stream processor will result in functional coupling and possibly a larger, potentially complex element. This could make it difficult and expensive to change or add to the raw data stream processing. Certainly it would not be as easy to make these kinds of modifications as it would be in the first design (Figure 5.1), where we can easily add and remove elements from the data stream. However, this convenience comes at the cost of performance.

This simple example illustrates that although functionality is critically important to a system, it has little influence on its structure. Similarly, the way a system is structured does have a deep influence on the properties a system possesses. In this example, functional responsibilities are explicitly assigned to specific elements. The responsibility for satisfying systemic quality attribute properties is assigned to the partitioning. Assuming that the resulting implementations based on these designs function properly, it is impossible to say which of these designs are better unless we understand which quality attributes are most important. This illustrates why it is important to clearly establish the relative importance of the architectural drivers with the stakeholder community, especially if it is obvious that some of the architectural drivers may be in tension with the others. When we begin architectural decomposition, architects must first consider the technical and business constraints. Of the architectural drivers, these are the most inflexible and will have the most dramatic impact upon the structure of the system—these are the load-bearing walls that are in place before design begins. Next architects must focus the quality attributes to guide the decomposition and systemic design. Architects select structures to promote the more important quality attributes first, and analyze the systemic effects on other quality attribute responses to balance the overall design. Of course as we decompose, architects must keep functionality in mind (customers are reluctant to pay for systems that do not work). However, as important as functionality is to any system, it typically does not influence structure as deeply as constraints and quality attributes, as this small example illustrates.

Example: The SmartMarquee

The context and decomposition concepts explained thus far will be illustrated in greater depth using the SmartMarquee system introduced in Chapter 3. Because this system will be used to illustrate a number of key design concepts throughout this section, Table 5.1 provides a more detailed treatment of the architectural drivers to support the examples presented here.

In practice, a far more comprehensive list of architecture drivers should be developed that includes use cases to describe key functionality, business constraints, and quality attribute scenarios. For the sake of brevity, Table 5.1 provides enough description to illustrate the key principles of decomposition.

SmartMarquee Context

For the SmartMarquee, we begin decomposition by establishing system context. Again, the architect must keep straight in mind the perspective from which he or she is designing the system. The perspective that an architect takes when beginning decomposition may vary, and there is no fixed rule. Generally, quality attribute properties may force architects to consider a particular perspective initially because each supports the analysis of various quality attribute properties. If performance, runtime configurability, interoperability, and other similar qualities are important, then it may make sense to start with a runtime perspective. Other qualities, such as modifiability and maintainability, might argue for beginning with a static perspective. No matter what perspective the architect begins with in the context, the design will have to be addressed from all perspectives as more detailed decomposition proceeds. Because runtime configuration is an important

Table 5.1   SmartMarquee Architectural Drivers

General Functional Requirements

The SmartMarquee will display graphical advertisements using various types of advertisement panes. A pane is a rectangular display area on the SmartMarquee display. Configuring panes: For any kind of advertisement pane, the user will be able to define a rectangular section of the display screen by specifying the x, y coordinate of the upper-left-hand corner, the height, and width of the rectangle. This rectangular section will be the advertisement pane.

- The SmartMarquee will be configured remotely via a configuration tool:
- The SmartMarquee will accept connection requests from remote configuration tools.
- The SmartMarquee will load configuration files from remote configuration tools.
- Upon receipt of a new configuration file, the SmartMarquee will reconfigure the display system to reflect the new configuration.

The SmartMarquee will support the following advertisement panes:

- Static ads: End users will be able to specify a graphic file to be displayed in the static ad pane. At runtime, the static ad pane will load the graphic and it will remain until the configuration is changed.
- Paging ads: Paging ad panes are similar to static ad panes, except rather than a single graphic ad, a list of graphic ads will be displayed. Each ad in the list of graphical ads will be displayed for a period of time configured by the user. After the configured display time has elapsed, the next graphic ad in the list will be displayed and so on until the end of the list is reached. Once the last ad in the list has been displayed for the prescribed display time, the paging ad pane will cycle back to the beginning of the list and repeat the process starting with the first ad graphic.
- Scrolling banner ads: For the scrolling advertisement pane, the user will specify a list of graphical advertisements of any size in the format JPG or GIF. At runtime, the horizontal banner pane will scroll advertisements first to last in the list, from left to right across the screen. For vertical banner panes, advertisements will scroll from top to bottom. When an advertisement graphic scrolls off the screen, it will go back to end of the list for display. Users must be able to specify the rate of scroll.
- Video ads: For the video pane, the user will specify a set of video clips in the format of MOV, MPG, or AVI. At runtime, the video pane will play each video clip in turn and then loop back to the beginning of the list of clips.

For all advertisement panes, the SmartMarquee software must proportionally resize each advertisement graphic, video, or text to fit the banner pane for the device it is running on. The only limitation as to which combinations or number of individual ad panels the user places on the SmartMarquee display will be the display area of the SmartMarquee device.

Technical Constraints

- Use standard Intel-based PC as computer platform.
- Provide ability to update application configuration at runtime using USB, wireless, and dial-in capabilities.
- Support for sound and no-sound options.
- Support the use of a large, flat-panel display. Use Windows XP or compatible variant.
- Use Java platform for application software, to include J2SE, Java language, and Java Runtime Engine.

Quality Attribute Requirements	
Quality attribute: The advertisement display space must be easily configurable.	
Stimulus:	A new ad space configuration is ready for installation.

(continued)

Table 5.1   SmartMarquee Architectural Drivers (continued)

Source:	User responsible for configuring the SmartMarquee advertisement space.
Environment:	System is deployed and the configuration change is made at runtime.
Response:	The system configuration is changed from any existing configuration, or from having no configuration at all, to the new configuration.
Response measure:	The current configuration is stopped (if it is running), the new configuration is loaded, and begins running within 3 minutes.
Quality attribute: Allow new advertisement pane types to be added in the future.	
Stimulus:	A new or custom ad pane type is required.
Source:	Customer using the SmartMarquee system.
Environment:	Code/compile time changes: These changes would be made by SmartMarquee software developers.
Response:	The new advertisement pane is designed, developed, and deployed to the customer. The new pane type is installed remotely using the SmartMarquee configuration tool.
Response measure:	The current configuration is stopped (if it is running) on the deployed SmartMarquee, and the new pane type is installed remotely and is ready for advertisement configurations to use it within 15 minutes.

quality for SmartMarquee, we can begin with the dynamic perspective. Recall from the system requirements, a deployed SmartMarquee is a stand-alone device with no direct user interface. Deployed SmartMarquee devices are configured with a configuration tool per the architectural drivers. In the context diagram of Figure 5.3, both the SmartMarquee and the configuration tool are shown.

Note that each of these context diagrams could have been shown separately; certainly separate architectural and detailed designs for these elements will emerge as more detailed decomposition proceeds. Including both the SmartMarquee and the configuration tool in the same context drawing is a matter of the architect's judgment. There is no right answer other than to ensure that the resulting representations are not cluttered and clearly communicate the design. The choice to put both elements in a single context diagram is effective because it is not a cluttered representation. Clutter is the biggest enemy of descriptive design representations, and reducing representation clutter should be of paramount concern for architects as they document their design decisions. Most architects have a bad habit of putting too many things into a single representation—in doing so they often mix perspectives. Architects should try to layer their representations, adding detail and information as they decompose. This not only results in clearer representations, but also helps to guide decomposition and analysis from coarse-grained designs to finer-grained designs. If the SmartMarquee and configuration tool are to be developed by separate parties, it may be useful to establish separate context diagrams early to ensure a clear separation of concerns. This is an especially good idea if the parties are geographically separated from one another. The greater the physical separation, the clearer the contextual separation, and the more detailed the interfaces between the elements must be. Again, this reduces clutter and confusion for the separate parties responsible for each of these elements and helps to establish clear responsibilities.

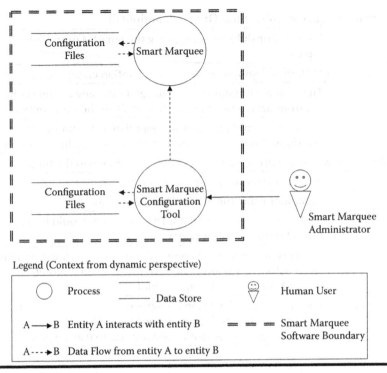

Figure 5.3 SmartMarquee system context from the dynamic perspective.

Figure 5.3 shows the SmartMarquee and configuration tool as processes. While only one process for each is shown at this level of decomposition, there will be more processes as we decompose each element further. There is a data flow relationship from the configuration tool to the Smart-Marquee that shows the configuration data moving from the configuration tool to the SmartMarquee. There are runtime data stores shown that are separately accessible by the SmartMarquee and configuration tool. A stakeholder is shown interacting with the configuration tool. Stakeholders will load graphical information and configure displays on a deployed SmartMarquee vis-à-vis the configuration tool. A boundary is drawn showing the SmartMarquee system context. One should note that this context is not cluttered, and the important relationships among the SmartMarquee, the configuration tool, and the external entities are clear. Overall, the context seems to aid in understanding, not detract. Checking perspective consistency, it should be obvious that all of the entities, elements, and relationships are visible from a dynamic perspective. Also note the use of a legend to describe each of the entities in the context diagram. The kind of notation that the architect uses should be clear to the reader and not open to interpretation, so a legend is a must. A nice habit for architects to adopt is to develop the legend first and refine it when writing down the design. For every new element and relationship architects draw, they should check the legend; if the element or relationship does not appear, they should add it to the legend or question what they had just written down. This is a design decision, so architects much be clear and explicit about it. Most often in practice a homegrown notation is used; however, architects should include a legend that clearly explains each of the entities and the relationships even if a standard notation is used.

In some cases, it may be necessary to create multiple context drawings from different perspectives to aid in understanding system boundaries, especially to meet the needs of different stakeholders. Figure 5.4 shows the SmartMarquee context from a physical perspective and how elements from the dynamic perspective map to physical system elements.

This physical perspective would be extremely useful for those engineers responsible for building and configuring the deployable SmartMarquee and configuration tool hardware, for establishing the network infrastructure requirements, and for understanding the deployment needs of the system. This drawing also tells software developers something about the hardware configuration that the SmartMarquee and configuration tool must execute upon. Again, these are typically technical constraints imposed upon the software design. In this context, drawing a clear separation of the SmartMarquee and configuration tool becomes necessary due to the different hardware platform each will be deployed upon. The SmartMarquee process and its data store are grouped and mapped to one computer; the configuration tool and its data store are grouped and mapped to another computer. In the physical perspective the connector between the SmartMarquee and configuration tool uses the TCP/IP protocol to communicate; however, the specific physical medium

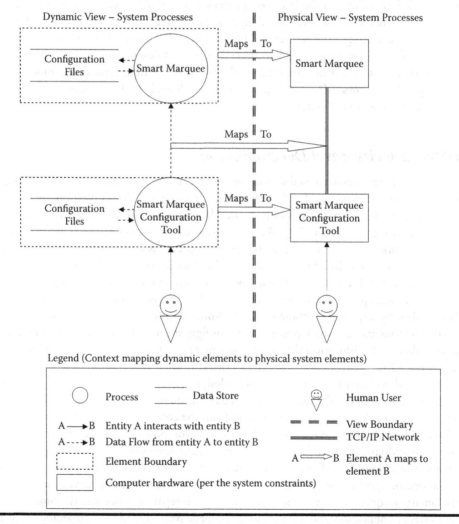

Figure 5.4   SmartMarquee system context from the physical perspective, showing how dynamic elements map to physical elements.

is left unspecified. This is done intentionally. If it is bound to a medium now, then it will be established forever—for better or worse. The choice was made here to defer binding this decision. The SmartMarquee and configuration tool must be able to use any kind of network medium—wired or wireless. The specific physical connectivity details will be established by downstream hardware designers; the only constraint imposed on this physical connection is that it can support the TCP/IP protocol. While the software is bound to a TCP/IP protocol, the specifics of configuration file structure and handshaking that must occur to transfer configurations will be decided later. However, if this system was to be developed with distributed teams, this protocol would have to be designed early and agreed to because both elements intimately depend upon it. This would become a contract between the parties developing the separate elements. The reader should note that this context is driven to some extent by the hardware constraints established in the architectural drivers.

In addition to the context drawings, the architect should provide a prose similar to the description provided here that explains the intent of the drawings—even if it seems obvious to the architect. Again, we do not want to leave any design decisions open to interpretation by the reader. Guidance for documenting architectures will be discussed in the next chapter; however, suffice it to say that establishing a consistent and accurate context and description is a critical first step in architectural design. It establishes the framework for all of the architectural decomposition and detailed design that follows. Mistakes and misunderstandings introduced here will have a long-lasting and deep impact to the system.

SmartMarquee First-Level Decomposition

Once the system context has been established, the architect can proceed with more detailed decomposition of the context elements. To illustrate the key concepts of decomposition and minimize the size of the example, we will focus only on the decomposition of the SmartMarquee process from the context diagram (Figure 5.3). We will begin decomposition of the system by continuing the decomposition that we started in the system context. Without violating constraints, the decomposition should be driven by the quality attribute scenarios. According to the architectural drivers listed in Table 5.1, one key quality attribute property that the system must possess is: "The advertisement display space must be easily configurable." This essential quality attribute requirement is described by a quality attribute scenario. Note the intertwining of quality attribute and functional requirements, namely, support remote configuration of the various advertisement pane descriptions. Again, this illustrates the point that a mere word, like *configurable*, simply does not mean anything. Quality attribute scenarios are critical to understanding the properties required of the system and essential for making the right design choices. Because we are supporting this loosely coupled notion of configurability, we will use this quality attribute scenario (Table 5.1) to guide the partition of the SmartMarquee process from the context diagram (Figure 5.3).

In this first-level decomposition, we continue with decomposition in the dynamic perspective. It is not a hard-and-fast rule that decomposition must continue in the dynamic perspective; it is a choice left to the architect for all the reasons stated earlier. Architects may decompose a system in detail from one perspective, or decompose the system from various perspectives simultaneously. Here the SmartMarquee process is decomposed into two separate processes, the SmartMarquee runtime (SMRT) application and a set of advertisement pane threads. As an architect we must explicitly assign the responsibilities to each of these elements of the design thus far. This must be done at each level of decomposition with care and discipline because the design only gets more complicated as we continue to decompose (which will be apparent as the example unfolds). The SMRT will interact with the configuration tool to upload configuration data. It is also responsible for starting the advertisement pane threads based upon the configuration file specifications received from the configuration tool. Note the specificity that is associated with the elements at this early stage. Too often in practice, architects will label a box as a "component," "module," or "element," but they never define what these structures really are. These are general terms that have no real meaning in the design space. A component can be a thread, a process, or even hardware in the vocabulary of different engineers. Modules are some kind of code structure, but what kind? Architects should be specific and remain consistent with perspective. If the architect is not specific, then it will be the implementer who defines the structure. These are simple disciplines in mindset that can make all the difference between clear, concise designs and muddy thinking and imprecise representations. This first-level decomposition shows a new element boundary that shows the connection with the configuration tool external to the element's context. Again, we use a legend to ensure that each element and relationship is clearly understood and consistent with respect to perspective.

SmartMarquee Assigning First-Level Responsibilities

It can be easier to see the responsibility of an element in a physical/mechanical device. Its separation from other elements and its contribution to overall function can even be obvious. However, this is not the case with software-intensive systems. After initial decomposition, the architect must explicitly assign responsibilities to the elements and partitioning. This is a commonly overlooked step in architectural design. In larger systems, it may be necessary to assign responsibility after the system context is established. This step was omitted in the SmartMarquee example for brevity, and this is a small system, but one could imagine an explicit assignment of responsibilities to the SmartMarquee process and the configuration tool. From the SmartMarquee context diagram in Figure 5.3 we explicitly assign responsibilities as follows:

■ The SmartMarquee process is responsible for accepting configuration data from the SmartMarquee configuration tool and configuring the display according to the configuration.
■ The SmartMarquee configuration tool provides applications that allow a system administrator to create SmartMarquee advertisement display configurations using existing graphics files and video clips and upload the configuration files to a deployed SmartMarquee device.

This may seem somewhat trivial, but if parts of the system will be developed by a highly distributed workforce, then it is prudent to explicitly assign responsibilities beginning with the context diagram. Complex systems that have context diagrams composed of many elements may be best served by having responsibilities explicitly assigned. If in doubt, err on the conservative side and write down the responsibilities beginning with the context.

Like perspective, assignment of responsibility starts with a disciplined mindset. Architects must cultivate the habit of specifically assigning responsibilities to elements and the partitioning as they design. Explicitly assigning responsibilities to the elements and relationships can help uncover errors in reasoning, ambiguous representations, and perspective inconsistencies. Design decomposition and assignment of responsibilities are shown here as separate steps because the written word necessitates it. These should be intertwined activities that architects do as they design, not something done as an afterthought only when forced to document the design. Every box or line drawn by the architect represents a series of design decisions. Every element selected is an assignment of functional responsibility, a line is a relationship between them, and the separation between them is a partitioning that promotes or inhibits the achievement of systemic quality attribute properties. These should be explicit regardless of the obviousness of the decision (and usually they are not obvious)—the architect's rationale must be captured. Table 5.2 is an example element responsibility table that lists the elements and their responsibilities for the first level of the SmartMarquee decomposition.

Table 5.3 lists the responsibilities of the relationships among the elements in the system this far. It is not necessary that separate tables be used for listing elements and relationship responsibilities. However, it is imperative that both are explicitly assigned and written in a clear, concise way. Assigning responsibilities this way can also help maintain traceability by mapping architecture drivers to responsibilities assigned to architectural elements, which can be further mapped to code. Explicit assignment of responsibilities can also help with estimation, project planning, test planning, and execution (examples of this will be demonstrated in Section 2 as the process of design is explored further). As the system changes and evolves, explicitly defined and documented responsibilities can provide insight into the cost and impact of change to the system. Finally, the rationale for this decomposition should also be explained. Again, there are many ways to capture this information—Table 5.4 is one simple way to document rationale.

Although prose may be sufficient in some cases, tables often work well, especially in larger systems, for concisely capturing and organizing responsibility information. What is definitely not sufficient is a picture of architectural structures alone. Although pictures may say a thousand words, the words they communicate to readers will be inconsistent and left to broad interpretation. Inconsistencies and ambiguities in the design will be resolved when the code is written and broad systemic properties will not be predictable. This is unacceptable when building complex software-intensive systems. In practice, design rationale is almost always left unstated. Again, it is usually through the partitioning that quality attribute requirements for a system are met.

Table 5.2   Element Responsibility Catalog for First-Level Decomposition

Associated Drawings: Figure 5.5	Perspective: Dynamic
Element	**Responsibilities**
SMRT	• This element is a thread or collection of threads. • Allow configuration tool to connect to SmartMarquee. • Coordinate configuration file downloads from the configuration tool to the SmartMarquee. • Instantiate, configure, and coordinate the operation of the advertisement panes.
Advertisement panes	• This element is a thread. • Size pane proportionally to fit any size SmartMarquee display. • Read advertisement graphics, text, or video clips and display content on the SmartMarquee display. • Resize graphics, text, or video clips proportionally to best fit the configured pane. • This element represents one of many.

Table 5.3   Relationship Responsibility Catalog for First-Level Decomposition

Associated Drawings: Figure 5.5	Perspective: Dynamic
Relationship	Responsibility
A ─────► B	• This relationship will be used to connect a SmartMarquee configuration tool to a SmartMarquee deployed in the field. This symbol indicates that element A connects to element B over a network connection. The connector envisioned for SmartMarquee will be a TCP/IP, socket-oriented protocol for transferring the configuration file from the SmartMarquee configuration tool to a deployed SmartMarquee. The physical network is not specified or implied.
A ----------► B	• This relationship indicates that element A instantiates or creates element B at runtime. After B is instantiated, this dependency is dissolved.

Table 5.4   First Level of SmartMarquee Decomposition Rationale

Associated Drawings: Figure 5.5 Associated Responsibilities: Tables 5.2 and 5.3	Perspective: Dynamic
This decomposition focuses only on the SmartMarquee process and omits a decomposition of the SmartMarquee configuration tool. This system was decomposed into a SmartMarquee runtime (SMRT) software and a set of advertisement panes. This partitioning was chosen to maintain separation of concerns between configuring the system, downloading files, and managing the displays (starting and stopping), and the details of displaying advertisement graphics. This eases runtime reconfiguration and allows for the easy addition of new kinds of advertisement panes.	

SmartMarquee Second- and Third-Level Decomposition

The first level of decomposition (Figure 5.5) is somewhat trivial. However, the rationale for this decomposition is important in supporting the reconfiguration quality attribute. This decomposition was selected to separate remote configuration concerns from those of advertisement display. The SMRT element is responsible for remote communication concerns, while pane elements display advertisement data. But this decomposition is naive and more work is necessary to complete the design. For example, as currently designed, in addition to remote communication with the SmartMarquee configuration tool, the SMRT element is also responsible for configuring, instantiating, and managing the advertisement pane threads. If one thread really was assigned all this responsibility, this would result in a monolithic structure. This approach would undermine the ability to satisfy the quality attribute requirement in Table 5.1: "Allow new advertisement pane types to be added in the future." The design is also silent regarding how advertisement configuration data is stored and shared once it is uploaded from the SmartMarquee configuration tool. It

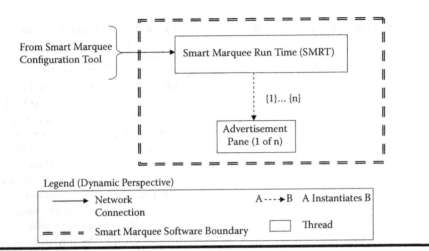

Figure 5.5 First level of SmartMarquee decomposition.

is never perfectly clear as to when the architect is done with design, but these are clear indications that more architectural design work is needed to answer these questions.

As the architect thinks about decomposing the system further, he or she may find it useful to focus on decomposing individual elements further. With this in mind, the focus shifts to the SMRT element. Figure 5.6 shows a second level of decomposition where only the SMRT element is further decomposed.

In this level 2 decomposition more detail has been added to the architecture design to address the concerns expressed with the SMRT element of Figure 5.5. The monolithic nature of the SMRT has been eliminated in favor of a decomposition that further decomposes the long list of responsibilities assigned SMRT. A new element boundary has been drawn that is actually the boundary of the SMRT element of Figure 5.5; however, this drawing drills down and shows the detailed decomposition of the SMRT. The advertisement pane elements are out of context in this drawing. It is important to note that it is not necessary; in fact, it is undesirable, and even impossible in many cases, to decompose the entire system at every level of decomposition. Many systems are too big to decompose in their entirety at every level of decomposition, and sometimes different parts of the system are decomposed by different teams of architects. Here the SMRT has been decomposed into three elements: SmartMarquee server process (SMSP), SmartMarquee display engine (SMDE), and a data store. Two new connectors have been introduced here as well. One connector shows data flow to and from the data store, and another connector shows that events are cast from the SMSP to the SMDE, and also from the SMDE to the advertisement panes. Note that the data store details have not been specified other than to indicate that this is local permanent (secondary) storage that serves as a repository for configuration information. Note that the design of the data store element could be deferred to the downstream detailed designers—this is the choice of the architect based upon his or her judgment and the larger organizational context in which the system is being developed. However, there is an inherit risk in this choice that the architect should be aware of. If the read/write protocol, file, and data structures are left unspecified by architects when this design is assigned to detailed designers, they will have to coordinate their efforts to ensure that the SMDE can read what the SMSP writes. Figure 5.6 shows that the SMSP is now responsible for accepting connections from the SmartMarquee configuration tool. Assume that there is a configuration loaded and running on the deployed SmartMarquee and a system administrator wants to configure the system. Upon accepting a connection request from

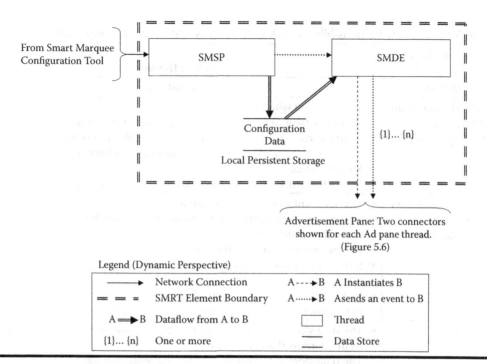

From Smart Marquee
Configuration Tool

SMSP

SMDE

Configuration
Data

{1}... {n}

Local Persistent Storage

Advertisement Pane: Two connectors
shown for each Ad pane thread.
(Figure 5.6)

Legend (Dynamic Perspective)

⟶	Network Connection	A ---▶ B	A Instantiates B
= = =	SMRT Element Boundary	A ······▶ B	A sends an event to B
A ⟹ B	Dataflow from A to B	▢	Thread
{1}... {n}	One or more	▬	Data Store

Figure 5.6   Second level of decomposition—focusing on the decomposition of the SmartMarquee RunTime (SMRT) software.

a SmartMarquee configuration tool the SMSP reads configuration data from the SmartMarquee configuration tool and writes the data to local persistent storage. Once all of the configuration information is stored in local persistent storage, the SMSP notifies the SMDE by way of an event that a new configuration is available. The SMDE then signals all of the currently running advertisement panes; upon receipt of the event, the advertisement panes terminate. The SMDE reads the new configuration file and instantiates the advertisement panes defined in the configuration. The element responsibilities assigned to the SMRT of Figure 5.5 are further refined and assigned to the SMSP, SMDE, and data store and are listed explicitly in Table 5.5, the element responsibility catalog for level 2 decomposition.

Again, the new connectors and their responsibilities are listed in Table 5.6. The rationale for this decomposition is to further divide the responsibilities assigned the SMRT to elements that will promote concurrent communications, pane management, and display of advertisement media. A simple table entry is used to record this information, as shown in Table 5.7. Finally, we can turn our attention to the structure of the advertisement panes. One possible decomposition is shown in Figure 5.7. The element catalog for this decomposition is listed in Table 5.8.

Again, the focus here is on the decomposition of the advertisement pane elements to address their design concerns in isolation from the SMRT (now decomposed further in Figure 5.5). This helps to eliminate confusion and allows the architect to focus his or her attention on a specific concern (such as a quality attribute requirement), further decompose an element, or otherwise focus on a specific part of the system. An element boundary is drawn around each of the advertisement panes showing their relationships to the other elements of the system. In particular, the instantiation and event relationships to the SMDE element are shown. These relationships have been established in the former decomposition, so we are bound to adhere to them here as well.

Table 5.5   Element Responsibility Catalog for the Second-Level Decomposition

Associated Drawings: Figure 5.6	Perspective: Dynamic
Element	**Responsibilities**
SMCS(derived from SMRT; level 1 decomposition)	• This element will be a single thread. • Allow configuration tool to connect to SmartMarquee. • Read the configuration file from the SmartMarquee configuration tool and store the configuration data to a local file on the SmartMarquee. • Notify the SMDE that there is a new configuration available.
SMDE(derived from SMRT; level 1 decomposition)	• This element will be a single thread. • Receive the new configuration notification from the SMCS. • Parse the configuration file. • Ensure that the configuration information is valid. • Stop any ad panes running in preparation for starting a new configuration. • Instantiate, size, and provide advertisement graphic file location information for the advertisement pane threads.
Data store	• The data store is a file or collection of files stored on a medium local to the deployed SmartMarquee. • The data store is the repository for the SmartMarquee configuration.

Table 5.6   Relationship Responsibility Catalog for Second-Level Decomposition

Associated Drawings: Figure 5.6	Perspective: Dynamic
Relationship	**Responsibility**
A ──────▶ B	• This relationship indicates that data moves from A to B. In the SmartMarquee context, element A is passive and B is responsible for opening, reading, and closing the connection. • This relationship will be used to connect a SMCS to the data store element and will allow the SMCS to write configuration data to the data store.
A ─────────▶ B	• This symbol indicates that element A sends an event to B. This connector will be used between the SMCS (A) and the SMDE (B). • In the SmartMarquee context, this connector is used so that the SMCS can notify the SMDE that a new configuration has been downloaded and is ready for the SMDE to begin the reconfiguration process. • This connector is also used between the SMDE and each instance of an advertisement pane to notify these elements that they should terminate their operation.

Table 5.7 Second Level of SmartMarquee Decomposition Rationale

Associated Drawings: Figure 5.6 Associated Responsibilities: Tables 5.5 and 5.6	Perspective: Dynamic
The rationale for this decomposition is to further divide the responsibilities assigned the SMRT to elements into two threats to separate the communications and advertisement pane management that will promote concurrent communications, pane management, and display of advertisement media. The SMSS is responsible for communicating with the SmartMarquee configuration tool and transferring and storing the configuration locally. The SMDE is responsible for pane instantiation. The configuration information for the panes will be stored in a common data store. The SMSS will be only one writer to this data store (with respect to the configuration data); the SMDE will read the configuration information, thus eliminating concurrent data access concerns.	

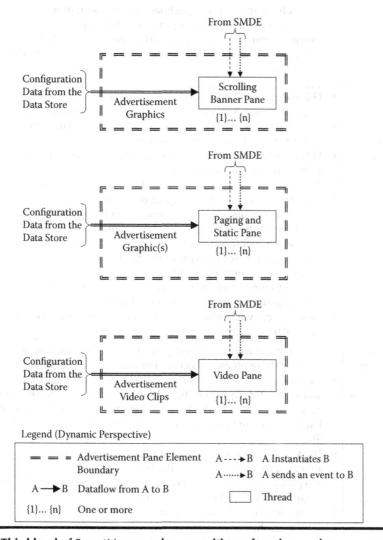

Figure 5.7 Third level of SmartMarquee decomposition—focusing on the same structures.

Table 5.8   Element Responsibility Catalog for the Third-Level Decomposition

Associated Drawings: Figure 5.7	Perspective: Dynamic
Element	**Responsibilities**
Static/paging ad pane (derived from SMRT; level 1 decomposition)	• This element will be a single process; however, there may be zero or many of these elements present in any given configuration. • This element is instantiated by the SMDE according to the specification in the SmartMarquee configuration file. • This element will read from the specified file on disk the list of pathnames of the graphics files. • The list of pathnames must have at least one pathname to a graphic file. A list of one pathname will define this element as a static ad pane. A list of two or more pathnames will define this element as a paging ad pane. • For each file in the list of pathnames, the element will read the associated graphics file, properly size the graphic, and display it for the specified period of time specified by the configuration. • This element will terminate its operation upon event notification from the SMDE.
Scrolling banner ad pane (derived from SMRT; level 1 decomposition)	• This element will be a single process; however, there may be zero or many of these elements present in any given configuration. • This element is instantiated by the SMDE according to the specification in the SmartMarquee configuration file. • This element will read from the specified file on disk the list of pathnames of the graphics files. • The list of pathnames must have at least one pathname to a graphic file. • Each graphic file is sized proportionally to best fit within the banner and will be displayed in the banner until the banner is full, at which point the banner will scroll ads. Horizontal ads will scroll left to right; vertical ads will scroll top to bottom. • Once an ad has scrolled off of the display area, it will wrap around. In a horizontal scrolling pane, ads will scroll off of the right and wrap around to the left of the display. Vertical ads will scroll off the bottom and wrap around to the top of the display. • This element will terminate its operation upon event notification from the SMDE.
Video ad pane (derived from SMRT; level 1 decomposition)	• This element will be a single process; however, there may be zero or many of these elements present in any given configuration. • This element is instantiated by the SMDE according to the specification in the SmartMarquee configuration file.This element will read from the specified file on disk the list of pathnames of the video clip files. • The list of pathnames must have at least one pathname to a video clip file. • The video player will be sized by this element to fit entirely within the allocated Video Pane space. If a list of video clips is provided, each clip will play in turn and the element will return to the top of the list and begin playing the clips again in turn. • If one video clip is provided, the element will loop the clip continuously. • This element will terminate its operation upon event notification from the SMDE.

Architects can add detail to designs in hierarchical decomposition, but not invalidate previous levels of decomposition. Each level of decomposition should flow consistently from the former. If the architect discovers that he or she cannot adhere to the constraints imposed by a decision made in higher-level decomposition, he or she must return to and address the problem in a former level of decomposition. In addition to these relationships, a read-only relationship is established with the data store for access to the advertisement information required to configure the pane and display the advertisement graphics. Fundamentally every advertisement pane is identical, which supports the quality attribute requirement that eases the runtime introduction of new pane types. Although there seems to be little impact to the runtime structures, it is impossible to determine what the impact would be upon the static structures. To examine how "modifiable" the system really is, we would have to shift to a static perspective. There are no new connectors or element types added here. Although another element and relationship responsibility catalog is not shown for this drawing, this information and the specific responsibilities of the elements and relationships should be precisely described by the architect. This information and the decomposition rationale have been omitted here for the sake of brevity.

Switching Perspective

So far we have been concerned with decomposition of the system in terms of the dynamic perspective. Now we will turn our attention to the static structures of the system. As stated earlier, it is impossible to say how modifiable this system is with respect to the quality attribute requirement "Allow new advertisement pane types to be added in the future." Although we know that there is little impact to runtime structures by adding new pane threads, we know nothing about the impact to static structures because we have been focusing on the design of the system from the dynamic perspective. To address this modifiability scenario, it would be helpful to look at the

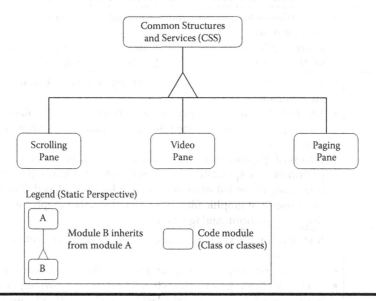

Figure 5.8   SmartMarquee class structure decomposition—switching to a static perspective and focusing on the structure of the display panes.

static structures of the advertisement panes. Figure 5.8 shows a decomposition of the advertisement pane from a static perspective.

This could be thought of as a first-level decomposition of the system in the static perspective, and essentially is a first look at how the code for part of the system might look. This is a simple and straightforward decomposition of the system to separate those concerns that are common to all advertisement pane types and those that are unique. The rationale for partitioning the advertisement pane this way is totally focused upon easing the development and integration of new advertisement panes. From the dynamic perspective we can analyze the impact a new pane might have on runtime structure, or how a new pane might be installed at runtime, but from the static perspective we address the cost of changing the system. The responsibilities for the elements and relationships are listed in Tables 5.9 and 5.10, respectively.

This decomposition isolates commonly used services and data structures in the CSS element, while the specific details of implementing a pane are left to the scrolling, video, and paging pane elements. Essentially this approach could allow for the formation of development templates for advertisement panes. This would significantly ease the development of advertisement panes, ensure their commonality, and eliminate the impact that new pane types might have on the overall architectural structure. Note that the use of the term *class* here should not be taken to imply a partition-

Table 5.9   Element Responsibility Catalog for the First-Level Static Decomposition

Associated Drawings: Figure 5.8	Perspective: Static
Element	**Responsibilities**
CSS	• Common methods for reading configuration and graphics data • Common methods for proportionally resizing graphics and video clips • Common structures and methods for creating and sizing panes
Scrolling pane	• Instantiating the scrolling pane according to the configuration specification • Reading advertisement graphics files, resizing, and scrolling them vertically or horizontally according to the configuration specification
Paging pane	• Instantiating the paging pane according to the configuration specification • Reading advertisement graphics files, resizing, and displaying them in the paging pane and for the period specified in the configuration specification • If a list of graphics is provided, each will be displayed in turn for a period of time specified by the configuration, returning to the beginning of the list when the last graphic is displayed. If only one advertisement graphic file is provided, then that graphic will be displayed without paging (statically).
Video pane	• Instantiating the video pane according to the configuration specification • Reading video clips, resizing, and playing them within the video pane • If a list of clips is provided, each will be played, returning to the beginning of the list when the last clip is played. If only one clip is provided, then it will be played continuously (looped).

Table 5.10 Relationship Responsibility Catalog for the Fourth-Level Decomposition

Associated Drawings: Figure 5.8	Perspective: Static
Relationship	**Responsibility**
Module B inherits from module A	• This is traditional object oriented inheritance. • Only single inheritance will permitted (consistent with the Java language constraint)

ing of the system where each class shown in Figure 5.8 maps to a single class in the strictest sense. Here a class could map to a collection of classes; often the term *package* is used to describe collections of classes. Another argument could be made that selecting class and inheritance mechanisms is too much detail for architectural design and may be a premature decision. The counterargument is that a key technical constraint is that the SmartMarquee must use Java as an implementation language; therefore, these structures are not out of order. For example, it may be inappropriate to bind architectural design decisions to object-oriented mechanisms if the implementation language is constrained to a structured language such as C. In this case it could be difficult for the implementation structures to match the design structures. Obviously this is very coarse-grained decomposition and more design (levels of decomposition) from the static perspective might be necessary to complete the design as was demonstrated with the dynamic perspective. At each level of decomposition, regardless of perspective, the architect must look for evidence that he or she is converging on a completed design. The key questions that architects should ask themselves to determine whether the architecture is complete include:

■ Are all of the responsibilities articulated in architecture drivers and any derived responsibilities that need to be addressed by the architecture assigned to elements or partitioning?

■ Is the downstream designer or implementer sufficiently constrained by the design? Can he or she use it to do detailed design or implementation so his or her design or implementation matches the architecture structurally?

■ Is the architecture sufficiently documented (documentation will be covered in more detail in later sections) so that the design is communicated in a clear, concise, and unambiguous way and designers and implementers can understand it?

The system may require more detailed decomposition in some perspectives and less in others. Note that relatively little decomposition was necessary for the SmartMarquee in the physical perspective due to its simplicity, and the technical platform constraints imposed dictate the partitioning.

What Happens and When Does It Happen?

At this point it may be apparent to the reader that the temporal relationship of what is happening, and when it is happening in the system as it executes, is not clear from these drawings. This is because representations of the dynamic perspective showing elements and relationships can only do one of the following:

1. Show the elements and relationships of the system at a single instant in time
2. Show all the elements and relationships that are possible at any time during execution

In practice, architects often create dynamic perspective representations that show all the elements and relationships that are possible during runtime execution. Although this can shed light on runtime structures, these views are usually insufficient for analyzing runtime properties of the system as it operates over time. However, these representations are often misleading as well because it is usually the case that the runtime structure morphs as the system executes. One representation technique is to pick an instant in execution time, called a mode such as start-up, shutdown, quiescence, peak load, and so forth, and provide drawings that show the elements and relationships that are visible at these instants in time. This is modal representation, where the various modes of systemic operation are represented by separate dynamic drawings. Modal representations are necessarily dynamic in terms of perspective. If using the modal representation technique, the architect should first identify the possible modes and then clearly document them as responsibilities. An excellent way to document modes is via functional use cases or quality attribute scenarios. After identifying and documenting a mode, the architect can create supporting representations to show the system structures at that point in time. This can greatly aid in designing and analyzing dynamic systemic structures and behaviors. Once the relevant modes are identified and documented, the architect should use these artifacts to analyze transitions between modes. These are usually points of interest in design. For example, assume that an architect identifies a start-up mode and a steady-state mode; these are described in documentation and representations are created showing the elements and relations visible during these modes of operation. The architect should then use the artifacts that document and represent the design of the system under these modal conditions to consider how the system transitions from the start-up mode to the steady-state mode. Modal transitions are usually tricky at best and are often a source of problems. As such, modes are worthy of deep analysis. Clearly representing these various modes of operation can help in the design and analysis of a software-intensive system. Other techniques that can be used are more traditional state transition diagrams, sequence diagrams, control flowcharts, and even prose descriptions. However, although these approaches can aid in analysis and provide insight, they do not depict dynamic structures and how the dynamic structures morph throughout execution. Often modal representation is used in conjunction with state transition diagrams, sequence diagrams, control flow, and prose—this is often the most effective approach analyzing the dynamic behavior of the system. These concepts are best illustrated by example.

In Figure 5.9, there is a modal representation of the SmartMarquee systems using four different dynamic representations. These series of representations illustrate the idle system after start-up loading an existing configuration, stopping the current configuration, and loading a new configuration from the SmartMarquee configuration tool.

Again, pictures cannot stand alone, so a narrative is provided to explain this modal behavior, and transition between modes:

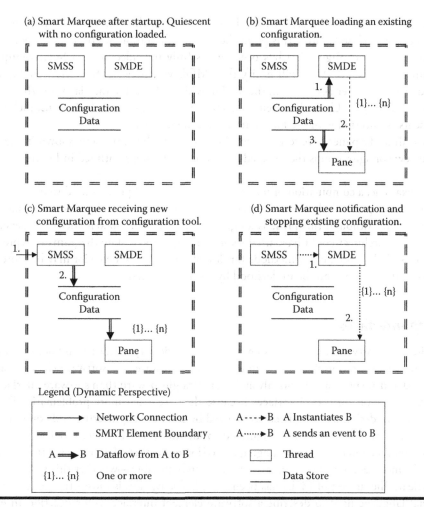

Figure 5.9   Modal representation of the SmartMarquee—showing how a configuration is loaded.

■ Figure 5.9a shows the deployed SmartMarquee after power-on and boot-up. The system automatically loads the SMSS and SMDE processes, which blank the display.

■ After power-on and boot-up the SMDE will search and load the current configuration as shown in Figure 5.9b. The process starts with the SMDE, which reads and parses the configuration file (step 1) from the local data store. For each pane specified by the configuration, the SMDE will instantiate the appropriate pane, passing along the pathname to the configuration information needed by the pane (step 2) during instantiation. After instantiation, the pane will read configuration information from the local data store.

■ At this point the system is in a steady display state running the current configuration. Figure 5.9c illustrates the uploading of a new configuration file from a SmartMarquee configuration tool (note this figure omits the connection process). Once the connection is established between the SMSS and the SmartMarquee configuration tool, the configuration data is sent to the SMSS from the configuration tool (step 1). As the data arrives, it is written to the local data store by the SMSS (step 2). At the conclusion of the data transmission, the network connection is closed, and at this point the new configuration has been uploaded.

■ Once the new configuration has been successfully uploaded from a SmartMarquee configuration tool, the SMSS will notify the SMDE via an event that a new configuration is ready (step 1). After notification, the SMDE will notify each pane via events that they must terminate (step 2). Upon the receipt of a termination event from the SMDE, each pane will close its connection with the local data store and terminate.

■ Once all of the panes have terminated, the system will be in the state shown in Figure 5.9a. The new configuration is then loaded by repeating the steps outlined in Figure 5.9b.

In this example, a combination of modal representation and prose is used to describe how the design addresses a particularly important set of architectural drivers related to the reconfigurability of the system. Although this prose is long, it is simple for any stakeholder to understand and descriptive. The architect could have used sequence diagrams or state diagrams to represent this behavior as well. Although other methods for describing dynamic behavior may be more precise, the resulting artifacts may not be understood by all stakeholders.

Defining Interfaces

The architect of a software-intensive system may have to identify hardware and network interfaces in addition to software interfaces. The interfaces for hardware and software elements are often standardized and are usually (but not always) more straightforward than software interfaces—our focus here will be on software interfaces because they are often more problematic. The importance of interface design has long been recognized by software engineering and computer science communities. Early research efforts attempted to identify formal interface definition languages (IDLs) and module interconnection languages (MILs) to precisely define the relationships among elements. In most research these terms are used interchangeably—whether this was the intent or not is unclear. The success of MILs has been mixed. Today, IDL is most often used in reference to a special language used to describe a software element interface. IDLs describe an element's interface in a programming language-neutral way. This allows two elements to communicate that do not share a common language. IDLs have enjoyed great success, and the IDL concept is used in Remote Procedure Call (RPC), Remote Method Invocation (RMI), CORBA, SOAP, .NET, and many other similar technologies. However, IDLs are typically used at a much finer granularity of design than is often required by architects. Various architectural description languages (ADLs) have been developed to describe architectures, but most do not address interfaces of the elements the ADL describes, or treat the interfaces in a very general way. General, industrial-strength ADLs, IDLs, or MILs for architectural design have not been widely embraced by the architectural design community at the writing of this text. However, the interfaces of the architectural elements define the scaffolding of the architecture. Without interfaces it is impossible to adhere to the element partitioning defined by the design, it is difficult to allocate elements to teams for construction, and it is hard to determine if the implementation adheres to the architecture. An interface is simply a boundary where two elements meet, interact, or pass information to one another. The characteristics of an interface depend upon the perspective taken. Runtime interfaces are formed by what is written in the code; that is, the interfaces of dynamic elements are related to, and defined by, the interfaces of the static elements. Sometimes this is simple and straightforward, as it is in an event sender/recipient relationship between two elements at runtime, or it can be more convoluted, as it might be if two elements communicate in an indirect way via shared memory. From a dynamic perspective, interfaces support data flow, events, message passing, remote method invocation, and so forth. From a static perspective, interfaces typically expose those services that are provided by an element. All elements have some kind of interface unless it is a completely self-contained monolithic structure. Even a monolithic embedded control program interacts with external sensors and displays—these are interfaces. Interfaces from the dynamic and static perspectives are related. More specifically, dynamic interfaces are realized by static structures, but they are not necessarily one-to-one. An interface in the static perspective may not be an interface visible at runtime. Imagine a simple system such as that shown in Figure 5.10a.

This is a static representation showing four elements. Elements A and B are related to one another vis-à-vis a uses relationship, as are elements C and D. Elements A and B are a functional group that is named "client," whereas elements C and D are another functional group named "server." Although it is temping to draw a line between the client and server functional groups, this relationship does not exist statically—and the dynamic relationships are not yet apparent in the static view. Clearly this is an important relationship to establish and reason about, especially if code modifiability of the client and server is a concern. However, when these modules are compiled, the interfaces and associated uses relation is no longer visible from the dynamic perspective and becomes some other runtime relationship (call-return, events, and so forth). When A and B from the static perspective are compiled and executed, the dynamic structures are realized. The

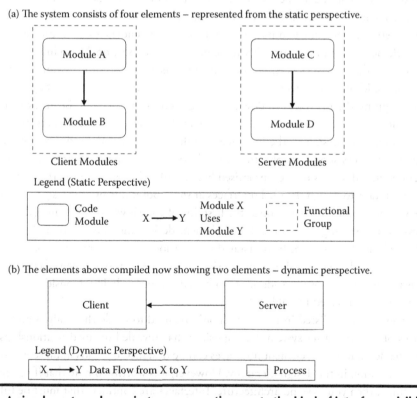

Figure 5.10 A simple system shown in two perspectives; note the kind of interfaces visible in each perspective. (a) The system consists of four elements, represented from the static perspective. (b) The system showing two elements, from the dynamic perspective.

dynamic structures become the client process in the dynamic perspective, and when C and D from the static perspective are compiled they become the server process in the dynamic perspective. In the dynamic perspective other interfaces and relationships become apparent at execution, such as data flow between the client and server, as shown in Figure 5.10b. Note that the relationships in the dynamic perspective depend upon the decisions made in the static perspective, but they are clearly not one-to-one relationships. Some views have very little pertinent interface information to document, and it may suffice to simply show the relationship. Figure 5.10 clearly illustrates this point. In Figure 5.10a it is essential that the interfaces define the exact services B provides to A and D provides to C so that the system will come together during construction and integration of these elements. However, in the dynamic perspective of Figure 5.10b the exact client and server interfaces are of far less importance; however, the relationship between the client and server elements (data flow) is critically important to understanding the runtime structures.

Interfaces can be two-way affairs. Most often architects only focus on what services a particular element provides, but elements also make assumptions about the context within which they exist. Elements expect that certain resources are available, that other elements behave in certain ways, that other elements provided resources in a timely way, and that certain data is available and correct. In this respect, interfaces are a formal definition of what an element provides other elements and what it requires from other elements in order to work. These provides and requires assumptions should be identified as the responsibilities are allocated to the elements during decomposition. Functional use cases can be exercised using a structured walk-through technique with the design to better understand assumptions, interactions, dependencies, and information exchanged between elements (techniques for this will be introduced in Section 2). Architects must design the interfaces, but the interfaces need not be as detailed as a method or function signature, although that would be ideal. If architects choose not to define detailed interfaces, they have deferred the task of designing the interfaces to downstream designers. This should be an explicit rather than implicit choice. If design of the interfaces is deferred to downstream designers, then this must be their first job. Once designed, the interfaces should be placed under strict configuration control. Changing interfaces should involve the oversight of a configuration control board to ensure that the architectural design is not compromised because of a change to an interface. If an architect or organization fails to design detailed interfaces at some point during the design process, the architecture will be compromised as soon as the first line of code is written. Defining detailed interfaces is necessary as a staging point for detailed element design and construction. This importance of well-defined interfaces cannot be overstated in situations where teams are geographically distributed. The design of interfaces should be considered a refinement step taken after much decomposition has taken place as a way to add more information to the design. Considerations for interface development are provided in Table 5.11.

The considerations listed in this table should be used to guide the analysis and refinement of interfaces of elements after system decomposition has revealed detailed relationships among elements. The detail to which element interfaces can be designed depends upon scope, scale, and the architect's position in the design hierarchy. However, it is worthy to note that if you have no interfaces defined, then you have no architecture. Interfaces are contracts that must be fulfilled by the builders of the elements. Interfaces in a very concrete way define the architecture. If interfaces are designed in a detailed way, they can be implemented first. These interfaces can be compiled and used to validate the overall syntactic structure of the architecture. This becomes the system scaf-

Table 5.11 Interface Design Considerations

Element name	Provide the name of the element or any suitable reference identification used.
Perspective	Dynamic, static, or physical.
Interface semantics	If possible, provide the exact interface signature and parameters that will be required and utilized by the interface. Provide example usages of the interface under various relevant conditions if possible, illustrating the interface semantics.
Provides assumptions	List what data and services this element provides to other elements. Detail the environmental conditions necessary for providing these data and services (if applicable).
Requires assumptions	List what data and services this element requires to provide the data and services required of this element. List the elements that this element is dependent upon. List the specifics of the data and services if available.
Preconditions	List any preconditions that must exist before a service can be invoked of this element.
Postconditions	List any postconditions that will result from utilizing a particular service provided by this element.
Security concerns	Describe any security issues, concerns, or mechanisms related to the interface and the services/data provided by it. Describe any undesirable uses of this interface that may compromise systemic security.
Availability concerns	Describe any availability issues or concerns related to the interface and the services/data provided by it. Describe any undesirable uses of this interface that may compromise the availability of the system.
Safety concerns	Describe any safety issues or concerns related to the interface and the services/data provided by it. Describe any undesirable uses of this interface that may compromise systemic safety.
Performance concerns	Describe any performance issues or concerns related to the interface and the services/data provided by it. Describe any undesirable uses of this interface that may compromise systemic performance.
Error mechanisms	Describe any error detection and handling mechanisms that are relevant to this interface. Especially describe their relationship to safety, security, and availability if relevant.
System resources	List any system resources that must be available and accessible to utilize the services and data provided by the interface. Examples include memory, storage, peripherals, sensors, processors, networks, and so forth.
Protocols	Describe any protocol and communication semantics or commercial standards that are used by this element and exposed through this interface.
Data items	List any messages, events, data structures, and so forth that are utilized by this element interface. Identify any local, global, and shared data. Describe other dependencies for any global and shared data.
Limitations	Describe any inherent restrictions or limitations to the services and data exposed vis-à-vis this interface.

folding on which all the other elements will rest. Elements can be stubbed* and used to introduce synthetic loads on the general system framework vis-à-vis the interfaces that define the architecture. This allows architects to test and validate various systemic quality attribute responses before production elements are built and integrated into the system.

Summary

This chapter starts with an explanation of what it is that architects do and their role in an organization. In addition to describing what architects do, a description of when architectural design occurs within the overall development process was provided. Finally, guidance on how to architect was introduced. It cannot be overstated that this is not intended to be a definitive statement on how to architect. Architecture design is guided by the intuition and judgment of the architect. The purpose here is to provide principles and guidance for how to think about decomposing a system, what to consider when decomposing the system, and how to capture key design choices and rationale. To best summarize this part of the chapter, it may help to see a road map of what happens during the architectural design activity in a short itemized list. Each of these topics has been covered in gory detail in the previous sections:

1. Create the system context: Select the initial perspective and stay cognizant of and consistent with the perspective, even as you switch perspectives throughout design. The context drawing and prose describe what is within the prevue of the architecture design space and what is external.
2. Start the initial decomposition: Using the context as a starting position, start decomposing the system using the architectural drivers. The most influential architectural drivers will be the technical and business constraints. They are in place before the first design decision is made—they are the load-bearing walls that may be impossible to move or can only be moved with great difficulty and cost. As decomposition begins, ensure that you are consistent with respect to perspective. Create legends before drawings and document elements, relationships, and rationale as you decompose. Assign responsibilities from the architectural drivers in an explicit way. Typically functionality is assigned to elements, while quality attributes are satisfied by the partitioning.
3. Iteratively refine the design: Further decompose each element as necessary, staying consistent with perspective. Switch perspectives to ensure a holistic design of the system is created, describing the system from all three perspectives: static, dynamic, and physical. Remember that each perspective may have many representations describing systemic structures. Continue to document elements, relationships, and rationale, and assign responsibilities as the system is further decomposed. When architectural decomposition is done depends upon the scope and the architect's position in the design hierarchy. In general, architects must know who they are constraining with their design and address their needs. The architecture must sufficiently describe what it is that the downstream designer and implementer must design or build.
4. Design the interfaces: As the decomposition of the system subsides, design the interfaces of the systems. The interfaces that are visible depend upon the perspective of the observers.

---

* A stub is a bit of code used as a surrogate for production-grade functionality. A stub may simulate the behavior of production code or be a temporary substitute for yet-to-be-developed code used for the purposes of debugging, testing, or validation.

While there is a clear relationship between static interfaces and dynamic interfaces, the relationship is rarely one-to-one and can be complex. Interfaces from some perspectives require little information to describe them, while interfaces from other perspectives for the same system are complex and require a great deal of information to adequately describe them.

Chapter 6

Documenting the Architectural Design

"What have I gained?" "Experience," said Holmes, laughing. "Indirectly it may be of value, you know; you have only to put it into words to gain the reputation of being excellent company for the remainder of your existence."

Sir Arthur Conan Doyle (1859–1930)

If you have made it this far, you have probably somewhat bought into the idea that software architecture is an important subdiscipline within the software engineering discipline. So far, key concepts and techniques have been introduced to enable architects to:

- Gather, organize, and analyze architectural drivers
- Understand the relationship between structure and systemic properties
- Decompose design into elements based upon the architectural drivers

This is the essence of architectural design. However, these things do not matter if the architect fails to adequately write down the architectural design. It would be prudent to again remind the reader that architectural representations are not the architecture of a system. Representations are a reflection of the actual structures or the structures you intend to build. Real software-intensive systems are often more complex than the best documentation is able to convey.

Architectural documentation is not the architecture any more than a written prescription from a medical doctor is the cure for a patient suffering from a bout of influenza. First the doctor must diagnose the patient correctly. If he or she gets this wrong, then the disease cannot be properly treated. Once diagnosed, the doctor must select the correct medication regiment. Finally, the patient must faithfully follow the directions for taking the medicine. Only when all these conditions are successfully met will the patient likely be cured of his or her ailment. If the diagnosis was wrong, then the prescribed medicine will not help. If the wrong medicine was prescribed, then following the directions on the prescription will not cure the ailment—in fact, it may kill the patient. If the right medicine was selected, but instructions for taking the medicine were not followed, then the patient will not be healed.

Architectural documentation is as important to building the right system as a prescription is in the medical healing process. First, architects must identify and organize the architectural drivers (diagnosis of the problem). They must then select the right structures to satisfy the architectural drivers (prescribing the right medication). The downstream designers and implementers must adhere to the architectural design to reap the benefits (following the prescription). If the architectural drivers are not identified, there is little chance that the architect will design the right ensemble of structures to satisfy the need. If the architectural design is not adhered to, then the promises made vis-à-vis the architect may or may not be fulfilled.

Again, using the medical analogy, there is also a third situation that is related to the subject of this chapter. If the prescription is unreadable or incorrectly documented, this could be misinterpreted by the pharmacist. Disaster could be the result for the patient. Although the disease may have been correctly diagnosed by the medical doctor, the incorrect medications, dosages, or regiment could be administered to the patient. Fortunately, this does not happen too often in the medical and pharmacological professions. However, this is one of the most common problems that occur when building software-intensive systems. The architectural design prescription is incorrectly documented, cannot be understood, or is misinterpreted by downstream designers and implementers. Just as in the medical analogy, the result can be disastrous when designing and building software-intensive systems. Well-documented architectural designs can help provide intellectual control over the complexities associated with construction of complex software-intensive systems. Although architectural documentation is the subject of entire textbooks, there is no one settled, standard way to document the architecture design of software-intensive systems. In the limited space of this chapter we will discuss a number of key issues that the architect must keep in mind as he or she writes down the architectural design.

Architectural Documentation Stakeholders

The essence of architectural documentation is that it is a means of communicating system design decisions and relevant information to stakeholders that need to know about them. It is impossible to communicate design decisions if they have not been made in a deliberate way or if the architect's thinking about the design decisions is not clear. Massive documents that attempt to capture all architecture design documentation for all stakeholders are large and unwieldy, not used, and quickly become obsolete. However, it is impossible to know what information to convey if we do not know what stakeholders we are communicating the design to and what their needs are. This is much easier said than done when creating architectural documentation for complex systems with diverse communities of stakeholders. Imagine an entertainer that walks before an audience that is expecting drama, stand-up comedy, and a demonstration of athletic prowess. This is a tall order for a single entertainer to fulfill, and creating architectural documentation often places similar demands on the architect. Identifying and interacting with the community of stakeholders for any given system can be a bewildering experience. Consider the needs of the following stakeholders:

Detailed Element Designers

This is one of the more obvious stakeholders for architectural documentation. Detailed designers are those engineers who design the elements (or parts) of the architectural design, to include code, special peripheral hardware, the infrastructure (networks, routers), and so forth. Detailed designers must be able to follow the architectural prescription so they can design the detailed artifacts from which the elements can be built. Sometimes detailed designers are also the builders of the architectural elements. This close coupling of designers and builders is somewhat unique in the construction of software-intensive systems. In fact, this is the norm rather than the exception. In the building construction industries, architects and structural design engineers do not pour cement or lay bricks—they design. This is not a statement based in snobbery—it is a statement of fact and highlights the high level of maturity achieved in these engineering disciplines. The designers in the building industries must create very detailed plans because they will not implement the designs. It is easy for designers of software-intensive systems to cheat on the documentation because they often implement their own designs. The assumption made by many designers is that because they will implement the design, they can keep the design details in their head and not waste time writing them down.

Detailed designers need to have a very clear vision of the system structures and will need to understand how their designs fit into the larger system. A properly documented architecture will clearly define the boundaries of the elements that downstream designers must design. Element boundaries, and the architecture itself, are defined by the element interfaces. If the detailed designers must design the interfaces, they must clearly understand the interface specification so they can design the detailed signatures for downstream builders/implementers. As engineers create the detailed element designs, they may uncover problems with various design choices made by the architect. These problems may ultimately impact systemic properties. When these problems are found, the architectural design should be revisited to study any impact that it might have on systemic properties and repair the design. Without a properly documented architecture, these kinds of problems cannot be found until after implementation begins or the system is deployed.

Builders/Implementers

Like detailed element designers, builders are another obvious stakeholder for architectural documentation. Builders are those engineers who implement the code, build special peripheral hardware that the software must interact with, or construct the system infrastructure. Builders and detailed designers are often one and the same. If builders are not the detailed designers, they must be able to read, understand, and follow the detailed designs. To prevent implementers from violating the architecture, information-hiding principles can be used. Detailed design specifications for the architectural elements can be assigned to builders and implementers and the larger architecture hidden from them. This can prevent them from introducing dependencies or otherwise changing the gross partitioning of the architecture. This can be challenging as well and requires a great deal of discipline. Because there is a large degree of separation between the implementation and the original architectural design, the transformation from architecture to detailed design becomes even more crucial. Conformance of the implementation to the architectural design is more difficult to ensure with each level of separation from architectural design levels, to detailed design levels, to implementation. Documentation plays a key role in communicating the design at each level of design granularity, and a key documentation challenge is to ensure consistency at each level of abstraction. If consistency is not maintained in this continuum, then the implementation will not match the architectural design, and the properties, functionality, and adherence to constraints that the architect promised may not be delivered in the implemented system. As construction commences, builders also may uncover problems with the architecture that result in structural changes to the architectural design. Builders like detailed designers must have access to the architects to resolve these kinds of problems. Without architectural design documentation, it is impossible to check implementation structures to ensure they match the detailed designs, and that detailed designs match the architecture designs.

Managers

In practice, managers are not often considered stakeholders for the architectural documentation because of the technical nature of architectural design; however, they should be. Managerial stakeholders are part of the organization building the system and the organization (or organizations) buying and using the product. The architectural documentation can help managers understand what will be built, the system scope, and how long it will take to design and construct the elements, and identify the likely technical challenges that may arise during design and development. Using this information, they can create organizational development plans and estimates, analyze risks, weigh technical trade-offs against costs and potential benefits, and allocate human and monetary resources to the project on a more informed basis. One of the most common mistakes that rookie architects make is that when they are asked to present the architecture to managing stakeholders, they tuck all their detailed class or structure diagrams under their arm and run down the hallway to the designated meeting room. In a desperate attempt to impress the VIPs in the room, the rookie architect will baffle managers with implementation details, technical jargon, and technical notation. This confuses managers and can frustrate the audience. The ensuing barrage of questions hurled at the poor architect can be intimidating to the point that he or she may consider a career change. Unfortunately, neither the manager nor the architect understands what the problem is; they both leave the meeting thinking that the other party simply does not "get it." Managers need information to help them determine how long it will take to build the product, how much it will cost, and what are the potential problems. For this reason, architects need to prepare architectural documentation that explains the technical details of the architecture in these terms.

Internal Procurement

If the system that the architect is designing uses commercial software elements, then it is essential that those responsible for buying the elements understand what the requirements are for the commercial elements and what they might require from the architecture. Often the architect is the same person who specifies the commercial software elements; in other cases they are different people or groups. Internal procurement specialists will shop around for the best fit and buy suitable software elements. However, if they do not have a prescription for the architect, or the prescription is wrong, or they cannot understand the prescription, it is unlikely that they will buy the right element.

Users

Not all users sit in front of terminals. However, these users are the easiest to satisfy with architectural documentation because they only indirectly care about architecture, so their need for architecture design insight is nearly zero. The system must function as specified, according to the quality attribute properties specified. However, end users continuously judge architecture vicariously by using the system and living with it day after day as they perform their job. Other users may have more technical insight into the system and may need more robust architectural documentation. For example, consider the user who is responsible for configuring end user accounts and security, backing up data, enabling or disabling user features, and so forth. These administrators are users, but they have very different needs than those of the end user, who generally cares very little about architectural design. These and other users can be very technically savvy and may even need some insight into the design. Imagine that the product will be used by another organization as part of a product it creates. In this case the user may be another architect, designer, or even coder. These users will need far more insight into the underlying design than an end user or administrator. A cardinal rule in requirements engineering is to identify the actual users of a system and their requirements. Never accept surrogates in place of real users unless an extraordinary situation forces otherwise. This is also a good rule for architects trying to identify the documentation needs of the users, and they should also keep in mind that not all users are the same.

Customers

Customers are not necessarily users of the system. For example, imagine that a wife sends her husband to the store for a chocolate cake mix. The husband, being sensitive to cost issues, buys the cheapest cake mix he can find. When he brings home the cheap cake mix, the husband is surprised to discover his wife's displeasure at his choice and he is unable to comprehend why she does not share his concern for cost. After all, other than flavor and color, how different can cake mixes be? Scolding him, she reminds him that she always uses the high-quality cake mix and chides him that it is worth the extra cost. She claims that the more expensive cake mix tastes better, has better texture, and even looks better! The cheap cake mix simply will not do. She then orders him back to the store to exchange the cheap cake mix for the expensive, higher-quality mix. In this example, the wife is the user and the husband is the customer. Assumptions were made by each party about the other party, based on their own experiences with the product. The customer assumed that the user cared about minimizing cost and that all cake features were the same. The user assumed that the customer knew that higher-quality cake mixes were important for the work she had to do and worth any extra costs. Customers buy systems but may not understand what is needed by the broader organization—this happens constantly in requirements gathering, analysis, and specification. Customers often assume they know what is best and guess at the rest. The architectural documentation can educate both parties and help clarify assumptions made by all stakeholders. The architect should strive to create architectural documentation with enough technical details to explain the underlying properties a system has for these kinds of stakeholders. Incorrect assumptions may deeply impact the implementation and result in irreversible consequences to the product and the entire stakeholder community. After all, in the example above one has to wonder what the husband's reaction would be if he knew the cake was for him. Would he have been satisfied with the qualities of the end product made with the cheap cake mix? A clear understanding of the expectations up front may have affected the choice the husband made at the grocery store. This kind of understanding can only be achieved by clearly identifying the stakeholders.

Maintainers

In practice, maintenance is generalized to mean helping users, fixing defects, or making significant systemic enhancements. Maintainers can be part of the organization that built the system originally, part of the organization that bought the system, a part of a third party responsible for system maintenance, or some combination of these. In most cases, maintainers spend more time with a system over its entire life cycle than the original designers and implementers do, and often understand its underlying structures better than the original designers (including the architect). Estimates place the average postdeployment maintenance costs for larger software-intensive systems between 60 and 80 percent of the total life cycle costs (Boehm, 1981)—other estimates are considerably higher (Coleman et al., 1995). Maintainers must have a deep understanding of the architectural structures, and there must be a change process in place that allows a system design to evolve in a structured way, not just focusing on changing code. They will be on the front line of changing the system and its architectural structures over the lifetime of a system. For these reasons they will need a detailed understanding of the architectural design. Change is a natural part of a successful system's life cycle, and the architecture documentation can be used to maintain and evolve the system in a predictable, deliberate, and orderly way. Maintainers not only need to change, fix, and upgrade the system elements, but also need to make sure the design documentation matches the as-built structures as well. Hopefully when a system is built, the design artifacts match the as-built structures. Over time the design documentation will erode as maintainers change the system structures if the design documentation is not maintained with the same zeal that real structures are changed. In practice, there always seems to be time to change code, but there is never enough time to update the documentation. As the design documentation drifts and no longer matches the as-built structures, the documentation will be used less and less. Eventually the as-built structures will only exist in code, computers, networks, and other system elements. At this point, the architecture is lost. The architecture can be recovered in some cases by studying code and rediscovering and documenting the as-built structures. Changes made after the architecture is lost will essentially be made blindly without understanding of systemic impact.

Installers

Some software-intensive systems or products must be installed by trained installers. Often deploying these systems is a complex undertaking requiring teams of technicians to assemble, configure, and install the system at the deployment location (or locations). Depending upon nature and scope of the system, installers may need very detailed architectural design insight or only a cursory understanding of the system design. The background of installers can vary as much as that of users. Some installers are like end users and have little need or ability to understand architectural structures, whereas others are highly trained and specialized experts. The architect documentation should address the installer's unique needs because the success of the system ultimately depends upon it.

Testers/Evaluators

If you plan on evaluating the architecture design, it will have to be thoroughly documented. Evaluators can use the quality attribute scenarios and use cases to perform structured inspections of the architecture design to ensure it meets the architectural drivers. The architectural documentation plays a vital role in architectural evaluation. Once implemented, the architecture documentation can be used by testers to measure test coverage by identifying elements to test and designing methods to test them. Depending upon the design, it might be possible to test various elements and relationships in isolation. Testers can use the architectural design to identify parts of the system for isolated unit (element) testing for a variety of purposes, such as supporting concurrent tests and development, limits and load testing, performance testing, and so forth.

Marketing/Sales

This is a stakeholder that few organizations realize have a stake in the software architecture design. Too often marketers and salespersons run out into the world and make promises that have no basis in what is possible back in the lab (and sometimes violate fundamental properties of mathematics, physics, or chemistry). Often marketing and sales professionals overestimate the flexibility of software. Unfortunately, architects and their teams of designers and implementers are left to fulfill the promises after the deal is closed. To prevent these situations, marketing and sales professionals must be made aware of what is and is not architecturally possible. They must also understand flexibility in realistic terms within the system and business context, as well as the costs associated with flexibility. A coarse-grained understanding of a system's key architectural structures and features is essential for marketing and sales stakeholders.

Not all organizations have all these stakeholders, and some organizations may have more stakeholders than those listed here. The above is only meant to be a general listing of potential architectural design stakeholders that should be considered by the architect. In small organizations some or all of these roles may be shared by a few people. This eases the documentation chore, but does not excuse the organization from thoroughly documenting the software architecture. Writing down the architecture enables analysis of the design—the very act of writing down the architecture design results in some analysis. Taking shortcuts with documentation can lead to mismatches between the design and implementation structures, undiscovered problems, interface mismatches, and many others. Identifying stakeholders is critically important when systems are designed and built by distributed teams and organizations. The greater the separation, the more critical the role documentation plays as a glue that is essential for knitting together the efforts of the distributed teams. Architecture design is about decomposing a larger thing into elements and integrating the elements together; essentially, we follow the age-old way that humans solve problems: divide and conquer. However, once we divide and conquer, it is essential that parties responsible for their constituent parts are able to tend to their own business of building the parts. Developing complex software-intensive systems with distributed teams is highly dependent upon partitioning a system in such a way as to minimize element dependencies—and therefore dependencies between the individuals or teams building the elements. To successfully accomplish this separation of concerns, elements must be documented in a self-contained way so that each individual or team knows what they are responsible for designing and building without having to comprehend the whole system. Certainly having to build a system with a distributed organization is a business constraint that should be a prime consideration for the architect as he or she decomposes the system. Understanding each participant's roles and responsibility in the design and construction of the system is critical for creating good self-contained chunks of documentation. Again, documentation's role in realizing the architecture of a system in the implementation cannot be underestimated, whether the system scope is small, big, or very big.

When to Document the Architecture

A very simple and useful device is to have a memorandum-book, so small that it can be easily carried in the pocket, to be used instead of your mind to keep note of any errand or any appointment that you may have. The Standard Diary, less than four inches long and less than two and a half inches wide, is one of the best for this purpose. In fact, such diaries as these, in their wide range of information, would seem to be all that one needs in practical life.

Anna C. Brackett (1836–1911)

Raise your hand if you like to write documentation. When to write design information down is a fundamental question that plagues architects, and it is a task that they generally dread and defer to the latest possible date. Software architecture documentation is often viewed as a one-time, monolithic task that must be done after the design work to satisfy a process geek somewhere in the organization. Generally architects equate time spent documenting their designs to time spent having to stoke the fires of hell. If architecture documentation is done as a monolithic task after design, then it will be arduous. However, good design and good documentation go hand in hand. One of the implied messages of Chapter 5 was that you should write down structures when deciding upon them, and record the rationale, right then and there, when the analysis and decisions are made. The heart and soul of documenting structures was discussed in Chapter 5; this chapter is more about the mechanics of documenting design and organizing the design document. Ideally, there should be a continuous ebb and flow between the design and documentation activities. If the architect waits to record this information until all of design is over, he or she will forget the details, the analysis, the trade-offs, and the rationale for the decisions made. Further, there will be a significant delay between when design is done and implementation can begin. What often happens in these situations is that detailed design or implementation ensues before the architectural design is written down. At this point, creating accurate design documentation is impossible. Architecture documentation should be grown with the architecture as it emerges from the fires of the design process. It is very difficult to know when architecture design is complete if it is not recorded as it is created. As the quote above suggests, a mere notebook could be the most valuable tool that an architect (indeed, any engineer) can carry with him or her. There was a time when there was no greater feeling as an engineer who had a brand new mechanical pencil in hand, a blank sheet of paper in front of him or her, and a problem to solve. The idea of learning how to render mechanical drawings by hand is all but a lost art. Once a fundamental skill taught to all engineers, rendering mechanical drawings has gone the way of the dodo bird, having been replaced by computer-aided drafting (CAD) tools. However, the engineering notebook is probably the most valuable tool that an architect of software-intensive systems carries with him or her in daily work. Continuously documenting the design is a habit that an aspiring architect would do well to adopt. One way to help develop this habit is to have an engineering notebook designed and structured to facilitate documenting architecture designs and decisions as they are made. The engineering notebook should not be the architectural documentation, but it will serve as the grist for what will become the architectural documentation. This is a place for recording information that is in a state of flux: to document thought experiments and analysis, record rationale as decisions are made, write down ad hoc notes and drawings, and so forth as the architectural design unfolds. The engineering notebook is the repository for all of the essential information that will make up the architectural design documentation. Creating the fit-and-finished final document is much easier if the engineering notebook is used faithfully by the architect. Periodically, as information and decisions crystallize, the architect should transfer information from the engineering notebook to the final document (or documents). In addition to plenty of ruled engineering paper for making notes and drawing ad hoc pictures to explore design ideas, the engineering notebook should also include templates to help architects capture information in a standard way. Figure 6.1 is an example of such a template. This is an architecture design drawing template that can be used to document structures consistent with the description given in Chapter 5.

A template like this can help architects organize their designs and remember to continuously consider perspective, include legends with their drawings, think about levels of decomposition, and maintain versioning information as they "rough out" the architecture design. The purpose of this template is not to use it electronically, but rather to use it with a nice sharp engineering pencil. Keep copies handy within the engineering notebook to quickly capture designs in a clear and consistent way to ease the documentation chore later. In the center of the template is a large ruled area for drawing the architectural structures. At the top of the right column is a place to enter the perspective: dynamic, static, physical, or mixed. If a mixed perspective is selected, a description should be provided to clarify the perspective. Below the perspective box is an area for giving the legend for the drawing. Again, it is advisable to draw the legend first. Every time the architect draws a line, box, circle, or any other shape, he or she should check to make sure it is in the legend. If not, then another element or relationship has just been added—this is a clue for the architect

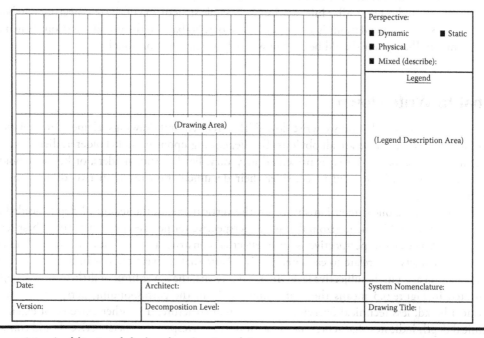

Figure 6.1   Architectural design drawing template.

to examine his or her decision. Is a new element or relationship really needed? Does the element or relationship already exist in another form? Is the new element or relationship consistent with respect to perspective? Across the bottom of the template, from left to right, are cells for entering the date and version of the drawing. The date is certainly applicable; because this is an idea notebook and not fit and finished documentation, versioning may not be necessary. In the next cells there is a place to name the architect and the level of decomposition. The decomposition level is important to include when there are multiple, related levels of architectural decomposition. The architect should develop a nomenclature to convey decomposition level that is meaningful and understandable to him or her. This may include systems, subsystems, elements, and so forth. In the bottom right of the template is a cell for listing the name of the system, element, subsystem, and so forth in addition to a cell for providing a title for the drawing. In addition to this template, the engineering notebook should also have blank tables such as those presented in Chapter 5 for creating element and responsibility catalogs and recording rationale (see Tables 5.5 to 5.7). These tables coupled with the templates described here provide a simple and powerful tool to design the architecture and capture the essential information throughout the design process. The architect should arrange this information in a ringed binder to suit his or her particular work style and habits. One binder per project—otherwise the binder gets cluttered. A recommended arrangement is to have a section of the notebook dedicated to recording design structures. To do this, consider placing the structure drawing template first (Figure 6.1), then an element responsibility table (e.g., Table 5.5), followed by a relationship responsibility table (e.g., Table 5.6), rationale for the design decisions (e.g., Table 5.7), and last, a section for interface definitions (Table 5.11). This pattern can be repeated, creating a section of the notebook where the architect can record design structure concisely and consistently as the ideas arise and decisions are bound. Other templates, such as those describing the architecture drivers, can be useful because they keep the key system requirements in front of the architect at all times. Other handy references can be included, such as unit conversions, formulas, rules of thumb, and an architect's journal of daily activities related to the system, project, and other similar information. A possible structuring of the engineering notebook based on these recommendations is shown in Figure 6.2. So back to the initial question: When do we document? The answer should be easy now: Early, often, and continually.

What to Write Down

The next question is: What do we write down? The architectural drawings, element and relationship catalogs, and rationale are all obvious. But depending upon the stakeholder audience we are targeting, the level of detail that is presented may vary. For key stakeholders, or key stakeholder communities, it can be helpful to consider their documentation needs in two dimensions, as shown in Figure 6.3.

Here we can see one dimension shown on the vertical axis as the technical depth needed by the stakeholders, and in the horizontal axis the perspective (or perspectives) that would best serve their needs. Once again, perspective is an intellectual construct that may lead to multiple documentation artifacts that relate to each perspective. Note that the vertical axis indicates the depth of information at a purely subjective level. In general terms, the lower limit of little technical depth illustrated in Figure 6.3 means the representations from the corresponding perspective should provide a broad, less technical overview of the system structure. The other extreme of extensive technical depth indicates that representations from the corresponding perspective should contain sufficient technical detail for engineers to design or implement system elements. Figure 6.3 is not

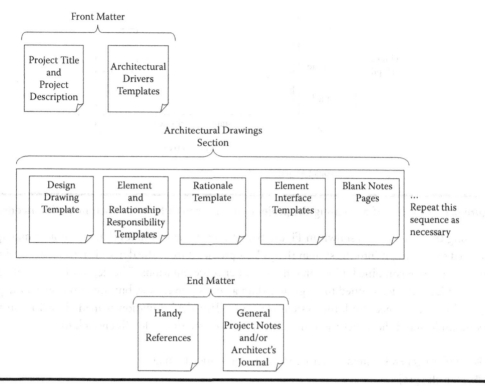

Figure 6.2   Engineering notebook organization.

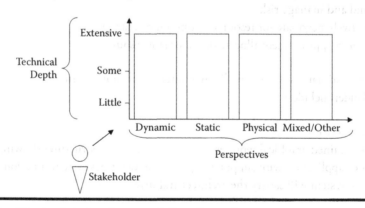

Figure 6.3   Architectural design documentation dimensions.

intended to be a precise tool for an architect to use straightaway. It is a way to think about and estimate what a particular stakeholder's architectural documentation needs are, help plan what will be written, and decide when it must be written. Using this as a guide, documentation artifacts can be planned, created, and packaged as a documentation suite addressing the needs of particular stakeholders or stakeholder communities, rather than a monolithic document that serves no stakeholder. As an example, let us consider a specific stakeholder. In Figure 6.4 the estimated documentation needs are shown for a project manager whose general responsibilities are to plan, budget, track, and direct the overall project development.

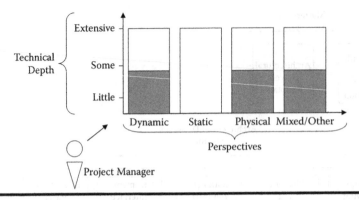

Figure 6.4   Example of estimating the project director's architectural documentation needs.

Using this approach as shown in Figure 6.4, the architect estimates that the project manager will need some insight into the system that is best provided from the dynamic perspective and the static perspective combined with some mixed/other representations. The depth of technical content is subjectively determined to be greater than a cursory overview, but not at the level of depth required by an engineer building system elements. This determination is made based upon the need to understand the structure of the system and key technical details enough to:

- Explain general system structure to peers and senior management
- Plan the project
- Track the efforts of engineers
- Understand and manage risk
- More effectively negotiate for resources from senior management
- Efficiently and appropriately allocate development resources

Based on this estimate, some of the likely content that might fulfill the need of the project manager stakeholder includes:

Dynamic perspective:
- Coarse-grained graphical representations of the runtime structures showing the key processes or application with supporting prose that describes system function, emphasizing how the system will satisfy the architectural drivers

Physical:
- Coarse-grained representations of the physical system infrastructure to illustrating placement and scope of key system infrastructure elements (networks, sensors, workstations, and so forth)

Mixed/other:
- Representations showing the mapping of elements from the dynamic to physical elements (computers), to teams responsible for implementation—can be done graphically, with tables, or with prose
- Descriptions of the key architectural drivers and a summary of how they are satisfied by various architectural decisions (perhaps using representations from the dynamic and physical perspectives to illustrate and explaining key design decisions)

This information would obviously be required as soon as possible so that the project manager could put plans in place. As projects evolve, the level of technical depth required by stakeholders from the architectural documentation may vary over time. In addition, information about the architecture will change over time as well. For example, information regarding the architectural structures will be sketchy early in the development life cycle, and therefore the information in the documentation that the project manager receives will likely change. As the architectural design matures, the project manager's documentation suite will have to be updated with new information because it might impact his or her planning and resource allocation. More depth of information may be required by the project manager as the design develops and problems are identified to help him or her understand and allocate resources and manage and mitigate risks. So the diagram of Figure 6.4 may change as the project and design unfold. Keeping this picture in mind can help the architect proactively plan for evolving stakeholder documentation needs to determine what design information is needed, when it is needed, and by what particular stakeholder.

Rather than recreate design artifacts, or create special design artifacts for a particular or emerging stakeholder, architects can plan to reuse artifacts. One strategy to do this is to think about architectural documentation as a set of horizontal rather than vertical artifacts. This eliminates duplication of documents, reducing the amount of writing and easing the maintenance of the architecture design documentation. These approaches are shown in Figure 6.5.

The vertical model is shown in Figure 6.5a, where the architect creates each document as a custom artifact for a single stakeholder or stakeholder group. A similar approach is proposed by Clements et al. (2003), although this approach depends upon the use of complex sets of view types to create documentation packages, rather than focusing on perspective and documenting the architecture throughout the design process. Although the vertical model shown here is greatly simplified, the successful application of this approach depends upon early planning and the disciplined continuous documentation of architectural design information. The use of an engineering notebook will help greatly in the adoption of a horizontal approach. In the horizontal approach, the architect (or the architecture team) creates each document in relative isolation. Reuse between documents is ad hoc, cut and paste. Formats may vary and changes of any kind (e.g., designs, architectural drivers, stakeholders) may impact any or all of these documents. In this case, the affected documents must be identified, the impact determined, and the location of the changes found, before the document can be updated to reflect reality. Duplicated information across documents is common, and keeping the information consistent as the designs evolve is nearly impossible. Most organizations today approach document production in this way. Is it any wonder why design documentation quickly gets out of step with the actual implementation and never really reflects reality? Adapting a horizontal approach can reduce the number of design artifacts that have to be produced, minimizing duplication of information. This can reduce the amount of time it takes for initial document production and ease the maintenance chore. A horizontal approach is shown in Figure 6.5b, where the architect (or architectural team) creates a stable of smaller fine-grained artifacts that follow a shared standard. Based upon the specific stakeholder needs, custom documentation suites can be assembled. The only new writing that may have to take place is any kind of "glue" that might be required to knit together the artifacts that comprise the suite. This reduces the amount of writing required and can contribute to a standard look and feel in the design documentation. Consistency is promoted in the horizontal approach because a common stable of artifacts are used to create the documentation suites. Document maintenance is eased because changes can be made to the artifacts and sent as updates to documentation suites in the field. A horizontal approach requires planning and discipline in creating architectural design artifacts. Again, identifying specific stakeholders or stakeholder communities and their particular architectural documentation needs cannot be overemphasized and is critical to knowing what to write down and when it is needed.

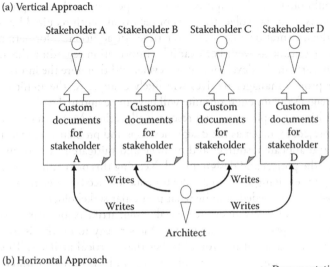

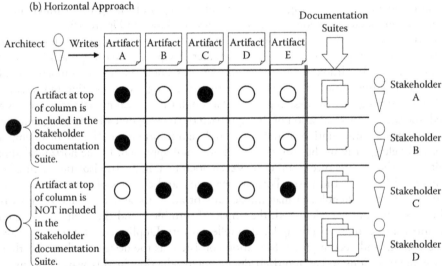

Figure 6.5   Vertical versus horizontal document production.

Documentation Tools and UML

At the writing of this text, the tools available for documenting the designs of software-intensive systems are abysmal in terms of choice and capability. The software tool business is a tough one to enter. The up-front development costs are high, and there is usually a great deal of inertia in the marketplace that a new tool must overcome. It is difficult for organizations to justify the costs of adopting new tools. For organizations adopting tools of any kind, there is the initial cost of buying the product, and continuing costs for licensing, support, maintenance/upgrades, and training for those engineers using the tool. Of course, there will be the indirect costs due to lost productivity as engineers learn how to use the tool on that first and even second project. Organizations with investments in legacy systems and tools are often reluctant to transition to new tools because of all of these costs. When adopting new tools or even upgrading existing tools, organizations are often forced to sustain and use multiple toolsets for an extended transition time—this is not a palatable choice in most cases. For these reasons, many would-be tool producers and consumers of tools are gun-shy of the tool market and tools in general.

Today the Unified Modeling Language (UML) in many ways has become the standard medium for documenting designs in the software engineering community, for better or worse. The popularity of object-oriented languages and standardized object-oriented design notations has provided an opportunity for object-oriented tools to capitalize in the marketplace. For the most part, UML provides a graphical notation; it remains, however, to provide a robust suite of tools for analysis, consistency checking, evaluation, or a means of automatically connecting the information expressed in UML with the code of the system or the larger architectural design constructs (Clements and Shaw, 2003). A variety of tools are available for designing software based on standardized UML notation. Many of these tools are very good at addressing detailed, object-oriented software design concerns. Some of these tools also have analysis tools, automatic code generation (for some application domains), and other handy features. The success of UML in supporting a broad range of detailed software design modeling cannot be disputed. However, UML was not designed to be used by architects for systemic design—it was developed to be used to document object-oriented software designs. However, engineers often use UML to document systemic designs and frequently lament that UML does not have a vocabulary that is well suited to documenting the designs of software-intensive systems. Attempts to adapt UML semantics to support software-intensive system designs have yielded mixed results in practice, and are obviously more effective in some domains than in others. UML is good for what it was created to do—capture detailed object-oriented software designs. However, the reader should realize that UML is not the end-all-be-all word on design documentation and has significant limitations in many situations. This is not intended to besmirch the good name of UML and its creators, or to discourage its use. Architects designing larger systemic structures often need more than UML can deliver. The idea of this critique is to make architects a bit smarter about using UML so they can use it more effectively. Some key issues of using UML to document systemic design follow:

■ UML is predominantly a design notation. It is not a formal notation with arithmetic rigor, syntax checking, and so forth—especially the way it is used 99.99 percent of the time in practice. As a design notation, designers can and frequently do misuse it. UML was created to document the detailed designs of object-oriented software. However, today engineers try to use UML to document system designs. In this respect, UML falls short because it does not capture nonsoftware structures very well. Users often contort the notation to do things that UML was never intended to do.

■ UML allows designers to create ambiguous designs, and Figure 6.6 is one classic example. In architectural design it is common to aggregate related structures, as is shown here, into a larger one, identifying common interfaces, exposing selected services and data, and so forth. This is applying information hiding to architectural structures and systemic design. However, the aggregation of classes and the uses relationship, as shown in packages FOO and BAR, really means very little. It could actually mean that every class in package BAR is related to every class in package FOO, but it is impossible to tell from this representation. Nothing is said about how the classes within each of these packages are related to one another. This makes some analysis difficult or impossible. For example, what effect will changes to these packages or the classes within them have systemically? It is impossible to know exactly what kinds of dependencies implementers will introduce when they try to implement this design.

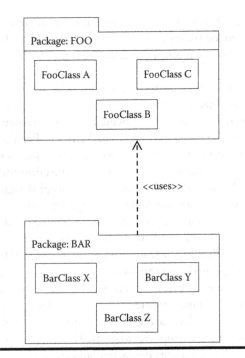

Figure 6.6   Example of confusing UML.

If modifiability is important, then this diagram will not support that analysis. UML modelers are often ambiguous about what things like packages mean in a design representation. There is an assumption that because package (or any other UML notation) is a UML construct, the reader automatically knows what it is. In this respect UML can promote a false sense of security. Furthermore, designers are often unclear about what they really mean in these kinds of drawings. Sometimes the packages are containers for source code; other times they are processes or threads. In some cases the perspectives are mixed in more insidious ways, where the designer indicates that the package itself is a runtime structure, then indicates that the boxes inside the package are classes (or vice versa)! Often designers do not know what the packages or the things inside represent. This reflects imprecise muddy thinking and poor design—not a problem with UML. UML is not bad, but designers do bad things with UML. Designers need to realize that designs rendered in UML do not magically mean something because they use symbols in the UML vocabulary. For example, one could string together valid English words like "Grass cross you real then under flavor give." Each word is a valid word in the English vocabulary, but semantically this sentence is nonsense—it means nothing. If architects choose to use UML, they must understand that they are still responsible for creating meaningful and communicative design representations. UML does not guarantee meaning by any virtue of its own, and in fact it leaves designers lots of rope to hang themselves with.

■ Architectural designs rendered in UML notation alone are not expressive enough for downstream designers, implementers, and other similar construction-oriented stakeholders. UML drawings still require the use of legends to explain the contextual meaning of lines, boxes, and so forth. Prose is still required with UML drawings to explain the rationale behind design decisions and to describe the behavior of the system. A common mistake made today by designers is to hand over UML drawings without legends or prose to downstream implementers and expect them to understand the design intent of the architect. This is a misuse of any notation, but it is especially common when UML is used. There is no formal guidance provided by UML regarding what to write down other than what is provided by the vocabulary of the notation. Engineers learn the notation of UML and how to create pictures of the design, but there is almost never any guidance about what or how to describe the design in prose. All the reader gets is the pictures! For all the reasons cited in the previous paragraph, UML pictures often leave much open to the interpretation of the developer. This is wholly inadequate in terms of providing the needed information for developers to follow the design in the implementation. A key assumption made by the creators of early object-oriented design methodologies seemed to be that code developers also created the designs. Obviously this is not the case today, yet this seems to be woven into the fabric of UML.

Many nontechnical stakeholders, who need some design insight, cannot understand UML designs. UML representations are not remotely comprehendible unless you are a computer scientist and an expert in UML. Many of today's software-intensive systems are far grander in scale, and there are often many layers of design before the developers write code to implement the design. Unless great care is taken, information will certainly be lost along the way from coarse-grained systemic designs to detailed software design to the point where the original design intent will be rendered meaningless. UML provides no mechanism to preserve this information. It is essential that designers move past mere hieroglyphics and cave drawings and include legends and prose with the design drawings.

■ UML is based on the object-oriented paradigm, which is not inherently bad by any means. However, this does come with a bit of baggage. One key assumption of object-oriented analysis and design is that modularity to support reuse (usually at the class level) is the most important aspect of all design. It should be apparent to anyone who has done a little system design that this is not always the case. Although UML (or any object-oriented design methodology, language, or tool) intrinsically promotes reuse, architects must keep in mind that this comes at a cost to other quality attributes. UML explicitly focuses on functionality and provides no guidance for designing for broad systemic quality attributes such as performance, security, interoperability, and any other quality attributes you can think of besides general reuse. It weakly supports design analysis and evaluation of these broader systemic quality attribute properties. Another important issue is situations where the system's implementation language is not object oriented. In these cases, many of the design constructs that are part of UML cannot be implemented in a non-object-oriented language, and the implementation will not follow the design. Promises made in the design will not be delivered in the implementation. Even the reuse promises inherent in the object-oriented paradigm, will be difficult to achieve if critical object-oriented design constructs (object encapsulation, inheritance, polymorphism, late binding, and so forth) cannot be implemented in code. If a structured language must be used to implement an object-oriented design, there are essentially three choices:

1. You can create the code mechanics that will implement the object-oriented design constructs in the structured language, which are used in the design.
2. The object-oriented design vocabulary (UML, for example) can be restricted as much as possible to avoid using constructs that are difficult or impossible to implement in the structured language.
3. Live with the fact that the implementation will not match the design.

■ A central theme of this text has been that understanding perspective is critically important as the architect designs the system, especially as he or she writes down the design. Perspective is not explicit in UML. In fact, UML implicitly emphasizes the static perspective and code structure. UML predominantly focuses on static structures, not on dynamic structures. UML provides notation for modeling interaction but not runtime structures. As such, it can be difficult to use UML representations to capture and reason about runtime structures and how they change throughout execution. Notation for modeling structures from the physical perspectives is extremely weak and coarse grained (even in UML 2.X), yet is often a critical part of systemic design and analysis of designs. Architects are usually forced to use a different design notation to capture dynamic and physical structures. This can be a major limiting factor in using UML to design systems, or even software where the design and analysis of dynamic structures are critical. Because UML is not explicit about perspective, architects must be even more diligent to maintain clarity and consistency in their thinking if they document their designs using UML.

■ There is no clear concept of hierarchical decomposition (and composition), which is necessary for systemic design and development. UML 2 is a little better, but still biased toward software concerns, and is not very expressive at capturing systemic structures and is still problematic in many ways. This is an essential technique when designing software-intensive systems, especially big ones.

■ UML has no explicit support for modeling legacy or commercial elements that are part of the broader system design.

■ UML has become complex over the years because it is trying to meet the needs for a very broad community of users. Currently UML is being extended to support model-driven architecture and automatic code generation; this includes new metamodels, data models, and many new constructs. In many ways, the notation is becoming a programming language in and of itself. Much of this has resulted in a very complex and somewhat convoluted notation and complex designs that rival the complexity of the very system being designed. Remember, designs are abstractions; as such, design languages and methods should help designers abstract away the right details and make it simpler for engineers to analyze complex systems and their systemic properties. In most cases, it is essential that tools are used to effectively utilize UML. This binds an organization to a design methodology, tool, and often a particular approach to design.

UML 2 has introduced component diagrams to help address some of the most prevalent deficiencies of UML 1 related to documenting software architecture. Component modeling diagrams now include several constructs to help architects: ports, provided/required interfaces, interface/component relationship diagrams, and subsystems. These constructs were introduced in UML 2 to help designers describe runtime and physical architectural structures common in systemic design. Component diagrams could be rendered in UML 1, but were implemented in terms of deployment diagrams, and the available vocabulary in UML 1 was weak for describing interfaces such as those shown in Figure 6.7.

Here we can see that we have a three-tiered system, but not much else. There are actually two different kinds of users in this system, with different interfaces to the middle tier that would be interesting to represent with a richer notation. However, because UML 1 does not support hierarchical decomposition/composition very well, any more details regarding these components would have required the use of class diagrams or a kluged application of the notation to show the detailed interfaces and underlying component details. Given UML 1 limitations, this would have been a fairly typical representation. The relationships shown here do little more than show basic dependencies. Another issue is we have no idea what the components are, and perspective is not explicit. The reader might infer that the perspective shown here is static due to the uses relationship, but because the identity of the components is unknown, we cannot be certain. The architect would have to include separate prose to indicate what the components are. In the vocabulary of UML 1,

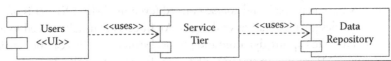

Figure 6.7   Example representing components in UML 1.

components are rectangular boxes, as shown here. However, if the architect wants to differentiate the components, it becomes difficult to do so without prose.

Component diagrams as defined in UML 2 provide the architect with a richer vocabulary to describe the architecture using components (artifacts in UML 2 parlance) and their interfaces with more detail that can be hierarchical if need be. Consider the same system architecture described in Figure 6.8 using the UML 2 component diagram.

Here the system components are shown, and their relationships to one another, as well as the interfaces the components expose. In this drawing, UML 2 components are used to describe the same n-tiered system as shown in Figure 6.7. Perspective is still not explicitly stated, and this is not improved by UML 2. However, in UML 2 it is assumed that component diagrams show threads, processes, data repositories, and so forth that "live" on (or map to) physical nodes. The notation specifies that components be documented with the rectangle rotation shown here, so if the architect wants to differentiate the components, it can be difficult to do so. It is essential to include the <<stereotype>> specification inside the component rectangle; forgetting this can leave the reader totally confused because a rectangle can mean component or class. This notation allows the architect to show interfaces for a component as well. The round circle on a line (lollipop) protruding from the component indicates that this is an interface provided by the element. The line with a cup protruding from the component indicates that this is an interface required by the component. The cup and circle is often called an interface socket, which is a bit of an overload because the term *socket* is often associated with the TCP/IP protocol; however, the actual interface may not be a TCP/IP socket or even a network at all. The interfaces are not bound to a particular protocol in this drawing, and the nature of the runtime interfaces is not articulated (e.g., data flow, events, RMI). Coarse-grained component diagrams like these can be further decomposed, and hierarchical levels of decomposition can be shown with the subsystem classifier. The subsystem classifier has been added to UML 2 and is a specialized version of the component classifier. Figure 6.9 expands the design of the service tier component shown in Figure 6.8.

Here, the internal workings of the service tier component are detailed. The outer box shows the boundaries of the service tier. Small boxes on the outer boundary map to interfaces external to the subsystem. In this case, the small open box at the left labeled "User Connect" maps to the customer and administrator components' connection point with the service tier component. At the right side of Figure 6.9 there are two connections to the database: one labeled "DB Connect" for handling user information processing requests, and the other "Admin DB Connect" for handling administrator information processing requests. Within the service tier subsystem, all client connect requests are handled by the "Connect" component. The connect component discerns between user requests and administrator requests. User requests are sent to the service broker, who checks

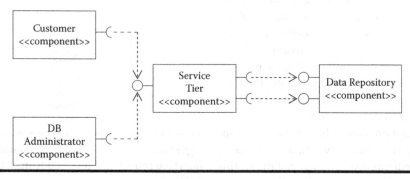

Figure 6.8   Example of UML 2 component diagrams showing interfaces and relationships.

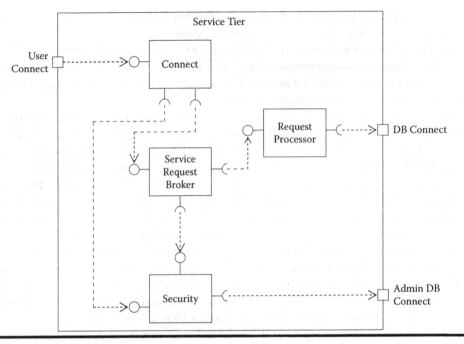

Figure 6.9   Example of UML 2 service tier subsystem documentation notation.

the type of request and the user's privileges with the security component. If the request is authorized, it is sent to the request processor. After an administrator connects to the system, the identity is validated by the security component. Once authorized, the administrator is directly connected to the database. At this point in the description, the reader should note that control and data flow are not depicted in this diagram. One might wonder (and rightly so) about the synchronicity of the components shown here and how data is returned to the user. Although UML has notation to show data and control flow (sequence or state diagrams), the component diagram here shows runtime structure. To show control or data flow between the components of a component or subsystem drawing, a kluge of the notation would have to be used. In general, there is very little information conveyed about the semantics of the interfaces in this representation, and much is left to the interpretation of the developer.

Although component and subcomponent notation can show relationships among elements and their provided and required interfaces, this is not enough information about the interface to sufficiently define the component boundaries for downstream designers and implementers. However, UML 2 provides another mechanism to show more interface details through the provided/required interface notation shown in Figure 6.10.

This diagram shows the service tier's connect component interface (Figure 6.9) using the provided/required interface notation. This notation is nothing new, and similar notation

Figure 6.10   Example of UML 2 component interface provided/required documentation notation.

has been used for many years in various object-oriented design notations. However, this leaves a lot to the downstream detailed designer or coder's imagination. Component interface descriptions can have additional compartments stacked below the <<component>> compartment for additional information. However, UML does not specifically guide designers to think in terms of an interface's description at the level of detail as those described in Table 5.11. Typically prose is still required to adequately describe an interface so that it is prescriptive enough for a designer or implementer to adhere to. Despite these enhancements, many of the original problems described above still remain when using UML to document systemic design. This becomes more difficult as the size, scope, and complexity of the system increase. These can be serious challenges to architects attempting to use UML 2.0 as a comprehensive notation for documenting the design of a software-intensive system. For these reasons, architects using UML often learn that they have to tailor the notation—use other methods, tools, and so forth to meet their exact needs. All notational vocabularies will have similar limitations, and UML is no exception. In many cases the problem with architectural documentation rendered in UML notation is not the fault of UML, but rather the fault of the architect thinking that notation and pictures rendered in UML can stand alone. The architect would have to include much more information than the UML notation alone provides to complete the design and create documentation that could be used for detailed design or construction of the components. UML can be a viable choice for an architect documenting an architectural design. However, the architect should be aware of the inherent weaknesses of UML (and any notation he or she uses). Essentially, all of the mistakes that can be made using an ad hoc notation can be made with UML just as easily. Using UML or any other notation standard does not relieve architects of having to pay close attention to the details of how their designs are rendered to ensure that they are an accurate prescription for downstream engineers and other stakeholders.

Although the guidance here can help the architect write sound architectural design documentation, it should only be viewed as a start. The body of knowledge about how to document the architectural design of software-intensive systems is constantly evolving, and there are a great many opinions, approaches, and evolving standards that the reader should explore. Because the topic of design documentation is so very large, this chapter is one point of view and should be viewed as an introduction to documentation essentials. Some noteworthy architectural documentation standards and approaches include:

- *Documenting Software Architectures: Views and Beyond* (Clements et al., 2003): *Views and Beyond* is the SEI's approach to software architectural documentation that is based on a multiview approach centered around model view types (static perspective), component-and-connector view types (dynamic perspective), and allocation view types (akin to the physical perspective, but broader in scope).
- ANSI/IEEE Standard 1471-2000: 1471 is a multiview approach to architecture documentation that is based upon establishing a conceptual framework that is used for architectural description and content definition.
- Open Process Framework (OPF) architectural documentation: The OPF is a documentation standard that is based in part on enterprise architecture framework concepts and two general families of artifacts: business engineering and application development documents. Under each of these headings various documents are prescribed for describing everything from business processes to technical designs. The OPF makes nearly exclusive use of UML for technical designs and is targeted more for the information technology domain.

Often in practice architects use collections of tools to document designs, such as Microsoft Word, PowerPoint, Visio, and other graphical representation tools. These tools are not bad, but unfortunately they are usually selected and woven together in an ad hoc way. This results in inconsistency, duplication, and a maintenance nightmare. The maintenance problem associated with this only becomes apparent after it is too late. One simple change can ripple across various documents written in Word, PowerPoint, and Visio—not to mention the impact to any artifacts maintained and any design tools that may be used. In extreme cases, engineers do not even know where to go to make the changes—usually there are many places to make changes. This situation is simply unavoidable today given the current state of architectural design tools; however, the impact can be minimized with a little early planning. To minimize these problems, consider the following guidelines:

- Adopt a standard set of tools and specify what they will be used to document. Plan the documentation suite using the defined set of tools. Accept no design artifacts in other formats, no matter how draconian this may sound.
- Plan documentation milestones throughout the project by which documentation (in whole or in part) must be completed. It is also a good idea to audit design documentation at these milestones.
- Agree to a standard artifact naming and configuration management scheme. Invest in a first-class configuration tool that will allow you to maintain the configuration of the design artifacts regardless of the tool or document type and format. Establish and configure a control process and select a tool to support that process. Keep all design artifacts under strict configuration control.
- Create standard document and artifact templates for the standard set of architecture design documentation tools. This will ease the documentation chore and will serve as an incentive for engineers to use the standard tool. Templates also help organizations produce documents with a consistent look, feel, and format that make navigating the document a bit easier for the reader. Templates also help let engineers know what to write and when they are done writing.

General Guidance for Technical Writing

There is no shortage of advice on how to write technical documentation. Indeed, many universities offer advanced degrees in technical writing, and numerous consultants are available to help with the chore of writing technical documents. Despite the importance and necessity of technical documentation, engineers and scientists have notoriously poor writing skills. If you read enough technical documentation, you will see common mistakes that technical professionals make when writing. Some of the most common errors include:

- Unclear context: Scientists and engineers often write as if everyone around them understands all of the technology, notation, context, and so forth that they understand. Often the technical design concepts themselves are not difficult, but the lack of context makes it impossible for a reader to understand design documentation.
- Poor organization: Scientists and engineers often organize documents around their own stream of consciousness rather than meeting the anticipated needs of the reader. Information is misplaced, out of order, or totally missing. This makes it difficult to use the documentation and frustrates the reader.

- Unclear purpose: There are a number of things that writers can do to make a document's purpose unclear. First, they can fail to establish context, as previously mentioned. However, another problem is that writers sometimes establish context, but then fail to stick to the context they have established. The prose is wordy, unfocused, and wanders around the topic rather than focusing on the topic at hand.
- Poor mechanics: As brilliant as scientists and engineers are, it is amazing how little attention they pay to format, sentence structure, syntax, grammar, spelling, and punctuation.
- Inconsistent use of technical terminology: Nothing is more frustrating to a reader and nothing will render a technical document more worthless than having to try to sort out inconsistent technical terminology. If a box is called a "widget" in paragraph 1, the same box should be called a "widget" in paragraph 2 unless there is a good reason to call it otherwise and the change in terminology is clearly explained to the reader.
- Acronym overload: Acronyms are a natural part of techno jargon. However, it is common for scientists and engineers writing technical documents to assume that the reader understands all of the acronyms as they do. The writer should assume nothing. For example, consider the simple acronym COM. In technical documentation, this acronym is often used to refer to Common Object Model, the center of mass, a serial data port on a personal computer, and many other things. Imagine the potential acronym overload in the following sentence: COM is used to structure the processes responsible for reading data from the sensor through the COM port and performing the COM calculation for the system. Obviously this is a staged and exaggerated example to illustrate a point, but acronym overloading is a common occurrence in technical documentation.

Architects should try to anticipate these problems and make the job of the reader as easy as possible. As you write, constantly consider the needs of readers, their attitude, and their technical depth of understanding. Decide before writing and assembling the document what the reader will know after reading your document. It is your job to adapt to the stakeholders reading the document—not for them to figure out or interpret what you are saying, why you are saying it, and whether it is relevant to their needs. The following techniques can help avoid some of these common problems.

Design the Document

Documents should be designed just as systems and software are designed. Most of the grist for architectural documentation should come from the architect's engineering notebook. If the engineering notebook practice is followed faithfully, then documentation is much easier to produce. Outlines are the critical first step in creating good, well-structured documents. An outline should list the major subject headings and a brief description of the anticipated content of each section. The subject heading outline is to documentation what interfaces are to architectural design elements. Given a subject heading and a general description of content sections, the document can be written in isolation, the sections can be reused in other documents, and individual document sections can be integrated with relative ease. If multiple documents must be created, then it is advisable to create a common template. This will ensure that the documents are consistent and that they share the same look and feel. Common information such as project overviews, legal notifications, nondisclosure notices, disclaimers, organizational/corporate information, and other similar information can be written once and included in the template.

Empathize with the Reader

Organize information logically from the reader's point of view. Assume that the reader does not have the context that you, the writer, possess. Always provide context no matter how trivial it may seem, and group similar design concepts together, explaining them in isolation before relating or intertwining them. Empathize with the reader. Put yourself in the place of the person trying to read and use your instructions. Try to anticipate what stakeholders know about the domain, how they view the system, what they know about the technology, what they need to know about the design, and how they might use the document. Include a reader's guide early in the document that describes who the document is written for and how to navigate the document. Describe notational and document standards that have been used and how to find relevant information. Provide cues that can help readers navigate and understand the information and organization of the document. Consistent headings, lists, and other formatting mechanics can convey information that greatly reduces confusion in the document. Templates help greatly in this regard. If documents share the same structure, then writers do not have to reinvent the document structure and the cues used within documents, and the reader will not have to learn how to read each document individually, but will learn the general structure of all of the documents. Writers should "telegraph" to the reader what lies ahead in the document by using forecasting statements to preview what is next. Combine forecasting statements with summary statements to review the information just presented and how it relates to what comes next. This greatly aids in transition from one topic or area of design to another. Consider the following example:

> In this section the structure of the server processes was introduced from the dynamic perspective [summarizing statement]. In the next section the server processes structure will be described from the static perspective and related to the dynamic structure shown in this section [forecasting statement].

These transitions are often too abrupt in technical documents because writers assume that readers understand the system exactly as the writer does. This dramatically disrupts the overall flow and readability of the document. The most astute reader will be confused (and frustrated) if the writer moves too quickly from one topic to another without providing cues that a change is about to happen and gently transitioning the reader through the document. Readers are often left scratching their heads, wondering how in one paragraph they were reading about one subject, but suddenly in the very next paragraph they seem to be reading about some unrelated, unconnected subject matter. Summarization and telegraphing are easy cues that the writer can provide that can gently prepare the reader for changes. Finally, to ensure that a document meets the needs of a reader, identify stakeholders that might use the design documents and ask them to review it. Obviously issues found with the document can be used to fix it, but they should also be used to further refine document templates to avoid similar mistakes in the future.

Pay Close Attention to Details and Assume Nothing

Have you thought through the architectural design in enough detail to describe the design in enough detail for the downstream designer or implementer? If you do not know what an element or relationship is, then the implementer will make something up. Ensure that the reader (especially the implementer) does not have to infer anything. If you cannot say what the elements are, what the relationships are, or you are having a hard time describing the temporal behavior and element interactions, it may be that the design has not been completely fleshed out. At this point, step back and revisit the architectural drivers. Step through the system using the key use cases to guide the analysis. Check the quality attribute responses using the quality attribute scenarios to guide the analysis. If there are missing details in the use cases or quality attribute scenarios, revise them and continue the analysis until the design is completely understood.

Reduce Large Numbers of Interactions by Grouping Related Interactions

Temporal steps or relationships are one of the more common things to document in technical documentation. Although seemingly intuitive, this is often one of the most problematic areas of technical writing. Writers tend to omit what seems to be trivial details and describe dynamic, temporal behavior from their point of view rather than the reader's. When describing large numbers of interactions or temporal steps, it can be helpful to group similar and related steps into phases. Each phase has a number of related interactions that are then sequentially numbered starting at step 1. A simple example is shown in Tables 6.1 and 6.2.

Table 6.1 shows a group of steps that describe temporal interaction between two elements. Even though this is a simple example, it can be difficult to understand the interaction; with a few more steps added to the interaction, or a bit of concurrency, this would quickly become difficult to understand. Table 6.2 shows the same steps; however, they are grouped into phases.

This modularizes the interaction and helps to eliminate clutter, especially when large numbers of steps are involved. Modularized phases can also be reused or referenced throughout the document rather than rewritten, reducing the amount of writing and contributing to consistency, and it is also much easier to add new steps later if necessary.

Table 6.1 A Series of Steps Describing an Interaction between Elements

1.	Server process listens for a connect request from client processes.
2.	Client process sends a connect request to the server.
3.	Server request acknowledges the connect request.
4.	Client receives the acknowledge message from the server.
5.	Server process spawns a process to service client requests.
6.	Client sends service request to client service process.
7.	Server acknowledges client service request.
8.	Client receives the server acknowledge message from client service process.
9.	Client service process processes service request.
10.	Client service process sends data to client.
11.	Client receives data.
12.	Client acknowledges the receipt of data.
13.	Client sends a close connection request to the client service process.
14.	Client service process acknowledges the receipt of close connection request.
15.	Client service process terminates.

Table 6.2   The Same Series of Steps Describing an Interaction between Elements Grouped into Phases

Phase 1: Client Connection	
1.	Server process listens for a connect request from client processes.
2.	Client process sends a connect request to the server.
3.	Server request acknowledges the connect request.
4.	Client receives the acknowledge message from the server.
5.	Server process spawns a process to service client requests.
Phase 2: Service Request Processing	
1.	Client sends service request to client service process.
2.	Server acknowledges client service request.
3.	Client receives the server acknowledge message from client service process.
4.	Client service process processes service request.
5.	Client service process sends data to client.
6.	Client receives data.
7.	Client acknowledges the receipt of data.
Phase 3: Connection Termination	
1.	Client sends a close connection request to the client service process.
2.	Client service process acknowledges the receipt of close connection request.
3.	Client service process terminates.

Simplify and Add Detail as Necessary

When solving a complex mathematics equation, a general rule is to first reduce the problem into in its simplest terms and solve those. The same can be said for describing complex design concepts. Explain design concepts by starting with general concepts and adding detail hierarchically to describe specific design concepts. Group designs of similar granularity together; avoid mixing detailed and coarse-grained design concepts together. For example, rather than showing a complex concurrent operation in one giant picture with many elements and relationships and explaining it in one large chunk of prose, consider first showing individual interactions separately, then explain their interaction separately.

Pay Attention to Mechanics

Few engineers like to write, so they tend to overlook simple writing mechanics that hamper the readability of their documents. Technical people tend to use jargon and technical language imprecisely. Many technical terms are overloaded and, without proper explanation and context, can mislead the reader. The writer should avoid vague and overloaded terms and phrases. Technical terms and phrases should be explained in context before they are used. Once the term or phrase is established, the writer should ensure that he or she remains consistent with the definition of the term throughout the document, or explains changes in context that may necessitate a different interpretation of a term or phrase. Similarly, acronyms should be spelled out unless they are absolutely obvious to all readers. For example, the term *laser* is actually an acronym that has become a word in modern English (Light Amplified by Stimulated Emissions of Radiation). Such terms do not need to be spelled out, but all others should be spelled out the first time they are used in a document, even if they seem obvious to the writer. Acronym lists and terminology glossaries are helpful; however, they can be disruptive to the reading process because readers must flip to an appendix each time they run across an acronym they do not understand. For this reason, it is highly recommended that writers spell out acronyms and explain terminology and phrases in the document the first time they are used. However, acronym lists and terminology glossaries can be useful as well and can be reused in various documents.

Engineers often tend to be wordy writers. Some writers seem to think that wordy sentences, paragraphs, and phrases make them sound more clever than a few simple ones, but wordy writing can make documents excessively long and can be frustrating to readers. Writing short, concise sentences and paragraphs is also one of the most difficult skills to develop as a writer. Table 6.3 lists a few of the most common mistakes that writers make that can lead to wordy technical documents.

The bad news is that although concise documents have fewer words, sentences, and paragraphs while preserving the meaning, they take longer to produce! The good news is that it gets easier with practice.

It is also common for some writers to write in short, choppy sentences that do not add to the meaning and readability of the document. Ironically, short, choppy sentence structure can contribute to wordy documents. Writers should try to identify these and combine them when possible. Consider the following examples:

We decided on a structure. The system would be built around a client/server pattern.

These two sentences can be combined to relate the same information in a more concise, coherent way.

We decided the system would be built around a client/server pattern.

Table 6.3 Examples of Common Wordy Phrases

Wordy Phrase	Concise Replacement
A majority of	Most
A number of	Few or many
In order to	To
Based on the fact that	Because
During the course of	While
For the purpose of	For
With regard to	About or concerning
In the event that	If
So as to	To

Some writers also confuse active and passive voice. This is a tough thing to keep consistent in a document, but if this writing style can be developed, it can dramatically help writers create concise documents that are easier to read. In the active voice, the subject of the sentence performs the action described in the sentence. In the passive voice, the subject receives the action. Passive sentences tend to be longer, complex, and less direct than active sentences. Consider the following sentence:

In using this structure, more advantages are provided.

This is a passive voice sentence that can be greatly improved if an active voice is used, as the following example illustrates:

This structure is more advantageous.

Engineers writing documents will often use the passive voice because it sounds more objective and scientific, but it results in wordy documents that are hard to read. Reading aloud can often help writers identify many of the mechanics problems described here.

Document Structure

Clearly documenting the architectural design of a complex software-intensive system can be a daunting task. The first recommendation provided in the previous section was that documents must be designed. Failing to design documents is one of the primary reasons that technical documentation is hard to read, maintain, and write in a clear, concise way. In this section an overall architectural design document outline is provided. This outline can be adopted, tailored to structure architectural design documents, or used as a basis for creating an architecture design document template. Although not suitable as is or for all situations, it can help with the most troubling aspect of architectural design documentation—designing the document. Each section of the outline will be listed and described in detail below.

Front Matter

At the front of the document there should be a title page, table of contents, revision history, and author information. A one-page executive summary can be included if necessary; however, this is not common in design documentation.

Section 1: Document Description

The purpose of this section is to describe who the intended audience is for the document, and to help them navigate and use the document. Each of the subsections of Section 1 is described below:

- Purpose and audience: Describe who the intended audience and organizations are and what they might use the document for.

- Document organization: Describe the overall organization of the document. List the major sections of the document and describe what concerns each section addresses.
- Common notation: List any notation that will be used throughout the document. This does not relieve the architect from including legends with his or her drawings, but provides an opportunity for the writer to list any notation conventions used to document the architecture. Include any standard notations (e.g., UML) and any tailoring that is commonly used in the document. Mathematical notation or formal modeling techniques used in the document should be described here as well.
- Terminology and definitions: Define any terms used throughout the document and provide context for terminology.
- References and relevant documents: List any other relevant documents that the reader might need to refer to, and most importantly, describe their relationships to this document and why the reader might want to (or need to) refer to them.

Section 2: Project Overview

The purpose of this section is to describe the project and its purpose and scope. Describe why the system is being built. Describe business, organizational, mission, or marketing concerns that are relevant to the project. List the relevant stakeholders, their organizations, and how they will interact with the system. Rather than list all the stakeholders individually, list the stakeholder communities, such as end users, maintainers, installers, and so forth. Each stakeholder or stakeholder community can be described in separate subsections.

Section 3: Architectural Drivers

In this section describe the architectural drivers for the system. If there are a lot of architectural drivers, it may be impractical to list them here, so it may be necessary to refer to a separate document that lists them. At a minimum, list the high-priority or critical drivers for the system (those that are very important, very difficult, or had a great deal of influence on the design). The architectural drivers can be listed in separate sections enumerated as high-level functional requirements, technical constraints, business constraints, and quality attribute requirements. Make sure to list the priority of the architectural drivers.

Section 4: System Context

The system context is the first step in design and should include at least one context drawing, as described in Chapter 5. In addition to the context drawing, include prose that describes the scope of the system being described by showing its relationship to external entities like systems, peripherals, organizations, and stakeholders as necessary to describe the context drawing. Describe the relative perspective of the context drawing or drawings. If an engineering notebook is used by the architect (as described in Chapter 5), the rough sketches there can be refined and used here.

Section 5: Level X Decomposition

In Section 5 we start with the first level of decomposition based upon the context established in Section 4. The X in the title of this section refers to the specific level of composition. Subsequent sections will show different, more detailed decomposition of the system. There are a variety of ways to document further decomposition of the system, depending upon the scope of the project. If the system is small, this section may describe all of the levels of decomposition. In projects of a larger scope, separate sections may be needed to describe each level. In projects of still larger scope, or projects with a highly distributed workforce, each section may be a separate document that will be referenced. If the architect is keeping an engineering notebook, he or she may have recorded many levels of decomposition. It may not be necessary to include each level of decomposition, but rather just the final decomposition. However, if this approach is taken, great care should be exercised that enough information is provided so that the reader is able to understand the detailed decompositions without the intermediate representations. For our purposes, we will assume that each section represents a single level of decomposition because this scales both up and down. Within this section, the following subsections should be included:

- Decomposition description: Describe what is being decomposed and relate it back to the context drawing. Describe the perspective of the decomposition.
- Primary representation(s): Include one or more drawings (or views) that represent the decomposition of the system, such as those described in section 5. If an engineering notebook is used by the architect (as described in chapter 5), the rough sketches there can be refined and used here.
- Description and rationale: Describe the primary representation and include rationale for the decomposition. Relate the architectural decisions to the architectural drivers by describing how the architectural drivers are promoted by the decisions and approaches taken. Describe any design trade-offs relevant to the design decisions in terms of the architectural drivers promoted and inhibited.
- Elements and relations: Include element and relationship responsibility catalogs as described in Chapter 5. If an engineering notebook is used by the architect (as described in Chapter 5), the rough sketches there can be refined and used here.
- Interface descriptions: If appropriate, describe specific interfaces for the elements. Whether detailed interfaces are described at any level of decomposition depends upon if there is enough detail in the decomposition.

Section 6: Mappings between Perspectives

If necessary, show mappings between structures in different perspectives. Show how specific structures in one perspective map to specific structures in other perspectives. Be careful in the mappings and use prose to describe any mappings you show.

Section 7: Document Directory

In this section include an index, glossary, and acronym list. Most word processing software will automatically generate indexes. Glossaries and acronym lists should be used to explain the terms and acronyms used throughout the document. If the writer spells out acronyms the first time they are used, an acronym list should still be included. If the reader forgets what a particular acronym means, he or she must search through the document to find the first occurrence of the acronym to find out what it means. If an acronym list is included, then the reader knows where to go should he or she forget an acronym. Although it is disruptive to have to flip to another section of a document to find out what an acronym means, it is better than having to search through the whole document to find the first occurrence. The combination of spelling out acronyms and including an acronym list can help prevent the reader from having to perform random searches to understand the meanings of acronyms.

Summary

Few architects like to document their designs. However, the maturity of the architect is readily visible in the quality of the design documents he or she creates. It is critical that architecture design documentation is able to clearly and concisely communicate the design to the appropriate stakeholders. If the design cannot be communicated to those that would build the system, then the design does not matter. Key points in this section include:

1. There are few tools available to architects designing software-intensive systems. One size does not fit all as far as tools, notation, or methodology is concerned when it comes to documenting systemic architectural design.
2. UML is a notation that is commonly used today to document software-intensive system designs. UML's key strength is that it is a standard notation and is quite good for documenting detailed object-oriented software designs. However, UML has some severe limitations when used to document systemic design, which was discussed at length. UML is not bad by any means, but engineers often do bad things with UML—several examples of this were presented and discussed.
3. Common documentation problems were discussed and approaches for avoiding these problems were presented.
4. General design document organization was discussed in terms of an outline that could be used to structure design documentation or create a design document template.

SECTION II

Chapter 7

The Architecture Centric Design Method

You can design the best architecture in the universe, but it is impossible to realize it if it cannot be communicated to stakeholders. You can design the best architecture in the universe, but it is worthless if it is not used to guide the creation of the system. This means that software design is an intimate part of the system or product development process. Unfortunately, having a development process or using a process framework does not automatically mean that you have a design process. Design should be part of the entire life cycle of software-intensive systems. The product or system life cycle is often thought of as a continuum of activities from requirements to design, implementation, maintenance, and decommissioning. However, an organization's development is not a series of seamless, sequential steps, but rather a set of individual processes, each addressing different needs, such as requirements, planning, tracking, configuration management, and so forth. Although many of these process areas have enjoyed a great deal of attention by researchers and practitioners, the least served of these is the process of architectural design. Although certain aspects of architectural design have received a lot of attention over the last decade or so, practitioners still struggle with fundamental practical matters, such as how and when to design, how to turn requirements into architectural designs, how to know when design is done, how to evaluate designs, and how to use designs throughout the life cycle. Architectural design is not exclusively a technical activity performed in isolation by architects. It is not an artifact. It is not just a milestone on a schedule. Design is a first-class member of the set of processes that comprise an organization's development and life cycle processes. An ad hoc design process is as dangerous as an ad hoc configuration management process—or any other process critical to project success and organizational well-being. Organizations are constantly bombarded with emerging methods, tools, and techniques, and they must figure out:

- If they are useful
- How to transition and use them
- How to make them fit with other processes and methods
- The estimated costs for adoption
- The return on investment

In other words, the not-so-trivial transition and implementation details of the method or process are left to the organization to interpret and work through. Since 1995, when architecture design concepts were first introduced, a few industrial-strength architectural methods have emerged that address specific aspects of architectural design, such as architectural requirements gathering and prioritization, design representation, design evaluation, and so forth. Some of these methods have provided great value to practitioners. However, adopting new processes, methods, and techniques can be a tough sell in many organizations. Just as elements of design can have mismatch, so can processes, methods, and tools when we try to bring them together in a project context. Similarly, many of these methods suffer from two key problems. First, they are intervention oriented; that is, they were designed to be applied in isolation from the design process or the overall development process. Organizations employing these methods must decide when and how to apply various architectural methods during the project—or weave together various (sometimes incompatible) architectural methods and processes within a project. Using these methods can be disruptive to the development life cycle without significant tailoring to fit the specific needs of the organization and project. Significant tailoring of the method (or methods) or development processes is often required to successfully use them. Unfortunately, very little guidance is available for tailoring architectural methods or the development processes. Less is available when it comes to weaving together technical methods and processes—sometimes brute force experience is the only teacher. Transitioning methods and changing organizational development processes is expensive, time-consuming, and risky. To most efficiently use architectural methods and organizational development processes, someone in the organization has to know a great deal about architectural design, the proposed method (or methods), and the organization's development processes. This can be a tall order to fill, time-consuming, and problematic. A second but related problem with these methods is that many of them were designed to be applied by a third party—usually a consultant. Some of these methods even have proprietary elements that require special training, tools, and expertise, much of which must be purchased at a premium. These hurdles have prevented many organizations in industry from adopting the best architectural design practices. Software development teams could benefit greatly from specific guidance about how to instantiate the architectural design process and how to weave it into an organization's existing development and life cycle processes.

This section of the text will introduce the Architecture Centric Design Method (ACDM). ACDM was developed to address these issues and provide a more comprehensive design process that can easily be meshed with existing process frameworks. ACDM provides techniques and structure for designing the architecture and then using the architectural design to guide the programmatic aspects of a project. Just as architectural design in the construction industry guides project planning, tracking, and construction, ACDM uses the design to guide the planning, tracking, and construction of a software-intensive system. ACDM is not a development process, but rather a design process that is intended to complement organizational development processes by weaving together design, development processes, and people into a cohesive, lightweight, scaleable design process. The goal of ACDM is to provide a design process framework that can easily be used with an organization's existing development and life cycle processes. ACDM provides detailed guidance for how to instantiate, utilize, and weave together ACDM with organizational development life cycle processes. To accomplish this, ACDM is geared toward organizations and teams building software-intensive systems and puts the software architecture front and center during all phases of the project or product life cycle. The method prescribes creating a notional architecture as soon as some of the preliminary requirements work has been completed. The architecture is developed early and quickly, and is iteratively evaluated and refined until the development team is confident that a system can be implemented and will meet the needs of the stakeholder community. In ACDM, the architecture design is used to estimate, plan, and track construction activities. ACDM provides templates, checklists, methods, and guidance for:

- Coordinating architectural design activities
- Eliciting, organizing, documenting, and refining the architecture drivers and the detailed system requirements
- Defining team structure
- Producing the architecture design
- Creating project estimates
- Identifying and mitigating technical risk
- Creating the project schedule
- Project tracking and oversight
- Managing change

In this and subsequent sections, the stages, methods, techniques, and guidance provided by ACDM will be explained in detail.

ACDM Overview

Among the key strengths of ACDM is that it forces architects to identify, organize, and analyze the architectural drivers—or architectural requirement—early in the development process. The architectural drivers are not all of the requirements or the details of the requirements; they are those requirements that will be most influential on the system or product structure. Once identified, the architectural drivers are used to guide the initial architectural design. The design is then evaluated in a structured way. The output of the evaluation is used to determine if the architecture is ready for production, or if experimentation and specific architecture drivers refinement is needed. If more experimentation is needed to mitigate issues uncovered in the evaluation, the team uses the output of the evaluation to guide the creation of experiments. After experimentation the architecture design is refined based on the results of the experiments, and it is evaluated again. This process continues until the architecture is deemed ready for production. The key difference between ACDM and other cyclical or iterative development methods is that ACDM iteratively refines the design based upon the output of evaluation, rather than iteratively creating operational prototypes to create a product. ACDM does not preclude traditional iterative operational prototyping, but focuses on iteratively developing the design. To achieve this in a predictable, repeatable way the ACDM follows eight well-defined stages. These stages are briefly described in Table 7.1.

During stages 1 and 2 teams will get the architectural drivers from the stakeholders and will establish the system scope. It may appear that stage 1 is identical to normal requirements elicitation processes. However, using ACDM the architectural team will explicitly press stakeholders to describe the system's architectural drivers rather than ad hoc requirements gathering. The elicitation in stage 1 is highly structured and geared toward gathering as much architecture driver information, from as many stakeholders, as possible. In stage 2 the team will consolidate, organize, and refine the architectural drivers and define project scope. Stage 1 is a big push to gather a lot of information quickly, but stages 1 and 2 are often iterative because it is usually impossible to meet with stakeholders once and get all of the architectural drivers. It is also difficult for designers to understand the nature of the architectural drivers, and they must often meet with all or some

Table 7.1 ACDM Stages

Stage	Description	Activities and Artifacts
1	Discover architectural drivers	Interact with stakeholders to discover and document the raw architectural drivers.
2	Establish project scope	Refine raw architectural drivers into an architectural drivers specification, and define the scope of the work.
3	Create/refine architecture	Create or refine the architecture design. After initial design the architect (or architecture team) will return to this step after experimentation (stage 7) to refine the architecture.
4	Architectural review	Review the architecture to discover and document issues that may compromise the satisfaction of the architectural drivers.
5	Production go/no-go	Prioritize and list the issues discovered during the architecture review and decide whether the architecture is ready for production or needs to be refined. If a go decision is made, the team goes to stage 8; otherwise, the team will experiment to refine the architecture.
6	Experimentation	Team designs and plans experiments to mitigate risks or issues that were discovered during the review to alleviate issues uncovered during the architecture review. Once planned, the team carries out the experiments and documents the results. Based on the results of the experiments, the team refines the architecture (stage 3) design base.
7	Production planning	The detailed element design and construction is planned based on the architecture design.
8	Production	The system elements are constructed.

of the stakeholders several times to define, refine, and negotiate the architectural drivers. This will continue throughout the design process as more is learned about the system and technology, and limitations are discovered. In stage 3 the architecture team will create the initial design. Later the team will return to this stage to refine the architecture design after stage 7. In stage 4 the team reviews the architecture, and in stage 5 the team has to decide whether the architecture design needs further refinement or if they should proceed into production planning. A key tenet of ACDM is to not dwell on the initial architecture design, but rather create the initial architecture quickly, review it to uncover technical issues, and refine it. If the architecture is deemed to not be ready for production to begin, the team will use the output of the review in stage 5 to plan and execute experiments in stage 6. The purpose of the experiments is to address specific issues that arose during the evaluation; thus, the architecture guides the team in discovering and mitigating risk. Once the experiments are executed, the team returns to stage 3, where the architecture is refined. After refinement, the architecture is reviewed again in stage 4. The team will iterate in stages 3 to 6 until the architecture is deemed fit for production. This iteration between stages is illustrated in Figure 7.1.

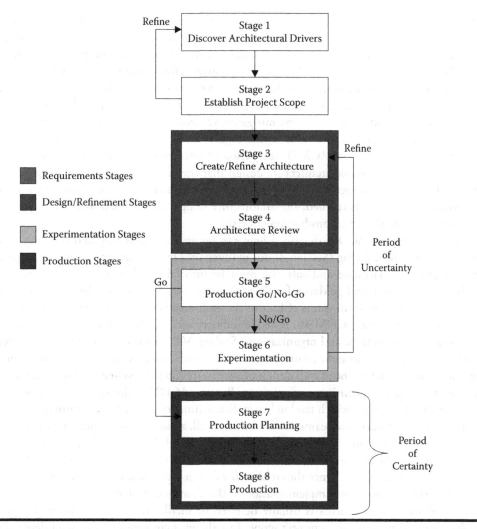

Figure 7.1   Graphic view of the ACDM stages showing architecture design, review, experimentation, and refinement iteration.

It is impossible to cross the chasm from what is needed by the stakeholders to a complete design in three steps (ask, design, develop). ACDM prescribes iteratively designing the architecture, not the system or product. Stages 1 and 2 and the iteration of stages 3 to 6 are discovery oriented, where the design team gathers information needed to build, refine, and eventually baseline the architecture. Early in a project, not much is known about the product, business context, or stakeholders. As such, precise production and cost estimates are not possible. As the various customer and developer groups are learning about the project, each other, and how to best work together, this time is characterized as the period of uncertainty in ACDM. A key concept of ACDM is to accept the fact that these unknowns exist and the architecture is used to reduce the period of uncertainty. Because of the period of uncertainty and the role architecture design has in mitigating the uncertainty, architectural design (like any kind of discovery) cannot be a one-time activity. ACDM provides specific techniques geared toward using the architecture to aggressively explore unknowns and overcome the period of uncertainty as quickly as possible.

Once the architecture is deemed fit for production, the architecture is baselined and the team enters the period of certainty. Once the architecture is solidified and risks have been identified and mitigated through experimentation, higher fidelity estimates and project plans can be created. Because the strength of ACDM lies in its iterative refinement of design, ACDM works best when the team defines the notional architecture and reviews it as quickly as possible. The benefit of this approach is that unknown and unclear requirements can be identified early; problematic technologies can be identified early and mitigated. Overcoming the temptation to create a perfect architecture in a single iteration is often the biggest challenge for design teams using ACDM. With the iteration built into ACMD, the period of uncertainty is overcome earlier. This helps design teams arrive at stable architecture design that they can have greater confidence in much sooner than creating a design in a big-bang fashion, or worse, in an ad hoc, chaotic manner. Once the period of certainty is reached, the architecture design itself is used to estimate production duration and is used to track production efforts.

The eight steps of ACDM described here can be used for designing and building new systems or, with some tailoring (Section 3), for maintenance projects or projects where a significant amount of legacy hardware and software must be utilized. In these cases, alternative ACDM staging must be used, and guidance for these situations will be discussed later in Section 3. The ACDM emerged from small teams of four to six team members and projects of one to two years in duration. However, as ACDM was tested in industry use, the method has evolved to accommodate larger teams, projects, and organizations. Scaling ACDM for various situations is discussed in Section 3. ACDM is an architecture design method and should be used by the core architecture team to create and refine the overall design of a software-intensive system and to guide managers in project estimation, planning, and tracking. Because ACDM addresses the needs of the chief architect and their teams, which tend to be smaller, scaling to larger projects is usually straightforward. In smaller projects and teams, ACDM works well, although the architecture design and the detailed design may be one and the same. The output of ACDM is the architecture design, which includes the documentation describing the partitioning of the system into elements (or subsystems) and their interactions. Once the architecture design is sufficiently refined, it is used to set the stage for detailed design and implementation of the elements. In many projects, detailed design of the various system elements is usually deferred to smaller teams or individual designers or implementers, depending upon project scope. Exactly what constitutes an element depends upon the scope of the system. Recall that the concept of scope and design hierarchy was introduced in Section 1. One architect's element can be an entire system unto itself, while for another architect an element might be one or several classes that work together to provide related services.

ACDM Roles

I'm not good in groups. It's difficult to work in a group when you're omnipotent.

The character Q, from *Star Trek: The Next Generation*

When groups of people work together on a problem, there is usually a time of chaos until the roles and relationships of the people on the team are established. Until then, members of the group will act independently; they will compete for position and status within the group, and will tend to be focused inwardly upon their own needs. Even in ad hoc groups where the roles and responsibilities are not formally established, after a period of time, individual members will coalesce into a team. Natural and fluid team operations will only ensue after (formally or informally) agreeing on leadership, rules, goals, methods, processes, and tools. At this point the group has become a team and we can think of the team as normalized. This does not mean that their processes, methods, and so forth are optimal, just that each team member has accepted his or her role, responsibilities, and the team standards for behavior. However, naturally overcoming these initial barriers can be very costly to an organization. Sometimes groups never normalize because one or more members or factions of the group refuse to accept or adopt their roles, responsibilities, and the group standards. These are dysfunctional teams, and when they reach this point, often outside authoritarian intervention is required to fix the problems.

When we think of designing the architecture of software-intensive systems, there is usually a small core of persons that are part of the architecture design team. In fact, *small* is the operative word that should be kept in mind when forming architecture design teams. Brooks (1995, pp. 44) indicates that design must proceed from one mind, or from a very small number of agreeing resonant minds. This does not mean that all projects need only one architect operating in a vacuum. Because most software-intensive systems are complex, a diverse group of engineers is usually required to successfully design and implement the system—architecture design teams are the norm, not the exception. What this means is that a design team needs a single, fully empowered leader—hopefully they are able to interact with management, marketing, and sales. The chief architect is responsible for the success (or failure) of the design team and the system or product design. No matter how small the team, structure is still needed to overcome difficulties in normalizing the behavior of the team. This is especially true in teams comprised of highly talented and well-compensated individuals. Architecture design teams are usually composed of the most talented engineers that an organization can muster. Unfortunately, normalizing the behavior of teams comprised of extraordinarily talented professionals can be very challenging—often it has been compared to herding cats! Asking a group of talented and experienced engineers to design a system is like asking a group of world-class artists to paint a picture. It is highly unlikely that they would agree on the medium, what style to use, or even how to paint the picture. The time before a team has normalized is a chaotic and resource-intensive period that is exacerbated if teams have little or no predefined structure. Natural selection is costly, and some teams never reach normalization; they remain dysfunctional. In the best case, dysfunctional teams can mature into a productive team, but often they are not as efficient as they could be, and the maturing process can be time-consuming. In the worst case, dysfunctional teams will implode, taking the project with them.

To build and maintain effective working relationships and maximize the productivity of the design team as quickly as possible, it is essential that each member of the design team understands his or her role and responsibilities to the team. ACDM provides team structure that is designed to help teams of talented designers normalize and become more productive faster than they would if allowed to naturally evolve without any structure. Without clearly defined responsibilities for team members, it is impossible to have defined, disciplined, repeatable processes, and teams tend to flounder and thrash while trying to figure out how to work together. This is a little like watching a pack of wolves and waiting for a leader to emerge. This can be a traumatic and tenuous time for the entire pack until a leader emerges and normal behaviors can resume. In unstructured teams where roles and responsibilities are not explicitly stated, it is nearly impossible to establish any processes and get consensus on anything. Often contentious relationships develop, team goals are unclear, expectations are unclear, and planning the next course of action is nearly impossible. In other words, this is a traumatic and tenuous time for the design team until a leader emerges and normal behaviors can resume. This results in wasted resources, frustration, and at some level will directly impact bottom-line concerns such as schedule and cost. Roles and responsibilities are a key element of ACDM. Although a number of roles are prescribed by ACDM, the organization should tailor the roles as necessary to meet its needs. If you are just beginning to use ACDM, it is recommended that you first try the defined roles (unless there are obvious mismatches) and tailor them after some experience. Before beginning a project, it is essential that roles and responsibilities are defined for each member of the design team. Each of the roles and their responsibilities are described here:

- Managing engineer: The managing engineer is responsible for coordinating the overall system design and development effort. Although they are responsible for the success (or failure) of the design team, they must also be able to listen to other members of the design team. They must be capable engineers and architects and able to confidently lead the design team without regularly resorting to draconian authoritarian means for leading the team. Such tactics do not work when leading talented engineers—the best engineers will simply leave under these conditions. They may also be the manager for the entire project as well; this is often a complementary role for this individual. However, in some large projects and organizations, there is a manager that is responsible for the design effort and other managers responsible for programmatic management activities. The managing engineer's scope of responsibility will have to be tailored and defined to meet the needs of the project and the organization. The managing engineer will plan, coordinate, track, and direct the overall activities of the design team. He or she is responsible for creating and maintaining the programmatic plans and schedules in both the period of uncertainty and the period of certainty.
- Support engineer: The support engineer is responsible for setting up and maintaining the design team's support tools and environments, such as development environments and tools, configuration management tools, test environments and testing tools, development infrastructure, Web presence, and so forth. He or she may also be responsible for the system or product infrastructure or environment. As such, support engineers will play a key role in the design of the system from a physical perspective.
- Chief architect: The chief architect is responsible for overall system design. He or she will work with all of the other members of the design team to coordinate the system design, beginning with gathering the architectural drivers, designing the architecture, reviewing it, refining it, and documenting it until production and deployment—preferably throughout the system or product life cycle. The architecture and the chief architect can provide enormous value throughout the system or product life cycle in managing change and evolution. The chief architect is responsible for coordinating the creation and maintenance of the architecture design documentation.
- Requirements engineer: The requirements engineer leads the effort to gather and document the architectural drivers. He or she will also help to manage the change and evolution of the architectural drivers—preferably throughout the system or product life cycle. The requirements engineer will also serve as the primary customer liaison. It is essential that the designing and developing organization presents a single, united face to the customer. Nothing can be more frustrating to customers than constantly receiving incongruent messages from the organization designing and building their product. The requirements engineer will also assist the quality engineer in coordinating architecture design review and in defining "black box" system or product tests. This testing will be explained in detail later, but in short, black-box element and systemic tests are derived directly from the architectural drivers without any insight into the underlying implementation.

■ Chief scientist: The chief scientist is the project technologist and is primarily responsible for coordinating the planning, tracking, and documentation of experiments that are used to refine the architecture design. While the chief architect focuses on the overall system or product's architectural design, the chief scientist focuses inwardly on technological issues that could impact the architecture. Generally, the chief scientist assists the architect with detailed technical issues concerning architectural design. In addition to a technical focus, the chief scientist assists the quality engineer in the architectural design reviews and in the development of "clear box" tests. This type of testing will be explained in detail later, but in short, clear-box tests are devised with an understanding of the underlying design and implementation details.

■ Quality process engineer: The quality process engineer ensures that ACDM and other defined processes are followed as prescribed to ascertain project quality goals are met. The quality process engineer is responsible for coordinating architecture design reviews as well as product test development, planning, and execution. The quality process engineer will work with the requirements engineer and the chief scientist to coordinate the architecture design reviews and in planning product or system tests. During architectural reviews, the quality process engineer is responsible for capturing, documenting, and tracking architectural issues uncovered during architectural evaluation, and that they are addressed and closed. The quality process engineer will also work with the team to establish the processes for configuration management, defect tracking, and so forth that the design team uses. These processes may also be used by the detailed designers or implementers throughout the production stage and for the life cycle of the system or product as well.

■ Production engineers: These are team members whose focus is on detailed design, implementation of the architectural elements, and integration of the elements to compose the system. The term *production engineer* has been selected deliberately to avoid bias toward software engineers, electrical engineers, IT engineers, or some other specific engineering community. Indeed, the production engineers of an organization may be software engineers, but the design teams often have software, electrical, mechanical, chemical, and many other kinds of engineers that play a role in the implementation of the system elements. In large organizations and projects, the production engineers may be a separate group or organization and may play a small role in systemic design. In smaller organizations and projects, all of the members of the design team may play a role as production engineers. Some production engineers may also participate in the design of the architecture, especially during stage 6 experimentation, when various proofs of concepts are developed to mitigate issues with the design. Production engineers also assist the quality process engineer in architectural design reviews and in system test as necessary.

The seven roles described here are the minimum required for a team using ACDM as prescribed. However, roles as they are described here do not necessarily map directly to a single person, but rather roles describe a group of related responsibilities and activities, as we will see as each stage is described. When piloting ACDM, roles were assigned in a variety of ways to best meet the organization's needs. In industry experiments using ACDM on medium to large projects and organizations, these roles were routinely filled by entire organizations and staffed by tens of engineers. In some cases, the roles were fulfilled by distributed engineers and teams. In smaller projects and organizations, architecture design teams were composed of three to five engineers, and the members of the team were responsible for more than one role. An interesting point to note is that there is an intentional separation of powers designed into these roles. There is a separation of design concerns between the managing engineer, the chief architect, and the chief scientist. The managing engineer has overall responsibility for the design team, and may even be the overall project manager. The chief architect has responsibility for the general architectural design and the representations of the design. The chief architect will also play a role to ensure that the architecture design is adhered to throughout the construction process. The chief scientist's role is that of a technologist on the team to ensure technical feasibility, mitigate risks through experimentation, and ascertain that the appropriate technologies are considered and utilized. To summarize these roles, the managing engineer's focus is globally on the system, its design, and even its production; the chief architect's focus is outwardly on the architecture design; and the chief scientist focuses inwardly on the technology of the system or product. This separation of powers is depicted graphically in Figure 7.2.

Another separation of concerns has been built into the area of architectural review and system test. These responsibilities are distributed among the quality process engineer (QPE), the chief scientist (CS), and the requirements engineer (RE). The QPE is responsible for test and evaluation but must work with the RE and CS to develop test plans and coordinate the architecture design reviews. This approach helps maintain objectivity in test and design reviews. From a test perspective, this separation of concerns allows the team to test the system from the stakeholder requirements and technical internal perspectives. The QPE is a neutral party from a technical standpoint. The RE contributes to test planning from the stakeholders' perspective. This is black-box testing in the ACDM context, where the system is treated as a black box and is tested only with respect to compliance with the architectural drivers—those of stimulus and response without internal insight. However, the chief scientist has insight into those potentially risky and problematic technical elements of the system that should be exercised through test. This is clear-box testing in the ACDM context. This separation of concerns addresses system testing objectively, inwardly (clear-box test), and outwardly (black-box test). To summarize these roles, the quality process engineer is responsible for coordinating design reviews and tests; the requirements engineer focuses outwardly on tests from the requirements standpoint; and the chief scientist focuses inwardly on testing

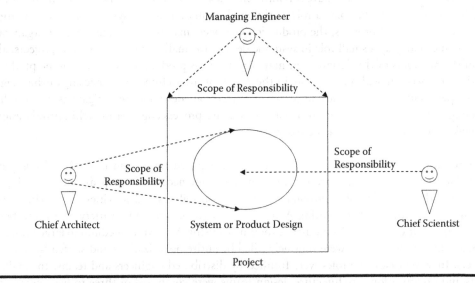

Figure 7.2   Representation of the relationships among the managing engineer, chief architect, and chief scientist with respect to the project and system/product design.

problematic elements, risky elements, or elements where high reliability, safety, and so forth are essential. This separation of powers is depicted graphically in Figure 7.3.

Other specialists may be required to be part of the design team to help in the design, construction, and test of some systems in some domains. Organizations should not hesitate to tailor these roles, their associated responsibilities, or add necessary personnel to the design team. Common examples of other kinds of expertise needed by the design team may include:

- Quality attribute specialists: It is often the case that software-intensive systems have extraordinary performance, security, or some other quality attribute requirement that is best designed into the system with the assistance of an expert in the quality attribute.
- Data engineers: Many systems today have very complex database systems that require specialized design attention from engineers who have expertise in designing and optimizing database structures.
- Infrastructure engineers: Software runs on hardware. Period. This sounds obvious, but you often have to remind software engineers and computer programmers of this fact. As such, the hardware infrastructures of computers, systems, networks, and peripherals are often complex and require the expertise of engineers who specialize in these areas. This is especially true in embedded systems domain. In the embedded systems domain, it is often necessary to remind engineers building the infrastructure that software design is a first-class citizen in software-intensive system design.
- Domain experts: Software is ubiquitous! It runs banks, customer relationship management systems, inventory control systems, cars, airplanes, refrigerators, and many more everyday devices and services we take for granted. It is typically impossible for software professionals to understand the application as well as domain experts. For example, it is common for

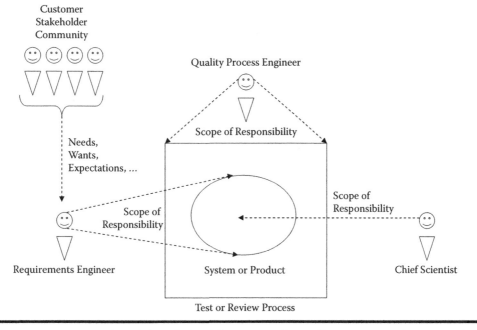

Figure 7.3   Representation of the relationships among the quality process engineer, requirements engineer, and chief scientist with respect to system/product test.

software engineers to write software for fly-by-wire control systems, even though they do not know how to fly. For this reason, domain experts are often required on projects. This can be as simple as just interviewing domain experts as part of the requirements elicitation processes in stage 1, but can be as complex as involving them full-time in the design, development, and test of products and systems.

The ACMD framework defines a number of specific techniques that are bundled in these staged activities to help architects coordinate the design process and help with the design activities. In the following chapters of this section, each stage of ACDM will be discussed in detail. At each stage various methods, templates, guidance, and lessons learned will be provided to help in the adoption and use of ACDM to design software-intensive systems.

Chapter 8

ACDM Stage 1: Discovering the Architectural Drivers

Purpose

The primary purpose of stage 1 is for the architecture design team to initiate one or more meetings with the client stakeholder community (or communities) to discover and document the system's architectural drivers, to include high-level functional requirements, business constraints, technical constraints, and quality attributes.

Preconditions

Before undertaking stage 1, the architecture design team must be established and the ACDM roles must be assigned to the architecture team members as described in Chapter 7.

General Activities

A summary of stage 1 activities, outputs, and responsibilities is listed in Table 8.1.

Techniques, Templates, and Guidance

- Architecture drivers elicitation workshop: This is a technique for structuring stakeholder and architecture design team interactions to gather the system/product architectural drivers.
- Master design plan template: This template is used to create the project plan. The plan is initially created in stage 1 and updated throughout the ACDM stages.

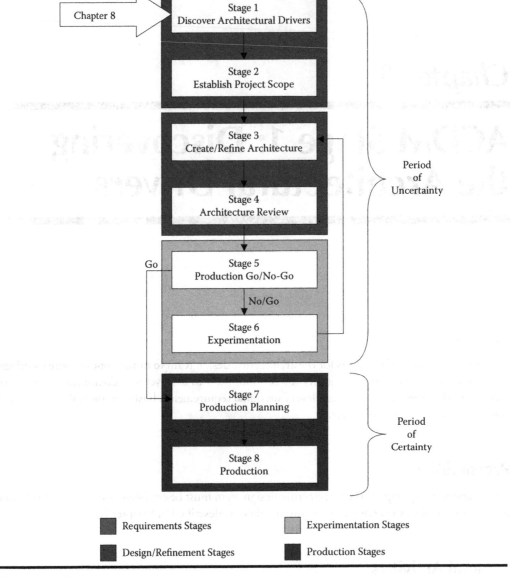

Figure 8.1   Stage 1.

■ Initial project plan estimation guidance: Various tables, checklists, and templates are provided to guide the creation of the master design plan.

Primary Artifacts

■ Initial draft of the master design plan
■ The documented, consolidated raw architectural drivers

Table 8.1 Stage 1 Activities, Outputs, and Responsibilities

General activities	Project introduction provided by the system stakeholders. Elicitation of the architectural drivers from the system stakeholders.
General outputs	The raw architectural drivers describing what the stakeholders expect of the system.
Role	**Stage 1 Recommended Responsibilities**
Managing engineer	Coordinate stage 1 activities. Create the initial master design plan. Assist the requirements engineer in planning the architecture drivers elicitation workshops. Track the workshop efforts. Update and replan the master design plan based on actual data from workshops.
Chief architect	Work with the requirements engineer to elicit the requirements from the stakeholders. The chief architect should focus on eliciting complete and measurable architecture drivers. Assist the requirements engineering in capturing and documenting the collection of raw architecture drivers.
Chief scientist	Work with the requirements engineer to elicit the requirements from the stakeholders. The chief scientist should focus on technical issues associated with eliciting the architectural drivers. Assist the requirements engineering in capturing and documenting the collection of raw architecture drivers.
Requirements engineer	Plan, coordinate, and facilitate the stage 1 architectural drivers elicitation workshops. Coordinate architectural drivers consolidation meetings. Compile the consolidated raw architecture drivers document.
Quality process engineer	Ensure that the ACDM (and other project processes) are being followed. Work with the requirements engineer to elicit the requirements from the stakeholders. Assist the requirements engineering in capturing and documenting the collection of raw architecture drivers. Coordinate a review of the raw architectural drivers document.
Support engineer	Work with the requirements engineer to elicit the requirements from the stakeholders. Install, configure, and maintain the tools necessary to support stage 1 activities and any tools that can be established now to support the remainder of the project.
Production engineers	In stage 1, minimal support is usually required from production engineers. However, if they have special implementation-oriented domain expertise in hardware, software, or other related engineering disciplines, they should be engaged and assist the team in the elicitation, capture, and documentation of architectural drivers.

Postconditions

- The initial master design plan has been created and is updated as required after each architecture drivers elicitation workshop.
- All or key stakeholders or stakeholder groups have been engaged using the architecture drivers elicitation workshop.
- The raw architectural drivers have been collected from the stakeholders and consolidated and documented. The focus of stage 1 is to collect data, not analyze or structure it.

Description of Stage 1

In stage 1, the architecture design team will meet with the system stakeholders to discover and document the architectural drivers. Stage 1 is not about refinement, analysis, or structuring the information that is garnered from the stakeholders, but rather about gathering as much information about what the stakeholders need and expect in the system. The goal of stage 1 is not to analyze and structure the architectural drivers. The goal is more about gathering as much information as possible regarding the architectural drivers. The encounters between stakeholders and the architecture design team are structured to make the most efficient use of valuable time spent with the stakeholders. Stage 1 is a divergent process in terms of the quantity of information that is gathered—more is better; the details will be sorted out later. In most cases it is unrealistic to assume that the architectural team could possibly get all the architectural drivers for a system of any consequence in a single meeting. Although stage 1 is divergent in terms of the quantity of information gathered, we want to avoid inconsistent and duplicate information as much as possible. However, this should be a secondary concern—quantity of information is the primary concern. Each engagement with the stakeholder community requires structure to make the most efficient use of time as well as avoiding duplication and maintaining consistency across the engagements as much as possible. During these engagements in stage 1, the architecture design team will use various methods and templates (described later) designed to provide structure, guide the discussion, and capture information about the architectural drivers. Once again, the architectural drivers include high-level functional requirements, business and technical constraints, and the quality attribute requirements. Collectively, they will shape the structure of the system, so it is essential that we get as much information as possible about them.

Because ACDM defines a framework for the design process, it focuses on design activities, not the total project planning activities. However, design can play an important role in project planning; this will be more obvious as the stages of ACDM are explained. Again, design is a process that takes time and resources. As such, it is essential that the design activities are planned with regards to the larger system project schedule. To plan the design activities, ACDM prescribes that a master design plan be created that describes how the design will be executed during the project. The master design plan, other planning templates, and guidance provided by ACDM were intended to supplement any existing overall project planning processes or methods an organization uses. However, if an organization has weak or ad hoc planning discipline, then the master design plan and the associated planning templates and guidance provided by ACDM can serve as a good start for organizations that want to improve their project planning and tracking processes. On small projects, the master design plan may be enough of a plan to guide the entire project.

Obviously stage 1 is the start of the project and the beginning of the period of uncertainty. Although precise construction estimates are impossible to derive with any fidelity at this point in a project, it is important to establish activity budgets at a minimum to use as a comparison against actual performance and to track progress during this period of volatility. An activity budget is a line in the sand, an allocation of time and resources to get some task done. Having activity budgets, even if they are very rough estimates (as they often are during the period of uncertainty), can provide a guide to let us know if we are getting behind. This can be an early indicator that our estimates were grossly inaccurate or we are experiencing unanticipated difficulties, and that we may need to replan the project or negotiate for more time or resources. The earlier in the project we can identify these technical and programmatic issues, the earlier we can intervene to correct the problem. If no plan or schedule is established (regardless of how volatile it may be in the early stages), we have nothing to compare our design activities against. It is impossible to determine if we are ahead of or behind schedule and if progress is being made. The period of uncertainty is present in any project regardless of whether ACDM is used. However, ACDM strives to reduce the duration of the period of uncertainty by (1) iteratively designing the architecture, (2) identifying issues by evaluating design, and (3) mitigating technical risk through experimentation. Uncertainty due to misunderstanding of the architectural drivers is a principal risk in many projects. The iterative design, evaluation, experimentation, and design refinement defined by ACDM help avoid many of the problems associated with big-bang or code-first-and-design-later approaches. Similarly, the master design plan is iteratively refined at strategic points during the design process as more information is gathered. As the design process progresses and the design matures, the master design plan is refined and estimation fidelity for production improves because we know more about the problem and the solution. At this point we are in a much better position to estimate duration, cost, difficulty, and so forth. As the team moves into the period of certainty, more accurate construction estimates can be projected because the design itself is used as a basis for estimation. Again, the master design plan can serve as input to an existing organizational planning process, or be used (with some modification) as the overall project plan itself.

The Master Design Plan: Planning the Design Strategy

Project plans that predict cost and schedule derived early in the life cycle are notoriously suspect because estimation is based almost entirely on gross assumptions, not on a stable architectural design. Still, plans are required to navigate the period of uncertainty to get an architecture design that can be used as a basis to plan construction. Essentially, ACDM prescribes incrementally planning and refining the plan as more knowledge is gained about the product, domain, stakeholders, and so forth. The initial focus of the plan is to address the period of uncertainty (stages 1 to 6). Once the architecture is stable, the focus is then on planning construction using the elements of the architecture as a basis for estimation and planning. ACDM calls for a creating a master design plan in stage 1 that initially focuses on planning the period of uncertainty stages, but the plan is updated frequently throughout the design process at prescribed strategic points as more is learned about the product/system. High-frequency updates are required because the project is highly dynamic in the period of uncertainty. The first activity to consider for the master design plan is planning the overall design strategy. ACDM calls for an architecture design team strategy meeting with specific activities and outcomes. During this meeting the team will meet to discuss, plan, and document the first crucial steps of the project. The purpose of the architecture design team strategy meeting is:

- Personal introductions: If the members of the architecture design team have not been formally introduced, the strategy meeting is a good time for the team to make formal introductions to one another. The architecture design team should also be formally introduced to the project management, the support staff, and so on.
- Reaffirm the team roles: The architecture design team roles should already be assigned. However, during the strategy meeting they should be reaffirmed to ensure that everyone knows what his or her role is on the team, and that all team members know what roles everyone has on the team.
- Project overview/introduction: At this point the architecture design team should be introduced to the project. Any related documentation such as requirements documents, requests

Table 8.2   Initial Strategy Meeting Planning Guidelines

Meeting Item	Description
Introductions	Architecture design team members introduce themselves. It is best if the managing engineer leads this meeting. It is a very powerful statement if a senior manager kicks off the strategy meeting by introducing the managing engineer and the chief architect for the team. This establishes each of their roles and authority formally to the group. Include support staff in the introductions and their responsibilities to the team as well.
Roles and responsibilities	Ensure that roles are assigned and that every team member understands his or her role and the responsibilities associated with the role. If each ACDM role is filled with multiple people, ensure that a primary and alternate(s) are defined for the role.
Project introduction	Provide a general description of what is known about the project at this point. Discussion may include: • Description of the customer, the market, general expectations of the customer • Description of how this relates to the developing organization's current business • Description of the customer stakeholder community • Distribution and discussion of available documentation, such as requirements, requests for proposals (RFPs), and so forth
Initial planning and milestones for stage 1	Stage 1 is essential for launching the project forward, and project planning at this point should focus on planning stage 1 activities. Consider the following items: • Architecture drivers workshops: How many will the team have to conduct? When will the team conduct them? When should the team complete them? • Tools: What support tools and infrastructure does the team need? When must they be in place and ready for the team to use? Tools may include configuration management, Web presence, communication, compilers, debuggers, test environments, and so forth. • Consolidating: How much time should the team allow for consolidating the raw architectural drivers? • Master design plan: How much time should the team allocate to create the Master design plan?
Initial planning and milestones for stages 2 to 6.	At this point, it will be impossible to establish the exact schedule for stages 2 to 6; however, it is appropriate to define schedule milestones and goals. In some cases the entire project duration has a hard-and-fixed delivery date, before the requirements begin. This becomes a key business constraint, and the architect design team must then set target dates within the established timeline to complete each stage.
Brainstorm project risks	At this point the team should brainstorm any potential risks that are facing the project. This list should be consolidated, prioritized, documented in the master design plan, and tracked.

for proposals (RFPs), or bids that relate to the project should be distributed to the architecture design team.

■ Discuss the master design plan: The managing engineer will work with the architectural design team to plan an initial strategy for interacting with the stakeholders. The managing engineer will use this information to begin the initial draft of the master design plan.

Experience with ACDM has shown that strategy meetings can be as short as a couple of hours or last up to a few days, depending upon the size and scope of the project. Strategy meetings are meant to be conducted by the organization developing the product and should not include customer stakeholders. This is a chance for the developing organization to coordinate its activities, before stakeholder engagements begin. A strategy meeting template is provided in Table 8.2 that can be used to guide these meetings.

While a complete template for writing the master design plan will be presented later, the primary activity to consider in the initial draft is the architecture drivers elicitation workshops. These are structured meetings where the architecture design team and the client stakeholders find out what they need and expect in the system/product and from the project. Before the architecture drivers elicitation workshops can begin, the architecture design team needs to get an idea of the breadth of stakeholders that are involved in the project. Until this is understood at some level, it is difficult to plan these workshops with any fidelity. This is a key consideration for planning stage 1, but also affects the planning for the rest of the project. The remaining stages of ACDM and the architecture design will be affected by the number of stakeholder groups the architecture design team has to engage to get adequate representation of the architectural drivers. The number of stakeholder interactions the architecture design team has to conduct is proportional to the time and cost of determining the architectural drivers of the system. It is prudent to track the reoccurring costs (time and resources) for conducting each workshop. This can help with the chore of tracking costs and effort, and help refine the plan. After each architecture drivers elicitation workshop, progress should be tracked with respect to the master design plan and the plan should be updated as necessary based on actual costs and effort it took to conduct the workshop. Figure 8.2 is a graphical depiction of stage 1 activities as described thus far.

The primary means of interacting with stakeholders to elicit systemic requirements is through the architecture drivers elicitation workshop. These are intense, structured, short-duration meet-

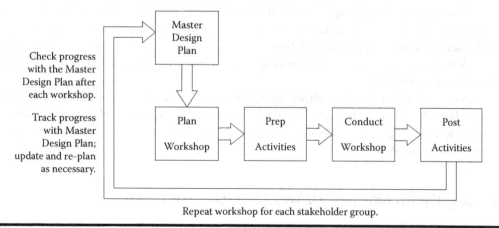

Figure 8.2 Architecture drivers elicitation workshop cycles.

ings designed to focus participants and gather data about the architectural drivers for the product or system. The architecture drivers elicitation workshops are designed to be conducted in one day; of course, this can be tailored as necessary. However, if the community of stakeholders is large, diverse, or geographically distributed, multiple workshops will be required to adequately capture the architectural drivers. Organizing stakeholders can be a daunting task in some organizations. The stakeholder communities should be partitioned into manageable groups that represent systemic interest groups and accommodate scheduling and logistics. Deciding on how many architectural drivers elicitation workshops to conduct, determining how much time it will take to do them all, the schedule, cost, logistics, and so forth will be a major part of the master design plan. In small organizations with few co-located stakeholders, it can be easy to coordinate workshops. However, in larger organizations with hundreds or thousands of stakeholders, or distributed stakeholder communities, it can be difficult or impossible to meet with all of the stakeholders. In these situations, the architecture design team should work with the stakeholders to create groups that will represent the interests of a particular stakeholder community in the system or product. For example, consider an organization that is building a new system to replace a legacy system that has hundreds of installers, hundreds of maintainers, a team of 20 trainers, and 10,000 end users. Assume that the new system will have similar kinds and numbers of stakeholders. Obviously it would be impossible for an architecture design team to meet with all of these stakeholders. However, if each stakeholder group provides a few representatives, we would have a manageable group of stakeholders that can provide valuable information about the architectural drivers from each community's perspective. In some situations, there may be stakeholders that the architecture design team would like to meet with but they are not available, or they are part of an anticipated market and do not exist yet. The classic case is when an organization is developing a new product or attempting to penetrate new markets for the first time. In this case the architecture design team should try to identify and engage surrogate stakeholders that can provide insight into the architectural drivers of concern for the anticipated stakeholder community. The point here is that wide coverage of stakeholders is highly desirable, and depth should be adequate enough to represent the larger stakeholder community's interest. Not enough breadth and some stakeholders' concerns will not be considered in the product or system design. Not enough depth and the interests of a given stakeholder community may not be addressed. Too much depth, and there may be duplication of information. There is no magic formula for determining if breadth and depth of stakeholder involvement is right. This is purely left to the judgment of the architecture design team, who must strive to understand the stakeholder organization, the system/product they need, and the business context in which it will be used. Table 8.3 contains a list of likely system/product stakeholders that can help the architecture design team identify stakeholders and plan architecture drivers elicitation workshops.

Each of the architecture drivers elicitation workshops are structured around the seven activities listed in Table 8.4. Each of these activities, the associated methods, and templates are discussed in detail in the following sections. Before the first workshop can be held, a considerable amount of planning must take place.

Planning the Architecture Drivers Elicitation Workshop

Planning each workshop is essential to ensure that they are conducted as efficiently as possible to maximize the time stakeholders and the architecture design team spend together. The

Table 8.3 Potential System Stakeholders

Stakeholders	Descriptions
Engineers and scientists	Concerned with efficient systemic design and construction. Engineers and scientists may have background in various domains directly related to systemic construction concerns, such as computer hardware, computer scientists, network, and software engineering. Engineers and scientists may have domain-related expertise in domains such as chemical, medical, aerospace, nautical, and other various types of engineering disciplines.
Developers	Concerned with detailed implementation of system elements. The term developers is often associated with software developers; however, in terms of identifying stakeholders, architects should think more broadly to include those who build software, network infrastructure, or computer or other systemic hardware. Engineer, scientist, and developer roles often overlap.
Designers	Concerned with designing systems and elements of the system. Designers may also be engineers, scientists, or developers, and often their roles often overlap. Designers may have varied backgrounds, depending upon the system and domain.
Integrators	Concerned with assembling elements into a complete system. Integrators are concerned with the efficiency of assembly of elements, avoiding element mismatch, coordinating construction, and resolving element mismatch as quickly as possible.
Testers	Concerned with testing system elements and the assembled system. Testers may or may not have in-depth engineering or technical expertise, but they must understand the system requirements to ensure that the system meets the specification. Testers need to understand the overall system's functional and behavioral requirements and must be able to ensure that the test coverage is adequate.
Maintainers	Concerned with system repair, reconfiguration, change, upgrade, and so forth. Maintainers may have varied backgrounds in hardware, software, and other similar domains needed for system construction, and also for system repair. Maintainers may come from the ranks of those responsible for designing and developing the system initially. Maintainers need to troubleshoot to find defects in the system or to understand how changes can be made in it, and be able to reason about the effects changes may have on systemic properties. Current architectural representations are critical for system maintainers.
Installers	Concerned with deploying or installing the system or system elements in the operational context. Installers must be experts in the technical details associated with element or system installation and configuration.
Trainers	Concerned with teaching others how to use, install, and maintain the system. Trainers may also have a varying amount of system or domain expertise, depending upon the kind of stakeholders they must train and the depth of knowledge/expertise the stakeholders must attain during the training. Trainers are typically interested in being able to configure, deploy, or otherwise use the system in a training mode. Training modes may include simulations, simulated data, artificial sensors and data streams, virtual environments, and so forth.

(continued)

Table 8.3   Potential System Stakeholders (continued)

Stakeholders	Descriptions
Procurement/ buyers	Concerns are typically cost, meeting functional specification, and timely delivery. Procurement specialists typically do not have in-depth technical or domain expertise, so they should not be relied on as a sole source for functional requirements, quality attribute requirements, and technical constraints. Although they may convey these requirements to the developing organizations, they are usually not the source of these requirements. Procurement specialists may impose business constraints because they often must enforce cost, schedule, and any regulations imposed on the procurement process.
End users	Generally concerned with using a system to do their job. The end user is typically the community of stakeholders that use the system to do some job, and are generally interested in a system that is easy to use, makes their job easier, and helps them to be more productive. Users are often concerned with usability. The end users are often the most varied group of stakeholders including users who are novices, experienced, unsophisticated, technically savvy, domain experts, and so forth. Each end user has different expectations in the functional services and behavioral properties of the system. All should be considered before design.
System administrators	Generally concerned with configuring the operational system, setting up and maintaining security parameters, performing backup, adding new users, and so forth. System administrators are a special kind of end user that is rarely considered in the stakeholder community, but are often critical to the system's day-to-day operation. Different systems from various domains may require a lot of system administrator support; in others, none at all. If systems administration support is required for a system, these stakeholders can provide important insight into the kinds of features and needs required for system administration so they can be designed into the system.
Managers	Concerned about product/system price versus cost (i.e., profitability), schedule, quality, and resources. Managers are present on both sides of the system. There are managers on one side buying the system/product, and managers on the other side designing and building the system/ product. However, managers on both sides of the system share the same concerns described above. Managers may or may not have technical backgrounds. Many managers come from the technical ranks and have a great deal of technical expertise. Managers will be the source of many of the system's business constraints.
Marketing and sales	Concerned about market share, closing the deal, product/system value, features, cost, and price. Marketing and sales professionals often secure work for an organization by bidding to build a system/product—often they have no idea if it can be built under the bidding price and schedule. This is a very dangerous situation. If there is no flexibility once price and schedules bidding is made, then architects should be part of the bidding processes to help provide more realistic bids. Marketers are interested in the features a system/product possesses so that they can show value and make the sale. In most domains, there needs to be closer cooperation between all the technical stakeholders and the marketing and sales forces.

Table 8.4   Specific Architectural Drivers Elicitation Workshop Activities

Activity	Who	When
Planning the workshop	Requirements engineer and managing engineer	Before the stakeholder architecture drivers meeting
Introductions and meeting overview	Architecture design team led by requirements engineer	During the stakeholder architecture drivers meeting
Product or system overview	Stakeholder representative(s)	During the stakeholder architecture drivers meeting
Identify operational descriptions	Design team and stakeholders led by requirements engineer	During the stakeholder architecture drivers meeting
Identify quality attribute requirements	Design team and stakeholders led by requirements engineer	During the stakeholder architecture drivers meeting
Identify business constraints and technical constraints	Design team and stakeholders led by requirements engineer	During the stakeholder architecture drivers meeting
Raw data consolidation	Design team coordinated by requirements engineer	After the stakeholder architecture drivers meeting

requirements engineer is responsible for planning and leading the workshop. In planning the workshop, the architecture design team should consider the following issues:

- Venue
- Stakeholders
- Agenda
- Project overview presentation
- Materials
- Meals
- Travel

The *venue* for the architecture drivers elicitation workshop is an important first consideration. It is strongly recommended that the workshop be conducted in person if possible rather than electronically via video teleconference (VTC), teleconferences, or some other similar technology. Experimentation using virtual meetings to conduct architecture drivers elicitation workshops has yielded mixed results. Once initial physical contact has been made between stakeholders and the architecture design team at a workshop, follow-up communications using virtual means are often much more effective. If possible, the venue should be conducted at a neutral site where the attendees are not likely to be called out of the architecture drivers elicitation workshop to attend to other business, handle problems, answer phones, and so forth.

It is essential that the *stakeholders* are contacted and invited to the architecture drivers elicitation workshop. Coordinating schedules among all of the stakeholders can be extremely frustrating. It is often a good idea to ensure that the manager of the client stakeholders is a champion of the architecture drivers elicitation workshop. Often he or she can set the date and ensure that the workshop is a priority for the stakeholders. However, the architecture design team must insist on adequate stakeholder representation at the workshop. The architecture design team should get a list of attendees as the workshop schedule solidifies, and they should verify each stakeholder's role in the organization and his or her relationship to the system/product. In a tactful way, the architecture design team should question any superfluous or missing stakeholders. Each workshop should be limited to 25 stakeholders or less. If you must use virtual meetings, plan on fewer stakeholders. Due to line delays, limited screen VTC space, and the general difficulty in coordinating distributed discussions, virtual workshops should be limited to fewer than ten stakeholders.

The requirements engineer should create a draft *agenda* so that all attendees have an idea of what is going to happen during the schedule for the architecture drivers elicitation workshop. This should be created and sent to the stakeholders in advance of the actual workshop. It is important to check with the stakeholders regarding the agenda, especially with respect to the duration of the start and stop times, and the duration of the workday and breaks. These are organizational and culturally sensitive issues. For planning purposes, the attendees should plan on spending eight hours in the architecture drivers elicitation workshop. For example, organizations in India, Germany, Korea, Japan, and the United States have very different working cultures, norms, and expectations from one another. To ensure that there are no surprises or social faux pas, prepare and send the agenda early, allowing the attendee organizations to comment, critique, and refine the agenda. Table 8.5 lists an agenda template that can be used as guidance to create a specific agenda for an architecture drivers elicitation workshop.

It is important that during the architecture drivers elicitation workshop the client stakeholders provide a *project overview presentation* to introduce the architecture design team to the system/product and the project. Rather than an ad hoc discussion of the system or product, the architecture design team should ask the client stakeholders to prepare a presentation in advance of the

Table 8.5   Architectural Drivers Elicitation Workshop Agenda Template

Architectural Drivers Elicitation Workshop

Location: <Insert location here>

Date: <Insert date here>

Start time: <Insert start time here>

End time: <Insert end time here>

Note: Please turn off cell phones for the workshop.

Activity	Who	Duration
Introductions	<Architecture team representative>	~15 minutes
Product or system overview	<Stakeholder representative(s)>	~1 hour
Break	All	~15 minutes
Operational descriptions	<Discussion led by architecture team>	~2 hours
Lunch	All	~1 hour
Identify quality attribute requirements	<Discussion led by architecture team>	~2 hours (breaks as necessary)
Break	All	~15 minutes
Identify business and technical constraints	<Discussion led by architecture team>	~1 hour
Summary and next steps	<Architecture team representative>	~15 minutes

workshop. In many cases, the client stakeholder organization already has written project proposals, presentations, or even customer written requirements specifications. While the team should read this material in preparation for stage 1 and the architecture drivers elicitation workshops, the client stakeholders should still plan on providing an overview of the system. Often when this presentation is made during the architecture drivers elicitation workshop, questions will arise from the stakeholders about the requirements, assumptions, and so forth that are very enlightening for all. It is best if the client stakeholders create a slide presentation for the project overview presentation. Table 8.6 provides a recommended outline for this presentation that can be shared with the attendee organization.

In addition to content, the architecture design team should also check to ensure that the presentation size is appropriate for the agenda. Often these presentations are too big, and as a result, the agenda is blown because it takes hours to get through the project overview presentation. If a project is very large and it makes sense to have multiple presenters, then the architecture design team may want to consider more than one day for the architecture drivers elicitation workshop or conduct multiple workshops. Again, this is the importance of planning the workshop, creating the agenda ahead of time, and getting the project overview presentation from the client stakeholders before the meeting. There should be no surprises for the architecture design team

Table 8.6   Project Overview Presentation Outline

Topic	Description
General business context	Describe: • Brief history of the company and market • Key market differentiators • Current need and how the proposed system will meet those needs and requirements
Key stakeholders	Describe the key stakeholders (organizations and individuals), their roles and responsibilities in the project. If the stakeholder will use the system, describe how.
General functionality	Describe the general function requirements of the product/system. Avoid lots of details and focus on describing critical, high-level functional requirements.
Technical constraints	Describe: • Hardware or software elements or products the system must use • Mandatory interoperation with other systems • Reuse of legacy elements (software or hardware) • Required technical standards and protocols
Business constraints	Describe: • Time-to-market demands • Cost limitations • Schedule demands • Regulatory standards and demand • Legal issues
Quality attributes	Discuss the general quality attributes requirements, such as performance, availability, security, modifiability, and so forth. Specifically indicate why these quality attributes are needed and by what stakeholder (or stakeholders).

or the attendees. Again, to make the time spent in the workshop as productive as possible, this preparation is crucial.

As the time for the first workshop gets closer, the architecture design team must consider the mundane but essential matter of logistics. Although not something we associate with design, successfully coordinating logistics in advance can make or break the workshop. Some key issues to consider (but not limited to) are *materials, meals,* and *travel.* Prior to the workshops, the required materials need to be in place for conducting the workshop. This is usually a bit more than making sure there are pens and paper. To minimize the amount of time required for eating lunch and snacks, it is advisable that meals be provided on site at the venue where the workshop is occurring. In addition to convenience, time will not be lost traveling to and from lunch and reconvening after lunch; this easily stretches one-hour lunch breaks to two-hour lunch breaks. A side effect of having lunch together is that it often promotes informal conversation among customer stakeholders and the architecture design team that can help with the workshop. A final detail is coordinating travel plans for all those involved in the workshop. Typically the architecture design team travels to the customer stakeholder location because there are typically more customers than architects, making it more cost-effective. Table 8.7 lists some of the considerations for materials, meals, and travel.

Conducting the Architecture Drivers Elicitation Workshops

Prior to conducting the first workshop, the architecture design team should establish the initial project plans and document them in the master design plan. The team should also have the product or system overview presentation from the client, and verify that it is of reasonable content and length for the duration of the workshop planned. Before the actual workshop begins, it is important that roles for the workshop are established; consider the following roles and responsibilities:

- Introduction and workshop overview: This should be done by the project managers and the managing engineer in some combination. The purpose of this is to set the tone and legitimacy for the workshop.
- Facilitator: The facilitator for the workshop will be the requirements engineer. He or she will manage the workshop and coordinate discussion.
- Timekeeper: A member of the architecture design team should be assigned as the timekeeper to ensure that the agenda is adhered to as closely as possible.
- Scribe/recorder: A member of the architecture design team should be assigned to record the proceedings electronically. If data is going to be recorded using flip charts, then it is a good idea to have two scribes. Also, keep in mind that recording information can be a tiring and tedious task; sharing the recording responsibility is a good idea.

It is important that the remaining architecture design team members in attendance that do not have an active role (such as those mentioned above) but focus on taking copious notes of the proceedings. With all of the logistics planned, the supplies ready, and the personnel in place, the team is ready to execute the first architecture drivers elicitation workshop.

Table 8.7   Logistics Considerations

Logistical Consideration	Description
Materials	• Note pads • Pens/pencils • Tape • Whiteboards • Whiteboard erasers • Flip charts • Overhead projectors • Slide beamers • Plastic overhead slides • Markers • PointersPower cables, regional power converters (110V to 220V, two-prong versus three-prong adapters, and so forth) • Tape recorders (if permitted and desired)
Communication	Because stakeholders will be in the meeting for a whole day, it can be helpful if they are able to stay in contact. Communications should be helpful, not a hindrance to the workshop. Ask stakeholders to turn off cell phones during the workshop and consider the following communication logistics: • Computer networks: Be careful. If network access is available in the meeting room, stakeholders will read e-mail. Have network access available outside the actual meeting room. • Message board and services: Provide a number that can be called where someone can answer and post the stakeholder's message to a message board or contact them directly.
Nourishment	Because the workshop is a focused activity that usually occupies at least one full day with a group of stakeholders, plan to have meals and snacks in close proximity to the workshop meeting room. Consider the following: • Morning snacks/pastries/fruit. • Coffee, water, juice, soda: It is a good idea to provide ample liquid refreshments all day. • Lunch: Try to avoid really heavy foods and big lunches because it can cause stakeholders to be really sleepy after lunch. Quick and light should be the rule. Do not forget to ask about dietary restrictions when planning meals (vegetarian, kosher, and so forth). • Snacks: Plan on snacks in the afternoon. This is important, especially if you follow the quick-and-light rule for lunch. Avoid ice cream and cakes, as they can make people too full and sleepy. Small cookies, fruits, veggies, crackers, cheese, and so forth are good choices for reenergizing stakeholders for the late afternoon.
Transportation	Time can be saved if transportation to and from hotels and airports is arranged and settled well in advance of the workshop. This can prevent stakeholders from having to leave earlier to find transportation, catch rides, or otherwise disrupt the workshop. Make sure to coordinate pick-up and drop-off locations.

Introductions and Workshop Overview

Before the workshop begins, make sure that you put the agenda up on a wall in a visible place and ensure that each participant has a pen or pencil and writing paper. The meeting begins with introductions of the customer stakeholders and the architecture design team. It is important to take attendance at the meeting to keep track of the stakeholders that have been engaged throughout stage 1. A simple sheet of paper that stakeholders can sign that lists their name, organization, e-mail/contact information, relationship to the system, and role on the project will suffice. After introductions, the architecture design team should establish ground rules for the meeting. Things to consider are:

- Turn off cell phones and pagers.
- Play nice: During the workshop, do not criticize attendee contributions. Encourage attendees to respect each stakeholder's point of view. Discourage attendees from interrupting stakeholders. Avoid side conversations and other undesirable behaviors that might disrupt the workshop.
- Stay focused: Encourage attendees to focus on the activities of the workshop, and emphasize that stakeholder participation is critical to the success of the workshop.

After establishing the workshop ground rules, the architecture design team should provide an overview of the architecture drivers elicitation workshop. This is best done by a short presentation that includes the following points:

- Purpose: The purpose of the architecture drivers elicitation workshop is to get requirements directly from the stakeholders of the system or product. A stakeholder is anyone who has a stake in the system/product concept, construction, operation, service, and deployment. It is important to directly interact with stakeholders to get architectural drivers. Explain to attendees what architectural drivers are those functional requirements, quality attribute requirements, and business and technical constraints that will dramatically influence early systemic design decisions.
- Outcomes: The outcome of the architecture drivers elicitation workshop is to collect the raw architectural drivers. The term *raw* means that drivers are accepted as is without analysis. This raw data will be used as input for analysis and creating the architectural drivers specification. This document will serve as the key input for architectural design, setting the exact project scope, establishing schedules, and determining costs.
- Methods: Various structured brainstorming methods will be used to elicit architectural drivers from the stakeholders. Some or all of the following methods and others may be used by the architecture design team to elicit the architectural drivers:
  - Open brainstorm: The audience will be invited to contribute specific information or add to information already collected at will.
  - Round-robin: Each audience member will be asked to contribute specific information in turn.
  - Silent contribution: Each audience member will be asked to contribute specific information on a written ballot where the identity of the contributors will be kept confidential.
- Stakeholders' role and expectations: Stakeholders should keep in mind that their participation is essential for these methods to work. They should be respectful of other members'

opinions and try not to interrupt speakers. They should avoid side conversations and yield to the facilitator when asked to.

■ Architecture design team's role: The architecture design team will lead and facilitate the architecture drivers elicitation workshop. They will record the architecture drivers, manage the conversation, and ensure that the workshop stays on schedule.

■ Questions: Invite the attendees at the architecture drivers elicitation workshop to ask any clarifying questions at this point.

If there are questions, obviously the architecture design team should answer them to the best of their ability. If a question cannot be answered, then record it as an issue and decide who is responsible for answering the question and when. It is best if there is a flip chart or area of a whiteboard set aside to capture issues that arise during the workshop that need to be resolved. If there are no questions, then refer the attendees back to the agenda and indicate the workshop will proceed to the product or system overview.

Product or System Overview

At this point the architecture design team will ask the client stakeholder representative to provide the product or system overview. Again, this should follow the outline provided in Table 8.6. It is important to capture information about the architecture drivers based on the presentation. Focus on each of the architectural drivers: high-level functional requirements, quality attribute requirements, and business and technical constraints. It can be helpful to keep separate columns on a piece of paper or separate pieces of paper for each architectural driver, or a similar technique if you are recording information on a laptop. It can help tremendously with consolidation if all architecture design team members use the same format to record the drivers.

Identify Operational Descriptions

Beginning with this phase of the architecture drivers elicitation workshop, the architecture design team will start to collect the specific architectural drivers. The information gathered here will complement what was described during the project or system overview. This acts as a check and balance to ensure that what was presented reflects the true need of the broader stakeholder community. During the operational description and successive steps of the workshop, the stakeholders will be asked to describe how they anticipate interacting with the system in an operational context. Essentially the architecture design team is trying to elicit the high-level functional requirements. It is important that the stakeholders describe how they might like to interact with the system and not propose solutions. This is especially difficult if the customer stakeholders are technically savvy. Some stakeholders often think they know the solutions to the requirements they propose and have their own ideas of technological solutions to a given problem. Although they may have an answer, it may not be the best answer and should not be accepted as a requirement. The architecture design team should carefully listen to the operational descriptions given by the stakeholders and try to identify when they are giving solutions rather than describing requirements.

Although a great number of techniques can be used to elicit functional requirements, recall that at this point we are interested in gross functionality, and it is highly recommended that we characterize systemic functionality through use case scenarios. So when considering requirements elicitation strategies and techniques, these ends should be kept in mind. In terms of requirements engineering, there are two general families of techniques that can be used to elicit requirements: active and passive. Active techniques involve directly engaging stakeholders to describe what they want in a system, whereas passive techniques involve observing stakeholders to see what they do and how they do it. Passive requirements elicitation techniques engage stakeholders vicariously through questionnaires, surveys, observation, surrogates, test instruments, and so forth. Once passive requirements data is gathered, it must be analyzed to determine the exact system requirements. Developing good data gathering instruments (questionnaires, surveys) can be very challenging and is well outside of the scope of this text. Passive requirements gathering is almost never used alone, and these techniques are almost always combined with active techniques. Recall at this point that we need to formulate coarse-grained functionality in terms of use cases, and later quality attribute requirements in terms of quality attribute scenarios. Gathering requirements in these forms would be extremely difficult to do using passive requirements elicitation techniques. In general, passive techniques are used far less in practice than active requirements gathering techniques. Active requirements elicitation techniques are most often used in practice, but can be very challenging in terms of coordination and application. Active requirements elicitation can collect a lot of raw systemic requirements, from lots of stakeholders, in a relatively short period of time. However, too often the interaction with stakeholders is ad hoc, and the requirements gathering and analysis phase of many projects never seem to converge—leading to "analysis paralysis." Common active techniques generally include brainstorming and interviewing stakeholders. Brainstorming is often most effective in initial requirements elicitation engagements if the brainstorming process is effectively managed. Unfortunately, brainstorming meetings are often formless, pointless discussions that can (and often do) degenerate into shouting matches. The requirements elicitation structure described here was built into ACDM to prevent this from happening and to make the most effective use of designer-customer time spent together. Interviewing is an effective follow-up technique after the initial data collection. We will see that interviewing is used in stage 2 to clarify requirements gathered in stage 1 that are not well understood. Questionnaires, a passive technique, can be used to complement active requirements gathering techniques. However, developing effective questionnaires can be a very complex undertaking requiring specific expertise to develop. Questionnaires have to be designed in such a way that they are easy for the stakeholder to navigate, as short as possible, and yet give stakeholders the ability to express their thoughts. If the questionnaire fails on any of these points, then the stakeholder may not complete the questionnaire, or the answers will be less than accurate.

The method that will be used here in the architecture drivers elicitation workshop is structured brainstorming. In fact, the entire workshop is a structured brainstorming session, from top to bottom, designed to elicit as much information about the architectural drivers as possible. To gather the information needed to construct use cases that will describe systemic functionality, operational descriptions will be developed with the stakeholders during the workshop. This information is elicited from stakeholders using the template shown in Table 8.8 to guide and focus the brainstorming activity.

This template can be projected on the wall or hard copies can be distributed to the stakeholders. This template is used to help stimulate and focus the stakeholders' thoughts and discussion on the functional aspects of the system. There are several ways the architecture design team can facilitate the brainstorming and interact with the stakeholders at this point. The requirements engineer should facilitate the discussion of operational descriptions. Consider the following approaches:

■ Open contribution: The architecture design team can ask the stakeholders to contribute operational descriptions at will. This can work if you are conducting the workshop in a

Table 8.8   Operational Description Template

Operational description title: Provide a name and description for the operational description.		
Describe stakeholder(s) role(s) proposing the description: List the relevant stakeholders here.		ID:
Operational Consideration	**Stakeholder Response**	
Provide a general description of the functionality.	Briefly describe the operation here. Allow stakeholder to explain the operation in his or her own words. Help stakeholders craft the description and ask clarifying questions to understand their language, domain, and the description.	
Describe what the stakeholder does now or would like to be able to do.	Explain what the stakeholder currently does now without the system/product; what they would like to do with the system/product; or what the system/product does now and how they would like to change what they do.	
Describe any input that is provided or is available at the time of initiation.	Describe any input that the stakeholders, device, peripheral, or other systems provide.	
Describe the operational context.	Describe the operational context that is relevant for this operational description. The architecture design team should press the stakeholders to think about and describe if possible: When the action initiated; any preconditions that must exist prior to initiation; the operational conditions at the time of initiation.	
Describe how the system/product should respond.	The stakeholder should describe how the system will respond in the ideal sense. It is not necessary to describe quality attribute responses in terms of timeliness, fault detection, or recovery in detail, as this will be discovered and documented as quality attribute scenarios. However, operational descriptions may serve as a starting point for describing the quality attribute scenarios.	
Describe any output the system/product produces as a result of the action.	List any and all outputs that will result from the operation. Outputs can be reports, data streams, hard copies, displays, and so forth.	
Describe who or what uses the output and what is the output used for.	Describe the consumers of the outputs. Consumers may be other stakeholders, devices, actuators, other systems, and so forth. Briefly describe what the output is used for.	

talkative culture; it will be disastrous if the stakeholders are unwilling to speak up. The facilitator (the requirements engineer) must ensure that each stakeholder is permitted to fully articulate his or her operational descriptions. Other stakeholders may be permitted to add to or clarify the description, but should not preempt or forcibly change the character of the operational description. The facilitator must aggressively manage this dialogue and try to capture each operational description as quickly as possible or other stakeholders will lose interest in the workshop. This will encourage bad behaviors like side conversations, leaving the workshop to answer e-mail, make phone calls, and so forth. It is best to make sure that each stakeholder has note pads, or preferably copies of the operational description templates, that he or she can use to capture his or her thoughts as stakeholders contribute their operational descriptions. In addition to managing the open discussion, the facilitator must also make sure that all stakeholders are able to participate. Some stakeholders are naturally more vocal and others are naturally quieter. If the facilitator notices that some stakeholders have not had an opportunity to contribute an operational description, the facilitator should personally invite them to contribute one if they would like to. Be gentle. Quiet people are often shy and reluctant to speak in public. Protect them from the more vocal stakeholders in the workshop as well. The facilitator should help stakeholders form the operational descriptions by asking probing and clarifying questions, but should not put words into the mouths of stakeholders. The facilitator must remain neutral at all times to avoid the perception that he or she is taking a side with a particular stakeholder against another stakeholder.

■ Round-robin contribution: If you are not sure that the stakeholders will volunteer operational descriptions using the open contribution format, it may be advisable to use the round-robin contribution format. In this format, the facilitator announces that he or she will start at one point in the room and in order will ask each stakeholder to contribute an operational description. Offer the opportunity for the stakeholders to pass if they do not have an operational scenario. Before beginning the round-robin, give the stakeholders some time to think of an operational description or two. This way the first stakeholder selected in the round-robin is not put on the spot. The facilitator should complete at least one complete cycle through all of the stakeholders, but may utilize as many cycles as necessary. The same facilitation rules apply here as do with the former format. Round-robin guarantees that every stakeholder is given the opportunity to contribute at least one operational description. It can also be easier to manage the discussion in the round-robin format. The problem with this format is that it discourages free-form discussion of ideas as they emerge. Another problem is that stakeholders often tune out of the workshop until it is their turn to contribute. After they contribute, they often tune out again.

■ Random polling contribution: This format is somewhere between the open contribution and round-robin approaches, except that the facilitator randomly picks the next stakeholder that will contribute. This format is often used when some participation is expected, but the architecture design team wants to guarantee some level of interaction and broad participation of the attendees to ensure all stakeholder communities are heard from. In general, the same facilitation rules apply here. This approach is often good for starting out the workshop and will usually morph into an open contribution format as stakeholders loosen up. This is fine provided the facilitator manages the interaction and transition at all times. Before beginning random polling, give the stakeholders a few minutes to think of an operational description or two. This way the first stakeholder randomly picked is not put on the spot. Allow stakeholders to pass. The facilitator should make sure that he or she engages all of the stakeholders and provides an opportunity for each stakeholder to contribute an operational description. Round-robin guarantees that every stakeholder is given the opportunity to contribute at least one operational description. It can be easier to manage the discussion in the random polling format. Random polling is also nice in that stakeholders have no idea who the facilitator is going to call on next, so they tend to stay in tune to the workshop better than they would in round-robin protocol. The problem with random polling is that it often has a parochial classroom feel during execution that does not often work with seasoned, cranky stakeholders.

■ Stakeholder interest polling contribution: In this format, the list of stakeholder interests such as users, maintainers, marketing, and so forth are publicly listed on a whiteboard or flip chart. Each stakeholder interest is asked to contribute operational descriptions based on the anticipated needs of the stakeholder interest. This method works when groups of stakeholders are present in a single workshop where each group has specific system interests. The biggest disadvantage of this format is that while the facilitator is interacting with one stakeholder interest, the rest are often tuned out of the workshop. Another disadvantage is that quiet members of a stakeholder interest group are often buried and never heard from during the workshop.

Whichever approach the architecture design team decides to use, decide before the workshop begins and explain the protocol, goals, and expectations to the stakeholders. These methods will have to be experimented with to discover which ones work best for the architecture design team. If the team has no facilitating experience at all, then the easiest format to use may be the round-robin one. The open contribution format is probably the most effective but requires very good facilitation techniques to manage the interactions. It is often the case that more than one method will have to be employed at various times, depending upon the culture, character, and social norms of the client stakeholder organization. As each operational description is captured it should be displayed prominently in the room. This can be done using a flip chart, or alternatively, the operational scenarios can be captured electronically using the template in Table 8.8 and projected in front of the room. Capturing the scenarios electronically is faster and easier to read than flip charts, but it is difficult for attendees to see them all. Each operational description can be recopied to a flip chart after it is captured electronically, but this is terribly inefficient. Another choice is to periodically make hard copies of the operational descriptions and distribute them to the attendees, but this wastes a lot of paper. Another option is to electronically capture and print the operational descriptions in a format that they can be read reasonably well. Hard copies from Microsoft's PowerPoint slide format can be read well enough when each is hung on the wall. However it is done, the operational descriptions captured should be in front of the stakeholders at all times so they can read them as the workshop proceeds. Having the operational descriptions in front of the stakeholders will often stimulate thoughts about the descriptions or help stakeholders formulate new ones. The scribe captures each operational description using the template listed in Table 8.8 as a guide. He or she should ensure that each operational description is given an ID; simple integers work, but other mnemonics can be used if desired to identify each operational description. Capture each operational description completely before starting a new one. If issues arise that are important but unrelated to the operational description, the facilitator should maintain a list of issues or "parking lot" where these things can be written down and handled later. This list of issues should be visible to all stakeholders as well. Again, it is important that members of the architectural design team that are not in active roles as a scribe or facilitator take detailed notes. These notes will complement the public information captures. A standard set of templates may be used by all of the note takers—this simplifies consolidation. It can be hard to visualize the room setup and positions of the attendees from a prose description like this. Figure 8.3 graphically shows a nominal architecture drivers elicitation workshop illustrating room setup and positions of the attendees. Note that Figure 8.3 shows flip chart scribes and an electronic scribe, but both probably will not be needed, depending upon how the information is captured and displayed.

The brainstorming will end when stakeholders grow quiet or begin to pass more frequently when asked to contribute an operational description. At this point the facilitators should double-check with the stakeholders to see if they have anything else to add and conclude the brainstorming.

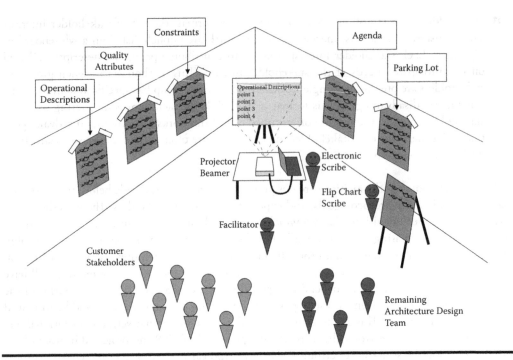

Figure 8.3   Graphical depiction of an architecture drivers elicitation workshop showing the room setup, attendees, equipment, and artifacts.

Then the operational descriptions need to be prioritized. This is done by giving each stakeholder in the architecture drivers elicitation workshop some number of votes that they can allocate any way they like to each operational description. The number of votes should be at least one-third to one-half the number of operational descriptions gathered during the brainstorming. This allows stakeholders more flexibility in ascribing importance than trying to rank the order of importance of operational descriptions from high to low. Voting can be done publicly or privately. Again, the facilitator must judge which is best for the stakeholder organization. If public voting is used, in a round-robin fashion, ask each stakeholder which operational descriptions they would like to place their votes on. Often the public dynamic of voting is constructive to the ranking process. However, if stakeholders do not feel that they can openly vote their conscience without interference, intimidation, or ridicule from other stakeholders, then the facilitator should opt for private voting. If in doubt, use public voting. In private voting, each stakeholder privately submits his or her votes for the operational descriptions on a piece of paper to the facilitator. At the end of private voting, the architecture design team tallies the votes and publishes them for the workshop attendees.

Identify Quality Attribute Requirements

In a way similar to the identification of the operational descriptions, the architecture design team will interact with the customer stakeholders to develop quality attribute scenarios. Again, brainstorming techniques will be used to facilitate and structure the interaction. Recall that one-word descriptions of quality attributes such as performance, security, modifiability, and so forth are meaningless. These requirements have the deepest influence on the structure of the system. Therefore, it is critical that the architecture design team gather enough information about the quality attribute requirements and prioritize them so they can be designed into the system. The most difficult aspect of eliciting quality attribute requirements is characterizing the behavioral properties associated with the desired quality attribute. The elicitation of quality attribute requirements from the stakeholder community is centered on the template shown in Table 8.9.

The quality attributes should be captured in a way similar to that of the operational descriptions. It is important that attendees see the template (Table 8.9) because it will help stimulate and focus the stakeholders' thoughts and discussion on the quality attributes and quantify them. The concept of quality attributes can be confusing for stakeholders, and the characterization strived for in ACDM can be especially difficult. It is therefore highly advisable that the facilitator provide a short description and example of what quality attributes are and why they will be characterized using quality attribute scenarios (explanation and examples were provided in Section 1). In Section 1, the six-part scenario was introduced as a way to characterize quality attribute requirements. However, during the workshop a streamlined format should be used in stage 1 to collect the raw data needed to create the full six-part quality attribute scenarios in stage 2 as part of the analysis of the architectural drivers. The full six-part scenarios can be developed during the workshop, but this tends to be cumbersome, and it often takes too long to get all six parts. While the facilitator is haggling with one stakeholder to develop all six parts of a scenario, the other stakeholders tend to disengage. It is important to maintain a quick pace and gather lots of information during the workshops. Therefore, it is highly recommended that the architectural design team strive to collect as much data about the quality attribute requirements in stage 1 as possible, and develop the six-part scenarios as part of the analysis in stage 2.

The requirements engineer should facilitate the identification of quality attributes. After the short overview and example of quality attributes and quality attribute scenarios, the session begins with the facilitator asking the stakeholders for a list of one-word quality attribute properties that the system must possess. This initial pass should focus on one-word definitions such as *performance, availability, security, modifiability,* and so forth—whatever comes to the mind of the attendees. This can be done in a one-pass round-robin contribution format or in an open contribution format. This should be recorded and visible to all of the attendees. Do not worry about precision, duplication, or defining what each word means at this point. In general, it should only take

Table 8.9   Quality Attribute Characterization Template

Stakeholder: Describe stakeholder role proposing the description.	**ID:**
Quality attribute: Select one of the one-word quality attribute descriptions from initial list generated by stakeholders.	
Reason for quality attribute: Explain why this quality attribute is needed in the system or product.	
Stakeholders' quality attribute story:	
Note: Ensure that the quality attribute story has a clear stimulus, response, and response measure. Stimulus (or stimuli): That which initiates the system to respond. Response(s) and response measure(s): The quality attribute response and the acceptable measure of response; the stakeholder should describe how he or she wants the system to respond to the stimuli.	
Other issues and concerns: List any relevant issues, such as the ability to achieve the response measure, or doubts about the response measure, potential constraints, and so forth, that arise during the discussion.	

a few minutes to generate a list of one-word quality attributes. Each of these words will be used as a basis to develop one or more quality attribute scenarios.

Once the list of one-word quality attribute properties has been generated, the facilitator will then ask the stakeholders which quality attribute they would like to explore first. Do not dwell on this, reach consensus as quickly as possible, or the facilitator should simply pick one that seems relevant to the system/product.

After a quality attribute word is selected, use the template listed in Table 8.9 to refine the quality attribute. Begin the characterization by recording the stakeholder(s) or stakeholder communities interested in this particular quality attribute, and then record the one-word description in the designated places in the template (Table 8.9). Invite the stakeholders to help characterize what this particular quality attribute word means. The same techniques used to elicit the operational descriptions can be used here as well: open, round-robin polling, random polling, or stakeholder interest polling formats. Once a stakeholder volunteers, we ask him or her to provide a brief quality attribute story. The quality attribute story should be a detailed account of how the stakeholder would like the system to respond (in terms of a quality attribute response) to some stimuli. It is critically important that the quality attribute story has one or more stimuli, a clear quality attribute response, and a quality attribute measure of the response. It can also be important to include any relevant environmental information. This is best illustrated by an example.

Assume that the architecture design team is working with a group who are building a new account data system for their banking operations. A stakeholder whose role is that of a maintainer is interested in a system that is easy to modify and proposes *modifiability* for the list of one-word quality attribute descriptions. When the facilitator asks the attendees which quality attribute to explore, the attendees indicate that they would like to explore modifiability. At this point, the facilitator would record the stakeholder's role and the one-word quality attribute description, *modifiability*, on the template. Next the facilitator will ask the stakeholder to describe what he or she means by "easy to modify" and invite him to characterize this system property from the perspective of his role as a maintainer. The stakeholder explains that his organization often acquires other banking operations and merges with other banks, and it is often a big chore to access the data of other banks because the format is always different. The stakeholder indicates that this kind of flexibility is needed to reduce merger and acquisition expenses and the time it takes to normalize operations between his organization and the acquired banking unit. This information should be captured in the template, explaining why this quality attribute property is important to the system. With the stage set, the facilitator must press the stakeholder for a specific story that illustrates how this property comes into play in an operational context. At first the stakeholder recalls several painful experiences, but the facilitator asks the stakeholder to describe how the new system should behave in the perfect world. The stakeholder indicates that after a typical acquisition or merger, the new system should allow those responsible for integrating the systems to easily read account data from the acquired unit's accounts without having to make code changes. This explanation contains stimulus information, environmental information, and some response information, but no response measure. Thinking in terms of response measures, the facilitator asks the stakeholder to specifically describe how he or she would want the new system to respond to these stimuli under these conditions. The stakeholder says the perfect system would allow the organization to merge legacy operations into the organization's standard operations in 30 days with no code changes or disruption to the operations of the newly acquired bank or the acquiring bank. The facilitator may want to explore what "no disruption to operations" means, or make sure that everyone understands "no code changes" in the same way. The facilitator should use these pieces of information to craft a complete quality attribute story that is recorded in the template. For example:

A savings and loan bank is acquired. After the sale is approved by the Federal Trade Commission, the system maintainers are able to merge the newly acquired bank's account data systems with the acquiring bank's account data systems. It takes 30 days or less to complete the merger of the data systems, and the integration of the data systems is completed with no changes to source code, and no interruption in banking operations from the acquired or acquiring bank's operations.

While this information was being recorded, the stakeholder indicated that he was concerned because the data formats are never known until after the acquisition, they are often proprietary, and sometimes there are many different data formats. It is typical during these discussions of quality attributes that such issues and concerns will arise that cannot be answered at this point and will require further investigation or experimentation. Rather than allowing attendees to drag down the discussion, or ignore them altogether, they should be recorded in the "issues and concerns" row of the template. An example template, filled out with this stakeholder's quality attribute information, is shown in Table 8.10.

Recall that there may be many characterizations of each quality attribute. This is because quality attribute words like *performance* and *security* can be characterized in many ways. For example, *performance* can mean transaction time, data throughput, response time, CPU processing time, scheduleability, and many other things. It is important that each of the relevant characterizations of the one-word quality attribute description is captured, but overloading a single characterization with every possible property of a single quality attribute is not a good idea. Use separate characterizations for each quality attribute characterization. Using the performance examples above, it might be a good idea to develop separate performance characterizations for response time and data throughput if they are sufficiently different. If there are different response measures, this is an indication (but not a rule) that it might be a good idea to use different characterizations.

This process is repeated for each quality attribute in the initial one-word quality attribute list. It is common to discover that there are duplicates in the initial list of quality attribute words. For example, assume that the initial list contained *modifiability* and *scalability*. After characterizing *modifiability*, the attendees realized that *scalability* is covered by the characterizations of the *modifiability* characterizations. It is perfectly reasonable to skip duplicate quality attribute words if it is okay with the stakeholder who proposed the quality attribute initially. Again, this illustrates why single-word descriptions are not enough to characterize quality attribute requirements. Once the quality attributes are characterized they must be prioritized. The prioritization should be done exactly as it was for the operational descriptions. At this point the bulk of the workshop is complete—all that is left is to record the significant constraints.

Identify Business Constraints

Recall that business constraints are indirect constraints on the design space. They are indirect in that business constraints do not specify that a particular technology is used to design or build a system, but impose cost, schedule, regulatory, legal, marketing, and other similar demands that will influence the design of the system. The facilitators should describe what these kinds of constraints are and invite the stakeholders to describe any business constraints that might be relevant to the system or product development. Table 8.11 can be projected or distributed to the stakeholders to help stimulate their thinking about business constraints.

Table 8.10   Example of Quality Attribute Characterization

Stakeholder: System maintainers	ID:
Quality attribute: Modifiability	
Reason for quality attribute: After acquiring other banking operations it is difficult to integrate the account data of other banks into our account data systems because the format, content, data types, and so forth are always different. The new system must possess the flexibility to easily merge/access account data from newly acquired banks. This will reduce merger and acquisition expense and the time it takes to normalize operations between this organization and the acquired banking unit.	
Stakeholders' quality attribute story:	
A savings and loan bank is acquired. After the sale is approved by the Federal Trade Commission, the system maintainers are able to merge the newly acquired bank's account data systems with the acquiring bank's account data systems. It takes 30 days or less to complete the merger of the data systems, and the integration of the data systems is completed with no changes to source code, and no interruption in banking operations from the acquired or acquiring bank's operations.	
Other issues and concerns: Often the data format of the acquired bank is proprietary and unknown until after the sale is approved. This is often late in the merger process, allowing much less time to integrate operations. Often multiple formats are used by the acquired bank—some standard formats, some proprietary. This further complicates the integration of operations.	

Business constraints are mandatory impositions that are largely nonnegotiable and often force the architect to make hard design choices. The business constraints should be recorded as they are described by the stakeholders.

Identify Technical Constraints

Technical constraints are less vague than business constraints and impose direct constraints on the design space. They are direct in that constraints specify that a particular technology is used to design or build a system, deeply influencing the design of the system. The term *technology* is used very broadly here to refer to computer languages, off-the-shelf hardware and software products, operating systems, peripherals, interoperability with legacy systems (hardware or software), and so forth.

Technical constraints are mandatory impositions on the design space and are largely nonnegotiable. The technical constraints should be recorded as they are described by the stakeholders. A template for recording the technical constraints is shown in Table 8.12.

Summary and Next Steps

Once the technical constraints are gathered, the workshop should be concluded with a summary and a discussion of the next steps that will be taken after the workshop by the architecture design team. The facilitator should explain that the information gathered during the workshop was the raw requirement for their (the customer stakeholders') system and that this information will be consolidated, later analyzed, and serve as input to the design process. It is important to let the

Table 8.11   Business Constraints Template

Consideration	Business Constraints
Cost limitations	How much over what period of time can be spent on the system or product?
Schedule limitations	What are the delivery schedules? One delivery? Incremental? What functionality must be delivered at what point in time?
Mandatory regulatory restrictions and demands	Are there any regulations imposed on the system, product, or organization designing and building the system, or the customer stakeholders' organization?
Legal restrictions and demands	Are there any legal impositions placed on the system, product, or organization designing and building the system, or the customer stakeholders' organization?
Market restrictions and demands	Does the target market impose any restrictions or demands on the system or product, especially if it could prevent entry into another market?
Organizational restrictions and demands	Do any of the organizations involved in the project have policies, processes, resources or lack thereof, or structural issues that could impose restrictions or demands on the design or construction of the system or product?
Logistical issues	Are there logistical issues such as deployment, transportation, supplier/supply chain, and similar that could impact the design of the system?

attendees know that some of the stakeholders present may be contacted for follow-up or to provide clarifying information. Explain that the raw data elicited during the workshop will be consolidated to remove duplicate information, and add or refine information where needed. Indicate that the raw consolidated architectural drivers will be shared with the broader stakeholder community before the architecture drivers specification is written and design commences.

Raw Data Consolidation

After the raw data is collected in the architectural drivers elicitation workshop, the architecture design team will need to consolidate the data into a single unified document. To efficiently consolidate the raw data, the requirements engineer will lead a consolidation meeting. At this meeting, the requirements engineer will lead the architecture design team in consolidating the raw architectural drivers. The only attendees for the consolidation meeting are the architecture design team members. Attendees should also come prepared to share their notes of the workshop. A scribe will be assigned to capture the corrections, additions, and modifications to the raw data collected during the workshop. The meeting should begin with a discussion of the purpose and goals of the system as presented by the client during the system or product overview. A consolidated statement should be agreed to as the purpose for the system or product being built. After this has been agreed to, the actual consolidation of the raw architecture drivers can proceed. An easy way to consolidate the raw architecture drivers is to project in the notes taken by the workshop scribe to the whole team. Beginning with the first operational description, the team members will compare their personal notes with the projected information and discuss any clarifications, additions, dif-

Table 8.12   Technical Constraints Template

Consideration	Technical Constraints
Computer operating system(s)	Are there any constraints to use a particular computer operating system? Are there any constraints to support multiple operating systems?
Computer platform(s)	Are there any constraints to use a particular computer hardware platform? Are there any constraints to support multiple hardware platforms?
Computer languages(s)	Is there a constraint to use a particular computer language?
Peripheral or network hardware	Are there any constraints that specify that particular peripheral devices or network hardware be used? Is there any custom hardware specified that must be used?
Commercial hardware or software products	Is there a constraint that specific commercial hardware and software products be used?
Tools and methods	Are there any constraints that specify that certain tools (e.g., design tools, process tools, programming environments) or technical methods be used?
Protocols, interfaces, standards	Are there any constraints that specify that certain protocols, interfaces, or standards be used or adhered to during development?
Legacy hardware and software	Are there any constraints that indicate that the new system/product must utilize or interact with any legacy hardware or software systems or elements?

ferences, or discrepancies that appear. This procedure is followed for each operational description, quality attribute characterization, business constraint, and technical constraint gathered during the workshop. Changes should be made publicly to a single version, which will be the consolidated raw architectural drivers. It is a good idea to archive the original documents and the individual notes from the workshop.

If multiple architecture drivers elicitation workshops are conducted, it is important that each workshop's raw data is consolidated. When all the workshops are completed, it is important that a similar consolidation occur for all of the workshops' consolidated raw architectural drivers. This is shown graphically in Figure 8.4.

The consolidation meetings are not that onerous and can save an enormous amount of time in stage 2 when writing the architectural drivers specification, which will be used to guide the design of the system in stage 3. Again, if all members of the architecture design team use the same templates, the consolidation step is much easier. Once the architectural drivers for a single workshop have been consolidated, the architecture design team can share them with the client stakeholders and ask for their feedback. The quality process engineer should coordinate this as a final check on the document and the quality of the raw data obtained from the stakeholders. Similarly, if multiple workshops are conducted, it is important to circulate the final consolidation to all of the client stakeholder groups to ensure their interests are represented. Again, this final review should be coordinated by the quality process engineer.

For a single workshop for a system of small scope and size, workshop data consolidation is trivial.

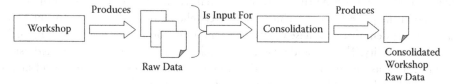

However, large scale data collection and consolidation takes more effort. However the effort more than pays for itself!

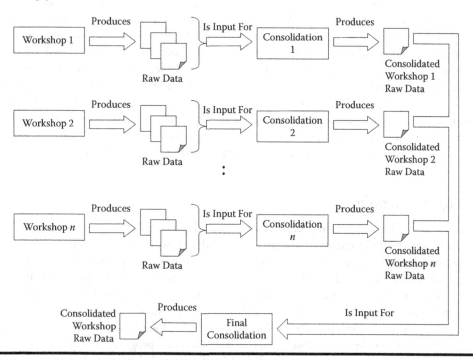

Figure 8.4   Architecture drivers consolidation.

Creating and Updating the Master Design Plan

Now that the entire architecture drivers elicitation workshop process has been explained, we revisit the master design plan. It should be a bit more obvious now what to consider when planning stage 1 activities and creating the initial draft of the master design plan. A checklist for creating the initial master design plan draft is provided in Table 8.13.

This checklist is not a formula for creating the master design plan, but rather a list of items to consider when writing the initial draft of the master design plan early in stage 1 before the workshops begin in earnest. The master design plan should be reviewed at the conclusion of each stage by the quality process engineer to ensure that it is current and of the appropriate quality. Certainly the master design plan described here could be extended into an overall project plan as well because many of the elements in the design plan are similar in spirit to those of a general project plan. Note that there are numerous sections that may have to be defined later; this is because the master design plan will evolve and grow as more information is gathered throughout the stages of the design process. What is known and unknown at the time of the initial draft of the master design plan will depend very much on the nature of the project and domain. Establishing an initial schedule is critical to tracking the efforts of the architecture design team. The primary activity at this time in the project is the architecture drivers elicitation workshops, and until more is learned about the system through these workshops, long-term construction costs are impossible to estimate with any fidelity. The cost and schedule for each workshop should be estimated using the template (Table 8.13) as a guide. In addition, the number of workshops that will be held should be estimated and included in the planning process and documented in the initial master design plan. After each workshop the actual time and cost information must be tracked, recorded, and the master design plan refined as necessary. This is standard project tracking practice, and it is critical that the managing engineer tenaciously track and manage the schedule during the entire period of uncertainty. This is the time when most project schedules go awry—it is chaotic, estimation is often nebulous, and tracking effort is highly subjective. In many cases the schedule will necessarily have to be a separate document so that it can be easily accessible, updated with actual effort, and facilitate changing (replanning) the plan. Regardless of the format or tool used to represent the schedule, it is important that the managing engineer makes provisions for recording actual performance numbers. This is essential for project tracking. There are numerous commercial tools that are available for creating and tracking the project schedule. At this point, the managing engineer may want to consider how he or she will track progress during the period of uncertainty.

Creating a Schedule

When creating a schedule, it is important to create one that helps the team track their effort over time. To better track the efforts of the architecture design team, the managing engineer may want to consider using earned value tracking to measure progress. Earned value tracking is a way that allows managers and stakeholders to monitor the progress of a project in terms of cost, schedule, and tangible performance measures. Traditional project management practices usually (and naively) compare actual costs with planned expenditures where cost can be time or resources. While this approach measures the actual effort and resources expended over some period against a planned effort and timeline, it confuses actual costs with actual progress. A very important measure is not accounted for: What was accomplished for the expended effort and resources over said period of time? For a given expenditure of time, what work has been completed, and how does this compare to what was planned by the team? Earned value takes into account the amount of work accomplished, the effort and resources expended, over some period of time to track progress. Admittedly, earned value can be difficult to use early in a project during the period of uncertainty, when the activities are less certain and it is difficult to estimate the duration of activities such as requirements elicitation, analysis, and design. Nonetheless, earned value can be used with the stage estimation tables provided for each stage of ACDM to estimate the period of uncertainty, establish cost and schedule budgets, and track progress. Using earned value can provide a more realistic view of progress and identify schedule slips earlier. The following steps describe how to create a schedule and establish earned value tracking for the period of uncertainty.

Step 1: Establishing the Work Breakdown Structure

The managing engineer must decompose stages 1 to 6, including design refinement iteration, into discrete tasks for each stage. For estimation and planning purposes, it is a good rule of thumb to initially plan on three refinement iterations. This data comes from industrial experience with

Table 8.13   Master Design Plan Document Checklist

Front matter	Provide any or all of the following as required: Name of producing organization and authors Document version and revision history Approval signatures Table of contents List of figures List of tables Applicable documents and references Executive summary
Project description	A brief description of the: Client organization and the organization designing and building the system (if they are different) Market/domain General project goals General project requirements and deliverables
General statement of work	The statement of work may be a separate document. If not, include the following items in the master design plan as a bare minimum: • Describe the role of the architecture design team on the project. • Describe the ACDM role assignments. • Provide any relevant organizational information, key project management and decision makers, and other authority and reporting channels as appropriate. • Describe what will be delivered (architecture drivers specification, architecture design, software, hardware, and so forth). The specifics may be discussed in the architecture drivers specification. If so, avoid duplication and just reference the architecture drivers specification. • Describe what activities will take place (architecture drivers elicitation workshops, architecture reviews, and so forth). For the customer stakeholder organization: • Describe any expectations required (must agree to attend architecture drivers elicitation workshops, review design, and so forth). • Provide any relevant organizational information, key project management and decision makers, and other authority and reporting channels as appropriate. Describe the minimal acceptable deliverables. (If this is described in the architecture drivers specification, avoid duplication and just reference the architecture drivers specification.) List any general expectations: • Describe who is responsible for paying for the product/system and how payments will be made. • Describe the product/system acceptance process (specific acceptance criteria will be developed later). Provide the general timeline for delivering the system/product.

(continued)

Table 8.13   Master Design Plan Document Checklist (continued)

General statement of work	Describe who may request changes to the baseline requirements (architecture drivers specification) and describe the change process (change request, negotiation, acceptance, approval, and so forth). Describe any relevant material needs and resources (office space, tools, computer equipment, environments, labs, and so forth) that are required, who needs them, when they will be available, and who will pay for them. Describe the consequences of failing to meet commitments (for all parties, not just the developing organization)—late fees, late deliveries, penalties, contract termination conditions, and so forth.
Description of the design process and strategy	Describe the overall strategy for designing and building the product. (Much of this comes straight from ACDM; however, describe any tailoring.) Describe each of the stages of design process that the architecture design team will use. For each stage describe: • The pre- and postconditions at each stage • The activities undertaken in each stage, and the roles and responsibilities of the architecture design team and the customer stakeholders in planning, conducting, hosting, and attending those activities • The artifacts produced at each stage
Schedule	Describe the schedule and key milestones for each stage of the project. Use Gantt, Pert, or any other scheduling mechanisms desired. Initially focus on the stage 1 activities because the rest of the schedule, budgets, and milestones will be based upon what is learned in stage 1. The schedule will be constantly refined at each stage. These are items that should be considered when developing the schedule: Project setup: See Table 8.14 for example setup items. Stage 1: Use Table 8.14 as a guide to estimate schedule and cost budgets. Stage 2: Use Table 9.2 as a guide to estimate schedule and cost budgets. Stage 3: Use Table 10.2 as a guide to estimate schedule and cost budgets. Stage 4: Estimates and budgets to be provided. Stage 5: Estimates and budgets to be provided. Stage 6: Estimates and budgets to be provided. Stage 7: Estimates and budgets to be provided. Stage 8: Estimates and budgets to be provided. If possible, estimate schedule and cost estimates and budgets for: • Stages 2–5 after stage 1 • Stage 6 experimentation after stage 4 • Stages 7 and 8 after a go decision has been made • Base refinement iterations (stages 3 to 6) based on the first iteration through these stages. As a rule of thumb, plan on three refinement iterations.

Table 8.14 Planning and Scheduling Considerations for the Initial Draft of the Master Design Plan in Stage 1

Workshop Planning *For each workshop consider the following:*	Time	Cost	Responsible Party
• Travel to and from workshop			
• Lodging			
• Workshop materials (reproduction costs, pens, paper, etc.) preparation			
• Venue			
• Food			
• Coordination and scheduling			
• Workshop team read-ahead and preparation time			
• Preparing workshop materials (instantiating templates, preparing the agenda, etc.)			
• Workshop raw architectural drivers consolidation			
• Updating the master design plan as necessary to reflect actual effort and cost expenditures			
Total *Time* and *Cost* of Architectural Drivers Elicitation Workshops *(average time and cost of a single workshop × number of workshops)*	**Total Time**	**Total Cost**	
Other Initial (Stage 1) Master Design Plan Considerations	Time	Cost	Responsible Party
Initial project setup (establishing the architecture design team; hiring; assigning roles; setting up support infrastructure, tools, configuration management, communication infrastructure and mechanisms, physical office and lab space)			
Creating the initial draft of the master design plan			
Consolidation of raw architectural drivers from all workshops			
Documenting the raw architectural drivers			
Circulating the consolidated raw architectural drivers document to the stakeholders for final comment			
Revising the raw architectural drivers document			
Updating the master design plan			

teams using ACDM. Each ACDM stage has defined preconditions, activities, outputs, and exit criteria. These are general specifications, but the specific tasks within each stage should be defined by the architecture design team for the specific project. Within each stage the tasks will form a series of detailed milestones whose "doneness" can be objectively measured. This activity is often referred to as developing the work breakdown structure (WBS).

Step 2: Assigning Completion Values

Once the WBS is established for each stage, the tasks associated with each stage must be assigned an estimated start and finish date and a completion value. The completion value is a numeric value that is assigned to each task and pertains to the value that the team earns when this task is completed. The completion value should be based on the estimated amount of time or the resources it will take to complete the task. For example, assume that we have a simple project consisting of four tasks. We estimate that task A will take up 50 percent of the budgeted time, task B will take 10 percent of the budgeted time, task C will take 5 percent of the budgeted time, and task D will take 25 percent of the budgeted time. Once the tasks and schedule are established, the architecture design team must come up with completion values for each of the tasks to implement earned value tracking. In this example, time will be used to determine the completion value. Therefore, a completion value of 50 is assigned to task A, a completion value of 10 is assigned to task B, a completion value of 5 is assigned to task C, and a completion value of 25 is assigned to task D. This is shown in Figure 8.5. These values are based directly on the percentage of estimated time to complete each task, but in practice this may be too simplistic. Completion values can be based on time as they are here, or resource costs, or a composite of time and resource costs. Some managers even like to apply subjective factors based on their experience that account for risk or difficulty in the completion value of each task. Determining the exact completion value is left to the judgment of the managing engineer and the architecture design team. It is important to consider cost as a factor even though it was not in this simple example. A task may take a short period of time, but it may be costly in terms of resources expended. The reverse is true as well; a task may take a long time, but may be relatively inexpensive. Costs and time can have a normalizing effect on the completion values. Remember, the completion value is the value of a task that is earned when it is completed and does not represent or track planned or estimated costs or time expenditures. With earned value tracking, estimated schedule and costs, actual schedule and costs, and the value of

Task	Estimated Duration	% of the Total Schedule	Task Completion Values
Task A	30 days	50%	50
Task B	6 days	10%	10
Task C	9 days	15%	15
Task D	15 days	25%	25
	60 person days total effort		100 = Total project earned value

Figure 8.5 Example of establishing the work breakdown structure, and estimating and assigning completion values.

a task are three separate measures that are used to measure progress. Table 8.5 illustrates a simple WBS and the assignment of completion values.

Step 3: Roll-Up Schedule

Once the WBS has been established and completion values have been assigned to the tasks, the managing engineer needs to roll up the schedule. This is a process of organizing the schedule, establishing and resolving dependencies, and calculating total estimated duration, total estimated resources, and total estimated earned value. Because ACDM requires that a certain set of tasks are undertaken and artifacts produced for each stage, it is only logical to organize the tasks by stage, if not done so already. There is a natural dependency between the stages, and therefore between the tasks of each stage. Within each stage, some of the tasks will depend upon one another (e.g., completion of task Y depends upon first completing task X), and others can be done concurrently. Guidance is provided by ACDM, but the actual dependencies will depend upon the specific way that the architecture design team executes each of the tasks within a given stage of ACDM. Once the dependencies are determined through the period of uncertainty (stage 6), the manager can then calculate the total estimated earned value, estimated duration, and estimated completion date for the period of uncertainty. A simple schedule roll-up example is shown in Figure 8.6 (dependencies) and Figure 8.7 (estimated earned value).

Step 4: Tracking Progress

To track the progress of the project the team, the managing engineer records the actual time and resource costs. In addition, as each task is completed, the team earns the value of the task. The completion values for each completed task are summed together, resulting in total earned value at some point in time. This is illustrated in Figure 8.8.

The completion value is awarded only when the entire task is complete. Establishing specific measurable exit criteria for each task makes it easier to track task completion, and thus credit the completion value of the earned value total of the project. In this way the earned value of the project can be determined at any given point in time using arithmetic rather than the subjective

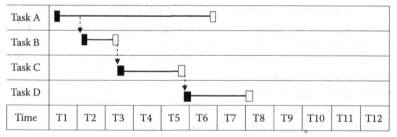

For the example, assume the following schedule dependencies, thus yielding the following schedule estimate:

	T1	T2	T3	T4	T5	T6	T7	T8	T9	T10	T11	T12
Task A												
Task B												
Task C												
Task D												
Time	T1	T2	T3	T4	T5	T6	T7	T8	T9	T10	T11	T12

Assume that each T*n* represents 5 days. Task A has no dependencies, but Task D is dependent upon Task C, and Task C is dependent upon Task B. Task B is dependent upon some event that occurs after the first 5 days of Task A. The total project duration will be 35 days.

Figure 8.6   Example of project tracking using earned value.

The following table shows the estimated earned value. This is derived from the schedule estimate shown in Figure 8.6

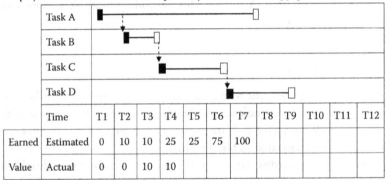

Time	T1	T2	T3	T4	T5	T6	T7	T8	T9	T10	T11	T12
Estimated Earned Value:	0	10	10	25	25	75	100					

Figure 8.7   Example of estimated earned value.

This example illustrates the estimated and actual earned value at time T4. The actual earned value at T4 is 10, when it should be 25, indicating the project is behind. Note that the project was behind at T2 and was probably the start of the slippage.

Time	T1	T2	T3	T4	T5	T6	T7	T8	T9	T10	T11	T12
Earned Estimated	0	10	10	25	25	75	100					
Value Actual	0	0	10	10								

Figure 8.8   Example of estimated earned value.

assessment of the engineers. The total earned value is the sum of all the task completion values. The estimated earned value at some point in time t is the sum total of the task completion values for those tasks that should be completed at time t. The actual earned value at some point in time t is the sum total of the task completion values for those tasks that are completed at some time t. Consider the example progress data plotted in Figure 8.9.

This figure shows the planned and actual earned value, and the planned and actual effort (time on task) expended on a project thus far at reporting interval T4. In this example the team has not met the estimated performance at T4; in fact, the project is behind as early as reporting interval T2. We can also see that despite being behind schedule, the team is spending more time on task (effort) than was originally planned. Effort does not equal progress. Using earned value, we can see that the team has not reached the planned earned value at time T4. This can be for any number of specific reasons, but generally the effort or time needed for one or more tasks was underestimated. At time T4, the team should have an earned value of 25, but rather the earned value at T4 is 10. Using this data, the managing engineer can see that the team is behind schedule, determine where the problem began, and begin planning corrective action. Corrective actions will typi-

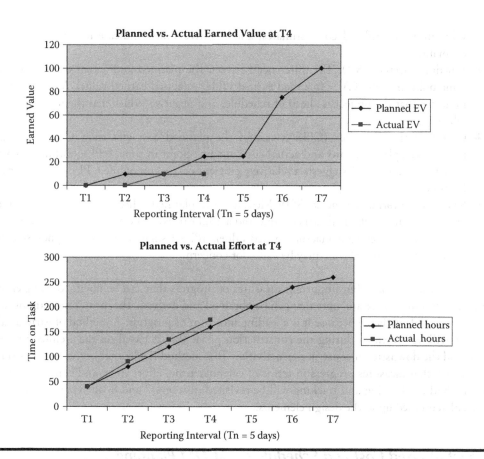

Figure 8.9 Example of tracking project performance using earned value.

cally include replanning after reestimating the work, negotiating for more time, adding resources (people, overtime, budget), renegotiating deliverables, or some combination of these. However, the task completion values should only be recalculated if there are changes in the nature of the task, or significant new risks or other similar issues uncovered that make the task more difficult, time-consuming, or costly to complete.

When using earned value tracking, it is important to balance the level of detail in the WBS. The goal is to reasonably and realistically estimate the cost of accomplishing each task (completion value) and measuring progress to determine when budgets are being exceeded. Providing too much detail creates too much data and results in a tracking nightmare—especially if replanning is necessary. Too coarse of granularity and progress comes in big lurches as long-awaited discrete step functions that do not portray an honest assessment of effort and progress. The direct measures from this approach include the planned and actual earned value of the project at some point in time, the estimated resources (time or cost) expended at some point in time, and the actual resources (time or cost) expended at some point in time. Using these primary measures, it is possible to derive measures that can be used to accurately assess the status of the project and predict its future state:

▪ Cost variance (CV): The difference between the planned and actual resource expenditures (time or costs) at some point in time. CV = (planned costs) − (actual costs). A positive value indicates inflated cost estimates, and negative values indicate underestimated cost estimates.

■ Schedule variance (SV): The difference between the planned and actual earned values at some point in time. CV = (planned earned value) – (actual earned value). A positive value indicates that the project is ahead of schedule, and negative values that the team is behind schedule.

■ Cost performance index (CPI): Measures the planned cost efficiency. CPI is the ratio between the planned costs and actual costs at some point in time. CPI = (estimated costs)/ (actual costs). CPI ≥ 1 suggests a relatively efficient cost factor, while CPI < 1 may be cause for concern.

■ Schedule performance index (SPI): Measures the planned schedule efficiency. SPI is the ratio between the planned earned value and actual earned value at some point in time. SPI = (estimated earned value)/(actual earned value). SPI ≥ 1 suggests a relatively good schedule performance, while SPI < 1 may be cause for concern.

These are a few basic, but important measures of progress that can be obtained using earned value, and certainly there are more that can be obtained and derived. The most important of these values is schedule variance because it is a leading indicator of progress. A method of earned value tracking will be presented during the construction phase that is based on the architectural elements and the downstream construction activities. This method is a less subjective progress tracking method that measures progress in terms of calendar time, effort time, and completed work. This method of planning and tracking will be revisited in stages 7 and 8 when earned value will be calculated based upon the design elements.

Impact of Fixed Cost and Schedule on ACDM Planning

Unfortunately, in many cases it is impossible to incrementally plan as described here. Sometimes total system construction schedules and budgets are part of a bidding process and must be provided or otherwise determined before the architectural drivers can be defined and explored in a meaningful way. In some organizations, estimates are routinely made without involving anyone from the architecture design team. In fact, sometimes estimates are made by sales, marketing, and accounting professionals with little or no technical expertise. In these cases, schedule and cost estimates become constraints on the project and the design team. There are always cost and schedule constraints in every project. What is at issue is the role the technical experts play in establishing realistic schedule and cost estimates, and how much they know about architectural drivers and technical risks before they must render their estimates. Ideally, there should be some flexibility in project cost and schedule estimates if they must be provided early in the project. Once the architectural drivers are understood, the technical risks are explored and mitigated, and the design is stabilized, high-fidelity construction estimates can be provided, and may be significantly different from initial estimates. When cost and schedule are predetermined and fixed, the architecture design team must determine how much of what the stakeholders want can be built in the predetermined cost and schedule constraints, rather than determining how much and how long it will take to build what the stakeholders actually want. This puts the architecture design team in a defensive position on the first day of the project, forcing them to negotiate for reduced project scope, less than optimal designs, compromised quality attribute properties, or some combination of these. This illustrates the importance of prioritizing the requirements. Without prioritization, it is impossible to know what kind of compromises can be made. In these situations, it is important that the architecture design team work with stakeholders to establish the *minimal acceptable delivery*. The minimal acceptable delivery is the minimal features and properties that the system must possess, delivered at some point in time in order for the project to be considered successful. The minimal acceptable delivery can be defined in conjunction with the ACDM methods designed to capture and prioritize the architectural drivers (operational descriptions and quality attributes). The minimal acceptable delivery typically affects the functional requirements and quality attributes because constraints are not negotiable by definition. Designers should try to question constraints to see if they are negotiable. If they are, then they are probably not constraints, but rather some kind of requirement. This is important to distinguish because constraints are often impediments to design with a negative impact on cost and schedule. To define the minimal acceptable delivery, the architecture design team must strive to define that set of functional requirements and quality attribute properties that the system/product must have, those that would be difficult to live without, and those that are nice to have. If the architecture design team is under difficult cost and schedule constraints, they can focus on the must-have and difficult-to-live-without features and properties. It should be obvious that these kinds of cost and schedule constraints will deeply influence the system/product design. This is a prime example of how business constraints indirectly influence design structure.

Impact of Preexisting Specifications on the ACDM Requirements Elicitation Process

In some situations, design teams are provided with requirements specifications that they had no part in developing. These situations can be challenging, especially if coupled with overly constrained cost and schedule constraints. In these cases, the architecture design team can mine the specification for the architectural drivers. In these cases, the designers should scour the specification and bin the requirements into functional requirements, quality attributes, and business and technical constraints. The architecture design team can develop use cases and quality attribute scenarios internally and review them with the stakeholders for clarification and to check understanding and details. This approach of mining for architecture drivers from existing specifications can be risky if the architecture design team is not experienced in the domain. If the architecture design team lacks domain experience, then they have no way of knowing if the specification is reasonable, accurate, or complete, and if the stakeholder community is well represented in the specification. Another approach is to conduct architecture drivers elicitation workshops to clarify and verify what is written in the requirements specifications. In this approach the architecture design team should analyze the existing requirements specification prior to conducting any workshops and bin the requirements into their respective architectural drivers as described before. As they do this, they should also identify:

- Poorly stated or unreasonable project/system/product goals and objectives
- Missing or poorly defined input and output
- Unclear or missing functional requirements
- Poorly articulated quality attribute requirements missing clear response measures
- Missing or poorly articulated quality attribute requirements
- Constraints that seem unreasonable or unclear

After reviewing the requirements specification, the architecture design team should then arrange architecture drivers elicitation workshops with those stakeholders that can help provide missing information and clarify information that is poorly articulated. This can reduce the number of workshops and focus the attendees' attention during them. Operationally, this can be done by beginning the brainstorming for the operational descriptions, quality attribute characterizations, and business and technical constraints by referring to what the requirements specification says, or does not say, or by pointing out what is unclear about what is written in the requirement specification.

Summary

Stage 1 is the first step in ACDM and focuses the architecture design team on identifying the stakeholder community and getting the architectural drivers from them. In addition to setting the architectural drivers for the project, the architecture design team will also establish the master design plan. Initially this plan addresses stage 1 needs, but will be continually refined throughout the stages of the design process. Stage 1 is comprised of the following key activities:

- Architecture design team strategy meeting: The architecture design team meets, possibly for the first time, to identify the client stakeholders, decide how many architecture drivers elicitation workshops are needed, and discuss initial planning issues. After this meeting the managing engineer will create the initial master design plan.
- Architecture drivers elicitation workshops: The architecture design team meets with the client stakeholders to elicit the architectural drivers. One or more workshops may be required. The raw architecture drivers are consolidated after each workshop, and when all the workshops have been completed, the consolidated raw architecture drivers from each workshop are once again distilled into a single, consolidated raw architecture drivers document.
- Create and update the master design plan: The initial draft of the master design plan will be created in stage 1. The most important element of the master design plan is the schedule. The schedule may be part of the master design plan document or in a separate document. The schedule should be updated after each workshop to reflect the actual time, effort, and cost to track progress. The managing engineer should consider using objective measures to track progress, such as the earned value techniques described in this section. During stage 1 little is known about the project, stakeholders, and deliverables, so change is inevitable during this initial stage in the period of uncertainty. The master design plan should be refined as necessary as more is learned about the domain, the stakeholders, and the architectural drivers.

Chapter 9

ACDM Stage 2: Establishing Project Scope

Purpose

The primary purpose of stage 2 is for the architecture design team to analyze the consolidated raw architecture drivers information gathered in stage 1 to clarify and refine the architectural drivers and firmly establish the scope of the system/product.

Preconditions

Before undertaking stage 2, the consolidated raw architecture drivers from stage 1 must be available.

General Activities
Techniques, Templates, and Guidance

- Templates and guidance for writing the architecture drivers specification
- Techniques and guidance for analyzing the consolidated raw architectural drivers

Primary Artifacts

- The architecture drivers specification
- Updated master design plan

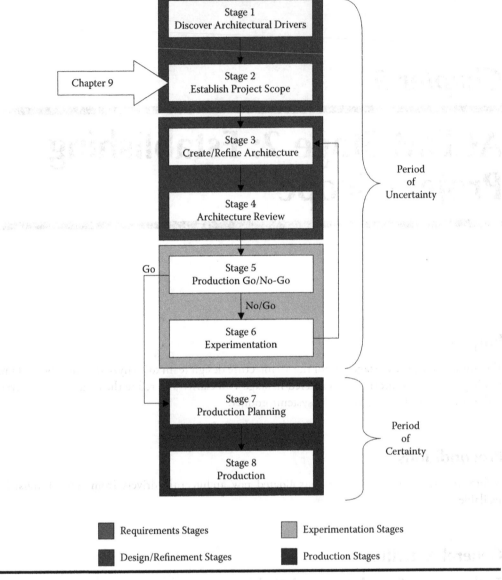

Figure 9.1   Stage 2.

Postconditions

The architecture drivers specification is completed and reviewed and formally accepted by the stakeholders.

Description of Stage 2

In stage 2, the architecture design team will analyze the consolidated raw architecture driver gathered in stage 1 and establish a baseline architecture drivers specification for the system/product.

Table 9.1 Stage 2 Activities, Outputs, and Responsibilities

General activities	Analyze the consolidated raw architectural drivers.
General outputs	The architectural drivers specification and the updated master design plan.
Role	**Stage 2 Recommended Responsibilities**
Managing engineer	Plan, coordinate, track, and oversee stage 2 activities.
Chief architect	Lead the analysis of the consolidated raw architectural drivers.
Chief scientist	Assist in the analysis of the consolidated raw architectural drivers and focus on technical issues, especially identifying early technical risks associated with the raw architectural drivers.
Requirements engineer	Responsible for writing the architecture drivers specification document.
Quality process engineer	Ensure that the ACDM (and other project processes) is being followed, and coordinate a review of the architecture drivers specification document.
Support engineer	Assist with analysis of consolidated raw architectural drivers and writing the architecture drivers specification document as necessary.
Production engineers	In stage 2, minimal support is usually required from production engineers. However, they may assist with the analysis of the consolidated raw architectural drivers and writing the architecture drivers specification document as necessary.

This analysis will also allow the team to better establish the scope, context, and size of the development effort. The architecture drivers specification is the primary input for the design activities in stage 3. While stage 1 is a divergent process where lots of information about the system is collected, stage 2 should be a convergent process that refines and structures information gathered in stage 1. In stage 2 the architecture design team will:

- Plan stage 2 activities and update the master design plan.
- Describe the high-level functional requirements by developing use case scenarios from the operational descriptions gathered in stage 1.
- Describe the quality attribute requirements by developing six-part quality attribute scenarios from the quality attribute characterizations gathered in stage 1.
- Analyze, clarify, and refine the constraints to ensure that they are commonly understood by the architecture design team and the customer stakeholders.
- Estimate and assign difficulty rankings to the architecture drivers.
- Identify and document early technical risks that may be candidates for experiments.
- Update the master design plan.

Each of these steps is discussed in detail in the following sections.

Stage 2 Planning

Stage 2 will begin with the team planning the activities of the stage and updating the master design plan to reflect the time that the architecture design team estimates they will take in stage

2. The managing engineer will lead the stage 2 planning meeting. Table 9.2 lists guidelines for planning stage 2 activities.

What is involved in each of these activities will become clearer as each activity is explained in detail in the following sections. The managing engineer should use Table 9.2 as a guide for the stage 2 planning meeting. The template can be projected and the members of the architecture design team should discuss the scheduling, duration, and any related issues associated with each of the items listed in Table 9.2. The managing engineer should review the role that each member of the architecture design team plays (Table 9.1) in stage 2, what activities each is responsible for, and what artifacts each must produce. Analysis is a notoriously open-ended activity, and "analysis paralysis" is a common syndrome that befalls many design teams that simply cannot stop the activity of analysis and move on to the next phase of work. The reasons for analysis paralysis are numerous, but a primary root cause for no one reason defines what it means to be done with analysis. This results in analyzing problems to death! Projects stuck in analysis paralysis have a difficult time moving on to design and construction. It is difficult to establish exact completion criteria for analysis that works for all domains, projects, and organizations. An organization building safety-critical medical equipment should probably spend significantly more time in analysis than may be required in other application domains. Analysis paralysis can be legitimately caused if the requirements are highly volatile. If the team finds that they are gathering a lot more new information in stage 2, then it might be the case that all of the stakeholders were not identified or engaged in stage 1. Another cause for volatility in the architectural drivers between stage 1 and stage 2 could be significant changes in the stakeholder community itself. Managing requirements will be discussed in detail later. However, in either of these situations, it is best to abandon stage 2 and reset. Revisit the architecture drivers elicitation workshop activities described in stage 1 rather than soldier on in stage 2 with analysis of volatile requirements that are no longer valid. Analysis performed on the

Table 9.2 Stage 2 Planning Meeting

Planning Consideration	Description
Updating the master design plan	Updating the master design plan should occur after the stage is planned, to record the estimated time and resources required in stage 2. The master design plan will also be updated at the end of stage 2 to record the actual time and effort expended in stage 2.
Analysis	Analysis is all of the activities required to: • Develop operational descriptions into use case scenarios • Develop quality attribute characterizations into six-part quality attribute scenarios • Refine and clarify the constraints Analysis might also involve meeting and interviewing the client stakeholders to clarify or add to information gathered in stage 1.
Architecture drivers specification	The key artifact produced in stage 2 is the architecture drivers specification that will describe the architectural drivers after analysis. This document will list the use case scenarios, the quality attribute scenarios, and the refined/clarified constraints.
Reviews	The master design plan should be reviewed within the team. The architecture drivers specification will have to be reviewed within the team and also circulated through the stakeholder community for their review and comment.

wrong raw architectural drivers will lead to an in incorrect specification, leading to poor or incorrect designs, resulting in a multitude of implementation problems. Some design teams want to perform the perfect analysis. This is only practical in the hallowed halls of academia. In the quest for perfect analysis, these teams would be satisfied with analyzing a problem forever—analysis as an end in itself rather than a means to an end. Perfection is the number one enemy of "good enough," and perfection is impractical and not necessary in practice. At ceremonies marking the 35th anniversary of the *Apollo 11* moon landing, Neil Armstrong remarked that when President Kennedy proposed putting a man on the moon the "unknowns vastly exceeded the knowns." This is the nature of many technical endeavors. The idea of analysis is not to make every unknown perfectly known, but to identify the important things we do not know and tackle those.

Analysis paralysis is a huge programmatic risk in stage 2, but there are three easy ways to help avoid it. First, the architecture design team should establish firm schedule budgets for analysis and only allow them to slip with great deliberation. Second, they should establish clear analysis completion criteria. Third, the architecture design team should do both. This third option is safest, and much of what is needed to do this is supplied by ACDM stage 2 templates and methods. If the analysis completion criterion is too stringent, then the time budget will be reached, triggering a warning. If the time budget is reached, the team can see if the actual analysis matches the completion criterion. If there are sufficiently large discrepancies between what was expected vis-à-vis the analysis completion criterion and the actual analysis that has been done, then it may be necessary to extend the analysis a bit or relax the completion criterion. Both an analysis schedule budget and completion criteria are effective ways to avoid and manage analysis paralysis. It is vital that the managing engineer is sensitive to the analysis paralysis phenomenon, is paying attention to what the team is doing in analysis, and is tracking the time spent in stage 2 analysis.

Analysis

Analysis is the key activity of stage 2. What analysis means for architectural design is that the design team must scour the consolidated raw architectural drivers collected in stage 1 and identify unclear, incomplete, missing, and conflicting architectural drivers. Each architectural driver must be clearly articulated so that it is understandable by the customer stakeholders and the architecture design team. Each architectural driver must be quantified to the greatest extent possible to set proper expectations for the system/product design. The high-level functional requirements and quality attribute requirements must be rated by the architecture design team in terms of how difficult they will be to implement or otherwise achieve. This will help in early technical risk identification. The collection of architectural drivers must be documented in the architecture drivers specification in a structured way that:

- Describes the high-level functional requirements in terms of use case scenarios derived from the operational descriptions gathered in stage 1
- Describes the quality attribute requirements in terms of six-part quality attribute scenarios derived from the quality attribute characterizations gathered in stage 1
- Describes the constraints in a clear and unambiguous way to ensure that they are commonly understood by the architecture design team and the customer stakeholders

The architecture drivers specification is an important document, but the act of creating the document (the analysis) is more important. This is not to say that the architecture drivers specification should not be written or compromised in any way. It is a critical communication vehicle that describes what the system will be designed to do, how it will do what it must do, and the constraints the design must adhere to. However, the architecture drivers specification is the culmination of the analysis. The quality and effectiveness of the document's content is dependent upon the quality of the analysis. The architecture design team should avoid just creating a pretty document based upon shoddy analysis. For this reason, analysis is more important than the architecture drivers specification as a document alone. This having been said, if the document can be read or inadequately describes the architectural drivers, then the analysis will not be properly communicated. Poor documents can be fixed if due diligence was exercised with analysis, but pretty specifications without substance can only be fixed with honest analysis work. Ensuring that the document is an effective communication vehicle is the job of the quality process engineer; ensuring the quality of the analysis is the job of the entire architecture design team.

A Guide for Developing Use Cases from Operational Descriptions

Use cases as described in Chapter 3 (Jacobson et al., 1992) will be developed to model the high-level functional requirements. The act of converting the data collected in the operational descriptions of stage 1 into fully developed use cases will also guide the team in the analysis of systemic functional requirements. The use case development described in ACDM differs from traditional use case modeling. It deliberately avoids the use of any specific graphical notation, is language and domain neutral, is architecture-centric, and broadly addresses entities rather than human actors and man-machine interaction to serve broader application domains. The optimal way to perform the analysis of operational descriptions is for the team to first agree on a template for guiding the analysis and modeling the use case—several templates are provided here for this purpose. The operational descriptions from stage 1 should each be assigned to one or more architecture design team members for analysis, thus making the analysis a parallel activity. Limit teams analyzing a single operational description to three persons. Having teams analyze operational descriptions can be beneficial, but analysis by committee can be difficult. In experiments with ACDM, analysis teams with more than three engineers seemed to take longer to complete their work than teams comprised of three or less. Teams larger than three found it difficult to reach consensus, schedule time to work together, and were more prone to fall into analysis paralysis. However, single engineers tend to miss some details and can become a single point of failure should they become ill or leave for greener pastures. Three is an optimal number of engineers, if possible.

The process of analyzing the operational descriptions and developing use cases should not be viewed as a one-pass activity, but an iterative activity where the use cases are analyzed, developed, and documented over time. It may be the case in the course of analysis that the stakeholders must be reengaged to confirm information, explore alternatives, define terms, gather more information, and so forth. As the analysis is completed, the full architecture design team should review each use case scenario. If there are a large number of operational descriptions, the architectural design team should first analyze those voted as most important by the stakeholders during the architectural drivers elicitation workshops. After review and acceptance, the use cases will be documented in the architecture drivers specification document with appropriate descriptive prose, which will be discussed later. To develop the use cases, each operational description should be analyzed in a structured way to ensure complete analysis. A common format should be used to document the use case to ensure that the same kind of information is developed and is recorded in the same format. This results in more complete, consistent analysis and significantly reduces the chore of writing the architecture drivers specification document. The following steps describe an approach to analyzing operational descriptions and developing use cases from them.

Step 1: Identify the Entities

The first step in modeling what is described in a raw operational description is to identify what entities (who or what) will be using something from, or providing something to, the system/product directly. Certainly an entity might include users, but the architect should try to think more broadly and identify the different kinds of entities that might come in contact with the system and what they will provide to, and require from, the system. Entities might include nonhuman things such as other systems, devices, sensors, and so forth. These may be elements and systems internal to or external to the design space or system/product context. As we will see, internal elements are typically within the design space, whereas external elements are often the source of technical constraints that must be adhered to in the design and implementation. As each entity is identified, define the provides and requires assumptions of the entity. Sometimes this is called an association in traditional use case modeling, but too often the exact nature of the association is imprecise, misused, or left unstated altogether. In practice, associations can be complex relationships such as business processes, sensor connections, protocols, interfaces, and so forth that should be exposed and analyzed for what they are as early as possible. Often these are the source of key technical constraints. The provides assumptions are those things that the entity will provide for the system, such as data, events, information, and so forth. The requires assumptions are those things that the entity expects from the system, such as data, events, services, information, and so forth. This is typically information that is omitted or implied in traditional "shall" requirements describing functionality. In practice, when traditional use case modeling is used, it is often the case that all we see is the interaction diagrams with actors, association lines, and boxes. This is not a rich description for the architect to make the early critical design decisions. To exacerbate the problem, the author often fails to provide a prose of the interaction diagram. The specific character of the entities in terms of their provides and requires association, and the related assumptions are omitted from traditional use case notation and modeling techniques. Use cases that explicitly list the entities' provides and requires associations and related assumptions can help architects discover missing information and hidden or invalid assumptions. Table 9.3 is a template that can be used to identify the entities from the data in an operational description.

Using this template engineers analyzing the operational description will name the entity and provide a pneumonic reference. If multiple engineers and teams will be performing the analysis, a numbering scheme for all entities should be devised and agreed to before the analysis begins. The engineer must then analyze the operational description and describe the entity to the fullest extent possible. Again, entities may or may not be human in nature. After describing the entity, the engineer must determine what the provides and requires assumptions are for the entity in the system/product context. Finally, the template (Table 9.3) provides a space to indicate what use cases the entity is involved in. Because entities may play in multiple use cases, it can get complicated if multiple engineers and teams are developing the use cases. One way to avoid duplication of effort is to ask each team or engineer to develop the entities first. The entity descriptions should be shared and reviewed by all of the engineers and teams developing use cases, and duplication where it occurs should be rectified and a common set of entities agreed to.

Step 2: Develop the Base Use Cases

Next, the actual use cases are developed from the operation descriptions using entities defined in the previous step. For each use case, decide what entities are involved. This will usually be an iterative process. As the use case is developed, entities may be discovered that were not identified as of yet. This should not be looked upon with frustration—this is exactly what should happen, as this is a process of analysis and discovery. The intent of the analysis process defined here is to help architects uncover missing information such as this early in the design process, rather than discovering it while writing code or, worse, after the system or product is deployed. When developing use cases, architects should initially focus on the normal course of events that occur when the entity or entities interact with the system or other entities of the use case. Do not consider erroneous or exceptional behavior initially—just focus on the base use case. The base use case should describe the system's normal response to stimuli from the entity and the entity's response to stimuli from the system. Describe the interaction between the entities and the system as a sequence of events. If new entities are introduced, ensure that they are defined using Table 9.3. Engineers should strictly avoid specific details of how things are done; be declarative and say what the system does in response to stimuli. Ensure that requires and provides assumptions are not violated. If you find yourself violating provides or requires assumptions, or making up new ones, then the entity should be reanalyzed, or perhaps clarification of the operational description is required. This might include engagement with one or more stakeholders to further clarify, refine, or gather more information about system requirements. Again, this should not be viewed with frustration, but as part of the analysis and discovery process. It is critically important that architectural use cases describing high-level functionality of the system are more than just pictograms commonly used in practice.

Too often the notation used to represent use cases is imprecise, especially in the definition of entities, their association and interaction with the system, and in the provides and requires assumptions. Although graphical notations can be useful, they should only complement prose

Table 9.3 Use Case Entity Description Template

Entity name: *One-line descriptive title*	**Entity ID:** *Mnemonic reference if desired*
Description: Describe the entity and its role in the system context. For example, is it a human, machine, sensor, actuator? Describe any special characteristics that it might have or lack. For example, consider a human entity: describe any education they have or lack. Or consider a sensor: describe any special characteristics the device may have, such as resolution, accuracy, or other figures of merit. Describe any relevant environmental conditions. For example, is it local, remote, internal, or external to the system design context?	
Provides assumptions: What does the entity provide to the system? Does it simply need to be present? Does it send data? Does it send requests? Does it sent events or interrupts?	
Requires assumptions: What does the entity require or expect from the system? Does the entity expect a service? Does it expect data, artifacts such as a report? Does the entity expect interrupts, events, and so forth?	
Identified use cases: List the use case titles that this entity is identified in. This may not be known when the entity is initially identified, but will become clear as the use cases are developed.	

descriptions. As the use case information is developed, graphical notation can be used to represent the use case if deemed necessary. However, the use cases develop and change over time, and the documentation burden is increased because information must be changed in multiple locations. This usually means that the information is not kept current. However, if a graphic aids in stakeholder understanding, the additional effort might be justified. Here tables are used to guide the development and capture use case models. Table 9.4 is a template to help guide the analysis of the operational descriptions and the development of use case scenarios.

Each use case should be given a meaningful title and a pneumonic reference ID as described in the template. Again, if multiple engineers and teams will be performing the analysis, a numbering scheme for entities should be devised and agreed to before the analysis begins. The template also provides an area to provide a short narrative description of the use case. The original operational description can be entered here, or some other brief description of the use case. List entities involved in the use case; use the use case descriptions derived thus far. Describe any preconditions or assumption that must be true before the flow of events described in the use case occur. The table then provides several rows to describe the primary use case flow of events. The flow of events should be listed as they occur, in temporal order, and described in terms of actions and responses between the entities and the system or product. It is important to avoid describing how the system renders service or behaves, but rather focus on the interactions and what the system or product does. After describing the use case, list any significant postconditions or assumptions that will be true after the flow of events.

Recall that the focus at this point is high-level functional requirements, so the engineer should make sure that he or she remains at a proper abstraction granularity. It is impossible to provide hard-and-fast rules for what is proper abstraction granularity for all domains, applications, and

Table 9.4   Use Case Development Table Template

Use case title: One-line descriptive title	Use case ID: Mnemonic reference if desired
General use case description: Provide a short narrative description.	
Entities involved: List entities involved. The entity identification table entries can be referenced. In any case, make sure that entities are defined before they are used here.	
Preconditions: Describe any preexisting conditions or assumptions prior to the start of the flow of events.	
Primary use case flow of events:	
1.	The flow of events should be described in terms of actions and responses between the entity and the system. Although not necessary, numbering steps is helpful.
N.	
Primary use case postconditions: Describe any relevant postconditions or assumptions after the flow of events.	
Alternate use case #_____ flow of events:	
1.	The flow of events should be described in terms of actions and responses between the entity and the system. Although not necessary, numbering steps is helpful.
N.	
Alternate use case #_____ postconditions: Describe any relevant postconditions or assumptions after the flow of events.	

projects of all size and scope. Some use cases may be important for design concerns, but may not be significant to architectural design. For example, if the engineer is describing how an entity interacts with a user interface in terms of what it provides to, and get from, the system vis-à-vis the interface, this is probably an appropriate level of abstraction for architectural design. However, if the use case is describing the details of the kind of widgets used and the color scheme of the user interface, this is probably not an appropriate level of abstraction. Although user interface design at this level is extraordinarily important, it is typically not relevant to architectural design and the early design decisions the architect must make. It may be prudent to defer the detailed design of the user interface to downstream engineers who are experts in interface design. To stay focused on the proper level of abstraction for architectural design and limit the number of use cases, engineers should constantly reflect upon the use cases as they are developed. The architecture design team should ensure that the use cases and the functional requirement represented by them are of interest and will be influential to system/product design. Functional requirements that may impact system partitioning decisions, assignment of responsibilities to architectural elements, key services provided by the system, and so forth and must be explored through use cases. If in doubt, model it! Ultimately, the use cases should describe what the stakeholder community wants the system to do and help the architect reason about the design choices he or she makes.

Step 3: Develop Alternatives to the Base Use Cases as Necessary

Once satisfied with the base use case, it may be necessary to extend the case to specify viable alternative use cases, such as error responses, fault recovery, or other alternative responses to stimuli. Modeling alternatives to the main flow of events may be necessary to describe how stakeholders want the system to respond to specific exceptions or events, or describe how the system responds when things go wrong. These situations could be modeled as separate use cases as well, but developing alternative paths can help avoid unnecessarily repeating information in use cases. If every base case and every viable alternative were modeled separately, this could result in an enormous number of use cases that the architecture design team would have to develop and manage. Extending base use cases to describe alternative paths avoids duplication of effort and information, saving valuable analysis time. Again, the architecture design team should focus on viable alternatives that might affect architecture design decisions and explore them by creating alternative use cases to describe them. This too will limit the number of use cases and alternatives. Focus on relevant alternatives, not every possible alternative to the base use case. The template in Table 9.4 provides a section to portray alternatives to the base use case described in the main body of the template.

This process should be repeated for each operational description until the high-level functionality of the system is adequately modeled vis-à-vis the use cases and their relevant alternatives. Architects should use the development of use cases as a means to analyze the operational descriptions elicited in stage 1 to refine and clearly describe the functional requirements from the stakeholder community. In stage 1, brainstorming was used to gather as much information, from as many stakeholders, as quickly as possible. Although these structured brainstorming techniques are very effective at gathering lots of information quickly, as the information gathered is analyzed, missing bits will be discovered. If the architecture design team finds that they are missing information, or information they have about an operational description is vague, they should not hesitate to interview the relevant stakeholder for clarification. Although brainstorming techniques gather lots of general information, interviewing techniques should be used by the architecture design team for very small groups or individual stakeholders and focus on asking very specific questions about some aspect of the requirements. Modelers must resist the temptation to make assumptions on the stakeholders' behalf. The development of use cases should involve engineers from the architecture design team and stakeholders working together as necessary. Iteration is important when modeling requirements with use cases. As the use cases are developed, they should be circulated or presented to the architectural design team for review, and their feedback used to refine the use cases. As the use cases are developed and reviewed, more entities may be discovered, functional requirements discovered, and the existing entities and related use cases may change as result. Early in the process of developing use cases there will be a lot of volatility and chaos as information is discovered and refined through the identification of entities and the construction of use cases. As the use cases are developed and iteratively refined and extended, requirements will begin to converge, coalesce, and stabilize. At this point, the initial model of the high-level functional requirements of the system will be done. In actuality, this is a baseline—a snapshot in time. The job modeling of requirements is not done until the system is retired. As functional requirements change over the life cycle of the system, use cases will serve as a point of reference and can be used to help architects manage change throughout the system's life cycle. As requirements and the system evolve over time, the use cases should evolve as well and be kept current with the as-built system.

Example of Use Case

To support analysis and adequately describe what stakeholders want, a properly articulated use case will:

- Be clear, concise, and fully descriptive
- Provide a generalized description of how the system/product will be used
- Describe how entities interact with the system/product
- Provide a description of the system/product responses to specific stimuli
- Be understandable by nontechnical as well as technical stakeholders

To illustrate these principles and show how the templates above (Tables 9.3 and 9.4) can be used to develop use cases, an example will be provided based on the SmartMarquee system introduced earlier in the text. Recall that the SmartMarquee's key functional requirement is to provide the capability to display text and graphical advertisement information, to include:

- A panel with scrolling banner (graphical) advertisements
- A panel that will display advertisements comprised of mixed text and graphics that will show each advertisement for a period, then page to the next one
- A panel that will display video advertisements

In addition to this, the system must also be remotely configurable by system administrators per the following requirement:

> Requirement 8: The SmartMarquee shall include a separate interactive tool that will allow administrators to define and configure advertisements. The support tool shall allow administrators to export configurations to a SmartMarquee locally or remotely.

Using these "shall" requirements as a basis, the architecture design team should work with the customer stakeholders as described in stage 1 to fully develop the architectural drivers. For the purposes of the example here, assume the architecture design team elicited the operational description in Table 9.5 from stage 1.

This operational description will be used to illustrate use case analysis. Note that this operational description is a powerful statement of what the customer stakeholder expects the configuration operation to be, but generates a number of questions that must be answered by deeper analysis.

Table 9.5   Example of Operational Scenario for SmartMarquee

Operational description title:		
Configuring the SmartMarquee		
Describe stakeholders' role(s) proposing the description:		**ID: 001**
System administrator		
Operational Consideration	**Stakeholder Response**	
Provide a general description of the functionality.	The ability for the system administrator to configure the SmartMarquee displays. A separate configuration tool is desired to configure SmartMarquee locally and remotely. The configuration tool provides an environment in which the advertisement graphics and video clips can be loaded and assembled into the panels and configured as a complete advertisement display package that can be loaded on a local or remotely deployed SmartMarquee.	
Describe what the stakeholder does now or would like to be able to do.	The system administrator is the stakeholder who will configure the SmartMarquee. He or she will respond to the need to establish or reconfigure advertisements on a SmartMarquee that is deployed locally or remotely. He or she will use a configuration tool to create, configure, and load the advertisement panels on the SmartMarquee.	
Describe any input that is provided or is available at the time of initiation.	The system administrator will have to have the advertisement graphics files (jpg and gif formats) or video files (mpg, avi, and mov formats) to create the advertisements. The system administrator must be able to load the graphics and video files onto the configuration tool.	
Describe the operational context.	The action will be initiated at the time reconfiguration is needed. While the advertisement display is being developed, the operation of the SmartMarquee will not be interrupted. Once the new advertisement configuration is loaded, the configuration tool must instruct the SmartMarquee to display the new configuration.Graphics and video files must be of the supported type and ready for loading. The SmartMarquee must be deployed and ready for use. If the SmartMarquee is remotely deployed, it must be accessible via a network connection. If the SmartMarquee is locally accessible, the system administrator must have access to the device's USB, disk, CD, or other similar media.The configuration is prepared in one location on the configuration tool, while the SmartMarquee is fully operational in the deployed location.	

(continued)

Table 9.5 Example Operational Scenario for SmartMarquee (continued)

Operational Consideration	Stakeholder Response
Describe how the system/ product should respond.	At the time of upload, the configuration tool will upload the new configuration to the SmartMarquee, while the SmartMarquee continues to display the former configuration. While continuing to display the former configuration, the SmartMarquee will examine the new configuration to ensure that it is valid. When the SmartMarquee determines that the new configuration is valid, it will stop the former configuration and start the new one.
Describe any output the system/product produces as a result of the action.	The output of the configuration tool is an advertisement panel configuration file that includes all of the panel position and size information and all of the associated graphics and video files. After upload, the SmartMarquee will stop the former configuration and display the new configuration.
Describe who or what uses the output and what the output is used for.	The SmartMarquee uses the output of the configuration tool to configure the public advertisement display. The output of the SmartMarquee is viewed by the public.

Step 1: Identify the Entities of the System

From this operational description, it is clear that the SmartMarquee will include a suite of at least two different products: the SmartMarquee application and device that displays the advertisements, and a tool that can create and load configuration information onto SmartMarquee devices. Although we must avoid making premature design decisions, the requirements for remote configuration, creating configurations will displaying advertisement, almost preclude the use of a single computer and application for the SmartMarquee. However, the details of how this is done are unimportant at this point, and we will focus on what the stakeholders expect in terms of configuring the SmartMarquee. To better understand the relationship between the stakeholders and the SmartMarquee, we begin with the identification of the entities listed in this operational description. There are three key entities in this operational scenario that we should analyze:

■ The system administrator who will make the advertisements and configure the SmartMarquee to display the advertisements
■ The SmartMarquee product that actually displays the advertisements
■ The configuration tool that is used by users to create advertisement configurations for the SmartMarquee

To guide the definition and documenting of these entities, we can use the entity definition template provided in Table 9.3. Using this template as a guide, we can define the SmartMarquee's system administrator entity as shown in Table 9.6.

In this example the entity identified follows the classic human actor as described in traditional use case modeling. The template calls for a description of the entity as well as the provides and requires assumptions. The provides assumptions list those things that the entity will provide to other entities (the system, entities of the system, or those entities external to the system). Those services and artifacts required by the entity are also listed in the template. Note that all this infor-

Table 9.6   Example of Entity: SmartMarquee System Administrator

Entity name: SmartMarquee administrator	Entity ID: E01
Description: The SmartMarquee administrator is a human user of the system that will be responsible for creating and configuring the advertisement display panes. This user may have training in graphical arts or marketing to create aesthetically pleasing advertisements, but no special computer training for the user of the system is assumed.	
Provides assumptions: The SmartMarquee administrator will provide: • Graphical files in gif or jpg format for advertisement development and system configuration • Video clip files in mpg, mov, or avi formats for advertisement development and system configuration • Textual information for advertisement development	
Requires assumptions: The SmartMarquee administrator requires the system to provide: • An environment to aid in the development advertisements • An ability to save, retrieve, and alter display configurations • A capability to configure SmartMarquee advertisement displays locally and remotely	
Identified use cases: Create advertisement configuration (UC01). Configure SmartMarquee display unit remotely (UC02).	

mation may not be immediately available from the operational descriptions elicited in stage 1, so the engineer should not hesitate to reengage this stakeholder to clarify or acquire missing information. It is normal to discover missing information during analysis; in fact, uncovering ambiguous or missing requirements information is the purpose of analysis. The entities listed in Tables 9.7 and 9.8 are not typical human actors but first-class entities in the system context. As such, their roles and the provides and requires assumptions for each must be analyzed and understood. These entities will be critical in developing the use cases that will be vitally important to understanding what the stakeholders expect from the SmartMarquee.

It is clear to see that some of these entities will interact with one another in a variety of use cases that we might explore and further develop. This illustrates the point that in practice, the thing that we call the system usually interacts with many entities in ways that is not always obvious during the initial requirements stages.

Step 2: Develop the Base Use Cases

Use cases help architects identify and describe the functional requirements of a system by developing stories about entities interacting with the system/product and each other. As an example, we will explore how an administrator creates an advertisement configuration. This use case is shown in Table 9.9 and was developed from the use case development template listed in the Table 9.4. Note that this use case only articulates the base use case. and therefore, no alternative use cases are listed in this example.

This is a fairly ordinary use case that describes an interaction between a human entity (system administrator) and another, nonhuman entity (SmartMarquee configuration tool). Note that the configuration tool is not the system but a nonhuman entity interacting in the system context.

Table 9.7 Example of Entity: SmartMarquee Configuration Tool

Entity name: SmartMarquee configuration tool	Entity ID: E02

Description:
The SmartMarquee configuration tool will assist a SmartMarquee administrator (E01) in the creation of advertisements for the SmartMarquee display unit (E03).

Provides assumptions:
The SmartMarquee configuration tool will provide:
- A graphical user interface (GUI) that will allow the SmartMarquee administrator to configure SmartMarquee unit's display with advertisements
- The ability to ingest graphical files (gif, jpg) and video clips (mpg, mov, avi) from the disk, USB jump drive, or network for the SmartMarquee administrator (E01) to configure advertisement panes for display on the SmartMarquee display unit (E03)
- The ability to configure a SmartMarquee display unit (E03) locally, i.e., run on a SmartMarquee display unit (E03)
- The ability to configure a SmartMarquee display unit (E03) via a USB jump drive, i.e., write SmartMarquee display unit (E03) configuration files to a jump drive
- The ability to configure a SmartMarquee display unit (E03) remotely, i.e., write SmartMarquee display unit (E03) configuration over a wireless or wireful connection

Requires assumptions:
The SmartMarquee configuration tool requires graphics and video files for advertisement configuration from external sources.

Identified use cases:
Create advertisement configuration (UC01). Configure SmartMarquee display unit remotely (UC02).

Table 9.8 Example of Entity: SmartMarquee Display Unit

Entity name: SmartMarquee display unit	Entity ID: E03

Description:
The SmartMarquee display unit is the system that will display advertisements to the public. Advertisements are created on the SmartMarquee configuration tool and sent to the SmartMarquee display unit, which will read the configuration and show, update, and change the display according to the configuration parameters.

Provides assumptions:
The SmartMarquee display unit will show advertisements depending upon the configuration file as:
- Horizontal or vertical scrolling banners
- A series of continuous, looped video advertisement clips
- A series of paging, static graphic, or text advertisement
- Live streaming stock quote data

Requires assumptions:
The SmartMarquee display unit requires a valid configuration file before advertisement displays can begin.

Identified use cases:
Configure SmartMarquee display unit remotely (UC02).
Stock stream provider operation (UC03)

Table 9.9 Example of Use Case: Creating a SmartMarquee Advertisement Configuration

Use case title: Create advertisement configuration.	Use case ID: UC01
General use case description: This use case describes how an advertisement configuration is created.	
Entities involved: E01—SmartMarquee system administrator E02—SmartMarquee configuration tool	
Preconditions: The assumption is that the SmartMarquee configuration tool is already installed on a stand-alone system (remote) or on a SmartMarquee (local).	
Primary use case flow of events:	

1.	E01 starts the SmartMarquee configuration tool application.
2.	The E02 application starts and the main menu is displayed.
3.	E01 elects to import several graphical files (mixed formats: jpg, gif) and video files (mixed formats: mpg, avi, mov) for advertisements.
4.	For each imported file, E02 prompts the user to specify the location of the file (network or disk to include local disk drives, CD, and USB jump drives). After specifying the location, E02 reads the files from that location and makes them available for E01's use in the development of advertisements.
5.	E01 elects to create a horizontal or vertical scrolling advertisement panel.
6.	E02 creates a resizable, movable panel for the user to size and place on the display.
7.	E01 then indicates it wants to associate graphics files it just loaded with the horizontal/vertical scrolling advertisement panel it just created.
8.	E02 prompts E01 to select graphical files. For each file, the graphic is resized to best fit the panel. Steps 7 and 8 are repeated for each graphics file associated with the horizontal or vertical scrolling advertisement panel.
9.	At the conclusion of creating the horizontal or vertical scrolling advertisement panel, E02 prompts E01 to select a scroll rate, i.e., the rate at which the graphics move across the display.
10.	E01 elects to create a paging static graphic and text advertisement panel.
11.	E02 creates a resizable, movable panel for the user to size and place on the display.
12.	E01 then indicates it wants to associate graphics files it just loaded with the paging static graphics and text advertisement panel it just created.
13.	E02 prompts E01 to specify the graphical files to associate with the panel. E02 allows E01 to resize the graphic and place it within the panel. Steps 12 and 13 are repeated for each graphic added to the panel.
14.	E01 then indicates it wants to create a text message for the paging static graphics and text advertisement panel it just created.
15.	E02 prompts E01 to enter the text to associate with the panel. E01 then creates a text message for the panel. E02 allows E01 to select font and font type, resize the font of the text message, and place it within the panel. Steps 14 and 15 are repeated for each graphic added to the panel.

(continued)

Table 9.9   Example of Use Case: Creating a SmartMarquee Advertisement Configuration (continued)

16.	Steps 10 through 15 are repeated for paging static graphic and text advertisement associated with this panel.
17.	At the conclusion of creating the horizontal or vertical scrolling advertisement panel, E02 prompts E01 to select a paging rate, i.e., the rate at which the static graphic and text advertisement are displayed before switching to the next advertisement.
18.	E01 elects to create a video advertisement panel.
19.	E02 creates a resizable, movable panel for the user to size and place on the display.
20.	E01 then indicates it wants to associate video files it just loaded with the video advertisement panel it just created.
21.	E02 prompts E01 to select video files. For each file, the video is resized to best fit the panel. Steps 7 and 8 are repeated for each video file associated with the video advertisement panel.
22.	E01 elects to save the configuration.
23.	E02 prompts E01 for a configuration name and a location to save the configuration.
24.	E01 enters the configuration name and location.
25.	E02 saves the information, including the graphics and video files, in a single-configuration file and indicates to E01 that the configuration is saved.
26.	E01 elects to exit the application.
Primary use case postconditions:	
At the conclusion of the use case there is a valid configuration file consisting of a scrolling banner pane, a static paging pane, and a video pane ready for export to a SmartMarquee display unit (E03).	

Clearly the configuration tool is within the project scope, that is, it is something that will have to be designed and implemented as part of the project. This use case also illustrates the delicate balance between ensuring that use cases describe interactions between entities and resisting the temptation to make design decisions prematurely—no matter how innocent or innocuous they may seem at the time. One could argue that the need for a separate configuration tool is obvious and is almost an indirect constraint imposed on the design because of the need to remotely configure SmartMarquees. This use case does not impose any specific design decisions in terms of the application partitioning, allocation to hardware platforms, look-and-feel decisions, and so forth. However, a counterargument could be made that the decision has been made in this use case that the configuration tool is a separate application with a graphical user interface and that this represents a set of decisions. To some extent, this "decision" is a way of addressing the constraint that a SmartMarquee be a stand-alone device. This may be a case where the requirements for the system or part of a system (a configuration tool or cases) are specified in terms of our experiences with similar tools, systems, or products. A balance must be maintained between making premature design decisions and genuine practicality of acknowledging the obvious need for various kinds of subsystems that may become apparent during requirements elicitation. Striking this balance must be left to the judgment of the architecture design team. This situation was purposely staged here to highlight the need for architects to vigilantly and constantly reflect, evaluate, and apply judgment as necessary to maintain this balance.

The use case listed in Table 9.10 describes an interaction between the SmartMarquee, configuration tool, and system administrator. Note that from an architectural design perspective the

Table 9.10   Example of Use Case: Remote Advertisement Configuration Upload

Use case title: Remote SmartMarquee configuration	Use case ID: UC02

General use case description:
This use case describes how advertisement configurations are loaded onto SmartMarquees remotely.

Entities involved:
E01—SmartMarquee system administrator
E02—SmartMarquee configuration tool
E03—SmartMarquee

Preconditions:
The assumption is that the SmartMarquee is deployed in a remote location, that is, the configuration and configuration tool are in one location, physically separated from the SmartMarquee that the system administrator wants to configure. There is a network connection between the configuration tool and the SmartMarquee. It is assumed that a configuration has been created and is stored on the configuration tool (see UC01).

Primary use case flow of events:

1.	E01 starts the configuration tool application.
2.	The E02 application starts and the main menu is displayed.
3.	E01 elects the option to load a configuration on E03.
4.	E02 presents a list of known E03 devices and prompts E01 to select an E03 from a list of known devices, or enter the address of E03.
5.	E01 selects a known E03 or enters the address of an unknown E03.
6.	E02 contacts the selected E03 device to ensure that it is accessible.
7.	E02 then prompts E01 for security information to authenticate access E03.
8.	E02 prompts E01 to select the configuration that E01 would like to load on the SmartMarquee.
9.	E02 sends the selected configuration data to E03.
10.	Once the transfer is complete, E03 notifies E02 that the transfer is complete.
11.	E03 checks the configuration to ensure that it is valid.
12.	E03 notifies E02 that the configuration is valid.
13.	E03 stops the current configuration (if one is running), reads the new configuration, and starts the display.
14.	E03 notifies E02 that the new configuration has been started.
15.	The connection between E02 and E03 is terminated.

Primary use case postconditions:
At the conclusion of the use case the configuration on E02 is sent to E03. The new configuration is validated by E03. The old configuration on E03 is stopped, and the new configuration is started and fully operational.

interaction between the SmartMarquee and the configuration tool is an extremely important part of this analysis. From this use case, we can see that there are quality attribute requirements for security (UC02 step 7) and reliability (UC02 steps 6 and 11). Although we do not delve into the specifics of these requirements in the use case, they will be analyzed in detail when the architecture design team develops the quality attribute characterizations into quality attribute scenarios. Clearly there are numerous alternative flows that should be explored in this use case as well. For example, how should the system respond if a SmartMarquee cannot be connected to (step 6), and what should happen if the configuration is invalid (step 11)? These and other important conditions should be explored with alternative use cases because they may impact the architectural design. Note that usability issues are not really described in this use case; clearly usability will be an issue in this context. Although usability will be important to the system's success, it will not be an architectural design issue. However, this use case can be used by downstream engineers as a starting point for analyzing usability requirements and designing the user interface. Finally, we will turn our attention to the online stock quote requirement that was listed earlier for the SmartMarquee:

> The system shall provide the capability to accept, process, and display continuous data streaming stock market quotes (in the Market Data Definition Language (MDDL)) in a scrolling banner panel consistent with the definition of a scrolling banner panel.

An interesting aspect of this requirement is that the streaming stock quote providers are entities external to the system boundaries, and as such are out of the control and design purview of the architect designing the SmartMarquee. The data they provide, the format it is provided in, the rate at which it is provided, and the availability of the data are direct constraints on the system. To ensure ease of interface of these entities, the requirements specify that a standard will be used (specifically MDDL). The operational description for this requirement is listed in Table 9.11. The streaming stock quote provider entity is described in Table 9.12. The base use case for the streaming stock quotes is listed in Table 9.13.

Once the base use case (or use cases) is established, variants can be explored to further shine light on the requirements. Note that there are a number of alternatives to the base case that need to be explored here. An alternative use case is shown in Table 9.14 to explore what happens if the SmartMarquee is unable to establish a connection with the streaming stock quote providers.

Clearly this use case analysis forces an architect to ask stakeholders how they would like the system to respond if a streaming stock quote server is not available. The alternative steps can be modeled separately or included with the same table as UC04 using the "alternative use case flow of events" section described in Table 9.4. One might argue that this case study is making design decisions regarding the system's fault/error handling. Again, this is not entirely true. The use case is describing how the system stakeholders would like the system to function when the streaming stock quote provider is not available. Admittedly, this is a fine line between quality attribute concern and functionality, but as stated earlier, quality attributes and functionality are often intertwined and sometimes closely coupled with one another. Another issue that becomes apparent in this analysis is the potential impact that performance may have on the system. The timeliness of the stock quotes might be an issue that could impact design. This can be fully explored when the quality attributes are analyzed. The point is that the system stakeholders may not have initially specified these behaviors, but through the analysis of the raw architectural drivers and the development of use cases, these issues become apparent. It is important that the architecture design team identify these missing or ambiguous requirements, and that they are able to work with the stakeholders to refine the requirements before design. The templates and methods described here provide a framework for that analysis.

Table 9.11   Example of Operational Description of the Streaming Stock Quote Requirement

Operational description title: Displaying streaming stock quotes	
Describe stakeholders' role(s) proposing the description: Marketing stakeholders	**ID: 002**

Operational Consideration	*Stakeholder Response*
Provide a general description of the functionality.	The ability for a SmartMarquee connected to the Internet to display stock quotes in a scrolling banner panel.
Describe what the stakeholder does now or would like to be able to do.	The system administrator should be able to specify a stock quote stream provider, or list of providers, and configure a scrolling-style display panel to scroll stock quotes as they are read from the stock quote stream provider.
Describe any input that is provided or available at the time of initiation.	The valid Internet address of a stock quote stream provider. The data stream from a stock quote stream provider.
Describe the operational context.	The stock quote stream display will be specified in the configuration. The SmartMarquee will negotiate the connection at start-up. The SmartMarquee will format and display the information at runtime. There may be costs and authentication associated with accessing the data stream from the streaming stock quote provider.
Describe how the system/ product should respond.	The streaming stock quotes will be similar to scrolling banner advertisement panels in operation and in their look and feel. If scrolling stock quotes are specified in an advertisement display configuration, on start-up the SmartMarquee will contact the streaming stock quote provider. Once the connection is established, the SmartMarquee will read the data stream from the stock quote provider, and format and display the stock quote data. Stock quotes will scroll across the screen in the banner panel from left to right, or top to bottom, as specified by the configuration.
Describe any output the system/product produces as a result of the action.	The output will be stock quote displays on the SmartMarquee.
Describe who or what uses the output and what the output is used for.	The output of the SmartMarquee is viewed by the public.

A Guide for Analyzing Stage 1 Quality Attribute Characterizations

After the constraints, the quality attribute requirements are often the most influential requirements for a system or product, and they will deeply impact the architect's design options and decisions. Many different ensembles of structures can solve a given set of functional requirements; however, only a few—sometimes one set of structures—can adequately solve the functional *and* quality attribute requirements. Designing systems to meet the quality attribute requirements is often where the architecture design team earns their salaries. In stage 1, the dialog regarding quality attributes was initiated from a simple list of one-word quality attribute requirements.

Table 9.12   Example of Entity: Streaming Stock Quote Provider

Entity name: Streaming stock quote provider		Entity ID: E04
Description: The stock stream provider is an organization with servers that will provide data streams of stock quotes from various market exchanges around the world.		
Provides assumptions: The stock stream provider provides a data stream in the Market Data Definition Language.		
Requires assumptions: The stock stream provider and the associated data stream are a fee service. Authentication for accessing the service is required.		
Identified use cases: Stock stream provider operation (UC03).		

Table 9.13   Example of Use Case: Streaming Stock Quote Provider

Use case title: Display real-time stock quotes	Use case ID: UC03
General use case description: This use case describes how the SmartMarquee display unit displays real-time stock quotes.	
Entities involved: E03—SmartMarquee display unitE04—Stock stream provider.	
Preconditions: A valid configuration is loaded on a deployed SmartMarquee display that includes a stock quote banner panel in the configuration. It is assumed that the use case will begin SmartMarquee start-up. It is assumed that the SmartMarquee display unit is connected to a network that provides access to one of the stock stream providers specified in the configuration. It is assumed that the fees have been paid and the appropriate accounts are established for the Marquee display unit to use the services of the stock stream provider(s).	

Primary use case flow of events:	
1.	On start-up, the SmartMarquee display unit (E03) reads the current configuration file. Among the advertisement panels specified in the configuration is a real-time stock quote banner panel.
2.	E03 configures the real-time stock quote banner panel on the display and reads the list of stock stream providers (E04) from the configuration file.
3.	E03 contacts each E04 to determine which ones are available.
4.	E03 selects the E04 that it will use during operation and establishes a streaming data connection.
5.	E03 starts the advertisement display application.
6.	E03 reads the stock quote data stream from E04.
7.	Upon receiving the data from E04, E03 displays the stock quote data in the appropriate panel.

| **Primary use case postconditions:** At the conclusion of the use case the SmartMarquee display unit (E03) is operational, connected to a stock stream provider (E04), and displaying stock quotes. | |

Table 9.14   Example of Alternative Use Case: SmartMarquee Is Unable to Connect to Streaming Stock Quote Provider

Use case title: Unable to connect to streaming stock quote provider	Use case ID: UC05
General use case description: This use case describes what the SmartMarquee display unit does if it is unable to establish a connection with the external systems providing real-time stock quotes.	
Entities involved: E03—SmartMarquee display unit E04—Stock stream provider	
Preconditions: A valid configuration is loaded on a deployed SmartMarquee display that includes a stock quote banner panel in the configuration. It is assumed that the use case will begin SmartMarquee start-up. It is assumed that the SmartMarquee display unit is connected to a network that provides access to one of the stock stream providers specified in the configuration. It is assumed that the fees have been paid and the appropriate accounts are established for the Marquee display unit to use the services of the stock stream provider(s).	

Primary use case flow of events:	
1.	On start-up, the SmartMarquee display unit (E03) reads the current configuration file. Among the advertisement panels specified in the configuration is a real-time stock quote banner panel.
2.	E03 configures the real-time stock quote banner panel on the display and reads the list of stock stream providers (E04) from the configuration file.
3.	E03 contacts each E04 to determine which ones are available.
4.	After attempting to contact all specified EO4s, none are available to provide service.
5.	A message indicating that "real-time stock quotes are not available" is placed in the real-time stock quote banner panel on the display, and E03 starts the advertisement display application.
6.	After a period of time, the E03 will attempt to establish contact with the specified EO4 per step 3 above. If contact is made, continue with step 7.
7.	Once contact is made, UC04 resumes with step 4.

Primary use case postconditions: At the conclusion of the use case the SmartMarquee display unit (E03) is operational. All advertisement panels are operational despite whether E03 is able to connect to a stock stream provider (E04). If the system is able to connect to an E04, real-time streaming stock quotes are displayed; otherwise, a message is displayed in the panel. All others (non-stock-quote banner panels) are able to function normally as described in UC04.

Working with the stakeholders, the architecture design team develops quality attribute characterizations to better describe the systemic quality attribute needs. In stage 2, we will analyze and clarify the quality attribute characterizations elicited from the stakeholders in stage 1. In addition to the quality attribute characterization, another place to look for quality attribute requirements is in the collection of use cases developed to describe high-level functionality. Often quality attribute requirements are woven into use cases—usually in the individual steps comprising a use case. For example, consider the display stock quotes use cases (Tables 9.13 and 9.14). Clearly an argument could be made that there are quality attribute requirements for performance, security, and availability associated with this use case and the alternate. For example, in terms of performance, how timely should the stock information be? Similar questions arise regarding security and availability as it applies to this functional concern. The hard part about analyzing quality attribute requirements is that the quality attributes are often associated with some aspect of functionality, and depending upon the functionality, the quality attribute response will be different. For example, in one part of a system, performance may refer to transaction throughput; in another part of the system, performance may mean user response time; and in yet another part of the system, performance may mean something else. This is why specific quality attribute scenarios have to be developed to fully describe a system's quality attribute responses to various stimuli under specific conditions. If there are a large number of quality attribute characterizations, the architectural design team should first analyze those voted as most important by the stakeholders during the architectural drivers elicitation workshops.

As an example, we will examine a stage 1 quality attribute characterization for *extensibility* as it pertains to the SmartMarquee product. This characterization was developed using the techniques described in stage 1 and documented using Table 8.9. The *extensibility* characterization for the SmartMarquee from stage 1 is shown in Table 9.15.

This information will be used to frame analysis of this quality attribute requirement. As a result of this analysis, the architectural design team will create the six-part quality attribute scenario for this quality attribute scenario. The six-part use case scenario template is shown in Table 9.16.

The six-part quality attribute scenario was introduced in Chapter 3. However, in the ACDM context the six-part scenario is developed as a part of analysis in stage 2 from the quality attribute characterizations elicited in stage 1. Just as with the use case templates, the six-part quality attribute scenario template will help the architecture design team analyze the details of the quality attribute needs that the stakeholders articulated in the quality attribute characterization. The analysis can be done in one of two ways. First, the architecture design team can work together in

Table 9.15 Example of Quality Attribute Characterization for the SmartMarquee

Stakeholder: SmartMarquee software developer	ID: XXX
Quality attribute: Extensibility	

Reason for quality attribute:
Customers or the marketplace will drive the need for new types or custom display and advertisement panels. It is important that the SmartMarquee product can respond quickly to market demand. As such, the SmartMarquee software, configuration tool, and hardware must be easily extensible to support the addition of new kinds of display and advertisement panels.
Stakeholders' quality attribute story:
A new customer would like to have a live video feed of the kitchen operations displayed on their store-front SmartMarquee display system with their menu, pictures of various dishes, and daily specials. The new live-video-feed panel hardware and software can be developed, tested, and shipped in 30 days. The SmartMarquee and configuration tool can be upgraded in the field by the customer, including installation of the new software and hardware (camera) to support the new panel.
Other issues and concerns:
Some customers have no training in computer technology, making the installation and configuration of the SmartMarquee difficult. How will we know if the camera will connect to the hardware easily and will be compatible with the hardware, operating system, and SmartMarquee software? How far away will the SmartMarquee be from the camera? Will cable length be a constraint? Can a wireless camera be used?

Table 9.16   Six-Part Quality Attribute Scenario Template

Title of scenario: Descriptive title if desired	**ID:** Mnemonic reference if desired
Quality attribute: The one-word quality attribute characterization	**Characterization ID:** The ID of the stage 1 characterization used as a basis for this scenario
Describe stakeholder role proposing the description: The stakeholder(s) or stakeholder communities interested in this quality attribute scenario.	
Source(s) of the stimulus	Description of the originating source(s) or potential sources of the stimulus or stimuli that will result in a system response.
Stimulus	Phenomenon, event, situation, etc., that prompts the system or stakeholders to react in some way or take some action. It might be a user request, an event or interrupt, an error, a request for change, and so forth.
Relevant environmental conditions	Description of any relevant environmental conditions that could affect the response and the measures of the response. It might include such conditions as normal operation, peak load, degraded operation, at development time, during operation, without interrupting operation, and so forth.
Architectural elements	System elements affected by the stimulus. Early in the development life cycle (prearchitectural design) the affected elements might not be known or may be a very high-level description. As design commences, scenarios should be refined and elements identified as they are known.
System response	Desired response of the system. This should be as specific as possible because this will be how the system will be designed to respond to the stimulus.
Response measure(s)	Measure by which the quality of the response will be measured. Response measures depend on the quality attribute. Response measures vary and may be in terms of person-hours, error detection, response time, recovery time, and so forth.
Associated risks	In the course of analyzing the quality attribute descriptions, the architectural design team may discover risks associated with satisfying the quality attribute requirement. These will largely be technical, but may include other issues that will influence later design decisions.

a meeting, using the template in Table 9.16 to guide the analysis, filling out each element of the template as a team until they are satisfied that the quality attribute requirement is fully described in the six-part format. Alternatively, each member of the architectural design team can be assigned one or more of the quality attribute characterizations, and the individual engineers can develop the six-part scenarios. After they complete the six-part scenarios, each team member should present their work to the architectural design team to critique and refine their six-part scenarios. The former approach works well if there are a few quality attribute characterizations (less than 50). If there are numerous quality attribute characterizations (more than 50), the latter approach works best. If the analysis meeting approach is used, this should be led by the requirements engineer.

Each quality attribute characterization should be read aloud and the six-part template projected. Members should be invited to contribute to filling out the six-part template, discussing issues as they arise. Make sure that a scribe captures the six-part scenarios and records any unresolved issues associated with the analysis. Table 9.17 shows the six-part scenario for the quality attribute characterization of *extensibility* shown in Table 9.15. A brief narrative of the analysis that led to this six-part scenario is described here as well.

Here we can see that the stakeholders interested in extensibility are those engineers that will be responsible for changing the system after it is deployed. The stakeholders in this case are those engineers that are hardware and software experts. Their interest in extensibility described in this particular characterization will affect the SmartMarquee hardware and software as well as the configuration tool software. However, notice that there is a stakeholder conspicuously missing from this characterization. The stakeholders proposing this characterization were those engineers that wanted to easily modify software and hardware to create a live-feed video panel. However, once the modifications are made, the upgrades will have to be installed in the field by the users of the SmartMarquee. It is also interesting to note that the configuration tool will be affected by these changes as well. Clearly the configuration tool software will have to be modified to configure live video feeds for the SmartMarquee, but it is unclear if this will also affect the configuration tool hardware. From a requirements and operational standpoint, the configuration tool might also need access to a camera to configure the panel properly. Note the issues and concerns that were described by the stakeholders in the quality attribute characterization. First, the user stakeholders may not have any computer expertise. This means that installation procedures, tools, and

Table 9.17   Example of Six-Part Quality Attribute Scenario for the SmartMarquee

Title of scenario: Live video feed		ID: YYY
Quality attribute: Extensibility	**Original characterization ID:** XXX	
Describe stakeholder role proposing the description: Maintainer and end user		
Stimulus	Need for a new live video stream panel to display live video in a SmartMarquee panel.	
Source(s) of the stimulus	Marketplace demand or individual custom customer development.	
Relevant environmental conditions	The SmartMarquee is already deployed. The hardware and software must be upgraded in the field.	
Architectural elements	The SmartMarquee application or applications. The SmartMarquee hardware. The configuration tool software and possibly hardware.	
System response	The SmartMarquees are already deployed and the software and hardware to support this feature must be upgraded by the customer without having to return the SmartMarquee to the factory and without the support of a SmartMarquee technician.	
Response measure(s)	The new live video feed panel can be implemented and tested within 30 days. The hardware and software upgrades to support this feature can be installed in 1 hour.	
Associated risks	It is not clear how many cameras a single SmartMarquee must support.	

mechanisms will have to be designed into these products to accommodate the user stakeholders' inability to perform complex software and hardware modifications or follow complex installation procedures. The stakeholders also expressed a concern about compatibility with respect to the camera, the operating system, and the SmartMarquee software. This is an especially important consideration when combined with the previous concern about the level of expertise of the stakeholder responsible for installing the upgrade. It is also not clear how far the camera will be from the SmartMarquee itself, and wireless cameras may have to be utilized or offered as an option. Another issue of concern that may arise during analysis is: How many live feeds should the Smart-Marquee support? This appears no where in the characterization of the quality attribute, but is an issue of concern worth noting at this point. Clear technical risks that emerge in the course of analysis should be recorded in the six-part template in the provided section. This risk is recorded in the template listed in Table 9.17. These risks will largely be technical in nature but may include other kinds of risks as well. The risks recorded here should be technical in nature—those having architectural impact. ACDM is a technical method, not a process improvement method. ACDM drives teams toward discovering and mitigating technical risks in a structured way through design or experimentation and refinement of the design. While ACDM can help organizations build better designs by providing structure for the process of design, it is not a method for measuring and improving organizational processes. This can be a fine line; if in doubt, record the risk.

The reader may have thought of other issues in addition to those described here. The point is that discovering missing information like this is the purpose of stage 2 analysis. This highlights the need for analyzing the raw quality attribute data elicited in stage 1 before architectural design, rather than marching off and binding design decision prematurely. All of these issues can deeply impact the design of the system and what is ultimately implemented. Relevant stakeholders should be consulted to clarify the quality attribute requirements or provide missing information; however, be prepared: the stakeholders may not have answers for these issues, concerns, or questions. Again, these issues may need to be explored through experimentation and refinement, addressed later in the design process.

In addition to the quality attribute requirements derived from the quality attribute characterizations, other quality attributes may also be important to consider. The architectural design team itself may have quality attribute requirements that they consider important in the product. The architecture design team should also contribute architecture drivers that they feel are essential to the success of the system or product. These can be quality attributes that the broader stakeholder community missed or those that serve the architecture design team. These are often quality attribute properties that are not important, or even visible, to end user or customer stakeholders, but are very important to the architecture design team, such as maintainability, modifiability, extensibility, and many others. Users or customers may not directly care about these quality attributes, but systems with these properties often have the potential to better serve end users and customers in the long run. While quality attribute concerns will generally be subordinate to those of the customers, they should be considered nonetheless, and may be able to be incorporated into the design and implementation with no undesirable side effects. Quality attribute requirements may also emerge from the analysis of the operational descriptions and the development of use case scenarios. Sometimes a single step in a use case can inspire the development of a quality attribute scenario. For example, consider Table 9.10, step 7:

E02 (configuration tool) then prompts E01 (system administrator) for security information to authenticate access E03 (deployed SmartMarquee).

This single action could inspire a series of security-oriented quality attribute scenarios. As such, it might be appropriate for the architecture design team to develop security quality attribute scenarios to explore how the system might validate the identity of an entity attempting to configure a SmartMarquee. These scenarios obviously would aid in the analysis of how the system should respond to stimuli under various conditions to ensure that the SmartMarquee could not be abused by a malevolent entity.

Refining the Constraints

Often during the analysis of the functional and quality attribute requirements, new, missing, incorrect, or incomplete constraints may be discovered. The business and technical constraints from the architecture drivers elicitation workshop should be reviewed at this time and refined as necessary (Tables 8.11 and 8.12). Note that while the use cases and quality attribute scenarios inherit the priorities originally set during the architecture drivers elicitation workshop, the constraints have no assigned priority. Because constraints must be adhered to, there is normally no option to negotiate whether they are part of the design. However, some requirements are often mistakenly identified as constraints. If there is any flexibility in a constraint, it must be further analyzed and explored with the appropriate stakeholders to ensure that it really is a constraint and to characterize the real nature of the constraint. Consider the following statement:

> The SmartMarquee must utilize the Java language to ensure portability across operating system and hardware platforms.

At face value, this seems to be a simple constraint that a particular implementation language must be used. However, on further analysis, is the real issue that the Java language must be used (constraint), or that the SmartMarquee be portable across hardware and operating system platforms (quality attribute requirement)? A constraint such as this should be further investigated to find out what the real need is. In some cases, architects are overconstrained. Consider the following statement in conjunction with the last one:

> The SmartMarquee must utilize a standard Intel/PC hardware platform and Microsoft Windows operating system to ensure portability.

This statement in conjunction with the last statement both point to a need for portability, which is a quality attribute requirement that should be characterized in terms of the stakeholders' expectations for what *portability* really means. However, the customer stakeholders have already made design decisions about how to achieve this requirement by specifying a particular hardware configuration, operating system, and computer language. Unbeknownst to the stakeholders, they may have needlessly constrained the design space in ways that may make it difficult to satisfy other functional and quality attribute requirements. If the real need is portability, then the architectural design team might be able to better satisfy this requirement without these constraints. Clearly, if Java is used, the cross operating system and hardware platform issues may be a mute point because Java provides both hardware and operating system portability. If a standardized hardware platform and operating system are used, then there might be flexibility in the language the architecture design team uses for the system. If the reason for the technical constraints specifying the use of Java, Intel/PC hardware, and the Windows operating system is that these are the standard language, operating system, and hardware platforms of the customer organization, then these might be valid constraints. Business constraints must be analyzed in a similar fashion; however, they tend to be less direct in terms of technical impact and more subjective in nature than technical constraints. For example, assume that the SmartMarquee must be delivered within a tight timeframe to hit a particular market window. Certainly, compressed schedules will affect the design of the system as well as the functionality and quality attribute properties of the delivered product. Market windows are typically determined by marketing research, focus groups, and crystal balls. Arguing for or against targeting an aggressive market is hard to do unless all parties are aware of the impact such a constraint has on the system or product. Aggressive schedules always impact design—the tighter the schedule, the less design and the lower the quality of the design. This might be a prudent trade-off to ensure that our product is first in the market. However, this may also leave us with a less than optimal product, lower-quality product, and may put the organization in a position where it will have to start designing the next version of the product from scratch. Constraints such as these have a dramatic impact, and design decisions made because of these kinds of constraints should be made with representation from management, marketing, and technical communities. From a purely technical standpoint, it is often prudent advice for the architecture design team to analyze the technical and business constraints and, where there are questionable constraints, negotiate for the weakest constraint possible. This maximizes the architecture design team's flexibility later in design stage.

Ranking Difficulty

Once all of the consolidated raw architecture drivers have been analyzed, refined, and documented as described here, the architecture design team has to rank the relative difficulty of each use case, quality attribute scenario, and constraint. The difficulty ranking process helps to identify potentially problematic functional architectural drivers. This additional prioritization has the effect of automatically identifying risky requirements and constraints that the architecture design team should pay particular attention to. For example, any use case or quality attribute scenario that was voted as high priority for the stakeholders and is ranked by the architecture design team as difficult should be a leading indicator of a problematic requirement. If it is impossible to determine the difficulty of a requirement, or the meaning of the requirement is not clear, it should be further investigated and rated as difficult by default until more is learned about the requirement. All constraints by definition are must-haves, and are therefore high priority. So any constraint that is ranked as difficult to satisfy has the potential of being problematic for the architecture design team. Early in a project, it may be difficult to precisely quantify the exact difficulty of a requirement or constraint; again, these should be further studied to better understand the nature of the requirement. However, some requirements will obviously be difficult to achieve, and some constraints will be challenging to adhere to. It would be easy if each architecture driver could be ranked in isolation, but the difficultly of a requirement or constraint must be ranked in context of the entire collection of architectural drivers. For example, it may be easy to meet a particular constraint C, and it may be easy to satisfy some functionality F, but meeting constraint C and providing functionality F may be very difficult. In this case, the architectural design team will have to decide whether both the constraint and functionality are rated as difficult, or if one of them is rated as difficult.

Difficulty ranking is best done in a group meeting with all the architecture design team members present. This meeting should be led by the chief scientist or the chief architect in order to focus on the technical details of each architectural driver and their potential impact on the design. The team will begin with the use cases and rank each one in terms of difficulty, then repeat the process with the quality attribute scenarios, and finally ending with the constraints. Again, difficulty ranking is somewhat subjective and is based upon the collective intuition of the architecture design team. For simplicity, it is best to limit the number of rankings: 1 = difficult, 2 = challenging, and 3 = easy. This simple three-tier ranking has proven very effective in experimentation with ACDM in industry. Each of these rankings is explained in detail below:

1. Difficult: Satisfying the architectural driver presents significant scientific or engineering challenges and unknowns. The architecture design team is unsure about how to satisfy this architectural driver or if they can satisfy it. They have little or no experience or expertise with the problem or domain. Little or no information exists about how to satisfy the architectural driver.
2. Challenging: Satisfying the architectural driver presents some scientific or engineering challenges and unknowns. Although challenging, the architecture design team generally understands how to satisfy this architectural driver. They understand the associated difficulties. There exists sufficient scientific and technical information about how to satisfy the architectural driver, or the team has sufficient experience and expertise with the domain or problem to satisfy the architectural driver.
3. Easy: Satisfying the architectural driver presents little scientific or engineering challenges or unknowns. The architecture design team clearly understands how to satisfy this architectural driver. This is a routine requirement or constraint, and copious scientific and technical information exists about how to satisfy it. The team has extensive experience and expertise with the domain or problem to satisfy the architectural driver.

As the prioritization commences with each architectural driver, the facilitator of the meeting should allow ample discussion among architecture design team members to fully describe their concerns and ranking associated with the architectural driver. The team must reach a consensus on the difficulty ranking for each. Because reaching consensus can be difficult on contentious ranking issues, establish an arbitration rule, such as resorting to a vote after discussion. A scribe should be assigned to capture the prioritization and document the concerns and issues influencing the ranking of each architectural driver. To ease the chore of capturing this information, the scribe should consider using the template in Table 9.18.

This table can be used to document the priorities of the use cases and the quality attribute scenarios. The associated ID for the use case or quality attribute scenario can be listed in the left column; in the next column the stakeholder importance priority is listed, in the next column the difficulty ranking, and finally, any discussion can be captured in the right-most column. Constraints are a bit different. First, they were not assigned IDs by the constraint templates, and second, they are not prioritized by the stakeholders—they are all assumed to be must-haves in the system context. An extension to the template is shown at the end of Table 9.18 for capturing the difficulty ranking for constraints. Using this template, a brief description of the constraint is provided. The architecture design team may alter the stage 1 templates to include constraint IDs if they like. If so, the ID can be entered in this template rather than a prose description. In practice and for the sake of clarity, it is usually a good idea to have separate prioritization tables for use cases, quality attribute scenarios, and business and technical constraints.

Table 9.18 Architecture Drivers Prioritization Templates

ID	Stakeholder Priority	Difficulty Ranking	Comments
Title: <Quality attributes scenarios/use cases prioritizations >			

Description	Difficulty Ranking	Comments
Title: <Technical/business constraint prioritizations>		

Documentation

Before stage 2 is concluded, the architecture drivers specification must be assembled. The word *assembled* was chosen quite deliberately. If the team has been disciplined in its documentation and the use of the templates described here (or defined by the team), then writing this document is more of assembling the templates into a document rather than writing the document from scratch. In addition to the architecture drivers specification, the master design plan must be updated and the activities of the next stages of the ACDM estimated. The requirements engineer is responsible for leading the effort to write the architecture drivers specification. However, all members of the architecture design team should participate in writing the architecture drivers specification. As always, updating the master design plan is the responsibility of the managing engineer.

Architectural Drivers Specification

More important than what an architectural drivers specification document is, is what it is not. It should not be the heavyweight, super-detailed requirements specification called for in traditional waterfall-oriented software development (e.g., MILSTD 2167A). The architecture drivers specification lists the coarse-grained requirements that will be used to design the architecture. For example, the architecture drivers specification should describe the specific needs for stakeholder interaction with a system or product, but should not specify the window color scheme, type of window widgets used, or other similar design or implementation details. A common problem that emerged when testing ACDM with practitioners was that the architecture design team cut and pasted the templates created in stage 2 into a single document. This is a start, but it is not the architecture drivers specification. Recall that after the architecture drivers specification is written, we must circulate it among the stakeholders for their comment before committing to design what is described in the document. This means that the document should sufficiently explain what the document is for, provide an overview of the project, and describe the architectural drivers. The architecture drivers specification should focus narrowly on the architectural drivers and avoid including an overabundance of programmatic information. The document can roughly be divided into the following sections: executive overview, purpose of the document, project overview and context, description of the requirements elicitation, and analysis. Following these sections, the architecture drivers specification should be divided into separate sections for each set of architectural drivers: high-level functionality, quality attribute requirements, and business and technical constraints. The document should conclude with a description of the prioritization process, followed by the actual prioritization of the architectural drivers. Each of these sections is described in detail below.

Executive Overview

The first sections of the document should include an executive overview (if necessary) and a "purpose" section. If an executive overview is required, this should be placed before the purpose section at the very front of the document. In terms of a hard copy document, the reader should see the executive overview after flipping a page or two at most. The executive overview should provide a very brief description of the entire contents of the document. The executive summary should address the following points as concisely as possible:

- Description of the project
- Description of the architecture drivers specification
- Overview of what architectural drivers are
- Summary description of key functionality, quality attribute requirements, and constraints (focus on the highest-priority architectural drivers)

It can be helpful to provide references for each of these to the appropriate sections in the document where the detailed information is located, should the reader want more details. The executive overview should be kept at a maximum of one or two pages of prose. Needless to say, it can be challenging to write the executive summary, but it may be all that senior managers ever read in the architecture drivers specification.

Purpose

The purpose section will provide a more detailed description of the nature and role of the architecture drivers specification and what it will be used for in later stages. Describe the intended audience for the document and what the customer stakeholder audience is expected to do with the document (review it), describe the review process, and include any key references. Refer to the process for changing the requirements listed in the statement of work.

Project Overview

Provide a general description of the project, the customer stakeholders, and the organization designing and building the system or product. Describe any pertinent marketing goals, business objectives, or other contextual information necessary and relevant for describing the project. If there is duplication of this information with what is written in the statement of work or master design plan, refer to those documents. Avoid duplication of information.

Architectural Drivers Overview

Describe the requirements elicitation and analysis process that produced the information in the architecture drivers specification. Provide a general overview of what architectural drivers are and their relative influence on the design of the system or product. Describe each kind of architecture driver: functional requirements, quality attributes, and business and technical constraints. Describe the process (architecture drivers elicitation workshop) used to elicit the raw architectural drivers. Describe the analysis of the raw architectural drivers and the distillation of this information in the architecture drivers specification. List those stakeholders and stakeholder communities involved in the process.

Functional Requirements

Start this section by describing how the functional requirements are articulated in terms of use cases from information provided by the stakeholder community. Describe the format of the use case templates used to document the use case scenarios to aid the reader in interpreting them. List each use case developed in stage 2. For each use case, provide a brief overview paragraph that describes the use case and any relevant contextual information to aid the reader in interpreting the case.

Quality Attribute Requirements

Start this section by describing what quality attribute requirements are, their importance to design, and how they are articulated in terms of use case scenarios from information provided by the stakeholder community. Describe the essential elements of a quality attribute scenario and the format of the quality attribute scenario templates that are used to document the quality attribute requirements. Again, this will aid the reader in interpreting the quality attribute scenarios. List each quality attribute scenario developed in stage 2. For each such scenario, provide a brief overview paragraph that describes the scenario and any relevant contextual information to aid the reader in interpreting the quality attribute.

Constraints

Start this section with a general description of constraints, explaining how they are premade design decisions. Differentiate between business constraints and technical constraints and describe their relative impact on the system or product design. Separate sections for each should be used. List the business constraints and then the technical constraints collected and analyzed in stages 1 and 2. Clearly distinguish between the business and technical constraints in prose and in format.

Prioritization

Describe how the functional requirements and quality attribute requirements were prioritized in terms of importance by the stakeholder community during the architecture drivers elicitation workshop. Also describe why constraints are not prioritized in terms of importance—by definition, constraints are inflexible and are the highest priority. Describe the difficultly ranking applied by the architecture design team, and how it expresses the relative difficulty of the architectural drivers. Include the ranking criterion that was used to judge the difficulty of the architectural drivers. Explain the significance of those architectural drivers that have been voted as important by the stakeholders and ranked as difficult by the architectural design team.

Minimal Acceptable Delivery

If the architecture design team has established minimal acceptable delivery criteria, the technical details should be discussed in the architecture drivers specification in terms of the priorities and the architectural drivers that comprise the minimal acceptable delivery. Programmatic information that is related to the consequences of not meeting the minimal acceptable delivery criteria should be left in the master design plan, as described earlier. Similarly, the master design plan will refer readers to the architecture drivers specification for the specific details of the minimal acceptable delivery criteria. Avoid duplication wherever and whenever possible.

Reviewing the Architecture Drivers Specification

Certainly, other pertinent information may be included in the architecture drivers specification, but these are the essential elements and will serve the purpose of communicating what the architectural drivers are for the system or product. This document will be used to show the customer stakeholders, collectively, what they asked. In large systems development, it is not uncommon for there to be disagreement among stakeholders and stakeholder communities about what the architecture drivers are and their relative importance. After writing the architecture drivers specification, the team should circulate it among the stakeholders for review. The quality process engineer should coordinate the review and collect comments. It is a good idea to distribute review templates with the architecture drivers specification, making it easy for stakeholders to comment on the document. Make sure the architecture drivers specification (and all documents you write) has page numbers, and it is a good idea to include paragraph numbers in the margin of the document. This makes it easy for the reviewers to refer to a specific section of the document for comment; it makes it easy for the architectural design team to understand what section a particular comment relates to, and eases the chore of revising the document. Include instructions in the review templates that explain how to reference sections of the document and provide meaningful feedback to the architecture design team. After receiving comments from the stakeholders, the team should review them and incorporate the changes. This might involve follow-up stakeholder interviews and analysis work. The review process should not be open ended, but have a definite deadline. There should be a small number of review cycles—one is best. Procrastination is human nature. If stakeholders know there will be many review cycles, they will wait until the last one to provide input. However, if they know there is one cycle with a fixed deadline, they will be more inclined to provide input sooner rather than later. Get client stakeholder management to reinforce the importance of providing feedback on the architecture drivers specification. In any case, indicate to the stakeholders before the reviews begin how many review cycles there will be and what the deadlines for review and comment are. After sending the document for review, remind the stakeholders frequently (but gently) of the review and comment deadline and that their input is needed and valued. After the stakeholders provide comment, thank them with a personally addressed e-mail, a snail-mail note, a phone call, or in person. This lets them know that their efforts are important and deeply appreciated by the architecture design team.

Updating the Master Design Plan

As indicated earlier, the master design plan will be updated continuously and will be used to track the efforts of the architecture design team. The managing engineer is responsible for ensuring that the master design plan is updated throughout the design process. As the design effort ensues, the managing engineer is responsible for frequently checking the schedule established for each stage of the project. This is especially important in the period of uncertainty. During this period, it is difficult to precisely estimate the activities of stages 1 through 6. However, it is critical that budgets for these activities are established and that actual time/effort expended is compared with the budgets. This is an early warning indicator of trouble, and when budgets are exceeded, the managing engineer must replan to determine the effects of exceeding the established budgets and overall project constraints. At this point the managing engineer should review/update the following elements of the plan:

Project description: After stage 2 activities, is the project description still accurate or does it need to be updated after analysis? Are the general project requirements and deliverables consistent with the draft master design plan written in stage 1?

General statement of work: Is the statement of work still accurate after stage 2 analysis? Have there been changes in the roles since stage 1? Are there any changes in the organization or management structures for either the customer stakeholders or the architecture design team? Are there any changes in expectations for either the customer stakeholders or the architecture design team? Have there been any changes in the general project timeline, budget items, or other resources and materials since stage 1?

Schedule: Update the schedule with the actual effort expended in stage 2, as explained in stage 1 for tracking earned value.

Summary

It is important the reader realizes that the templates and methods provided here are not just documentation, but are intended to guide in the analysis and structuring of the raw information gathered in stage 2. If the architecture design team just fills out the templates in this section without engaging their collective brains, these methods will not work and will not help. Concentrating on documentation artifacts is the same as creating form (pretty documentation) without substance (meaningful analysis and structure). It is essential to understand that these templates and methods are not the definitive word on analyzing the raw architectural drivers—they are necessarily generalized to be broadly applicable in many application domains and business contexts. There is no one-size-fits-all recipe for analysis, so do not look for one here (or anywhere for that matter). Thoughtful consideration and reflection is required to instantiate ACDM and in the tailoring of the methods and templates described in stages 1 and 2 thus far. The best that any template or method can do is guide the intuition and analysis activities of the engineers designing and building the system or product. Methods and templates are not intended to be recipes; they cannot replace honest, intellectual discernment, judgment, and hard-earned experience. With this caveat, ACDM provides a great deal of guidance in the technical and programmatic work associated with eliciting, analyzing, and documenting the architectural drivers. ACDM provides a powerful starting position to ease the chore of how to organize the talent to analyze and structure the mess of data gathered in stage 1 to quickly converge on a clear vision of what is needed in the product or system. Although tailoring and instantiation of ACDM are certainly required, the organization does not have to start with a "blank sheet of paper" when planning the analysis activities. To summarize, stage 2 is comprised of the following key activities:

- Stage 2 planning: Stage 2 starts as all ACDM stages do—with a bit of planning. Stage 2 focuses on the analysis of information gathered in stage 1, which is inherently difficult to plan. Nonetheless, it is critical for the architecture design team to establish a budget for analysis to avoid analysis paralysis—those never-ending cycles of analysis and refinement. Specific activities and templates are provided to guide the activities of the architecture design team.

- Analyzing the raw architecture drivers: The key activity of stage 2 is to take the information gathered in stage 1, analyze it, and turn it into a clear, concise description of what the user wants. During analysis, the operational descriptions are analyzed and cast as use cases. The quality attribute characterizations are analyzed and cast into six-part quality attribute scenarios. The constraints are also analyzed for inconsistent constraint, overly constraining specifications, invalid constraints, and so forth. Analysis concludes with the architecture design team assigning a difficulty ranking to each of the architectural drivers. Those architectural drivers that were voted as important by the stakeholders (in stage 1) and were ranked as difficult by the architecture design team could be potentially problematic and may warrant early exploration.

- Architecture drivers specification: As the analysis of the raw consolidated architectural drivers concludes, the architecture driver specification must be written. This effort is led by the requirements engineer, but should involve all the members of the architecture design team as authors. The architecture drivers specification should be circulated around the customer stakeholder community for review and comment. After customer stakeholder review and comment it is ready for initial architectural design in stage 3.

- Update the master design plan: The master design plan should be updated as various tasks are completed to reflect the actual time, cost, and effort. Again, if the managing engineer is using earned value as described in stage 1, he or she will see a picture of project progress emerging. The managing engineer should use this information to adjust the project schedule, resources, and so forth to ensure that the project is progressing at a satisfactory rate.

Chapter 10

ACDM Stage 3: Create/ Refine the Architecture

Purpose

The primary purpose of stage 3 is for the architecture design team to create the initial architectural design, or refine the architectural design based on the results of the architectural evaluation. If this is the first iteration in stage 3, then the initial notional architecture design will be created. Once the architecture is designed in stage 3 it is evaluated in stage 4. After the evaluation of stage 4, the team will make a decision to build the system or continue refining the design. Stage 5 is where this decision is made. If the decision is to continue refining the design (stage 5), then issues uncovered in the evaluation are addressed in stage 6 through experimentation. After stage 6 experimentation, the architecture design team then returns to stage 3 to refine the architecture design based on the issues uncovered during the evaluation. The team then conducts another evaluation of the refined architecture, and then moves on to stage 5 to once again decide if the design is ready for implementation or if more refinement is needed.

Preconditions

For the first iteration of stage 3 the architectural drivers must be analyzed and documented as described in stage 2 vis-à-vis the architecture drivers specification. If this is the second (or n^{th}) time through stage 3, the issues raised in the stage 4 evaluation must have been addressed by the architecture design team through stage 6 experimentation.

General Activities

Techniques, Templates, and Guidance

- Element and relationship catalog templates (Section 1 of the text)
- Rationale templates (Section 1)
- Decomposition guidelines and example (Section 1)
- Architecture design drawing template (Section 1)
- Architecture documentation guidance and outline (Section 1)

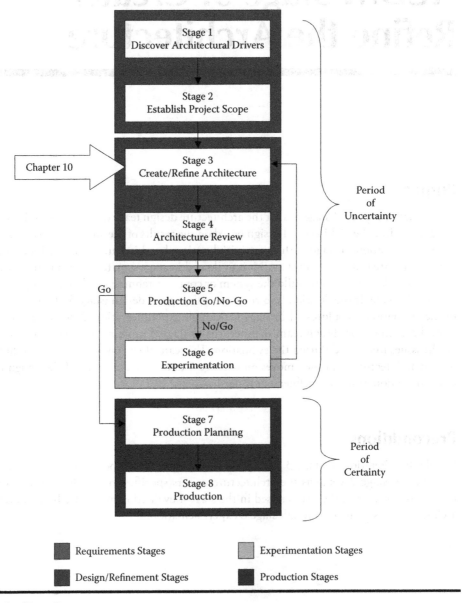

Figure 10.1   Stage 3.

Table 10.1   Stage 3 Activities, Outputs, and Responsibilities

General activities	Design the initial architecture or refine the architectural design, or refine the architecture design based on the output of the design evaluation (stage 4).
General outputs	The initial architectural design or the refined architectural design and the associated documentation artifacts.
Role	**Stage 3 Recommended Responsibilities**
Managing engineer	Plan, coordinate, track, and oversee stage 3 design activities. Assist the chief architect with the design, design representations, and writing/updating the architecture design document. Assist quality process engineer with reviews.
Chief architect	Lead the architectural design activities. Create the design representations and the architecture design document. Assist quality process engineer with reviews. Assist the managing engineer in planning and coordinating the design activities of stage 3.
Chief scientist	Assist the chief architect in the design of the architecture and in representing the design, with particular emphasis on detailed technological concerns, issues, and implementation details that may impact the architecture design. Assist quality process engineer with reviews. Assist the chief architect with the design representations and writing/updating the architecture design document.
Requirements engineer	Manage requirements change throughout the design. Maintain communications with the stakeholder community. Assist the chief architect with the design, design representations, and writing/updating the architecture design document. Assist quality process engineer with reviews. If required, work with the chief architect to create/update and maintain a requirements traceability matrix.
Quality process engineer	Ensure that the ACDM (and other project processes) are being followed. Lead and coordinate the review of the architecture design documentation in terms of completeness, not for design correctness. Assist the chief architect with the design, design representations, and writing/updating the architecture design document.
Support engineer	Assist the chief architect with the design, design representations, and writing/updating the architecture design document. Assist the quality process engineer with reviews.
Production engineers	Assist the chief architect with the design, design representations, and writing/updating the architecture design document. Assist the quality process engineer with reviews.

Primary Artifacts

- The initial or refined architectural design documented in the architecture design document
- Updated master design plan
- Traceability matrix

Postconditions

- The notional architecture design is completed (first time through stage 3), or the architecture design is refined based on experiments conducted in stage 6 (n^{th} time through stage 3).
- The notional architecture design is documented (first time through stage 3), or the architecture design documented is updated after refining the architecture based on stage 6 experimentation (n^{th} time through stage 3).

Description of Stage 3

Architecture design is dictated by engineering and design principles presented throughout Section 1 of this text. However, all design is also driven by intuition, experience, creativity, and inspiration. A key concept of this text is that design instinct should be tempered by design principle. Because of this, it is highly unlikely that the design of software-intensive systems will ever be a simple recipe that one can follow for all domains and business contexts. By now it should be clear that the design process is wrapped up within the larger product/system development processes of an organization (or organizations). This text provides the engineering and scientific principles for architecture design as they are understood today, and provides a framework for establishing and executing the architectural design process. Later (Section 3) guidance will be provided for using the ACDM within a larger organizational development process and wedding ACDM with existing process frameworks. Design is the key activity of stage 3. The primary purpose of stage 3 is twofold. The first time through stage 3 the architecture design team will design the initial or *notional* architecture based on the architecture drivers specification created in stage 2. Once the architecture is designed in stage 3 it will be evaluated in stage 4. After the evaluation, the architecture design team must decide whether the design is ready to commit to construction stages or needs refining. This decision is made in stage 5. If the decision is to continue refining the design, then issues uncovered in the stage 4 evaluation are explicitly addressed through structured experimentation in stage 6 and tracked until resolution. In subsequent iterations through stage 3, the architecture design team will refine the architecture design based on the results of architecture evaluations conducted in stage 4. After refinement, the design process continues with another stage 4 evaluation, and so on until the design is ready for production stages. While these appear to be separate, distinct steps, often these stages blur together. After the stage 4 evaluation, the stage 5 production or refinement decision, stage 6 experimentation, and refinement in stage 3 happen quickly and are somewhat concurrent. Quick is good, but as we will see, there are specific preconditions and exit criteria for each stage that are not onerous, but help the team ensure that each stage is completed and the maximum benefit from ACDM is realized. As data is available from experimentation, the architecture is refined. The reader should be reminded that ACDM stages are intended to group related activities, not to necessarily impose rigid temporal dependencies. However, the first iteration through stages 3 to 6 tends to be very sequential in nature. After the notional architecture is created and evaluated, experimentation is conducted; subsequent refinement and evaluation iterations tend to be more concurrent. While guidance is provided, planning and execution of these iterative stages must be left to the judgment of the organization and the architecture design team. Although the focus of stage 3 is design, we will not revisit the detailed techniques and examples of design already discussed in Chapter 5. In reality, the chief architect and chief scientist will be leading and performing most of the architectural design as described in previous sections of the text, providing guidance for how to design and document the architecture. The reader should revisit these sections of the text, because most of those concepts, principles, techniques, and templates will be directly applied here in stage 3.

Stage 3 Planning

Stage 3 begins with the team planning the activities of the stage and updating the master design plan to reflect the time that the architecture design team estimates they will spend designing the architecture. The managing engineer must work with the team to establish a design budget for the initial design and subsequent refinement of the design undertaken in stage 3. Design can be one of the most challenging activities to plan because it is an activity that depends to a large extent on intuition and creativity. As such, it is important that the architecture design team establish completion criteria for the design. This will be discussed in detail later, but completion criteria for design should be incorporated into the overall master design plan. As in previous stages, the managing engineer leads the stage 3 planning meeting, as he or she did in previous stages. Table 10.2 lists guidelines for planning stage 3 activities.

Although ACDM attempts to structure the design process and shorten the period of uncertainty, the design process can be notoriously unpredictable. As such, it is essential that the managing engineer establish schedule and resource budgets for design and aggressively manage the process and track the schedule to quickly identify problems and overruns as early as possible. The first time through stage 3, creating the notional architectural design will be the most problematic in terms of adhering to a predicable schedule. As the team refines the architecture in subsequent iterations through stage 3, the refinement activities tend to be shorter and more predictable than the initial design of the notional architecture. When planning for stage 3, there are three key activities to take into consideration. First is the initial design or design refinement activities. Significantly more time must be provided for initial design to allow for the natural design process to play out. This work will be conducted by a smaller number of designers or even by the chief architect alone, depending upon the scope and scale of the system being designed. A second, but concurrent activity is writing down the architectural design. Tools will be required to capture architectural information. This could be as simple as a standard word processor and drawing package, but may be a complex workbench of tools that must interoperate and allow cooperative designers to work on the design together. These tools should have been installed, configured, and readied by the support engineer in stage 1. The support engineer will continue to support and configure the design toolset throughout the design process. If the design toolset has not been readied, the support engineer must do so before stage 3 begins. It is essential that these tools are readied as soon as possible because they are crucial for ensuring that artifacts that are produced for representing the design are adequate, consistent, and ease the chore of capturing architecture information. Architecture documentation can be planned before stage 3 begins, and the architecture design team can begin training with the toolset before they actually must use them. Again, it is strongly recommended that the architect keep an engineering notebook. The engineering notebook typi-

Table 10.2 Stage 3 Planning Meeting

Planning Consideration	Description
Updating the master design plan	Updating the master design plan should occur after the stage is planned, to record the estimated time and resources required in stage 3. The master design plan will also be updated at the end of stage 3 to record the actual time and effort expended in stage 3.
Initial architecture design	This is the primary activity of stage 3 if this is the first iteration through stage 3. Considerably more time should be allocated for initial design than subsequent refinement iterations. The architecture design team should also establish completion criteria for the initial design.
Refining the architecture design	After the initial architecture is designed and evaluated, issues that are found during the evaluation will be used as a basis for experiments. After experimentation, stage 3 is revisited and the architecture is refined based upon what was learned from the experiment. Refinement iterations in stage 3 tend to take considerably less time than the initial design of the architecture the first time through stage 3. The architecture design team should also establish completion criteria for refinement of the design.
Architecture design documentation	If this is the first iteration in stage 3, the key artifact produced is the architecture design document. In subsequent iterations, the architecture design document will be updated, refined, and complemented with other sections or documents to meet the needs of the broader stakeholder community.
Reviews	The master design plan should be reviewed within the team. The architecture design document should be reviewed for format, content, and quality, but not for the fitness of the design itself.

cally includes design representations, rationale, element and relationship responsibility tables, and so forth, which are the grist for the architectural design document. If the continual documentation approach described earlier (Chapter 6) is used, most of the architectural design documentation will emanate from the engineering notebook. The architecture design document will wrap this information up into a cohesive document that explains the design of the system as described in Section 1 of the text. The architecture design document may be a simple word processor document of 20 pages, a suite of design products, or a complex online document that is accessible by hundreds of downstream designers.

After the notional architecture is designed and evaluated, planning subsequent iterations through stage 3 is considerably easier because the refinement is based on specific experimentation data gathered to address issues uncovered in the evaluation of stage 4. Refinement can be as easy as clarifying a relationship between two elements in the design or expanding the detail of the initial design, or may involve significant redesign of the architecture. From a planning perspective, these are discrete tasks that can be planned with much greater ease than the initial creative step of designing the notional architecture. Most of the refinement work will center on updating the architecture representations and prose descriptions by adding detail or changing representations and descriptions to reflect the better understanding of the architecture gained through experimentation.

Again, the underlying philosophy of ACDM is to use the architecture as the blueprint for the entire project, not just as a technical artifact developed once and ignored in subsequent design and implementation. Architects that design buildings and bridges create models of the thing they plan to build early in the project life cycle. These models become the basis for all project planning and oversight, guiding detailed design and construction, and act as a communication vehicle with the stakeholder community. This is the driving principle and philosophy of ACDM for the design and construction of software-intensive systems. However, a key concept behind ACDM is not to spend too much time creating the notional architecture—this cannot be overstressed. This might seem to contradict ACDM's underlying dependency on software architecture for guiding all other aspects of the project. This is because ACDM prescribes iteratively refining the architecture until it is deemed to be fit for purpose (according to guidelines that will be explained later in stage 4). This can be thought of as the dialog between the building architect and the customers and users of the facility he or she is designing. The initial model of the building created by the architect is rarely perfect, but it is a mechanism for facilitating communication between the designer and the various stakeholders. In organizations that piloted ACDM, the hardest practice to institute was to get the architects to quickly design the notional architecture and let the iterative nature of the design process play out. Most engineers simply cannot live with the idea that something they designed is less than perfect, but an essential concept and practice of ACDM is not to spend an inordinate amount of time in stage 3 developing the notional architecture. The chief architect and the architecture design team should assume that the notional architecture is a rough draft, and that it will be evaluated and refined in a very structured way, as we will see in stages 4 to 6, and again in subsequent iterations in stage 3. Dwelling on the initial design can be dangerous because the time may be wasted because there is no way that an architect can effectively identify and address all of the potential unknowns and problems with the design in the first attempt. If the architect can get it close to what is needed quickly, the evaluation process (stage 4) will then help identify unknowns, issues, and outright problems with the design. Those specific issues can then be addressed through targeted, planned experimentation. Field trials of ACDM demonstrated that architectural design teams converged on a much higher-fidelity, better-understood design (on average) 40 percent faster than they did with previous one-pass design approaches. One-pass design approaches also do not have provisions for structured evaluation, experimentation, and refinement. In addition to completing the design more quickly, the architectural designs were far more complete, consistent, and correct, and exhibited a better balance of systemic qualities than were realized in one-pass design approaches.

Designing the Notional Architecture

In the first pass through stage 3 the development team uses the architectural drivers as a basis to design the notional architecture. Often the initial design leaps from the architecture drivers specification into the head of the architect and onto paper with relative ease. This is common in domains where systems or products are similar, or with architects possessing deep experience with a particular class of systems. However, like a writer struggling to find words amidst the dreaded writer's block, architects are often faced with "designer's block," where the initial partitioning of the system seems to be a daunting task. Each of these situations has its dangers. In the first case, architects may make casual assumptions and repeat past mistakes or overlook details that seem obvious at face value. In the latter case, architects may be unsure of the initial, crucial choices they make. It is important that architects remain faithful to a principled design approach for initial decomposition no matter how familiar or foreign the design landscape may seem.

Establish Context

Despite the popularity of object-oriented design, the design of software-intensive systems still tends to rely heavily on hierarchical decomposition. Architects often must consider hardware and software elements and how they work together as an ensemble. Sometimes the hardware and software will be selected or will be a constraining factor. In other cases, the architecture design will become a specification for downstream hardware and software designers who will design and build the product or system elements. To begin the initial partitioning, the architect should create a clear context drawing that establishes the system boundaries as described in Section 1. This is illustrated by example in Figure 10.2.

In the simplest case, the architect can start with a box that represents the entire system (keeping perspective in mind), surrounded with a dotted line that represents the system boundary as shown in step 1 of Figure 10.2. As previously described, the most influential architectural drivers on the design will be the constraints. Focusing on the technical constraints, the architect should determine where the technical constraints fit into the system context. Software applications, databases, hardware, events, data streams, sensors, and so forth external to the system that are predetermined by constraint should be represented using consistent notation clearly described by a legend. These should be shown outside of the dotted system boundary, as demonstrated in Figure 10.2, step 2. Typically these are the technical constraints that the architect will have the least amount of control

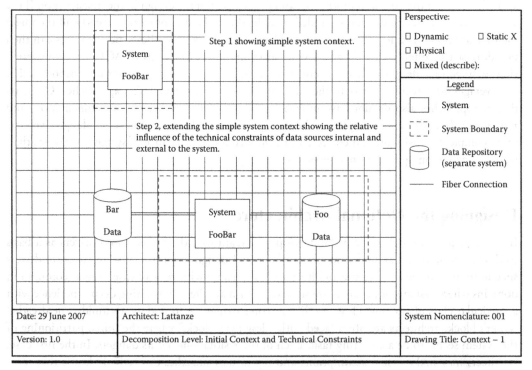

Figure 10.2   Example of architectural context drawing showing constraints.

or influence over. Next the architect should similarly represent those constraints that are within the system boundaries, as shown in Figure 10.2, step 2. These constraints tend to be somewhat more flexible than external constraints. As an example, consider a database external to the system boundary that houses data critical for the system operation. Often databases external to the system boundary have table structures that are established a priori, and the architect must live with whatever that structure is and design around those existing constraints. In other cases, the architect may have to design a system that stores data, and there may be a technical constraint to use a particular database technology and infrastructure. Although technically constrained to use this technology, the structure of the tables are usually not predetermined, but are part of the design of the system. Certainly, this is not a hard-and-fast rule, but it is a general trend that the architect would be wise to identify as he or she begins the initial system decomposition and design. In other cases, it may clear during initial partitioning that a commercial product will be used in the system design. For example, if there is a requirement to store considerable amounts of data, it is relatively obvious that a relational database will be used. It may also be obvious that a particular database technology product should be selected to satisfy this need. However, once selected this can be a self-imposed technological constraint for the lifetime of the system or product. If we ever want to move away from the specific product selected, it may not be easy, depending upon other design choices that are made. The architect should defer binding these kinds of decisions until later detail decomposition and design of the system, rather than prematurely limiting design choices. If these decisions are made too early, they can limit options that the architect may have in the design space. Frequently, architects select hardware, operating systems, and other similar technologies—and even purchase the products—before the initial design is complete! In this case, what was a choice now becomes a hard-and-fixed constraint on the design space. Again, this is not a fixed immutable rule. Sometimes we must bind these choices early, but the architect should strive to defer these decisions as long as possible, at least until after initial decomposition is complete and some detailed composition is accomplished. At some point during decomposition, if the architect finds it impossible to make design choices because the particular hardware, operating system, language, and so forth are unknown, it may be time to bind these decisions. Guidance for selecting suitable commercial elements and designing with legacy elements is discussed further in Chapter 16.

When establishing the initial system context, the architect must keep perspective in mind as he or she establishes the system boundary. The concept of perspective was introduced in Section 1, and its importance has been stressed throughout the text. The importance of establishing and maintaining an intellectual grasp of perspective cannot be overstressed when the system context is being established and in the subsequent decomposition of the system. Context diagrams are often rendered in the dynamic or physical perspective. Figure 10.2 shows the system from the physical perspective. Note that each element in the drawing is consistent with this perspective. Multiple context drawings can be created if necessary to represent different perspectives. If the architect is focusing on software architectural design, often the hardware or infrastructure is established as a constraint, so the physical context drawing is a graphical representation of the hardware constraints. However, if the architect is designing the hardware and software, care must be taken, as one may constrain the other. For example, if the architect designs/selects the hardware platform and infrastructure first, this may constrain the software, as described earlier. If the software is designed first, this may be a constraining force on the hardware. One could argue that portable software could run on any hardware or infrastructure, but again, this becomes a quality attribute requirement or even a constraint on the software design space. In many cases it may be common sense to define the hardware and infrastructure first, but not always, and the architect should never assume that one or the other should always be the first design concern in all cases.

As the architect decomposes the design from the context drawing, he or she should carefully describe his or her decisions by using representations, prose, and recording the rationale for decisions as faithfully as possible. The initial design can be an extraordinarily dynamic and chaotic period of time in a project, where design decisions are made and change quickly and frequently. For this reason, it is highly recommended that architects keep an engineering notebook or similar low-tech artifact that allows them to capture this kind of information quickly, anywhere they may be. It is not recommended that online or other automated tools be used to capture initial design information—they are too slow, inflexible, and are often inaccessible. A physical notebook can be tucked under the architect's arm, and while they are having coffee with a colleague and a great idea comes to mind, they can write it down immediately. Because design is a creative and often serendipitous process, the tools that an architect uses to capture these precious bits of inspiration and insight must be equally spontaneous and available. A simple notebook and pencil is often the best choice. The templates provided in Chapter 6 for the engineering notebook can be used to better organize information, but in general, the architect must use a medium to quickly and freely record ideas, sketch out system structures, and so forth. However, once the design begins to take form, the architect must transfer the rough sketches, ideas, rationale, and prose to a more formal document. Often an automated tool (or tools) is best for writing the finished document. This usually includes a combination of word processor and drawing technologies.

Iteratively Decompose

Once context has been established, the architect will begin decomposing the elements from the context drawing(s). Each element will be iteratively decomposed until the architecture is fully designed. After the technical constraints, the quality attribute requirements will exert the most influence over the design of the product or system. It follows then that the first levels of decomposition from context should be guided in large part by the quality attribute requirements. Obviously, as the architect decomposes the system to adhere to the constraints and balance the quality attribute requirements, he or she must also design a system that meets the functional requirements. So while design may be driven by constraints and quality attributes, the architect must constantly strive to balance these concerns with functionality. There may be relatively few levels of design decomposition, or there may be many, depending upon the scale, scope, and domain of the system or product being developed. Some perspectives may require more decomposition than others. For example, the hardware for a system (physical perspective) may be trivial, requiring off-the-shelf computer systems and infrastructure elements, and thus requiring very little decomposition at all. On the other hand, the software (static perspective) for the same system may be complex and require many levels of decomposition. Again, the reader should not assume that this is a hard-and-fast design rule or assumption valid for all situations and domains. Consider a sophisticated digital video camera that consists of complex custom hardware with advanced features provided by software. In this case, the system is not physically big but is very complex in both its hardware and software elements. Such a system may require many levels of decomposition in all perspectives to adequately design such a complex system.

In some cases decomposing the system may be accomplished by starting with a well-defined pattern, as described in Section 1; however, patterns are only starting propositions for design. For example, a system may fit a client/server pattern, but there are a great many details that must be decided to complete the design in terms of the hardware, infrastructure, software applications, and allocation of software to hardware and other infrastructure. Again, perspective is an important consideration when thinking about decomposition in terms of patterns. Recall that patterns have:

- Perspective
- Defined elements and responsibilities
- Defined relationships among elements
- A common topology
- Semantics for using the pattern
- Quality attribute properties that are promoted, while others are inhibited

Understanding the perspective from which a pattern is visible can shed light on the quality attributes promoted and inhibited by the pattern. Consider the layered pattern as an example. In this pattern, each layer consists of services that represent code-oriented structures such as libraries (static perspective). From the static perspective we can reason about code-oriented changes (modifiability). Layering promotes various flavors of modifiability because changes can be isolated to a layer without affecting adjacent layers of the structure. However, it is difficult to reason about performance of this structure from the static perspective. In general, if layered structures are compiled (static perspective), the layers collapse into processes or threads (dynamic perspective). In general, we do know that the extra layers of abstraction translate into code, which tends to inhibit systemic performance. However, to understand systemic throughput, response, and other performance-oriented issues, we must study the structure from the dynamic perspective. This may even reveal different patterns or ensembles of patterns. Perspective is essential to selecting and analyzing patterns and ensembles of patterns during initial system decomposition and in subsequent decomposition of the elements of design. For example, consider the client/server pattern once again. A client/server design is clearly visible from the dynamic perspective, but we have no equivalent representation from the physical, dynamic, and static perspectives. In this case we know that during design, we will have to decide what the physical system will look like and how clients will physically connect to and communicate with servers (physical perspective). It may be difficult to discriminate between client and server elements when designing the code structures (static perspective) of a client/server system, but again, this will be essential for the overall design of the system. All that the pattern provides is client and server elements and semantics about how clients and servers interact. We also know from the pattern that systems like this tend to scale fairly well in a number of ways, support certain kinds of modifiability, and that performance and availability are relatively inhibited. The architect is responsible for designing the details and addressing the shortfalls inherent in the pattern if they pose a problem. The design of the client/server from the physical perspective must be more fully developed to show the server hardware and communication infrastructure, and how applications map to these physical elements. Certainly the dynamic perspective will have to be elaborated with more details than just clients and servers, and describe the detailed runtime process and interactions and how processes are allocated to hardware. Of course, the static structures of the system are essential for facilitating construction of the software. Whether patterns are used or not, early levels of decomposition will be coarse grained, and subsequent levels of decomposition will add more detail to the architecture design. Systems rarely exhibit a single pattern. A single element may be decomposed into another pattern or ensemble of patterns and structures, adding more detail to the design of the system or product. Recall from Section 1 that patterns are repeated in practice. Patterns are not only found in textbooks. Patterns are often found in practice and are often unique to a particular application, domain, or organization. Analyzing the designs of related systems or legacy systems can uncover structures, patterns, tactics, and ensembles that repeat and are regularly reused by engineers building similar kinds of systems. This can provide valuable hints for the architect as he or she thinks about how to decompose the system or look for opportunities for strategic reuse.

Refining the Notional Architecture

In subsequent iterations through stage 3 the development team uses the output of the evaluation in stage 4 to define experiments and refine the architecture design. To describe the refinement process, we really need to look ahead at some of the other stages of ACDM. In particular, we have to understand a little bit about stages 4 to 6 before we can understand how we revisit stage 3 and further refine the notional architecture. Each of these stages is briefly introduced in the following timeline of events so that the iterative refinement of the architecture design built into ACDM can be explained through example:

- Initial stage 3 activities: The first time we visit stage 3, the architecture design team creates the notional architecture. This should be done as quickly as possible, realizing that the design and documentation will be further refined literately. The design and documentation must be completed to a level of detail that has enough information that engineers can understand the fundamental design decisions and structures.
- Stage 4 activities: In stage 4, the architecture design created in stage 3 is evaluated. Initial designs should be evaluated by the team internally. It is highly recommended that architecture designs be evaluated by a broader group of stakeholders, including customers, users, maintainers, and other relevant individuals from the stakeholder community. This is not always possible, but should be considered because it can provide the architecture design team with valuable insight into the fitness of the design and introduce customer stakeholders to the system design. The output of the evaluation process is a set of issues that must be addressed by the architecture design team.
- Stage 5 activity: The primary activity of stage 5, which is brief, is to decide whether to continue with architecture design refinement or press on to the production of the product or system. This decision is based upon the types of issues uncovered in stage 4.
- Stage 6 activities: Stage 6 is undertaken when the architecture design team decides that the architecture design requires further refinement (stage 5). In stage 6, each issue is addressed by the architecture design team. Some of the issues uncovered in stage 4 will be *risks* that must be addressed by *experimentation*; others will be *investigation items* that will be resolved by *information gathering activities*.
- Stage 3 activities (revisited): Armed with the information gathered in stage 6, the architecture design is refined. This includes updating and refining the design and the corresponding documentation.
- Stage 4 activities (revisited): The refined architecture is evaluated.
- Stage 5 activity (revisited): The output of the second evaluation is analyzed, and a production or refinement decision is made.

The iteration described above continues until a production decision is made in stage 5, at which point stage 7 production planning is undertaken. Each of the activities in stages 4 to 6 will be explained in detail in subsequent chapters of the text. The purpose here is to explain how stage

3 is reentered after initial design, and to highlight the differences between initial design in stage 3 and subsequent refinement of the design in subsequent stage 3 iterations.

Element Interfaces

As the architecture is refined through successive decomposition, the element interfaces must be defined. Essentially, interfaces are agreements between elements that define the rules for their relationships. As mentioned in Section 1, it is highly recommended that the architect design to the level that he or she defines the element interfaces. Interfaces are key to defining the element boundaries, interactions, services, and the very skeleton of the architecture. A common question architects have is: How detailed should the interfaces be? The more detailed they are, the better it is, but detailed interfaces for large systems may be impossible. A well-defined interface codifies the element's boundary and establishes rules for interaction, as well as what services and data it requires and provides. Designing element interfaces is a definitive end to architectural design and firmly establishes the architecture design infrastructure. There can be dire consequences if interfaces are not established. Ill-defined interfaces increase the chances that designers and implementers will violate element boundaries or introduce dependencies between elements not explicitly defined in the architecture. This may be done because the architecture design does not specify the interfaces, is unclear in terms of what the interfaces should be, or the design documentation is ambiguous. Any of these situations will compromise the architecture design.

As an example, consider a situation where two elements are being produced by two different teams or individual engineers. Assume that the two elements are dependent upon one another for data and services, and the architect fails to define the detailed semantics of these interactions. In short, the interfaces for the elements were not designed by the architect. Implicitly, this means that the agreement for how the two elements will share data, services, control, and so forth has been deferred to downstream designers. In this case, the architect may not understand or be aware of the resulting interfaces that will emerge between these two elements. As a consequence, it may be difficult to verify that the architectural structure of the implementation will possess the properties promised by the design. The issue of the interface is less about functionality and more about whether the emerging relationships between the two elements will be able to support the quality attribute requirements (whether it will be fast enough, able to support modifiability, and so forth). Ill-defined interfaces can affect the organization as well. Again, assume that we have two elements whose interfaces are ill-defined. The team now must haggle among themselves to define the semantics of the interfaces for the elements. When this happens, teams usually spend inordinate amounts of time in meetings trying to define interfaces and agree upon them. As the number of engineers involved gets larger, the problem becomes more difficult. In extreme cases, teams implementing components will not want to yield for a variety of reasons, such as a perceived loss of control or autonomy, potential loss of funding, and so forth. Some of these reasons may be valid, and some may not be, but this behavior is always destructive to the organization and is a drain on project schedules. More importantly, the resulting compromises may undermine the original partitioning established by the architect, compromising quality attribute characteristics expected in the implementation. A more serious situation is when the detailed designers or implementers do not explicitly agree on interfaces and begin development or procurement of system elements. In these cases, the interface mismatches will be addressed after code is written, hardware is purchased, or other significant investments are made that are hard or impossible to resolve.

There are two general approaches that the architect can take when defining interfaces. First, the architect or the architecture design team can define interfaces themselves, or they can defer the definition of the interfaces to others, but guide their definition. The first option is obvious; the second is less obvious. In the second case, the architect may choose to allow other downstream designers to define interfaces, but they must guide the effort and must reserve the final say as to when they will be defined and how. The architect then must place the interfaces under strict configuration control and ensure that all of the properties promised by the architecture will be realized in the implementation. At this point, the interfaces are no longer in the hands of the detailed designers or implementers. Changing the interfaces should be done only with great care and deliberation with the oversight of the architect, architecture design team, or similar configuration control body. If interfaces are defined early and explicitly, teams can develop the elements in relative isolation, and the integration of the elements into a system will be relatively easier.

Traceability

The term *traceability* or *requirements traceability* is often used to describe a mapping between requirements and the part of the system that satisfies or otherwise addresses the requirement. This is not typically required in commercial organizations, but is a routine part of government work—in particular, U.S. Department of Defense work. Unfortunately, definitively mapping a requirement to a system element is not as easy as it may seem, and can be a daunting and frustrating task. Without an architecture design, it is nearly impossible to provide requirements traceability. However, if traceability is required by the customer stakeholder, this is far easier if we begin documenting traceability from the initial architecture design. The further you get from the initial architecture design, the harder it becomes to map requirements to elements that satisfy them. Recall the steps of architecture design from the guidance provided in Chapter 5:

1. Establish context.
2. Partition the system based on the context.
3. Assign element and relationship responsibilities.
4. Document rationale, element responsibilities, and relationships.
5. Switch perspective as necessary.
6. Repeat steps 2 through 5 until the interfaces are designed.

To document requirements traceability, this simple process can be modified to contain one additional step in between steps 3 and 4, where we document the traceability. Because the architecture design is driven by architectural drivers, it is easiest to establish traceability at this point, before detailed design and implementation. As the system is partitioned and the element and relationship responsibilities are defined, the additional step that must be taken is to identify the specific architectural drivers that are addressed by the partitioning, elements, or relationships. Most traceability centers on mapping functional requirements. Functionality typically maps directly to elements, but quality attribute requirements are most often satisfied by the partitioning of elements. Both can be captured. The mistake that is most often made by organizations is that they do not begin requirements tracing at the earliest stages of design. Once a system is partitioned into many elements, those elements are transformed into detail design elements, and finally the detailed design elements become code, data, and hardware. At this point it is nearly impossible to map a single requirement to a line of code, circuit, database, and so forth. Consider the example in Figure 10.3.

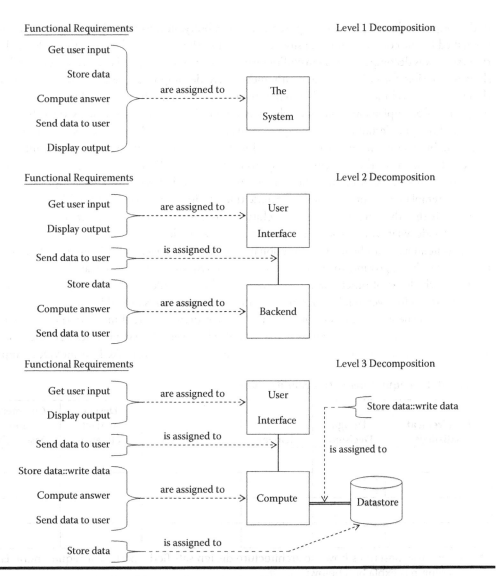

Figure 10.3   Example of architectural context drawing showing constraints.

At the first level of design/decomposition we see the equivalent of a system context drawing before decomposition of the system really begins. Here the functional requirements are assigned to "the system" for satisfaction. In the next level of decomposition (level 2) we see that the system has been partitioned into two elements: user interface and back end. As specific responsibilities are assigned to these two elements and connector, the architect can also indicate which functional requirements are satisfied by them. Note that there may be multiple elements that satisfy a single requirement, as shown in Figure 10.3, level 2. The connector satisfies the "send data to the user" requirement, as does the back-end element. Consider the final level of decomposition. Here the back-end element is decomposed into a compute element and a data store element. A new connector is added between the compute and data store elements. Also note that "store data" requirement has been changed to include a "Store data::write data" requirement. The "write data" part of the "store data" requirement is a derived requirement worth noting because a connector is dedicated to this responsibility. In terms of requirements traceability, however, the "store data" requirement is satisfied by the compute and data store elements and the connector between them. Note that as the system was decomposed, responsibilities were also decomposed, and the elements and relationships responsible for satisfying the requirements were decomposed as well, thereby confounding the chore of traceability. This is what makes requirements traceability impossible to do in detailed design or after implementation, and why it is essential to begin requirements traceability with the initial design. Certainly tracing requirements as they were in Figure 10.3 is cumbersome and would be impractical in practice; however, Table 10.3 illustrates an example traceability matrix that can be used with the element and responsibility catalogs discussed in Section 1.

Another option is to modify the element and relationship responsibility templates, and the rationale template presented earlier, to include traceability information as well. The risk with this approach is that these templates may get cluttered as a result—the architecture design team will have to decide what will best serve the project and stakeholders.

As difficult as it can be to trace functional requirements to elements of design and implementation, it can be impossible to trace quality attribute requirements. As indicated earlier, elements tend to be the locus of functionality, and therefore they will address the functional requirements in most cases. However, quality attribute requirements are often satisfied by the partitioning, not the specific elements themselves. Quality attribute requirements are difficult to trace if the rationale for decomposition and design is not captured. However, ACDM provides guidance for how and when to capture this information. As the system is decomposed, ACDM provides templates

Table 10.3   Requirements Traceability Matrix

Requirement Satisfied[a]	Design Decision[b]	Element[c]	Relationship[d]	Design Artifact Reference[e]	Comments and Description[f]

Note: Each row describes how the architecture design satisfied a particular requirement. Each column is explained below:

[a] This column lists the requirement that satisfies the design decision, element, and or relationship described in this row. The requirement may be a specific functional or quality attribute requirement, or a derived requirement related to a specific functional or quality attribute requirement.

[b] This column describes the design decision that satisfies the requirement. Typically (but not always) design decisions include partitioning choices, but may include other decisions made by the architect that directly affect quality attribute responses.

[c] This column lists the element that satisfies the requirement.

[d] This column lists the relationship that satisfies the requirement.

[e] This column lists the reference in the architecture design document for the design decision, element, or relationship.

[f] This column is for the architect to describe how the design decision, element, or relationship satisfies the requirement.

to capture decomposition rationale and design decisions. As this design information is captured, it can be relatively easy to map these design decisions back to the quality attribute requirements that motivated them in the first place, thereby maintaining traceability of these critical requirements.

When Are We Done with Design?

It is never perfectly clear as to when the architect is done with design, and this is an intuition that the architect must develop. However, guidance is provided here to help architects develop this intuition. It is also impossible to establish a criterion that definitively describes when the architecture design is complete and works for all domains and business contexts. At a minimum, the architects should review the design with downstream designers and implementers to ensure that they understand the architecture design and what they are responsible for designing or implementing. To a large extent, when architectural decomposition and design is done depends upon the scope and the architect's position in the design hierarchy. In general, the architecture design is done when it sufficiently constrains the downstream element designers or implementers. Guidance for completion includes the following:

- The system is partitioned into elements with relationships among them and is documented from the static, dynamic, and physical perspectives, describing the architecture of the system.
- The rationale for the decomposition and design decisions is documented.
- The elements and relationships are documented in element-relationship catalogs as described in Section 1.
- For each element, the responsibilities are defined and documented.
- For each element, the data and services required by the element to meet its responsibilities are defined and documented.
- For each element, the data and services provided by the element are defined and documented.
- The interface(s) for each element is defined, or the plan for its definition is established, documented, and agreed to by all involved.

The initial architecture design may be incomplete before moving on to stage 4 and evaluating the design—this is OK. The architecture can be refined as more is learned through the evaluation process. Once the baseline architecture is established, the detailed designers can focus inwardly and design the details of how each element will work. Architecture design does not replace detailed designs; detail designs and architecture design complement one another. Detailed design is the necessary next step in system development after the architecture design is stable. Detailed design is done in the production stages (stage 7 and 8). However, the architecture design forms the contextual framework in which the detailed designs of the elements are created. The detailed element designs must adhere to the architecture design to ensure that the properties promised by the architecture can be realized in the implementation.

In general sense, architects must know who they are constraining with their design and sufficiently describe what it is that the downstream designer and implementer must design or build. The initial levels of decomposition may be somewhat trivial, but the rationale for the decomposition is important in satisfying the architectural drivers and will guide the work of the detailed designers and implementers. The architect must clearly define what the downstream designer has to design, the boundaries for the elements they are responsible for, the element interfaces and responsibilities, and the semantics for the design. The same is true for engineers responsible for implementing the elements of the design. Architects should think in terms of restricting the visibility that downstream designers and implementers have of the overall architecture design. To do this, clear element boundaries must be established, and the best way to achieve this is through well-defined element interfaces. The architecture design team does not need to produce all the architecture documentation for all the stakeholders because the design will likely be in flux as it is refined in successive iterations. If this is the first time the team has visited stage 3, they should focus on creating artifacts to support the evaluation of the architecture in stage 4. As the design matures after each refinement iteration, the complete complement of required architectural documentation for the broader stakeholder community will have to be planned and written. Again, templates were provided in Chapter 6 that can help develop a strategy for developing document content and staging the delivery. In addition to creating the architecture documentation, the team should plan on reviewing it to ensure that it is complete, consistent, descriptive, and so forth.

Updating the Master Plan

As design proceeds, the managing engineer must track the activities of the architecture design team and replan as necessary. As stage 3 concludes, it is a good time to update the master design plan, but effort tracking, actual performance, and earned value should be calculated and updated with greater frequency than at the beginning and end of stage 3. Design is unpredictable, and it can be difficult for teams to conclude design activities—engineers never seem to want to finish the design. The managing engineer must work to establish a schedule budget for initial design and press the architecture design team to stick to it. Once the initial design is complete, subsequent iterations tend to be more predictable. However, it can be difficult to know when to stop the refinement iterations of stages 3 to 6. To help conclude initial design and refinement iteration, it is prudent if the team develops completion criteria for the initial stage 3 design and for ending the refinement iterations and moving on to the production stages. The master design plan is a good place to record this information.

Summary

Stage 3 is the beginning of the design refinement iteration that is built into ACDM. The activities in this chapter are dependent upon the principles introduced in Section 1 for architectural drivers, structures, design, and documentation. In this chapter, the details of how to design were not discussed because they were addressed in Chapter 5; the focus here was on the process of design in the context of ACDM using principles introduced in Chapter 5. Initially, the first time the architecture design team undertakes stage 3, they will design the notional architecture. Once created, the architecture design team will evaluate the architecture to identify risks (stage 4). If the decision to further refine the architecture design is made (stage 5), the architecture design team will conduct experiments (stage 6) to mitigate risks uncovered during the evaluation. After experimentation, the team will start another iteration in stage 3 to refine the architecture. Again, these stages are not necessarily discrete steps, but there are clear activities, guidelines, and checklists associated with each stage of the method to guide the activities of the architecture design team. To summarize, stage 3 is comprised of the following key activities:

■ Stage 3 planning: Stage 3 begins with the managing engineer leading the architecture design team in planning initial creation of the architecture design, or the refinement of the design after evaluation and experimentation. In general, greater time should be budgeted for initial design and less for subsequent refinement activities.

■ Initial design: Much of the detailed design techniques presented in Section 1 are applied here to design the notional architecture. In addition to design techniques, it is essential that the architect faithfully record his or her rationale, design decisions, and representations as they are made. This significantly reduces the documentation overhead later. The initial documentation may be less formal in the initial design, but it must completely capture the notional architecture, rationale for the choices made, and so forth (as discussed in Chapter 6), as the information is known.

■ Design refinement: Experiments are designed to address risks uncovered in stage 4. The results of these experiments (conducted in stage 6) are used to refine the design. This also includes refining the amount of detail of the design and refining the documentation. While the initial documentation can be less formal, it should be iteratively refined as the architecture is refined, until it is in an acceptable format for downstream designers or implementers.

■ Architecture design document: The architecture design team will iteratively document the architecture as it is refined. Documentation techniques and the contents of architecture design documentation were discussed at great length in Chapter 6.

■ Update the master design plan: The master design plan should be updated as various tasks are completed to reflect the actual time, cost, and effort. Again, if the managing engineer is using earned value as described in stage 1, he or she will see a picture of project progress emerging. The managing engineer should use this information to adjust the project schedule, resources, and so forth.

Chapter 11

ACDM Stage 4: Evaluate the Architecture Design

Purpose

The primary purpose of stage 4 is for the architecture design team to evaluate the initial architectural design, or reevaluate the refined design after architectural evaluation and experimentation.

Preconditions

Before undertaking stage 4 the architecture design must be sufficiently complete to facilitate the design evaluation. At a minimum, the architecture design must be designed and documented in preliminary fashion with representation from the three primary perspectives. In addition to drawings, there must be sufficient prose to describe the design and its rationale.

General Activities
Techniques, Templates, and Guidance

- Evaluation planning templates
- Evaluation guidance
- Issue recording template

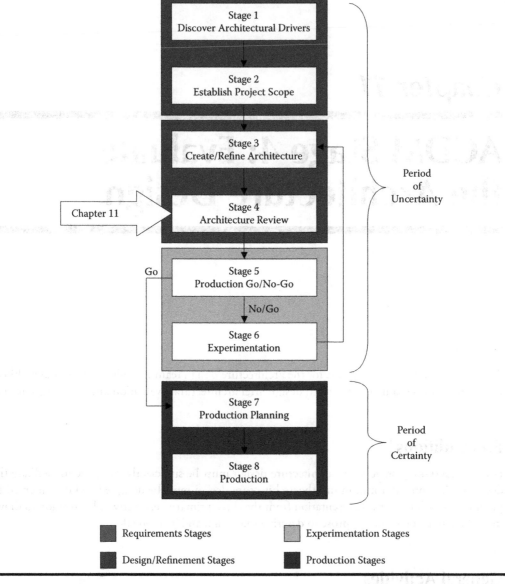

Figure 11.1   Stage 4.

Primary Artifacts

The primary artifact is a list of issues (issue recording template) resulting from the evaluation workshop.

Postconditions

Architecture design is evaluated and key issues identified and documented.

Table 11.1   Stage 4 Activities, Outputs, and Responsibilities

General activities	Evaluate the architecture design.
General outputs	A list of issues uncovered during the evaluation that impact the design's ability to satisfy the architectural drivers.
Role	**Stage 4 Recommended Responsibilities**
Managing engineer	Plan, coordinate, track, and oversee stage 4 design evaluation activities. Assist the quality process engineer with coordinating and executing the architecture design evaluation. Participate in the evaluation as a questioner.
Chief architect	Trace through and answer analysis questions about the architecture design during the evaluation.
Chief scientist	Assist the chief architect in tracing through and answering analysis questions about architecture design. Participate in the evaluation as a questioner.
Requirements engineer	Participate in the evaluation as a questioner.
Quality process engineer	Ensure that the ACDM (and other project processes) is being followed. Facilitate and coordinate the review of the architecture design evaluation. Participate in the evaluation as a questioner.
Support engineer	Participate in the evaluation as a questioner.
Production engineers	Participate in the evaluation as a questioner.

Description of Stage 4

Edward Yourdon predicted that design evaluations would be manual processes until the mid-1990s, when design reviews would be done by automated design workbenches (Yourdon, 1989b). Unfortunately, he was wrong. We still cannot agree on an architectural design notation or common standard for what constitutes a complete design for software-intensive systems. There are promising concepts being explored in labs and universities around the world. However, the current state of the practice with respect to automated design tools for designing software-intensive systems is extremely limited at the writing of this text. The author of this text will make no bold predictions about when design evaluations will be a "push button" activity like compilation is today for many systems. Rather, a design method is described in this section that will be used by the architecture design team to evaluate architecture designs without the aid of any tools other than word processors, PowerPoint, Visio, or similar commonly available tools.

The purpose of stage 4 is to conduct an evaluation of the architecture design to determine if the design is fit for purpose with respect to the architecture drivers, and to raise issues that may compromise satisfaction of the architecture drivers. An issue is a discrepancy raised during the evaluation of the architectural design that may compromise the ability of the system or product implemented from the design to achieve the architectural drivers. The goal of the stage 4 evaluation workshop is to identify issues, not fix them. Evaluating, reviewing, or otherwise scrutinizing the work products of software-intensive systems is not new; however, historically the focus of structured evaluations has been on code-oriented artifacts. Examples include Fagan inspections (Fagan, 1976), Yourdon structured walk-throughs (Yourdon, 1989b), and more recently, the Software Engineering Institute's Architecture Tradeoff Analysis Method (ATAM) (Clements et al., 2001). These methods were developed to be used without specific regard to the larger development context and processes the organization uses to design and develop software-intensive systems. While this is a strength, the weakness is that the organization must figure out how to instantiate the method, tailor it, and weave it into the organization's design and development processes. As we will see, the method presented here for evaluating the architecture is unique in that it has been developed for ACDM to support iterative refinement of the architectural design. Because ACDM is an architectural design method, the evaluation method described here is a design evaluation method and does not address the evaluation of code, detailed hardware designs, or other similar detailed artifacts. However, other methods for scrutinizing these detailed design and implementation artifacts can be used during the production stages, and recommendations for their use will be provided in these stages.

By now, the reader should realize that functionally correct code is certainly important to the success of the system. Unfortunately, it is only part of the picture when determining the overall fitness of a system or product. Architecture design embodies the earliest design decisions made by the organization, and it is where we turn the corner from what is needed to how it will be built. These decisions have the greatest impact on all of the ensuing detailed designs and implementation, whether we are concerned with code or other infrastructure elements such as networks, hardware, or any other peripheral devices. Architectural design is critical for ensuring that a system or product possesses the functionality and quality attribute properties, and adheres to the constraints specified by the broader stakeholder community. For software-intensive systems, it is essential that these decisions are as good as they can possibly be. In most cases, there is no perfect architecture, only perfect compromise because a system possessing all of the desired properties and functionality would be very difficult to build within acceptable cost, schedule, and technical constraints. The word *good* often means that acceptable compromises or trade-offs in functionality and in the various quality attribute properties are made by the architect.

Comparison of Evaluation Methods

The closest relative to the ACDM's architecture evaluation method is the SEI's ATAM. The ATAM is a method for evaluating software architectures relative to an organization's quality attribute goals, and exposes architectural risks that potentially inhibit the achievement of an organization's business goals (Clements et al., 2001). The ATAM is designed to reveal how well an architecture satisfies quality goals, but it also provides insight into how those quality goals interact with each other—how they trade off against each other. Although ACDM's evaluation method and ATAM share some common principles, ACDM's evaluation method, used to evaluate architecture designs, is decidedly different in a number of ways. The reader should keep in mind that this is not a condemnation of ATAM. Indeed, the ATAM represents a quantum leap in design evaluation, but the underlying context and philosophy motivating the ATAM and the ACDM evaluation method are fundamentally different. The key differences between ATAM and ACDM are briefly explained below.

ATAM focuses on using quality attribute scenarios to evaluate the fitness of an architectural design. Functionality is only vicariously evaluated in ATAM through quality attribute scenarios similar to, but not as rigorous as, those developed in stage 2 of ACDM. However, unlike ATAM, the ACDM method explicitly evaluates the architecture design with respect to functionality vis-à-vis the use case scenarios, rather than focusing solely on quality attributes. Although functional evaluation is often trivial in comparison with quality attribute evaluation, functionality matters and must be evaluated explicitly.

Another key difference is that in the ATAM evaluation method, the quality attribute scenarios (which are the basis of the evaluation) are developed after the design work is completed. Although this is certainly better than no evaluation at all, and is actually quite helpful if an organization never considered the broader quality attribute requirements in its design, it can result in massive rework of the design after the evaluation. The evaluation method described in ACDM is woven into the design process where the architectural drivers discovered and analyzed in stages 1 and 2 are used to design the architecture in stage 3. The architecture drivers are then used to evaluate the architecture in stage 4. Because the ATAM was designed with the assumption that designers did not explicitly consider the quality attribute scenarios before design, the method guides evaluators in the discovery of the quality attributes as part of the architecture evaluation. This often takes a considerable amount of effort and time, and reduces the amount of time that evaluators and stakeholders can spend evaluating the architecture. ATAM has two primary phases that each take at least two full days or more on average, with a hiatus between the two phases of a few weeks in duration. There is often a considerable amount of preparation and coordination involved in conducting an ATAM evaluation because it is usually an activity that is outside of the normal development processes. This can make ATAM evaluations costly, heavyweight, and often waterfall-like in nature. In practice, ATAM is most often used by large organizations and projects with commensurately large staffs and budgets, building large systems in a more or less waterfall fashion. Because of the resource and schedule costs of ATAM evaluations, they tend to be one-time affairs. Another unintended consequence of this is that using ATAM in smaller organizations is often cost-prohibitive. The evaluation method built into ACDM stage 4 has the advantage of being more tightly coupled with the design process, where much of the work that must be done during an ATAM evaluation is already completed prior to the design process, thus reducing the cost of an evaluation. ACDM evaluations are lightweight in comparison to ATAM evaluations, and ACDM evaluations can be iterative due to the reduced impact on cost and schedule. In fact, iterative evaluation is *prescribed* in ACDM and is an essential part of what makes the method effective. On the down side, ACDM evaluations of stage 4 cannot be performed in isolation.

The output of an ATAM evaluation is essentially a report that lists the risks discovered during the evaluation and is turned over to the designing organization without specific guidance about what to do with the information. Evaluation is an essential part of the ACDM design method. As such, ACDM provides specific guidance for what to do with the output of a design evaluation. The output of the ACDM evaluation is part of the design process and used in a structured way to develop and refine the architecture, rather than find mistakes after the design is thought to be totally complete.

The ATAM is a method best suited to those organizations that want to ensure that they have an architecture design that is fit for the intended purpose, but do not necessarily have an architecture-centric approach to designing and building systems. The ATAM can work as a stand-alone method that can be applied anytime there is a completed design—whether the quality attributes were considered before design or not. The underlying philosophy of ACDM is that it is nearly impossible to design the right architecture the first time, so ACDM incorporates design evaluation as part of a more comprehensive, iterative architecture-centric approach. In ACDM, the organization must first discover the architectural drivers before design (stages 1 and 2); the architecture drivers motivate the design and serve as input to the architecture evaluation method described in stage 4. This is shown graphically in Figure 11.2.

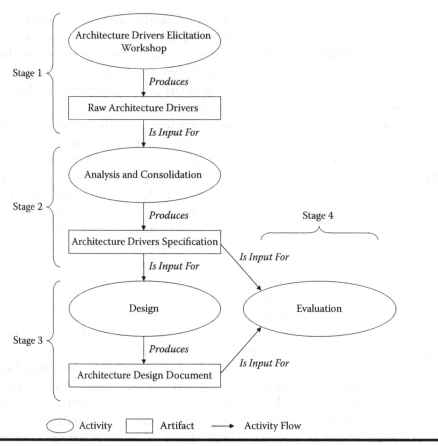

Figure 11.2 **The relationships among stages 1, 2, and 3, the artifacts they create, and the evaluation of the architecture in stage 4.**

Stage 4 Planning

Stage 4 planning involves determining the amount of time that the architecture design team anticipates that they will spend evaluating the architecture. The key element of this is planning and executing the architecture design evaluation workshop. The first evaluation of the architecture typically takes longer than subsequent evaluations. Evaluations can be undertaken by a small group of stakeholders comprised mainly of the architecture design team and others that are part of the organization developing the system, and perhaps a few key customer (external) stakeholders. Evaluations with a larger makeup of external stakeholders (called external evaluations here) are usually more elaborate affairs to coordinate and generally involve a broader community of customer stakeholders, as well as stakeholders from the internal developing organization. It is recommended that initial evaluations of the architecture design are internal, and that an external evaluation is conducted before a decision to advance to production is made. Early internal evaluations, when the architecture design is still relatively immature, can uncover glaring issues that can be addressed without have to involve a lot of stakeholders at a greater cost and with more logistical difficulty. As the architecture matures, the architecture design team may consider including external stakeholders to evaluate the architecture, especially if they can help scrutinize potentially problematic aspects of the design. One of the first planning decisions that the architecture design team must make in stage 4 is whether the evaluation should be internal or external. Once this decision is made, the evaluation workshop's detailed logistics can be planned. As in the other stages of ACDM, planning stage 4 is led by the managing engineer. Table 11.2 lists a number of items to consider when planning the evaluation of stage 4.

A key activity that will drive stage 4 planning is the evaluation workshop. Like all meetings, preparation and structure can make the meeting productive or a total waste of time. However, the actual evaluation workshop may be quite different in terms of planning, preparation, and execution, depending upon whether it is an internal or external evaluation. Internal evaluations may impose less of a logistical demand than external evaluations, where numerous external customer stakeholders may be involved in the evaluation workshop. Certainly there may be many shades of gray between what constitutes an internal and external evaluation. Table 11.3 is a list of considerations for planning the evaluation workshop. This includes items such as travel, lodging, and so forth that may not be applicable for an internal evaluation.

The architecture design team will have to apply their own judgment as to what to plan for, but Tables 11.2 and 11.3 list some items to consider when planning for the evaluation workshop. The quality process engineer is responsible for planning the architecture evaluation, facilitating it, and ensuring that the postactivities are carried out to completion before moving on the stage 5. Once the initial planning for the evaluation workshop is complete, the managing engineer must update the master design plan and the schedule (recall that the design schedule may be separate from the master design plan) to reflect the estimated time that will be spent in stage 4.

Table 11.2 Stage 4 Planning Meeting Considerations

Planning Consideration	Description
Updating the master design plan	Updating the master design plan should occur after the stage is planned, to record the estimated time and resources required in stage 4. The master design plan will also be updated at the end of stage 4 to record the actual time and effort expended in stage 4.
Evaluation preparation	These are the activities associated with preparing for the architecture design evaluation workshop. This may differ depending upon whether the evaluation is internal or external. Specific considerations for evaluation preparation are provided in Table 11.3.
Evaluation workshop	This is the amount of time spent in the actual design evaluation. Typically ACDM evaluation lasts a day or less; however, in industry trials a few evaluations span two days for large systems with large external stakeholder groups. A sample evaluation agenda is provided in Table 11.4.
Postevaluation activities	After the evaluation, the issues uncovered during the evaluation must be recorded in the issues action document, and the resolution action determined by the chief architect.

Table 11.3   Evaluation Workshop Planning Considerations—The Evaluation Is Planned, Facilitated, and Executed by the Quality Process Engineer

Consideration	Comments
Attendees	Decide who will attend the evaluation workshop. Earlier evaluations should be internal; later evaluations should include customer stakeholders if they are available.
Homework	The architecture design and the architecture drivers specification should be sent to the stakeholders who will attend the evaluation workshop. They should be asked to read through the architecture to get familiar with the documentation and the design. Homework may be omitted if the stakeholders do not possess the technical wherewithal to evaluate the architecture. However, the architect should consider providing these stakeholders with read-ahead material to familiarize them with the general design. If stakeholders are unfamiliar with the evaluation process, send them information explaining the process, expectations, and outcomes.
Venue	Decide where the evaluation workshop will be conducted. Internal evaluations can be held at a place convenient for the architecture design team, but should not be interrupted. If a significant number of external stakeholders will attend the evaluation, a neutral site should be considered if possible to minimize interruptions. Ask attendees to plan on spending the allocated time for the evaluation uninterrupted (no cell phone interruptions, impromptu meetings, answering e-mail, etc.). An uninterrupted evaluation is faster, more productive, and results in a higher-quality evaluation. So that attendees are not totally isolated, consider providing a message board or a phone number that can be called where someone can answer and take messages for attendees. Ensure that attendees are aware of this phone number before they arrive at the evaluation. If needed, make sure the room is suitably equipped with power cables, regional power converters (110V to 220V, two-prong versus three-prong adapters, and so forth), and network access.
Materials	Plan on having a projector/beamer to view the architecture designs, and hard copies as necessary. Ensure that meeting materials are available as necessary, such as note pads, pens/pencils, flip charts and tape, whiteboards and markers and erasers, overhead projectors and plastic overhead slides, pointers, and tape recorders (if permitted and desired).
Travel and lodging	If stakeholders must travel to attend the evaluation, plan and budget accordingly for travel time and lodging costs.
Nourishment	Consider providing cold drinks (juices, water), coffee, meals, and snacks as necessary. The cost of providing nourishment at the venue will more than pay for itself in time lost as attendees venture off on scouting trips for drinks, lunch, and snacks.

The Psychology of Design Evaluations

The design evaluation described here is essentially a structured, social, peer-oriented evaluation of the design decisions and architectural documentation developed by the architecture design team. As introduced earlier, organizations using ACDM are encouraged to develop the initial design quickly and evaluate it so that it can be refined based on the issues uncovered during the evaluation workshop. To facilitate iteration, reduce the total cost of evaluation, and rapidly improve the quality of the design, internal and external evaluations are strongly recommended. Internal evaluations use an evaluation team composed predominantly of the architectural design team and other technical stakeholders. Internal evaluations should be used after the notional architecture is created and is focused on the essential design decisions, like initial partitioning, technical approaches, and how key quality attributes and functional requirements will be satisfied by the design. Preparation for the internal evaluation workshop is not usually as onerous as that for an external evaluation workshop. Design evaluations can be hampered or completely undermined by various behaviors and organizational syndromes that are due to human nature and the natural conflict that arises when scrutinizing design artifacts. A few of the common behaviors and syndromes prevalent in organizations and their effects on the evaluation are discussed below.

My Baby Is Not Ugly!

No one likes to be criticized personally, but most adult human beings would never take a swing at another human being if they were called a dirty rotten scoundrel. Most adults would even walk away from a situation where their husbands, wives, mothers, and fathers were insulted. However, the most mature and sophisticated person may be inclined to get pretty defensive, or even downright physical, if you insult his or her children. A design is a labor of love for most engineers, so when they present their design (their baby) to a group of cynical stakeholders who systematically criticize it (your baby is ugly), we should not be surprised if they get a bit defensive. In its extreme, this attitude can undermine evaluations because stakeholders will not want to offer criticisms if they feel that the designer will get offended by the criticism and bite their head off. Passionate discussion is productive and shows that both the designer and customer stakeholders care about getting the best possible designs, but when passionate becomes personal or valid criticism of a design is taken personally, passionate discussion can become destructive behavior.

Apathy

Apathy is the opposite of productive passionate architecture evaluation and discussion. Apathy results when members of the architecture design team do not apply their best efforts and talents to the evaluation of the architecture. In some design teams and organizations, the evaluation process is viewed as a bureaucratic hoop the team must jump through to get on to more productive work. If an architecture design team has apathy toward the architecture evaluation in stage 4, then ACDM as a design process will not work properly. The quality of the architecture is directly dependent upon the quality of the evaluation process. Apathy can result from burnout due to aggressive schedules, impossible requirements, and lack of interest in the products, technologies, or products being created. Apathy can also result in organizations that place a high premium on team harmony. Team harmony is a great thing, but not if opposing viewpoints and passionate debates (like those that often result during evaluation workshops) are discouraged. In the name of harmony, those with dissenting points of view will keep their mouths shut and after a while they become apathetic toward evaluation, the project, and even the organization. A similar source of evaluation apathy is in organizations where critiques and criticisms are generally discouraged. Apathy can also be a big problem with stakeholders who are not technically oriented, but whose participation in the evaluation workshop is essential. These stakeholders need to be reminded how important their contribution is to the success of the system or product design and development. Their role and expectations in the evaluation workshop must be clearly articulated.

I Am Just Smarter Than You

Sometimes during evaluation workshops, designers will respond to inquiries made by stakeholders regarding their designs. When stakeholders attempt to point out issues with the design, sometimes technocrats will say that the stakeholder simply does not understand the technical or design concepts. Architects (and other technologically inclined stakeholders) can overestimate their own abilities and underestimate the insights and criticisms of other stakeholders. The "I am just smarter than you" attitude and syndrome presents significant challenges in some organizations. Ronald Reagan was famous for his quote regarding his trust of the former Soviet Union in regards to their promise to dismantle nuclear weapons: "Trust but verify." The evaluation workshop is an opportunity to scrutinize the design and confirm the architecture design decisions made by the architect and the architecture design team. As such, the architecture design team has the responsibility to communicate their design decisions to the satisfaction of the stakeholders during the evaluation. Sometimes this may mean fixing confusing representations, adding prose, or admitting that there are indeed problematic design decisions or omissions in the design. Remember that the architecture design is a communication vehicle first and foremost. In the ACDM context this is especially important because the architecture design is used to guide detailed design, construction, and the programmatic management of the project as well.

Let's Just Skip It

If you combine the confidence of the "I am just smarter than you" syndrome with apathy you get the "Let's just skip it" syndrome. Sometimes architects and design teams are overoptimistic and overconfident in their designs and underestimate the trouble that they can get into with substandard designs. Overconfidence has been prevalent in software engineers since the abacus was invented, and most of the major process improvement authors of the last 25 years have written about the dangers of overconfidence. Architecture design teams using ACDM tend to be very cautious and thorough when creating and evaluating the first architecture design. However, as teams gain more confidence in the method and more experience as architects, they are often tempted to bypass the evaluation step. This is common if the team is under schedule pressure (which is all the time in practice). A single defect found and fixed before the production stages can more than justify the cost and effort of sticking to the evaluation and refinement strategy defined by ACDM. According to Martin (1984) and other similar studies from the process improvement community, in large information systems 50 percent of errors found after deployment are traced back to analysis and design. According to Boehm and Victor (2001), the cost-escalation factor for defects found after design is 5:1 for small- and medium-sized systems (it costs five times as much to find and fix defects after design). For large complex systems the ratio balloons to more than 100:1. This data reveals that early design evaluation is a cost-effective way to remove costly defects. Another insight of this study revealed that good architectural practices can significantly reduce the cost-escalation factor. This Boehm and Victor report concludes that peer reviews (including architecture design reviews) are credited with finding 60 percent of systemic defects before implementation. When it comes to architecture design evaluation, rather than an attitude of "Let's just skip it," it seems the data would indicate that a "Let's just do it" attitude is much wiser.

Hang 'em High

In some corporate cultures, mistakes of any kind are not tolerated. Certainly blatant incompetence or negligent behaviors should not be tolerated, but some organizations and the engineers in it are overly sensitive to anything perceived as a mistake. This can be a highly destructive culture for the design evaluation process and must be overcome if organizations want to iteratively refine architectures using ACDM. The evaluation process not only uncovers issues with the architectural design, but the person responsible for them is right in front of the room! That is convenient in organizations where blame must be assigned as part of the corporate culture. Unfortunately, this often causes the architect to retreat from admitting to any issues that may be uncovered, or discussing the architecture design in a candid way that will lead to finding potential problematic design decisions. In situations like this, apathy will likely result as well.

Let's Fix It Now

Engineers are problem solvers and will not hesitate to begin solving problems as soon as they are discovered. This single characteristic of technical people can significantly undermine the productivity of the evaluation workshop and the evaluation schedule. As problems are discovered during the evaluation, the temptation to solve them on the spot can be overwhelming for the members of the architecture design team. Fixing problems is not the objective of a design evaluation; finding problems is the purpose of it.

Story Time

Another common misbehavior in social methods such as those used in design evaluation workshops is for attendees to head off on tangents about past experiences or discuss organizational and process-oriented issues not directly related to the design. This too can severely undermine a design evaluation workshop and swallow up huge amounts of time if not properly managed and discouraged.

The architecture design team would do well to be aware of these misbehaviors and syndromes within their teams and organizations so that they can be addressed or avoided whenever any kind of evaluation is used. The ACDM design evaluation process was designed and structured in a number of ways to help avoid some of these syndromes. First, ACDM includes broad stakeholder involvement early in the design process, helping to avoid the apathy and "Let's just skip it" syndromes. Stakeholders are involved and provide the grist for design vis-à-vis the architectural drivers and tend to be more engaged in the process of design. Because ACDM design activities are structured around a central architecture design team, ownership of the architecture design is distributed and not the brain child of a single architect. This helps to avoid the "My baby is not ugly" and the "I am just smarter than you" syndromes. The structured nature of the design evaluation process helps to keep attendees focused, avoiding the "Let's fix it now" and story time syndromes. Finally, a fundamental philosophy of ACDM is that the notional architecture is designed quickly and iteratively refined—problems with the design are not only anticipated, but are expected and welcomed because this is how the architecture is designed and refined. This goes a long way to avoid the "Hang 'em high" syndrome. Other more specific ideas and techniques will be presented to help prevent these attitudes and the resulting destructive behaviors as the detailed steps of the evaluation workshop are presented.

Conducting the Architecture Design Evaluation Workshop

Given that the planning of the stage 4 logistics is complete, the actual evaluation workshop must be planned. The ACDM design evaluation workshop is a social process structured around seven discrete steps that each consist of specific well-defined activities. These steps should be used to form the evaluation workshop agenda and plan the timing of the specific activities of the workshop. Each of these steps will be discussed in great detail throughout the rest of this chapter, but Table 11.4 provides a template that can be used to create a specific agenda for the evaluation workshop. Each of the elements in the agenda, as well as estimating the timing for each activity, will be cleared as each step is elaborated upon.

Note that there are no times for each step provided in the template in Table 11.4. This is because the duration of each step may depend upon the size and scope of the system and the number of attendees. As a rule of thumb, two-thirds of the time spent in the evaluation workshop will be spent in step 6, analyzing the system structures with respect to the quality attribute scenarios. In industrial trials using ACDM, only one rather large IT system took more than one day to complete the evaluation. This sounds like a long time, but in using ACDM the organization found that the evaluation of the architecture design was three days to one week less than the former ad hoc design review process they were using. They also found that the ACDM approach resulted in a more thorough evaluation, the resulting architecture was of a higher quality, and the outcome of the evaluation was more predictable and repeatable than other evaluation methods they had used. Prior to the evaluation workshop it is important that the evaluation roles are established for the architecture design team members. This is important for internal and external evaluations. However, establishing roles is especially important if a significant number of external stakeholders are present during the evaluation workshop. The roles in an evaluation include:

- Facilitator
- Architecture presenter
- Scribe
- Evaluation process enforcer
- Timekeeper
- Questioners

In small teams or internal evaluations, these roles may be combined or tailored to best fit the needs of the organization, the architecture design team, and the context in which the design is being evaluated. However, for external evaluations, especially with large numbers of stakeholders, each of these roles becomes very important in managing the proceedings of the evaluation workshop. Each of these roles is explained in detail below.

Table 11.4   Architectural Design Evaluation Workshop Agenda Template

Architectural Design Evaluation Workshop

Location: <Insert location >

Date: <Insert date >

Start time: <Insert start time >

End time: <Insert end time>

Note: Please turn off cell phones for the workshop.

Step	Activity	Who
1.	Introductions	Managing engineer Quality process engineer
2.	Review business context and business constraints	Chief architect
3.	Review the technical requirements and constraints: • Functional use cases • Quality attribute scenarios • Technical constraints	Chief architect
4.	Architecture overview presentation	Chief architect
5.	Functional analysis	Quality process engineer Chief architect
6.	Structural analysis	Quality process engineer Chief architect
7.	Summary: Review recorded issues	Quality process engineer

Facilitator

The facilitator will lead the evaluation workshop and keep the attendees focused on the evaluation process and activities. The facilitator role is filled by the quality process engineer. The exception to this is any introductions and opening statements that are typical when there are a significant number of external stakeholders present. To establish the importance and tone of the evaluation, it is recommended that the managing engineer provide the opening statements and conduct the introductions.

Architecture Presenter

The architecture presenter will present the architecture, explain the design decisions to the evaluation workshop attendees, and respond to questions about architecture. The chief architect will fill the role, but he or she should feel free to call on other members of the architecture design team as needed to address questions. For example, the chief scientist or other engineers aiding the chief architect with the design may better understand the technical details of a particular element of the design.

Scribe

The scribe will record the proceedings of the evaluation workshop. In particular, he or she will record the issues as they are raised during the evaluation. The scribe can be filled by any member of the architecture design team that is not already filling a role. Although the role of a scribe can be delegated to a staff member not on the architecture design team, this is not recommended. Because much of the discussion during the evaluation workshop will be technical in nature, and in some cases may include deep technical details, it is helpful if the scribe is technically savvy and preferably somewhat familiar with the architecture design. This will speed up the recording of issues and other information discussed during the evaluation workshop and will ensure that the information recorded is accurate.

Evaluation Process Enforcer

To ensure that the evaluation process and any tailoring of it is followed, it can be helpful if someone is assigned to monitor the proceedings and ensure that the process is followed. Although it is essential that a disciplined and repeatable evaluation process is followed, this role may be overkill for internal evaluations within the architecture design team. However, this role can be very important when a significant number of external stakeholders are present, especially if the number of attendees is large (20+). Managing evaluation workshops with large numbers of stakeholders can be extremely chaotic, so it is a good idea to keep a simple checklist of steps and have someone monitor the proceedings to make sure that nothing is missed. The obvious choice for this role is the quality process engineer, but because he or she will be extremely busy with facilitating the evaluation workshop, his or her filling of this role may be impractical. It is very easy to miss a step, forget to record something, or overlook some other detail in the heat of facilitating the workshop. This role can be filled by any member of the architecture design team that is not already filling a role, but he or she should be thoroughly familiar with the evaluation process and any tailoring that the organization has adopted.

Timekeeper

The timekeeper role is of a similar stature as that of process assurance. Although it is essential that evaluation workshops adhere to a predefined schedule, a single person dedicated to watching the clock may be overkill for internal evaluations within the architecture design team. Again, this role becomes important when a significant number of external stakeholders or a large number of attendees are present. Groups often get lost in discussion during evaluation workshops and time passes without notice, which results in not covering all of the requirements and constraints or taking too much time in the evaluation. Never assign the timekeeping role to the facilitator—it is impossible to track time and focus on managing discussion and the proceedings of the workshop. Anyone with a watch can track time.

Questioners

Everyone present during the evaluation workshop may ask questions at the appropriate time and are questioners. The role of all attendees is to listen to the explanations of the design provided by the architect, and evaluate what is said by the architect, what is seen in the representations, against the requirements and constraints. The questioners will ask the architect for more information or clarifications, or challenge decisions that the architect made. These may become issues that will be resolved after the evaluation workshop.

What is not mentioned here, but should be an obvious precondition for the evaluation, is that the architecture design documentation must be in a state that can be evaluated by the stakeholders. If ACDM stages 1 to 3 have been followed, then the architecture is probably ready for the evaluation. For an internal evaluation, this may be as simple as having the electronic version of the design available for the architecture design team and projecting it during the evaluation workshop. However, for the evaluations where there are a large number of attendees, the architecture designs might need to be available electronically for projecting, and also in hard copy for attendees to scrutinize. In addition to the architectural design, the architecture design team must make the architecture drivers specification available to the attendees. Again, electronic, hard copy, or both should be used to best meet the needs of the evaluation and the stakeholders. As mentioned earlier, the architecture drivers and the architecture design should be distributed prior to the evaluation workshop. This is simple if it is an internal evaluation, but more difficult if the evaluation will include a significant number of external stakeholders. If hard copies are used and there is a large audience, consider assembling a packet for the stakeholders that lists the evaluation workshop agenda, the architectural drivers, and the architecture design. This simplifies distribution and, if properly designed, can help stakeholders navigate the information and speed the evaluation along.

Once the roles for the evaluation have been set, the venue for the workshop scheduled, and the agenda established, the evaluation workshop can commence. For evaluations with external stakeholders, make sure that the meeting venue is prepared. Ensure that there is adequate seating, and the room arrangement is comfortable for attendees, facilitators, and presenters. Make sure that the room is equipped with whiteboards, flip charts, markers, pencils, pens, paper, and so forth. Ensure that the projector and commensurate cabling are in place and that all is functioning properly. Have cold drinks, coffee, snacks, and so forth ready for the attendees in a location that is not likely to disrupt the evaluation when someone gets a drink or snack. It is also a good idea to copy the day's agenda to a whiteboard or flip chart, and that it is visible to all of the attendees. Certainly all of these preparations may not be needed at this level of formality for internal evaluation workshops, but these should serve as guidelines for these kinds of evaluations as well. At this point the evaluation workshop can begin. The steps of the evaluation are explained in detail in the subsequent sections.

Step 1: Introduction

The formality of the introduction will vary depending upon whether the evaluation is internal or external. If the evaluation involves external stakeholders, the architecture design team should plan on providing an overview of the evaluation process to the attendees. In addition, it is essential that the architecture design team explicitly explain what the stakeholders' role is in the evaluation. For evaluations with external stakeholders, the evaluation should begin with the managing engineer welcoming everyone to the evaluation workshop and introducing himself or herself and the architecture design team. The managing engineer should then invite the attendees to introduce themselves. Following the introductions, the quality process engineer should explain the evaluation process to the attendees and their role in the evaluation workshop. It is extremely important that the quality process engineer explain what is expected of the stakeholders to keep them engaged in the evaluation process and avoid apathy. This is also a good time to gently explain to stakeholders what behaviors are to be avoided during the evaluation workshop. The quality process engineer should explain the following points:

■ Role of the attendees: The role of the attendees is to ask questions about the architecture with respect to the functional and quality attribute requirements, and the technical and business constraints. The evaluation process and questioning will be structured and facilitated by the quality process engineer. The chief architect will be responsible for describing the design decisions and responding to any questions that the attendees may have about the architecture (including architecture design team members). The chief architect may defer questions to other members of the architect design team for clarification or explanation. If the group feels that the architecture design does not adequately address a functional or quality attribute requirement, or satisfy a constraint, any attendee may raise an issue. Issues will be recorded and addressed after the evaluation workshop.

■ No dumb questions: Attendees must understand that the evaluation process will not work if they do not critique the architecture design, or if they hold back their thoughts and fail to express their concerns. Attendees should not feel inhibited by their lack of technical expertise, which might lead them to ask what they might perceive as a "dumb question." Attendees should be reminded that there is no such thing as a dumb question, and this should not be a factor that inhibits them from asking questions. The facilitator should try to foster an open environment where attendees feel that they can ask any question they like. It can be challenging for the facilitator to achieve and maintain this openness in some corporate cultures (advice for facilitators is provided at the end of this chapter).

■ Yield to the facilitator: The quality process engineer will facilitate and lead the evaluation of the architecture design. His or her role is to ensure that the architecture is evaluated and that everyone's voice is heard. To cover all of the material within the evaluation workshop time constraints, he or she must ask that participants yield to the facilitator. If there are a lot of stakeholders present, the facilitator may institute a hand-raising rule where the attendees must raise their hands to contribute.

■ Avoid side conversations: It is important that every stakeholder's voice is heard during the evaluation workshop. Side conversations during the workshop make it very hard to focus on the evaluation and to hear what the current speaker is saying. Please step out of the room if the side conversation is necessary, or better yet, share what you have to say with the group.

■ Stay focused: Remind attendees that they should try to stay focused on the current topic of discussion during the evaluation. If an attendee wants to refer back to something discussed in the past, he or she should ask the facilitator how to address this. The facilitator will decide to either handle it right away or defer it. The facilitator will ask the scribe to record the matter so that it is not forgotten. Attendees should be reminded to stay on the topic of evaluating the architecture design and avoid tangential discussing of organizational politics, process matters not concerning design, and war stories. These may be interesting discussions, but they will take time away from the evaluation of the architecture. The facilitator should remind the attendees that he or she will ask those who engage in these kinds of discussions to table them. Finally, the facilitator needs to reinforce the message that the attendees need to be present mentally and physically. For this reason, the attendees are asked to turn off cell phones, not to answer e-mail, and refrain from leaving the evaluation workshop to tend to other business unless it is absolutely necessary. When stakeholders are not present (mentally or physically), we miss their valuable contributions during the evaluation. Further, it can be disruptive when they return to the evaluation workshop and bring up points already discussed or want to catch up with the proceedings.

■ Find issues, do not fix them: Frequently when evaluating architectural designs, attendees are tempted to try to solve problems when issues are raised—this includes members of the architecture design team. This is a chronic problem with teams inexperienced in design evaluation. Problem solving during the evaluation workshop will quickly lead to schedule overruns, and this must be strictly managed by the facilitator. The facilitator must remind the attendees that the purpose of the workshop is to evaluate the design to find issues, not fix them. If the facilitator finds the group discussing solutions to an issue, he or she must ask the participants to table the discussion.

■ Go easy on the architect: The evaluation in stage 4 can be a stressful time for the chief architect, especially the first evaluation. Attendees in both internal and external evaluations should be reminded that the architecture design is the product of the entire architecture design team, not just the chief architect. Evaluation workshop attendees need to understand that the evaluation in stage 4 is a critical process for improving the design, not a court of law for indicting the architect. The evaluation is productive only if the work products are critiqued, not the designers personally. If the evaluation becomes a place to hang designers, then problems will never be found in workshops. Under these conditions, evaluations will eventually cease all together, and the fundamental mechanism that makes ACDM work will be undermined.

It is strongly recommended that the quality process engineer use a short presentation to explain the evaluation process. After it is developed, it can be reused in future evaluations. Table 11.5 provides an outline for creating this presentation. The presentation should be developed by the quality process engineer and tailored to meet the organization's needs. However, specific material for this presentation can be found in this and other sections throughout the text.

This presentation should be about 6 to 12 slides or so and take approximately 15 to 30 minutes to deliver, including questions. Again, this presentation should not be needed for internal evaluations, but this is a decision that is best left to the judgment of the architecture design team. Sometimes it is useful to give such a presentation for the first internal evaluation to set the tone and guidelines for evaluations, but skip it for subsequent internal evaluations, only referring to it when necessary.

Step 2: Review Business Context and Business Constraints

The chief architect will lead the evaluation and trace through the architecture design artifacts, beginning with the review of the business context and the business constraints. These should have been discovered in stage 1 and analyzed in stage 2, but the impact they had on the design in stage 3 should be discussed at this time during the evaluation workshop. While technical constraints are hard-and-fast design decisions made before the design even begins, business constraints are far more subtle, but their impact on the design is no less dramatic. Reviewing the business constraints is a critical first step in the evaluation process because they often describe the overall business context that will help shape the design of the system. This step should be done for external evaluations, but also should be part of the first internal evaluation. The business constraints, and indeed the broader business context, might include:

■ Budget: An ever-present constraint in any project is budget. Specific fiduciary limitations should be understood prior to design of the system because they will necessarily impact the design decisions that the architect will make. For example, if budgets for a project are tight, the architect may not be able to design a system that is as flexible or one that possesses anything other than the basic functionality and properties required. If the architect ignores the budget during design, he or she may well design something that cannot be built with given resources.

Table 11.5   Evaluation Process Overview Presentation Outline

Number of Slides	General Content
1–2	**System/product introduction:** Briefly introduce the system or product being built and the key project stakeholders and their relationship with the system or product.
1–2	**Overview of architecture design:** Describe the role and importance of architectural design. Explain the architectural drivers, where they come from, and their relative influence on the design decisions and how they shape the architecture. Stress the importance that technical constraints and quality attribute requirements have on the design of the system or product.
1–2	**Overview of ACDM:** Describe the design process using ACDM. Explain how the underlying philosophy of ACDM is to iteratively refine the architecture design after evaluation, using the output of the evaluation to guide the refinement. Describe the current stage of the method (stage 4), what has happened before this stage, and what will happen after this stage.
1–2	**Overview of the evaluation process:** Describe each step of the evaluation process, highlighting the purpose and the outcomes. Refer to the agenda. Describe the primary artifact created during the evaluation—a list of issues that will be discovered during the evaluation. These will be reviewed and summarized at the conclusion of the evaluation.
1	**Roles and responsibilities of attendees:** Explain the roles of the attendees, including those who are on the architecture design team and the other stakeholders in attendance. Ensure that attendees understand what their obligations are to the evaluation process.
1	**Rules of engagement:** In a gentle way, inform the attendees of the kinds of behaviors that are not helpful during the evaluation process.
0 or 1	**Questions:** Provide an opportunity for attendees to ask questions. Include a closing slide if desired.

■ Schedule: Hand in hand with budgetary constraints is schedule constraints. Schedule constraints may have many different origins, which were discussed in Section 1 of the text, but regardless of origin the architect must understand schedule limitations before design. Again, the architect may design a system that cannot be built within the schedule constraints. A delivery deadline is one kind of constraint, but schedule constraints may also include delivering incremental functionality at a set of specified deadlines. This kind of schedule constraint can deeply impact the design decisions the architect makes and may drive up the costs of designing and building the system. If the system is to be delivered in an incremental way, the architect must design a system that will accommodate the changes over time, or the system may have to be redesigned at each delivery. Up-front design will cost more in terms of money and time, but may save both in the long run. Designing with only the initial delivery and associated capabilities in mind will result in deploying the system faster, and maybe initially inexpensively, but the system may have to be substantially redesigned for the subsequent deliveries. Neither choice is right or wrong, but the architect must understand what the customer stakeholder wants and when. This will be the business constraint that he or she must design to. Note the relationship between schedule and budget here. The old adage is: better, faster, cheaper, … (pick any two). One of these variables must remain flexible or architects may find themselves in a no-win, overly constrained situation. Another point to keep in mind is that time does not equal money. Time costs money, but you cannot always buy time if it is not available. This can play out in many interesting ways in a real business context. Consider the year 2000 bug (commonly known as the Y2K problem) as an example of an interesting schedule/budget relationship. In this case the year 2000 was approaching and no amount of money could buy more time. Many organizations paid huge sums of money and hired armies of programmers to fix Y2K-related problems. However, many found that more resources would not help fix the problem in time, and what they really needed was, in fact, more time. Similar relationships may be present in the schedule and budget constraints and should be presented at this time.

■ Human resources: In many cases, organizations are constrained by the available human resources or are otherwise constrained in how they can use the available workforce. In some cases, organizations may not have enough personnel or talent available to design and build a particular system. In other cases, there may be restrictions upon how many hours an employee may work in a given week. In many European countries the government has imposed mandatory 35-hour workweeks, with no overtime unless an onerous government process is followed to obtain permission for it. Such a situation can be made more difficult if there is a shortage in the labor force of personnel with the prerequisite talent needed to design and build the system. This can severely hamper how much product or system an organization can deliver and the timeliness of the delivery. In other cases, an organization is faced with having to build a system for which it has limited expertise or experience. In these cases it may be difficult to hire the necessary talent, and such a constraint may force a more conservative design to reduce risk. Obviously, such constraints could impact the architectural design of the system in dramatic ways. As these constraints are revisited during this part of the evaluation workshop, their impact on the design should be discussed as well.

■ Organizations: As described earlier, organizational structures can be the source of design forces and deeply influence designs as well as how systems are built, deployed, and maintained. An organization responsible for designing a product or system (especially big, complex ones) may be required to utilize specific vendors or other subcontractors for design, development, test, maintenance, configuration, deployment, and so forth. In one example during industry trials of ACDM, an organization was responsible for designing and building engine control systems for the automotive market. This organization was based in an Asian-Pacific country where the hardware was built. However, the software was written in yet another Asian country. The product (hardware and software) was distributed to final assembly plants around the world, where the product was installed and configured on the assembly line. In addition to the product having to serve a dozen or more different automobile models, regional differences in emission laws and safety requirements had to be accommodated. All of these organizations spoke different languages and had different national as well as corporate cultures. The organization designing the engine control system found it difficult to communicate its design decisions to all of the organizational partners. In addition to all of the inherent technical challenges, the various organizational structures created a formidable set of constraints that were very costly for the organization to overcome. The system designers did not account for these constraints, and they led to a number of problems throughout the product life cycle. The development of the product alone was costly, and late with a 200 percent schedule slippage. Business constraints such as these should be clearly outlined.

■ Marketing and business: Marketing and business concerns are simple: tell the world about the product, system, or services; sell it for more than it costs to produce; and make money.

Unfortunately, marketing and business goals are never as straightforward as they appeared to be in your undergraduate business class. Marketing and business goals are of two types: those internal to the developing organization, and those external to it. In the case where the organization is developing a product for another, external organization, both have business goals they want to achieve. The external organization wants a product that does what it wants the product to do, possesses certain properties, costs a certain amount, and is delivered within an acceptable timeframe. All this is to achieve some business or mission objective within the external organization. The developing organization must market its ability to do this, and then deliver as advertised to stay in business. This is the simplest case. In other situations, the developing organization is developing products for the broader consumer marketplace and often has to "guess" about what will sell. In this case, marketing and designers should work hand in hand to understand market window constraints, technical feasibility, and cost to derive a meaningful product or system definition. In still other cases, the developing organization is part of an internal technology organization and provides technical goods and services for the organization to use in the course of conducting business. A good example of this might be a bank's internal IT group responsible for designing, building, and maintaining the expansive data processing systems they need to conduct daily business operations. Marketing and business constraints are often poorly communicated to designers in terms of their origin and why they were established. Marketing and business constraints are often manifested in terms of schedule and cost constraints, but may be more complex than simple currency and calendar days. Consider a developing organization that is building a product for several external customers. Each product is different, but has many of the same features and properties. A business goal of the developing organization may be to design and build a product line to satisfy the needs of all the external customers. Such an approach could save enormous amounts of resources if properly executed. This is a business constraint that translates into saving money and time, but it is not straightforward, and the impact to the architecture design is huge. At this time the architect should review the marketing and business constraints and their impact on the design.

■ Legal/regulation: In many business contexts, developing organizations must adhere to regulations and legal requirements. These constraints can impact the design and influence the way that the system is built. For example, avionics systems must undergo a rigorous review, verification, and validation process established by governments around the world. Product liability concerns may also be a large source of design constraints in our modern litigious societies. Other systems are subjected to safety standards, such as those established by underwriters laboratories and others, to ensure that products fail safely or not at all. Any legal and regulatory constraints imposed on the architecture design team should be reviewed at this point and their impact on design discussed.

Any issues that arise during the review of the business context and the business constraints should be recorded by the scribe.

Step 3: Review the Technical Requirements and Constraints

At this point in the evaluation, the architecture design team will review the key functional and quality attribute requirements, and the technical constraints. The purpose of this step is to refresh the attendees' understanding of the key technical requirements and constraints motivating the design. The architect should review the functional use cases, the quality attribute scenarios, and the technical constraints as they appear in the architecture drivers specification. To maintain consistency across evaluations, they should be presented in this order:

- Functional use cases: There are a couple of ways to review the functional use cases. Certainly each one could be read, but this may take a very long time and would be appropriate when there are large numbers of use cases. Recall that the architectural drivers specification was distributed prior to the evaluation workshop. An alternative approach is to walk through the first functional use case, so that the attendees understand the format and content of the use cases. For each subsequent use case, read its title and ask the attendees if they have any questions. Wait for a few moments, allowing them to read through the use case. Ask attendees if they understand the use case and wait a few more moments. Provide closure by indicating that if there are no questions, you would like to go on to the next use case. Do not rush this too much because it can give attendees the feeling that you are trying to hide something. This approach significantly reduces the amount of time it takes to review the functional use cases.
- Quality attribute scenarios: Review quality attributes with the attendees once again. Emphasize why they are important and why we use quality attribute scenarios to characterize quality attribute requirements rather than one-word descriptions. As with functional use cases, each quality attribute scenario can be read to the stakeholders. Alternatively, an approach similar to that described for functional use cases can be used, where the architect reads through the first scenario. For subsequent cases, the architect invites the stakeholders to read through each scenario by themselves, offering comment as they see fit.
- Technical constraints: Technical constraints are typically straightforward in comparison to the other architectural drivers and should be reviewed by the architect, inviting the stakeholders to comment where necessary.

For internal evaluations, it may suffice to only review the technical requirements for the first internal evaluation, and then only review technical requirements that change or are refined in subsequent internal evaluations. The technical requirements should always be reviewed as described here when a significant number of external stakeholders are present at the evaluation workshop. Any issues that arise during the review of the technical requirements and constraints should be recorded by the scribe.

Step 4: Architecture Overview Presentation

Finally, the architect gets to show everyone their work of art! In this step the architect will provide an overview of the architecture that they and the design team have created. It is best if the architect can project the design for all to see. If there are a large number of attendees, the architect should refer them to the architecture design specification for details as he or she leads the attendees through the overview. The purpose of the architecture overview presentation is to inform the attendees of the key architectural decisions that have been made and to introduce them to the design documentation. The architect should focus on explaining the architecture from the three key perspectives discussed throughout the text: static, dynamic, and physical. As the architect walks through the presentation, he or she should ensure that the stakeholders know what perspective they are looking at and are keeping pace with the architect. The architect is also advised to make sure to explain when he or she switches perspectives throughout the presentation. For each perspective, it is helpful for the architect to first explain the primary representation. For each representation, the architect should explain the responsibilities assigned to each element and relationship. For this, the element-relationship responsibility tables can be used. If this is too much information to display, the architect should refer the attendees to the documentation. During the architecture overview presentation, it is important that the architect is not interrupted unless it is for simple clarifying questions. This is not the time to grill the architect—this is the time for the attendees to understand what the architect has designed. This means that the facilitator must make clear to the attendees that this is not the time to ask questions yet, but rather, they should give the architect the chance to explain the design. The facilitator must protect the architect at this time by asking attendees who begin to ask detailed technical questions about the architecture design and how it satisfies various requirements and constraints. Attendees who jump ahead as described here should have their comments recorded and revisited at the appropriate time during the evaluation. The architect should not be allowed to filibuster the evaluation by taking hours to present his or her design. At this point, the architect should focus on presenting an overview of the architecture and explaining the documentation. The architect should not be concerned with explaining how the design satisfies each and every requirement and constraint at this time.

Guidelines for preparing the architecture presentation are given by the template in Table 11.6. This presentation should be limited to 45 minutes to an hour, if at all possible. Again, this is just an overview to familiarize the audience with the general structure of the system and the documentation. The architect should follow the guidance provided earlier in the text for creating architectural representations and documenting the architecture. Ensure that the representations are consistent with the stated perspective, and that every drawing has a legend, or a master legend for all drawings is provided somewhere. The architect should maintain consistency among the representations and what is indicated in the legends. Because this is a presentation, there will only be limited space for prose to describe the representation. However, it is helpful if there is a reference in the slide to where the representation and the accompanying prose are located in the architecture design document. Ensure that the representations shown in the presentation are consistent with those in the architecture design document. Nothing is more frustrating to an audience than when they see drawings in the presentation that appear nowhere in the documentation. For internal evaluations, it may suffice to provide a complete architecture overview presentation for the first internal evaluation, and then focus on those elements or parts of the architecture that are changed or refined in subsequent internal evaluations. A complete architecture overview presentation should always be provided as described here when a significant number of external stakeholders are present at the evaluation workshop.

Step 5: Functional Analysis

In ACDM design evaluations, the functional requirements are first analyzed to ensure that the design will meet the required functionality. Another reason for beginning with the functional requirements is that analyzing a design with respect to functionality serves the purpose of familiarizing the attendees with details of the design. As steps 4 to 6 unfold, the attendees are exposed to more detail at each step. At the end of the evaluation of the functional use cases (step 5), attendees should be thoroughly familiar with the overall architecture design. Functionality has little influence on structure, but in evaluating the system with respect to

Table 11.6   Architecture Design Presentation Guidelines

Number of Slides	General Content
1–2	Architectural drivers: Describe the most influential architectural drivers and their impact on the design. Describe any key challenges in meeting the architectural drivers.
1–2	Design strategy: Describe any key structures or design approaches or general philosophies used by the architectural design team to design the architecture. Describe how the design strategy helped to satisfy the architectural drivers.
1–2	Design context: The architect should show the system context as described in Section 1 of the text. Highlight important entities internal and external to the system context. Explain general flow of data, control, events, and so forth to and from the system context.
4–10	Architectural: Present the key architecture representations. The architect should be careful not to present too much detail, but rather focus on a general overview to familiarize the audience with the key structures of the design. The architect should first show the system context, and from there show at least one representation of the system from the three essential perspectives: static, dynamic, and physical.
0–3	Legacy and external influences: Discuss any legacy or commercial elements, systems, products, services, standards, protocols, frameworks, or other similar items that are part of the design. Indicate their position in the architecture, why they were utilized, and the strategy for incorporating them in the design. Pay particular attention to addressing architectural mismatch, especially as the system evolves. If there are none of these items, or they are adequately addressed by the architectural views, then omit this part of the presentation.
0–3	Key issues and challenges: Describe any key issues or challenges that the architect would like attendees to pay particular attention to during the evaluation. Include any concerns with current design decisions, any unknowns, or any anticipated problems in moving ahead with detailed design and production.

the key functional use cases, is a critical aspect of system design. The quality process engineer will facilitate the functional analysis, and the architect will conduct the walk-through of the design. The functional analysis of the architecture design is driven by the functional use cases discovered and refined in stages 1 and 2. Functional analysis begins by selecting one of the functional use cases to analyze. The functional use case can be selected by consensus, by the architect, by voting, by priority, or some other method. It is recommended that priority be used to guide the order of functional analysis. Because there may be a large number of functional use cases, it may be impossible to analyze all of them. In this case, it makes sense to focus on the highest-priority or most difficult use cases. A key point to remember is that the architecture design team should decide upon the process of how functional use cases will be selected for analysis, and how many functional uses will be analyzed before the evaluation workshop. If the team fails to do this, chaos will be guaranteed to break out during the evaluation workshop. The functional analysis is a kind of structured dialog between the architect and the attendees, facilitated by the quality process engineer, and centered on the functional use cases. An example of this dialog follows:

- The quality process engineer reads the functional use case in its entirety.
- The quality process engineer asks the attendees if there are any questions regarding the use case. If there are, then they are addressed, or any issues are recorded by the evaluation scribe. If there are none, then the analysis continues.
- The quality process engineer asks the chief architect to trace through the design, showing how it supports the use case. The quality process engineer reminds the attendees that they should feel free to ask questions at any point during the architect's explanation.
- At this point the chief architect takes the floor. The chief architect will use the design artifacts and show where the entities described in the use case are located relative to the design (usually indicated in the context drawing). The architect should show inputs from the entities to the system, highlighting the roles of the various elements in the design. The architect should show how the system generates output, what elements receive the input from what entities, how the elements interact, and how and what entities receive the output.
- As the chief architect traces through the design, the quality process engineer will facilitate by stopping the architect and allowing the attendees to ask questions. If an architect is unsure how the design addresses a particular concern raised by an attendee during the evaluation, this will be recorded as an issue by the evaluation scribe. For example, assume that the architect is explaining how the system is designed to read the value of a sensor and make continuous adjustments in a chemical process based on the value of the temperature. At some point during the explanation, a stakeholder raises his hand and asks, "What happens if the sensor breaks? What temperature reading will you get? Can the system detect a faulty sensor?" The architect (with a puzzled look on her face) says that she did not consider what would happen if the sensor was faulty. The quality process engineer would point this out as an issue and it would be recorded by the evaluation scribe. No one may deny the recording of an issue. All issues and actions taken to address them are part of stage 5 activities. To ensure that all of the relevant information is captured as quickly and accurately as possible, an issue recording template is provided in Table 11.7.
- The facilitator (quality process engineer) is responsible for stopping the analysis and ensuring that the issue is accurately described and all of the associated information is completely captured. Issues can be related to design decisions that appear to be less than optimal, unclear or incomplete documentation, incorrect assumptions, incorrect or missing requirements, and so forth. Working with the scribe, the quality process engineer will facilitate discussion with the attendee(s) who raised the issue and the chief architect to ensure that the information is captured accurately and as quickly as possible. Once the issue is completely recorded, the facilitator will ask the architect to continue with the analysis. If possible, the issue recording template should be projected for all to see. This can be difficult if the architecture design is also being projected, unless the room has multiple projectors. Alternatively, the issues can be captured electronically and hard copies made available to the attendees or copied to flip charts and hung on the walls. However, this alternative presents its own operational challenges. The point is that the issues should be visible to the attendees at all times because this can help spur on the analysis and can help attendees formulate more questions. The logistics of how the architecture design and issues are projected to the attendees should be decided before the evaluation workshop. While only general guidance is provided here, the exact situation may dictate that different approaches be used for internal and external evaluations and for different venues in which the evaluation workshop is conducted.
- Issues are what they are. They are neither good nor bad; they are not an admission of good or bad design, right or wrong approaches, or guilt. How each issue is addressed is decided

Table 11.7   Issue Recording Template

Issue reference number	Provide a reference number or mnemonic.
Issue Origin	
Functional use case or quality attribute reference **Other**	Circle the appropriate issue origin from the list in the left column. List the reference number or mnemonic for the functional use case or quality attribute scenario. If the issue is not related to a functional use case or quality attribute scenario, circle "other" and describe it here.
Documentation or representation references: Describe the documentation or representations associated with the issue. This can be a reference to a particular figure, slide, section, or entire document. Try to be specific because this information can be critical for reconstructing, analyzing, and addressing the issue after the evaluation.	
Description: Describe the issue here, matching the words of the attendee raising the issue as closely as possible. Provide additional references or data as appropriate. Avoid uncommon acronyms and abbreviations, as they are often not understood after the evaluation. Issues can be related to design decisions, unclear or incomplete documentation, incorrect assumptions, incorrect or missing requirements, and so forth. When in doubt, capture it as an issue. It can be studied after the evaluation.	

after the evaluation workshop by the architecture design team in stage 5. Sometimes after raising an issue, it can be pointless to continue analyzing the use case if the issue is a "show stopper." If this is the case, the facilitator or architect may suggest moving on to the next use case, or the attendees may start fixing the design to address the issue.

This dialog continues until all of the functional use cases (or some subset that were agreed to prior to the evaluation workshop) are evaluated. For internal evaluations, it may suffice to provide a complete architecture overview presentation for the first internal evaluation, and then focus on those elements or parts of the architecture that are changed or refined in subsequent internal evaluations. A complete architecture overview presentation should always be provided as described here when a significant number of external stakeholders are present at the evaluation workshop. Asking insightful questions about the architecture design can be tricky for those new to evaluating architectures. The information typically comes from the architect fast and furious, and it can be easy to be dazzled by the quantity and complexity of the information. Unfortunately, like deer in headlights, it can be easy to miss serious issues that need to be pointed out. For this reason, attendees should not hesitate to ask the architect to slow down or stop for a moment to give them a moment to reflect about what was said, what they are looking at, and how this relates to satisfying the architectural drivers. The facilitator should not hesitate to acquiesce to this request because the quality of the evaluation depends upon the attendees understanding the architecture so they can critique it. Specific guidance on questioning is provided a bit later in this chapter.

An equally tricky task for the chief architect is how to trace through the design and show how the system satisfies a functional use case. For functional analysis, the context drawings and dynamic and physical views seem to be used most often. This is logical because functional use cases describe runtime interactions with the system or product, and systemic behavior is described using the dynamic perspective. However, it is often the case that the dynamic behavior also involves hardware, networks, and so forth. For this reason, when analyzing functionality, physical views are often helpful as well. Dynamic and physical views are often useful for depicting and analyzing control and data flow through the system, and are very useful for tracing operational threads through a system. While static views are useful for analyzing system construction concerns, and especially various quality attribute concerns, they tend to play a minor role in the analysis of functionality. Context drawings are useful as a starting point for analysis. Using context, the architect can show how data, events, messages, and so forth enter the system as input and leave as output. A strategy for tracing an operational use case might include the following:

- Identify the entities in the use case. Review the entities and ensure that attendees understand who or what they are. Recall that entities can be animated things such as human beings (users or other stakeholders), or inanimate objects like sensors, peripherals, and other similar devices. The entities should be defined if the use case templates provided in this text were used when creating the functional use cases.
- Show the entities' position in the design at the start of the use case. The context drawing is often useful for showing these relationships.
- Show or explain how the preconditions defined in the functional use case are true in the design at the beginning of the trace.
- Trace through each step of the functional use case. Show how control, data, events, and so forth move through the system, and how elements interact to satisfy the use case. For those elements that participate in the use case, list their responsibilities and the relationships between them. This should be available in the element-relationship responsibility tables. Restate these responsibilities and refer the attendees to the documentation for the details. Trace through each alternative step of the use case as applicable. In terms of representations and tracing use cases, it can be helpful if the architect starts by showing the physical design of the system, then the dynamic structures (threads, processes, data flow, and so forth). Finally, show how the dynamic structures map to physical elements of the system. This takes a little more effort and organization, but provides a clearer context for the audience and makes the trace less confusing because the mapping between software and hardware elements is made clearly and explicitly. This extra effort is worth it because it helps increase the effectiveness of the evaluation, and ultimately saves time because one explanation at this level of detail will serve all of the subsequent analysis. Sequence diagrams can also be helpful when tracing through use cases, but the problem with traditional sequence diagrams is that the elements of design and their relationships are lost. However, it can be extremely effective if the architect shows these relationships as described here and then shows their interaction using sequence diagrams. Ensure that the elements and entities in the sequence diagrams (boxes at the top of the vertical lines) match those in the architecture representations. Examples and counterexamples are shown in Figure 11.3. As a matter of presentation style, architects should discipline themselves to pause often as they trace through the design to allow attendees time to reflect upon what they are seeing, hearing, and reading. A good general rule is to provide ample time and opportunity for attendees to ask questions.
- Address questions as they arise. Ensure that as issues are raised by the attendees, they are captured by the scribe in a way that the architecture design team will understand later. Include the functional use case reference number with the issue. The facilitator should prevent attendees from bombarding the architect, and allow the architect to address each ques-

The intent of this example is for the sequence diagram on the right to describe the behavior of the dynamic representation on the left. The problem is the elements from the dynamic representation do not match those shown in the sequence diagram. The sequence diagram shows an entity (stick figure) not shown in the dynamic representation and the other element names do not match anything in the dynamic representation. The interactions in the sequence diagrams do not match those shown in the dynamic representation either. These differences lead to confusion.

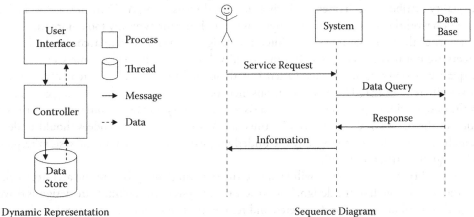

Dynamic Representation   Sequence Diagram

Here the elements and interactions in the sequence diagram match the elements and relationships shown in the dynamic representation making it much easier to understand the structures and the interactions between them.

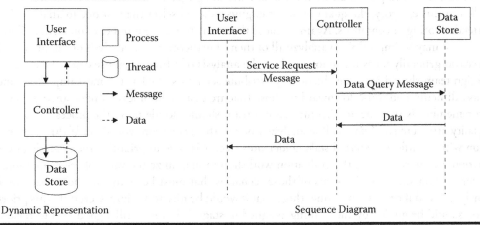

Dynamic Representation   Sequence Diagram

Figure 11.3   Examples of sequence diagrams and architectural representations.

tion and document any associated issues in their entirety before moving on to the next question.

■ Explain how the postconditions specified by the functional use case are true after the trace.
■ Allow a few moments for attendees to reflect on the functional use just presented and traced through. Ask attendees if they have any final questions before moving on to the next use case.

This strategy should only be viewed as guidance, not as the definitive way of tracing through a design. However, in the absence of any experience with design evaluations, this may serve as a good starting point for analyzing how a design satisfies functional requirements.

Step 6: Structural Analysis: Analyze the Systemic Structures Using the Quality Attribute Scenarios

After evaluating the ability of a design to meet the functional requirements by analyzing the use cases, the structural elements of design are evaluated with respect to how well the design satisfies the quality attribute requirements. During industrial trials using ACDM, in stage 4 during the evaluation workshop, the structural analysis of the architecture typically took more time than any other part of the evaluation, so the architecture design team should plan accordingly. Recall that systems are not partitioned to satisfy functionality, but are partitioned to satisfy constraints and the quality attribute requirements. Often it is these quality attribute requirements that become market differentiators and help organizations meet broader business and marketing goals. Evaluating the design with respect to how well it satisfies the quality attribute requirements is the culmination of the design evaluation activities thus far. At this point the attendees should understand the architecture well enough to study the underlying structures to see how the system responds to various quality attribute stimuli.

The quality process engineer will facilitate the structural analysis, and the architect will conduct the walk-through of the design. The structural analysis of the architecture design is driven by the quality attribute scenarios discovered and refined in stages 1 and 2. Structural analysis begins by selecting one of the quality attribute scenarios to analyze. It is strongly recommended that the first quality attribute scenarios analyzed are those that were rated as high priority by the stakeholders and as being difficult by the architecture design team. If there are several scenarios that fall into this category, the quality process engineer should select the first one to analyze through attendee voting or consensus. Again, because there may be a large number of quality attribute scenarios, it may be impossible to analyze all of them. Furthermore, the analysis of a quality attribute scenario generally takes much longer than the analysis of a functional use case. The architecture design team should focus on the quality attribute scenarios rated as the most important and the most difficult, and work downward to those that are easier and of lesser importance. A key point to remember is that the architecture design team should decide upon the process of how many quality attribute scenarios will be analyzed before the evaluation workshop. If this is an evaluation with significant external stakeholder presence, it is wise to prioritize the analysis of quality attribute scenarios before the evaluation workshop to maximize the value of the evaluation. This prioritization should be in terms of those scenarios that must be analyzed, those that should be analyzed, and if time is remaining, those that it would be nice to analyze. Certainly this prioritization should be guided by the ranking assigned in stage 2, but it is still a good idea to review this prioritization with the attendees to ensure this does not circumvent their concerns. If the evaluation is internal, the architecture design team can conduct the analysis of the scenarios in multiple sessions, ensuring complete coverage of the quality attribute requirements. Similar to functional analysis, the structural analysis is a kind of structured dialog between the architect and the attendees, facilitated by the quality process engineer, but centered on the quality attribute scenarios. Because the format of the quality attribute scenarios is different from that of functional use cases, and concerns represented by them are different, the dialog and ensuing analysis are different. An example of this dialog follows:

- The quality process engineer reads the selected quality attribute scenario in its entirety.
- The quality process engineer asks the attendees if there are any questions regarding the scenario's stimulus, the source of the stimulus, the environment, associated artifacts, response, or response measures. If there are issues with any of the scenario's constituent parts, then

they are addressed and are recorded by the evaluation scribe. If there are none, then the analysis continues.

■ The quality process engineer asks the chief architect to trace through the design, showing how it supports the quality attribute scenario. The quality process engineer reminds the attendees that they should feel free to ask questions at any point during the architect's explanation.

■ At this point the chief architect takes the floor. The chief architect will use the design artifacts and show how the system will respond to the stimulus described in the scenario. Often this can be much more difficult than describing how the design satisfies functional requirements. The kinds of representations used and the way that the information is presented to the attendees will depend upon the quality attribute being analyzed. General change-oriented scenarios (modifiability, extensibility, scaleability) will require that the architect explain how to make changes to the system and the amount of resources that will be required to make the changes. If these are code-oriented changes the static perspective will be required, but runtime changes will require the use of the dynamic perspective to analyze how and when the changes are made. Physical perspectives are applicable to both situations. If the quality attribute scenario addresses some aspect of performance, the analysis may be very similar to analyzing functionality, except that correct function is assumed and the timing of the functionality is scrutinized. Tracing through quality attribute scenarios can be much more difficult for the architect and is a real test of how well the design is conceived and documented. To help stay focused during the analysis of a quality attribute scenario, the architect may want keep the following in mind: *given the stimulus, from the stated source, under the stated environmental conditions, affecting the artifacts indicated, describe how the system will or will not respond as described, consistent with the response measure specified by the scenario.*

■ As the chief architect traces through the design showing how the system responds to the quality attribute stimulus indicated by the scenario, the quality process engineer will facilitate by stopping the architect and allowing the attendees to ask questions. If an architect is unsure of how the design responds to a particular quality attribute stimulus, this will be recorded as an issue by the evaluation scribe, just as it was during functional analysis. Once the issue is recorded, the architect continues with the evaluation. The same guidance for capturing issues while analyzing the functional use cases also applies when analyzing the quality attribute scenarios.

It can be difficult for an architect to describe how the system will respond to quality attribute stimuli. Some responses are not precisely measurable. For example, assume that the architect must explain how a particular modification can be made to a system, within a specific time period, with a given set of resources. Accurately predicting and proving the cost of change and the amount of time it will take is as difficult as estimating the amount of resources required for original system construction. These measures require judgment, experience, and intuition. In these cases, the architect must show how changes will be made, and the relative cost in orders of magnitude to the best of their ability, based on the architect's judgment and experience. If the attendees are not satisfied, then they may raise an issue. In some cases quality attribute analysis is not always exact, and in other cases the analysis can be relatively precise. For example, consider a performance-oriented quality attribute scenario. Depending upon the kind of performance, there are a number of formal analysis frameworks that are available for analyzing performance that can be applied to the architectural design evaluation. However, analyzing systemic modifiability is a bit more challenging because there are no rigorous frameworks for describing and analyzing modifiability.

So, analyzing designs with respect to quality attribute requirements with more rigorous analysis frameworks can be more exact than analyzing quality attribute requirements that lack analysis frameworks. However, this does not make quality attributes lacking formal analysis frameworks less important than those with more formal analysis frameworks. The onus is on the architect to show how the architecture design satisfies all of the quality attribute requirements with the design artifacts at hand. This leads to another difficultly when analyzing quality attribute requirements. It can be challenging to make effective use of the design representations to analyze quality attributes and explain the design to the attendees in a meaningful and understandable way. Functional analysis tends to focus on the dynamic and physical representations of the system and is often more straightforward—stuff goes into the system, there is computation, and stuff comes out of the system. However, the analysis of the quality attribute scenarios often requires the use of representations from all of the perspectives, and different types within each perspective, and the flow of events is not always precisely laid out as it is in a functional use case. Again, this makes sense because quality attribute requirements largely define and affect the structure of a design. Analyzing quality attribute responses can be challenging, and often takes much more time than it does to analyze functionality. A strategy for analyzing quality attribute scenarios might include the following:

- Identify the perspective(s) that will best explain how the design responds to the stimulus described in the quality attribute scenario. Table 11.8 lists a few common quality attribute concerns and the associated perspectives that might best explain how the system responds in terms of the quality attribute concern. This table is not a complete listing of all of the quality attribute concerns and all of the types of representations that may be required to describe how a system or product will respond to quality attribute stimuli. This table should serve as an example for the kinds of representations that may be required during an evaluation workshop, and to once again stress the importance of perspective. The architect should ensure that he or she describes the perspective(s) and the representations selected to the attendees, and how they will be used to describe the system responses to the quality attribute stimulus described in the scenario. Never assume that the attendees understand or appreciate the perspective(s) of the representation you are showing them—the architect should explain his or her reasoning even if it seems obvious.
- Identify the source of the stimuli relative to the architecture design, and especially the artifact specified in the scenario. Often it is best to start by showing the source relative to the system by starting with the context diagram and working into the detailed representations from selected perspectives. Certainly, although this may be obvious for engineers familiar with the design, it may not be for attendees that are not familiar with the design or lack technical expertise. Again, play it safe and do not assume that the attendees understand the source, its origin, or where it stands in relation to the design. For internal evaluations, ask the members of the architecture design team if they understand the source, its origin, and where it fits into the architectural design. For external evaluations, explain it.
- Identify and explain the specific artifact(s) described in the quality attribute scenario and show its position in the design. If the artifact is an element or relationship, briefly explain or review the element-relationship responsibilities and refer the attendees to the architecture design document for details. Show the impact that the stimulus has on the artifact(s) of the design. In some cases the artifact listed in the scenario is not specific enough (e.g., "the system"), or it does not appear in the perspective selected. The architect should resolve these discrepancies before continuing with the analysis by fixing the scenario or

Table 11.8   General Quality Attributes and the Related Perspectives

General Quality Attribute Concerns	Perspectives
Throughput, response time	Dynamic: Task structure and relationships, sequence diagrams, state charts, data flow (including transactions, events, messages, and so forth), control flow. These representations can help evaluate how long it will take a system to process, respond, or react to input. Physical: Networks, computer systems, peripheral devices. These representations can help evaluate what hardware and mechanical devices contribute to timing and throughput.
Scheduleability	Dynamic: Task structure and relationships, sequence diagrams, state charts, data flow, control flow. Other representations to support the analysis of scheduleability might include task/process/thread priority, scheduling strategies, concurrency, anticipated event arrival rates, and so forth. Some of these representations might be from the static or even physical perspective.
System changes	Static: Code structures, data format, and other representations from this perspective will be required to show what will change and how to change these structures, and to help evaluate the cost of change. Physical: Networks, computer systems, peripheral devices. These physical representations are required to evaluate the impact of change on the physical elements of the system or product. Dynamic: If changes happen at runtime, the task structure, task relationships, sequence of events, and so forth may have to be analyzed to evaluate when, how, and the effect of changes on the runtime structure of the system.
Runtime fault detection, recovery, safe operation	Dynamic: The task structure, task relationships, sequence of events, and so forth will play an important role in the analysis of how well the design addresses these quality attribute concerns Static: Analyzing code structures can be essential when evaluating how well a design can detect faults and handle them in a predictable way. Physical: The design of networks, computer systems, peripheral devices, and so forth is an essential part of systems with these quality attribute concerns. These physical representations are essential when evaluating systemic response to faults.
Authentication, data security, intrusion detection	Dynamic: The task structure, task relationships, sequence of events, and so forth will play an important role in evaluating how users log in to the system and use it during operation Static: Various access policies are implemented in static code and data structures. Physical: Evaluating networks, computer systems, and peripheral devices are essential because they may be responsible for permitting or denying access to system services and data.

explaining the difference in perspective. If the artifact is not as specific as it should be, add details to the scenario and ensure that the attendees understand the information added. This should also be updated in the architecture drivers specification. If the artifact appears in a different perspective than those selected earlier to analyze the scenario, the architect should explain and clarify the relationships between the artifacts in the different perspectives. For example, assume that for a given scenario the artifact affected by the stimulus is a process that appears as a single box in a dynamic perspective. This is easy for attendees to understand and visualize, and it is easy for the architect to present and explain. However, let us assume that the quality attribute of interest is modifiability in terms of how easy it might be to change an application to run on different kinds of hardware. Assume that the scenario response and response measure state that the code for the process should be modified to accommodate the new hardware within a specific period of time. If the application code must change in response to this scenario, the architect will have to use representations from the static perspective to analyze how long this change will take. The single application shown in the dynamic perspective is gone, and now the architect is showing something that looks like a giant layer cake in the static perspective. This can leave some attendees scratching their heads. Clearly the dynamic representations of the application are not suitable for analyzing how easy it is to change the code that makes up the process. But in switching to a static perspective to study the code, the architect has to make sure that he or she takes the attendees with him or her. The architect must explain how the artifact is the same, but looks different from the various perspectives, and how each perspective helps us analyze different quality attribute responses.

- Describe how the system will respond by using the design to guide the analysis. If it is a modifiability-oriented scenario, show what structures will change due to the stimulus and the relative ease and cost of those changes. If it is a performance-oriented scenario, show how data moves through the system and the anticipated timing of the data movement. The architect should make sure that he or she explains response measures as well as responses. Some of the response measures will be based on data from precisely designed experiments. Other response measures will be less precise and based on heuristics, general industry guidelines and data, or even antidotal experiences.
- As the analysis wraps up, the architect should allow a few moments for attendees to reflect on the scenario and ask any final questions before moving on to the next scenario.

These steps should not be viewed as a recipe for how to analyze a quality attribute scenario, or how to walk an audience through the design and explain how it reacts to quality attribute responses. Successfully presenting and analyzing an architecture design as described here is highly dependent upon solid communication skills. These guidelines can help, but learning how to do this effectively takes practice. Rather than memorizing specific steps and activities, the architect is advised to internalize the spirit of these steps and practice them until they become second nature. This serves the purpose of improving the quality of the evaluation, but also helps make a better architect.

Step 7: Summary: Review Recorded Issues

After the last quality attribute scenario is analyzed, the quality process engineer should ask the scribe to review the list of recorded issues. Each one should be projected, or hard copies should be made available for all of the attendees. Each issue should be read aloud. After reading the issue, the facilitator should then ask the attendees if there are any comments or clarifications regarding the issue. The issue should be amended with additional information as necessary. The issues should be reviewed for both internal and external evaluations because this is the key output of stage 4 and is the primary input for stage 5. For external evaluations, the facilitator should remind the attendees that each of these issues will be studied, and a specific strategy for addressing each will be devised. It is essential that all of the attendees get a copy of the recorded issues after internal reviews because they will need this information for stage 5. However, it is also a good idea to circulate the recorded issues to all of the attendees for external evaluations as well.

Advice for Questioners

The most difficult task for architecture design teams to learn, adopt, and master seems to be developing effective questioning techniques. The most problematic area of the evaluation method described here (and with ATAM) is that of questioning. It can be hard to know when to challenge the architect, how much design detail to explore, and when to raise an issue. Although any attendee can ask questions during the evaluation workshop, often the most critical technical scrutiny comes from the architecture design team itself. While technically astute, it can be hard to know what to look for in design, how to start asking questions, what to focus on and when, what to ignore, and how to determine if something is an issue to be raised. This is especially true for stakeholders participating in their first evaluation. The quality of the evaluation process (internal or external) is critical to ACDM and is highly dependent upon the quality of the questions asked by the participants of the evaluation workshop. Unfortunately, asking insightful and probing questions seems to be more of a black art than a rigorous science. This is partially true because the design of software-intensive systems is not a rigorous formula as of yet—and it may never be. However, based on experience with scenario-based evaluation techniques such as ATAM and ACDM, some guidance is provided here as to what the readers should focus on and when, and how they should formulate good, probing questions during evaluations.

Scrutinize Consistency

Inconsistencies are usually detected in the architectural documentation. Scrutiny of the architectural documentation begins in advance of the actual evaluation workshop. It takes practice to learn how to read design documentation with a critical eye, but with practice inconsistencies are as obvious as a large neon sign on a moonless night in a dark alley. Intuitively one may think it is a simple matter of addressing documentation and representation inconsistencies by simply fixing the prose or diagram, or adding missing information. Occasionally this is the case, but this is the exception rather than the norm. Inconsistencies in documentation nearly always reflect inconsistent thinking in the mind of the designer, and it is directly reflected in the design artifacts. Inconsistencies occur most often in drawings and diagrams that show elements and relationships that are inconsistent with the stated perspective. If perspective is not consistent in the mind of the architect, then it will never be right in the documentation. For example, consider the case of classes shown in a dynamic representation. This is a case of implicitly mixing perspectives that may indicate that the architect does not understand the design or notation, or the design may not be completely thought through. At the very least, there is an inconsistency with the representation.

The questioner should challenge the architect to explain inconsistencies such as these (usually the responses are entertaining). Sometimes this is a completeness problem—the design is not done. This frequently happens in early evaluation cycles in ACDM. In other cases, architects will not be consistent in their use of notation—whether a standard notation like UML is used or not. Sometimes the nature of elements and relations are not specified; there are no element-relationship responsibility tables. Elements and relations are not identified as to whether they are processes and data flow, threads and control flow, classes and call-return, or something else. Look for a legend that explains the elements and relations. If there is no legend and the elements and relations do not have names associated with them, then it is almost a certainty that the architect does not have a clear idea of what the elements and relationships are. If he or she does not clearly establish this in the design, then it will be determined later during detailed design or implementation, when it is too late to guarantee broad systemic properties. If the perspective of the drawings is not clear and the elements and relationships are not named, then it is impossible to understand the design or evaluate its fitness for purpose. Certainly this must be raised as an issue. Another problem with consistency is having objects like lines and boxes mean different things in a single representation. Architecture representations can be complex, and it can be difficult for the architect to come up with creative ways to represent different elements of the design. However, it is critical that if a square box is used to represent a process, then it always represents a process in the same representation. It is best if a consistent notation can be applied across the entire suite of architecture design documentation, but this is often impossible. If different colors are used by the architect, then they should be used consistently. If hard copies are handed out to evaluation workshop attendees, they must be in color as well so the representations can be read and understood. Representations require prose, but the prose description of a representation must match any diagrams, figures, tables, and so forth the prose attempts to explain. The terminology used in the representations must also be consistent with the prose. If there are enough of these kinds of inconsistency problems, it may warrant postponing the evaluation until these issues are resolved, especially if an external evaluation is planned.

Too Much or Too Little Detail

It can be confusing to know if there is too much or too little detail in the architecture design. To these ends, some guidance is provided here in terms of how much detail is a reasonable level to expect in architecture designs to facilitate evaluation. Recall that architecture design is about partitioning and defining the elements, the relationships among the elements, and explicitly assigning responsibilities to the elements and relationships. As indicated earlier, the level of details addressed by the architecture design depends upon the scope of the project, the size and scope of the system or product, the business context, and the architect's position in the design hierarchy. Because of this, it is impossible to give precise instructions for what is too much or too little design detail for the architecture, and how much detail will be required during an evaluation. Evaluating how elements provide the various services may be more detailed than necessary but should not be summarily dismissed. No detail is too miniscule if it affects broad systemic properties. Some elements will require more detailed design than others to ensure that the system implemented from the design functions and behaves as specified. Similarly, different kinds of analysis may require different levels of design detail. For example, if modifiability is an important quality attribute requirement, or if the system elements will be built by highly distributed teams, then it may be necessary to evaluate the detailed element interfaces to ensure that the design will meet these requirements. However, for the same system, analyzing functionality may be a simple matter of scrutinizing the gross partitioning and the responsibilities assigned to the elements with little more detail than what is provided by the context drawing. In this case, overall functionality can be reasonably ensured by scrutinizing the coarse-grained design decisions. The design on the element internals can be reasonably deferred to downstream designers and implementers with reasonable confidence. Of course, this does require some judgment on the part of the questioner. However, if in doubt, ask! After all, this is your job as a questioner.

If during an evaluation the questioner cannot reasonably determine if the architecture will respond (quality attribute) or provide the desired service (use case), then press the architect for more details. If the details are not available, or the architect is unable to express his or her design decision, then the questioner should explore why. Is the problem that these design decisions were not adequately explained by the architect? Is insufficient data or experience available to answer the question? Is the problem that the response cannot be precisely measured? The questioner should try to determine why the response cannot be described. If an issue is raised, make sure to include this information on the issue recording template, as it can help address the issue later. Addressing the issue may be as simple as fixing the representation and documentation, or it may involve more detailed design work, or perhaps going back to the stakeholders and revisiting the requirements.

Guidance on Questioning during Functional Analysis

As described earlier, functional analysis tends to be a bit more straightforward than structural analysis because what the entities do and provide, and how the system responds are listed in the discrete steps of the functional use cases for all to see and review. However, it can still be a tricky matter to probe the design and gain insight as to whether it will satisfy the functional requirements. The essence of functional analysis is to ensure that the design will result in a correct implementation. Although there are many opportunities for functional defects to be injected between architecture design and implementation, we want to avoid errors due to architectural design problems. These are the most difficult and expensive to fix. As the analysis of a functional use case begins, scrutinize the use case text carefully. If the use case is wrong, incomplete, or inconsistent, the design may be wrong, and any implementation based on the design will be wrong. What often happens during functional analysis is that steps are missing in the use case, or the steps occur out of order. Hopefully these problems are discovered by the designer and corrected during stage 2, but sometimes they are not uncovered until the evaluation. Missing or out-of-order steps in the functional use cases can affect the design and evaluation of the architecture. As functional analysis proceeds, questioners should scrutinize the steps of the use case as closely as they scrutinize how well the design satisfies the use case. It can be a challenging task to check the use case and scrutinize the design, but this becomes easier with practice. In the moments before the architect traces the use case through the design, read the use case, paying particular attention to the steps of the use case and their ordering. This can be especially helpful for the evaluation if the questioner has domain experience in doing what is described by the use case. Again, this is the power of community evaluations using structured, social evaluation methods. Another problem with use cases is in that pre- and postconditions are not specified, are incorrect, overlooked, or not given serious attention. Questioners should reconsider the pre- and postconditions to ensure they are understood, seem to be reasonable, and are based on reasonable assumptions. If they are not correct, then the steps of the use case may not matter—the entire use case may be invalidated. Ensuring that pre- and postconditions are met is an essential part of functional analysis. Before the steps of the use case can be executed with predictable results, the preconditions must be true, and after executing the steps of the use case, the postconditions must be true. If it cannot be shown that the pre- and postconditions hold, then the use case is essentially invalid. The questioners must press the architect to describe how the design satisfies these conditions. If it is not clear after the architect's explanation, then the questioners have the responsibility to raise an issue.

Guidance on Questioning during Structural Analysis

If questioning the architect during functional analysis is as tricky as algebra, then asking good, probing questions during structural analysis is like multivariable calculus. This is because the stimuli, artifacts, environmental variables and conditions, responses, and response measures may be difficult for the architect to represent and describe. Furthermore, while analyzing structures with respect to one quality attribute response, other quality attribute responses can be affected. It is often the case that when analyzing a quality attribute scenario, the architectural decisions made regarding the primary quality attribute responses are deemed satisfactory with respect to the response measures described in the scenario. However, those same design decisions can ultimately be unacceptable because of their negative impact on other system quality attribute properties. This can make evaluating the architectural structures difficult. This is also why analyzing designs with respect to quality attribute requirements often takes so much more time than analyzing functionality.

In beginning the analysis of a quality attribute scenario, questioners should first scrutinize the scenario. Check each part of the scenario: source, stimulus, artifact, environment, response, and response measure. Are they understandable and consistent? If they are not clear, are unrealistic, or wrong, then it will make the already difficult task of evaluating the design structures nearly impossible. Questioners should not be afraid to ask clarifying questions about the scenario, even if they seem obvious. Dumb questions are often not dumb at all—many consultants earn handsome salaries by asking dumb questions. Architects and other technical experts are often so focused on details that they can miss the obvious. Scenario response measures can be problematic in many ways. They are often mischaracterized, poorly articulated, inconsistent, and not properly quantified. If the response measures are not precisely quantified, establish some hypothetical measures in three degrees. In terms of measures that are: (1) very difficult to attain, (2) challenging to attain, and (3) relatively easy to attain. This will give the evaluators some range of reference to determine how fit the architecture is in its response to the stimuli described by the scenario. The architecture design team will then have more data to support their follow-up analysis of the scenario after the evaluation workshop. Another issue to beware of is the scenario's real quality attribute concern. Sometimes the quality attribute referenced by the scenario does not match the indicated responses and response measures. This can provide a false sense of what is important to pay attention to during analysis. Consider the example scenario snippet in Table 11.9.

Note that the quality attribute of interest cited in this scenario is usability. However, look closely at the response: "The new and legacy data formats are interpreted or recognized by the system and are easily imported and correctly merged into the database system." Certainly if the system did this, it would be more usable. However, is this an issue that can be addressed by usability tactics, strategies, and structures? Probably not. Consider the response measure: "No modification to the code or reconfiguration is required." Clearly this response measure is not visible to the user. Again, although a system that is able to respond this way may be deemed more usable, there is a huge difference between what is normally thought of as usability and the response measure

Table 11.9   Example of Scenario

Quality attribute	Usability
Source(s) of the stimulus	End user
Stimulus	User wants to merge new data and legacy data into the current database system
Environment	During normal use and operation
Architectural elements	The new and legacy data sources and the system's existing database
System response	The new and legacy data formats are interpreted or recognized by the system and are easily imported and correctly merged into the database system
Response measure(s)	No modification to the code or reconfiguration is required

described here. This response measure seems to indicate that data and format compatibility are the real properties needed in the system, and the attendees should be focused on trying to analyze the structures in the design that support this kind of compatibility. However, when attendees see *usability* listed in the scenario, their collective attention may be focused on the user interface element and the related structures. Often in cases like this, the real quality attribute concern is never identified or analyzed. As the analysis of the scenario begins, the questioner should focus on creating a mental picture of the stimulus and the source, and their relation to the design of the artifact under the environmental conditions described by the quality attribute scenario. This is the context of the scenario as shown in Figure 11.4.

This can help ensure that the scenario is clear and consistent in the mind of the questioner. If the picture is not obvious and it is not clarified during the architect's explanation and presentation, then the questioner should engage the architect and press him or her to establish these relationships. If the scenario context cannot be adequately established, then the questioner should consider this an issue.

The essence of structural analysis is for attendees to evaluate the partitioning decisions and the structures selected by the architect to measure how well they satisfy the response measures described in the quality attribute scenario. This is trickier than it sounds because it is impossible to evaluate a set of architectural decisions with respect to a single quality attribute. For example, those structures that may promote modifiability may also inhibit the performance of the system. So during the evaluation of a quality attribute scenario, we must also consider the relative side effects on other quality attributes of architectural decisions selected to promote a given quality attribute. Certainly any significant trade-offs should be raised as an issue, especially if it is not clear if it is the right trade-off, or if the trade-off was made implicitly by the architect. As the architect begins to trace through the design, questioners should think in terms of what structures were selected by the architect and why. Sometimes they are obvious, such as well-known patterns visible in the design with well-understood properties. This

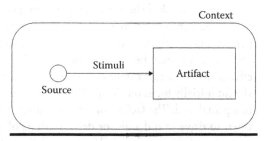

Figure 11.4   Quality attribute scenario context.

can help questioners determine the effect that the design choices will have on systemic quality attribute properties. For the various structures and ensembles of the design, questioners should try to create a mental list of the quality attribute properties that the structures promote and inhibit. If you are like the author, maybe you are a bit scatterbrained at times and find it hard to focus during evaluation workshops. So it can be useful to jot down the scenario context shown in Figure 11.4 on a scratch pad and add information like this to the scenario context as the architect traces through the design. It is usually not enough for the questioners to restrict their attention to one structure because most architectural designs are composed of ensembles of structures. Questioners should try to evaluate the aggregate ensemble of structures and determine the net effect they will have on the system's overall quality attribute responses. For example, while a client/server structure inhibits security, an encrypted connection between the client and server can offset some of the inherit weakness of the client/server pattern's ability to promote security. The net effect of these design choices on security should be evaluated, not just the effect one of these structures in isolation has on the quality attribute. Questioners may be inclined to ask: What kind of encryption algorithm was used, and does it sufficiently protect the data? If the architect does not know, then this might be an issue. Another question might be, Does this strategy provide the right kind of security, or does the system also need to authenticate users, detect intrusions, or something else? If these other aspects of security are not addressed by the scenario being evaluated, or other quality attribute scenarios, a questioner should be suspicious and should be motivated to press the architect about other aspects of security if they are not addressed in the collection of quality attribute scenarios. The problem may not be design oriented, but perhaps the security requirements were not understood well enough to design the system's security mechanisms.

Initially, questioners should evaluate the design choices the architect made with the desired responses and response measures described in the scenario being analyzed. However, questioners should also realize that there will be side effects on other quality attributes, and they should pay attention to those as well. This multidimensional nature of structural analysis is what makes analyzing design structures so challenging. For example, while the design choices above improve security, the net effect of using the client/server pattern and encryption tactics will be negative on performance. This is an engineering trade-off. Perhaps this trade-off was made consciously by the architect, but perhaps not. Maybe this trade-off was made consciously by the architect, without studying the impact to performance. All of this is fertile ground for the questioner to formulate probing questions and raise issues. The questioner should ask the architect if this is a reasonable trade-off and if he or she has studied or modeled the performance impact of encryption and latency between the client and server elements. The questioner should scan the collection of quality attribute scenarios to see if there are performance-oriented scenarios. If not, then it might be appropriate to ask if there are any performance requirements. If there are performance scenarios, it may be appropriate to note the performance issues and raise them now, but defer detailed performance analysis until the performance scenarios are analyzed. If there are not performance scenarios, this may be an issue worth raising. Although it is important to pay attention to the effects that structures have on other quality attributes and the inherent trade-offs, the analysis should initially focus on the quality attribute primary response measures described in the scenario being analyzed. The facilitator must pay attention to the analysis dialog and help the group decide when to drive into details, or defer analysis of quality attribute side effects until the appropriate scenario is being analyzed. There is a delicate balance to strike between analyzing the primary quality attribute response and analyzing the side effects impacting other quality attributes. Unfortunately, it is impossible to give precise rules for when to cut conversation off and defer discussion on these matters until later, but it does get easier with practice. The facilitator is responsible for using his or her judgment, watching the clock, and maintaining this precarious balance. One rule of thumb for managing the analysis of secondary effects is that if secondary quality attribute effects are covered by other quality attribute scenarios that are planned to be analyzed during the evaluation workshop, then consider deferring the discussion until those quality attribute scenarios are analyzed. The facilitator should record the issue publicly, but defer the detailed analysis until later. However, once deferred, the facilitator owes it to the attendees to make sure those scenarios addressing those quality attributes are analyzed later in the evaluation. If effects on other quality attributes are discovered while analyzing a quality attribute scenario, but there are no scenarios to address these quality attributes, then this is an issue. Certainly this may not be a problem if the quality attribute is not important or the effect is minor, but this can be decided later—the issue should be raised.

Advice for Facilitation

Communication is a complex process of sharing, interpreting, and receiving information. The process of communication is one that is deeply affected by culture (corporate and societal), personal character traits, and the environmental setting. Good communication is essential for productive design evaluation workshops, and sound facilitation is essential for encouraging attendees to communicate during the workshop in a constructive way. Much has been written about the "soft skills" required to facilitate group communication. Unfortunately, a complete treatment on the topic of facilitation is beyond the scope of this text, but good facilitation skills are essential to the evaluation process and are critical to productive evaluation workshops. This is especially true for evaluations that have a significant number of external stakeholders in attendance. Nothing can destroy an evaluation faster than a poorly facilitated evaluation workshop. To these ends, a few guidelines are provided here to help facilitators manage the evaluation process. If you are already a skilled facilitator, these guidelines can help you transition into the role of facilitating an architecture design evaluation workshop. If you are experienced at facilitation, this will be an easy transition. However, if you have never facilitated a meeting, get some training, practice, or preferably both before you attempt to lead an external architecture design evaluation workshop. Your results may vary, but in the author's experience, inexperienced facilitators are eaten alive by blood-thirsty engineers during design evaluations. This can undermine the productivity of the evaluation, leave the architect unprotected from the onslaught of questioners, and may leave the attendees with a bad evaluation experience. As a result, design evaluations may be avoided in the future.

Be Impartial

The facilitator for ACDM design evaluation workshops is the quality process engineer. This choice was made for two primary reasons. First, the fitness of a design for its intended purpose is a quality issue that is judged through the evaluation process. Therefore, it seemed to make sense that the quality process engineer should have ownership of the evaluation process because the quality (goodness) of the design is his or her responsibility. The second reason is that they are somewhat impartial with respect to the design decisions. Note that the quality process engineer does not have specific responsibilities associated with designing the architecture. This is left largely to the chief architect and chief scientist. While the quality process engineer coordinates and leads reviews of the design artifacts, he or she does not design. Certainly, this separation may be impractical in some smaller teams, and the issue of tailoring ACDM will be addressed later, in Section 3. This separation of concerns was intentionally designed into ACMD so that quality process engineers could look upon the design artifact with some degree of impartiality. Certainly they are part of the architecture design team, and as such, they do share ownership for the design and its creation. This may appear to be a contradiction and a conflict of interest. However, this is a little like a police officer who is a citizen of a town, but is also responsible for maintaining the order of the town's citizenry. One could argue there is a conflict of interest for the police officer. However, there is also a certain motivation for him or her to ensure that the town (or the architecture in the case of the quality process engineer) is an orderly and tranquil place to live because he or she is also a citizen of the town. This same philosophy was applied to the role of the quality process engineer and his or her relationship to the design. This impartiality with a commensurate level of ownership is an important team dynamic built into ACDM. With the roles and responsibilities of the quality process engineer as a facilitator, some guidelines for facilitating design evaluation workshops follow.

Listen

The best facilitators say very little relative to their role as a meeting leader. During well-facilitated meetings, facilitators manage the discussion of the participants to keep the meeting focused on the task at hand—evaluation in the case of ACDM, stage 4. Facilitators must discipline themselves to stay engaged throughout the evaluation and listen to both content (verbal) and feelings (non-verbal) expressed by the attendees. Unlike other attendees, the facilitator cannot drift off for a few minutes for a mental break by day dreaming. Listening is an active behavior, not a passive one. Facilitators should listen to what is said by the attendees, and if it seems their message is unclear or that other attendees are disengaged, the facilitator may want to reiterate the attendee's message. This is important if the facilitator feels that an important point or issue was discussed but missed by the attendees. While the facilitator may sense that the speaker's message was not understood by the attendees, he or she cannot just interrupt the speaker and say, "Hey boneheads! Listen up!" Although this approach might work in a military bootcamp, this could alienate some attendees during a design evaluation workshop. This matter should be approached a bit more delicately. The facilitator should wait for an opportune moment to interrupt the speaker and say something like, "Joe, hold on for a minute. Let me test my understanding, I think you just said … Is this correct? Do I understand you properly?" This approach does not indict the attendees for not paying attention, but rather, the facilitator takes responsibility for not understanding what was said (even if he or she did understand the message) by saying, "Let *me* test *my* understanding." In addition to listening to actual spoken messages, facilitators must also listen for implied messages and make them explicit in a sensitive way to the attendees. For example, if the facilitator sees an engineer shaking his or her head as the architect explains the design, the facilitator may inject by saying, "Joe, I sense that you are not comfortable with that approach. What is your experience?" There are a variety of similar techniques a facilitator can use to engage the audience, such as:

- Clarification and paraphrasing: Clarification is the technique used above, where the facilitator will wait for a speaker to finish, or wait for an opportune moment to interrupt a speaker and begin by saying, "Let me test my understanding." After this statement, the architect will restate the point that the speaker just made and ask if this is what was meant. This is useful if a speaker is inarticulate or having a difficult time making his or her point, or if the speaker is stringing together many ideas. Paraphrasing can be used to aid in clarification to rephrase a confusing explanation in a concise way or consolidate a long list of points made. The facilitator is advised to be judicious in his or her use of clarification and paraphrasing. It is impossible to clarify every single point made, and it can be annoying and disruptive to the discussion. When paraphrasing, the facilitator should be careful not to insert his or her own meaning or opinion in the paraphrased message, as this may jeopardize his or her impartiality. When paraphrasing, always confirm the paraphrased message with the speaker by saying, "Did I understand you?" or "Did I get that right?"

- Reflecting: At certain points, a speaker may make a list of assertions about the design. Rather than accepting them and moving on, the facilitator may challenge the group by asking them, "What does everyone else think about what Joe just said?" or "Does anyone else have a different viewpoint?" After challenging the group, the facilitator should wait for a few moments and allow the attendees to reflect. If no one offers a counterpoint, then move on. Caution should be used with reflecting. Too much reflection slows down the pace and tempo of the evaluation workshop and attendees may disengage.

- Redirection: Facilitators are often viewed as experts, and attendees will ask questions of facilitators. If the questions are procedural in nature—about the evaluation process, what will happen next, who is responsible for certain activities—the facilitator should not hesitate to answer. However, if the facilitator is asked a design question relating to a choice the architect made or comment made by another attendee, it can be risky for him or her to answer, and he or she may be missing an opportunity to engage other stakeholders. The risk is that if facilitators start answering questions like these, they may lose their impartiality and squelch discussion on the topic. When questions are asked like this, it is an opportunity for the facilitator to encourage thought and debate by redirecting the question back to the attendees by saying, "That is a great question, what do others think about this question?" Facilitators should moderate their use of redirection. Too much redirection may make the facilitator appear to not possess any substantial understanding of the material, or to be totally context-free during the evaluation. Sometimes the attendees need your candid opinion, but facilitators should offer opinions in such a way as to not hamper debate and other opinions, by saying, "My opinion is ..., but my opinion is not as important as yours. What do you [attendees] think?"

- Confirmation: Confirmation is a subtle technique that can be used to get group consensus and confirmation on open points and issues. Often an attendee will state an opinion, point of view, or fact that is not openly acknowledged by the group, but one that is commonly agreed to. If the facilitator senses this, he or she can say, "It sounds like we all agree on this. Is that true?" The facilitator should then pause after asking for confirmation. This technique can settle informally agreed matters once and for all in an open way and can be useful for formally establishing assumptions. However, the facilitator should be careful to check with the group to ensure that the issue is commonly agreed to by asking, "Is this a matter we all agree to?" At this point, the confirmation becomes an implicit vote, squelching further discussion on the matter. Some stakeholders may feel alienated. If the facilitator senses this is a problem, he or she should call for an explicit vote on the matter. The confirmation technique should not be used to silence debate. If there are dissenters, their points of view and the ensuing debate should be welcomed.

These simple techniques, when properly applied, can dramatically improve the quality of a design evaluation. However, it is impossible for facilitators to engage the attendees and use any of these techniques if they are not actively listening every minute of the evaluation workshop and tuned into every message attendees transmit. So these techniques fundamentally depend upon the listening skills of the facilitator. Active listening is a powerful technique that builds credibility, increases understanding, encourages participation and openness, and can help detect and diffuse conflict before it gets out of control. Most importantly, the attendees feel that their time is being honored and their participation in the evaluation is valued. After all, we all like to be listened to.

Protect the Vulnerable

Be sensitive to those attendees exposing their artifacts or offering comment—they are vulnerable. Speaking in public is a huge risk for some people, but what they have to say is very important to the evaluation of the design. Do not let others belittle their comments, stop them from speaking, or intimidate them. Architects are showing the world their baby—the architectural design. Try to be sensitive to the fact that they are vulnerable to attack by evaluation workshop attendees. Try to ensure that attendees critique the design, not the architect.

Pay Attention to Nonverbal Cues

Many experts in communication have determined that verbal communication is only about 30 percent or so (depending upon the study and researcher) of total interpersonal communication. Nonverbal communication is a combination of body language that includes posture, gestures, facial expression, and repetitive movements (like squirming and fidgeting). Nonverbal communication may also include vocal inflection and the general attitudes of the communicators. The tone and inflection of our voices convey messages along with our choice of phrases and language, and the real message is often reinforced with body language. Facilitators must pay attention to nonverbal cues during evaluation workshops and understand the real messages being communicated. Obviously, facilitators need to observe the nonverbal cues of the attendees as they speak to understand the real messages and dynamics of the evaluation workshop dialog. Some attendees may be bored, tired, hungry, impatient, anxious, and so forth, but they never articulate these messages verbally. However, an observant facilitator can pick up nonverbal cues that may indicate that there are issues, and the facilitator should address them openly with verbal language. For example, if a facilitator sees an attendee dosing off and another staring out the window, this may be an indication that the attendees are tired and bored. The facilitator can address this openly by calling for a break, or if a break is inappropriate, he or she can say something like, "I know everyone is tired, but I need your attention for a few more minutes, so please bear with me." Nonverbal cues are twofold. Facilitators need to be aware of the nonverbal cues they project as well as the unspoken messages communicated within the group. An improperly placed nonverbal cue may send a signal of disinterest, partiality, impatience, or anger, even though these messages were not explicitly spoken, and in some cases were not even intended. Some nonverbal cues are unintended habits and send messages that are not true. The author has a bad habit of twirling pens, pencils, and markers in his hands. It is an innocent nervous habit, but can be interpreted as boredom or impatience.

Manage Unproductive Behaviors

Facilitators need to be aware of the group dynamics during an evaluation workshop and remain vigilant against bad behaviors that could undermine the evaluation. For example, facilitators may have one person who tries to dominate the evaluation and discussion, another who may have a war story for every comment or situation, and still others who say absolutely nothing. All of these behaviors are unproductive to one degree or another and need to be managed. Facilitators must correct inappropriate behavior as soon as possible. If they do not, then they are implicitly rewarding the unproductive behaviors. A few guidelines for dealing with unproductive behaviors follow:

- Engaging the ghosts: It is important that everyone participate in the evaluation, but there are always those who say nothing and are like ghosts hiding in the corner. Facilitators should recognize the ghost and invite his opinion by saying, "Joe, we haven't heard from you yet today. Do you have anything to add?" Note that this is a deliberate closed-ended question that gives the participant the option of simply saying no. This is intentional and respects the person's right to not participate, but it specifically invites him to. Silent individuals or subgroups can be drawn into participation by explicitly polling each person in turn and asking for his or her input on the topic.

- Please shut up: Sometimes the art of facilitation boils down to being able to tell someone to shut up in such a way that they are not offended and will indeed shut up. During an evaluation workshop, each attendee must have an opportunity to voice his or her concerns, opinions, and ideas fully. Facilitators must not let the discussion be dominated by a few, nor must they tolerate interruptions by other participants. Be direct. For example, "Joe, we've heard your issue with this design decision. Let's see if anyone else has anything to add to what you have said." Talkers can also be allies in drawing out the ghosts. During a break, recruit the talkers to help engage the ghosts. Ask the talkers what ideas they may have for engaging the ghosts. Suggest that you may intentionally not engage them (the talker) at times to give others an opportunity to speak. If one person monopolizes the discussion, other participants leave the evaluation workshop feeling that they did not have an opportunity to speak and that their time was not honored. People leaving with such feelings will probably not attend another evaluation.

- Side conversations: There should only be one evaluation workshop, and one person should speak at a time. Facilitators should stop side conversations as soon as they start. Standing next to the persons involved can silence side conversations. Sometimes a more direct approach is required. If the disruption persists, speak to the persons involved during a break to ensure there is not another problem.

- Be there or be square: Participation has to be full-time. Poor or sporadic attendance will undermine the evaluation workshop. As discussed earlier, reinforce the attendance message, ask attendees to turn off cell phones, and discourage attendees from answering e-mail during the workshop proceedings.

- Stay on topic: The facilitator controls the agenda and is responsible for adhering to the schedule as closely as possible. It is easy for attendees to degenerate into office politics or get sidetracked by discussions that are only marginally related to the evaluation. Facilitators should stick to the agenda and evaluation process. Do not let tangential discussions consume the evaluation workshop timing budget. Stop discussions that are not related to the topic with phrases such as "This is a good question, but this is not related to the evaluation;

let's record this for later discussion and get back to the evaluation." Record the key points of the discussion in the "parking lot" and continue with the evaluation. A parking lot is a place on a whiteboard or flip chart somewhere in the room where issues not related to the evaluation are recorded for later discussion.

■ Stay out of the weeds: It is easy to get bogged down with details during an architecture evaluation workshop. As introduced earlier, engineers will naturally want to explore details and solve problems that are not relevant to the evaluation of the architecture design. The facilitator must pay particular attention to the details being discussed and control the level of detail and curb problem solving during the evaluation workshop.

Know Thyself

When assuming the role as facilitator and preparing for evaluations, facilitators are strongly encouraged to examine their own leadership and communication styles. Be as honest as possible with yourself; assess your strengths and weaknesses. If you find it painfully difficult to speak publicly, ask someone to stop talking, or press a group of engineers to focus on the evaluation, then facilitation will be hard for you. These are things that a facilitator may have to do 20 times during a single evaluation workshop. Facilitators need to be reminded that they often set the tone and character for the evaluation, and the energy they pump into the workshop is critical for ensuring that the evaluation is productive. Attendees feed off of the energy the facilitator brings into the evaluation, or they will starve from the lack of energy brought by the facilitator. This having been said, facilitators are best when they are themselves and try not to be pretentious or portray a false image to the attendees. This will be interpreted as being disingenuous and will impact the credibility of the facilitator and could undermine the evaluation. A good sense of humor can be extremely helpful to facilitators, and humor can be an effective communication tool if used appropriately and not overdone. Humor can put the attendees at ease and help them feel more comfortable and open up during the evaluation. Self-deprecating humor can be helpful in putting attendees at ease and putting a human face on the facilitator, but facilitators should always avoid ridicule or sarcasm of any attendees. What may be humorous to one person could be offensive to another, and humor is highly dependent upon culture. If the facilitator is dealing with cross-cultural teams, the best advice is to avoid humor until he or she better understands the cultures he or she is dealing with or risk an embarrassing social faux pas. Attitude is a critical element for successful facilitation. The best facilitators have a lot of energy and always project a positive attitude, especially in stressful situations. While successful facilitators will aggressively manage the evaluation workshop and focus on results, they must balance these goals and be sensitive to the needs of the attendees.

Updating the Master Plan

Planning and tracking the activities of stage 4 design evaluation is more straightforward and easier to quantify than the activities in the preceding stages of ACDM thus far. As stage 4 concludes, the master design plan should be updated, with the actual effort spent evaluating the architecture design.

Summary

Stage 4 is a critical stage in the ACDM where the architecture design is evaluated and the output will be used to determine if a system is ready for production or will be used to refine the architecture design. The evaluation method described in stage 4 evaluates the architecture design created in stage 3, based on the architecture drivers specification developed in stage 2, from the architecture drivers elicitation workshops held in stage 1. Stage 4 is a pivotal stage in the ACDM, and although mistakes can be made in stages 1 to 3, stage 4 is not so forgiving. If the evaluation in stage 4 does not uncover the design defects, missing requirements, or documentation problems, then these defects may find their way into the implemented system or product. The objective of the evaluation workshop is not to fix problems, but identify issues. An issue is a discrepancy in the architectural design or design documentation that may compromise the fitness of the design with respect to the architectural driver. The purpose of the evaluation workshop is not to determine if issues are risks, problems, trade-offs, and so forth. The evaluation workshop is not a forum for addressing issues and fixing design defects. Classifying the issues and addressing them is an exercise left to stage 5. All of these activities take too much time if done during the evaluation workshop, and drive up the cost of evaluating the architecture design. The sole purpose of the evaluation workshop, and stage 4 in general, is to determine how fit the architecture design is with respect to the architecture drivers and raise issues that may compromise the design's ability to satisfy the architecture drivers. What these issues are, their potential effects, and how they will be addressed is dealt with in stages 5 and 6 of ACDM. The evaluation method described here can be used for internal evaluations conducted within the architecture design team, or can be used with broader groups of stakeholders as necessary to evaluate the design. The method uses the functional use cases, the quality attribute scenarios, and the constraints documented in the architecture drivers specification in stage 2 as a means for testing the architecture design. Stage 4 is comprised of the following key activities:

- Stage 4 planning: Stage 4 begins with the managing engineer estimating the duration and resources required for the evaluation workshop. In general, greater time should be budgeted for external evaluations than for internal evaluations. Evaluation planning templates were provided to guide the estimation of the time and resources, and for planning the logistics of the evaluation. Evaluation workshops are typically short in duration. Experience with ACDM has shown that ACDM evaluation workshops can take anywhere from a few hours to two days.

- Internal evaluations: Internal evaluation workshops are evaluations of the architecture design that are conducted by the architecture design team. Internal evaluations are easier and less expensive to conduct, but also suffer from not having the broader participation of other stakeholders. It is strongly recommended that at least the first evaluation be conducted internally because the design is relatively immature, and the cost of external evaluations is relatively high in comparison to internal evaluations.

- External evaluations: External evaluations involve a significant number of stakeholders external to the architecture design team. Typically the number of attendees at external evaluation workshops is higher than the number of attendees at internal evaluations. The cost of an external evaluation is higher than that for an internal evaluation, and it is much more difficult to facilitate. Because of this, the architecture design should be relatively mature before conducting an external evaluation. However, the benefit is that with more stakeholders engaged, the architecture design is scrutinized more closely, and stakeholders with domain experience can bring their experience to bear on the evaluation. It is strongly recommended that at least one external evaluation be conducted if possible and practical.

■ Update the master design plan: The master design plan is initially updated at the beginning of stage 4, with the estimates of the time and resources required to conduct the evaluation workshop. At the conclusion of the evaluation workshop, the master design plan is updated with the actual time and resources expended during stage 4.

Chapter 12

ACDM Stage 5:
The Go/No-Go Decision

Purpose

The primary purpose of stage 5 is for the architecture design team to analyze the issues uncovered in stage 4 during the architectural design evaluation and devise concrete strategies for how to address each issue. Each issue will be analyzed, and a specific deposition action for each will be decided upon. The team will then decide whether the design is ready for the production stages, or if the architecture design should be further refined and evaluated.

Preconditions

Before undertaking stage 5, the architecture design must have been evaluated and the issues from the evaluation recorded and available to all of the architecture design team.

General Activities
Techniques, Templates, and Guidance

- Issue deposition document template
- Go/no-go decision guidance

Primary Artifacts

The primary artificat is the issue deposition document.

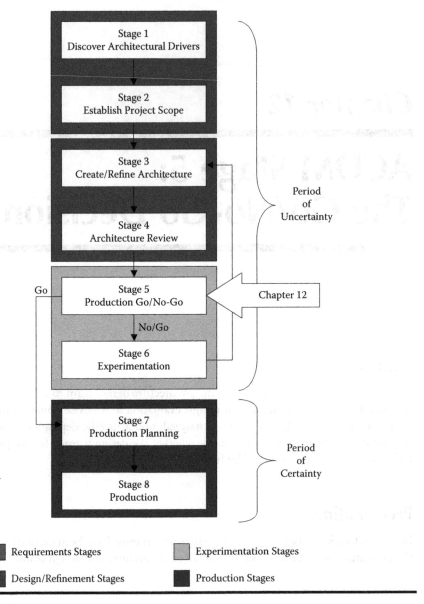

Figure 12.1 Stage 5.

Postconditions

- There is a concrete strategy for how the issues uncovered during the stage 4 evaluation will be addressed by the architecture design team.
- A decision is made as to whether the team will further refine the architecture design through experimentation (stage 6), or if the team will begin planning the implementation of the design in the production stages (stages 7 and 8).

Table 12.1 Stage 5 Activities, Outputs, and Responsibilities

General activities	Evaluate the list of issues uncovered in architecture evaluation (stage 4) and determine how each issue will be addressed. Make a go/no-go decision. A go decision means the architecture is fit and ready for production; a no-go decision means that the architecture needs further refinement.
General outputs	Issue disposition document. A go/no-go decision.
Role	**Stage 5 Recommended Responsibilities**
Managing engineer	Plan, coordinate, track, and oversee stage 5 design evaluation follow-up activities. Arrange and lead the issue analysis meetings.
Chief architect	During issue analysis meetings, propose how the various issues will be addressed.
Chief scientist	Work with the chief architect during issue analysis meetings to propose how the various issues will be addressed.
Requirements engineer	Participate in the issue analysis meetings. If requirements traceability is important, the requirements engineer may track the issues raised, map their effect back to the requirements, and track the issues to resolution.
Quality process engineer	Participate in the issue analysis meetings. Ensure that each issue raised during the architecture design evaluation (stage 4) has been addressed. Compile the issue disposition document, coordinate its review, and circulate it among the stakeholders for comment.
Support engineer	Participate in the issue analysis meetings.
Production engineers	Participate in the issue analysis meetings.

Description of Stage 5

Stage 5 is a key intersection in ACDM. Although this stage is typically much shorter than the other stages, the activities of stage 5 are critically important for establishing what the architecture design team will do next. Again, at this time the team is still in the period of uncertainty and will decide if their design is ready for production planning and implementation, or whether they need to continue refining the design. In other methodologies, decisions such as these are implicit and based on the instinct of the architect and other technical experts. Judgment is still required to render this decision in the ACDM context. However, in ACDM the decision to continue refinement or begin production is based on the issues uncovered in stage 4 and their analysis in stage 5. If the decision is made to continue refinement, the issue analysis will guide the refinement of the design. Specific actions to gather data, resolve issues, and refine the design are planned and executed in stage 6, before the architecture design is refined by returning to stage 3. After the design is refined, the team will again evaluate the design (stage 4) and again determine if the design is ready for production or if further refinement is required (stage 5). This is the iterative design refinement built into ACDM.

Stage 5 Planning

Stage 5 planning involves determining the amount of time that the architecture design team antici-pates they will spend analyzing the issues that were uncovered during the architecture design evalu-ation in stage 4. After the first evaluation of the architecture there are typically many more issues that will require further discussion and analysis, so the first iteration through stage 5 can take longer. Also, if this is the first time that the team has done this kind of analysis, it may take longer. In these cases, the managing engineer should include some buffer for the issue analysis meetings. Unlike stage 4 activities, the issue analysis activities in stage 5 are more difficult to predict. As such, the engineering manager should try to establish schedule and resource budgets and aggressively try to stick to them throughout stage 5. It is difficult to provide concrete checklists for planning the issue analysis meetings because their duration depends upon the number of issues uncovered during the analysis, the complexity of the issues, and the size and scope of the project. As the architecture matures in successive refinement iterations, stage 5 becomes much easier and will take significantly less time. In smaller projects, stage 5 can last one afternoon; in large projects, stage 5 can take weeks. A general rule of thumb is difficult to establish for the duration of stage 5—the more issues raised in stage 4, the more time it will take to wade through them and assign actions to each. For reasons that will be discussed, issue analysis is best when conducted within the architecture design team. One side effect of this is that the planning and execution of the issue analysis meetings is much easier than having to coordinate meetings with stakeholders from all over the planet. However, if the architecture design team is a distributed design team, this may not be the case (issues associated with distributed design and development using ACDM will be discussed in Section 3 of the text). As in the other stages of ACDM planning, stage 5 is led by the managing engineer. Table 12.2 lists a number of items to consider when planning the evaluation of stage 5.

A key activity that will drive stage 5 planning is the analysis of the issues uncovered during the evaluation workshop. Unlike other ACDM meetings, where detailed structure and agendas are provided, it is much more difficult to predict the exact agenda of issue analysis meetings. Like all meetings, preparation makes the meeting productive; some guidance for structuring these meetings is provided here. The good news is the task of analyzing each issue and deciding upon a course of action for each is relatively straightforward. However, teams can get into lengthy debates over how particular issues should be addressed, so reaching consensus on these matters can be challenging. In field trials with ACDM, architecture design teams tended to get good at analyzing issues relatively quickly, and stage 5 tended to progress very quickly. The go/no-go decision can be another chal-lenge that the team will have in stage 5. General go/no-go criteria are provided here, but ultimately the architecture design team will have to apply their own judgment as to whether to refine the archi-tecture or press on to production. The architecture design team will have to amend these criteria with their own go/no-go factors. The go/no-go decision is highly dependent upon many contextual factors that will influence the criteria used to determine whether to build or continue refining the architecture design. The quality process engineer is responsible for ensuring that each issue uncov-ered in the stage 4 evaluation is analyzed and a plan for addressing the issues is developed. This plan is called the issue deposition document. Although this is called a plan, it is really a simple list of the issues and how each one will be addressed. It is the quality process engineer's responsibility to write this document and see that it is internally reviewed, as well as circulated among the broader com-munity of stakeholders. Feedback from the various stakeholders may warrant more issue analysis meetings to address their feedback. Once the initial planning for stage 5 is complete, the managing engineer must update the master design plan and schedule (recall that the design schedule may be separate from the master design plan) to reflect the estimated time that will be spent in stage 5.

Table 12.2   Stage 5 Planning Considerations

Planning Consideration	Description
Updating the master design plan	Updating the master design plan should occur after the stage is planned by the managing engineer. He or she must establish a schedule and resource budget for conducting the issue analysis meetings. These estimates should be recorded in the master design plan or schedule. The master design plan must be updated at the end of stage 5 to record the actual time, effort, and resources expended in stage 5.
Planning the issue analysis meetings	Planning for the issue analysis meeting(s) is relatively trivial when compared to the architecture drivers elicitation workshops or architecture evaluation workshops. A more difficult matter can be planning how many issue analysis meetings to have. Specific planning guidance is difficult to provide because the number of meetings is dependent upon the number of issues, the complexity of issues, and the size and scope of the project.
Issue analysis meetings	The issue analysis meetings are the primary activity of stage 5. During these meetings, each issue will be reviewed and analyzed, and a course of action for each decided upon. At the last of the issue analysis meetings, the team will make a decision as to whether to continue refining the architecture (no-go) or to move on into production (go).
Reviews	The issue disposition document should be reviewed and circulated among the broader stakeholder community for comment.

The Issue Analysis Meeting

The issue analysis meeting is the forum where the members of the architecture design team review each of the issues that were raised during the evaluation workshop, and a course of action is decided upon to address the issues. The meeting is led and facilitated by the managing engineer. The quality process engineer acts as a scribe for the meeting and is responsible for recording the course of action decided upon for each issue. After the issue analysis meeting, the quality process engineer is responsible for compiling the information into the issue deposition document. Although this is called a document, it is more like a concise list that describes the actions that the team will take with respect to addressing each issue uncovered in stage 4. The issue deposition document is a kind of mini action plan for how the team will resolve the issues associated with the design.

The issue analysis meeting is a simple affair to conduct. The architecture design team should have access to the issues—ideally the issues would be projected during the meeting. The quality process engineer should be prepared to capture the deposition of each issue as it is decided. A deposition is a decided course of action that will be taken with respect to a specific issue from the issue recording template used in stage 4. Table 12.3 is the template that can be used to record issue depositions as they are decided during the issue analysis meeting. This template is partially filled in with an issue to illustrate its use.

Prior to the meeting, a brief description of the issues should be cut and pasted into the issue deposition template. This is not necessary, but it tends to ease the recording of depositions, prevent attendees from flipping through documentation to find specific issues, and can help speed the issue analysis and decision making along. Although any kind of similar table can be used to capture the issue depositions, this template has a number of important features worth reviewing. Start with the left-most column labeled "Issue No.," the reference number of the issue as it was captured on the issue recording template during the evaluation workshop. This will allow the architecture design team to refer to the issue recording document to review the context in which the issue was raised and any supporting information. In the next column, labeled "Issue Description," a brief description of the issue should be listed. This short description may be enough to jog the collective memory of the architecture design team to determine what the deposition should be and prevent the attendees from having to go back to the issues recorded during the evaluation. In short, this could save time for trivial or obvious issues. In the next column, labeled "Action," the team will decide what course of action will be taken to address the issue. A few general categories are provided in the template:

■ No action required: Often when issues are raised during architecture evaluations, the issues may not be related to the design or they may be trivial in nature. After analysis, the architecture design team may decide that the issue is really not an issue at all. Provide an explanation in comments.

■ Repair, update, or clarify the documentation: Often when issues are uncovered during evaluations, the fundamental design decisions are sound, but the documentation poorly captures and describes them. This can lead to misinterpretations and issues being raised during the evaluation workshop.

■ More technical information required: Sometimes questions are raised during the evaluation that the architect (and the architecture design team) cannot answer without additional research. This deposition is indicated when the architecture design team feels that a document or Web search will yield information that can satisfactorily address the issue. This deposition is different from the experimentation deposition in that prototyping or other similar kinds of tests and trials are not required.

■ More information on architectural drivers required: Despite the efforts to accurately capture and analyze the architectural drivers, architecture design teams can still get them wrong. Often problems with the architectural drivers are uncovered during the evaluation. To address these issues, the responsible engineer may have to go back to one or more stakeholder communities to get more information to clarify the architecture drivers.

■ Experimentation required: This is the deposition from which stage 6 gains its title. Experimentation in the ACDM context is used to address specific technical issues that cannot be resolved in any way other than by testing concepts, technology, or various design approaches. The word *experimentation* is used rather than *prototyping* because of the negative connotations associated with prototyping, which will be discussed in stage 6.

These are a few recommended, general depositions that should be considered by the architecture design team, and certainly the team may want to add to this list or remove some of those items provided here. Also note that in the example shown in Table 12.3, two actions are specified in the deposition column. In reality, any number of deposition actions can be specified for any given issue. However, any deposition (especially multiple actions) should be explained in the "Comments" column. As each issue is analyzed during the issue analysis meeting, any comments related to the deposition should be recorded in the column labeled "Comments." Any comments provided will help the engineer responsible for resolving the issue recall any important data or facts related to the deposition of the issue. The final column, labeled "Responsible Engineer," should be used to list the engineer that is responsible for addressing the issue in stage 6.

During the analysis of the issues the engineering manager will facilitate the meeting and will begin by directing the attention of the architecture design team to the first issue on the list. The engineering manager will invite any discussion on the issue and specific actions that should be taken to address the issue. In the most ideal case, the architectural design team will reach consensus regarding the deposition of issues; however, in some cases how issues are addressed can become a point of contention. It is very important for the team members to avoid fixing the architecture during this meeting. If this occurs, the meeting will quickly get out of control. The purpose of this meeting is to decide upon specific courses of action to take to address issues uncovered in stage 4. These activities will yield information that will enable the team to refine the architecture from a position of knowledge, not conjecture. In situations where the team cannot reach consensus on a course of action for a specific issue, the facilitator (engineering manager) should be prepared to present the options for deposition and bring the matter to a vote before the architecture design team.

Each issue will have a responsible engineer assigned to execute the planned action, and eventually report his or her findings back to the architecture design team. Responsible engineers can be assigned during the meeting as each issue is addressed, or assigned after the actions are assigned to the issues. There are two general options for assigning engineers to address the specific issues. In some situations it is appropriate to allow the various members of the architecture design team to volunteer to be responsible for specific issues. In other cases, it may be prudent for the managing engineer to appoint engineers to address specific issues. To ensure that the engineer's skill set matches the needs of the issue he or she is assigned to, the managing engineer should seek the council of the chief architect and the chief scientist. Whether responsibilities for the issues are assigned before or after the meeting, by volunteer, or by the managing engineer, it is important that the managing engineer monitors and balances the workload among the members of the architecture design team. To better manage workloads, it may be wise to refrain from assigning responsible engineers to issues until all of the actions are decided upon. After the issue depositions have been determined, the total workload to address the issues will be better understood, and the managing engineer can then balance the workload among the architecture design team. In some situations, it may be the case that issues must be resolved by an external expert. In these cases, the responsible engineer might be another organization, commercial vendor, or a consultant.

Each issue captured during the evaluation workshop will be addressed in turn until the entire list has been discussed and specific depositions assigned to each. Once the last issue has been analyzed, and actions assigned, the scribe (quality process engineer) will review the deposition for each issue for the attendees to ensure that all of the required information has been captured accurately. In some situations multiple issue analysis meetings may be required. This can be because circumstances dictate that external parties must be included in the issue analysis, there are a lot of issues, the issues are complex and require a significant amount of time to analyze, or some combination of these. There are two approaches that can be used to handle these situations:

- Multiple sequential issue analysis meetings: The obvious approach is to schedule sequential analysis meetings where some subset of the total number of issues is addressed in each meeting.
- Concurrent sequential issue analysis meetings: Another, not so obvious approach is to conduct concurrent analysis meetings. The list of issues is partitioned, and smaller working groups are assigned to analyze each group of issues. The managing engineer will delegate his

or her role as facilitator to other members of the architecture design team, who will each be responsible for facilitating the issue analysis meetings. Each working group should consist of two engineers who will be responsible for analyzing the issues assigned to them. As each working group is finished, they must brief the managing engineer, chief architect, and chief scientist on the contents of the issue deposition template created by the working group.

Each of these approaches has pros and cons. Multiple sequential issue analysis meetings will take more time, but all members of the architecture design team participate in how the issues will be handled. This usually results is a consistent analysis and better deposition decisions. Concurrent sequential issue analysis meetings are definitely faster and may be necessary for large projects, or for projects with lots of distributed teams and organizations participating in the design. However, not all members of the architecture design team will be able to participate in the issue analysis. This can compromise the quality of issue analysis in some cases. Another danger is that some issues are interdependent and must be addressed together. If these issues are addressed by different groups, there can be conflicting dispositions as a result or duplication of effort. The architecture design team will have to apply their judgment to decide what is in the best interest of the project.

The Go/No-Go Decision

After the last issue analysis meeting (or if there is only one issue analysis meeting), the architecture design team must make a go/no-go decision where the architecture design team decides whether the design is ready to use for detailed design and production or needs further refinement. If an issue is left unaddressed in stage 5, it must be addressed during detailed design and implementation. In some cases this is fine; in other cases it can be catastrophic. Each issue should be analyzed as to its effect on the implemented system if left unaddressed or unresolved now. Some issues may be subjective and difficult to precisely quantify. In terms of the go/no-go decision, the team must honestly assess the state of the architecture, through the issue deposition document, to determine whether the architecture needs more refinement or if they feel confident that the design is ready for detailed design and implementation. In some cases, this decision need not be all or nothing. Perhaps the overall structure is sound, but more refinement is needed on particular elements of the system. In this case, it may make sense to advance the production of certain elements, while other elements are further refined. Again, care should be exercised if this course is taken, as it can be disastrous if improperly executed. If potential refinements to the design affect the underlying architectural structure or the elements that are currently in production, then chaos will ensue. Piecemeal production and architecture refinement should be considered fully before undertaking this approach, as ripple effects can be devastating. These special cases will be discussed in Section 3 of the text, when instantiating ACDM will be addressed. If the business context (schedule, cost, resources, market conditions, etc.) will permit, then it is advisable to err on the side of caution and completely refine the architecture. After the first refinement iteration (stages 3 to 6) it is entirely possible that subsequent refinement iterations can happen in a relatively short amount of time (weeks, days, or even a single day). Subsequent refinement and evaluation iterations tend to be much easier and less taxing on resources than early iterations are. A penny's worth of prevention in design is worth a pound of cure once implementation has started or the system/product is deployed.

Are We There Yet?

The following are some signs to look for when making a go/no-go decision:

- If there are no experimentation or requirements-oriented issues (action types 4 and 5 according to Table 12.3) and only minor technical clarifications (action types 3 according to Table 12.3), the architecture might be ready for production. However, even minor experimentation depositions can lead to changes in the architecture that can affect downstream designers and implementers. These types of issues tend to be the most severe and generally have the broadest impact on the design and the resulting implementation. If a lot of issues must be resolved with these deposition types, this is an indication that the design is immature and not well conceived, and it is a good idea to continue to refine the architecture.
- In addition to the architectural decisions, the quality of the architecture design documentation must also be evaluated as part of the go/no-go decision. In some situations, the design may be sound, but the downstream designers and implementers cannot understand its documentation. This is why it is a good idea to review the design with downstream designers and implementers, especially if they are not part of the architecture design team or had little to do with designing the architecture. Reviewing the design with detailed designers and implementers is an explicit activity in stage 7, but unfortunately in practice, it is one that is often omitted in the interests of time. The architecture design documentation must sufficiently describe the design, the element boundaries, and the overall framework so that downstream designers and implementers can design and build the system. If the documentation does not sufficiently describe the design, then the designers and implementers will not be able to use it to guide their work, and the system or product will not match the architecture design. If this happens, then promises made vis-à-vis the architecture design will not be realized in the implementation. If there are only minor documentation issues (deposition type 2 according to Table 12.3), then the design might be ready for the production phases. However, if there are a lot of documentation issues, then perhaps the design documentation should be further refined. If there are a lot of issues where the technical details were not clear because of the documentation (deposition types 3 according to Table 12.3), this is an indication that the

Table 12.3   Issue Deposition Template

Action types:

1 = No action required. Provide an explanation in comments.
2 = Repair, update, or clarify the documentation (prose, drawings, tables, and so forth).
3 = More technical information required. Provide an explanation in comments.
4 = More information on architectural drivers required. Provide an explanation in comments.
5 = Experimentation required. Provide specific description of experiment in comments.

Issue No.	Issue Description	Action	Comments	Responsible Engineer
1	Unsure of connectors between the Foo element and the data repository.	2, 5	Check drawings and clarify the dynamic representations after experimentation.	Joe Smith
:	:	:	:	
:	:	:	:	

documentation is weak, but it also may indicate that the design decisions are problematic. This should be studied and the documentation should be tightened up, and possibly the design itself should be further refined before proceeding into production. In general, the architecture design team will get a sense of the quality of their design documentation during the evaluation workshop. If the architect has to draw a significant number of supplemental pictures during the evaluation to explain the architecture, this can be an indication that the architecture documentation is weak. Again, this will make it difficult for downstream designers to adhere to the architecture. However, caution is advised in assuming that documentation problems are only problems with pictures and prose. It is usually the case that in refining the architecture documentation, deeper design problems will be uncovered that will require more analysis and design work. Problems in design documentation usually result from designs that are immature or not well thought out.

■ If there are numerous requirements issues, this can be an indication of two kinds of trouble. If radical new architecture drivers or major changes to existing architecture drivers emerged during the evaluation, this could be an indication that (1) stages 1 and 2 were not executed properly with the right stakeholders, or (2) the business context is volatile. ACDM refinement iterations are relatively quick, so numerous changes between requirements elicitation and architecture design and evaluation are indications of a highly volatile requirements environment. In either case, if there are numerous requirements changes or requirements-oriented issues, these can have a major impact on the fundamental architectural structures. Some of the key indicators that stages 1 and 2 were not executed properly include architecture drivers that lack detail, available stakeholders that were not engaged, and a poorly written architecture drivers specification. All of these situations amount to not having enough information to motivate the design decisions. Indications of a volatile business context include changes in key stakeholders, dramatic changes in the marketplace, changes in business models (internal or external), and dramatic changes in key technologies used in the design. If the architecture design team suspects that any of these situations are causing requirements issues, then the team should step back from the design and revisit stages 1 and 2, if necessary, to understand the architecture drivers. If the team continues with production in the face of these kinds of problems, then they will probably develop the wrong system.

The architecture design team will develop an intuitive sense of whether the architecture is ready for production during the evaluation workshop. If issues arose because the architect was unable to answer questions regarding the architecture, there were conflicting answers, or key parts of the architecture are yet to be defined, then these are all indications that more refinement is necessary. The issue deposition document should be circulated among the architecture design team and the stakeholders for final comment. Prior to circulating the context-free issue deposition template for review to the broader stakeholder community, the team should have the quality process manager add some prose explaining what the template is, and perhaps an executive summary. This will provide context for readers unfamiliar with the purpose of the document, but keep it brief. Writing the issue deposition document is the responsibility of the quality process engineer, and this document will be used to track the resolution of each issue in stage 6. The issue deposition document should also describe the go/no-go decision made by the architecture design team and the next steps in the design process.

In field trials of ACDM it was discovered that it was most productive if the issue deposition document was written exclusively by the architecture design team members. It can be difficult for the architecture design team to reach consensus about how to address each issue. If there are numerous attendees in the issue analysis meetings and many authors of the issue deposition document, it can be impossible to reach consensus about how to address each issue. This is especially true if attendees or authors do not understand the design. If attendees at the issue analysis meetings lack technical expertise or an understanding of the architecture design, they may drift off and not contribute anything to the analysis of issues. This is a waste of resources and should be avoided. If authors of the issue deposition document lack technical expertise or an understanding of the architecture design, they may not be able to write well-formed action plans for stage 6. However, because it is recommended that the issues and their deposition are decided by a relatively small number of people, stakeholders that attended the evaluation workshop (in particular external attendees) may feel that their issues were not addressed. For this reason, it is important that the issue deposition document be circulated among the broader stakeholder community for their comments. This will help avoid feelings of disenfranchisement from the process.

Updating the Master Design Plan

As stage 5 concludes, it is a good time to update the master design plan to reflect the actual time spent in stage 5. It is worth mentioning at this point that the estimated and actual effort spent in each stage are data that can be used for planning subsequent projects using ACMD. Again, the managing engineer should track effort, actual performance, and earned value with an appropriate frequency to take corrective action and replan as necessary. Because stage 5 is often short in duration, it may be appropriate to plan stage 5, but only update the plan at the conclusion of the stage. A good rule of thumb is that the managing engineers should track the project with no more than a two-week granularity. The period of uncertainty in any project is unpredictable, and the earlier that problems can be detected, the earlier they can be addressed, stakeholders can be informed, and replanning can begin. The managing engineer must work to establish a schedule budget because estimation is difficult during the period of uncertainty, and aggressively track the team's effort against the schedule budget. This is often the best that can be done given the unknowns that are inevitably present during the period of uncertainty. ACDM reduces the duration of the period of uncertainty, but does not eliminate it. Not establishing, following, and updating the master design plan severely hampers the effectiveness of ACDM. It can be difficult to know when to stop the iteration refinement of stages 3 to 6. If the team does decide to move into production or continue with refinement then the factors that contributed to this decision should be recorded in the master design plan. Not only does this capture key programmatic and design decisions for posterity (useful after deployment and maintenance), but this information can help future projects using ACDM. In addition to recording the go/no-go decision and the rationale for this decision, the team should record objections. This is not an opportunity for a member of the architecture design team to say "I told you so," but rather a way to track the impact of objections on future projects and evaluate their significance when the team develops more products and systems using ACDM.

Summary

Stage 5 is all about classifying the issues and deciding how they will be addressed by the architecture design team. Stage 5 is comprised of the following key activities:

- Stage 5 planning: Stage 5 begins with the managing engineer estimating the duration and resources required for the issue analysis meetings. In general, greater time should be budgeted for the first analysis meetings.
- Issue analysis meetings: These can, and should, be discussion-oriented meetings largely facilitated by the engineering manager, but are dependent upon the technical expertise of the entire team. Although external stakeholders could participate in the issue analysis meetings, in most cases they will be attended by members of the architecture design team. There will be at least one issue analysis meeting, but there could be several. At the end of the last meeting the engineering manager should put the go/no-go question to the vote. The architecture design team should vote on whether more refinement and evaluation is required, or if the team is ready for production.
- Update the master design plan: The master design plan is initially updated at the beginning of stage 5 with the estimates of the time and resources required to conduct the issue analysis meetings. At the conclusion of the evaluation, the master design plan is updated with the actual time and resources expended during stage 5. Because of the discussion-oriented nature of the issue analysis meetings, the engineering manager should try to aggressively stick to the schedule budgets established at the beginning of stage 5. The go/no-go decision and the factors contributing to the decision the team makes should also be recorded in the master design plan.

Chapter 13

ACDM Stage 6: Experimentation

Purpose

The primary purpose of stage 6 is for the architecture design team to resolve issues uncovered during the evaluation in stage 4 by carrying out the actions described for each issue in the issue deposition document developed in stage 5. Each action will be planned, executed, and tracked until resolved.

Preconditions

Before undertaking stage 6 the architecture design team must have developed the issue deposition document and assigned responsible engineers to each issue for experimentation.

General Activities

Techniques, Templates, and Guidance

See the experimentation template.

Primary Artifacts

The primary artifacts consist of a collection of completed experimentation templates that contain the data that will be used to refine the architecture design.

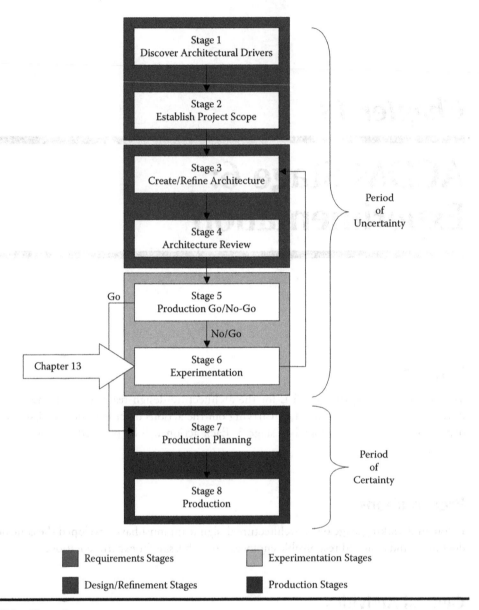

Figure 13.1   Stage 6

Postconditions

The experiments have been conducted for each issue according to the issue deposition document, which will provide the data that will be used to refine the architecture design.

Description of Stage 6

In industry trials with ACDM, practitioners often referred to stage 6 as the fun stage because it is an opportunity for the members of the design team to do some interesting technical exploration.

Table 13.1 Stage 6 Activities, Outputs, and Responsibilities

General activities	Responsible engineers will plan and carry out the specified activities for the issues they are responsible for and record the results of their work.
General outputs	Experimentation results.
Role	**Stage 6 Recommended Responsibilities**
Managing engineer	Plan, coordinate, track, and oversee stage 6 experimentation. Participate in experimentation as a responsible engineer as necessary.
Chief architect	Work with the responsible engineers to resolve issues from a detailed technical perspective. Participate in experimentation as a responsible engineer as necessary.
Chief scientist	Work with and directly assist the responsible engineers as necessary to plan experiments and resolve issues from a detailed technical perspective. The chief scientist will collect the experimentation plans from the responsible engineers. The experimentation plans will be used to track stage 6 experimentation efforts. Participate in experimentation as a responsible engineer as necessary.
Requirements engineer	The requirements engineer will monitor the stakeholder community for changes and breaking developments in the architecture drivers. He or she will also follow the experimentation and the resolution of issues and their impact on satisfying the architecture drivers. Participate in experimentation as a responsible engineer as necessary.
Quality process engineer	Ensure that each issue action is addressed to completion.
Support engineer	Support the responsible engineers in their experimentation. Participate in experimentation as a responsible engineer as necessary.
Production engineers	Participate in experimentation as a responsible engineer.

However, this technical exploration is not the aimless prototyping so common in practice. The technical exploration called experimentation in ACDM is designed to specifically address those issues that were uncovered during the evaluation of the design in stage 4. In stage 5, the architecture design team decided how each issue would be addressed, but in stage 6 the specific experiments are designed, executed, and the data collected to address each issue. There may be many reasons for experimentation, such as:

- Continuing to decompose various elements of the notional architecture to better understand underlying details that may have systemic impact
- Validating basic assumptions in requirements or the design
- Creating and experimenting with alternative architectural approaches
- Exploring technologies, requirements, and domains that are not well understood
- Validating ensembles of elements whose quality attribute properties and functional behaviors are not known or cannot be validated unless they are tested through real artifacts

- Market research for commercially available components, and testing those components for feasibility and to verify the claims of the maker to ensure they are fit for purpose
- Building and testing the architectural infrastructure, specific elements, or relationships

There are many ways in which experiments may be conducted. The author is very deliberate in the use of the word *experiment* rather than *prototype*. Experimentation is a planned activity following the scientific method. The experimenter has a hypothesis and seeks to design experiments to validate or refute the hypothesis. Prototyping (especially in the software industry) tends to be more ad hoc and open ended. Prototypes often become products with unknown structure and unpredictable functional behavior and quality attribute properties. In the ACDM context, experiments are not limited to writing code, breadboarding hardware, or other similar activities associated with technical exploration. Certainly, experimentation includes these activities, but experimentation is used in a wider sense to include a broad range of activities designed to gather the necessary data to address issues uncovered during the evaluation.

Stage 6 Planning

Stage 6 planning involves determining the amount of time that the architecture design team anticipates that they will spend resolving the issues that were uncovered during the architecture design evaluation. After the first evaluation of the architecture there are typically many more issues that will require time to resolve, so the first iteration through stage 6 can take significantly longer than subsequent iterations through stage 6. Stage 6 activities can be hard to accurately predict, especially if there are tough technical issues that need to be addressed through experimentation. As we will see, ACDM provides templates for estimating and putting some bounds on each experiment. The estimates for each experiment can be rolled up to create much more unpredictable estimates for experimentation than organizations prototyping products in an ad hoc way. As such, the engineering manager should try to establish some schedule buffer for stage 6 activities if there are a significant number of issues to address and technical experiments to conduct. As the architecture matures in successive refinement iterations, stage 6 will take significantly less time and become more predictable. The overall planning for the activities revolves around the experiment plans that will be developed by the responsible engineers. Responsible engineers are in charge of developing a short experimentation plan for each issue they are responsible for. The collection of experimentation plans will be used by the managing engineer to plan the stage 6 schedule and determine the resources required, significantly improving the stage estimation. Table 13.2 lists the key activities of stage 6.

Each responsible engineer is also responsible for recording the amount of time he or she spends on each experiment. This is critical information for the managing engineer as he or she tracks the progress of the team during experimentation. It is impossible to provide specific guidance for planning experiments because the nature, duration, and resources required for experimentation are highly dependent upon the nature and complexity of the issue. However, certain courses of action tend to take more time than others. Referring to the issue deposition document, we can see that some activities are more open ended and riskier than others, as shown in Table 13.3.

In some cases, certain issues may require complex interactions to resolve and can present a significant challenge in planning experimentation, and may present unique risks to the project. For example, consider the need for a complex, novel user interface that must be easy to use, multicultural, and configurable. Getting this right will involve working with stakeholders who

Table 13.2 Stage 6 Planning Considerations

Planning Consideration	Description
Updating the master design plan	Updating the master design plan should occur after the stage is planned by the managing engineer. He or she must establish a schedule and resource budget for planning and conducting the experiments. Planning the experimentation schedule is based upon the experimentation plans developed by the responsible engineers.
Experimentation planning	Each responsible engineer will develop a short plan for how he or she will perform the action described for each issue he or she is responsible for according to the issue deposition document. Once the experiments are planned, they are sent to the managing engineer, who will use these short plans to plan the stage and update the master design plan.
Experimentation	Each responsible engineer will conduct the experiments specified in his or her experimentation plans. He or she will collect all relevant technical data and will also track the time spent on each experiment.
Experimentation review meetings	One the experiments are concluded, the team will share and review the outcomes and the data collected during the experiments.

will use the interface to test design concepts to ensure they are easy to use. In addition, experimentation with various design structures will be required to get a configurable, multicultural user interface. Because this involves significant interaction with external stakeholders (possibly scattered all over the planet), this experimentation can be highly unpredictable to plan. In practice, situations like this often go unnoticed because prototyping is usually an ad hoc activity, so traditional planning does not account for the effort required to mitigate these kinds of technical risks. ACDM presents these issues, which is a significant improvement. However, mitigating each of these issues still requires an honest assessment of the amount of time and resources it will take to satisfactorily resolve the issue. Unfortunately, in practice, situations like this are often the norm rather than the exception, and should be carefully considered when planning stage 6. Although the responsible engineer creates the experimentation plan, it should be scrutinized for a "sanity check" to ensure that nothing was missed. Issues should be scrutinized for situations such as these during the planning of the experiments. Once the initial planning for stage 6 is complete, the managing engineer must update the master design plan or schedule (recall that the design schedule may be separate from the master design plan) to reflect the estimated time that will be spent in stage 5.

Experimentation Planning and Execution

In stage 6, the architecture design team will further refine the architecture design through experimentation. Strictly speaking in stage 6, the design itself is not refined. In stage 6 data is gathered through planned, focused experimentation that will be used to refine the architecture

Table 13.3   Experiment Planning Considerations Based on Action Type

Action	Description	Planning Considerations
1	No action required	Because there is no action required, there is no time or resources required to resolve these issues.
2	Repair, update, and/or clarify documentation	The extent to which the documentation needs to be revised will dictate how much time is required for resolving this issue. In general, documentation problems require the time of one or two engineers to correct. Typically no special tools or environments are required to resolve these issues. Plan on reviewing changes to the document to ensure that the issues are addressed satisfactorily.
3	More technical information required	This issue is typically resolved by reading textbooks, product literature, or research on topics that will shed light on how to address the issue. Typically no special tools or environments are required to perform the actions to resolve these kinds of issues. In some cases responsible engineers may have to conduct site visits, attend conferences, and get product demonstrations to obtain the necessary technical information. A risk is that the necessary information may not exist, in which case the organization is facing a potential technical risk that must be resolved through experimentation.
4	More information on architectural drivers required	Addressing these issues involves interacting with the appropriate stakeholders to get new information or clarify existing information. If there is no specific identifiable stakeholder other than an anticipated market for a product or system, clarifying the architectural drivers may involve market studies or human interaction testing, which can be time- and labor-intensive, and may involve the need for domain experts, special tools, and environments.
5	Experimentation required	This action refers to building small executable models or prototypes to verify design approaches and related technical concepts. These actions may involve: Writing software; breadboarding hardware elements; buying, testing, and analyzing software and hardware components; testing and analyzing legacy elements; special and extensive test environments and tools may be necessary and are often required. In addition, special expertise may be required to aid in the experimentation. This action is often the most expensive in terms of time and resource requirements.

when the team returns to stage 3. This is splitting hairs a bit. As mentioned earlier, the iteration between these stages can happen very quickly. There does not need to be a big ceremony at the beginning and conclusion of each stage. To refine the architecture, engineers responsible for resolving issues will create very specific plans that describe what they will do in their experimentation. The general course of action that will be taken to resolve the issues was decided in stage 5 and recorded in the issue deposition document. The experiment planning effort is led by the chief scientist, who is responsible for overseeing the technical details of the experiments. However, responsible engineers will develop the experimentation plans describing how they will address the issues they are responsible for. These plans are lightweight descriptions of the experimentation activities the engineers will undergo to address the issues uncovered in stage 4. Experimentation plans in the ACDM context serve two main purposes. First, planning experiments with specific goals in mind keeps the responsible engineer, and the entire design team, focused on uncovering only that information required to address the issues and refine the architecture design. The difference between ACDM experiments and traditional prototyping is how the team decides what to prototype and planning the activities. Prototyping is nothing new, but the problem with unplanned prototyping is that too often the prototypes become the product that is delivered. This happens because systems are not designed before engineers start prototyping. The prototyping activities are not deliberately planned, and project time is consumed with prototyping. At some point, the developers realize they are out of project time and decide to clean up and ship the prototype. Prototypes typically do not include the same level of quality as production artifacts do. Besides the obvious functionally oriented quality problems, software-intensive systems and products that evolve from prototypes are comprised of architectural structures that evolve and are largely unknown. In this situation, unpredictable systemic properties emerge as well—both functionally and in terms of quality attribute properties. Systems like this are hard to maintain, tune, extend, and so forth. It can be hard for new engineers to learn about and comprehend the system because the overall structure is not well known. All software-intensive systems have architectures whether they were deliberately designed or not. If the architecture is not deliberately designed, but rather emerges as a consequence of grinding out code, adding a bit of hardware here and there, and generally tweaking until it works, you will still get an architecture. Unfortunately, you might not like what you get! Planning experiments to address specific issues raised during evaluation of the design prevents the common problem of endless prototyping where prototypes eventually transmogrify into products and systems. A second reason for planning the experiments is that the engineering manager can use the small experimentation plans created by the experimenters to create a schedule for stage 6, track the effort, and update the master design plan. Because experimentation can be notoriously unpredictable, the small individual experimentation plans help the managing engineer create more reliable plans and track the effort with greater fidelity.

Experimentation Templates

To help engineers create consistent, simple, lightweight experiment plans, a template is provided in Table 13.4 for creating experimentation plans. Experimentation often includes hardware-oriented prototyping of design elements to learn about technologies and design decisions, especially potential problematic decisions. However, in addition to these traditional kinds of experiments, experimentation may include:

Table 13.4   Experiment Planning Template

Preexperiment	
Experiment title:	Experiment ID:
Issue ID/description:	Responsible engineer:
Issue deposition (check one): • Repair, update, and/or clarify the documentation (prose, drawings, tables and so forth). • More technical information required. • More information on architectural drivers required. • Experimentation required. • Other (describe):_____	
Purpose:	
Description of the experiment:	
Artifacts created:	
Completion criteria:	
Resources required:	
Estimated duration and key milestones:	
Postexperiment	
Summary of the findings:	
Actual duration:	
Actual resources:	
Responsible engineer's recommendations:	

- Investigating ways to repair documentation and better represent the design
- Information and document searches to better understand design approaches, technologies, domains, and so forth
- Procuring and experimenting with commercial hardware and software elements and tools
- Interacting with stakeholders to better understand the architectural drivers

It is important to plan these activities as well as traditional hardware- and software-oriented experimentation. Planning all of the experimentation work helps the managing engineer plan and track the work of the engineers during stage 6, as well as provide assurance that issues are being addressed. Planning the experiments also allows the chief scientist and chief architect to review the technical aspects of the experiment to ensure that it will satisfy the technical demands of the issue. The experiment planning template of Table 13.4 is divided into two main sections containing information that should be provided before the experiment and information that should be provided after the experiment has been conducted. Each element of the experiment planning template is explained below. Preexperiment information includes:

- Experiment title and ID: It is useful to provide a name or an ID for the experiment. Alphanumeric IDs are useful when there are a lot of experiments; however, titles tend to be more descriptive.
- Issue ID/description: It is important to include the issue that is being addressed by this experiment so that the quality process engineer can map experiments to issues and ensure that each issue is addressed to completion. The issue ID or description should be the same here as it appears in the issue deposition document.
- Responsible engineer: This is the name of the engineer responsible for designing, planning, and conducting the experiment.
- Issue deposition: The issue deposition here should be the same as that listed in the issue deposition document.
- Purpose: Describe the purpose and intent of the experiment and what information is to be collected and why.
- Description of the experiment: Describe the exact procedures of the experiment. Be clear about what will be done and include any relevant information, such as what code will be written, what hardware will be built, where information searches will be conducted, how stakeholders will be engaged and how often, how the experiment will be instrumented, and how data will be collected.
- Artifacts created: Describe any anticipated artifacts that will be created as a consequence of the experiment. Artifacts may include software, hardware, data, reports, and so forth.
- Completion criteria: Describe the completion criteria for the experiment, that is, describe when the experiment is completed. Completion criteria could be as simple as information gathered or as complex as describing various anticipated outcomes, any of which may signal the end of the experiment.
- Resources required: List any material resources required to support the experiment. This includes hardware, software, tools, testing environments, special support personnel, and so forth.
- Estimated duration and key milestones: The responsible engineer must estimate the approximate duration of the experiment. It is a good idea to include important milestones for longer and more complex multifaceted types of experiments.

Postexperimentation information includes:

- Summary of the findings: At the conclusion of the experiment, the responsible engineer should describe the results. Reference any relevant artifacts. Describe any major deviations from the anticipated outcomes.

■ Actual duration: List the actual time spent on the experiment. Indicate any deviations in the schedule and explain the reasons for them.
■ Actual resources: List the actual resources utilized on the experiment. Indicate any deviations from the anticipated resource and explain the reasons for them.
■ Responsible engineer's recommendations: The responsible engineer should describe any recommendations regarding how to refine the architecture to resolve the issue based on the experiment.

Certainly an organization can tailor this basic template in any number of ways to better meet the specific needs of the project and organization. During industrial trials with ACDM, the experiment planning template was among the most popular, but also one of the most tailored in the ACDM repertoire of templates and checklists. Some organizations added significantly more information to the experiment planning template, while other organizations reduced the amount of information. However this template is tailored, it is critically important that it captures the following information:

■ The goal of the experiment and how the experiment will resolve a specific issue that was raised in the evaluation
■ The duration and required resources for the experiment
■ A description of what the engineer will do to conduct the experiment
■ A descriptions of the results of the experiment
■ Experiment completion criteria

The Process of Experimentation

To begin stage 6, the managing engineer assigns to the architecture design team a schedule and deadline for the development of the experimentation plans. Each of the responsible engineers will complete one experimentation plan for each issue he or she is assigned. There will be one plan for each issue that has an action assigned to it, unless "no action" was the deposition decided upon for the issue in stage 5. Once completed, the experimentation plans should be reviewed. The entire team can review the experimentation plans, but at a minimum the managing engineer, chief scientist, and chief architect should review them. The chief scientist and chief architect should review the plans to ensure that the technical approaches are sound and provide the responsible engineer with technical feedback regarding his or her plans. The managing engineer should review the plans from a programmatic perspective. He or she will create a schedule for the entire stage 6 activities based upon the individual experimentation plans. The collection of experimentation plans represents a detailed portfolio of the activities that will be undertaken in stage 6. This can be rolled up into the plans for stage 6, and to manage the uncertainty of experimentation. In cases where there are large, complex experiments, it may be necessary to assign several engineers to a single experiment. In these cases, these experiments should be treated as miniprojects with small teams assigned whose sole purpose is to devise, plan, and execute the experiment to resolve the related issue. The team of engineers assigned to resolve the issue will develop a single experimentation plan. It is best if a lead engineer is assigned who is responsible for leading the effort and the experimentation plan. In other cases, experiments may be dependent upon one another. For example, the output of one experiment may be necessary for planning and executing another experiment. In other cases, the output of one experiment may indicate whether another experiment is necessary. If at all possible, dependent experiments should be assigned to the same engineer or the same small team of engineers to address all of the related issues and dependent experiments. This simplifies coordination and communication among engineers.

Experimentation Approval

Several organizations using ACDM decided to institute an experiment approval process. This is presented here as an option to provide more oversight of experimentation activities, not as a necessary or prescribed activity of ACDM. In one organization, after the experimentation plans are completed by the responsible engineers, they are sent to the managing engineer. At this point plans would be scrutinized by a small board of technical leaders. Each plan has to be reviewed and approved before the responsible engineers are allowed to execute the experiments. This is a heavier-weight process than the author had in mind for ACDM experimentation. However, this particular organization had a very difficult time controlling prototypes and prototyping activities—nearly every product in recent memory was developed as a prototype. This was a costly and unpredictable proposition that resulted in numerous products of dubious quality. After instituting this process, the organization was able to better predict and control project costs and provide technical and managerial insight into what the engineers were doing. Recall that the purpose for experiments in ACDM is to refine the architecture design in a disciplined and predictable way. Although this level of rigorous control was not designed into ACDM, some kind of scrutiny and approval of experiments is a really good idea. A key reason for iteratively refining the architecture design is to minimize costs and reduce the time spent in the period of uncertainty. Prototyping is an activity that is a notorious schedule and cost drain on projects, typically because it is unbounded, uncontrolled (for a while at least), and unfocused. So it only follows that experimentation should receive some management and technical scrutiny, and that experimentation activities are approved. No one likes to have his or her liberty trampled upon. The exact process used to review and approve experiments will vary from organization to organization, but a little common sense oversight usually goes a long way. There are often political considerations that must be considered when instituting such an approval process that are outside of the scope of this text. It is important to note that the experimentation planning and approval process (if implemented) should not be an onerous one—this can have a demoralizing effect on engineers. The actual planning step should be based on a simple template like that shown in Table 13.4, which captures essential planning information. Nominally, it should be possible for the experiment plans to be created (and approved if necessary) by the responsible engineers in hours, or at most a few days.

Conducting the Experiments

Once the experiment plans are complete, the managing engineer will use this information to plan the stage, update the master design plan, and schedule. All plans should be archived and kept under configuration control. At this point, the responsible engineers should execute their experiments according to their plans. Table 13.5 is an example of an experiment plan with the preexperiment information filled out.

If significant deviations or problems are encountered during experimentation, responsible engineers should inform the managing engineer and chief scientist, and corrective programmatic action can be taken or assistance can be rendered. In some cases, the existing experiment plan has to be altered, and in other cases the experiment has to be replanned. As experimentation com-

Table 13.5   Experiment Planning Template: Pre-experiment.

Pre-Experiment:	
Experiment Title: Vision Processing	Experiment ID: R10
Issue ID/Description: Stage 4 issue: The vision processing and navigation responsibilities are not clear in the architectural design	Responsible Engineer: Jiyeong Yoon
Issue Deposition (check one): ☐ Repair, update, and/or clarify the documentation (prose, drawings, tables and so forth). ☐ More technical information required. ☐ More information on architectural drivers required. ☐ Experimentation required. ☐ Other (describe): _____	
Purpose: The purpose of the experiment is to clarify the roles and responsibilities of the vision processing and navigation elements and to verify the interaction between them by build a small model to test performance and communication.	
Description of the Experiment: The experiment will include building a skeleton of the vision processing and navigation elements. This will include minimal functionality for both elements. For the vision processing elements, the services that will be implemented will only include image capture and color determination. For the navigation element, only the color search service will be implemented. The experiment will fully develop the communication required to test how these elements will interact to verify the assumptions in the architectural design.	
Artifacts Created: Code for the navigation and vision processing elements and the associated software to facilitate communication between the elements.	
Completion Criteria: The elements are implemented, are able to communicate, and the basic color search function is tested.	
Resources Required: 1 Engineer. Robot simulator. Access to robot hardware for testing.	
Estimated Duration and Key Milestones: 1 Week.	
Post-Experiment:	
Summary of the Findings:	
Actual Duration:	
Actual Resources:	
Responsible Engineer's Recommendations:	

mences, the responsible engineer must record the results of the experiment and complete the rest of the postexperimentation data required on the plan. An example of a plan filled in with this information is provided in Table 13.6.

This information and all of the associated experimentation artifacts should be archived and kept under configuration control. In many organizations, the results of prototypes are never formally recorded, and the results of the effort are lost when the engineer forgets what he or she did, or he or she moves on to another position or organization. The experimentation plan template in Table 13.4 is designed to preserve what was done and the results of the experimentation effort for the life of the project. Gaining information through experimentation costs time and money, and it is really stupid to just throw it away, but this is a common approach in organizations building software-intensive systems today! As the experimentation gets under way, it is the managing engineer's responsibility to track the experimentation effort from a programmatic standpoint and take corrective actions as necessary. Again, the granularity with which the experimentation effort is tracked will depend upon the duration of the experiments. It is a good idea to track experimentation activities more frequently (one-week intervals) because experimentation tends to be a volatile activity and problems can quickly arise that may adversely impact schedule and cost. It is important that an objective completion criterion be established and adhered to for each experiment. When this criterion is met, the experiment is done—period. If not, experimentation will never end and prototypes will turn into products and systems.

The chief scientist's role in experimentation is that of a mentor and advisor to the responsible engineers. The chief scientist will monitor the progress of the experiments from a technical standpoint and assist the engineers as necessary. Certainly the chief scientist can participate as a responsible engineer, but on larger projects his or her time may be better spent helping the responsible engineers plan and execute their experiments. When problems with experiments arise, the chief scientist will assist the team in resolving the problems. The chief scientist oversees the technical aspects of the experiments and guides the technical activities of the responsible engineers, and will mentor them in designing, planning, and executing the experiments. As the experiments unfold, the chief scientist has a vested interest in monitoring them and helping the responsible engineers complete them. The chief architect will also monitor the outcomes of the experiments and may begin thinking about how the design will be affected by the information gathered through the experiments. The quality process engineer's role in experimentation is to ensure that each issue is addressed according to the issue deposition document. The requirements engineer also has a vested interest in tracking the outcomes of the experiments because their outcomes may dictate which requirements need to be renegotiated.

Postexperimentation

Once the experimentation has been completed, the team will conduct an experiment review meeting to review the results of the experiments. This meeting can be conducted all at once, when all of the experiments have been concluded, or continuously, as experiments are completed. This meeting is attended by the architecture design team and any other engineers that may have been involved in the experimentation. During the meeting, each issue in the issue deposition document is reviewed. For each issue, the responsible engineer will present his or her experiment plan for addressing the issue. He or she will discuss the technical details of the experiment, the results obtained, and recommendations. The attendees should be invited to comment on the experiment. The quality process engineer will preside over, and serve as the scribe for, the experiment review

Table 13.6   Experiment Planning Template: Post Experiment

Pre-Experiment:	
Experiment Title: Vision Processing	Experiment ID: R10
Issue ID/Description: Stage 4 issue: The vision processing and navigation responsibilities are not clear in the architectural design	Responsible Engineer: Jiyeong Yoon
Issue Deposition (check one): ☐ Repair, update, and/or clarify the documentation (prose, drawings, tables and so forth). ☐ More technical information required. ☐ More information on architectural drivers required. ☐ Experimentation required. ☐ Other (describe):	
Purpose: The purpose of the experiment is to clarify the roles and responsibilities of the vision processing and navigation elements and to verify the interaction between them by build a small model to test performance and communication.	
Description of the Experiment: The experiment will include building a skeleton of the vision processing and navigation elements. This will include minimal functionality for both elements. For the vision processing elements, the services that will be implemented will only include image capture and color determination. For the navigation element, only the color search service will be implemented. The experiment will fully develop the communication required to test how these elements will interact to verify the assumptions in the architectural design.	
Artifacts Created: Code for the navigation and vision processing elements and the associated software to facilitate communication between the elements.	
Completion Criteria: The elements are implemented, are able to communicate, and the basic color search function is tested.	
Resources Required: 1 Engineer. Robot simulator. Access to robot hardware for testing.	
Estimated Duration and Key Milestones: 40 Hours.	
Post-Experiment:	
Summary of the Findings: Another element was required to manage the inter element communications since many of the interactions between vision processing and navigation must be asynchronous.	
Actual Duration: 36 Hours	
Actual Resources: As stated.	
Responsible Engineer's Recommendations: The responsibilities of the vision processing and navigation elements remain unchanged. However, it is strongly recommended that the design be modified to include a separate run-time element that is responsible for coordinating communications between vision processing and navigation. The communication between the elements is also far more complex that show in the original design. The design should be amended to show the communication between vision processing and navigation more accurately	

meeting. He or she will record any comments or follow-up actions deemed necessary, and will ensure that each issue in the issue deposition document has been addressed to the satisfaction of the group. If at all possible, it is highly recommended that all members of the architecture design team be present during the experiment review meeting. The information gleaned from the experiments provides critical insight for understanding the design, the technical details, and the impact on the project schedule. The chief architect will use this information to refine the design; the chief scientist needs this information to verify the technical feasibility of the design; and the managing engineer needs this information to estimate, plan, and schedule the remainder of the design process until a production decision is reached. Once the experiments have concluded and they have been reviewed, the team will essentially return to stage 3 to refine the design. The existing design will be refined based on the outcomes of the experiments. Again, the responsibility for changing the design rests with the chief architect, who works with the entire team to update and refine the design. Design refinements can be anything from simply changing documentation to completely redesigning the architecture. After the design is refined, it is evaluated again in stage 4. The issues uncovered in the second evaluation are again analyzed in stage 5, and another go/no-go decision is rendered based on this analysis. In industrial trials with ACDM, teams typically converged on a design that was ready for production after three refinement iterations. This is a heuristic, not a rule based in rigorous mathematics. A few project teams converged after two iterations, but some of these teams found problems when they were in implementation. In postmortem analysis, it was generally agreed that a hasty production decision was made, which led to the design problems uncovered in production phases. Teams building similar kinds of systems found two iterations acceptable, whereas teams with more unknowns tended to iterate three or more times. Still fewer organizations took four or more iterations. On closer examination, these projects did not follow the guidance in stages 1 and 2 and had very weak architecture drivers specifications. The ensuing designs were exceedingly weak, resulting in more iteration than necessary. The importance of the iteration described in ACDM is illustrated in Figure 13.2.

In this figure we can see that all system or product design begins with stakeholders in a given business context. From this business context and from the minds, hearts, and mouths of the

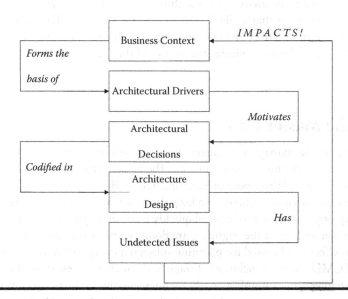

Figure 13.2   Impact of issues that become design problems

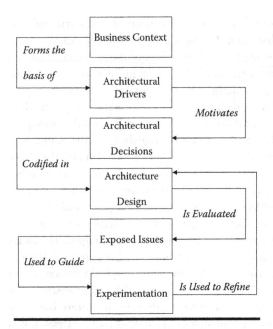

Figure 13.3 The impact of iterative evaluation and refinement

stakeholders, the architecture design team will gather the architectural drivers. These will motivate the design decisions of the chief architect and architecture design team. The decisions made by the chief architect and design team are codified in the documented architecture design. This is how the design is communicated to those who will commit the design to implementation. Therefore, as Figure 13.2 shows, issues with the design will directly impact the ability of the system to satisfy the stated needs of the stakeholder in the given business context. There are lots of opportunities to make mistakes in the transformation from idea to architecture design to implementation. The wrong stakeholders could be engaged, the architecture drivers may be ill-formed or erroneous, problematic design decisions could be made, and the design could be poorly documented. An error in any one of these steps could compromise the design. ACDM adds a simple verification and refinement step to this cycle, as shown in Figure 13.3.

Here we can see that the same stakeholders and business context give rise to architectural drivers, and they still motivate design decisions that are documented as the architecture design. We still have the opportunity to make all of the same mistakes. However, the key difference in Figure 13.3 is the use of evaluation to guide experimentation, and the use of experimentation data to refine the design. In ACDM we resign ourselves to the fact that errors will be made in engaging the stakeholders, defining and analyzing the architecture drivers, and designing and documenting the architecture. The irony is that while ACDM assumes that there will be defects, it is structured to aggressively detect and manage the maturation of the design through iterative evaluation and refinement cycles. This helps to minimize the impact of the costly early defects that creep into the design process.

Updating the Master Plan

Throughout stage 6 the managing engineer should closely monitor the actual performance of the engineers as they carry out the experiments. The master design plan should be checked and updated to reflect the actual time spent in experimentation. Because experimentation is notoriously unpredictable, greater attention is needed to keep the schedule under control. Again, experimentation, like prototyping, can get out of control quickly if the managing engineer and chief scientists do not stay in touch with what the engineers are doing as they experiment. Estimated and actual experimentation effort can be used for planning subsequent stage 6 iterations and planning other projects using ACMD. At the conclusion of stage 6, the team will return to the activities of stage 3 to refine the architecture, beginning another refinement and evaluation iteration.

Summary

Stage 6 is often referred to as the fun stage, where engineers get to experiment to resolve the technical issues uncovered in stage 4 and documented in stage 5. Stage 6 is comprised of the following key activities:

- Stage 6 planning: Stage 6 begins with responsible engineers creating experimentation plans to address each issue deposition established in stage 5. The experimentation plans are short descriptions of how the issues will be resolved. The experimentation plans are reviewed by the managing engineer, who uses them to create the stage schedule. The chief scientist and chief architect review the experimentation plans for technical merit.
- Experimentation: The responsible engineers will conduct the experiments according to the experimentation plans. As experiments are conducted, experimentation data is collected and recorded by the responsible engineers. The responsible engineers will also update the experimentation plans with actual performance data and experimentation results as the information is available.
- Experiment review meeting: This meeting is conducted by the architecture design team to share and review the results of the experiments and provide an opportunity to allow team members to provide comment on the various experiments.
- Update the master design plan: The master design plan is initially updated at the beginning of stage 6 with the estimates of the time and resources required to conduct experiments based on the experimentation plans. At the conclusion of stage 6, the master design plan is updated with the actual time and resources expended on experimentation.
- Archive the results: It is essential that the experimentation plans, the resulting artifacts, and the results of the experiments are recorded and archived.

Chapter 14

ACDM Stage 7: Production Planning

Purpose

The primary purpose of stage 7 is for the architecture design team to use the architecture to plan the subsequent design and implementation of the system or product. ACDM does not prescribe specific methods, detailed design, or development process frameworks, but ACDM does provide guidance and techniques for planning the postarchitecture design activities based on the design.

Preconditions

Before undertaking stage 7, the architecture design has to be fully stabilized through iterations of design, evaluation, and refinement.

General Activities
Techniques, Templates, and Guidance

- Architecture familiarization workshop guidance
- Element-wise Wideband Delphi estimation technique
- Production estimation template
- Implementation and design schedule guidelines

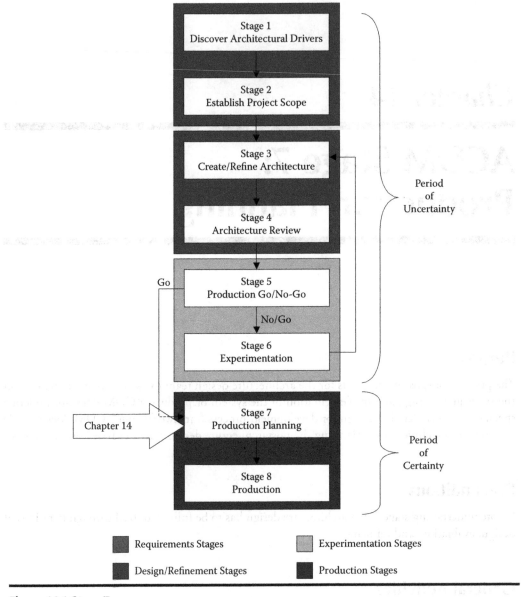

Figure 14.1 Stage 7

Primary Artifacts

The primary artifact consists of detailed design and implementation schedules.

Postconditions

The team will create a production schedule that can be used to plan and track the product or system's detailed design and implementation activities.

Table 14.1 Stage 7 Activities, Outputs, and Responsibilities

General activities	Present the architecture to the detailed design and implementation engineers. Estimate the amount of time and resources required to develop the product.
General outputs	Documented production schedule.
Role	**Stage 7 Recommended Responsibilities**
Managing engineer	The managing engineer is responsible for planning, coordinating, and leading the development of the production schedule. The managing engineer is also responsible for ensuring that the team documents the production schedule and any associated planning documents required for production.
Chief architect	Present the architecture design to the detailed designers and implementers. Assist the managing engineer in conducting the Element-wise Wideband Delphi estimation and in developing the production schedule from these estimates.
Chief scientist	Assist the architect in presenting the architecture design to the detailed designers and implementers. Assist the managing engineer in conducting the Element-wise Wideband Delphi estimation and in developing the production schedule from these estimates. The chief scientist is responsible for planning integrated system/product test.
Requirements engineer	Assist the managing engineer in conducting the Element-wise Wideband Delphi estimation and in developing the production schedule. The requirements engineer is responsible for planning integrated system/product test.
Quality process engineer	Lead the Element-wise Wideband Delphi estimation and develop the production schedule from these estimates. The quality process engineer is responsible for planning integrated system/product test.
Support engineer	Assist the architect in presenting the architecture design to the detailed designers and implementers. Assist the managing engineer in conducting the Element-wise Wideband Delphi estimation and in developing the production schedule from these estimates.
Production engineers	Attend the architecture presentation and ensure that the design is understood before moving into design.

Description of Stage 7

Stage 7 represents a departure from the period of uncertainty and a transition into the period of certainty, where the design structures of the system have been established and stabilized by successive iterations of design, evaluation, and refinement. Once the architecture design team concludes that the architecture is sound and the key technical issues have been sufficiently addressed, they will decide to begin planning for production. The term *production* in the ACDM context refers to detailed design of the architectural design elements, implementation and unit testing of the elements, integration of the elements, testing of the ensemble, and installation or delivery of the system or product. Production may mean building the whole system/product all at once, or it may mean that the system/product is produced incrementally. ACDM supports the notion of iterative product development and integration; however, as previously mentioned, care should be exercised when designing and building a system or product in a piecemeal fashion. If design elements or functionality is to be produced and delivered incrementally, it is important that the architecture supports the integration of subsequent elements or functionality into existing structures. The system or product must be designed to support the integration of new elements to support new functionality, while continuing to satisfy the key architectural drivers of the system. This is difficult to do if the structures of the system were not designed to accommodate incremental development and delivery. Those that can be most subtly affected are the quality attributes and constraints. Quality attribute responses can change over time as new functionality is added to the system, and if care is not exercised, constraints can be inadvertently violated. For example, consider a simulation that is developed with some initial functionality where additional capabilities are to be integrated and delivered over time. As the new capabilities are integrated into the systems, stakeholders may notice that the system seems slower with each delivery. This example is quite common in these types of systems. In this example, the system was designed to support some initial functionality and meet stringent performance requirements. However, it was not designed to specifically accommodate incremental integration of new capabilities and features. As a result, when the new capabilities and features are added, performance can suffer and the original systemic structures morph and begin to decay as they are modified to accommodate new requirements and tweaked to improve performance. Because there is natural tension between modifiability and performance, this can be a difficult accommodation unless designed into the system. As performance demands increase, the ability to accommodate modifiability becomes more challenging—and creating a design to accommodate both quality attributes and functionality becomes more time-consuming and expensive. This will also incur more time and cost in the implementation. These problems can be compounded if the design documentation is not maintained as changes are made. Eventually the architecture will erode to the point that it will be lost, and no one will understand the underlying structures. This example illustrates the need for precisely describing quality attributes like modifiability, estimating the effect they have on the system, and making sure that the system is designed to accommodate change. The impact that incremental delivery will have on the system should not be underestimated and should be anticipated by the architect and accommodated for in the design. If not, stakeholders must be willing to pay for redesign of the product at some point when new functionality is delivered. All systems eventually erode to the point that they must be redesigned; however, some change can be anticipated and systems designed to accommodate the change. If we choose not to spend the time and money now to design and build systems that can accommodate anticipated changes, then we can expect to pay more for redesign later in the life cycle. If production of the system is iterative, any critical issues that could impact the stable elements of the system should be resolved before moving into production. If there are remaining issues, the architecture design team should ensure that they are identified and isolated to a single element or region of the architecture design, thereby limiting potential ripple effects as the element is further refined.

Stage 7 is where the architecture design team prepares to deliver the design for implementation and transition from architecture design-oriented activities to production-oriented activities. Stage 7 will begin with a presentation of the architecture design to the downstream detailed design or implementation engineers. For this, the architecture design documentation should be well established. The design document should be ready for use to create production schedules and guide the work of detailed designers, integrators, or engineers responsible for implementing elements of the system or product. The primary activity of stage 7 is to use the architecture design to create a detailed production schedule. These activities are designed to set the context for production. Stage 7 techniques, templates, and guidelines are designed to help the team develop a more predictable production schedule and help ensure that the implementation matches the design. The schedule artifacts created in stage 7 will be used to track production activities in stage 8. Stage 7 has few technical activities prescribed for the stage, but rather focuses on using the design to guide the programmatic aspects of the project that are critical in the overall product/system development scheme.

Stage 7 Planning

Stage 7 planning involves determining the amount of time that the architecture design team anticipates they will spend developing the production schedule and reviewing the architecture design with the production engineers. These are the two key milestones in stage 7. Although stage 7 can be relatively brief in comparison to other stages of ACDM, explicitly planning these activities is still important to the architecture design process. While the method for deriving the production schedule prescribed by ACDM is relatively lightweight, the team may be required to write other planning documents to support system/product production. These may also be part of stage 7 and included in the stage planning.

The Architecture Familiarization Workshop

The downstream detailed designers and implementers will understand the architecture design at varying levels of detail, depending upon their relationship with the architecture design team. However, it can be useful to involve these engineers in estimating production schedules, including detailed design, implementation, test, integration, and so forth of the system elements. Before these engineers can be asked to provide estimates, design, and build the system, we will have to familiarize them with the architecture design. The forum for design familiarization is the architecture familiarization workshop. The nature of this workshop will vary depending upon how separated the detailed designers and implementers are from the architecture design team, and

Table 14.2   Stage 7 Planning Considerations

Planning Consideration	Description
Updating the master design plan	Updating the master design plan should occur after the stage is planned by the managing engineer. In relative terms, the activities of stage 7 are not long in duration, but these activities must be planned, and schedule and resource budgets for stage 7 established.
Architecture familiarization workshop	The chief architect will arrange a technical presentation for the production engineers and any other engineers that play a role in the detailed design and implementation activities.
Element-wise Wideband Delphi estimation	The estimation is lead by the quality process engineer. The technique used is Element-wise Wideband Delphi estimation. All of the members of the design team will participate in the estimation exercise.

this is often dependent upon the size and scope of the project. In some situations the production engineers (detailed designers or implementers) have been on the architecture design team and participated in the design, experimentation, and refinement of the design; thus, the architecture familiarization workshop is trivial because the production engineers are intimately familiar with the architecture design. However, there are other situations where the production engineers have not been part of the architecture design team and did not participate in the creation of the design. In these cases the workshop may be more extensive because it will take longer to familiarize the production engineers with the architecture design. In either case, the designers and implementers must understand the architecture design so the implementation adheres to it.

General Planning Guidelines and Considerations

The first consideration for planning and conducting the workshop is identifying who will be responsible for detailed design and implementation. The architecture design team must determine what engineers are responsible for what elements of the architecture design, and then determine how much they know about the elements they are responsible for and how well they understand the overall design. The decision to assign these responsibilities is usually the responsibility of the managing engineer working with project management or other organizational management. If the architecture design team has been closely coupled with those responsible for the detailed design and implementation, as they often are in small teams, projects, and organizations, then a massive architecture familiarization workshop is a waste of time. In some cases, the architecture design team is also responsible for detailed design and even implementation, in which case an architecture familiarization workshop may be a waste of time. However, as project scope and organizations get larger and teams become distributed, a more formal architecture familiarization workshop is a necessity. In these cases, workshop planning will be a lot like an architecture review where there are a considerable number of external stakeholders. Planning and logistics concerns for the workshop are listed in Table 14.3.

In cases where the system scope and design are relatively large, it may be necessary to assign teams of engineers to the elements for detailed design and implementation. Some of these teams may have never seen the architecture design at all. This is especially true if some of the elements will be outsourced for production. In these cases, element specifications must be extremely detailed so that production engineers can design and build the element. In outsourcing situations, precise specifications can help the architecture design team validate that the element meets the specification. In cases where system scope and design are large, it can be helpful if the design documentation is partitioned into manageable chunks for each team. This will restrict the team visibility and focus their attention on the element(s) they are responsible for. This can reduce the chances that they will violate the overall architecture structure by introducing dependencies not specified by the architecture design. If there are multiple teams of engineers, it can be useful to plan for multiple concurrent workshop meetings rather than trying to brief all of the production engineers in one big meeting. In projects of large scale and scope, a better strategy might be to:

■ First begin with a general presentation of the overall architectural design. All of the production engineers should attend this presentation to understand context and provide general familiarization with the design.

Table 14.3 Architecture Familiarization Workshop Planning Considerations

Consideration	Comments
Attendees	Decide who will attend the evaluation workshop. Earlier evaluations should be internal; later evaluations should include customer stakeholders if they are available.
Element assignments	The architecture design team must assign elements to engineers before the architecture familiarization workshop. If the system scope and design are relatively large, it may be necessary to assign teams to elements. In some cases, various elements may be outsourced to other organizations for design and production.
Homework	The architecture design and architecture drivers specification should be sent to the production engineers well in advance of the workshop to allow adequate time to review the design. Ask engineers to be prepared to ask any clarifying questions about the architecture design. If the system scope and the design are relatively large, consider partitioning the design documentation into manageable chunks for each team designing and implementing the elements.
Venue	Decide where the workshop will be conducted. As always, encourage participants to refrain from e-mail or cell phone conversations during the workshop. Make sure the room is suitably equipped with presentation projectors, whiteboards, flip charts, and so forth. Ensure that power cables, regional power converters (110V to 220V, two-prong versus three-prong adapters, and so forth), network access, and so forth are available as necessary.

■ After the general design overview, the engineers can break into separate, concurrent workshops. Each workshop will focus on some part of the design and will be attended by those designers and implementers responsible for that part of the system.

The architecture familiarization workshop is essentially an opportunity for the architecture design team to communicate the design to the detailed designers and implementers. The chief architect will be responsible for presenting the architecture design to the engineers. In cases where there are multiple concurrent presentations, other members of the architecture design team should be assigned to present the various parts of the system to production engineers. During the architecture familiarization workshop, the following topics should be reviewed in detail:

■ Architectural drivers: The architect should review the most influential architectural drivers and describe how they motivated the design.
■ Overall design strategy: The architect should review any general design approaches or guiding principles used by the architectural design team to design the architecture and how this strategy helped to satisfy the architectural drivers.
■ Present the architecture design: If the design will be described in totality to the detailed designers and implementers, then begin this presentation with the context diagram and continue to present the design from the various perspectives. If the design will be described

generally, followed by specific presentations for the individual teams building the elements, start with the context and then proceed to a level of detail that will show the elements and team responsibilities. The chief architect should explain the rationale for the partitioning and how it satisfies the architectural drivers. From this point the production engineers will have a good sense of general context and their role in the overall system design. As each element is explained in detail, the architect should begin with a description of the element's functional responsibilities. Following this discussion, the architect should explain the element interfaces. If the interfaces have not been designed in detail, the relationships among the elements should be explained, along with the responsibilities of the relationships. This will help the production engineers as they design and implement the interfaces of the elements. This is essential because the interfaces between the elements and the runtime relationships between the elements essentially form the scaffolding of the architecture. The architect should ensure that he or she describes the system from the various perspectives, and he or she should always be explicit about the perspective being presented to the attendees. Throughout the review of the design, the architect should be sure to reference the engineers to the appropriate section of the design document that describes the details. At no time should design information or representations appear in the presentation that do not appear in the design document. Certainly the information in the presentation will be a subset of the architecture documentation, but the representations, notation, and information in the presentation must be consistent with the documentation. Table 14.4 provides an outline to help guide the preparation and delivery of the design presentation.

The Production Schedule

In general, ACDM prescribes estimating the size, effort, and resources associated with producing (buying or building, testing, and so forth) each element of the architecture and then rolling up the element estimates into an overall system production estimate. A key feature of ACDM is the use of the architecture design to create a production plan that guides implementation efforts. The first step in planning is to decompose the overall project into a set of well-defined tasks. To create a schedule, each task is estimated as to how long it will take to complete. ACDM uses the architecture design to decompose the overall project into a set of tasks that maps directly to the elements of design. The schedule is then created by decomposing the construction of each element into a set of tasks, that is, the construction of each element will become a major task on the schedule. This concept is illustrated graphically in Figure 14.2.

Like so many aspects of design discussed in this text thus far, estimation depends upon perspective. When estimating the constituent activities associated with production, different perspectives must be utilized. This illustration shows that the schedule is derived from the design using the static perspective. The assumption in the example shown in Figure 14.2 is that the focus of this estimation is of software development costs. In most cases the static perspective is the most useful for estimating software construction schedules. However, other perspectives may be better suited for estimating hardware production, procurement activities, and so forth. For example, consider an engineer that must estimate the schedule for producing and installing a system's server and network infrastructure. The physical perspective that represents the hardware, including servers, routers, wireless hubs, cabling, and so forth, might best serve this engineer for estimating the work. Just as architectural designs must include different perspectives to adequately capture and represent design decisions, production estimates may require the use of different perspectives to create

Table 14.4   Architecture Familiarization Workshop Presentation Guidelines

1	Introductions	Welcome and participant introductions
2	Architecture drivers overview	Describe the functional requirements, quality attributes, and business and technical constraints at a high level of detail. Refer the production engineers to the architecture drivers specification for more detail.
3	Design context	Describe the context for the design. Explain what is inside and outside of the system scope. Describe any key external technical constraints, such as legacy systems, interfaces, and so forth.
4	Overall decomposition	Describe the overall decomposition of the system. Although the overall decomposition can be shown from multiple perspectives, this may not be necessary or efficient because the various perspectives will be discussed during the detailed discussion of each element. This is not a rule, but rather the architect should judge between a timely presentation and a thorough presentation. Discuss the rationale for the decomposition and briefly describe the relationships and their responsibilities. If teams are assigned to the elements, this is a good time to separate the teams into breakout groups where each element will be discussed in detail. Representatives from the architecture design team should be assigned to describe the elements to various production teams.
5	Element details	Describe each element. For each element, begin with the functional responsibilities assigned to it. Describe the element from the various perspectives and show its relevance in the overall design. Describe the interfaces to the element and their responsibilities. Describe any relationships between the element and other elements it is connected to.

accurate schedule estimates. The production schedule for each module in the architecture design is estimated by the architecture design team. The production engineer responsible for this element must be included in this estimation as well if he or she is not already part of the architecture design team. Element estimates are in terms of schedule time and number of engineers. Simply put, this equates to calendar time × number of engineers = engineering hours. This information can be used to calculate the cost to produce the elements of the system. A template will be introduced to guide element estimation. Once each element's production costs have been estimated, the collection of element estimates is used to create the production schedule. For each element that must be built, the architecture design team must consider each of the following activities as they decompose the task of building each element into constituent tasks:

■ Detailed requirements gathering: It may be the case that the production engineers may have to spend more time and resources gathering more detailed requirements associated with the elements. For example, consider the case of a user interface. The detailed design and implementation of this element may necessitate more detailed requirements elicitation and analysis than what is provided by the architecture drivers specification.

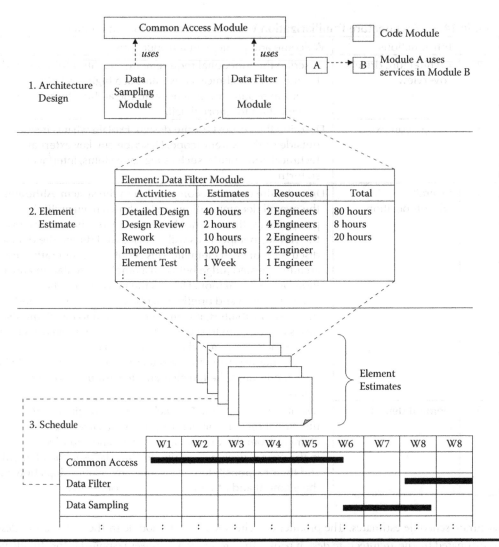

Figure 14.2   Partial design illustrating decomposition of a design element into schedule elements. The design perspective represented here is from a static perspective.

- Detailed design: This is the amount of time spent designing the element and documenting the design.
- Implementation: This is the amount of time and resources necessary for writing the software, fabricating the hardware, and so forth.
- Element test: This is the amount of time spent testing the element. This may include setting up testing environments, setting up test harnesses, planning tests, executing tests, and so forth.
- Rework: Some buffer should be added to the schedule for some rework to fix defects with the element after element test.

For elements that are purchased rather than built, the architecture design team must consider the following in planning for the use of purchased elements:

- Ordering and delivery time: This is the amount of time that it will take to order and deliver software, hardware, and so forth.
- Qualification of the element: This is the amount of time and resources that may be required to ensure that the element meets the advertised specification. There should be no significant issues at this point because any significant specification issues should have been uncovered and resolved in stage 6 experimentation.
- Training and experimentation: This is the amount of time and resources that may be required to overcome any learning curves associated with using the element. There should be no significant issues at this point because training and experimentation issues with the element should have been resolved in stage 6 experimentation.
- Configuration or installation: This is the amount of time and resources that may be required to configure or install the system software and hardware or any associated tools that may be required to use the element.
- Use of alternatives: If necessary, to mitigate any risks associated with using the element, planners should consider the time and resources required to utilize any suitable alternatives to the first-choice product.

As the elements are completed, they will have to be integrated into an ensemble that will be the system. For integration planning, the following should be considered:

- Integration tools and environments: This is the amount of time required to set up the integration environment and any associated tools to facilitate integration of the elements. This may include systemic test harnesses, data configuration, tool setup, and so forth.
- Assembly and installation: This is the time it takes to assemble the elements (hardware and software) and install or deploy the system or product.
- System test: This includes any time and resources required to test the fully integrated system.
- Rework: It is a good idea to build a buffer into the integration schedule for any rework that might be necessary to fix any defects after system test.

Tables 14.5 to 14.7 may be helpful in guiding the creation of the production schedules.

The purpose of these tables is to serve as worksheets for the architecture design team and the production engineers responsible for the elements to guide their estimation. Not all possible estimation considerations are listed in these tables, and not all of those listed may be applicable in all situations. These tables are meant to serve as starting positions only—you should tailor as necessary. These tables allow the architecture design team to estimate the amount of time it will take to produce the element based on the amount of time each subtask will take. Essentially each table represents an element that becomes a major task in the overall schedule. Each row in the table represents a subordinate task to building the element. Each subtask is estimated in hours—a specific estimation technique will be presented later. The hours for the subtask are multiplied by the number of engineers assigned to the specific subtask, resulting in the total subtask engineering hours. At the end of the worksheet, the total engineering hours required to produce the element can be calculated by adding together all of the subtasks. The collection of worksheets then becomes a work breakdown structure based on the elements of the architecture and a strong starting position for creating a production schedule. Monetary costs and overall schedules can be derived from these estimates. Once the estimates have been agreed upon, the managing engineer can use these worksheets as a basis to create detailed production schedules based on the elements

Table 14.5 Element Construction Planning Worksheet

Element name/ID:			
Responsible engineer/team lead:			
Considerations	**Estimated Time**	**Estimated Number of Engineers**	**Task Engineering Hours**
Detailed requirements • Stakeholder meetings • Documenting detailed requirements • Analysis of requirements			
Detailed element design • Element design • Design documentation • Design review • Rework			
Element implementation • Coding • Code inspection • Fabrication			
Element test • Software or hardware element test Rework Element qualification, certification, acceptance			
Other			
Total engineering hours:			

of the architecture. The information in these sheets can be used to resolve dependencies between tasks, calculate production costs, allocate resources, and generally plan the overall production effort. Schedules created directly from the architecture design tend to be far more accurate than estimates and schedules created before the architecture design is complete, or those that do not use the architecture design as a basis for estimating production schedules. This concept is analogous to architects in the building construction industry who create models for stakeholders. These models are used to communicate ideas to stakeholders and design decisions to detailed designers and builders. These models become the basis for planning and scheduling construction concerns as well as the basis for design and implementation. This same philosophy is embodied in ACDM.

Element-Wise Wideband Delphi Estimation

Some organizations have established estimation methods that are used to estimate project costs and duration. These may be used provided that they take into consideration all of the points mentioned thus far. In organizations where there are no established estimation processes or methods, estimation can be a huge challenge to overcome. To estimate production schedules based on the

Table 14.6 Element Procurement Planning Worksheet

Element/product name/ID:			
Responsible engineer/team lead:			
Considerations	Estimated Time	Estimated Number of Engineers	Task Engineering Hours
Supplier site visits • Product demonstration and evaluation			
Element ordering and delivery			
Element qualification			
Experimentation			
Training			
Configuration/installation			
Other			
Total engineering hours:			

Table 14.7 Element Integration Planning Worksheet

Element name/ID:			
Responsible engineer/team lead:			
Considerations	Estimated Time	Estimated Number of Engineers	Task Engineering Hours
Element integration • Laboratory integration • Site integration			
Transportation deployment			
System test			
Initial site testing			
Operational testing			
System qualification			
Site rework and tuning			
Other			
Total engineering hours:			

architecture design, ACDM recommends the use of *Element-wise Wideband Delphi estimation,* which is a tailored version of the traditional Wideband Delphi estimation (Boehm, 1981). The original version of Wideband Delphi estimation was developed in the 1940s at the Rand Corporation and was dubbed a forecasting tool for estimating system development costs. It has since been adapted for use in many domains, and has proven to be an effective estimation tool for software development projects. Element-wise Wideband Delphi is just such an adoption of traditional Wideband Delphi estimation techniques to estimate element production efforts. By estimating each element's production effort we can predict the overall system or product production effort and cost. Element-wise Wideband Delphi is a consensus-based method that focuses all the team's expertise to derive element estimates. Although any estimation method can be used, if an organization does not have any formal estimation process or methodology and are adopting ACDM, it is strongly recommended that it use Element-wise Wideband Delphi estimation initially. As the organization gains experience with ACDM and estimation in general, it can tailor the estimation process as it deems necessary based on experience. What follows is a description of Element-wise Wideband Delphi estimation.

1. Assign responsible engineers: For each architectural element, a responsible software engineer should be assigned if they have not been already. The element's responsible engineer is responsible for leading the construction of the element—this includes coordinating production estimates.

2. Element estimates: The effort required to build each element is estimated by the team responsible for building the element. Because of the nature of consensus-based estimation, it is best if three or more engineers estimate the effort to build each element. In small teams this may mean that members of the architecture design team estimate the effort to build each element. However, it is possible in larger projects for the elements to be turned over to teams for production. In this case, each member of the element production team estimates the effort to build the element. The team responsible for producing the element should create an element estimation form for their element(s). Tables 14.5 to 14.7 can be used as a basis for creating element estimation forms. Each engineer should use the same estimation form so that the element estimates are consistent. It is a good idea for the team to review and reach consensus on the estimation forms before estimation.

3. Consolidation and review: The engineer responsible for the element will collect the estimates for each element and consolidate them. The estimates can be analyzed and presented in any number of ways. At a minimum, the responsible engineer should tabulate the raw production estimates from each engineer for each subtask to include the following data: the high estimate, the low estimate, the average estimate, and the standard deviation for each subtask. Figure 14.3 illustrates an element estimate consolidation process.

   An example of consolidated estimation information is shown in the graphs in Figure 14.4. This information and the associated graphs are easy to compile with a spreadsheet or similar tool. All of the team members will estimate each subtask of the element, but the data for the estimation should be kept anonymous to avoid any preconceived notions that may be associated with persons performing the estimation. Once consolidated, the data should be reviewed with all of the members of the architecture design team or the element production team, and schedule negotiations can begin.

4. Negotiation: After consolidation, the responsible engineer should present the element subtask estimation data to the team that made the estimates. The estimates should be compared and points of deviation identified and discussed as a group. Plotting the standard deviation

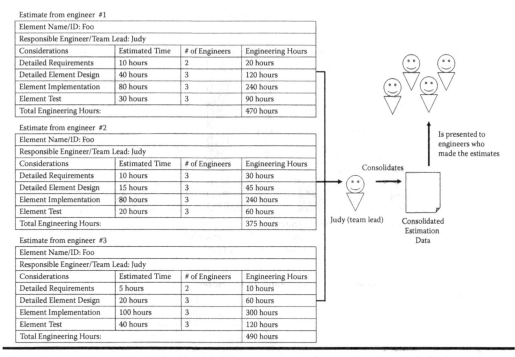

Figure 14.3   Consolidated Estimation Data

can quickly highlight significant differences in estimates. Where there are differences, the team should discuss the reasons for them in subtask estimates and try to reach consensus where possible. Where compromise is not possible, consider using the average estimates.

5. Revise and roll-up: Any changes to the estimates should be made on the element estimation sheets. The revised estimation sheets should then be sent to the managing engineer, who will "roll up" all of the individual element estimation sheets and compile them into a production schedule for the project. This includes resolving any dependencies and computing production costs as necessary.

The estimates described above can be rolled up at the project or program level to create a Gantt chart, PERT charts, or any other standard schedules. The managing engineer is responsible for creating the production schedule, but all members of the architecture design team and any engineers who are part of the architecture design team may participate in its creation through the estimation process described here.

Test Planning

During production planning, the requirements engineer must create plans for testing the system or product. Integrated system or product test should be planned by the quality process engineer, chief scientist, and requirements engineer. These roles are responsible for system test. The chief scientist should focus on testing the system in terms of detailed technical elements that should be tested (clear-box test). The requirements engineer should focus on testing the system in terms of the requirements (black-box test). The quality process engineer is responsible for overall test planning and execution. Once a test is planned, the test activities should be estimated; the form

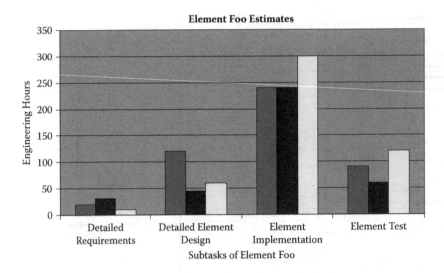

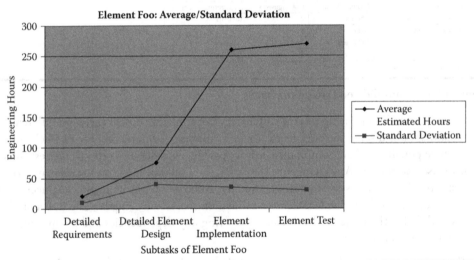

Figure 14.4 Example Consolidated Estimate Graphs

in Table 14.7 can help guide test estimation and planning. It is essential that the requirements engineer use the architecture drivers specification as a basis for planning tests. Remember, the architectural drivers represent the business goals of the client stakeholder. In addition to developing tests to validate functionality, the quality attributes properties and adherence to constraints must also be validated. Some quality attribute properties and constraints can be tested and validated through operational testing. However, others (such as modifiability) can only be validated through inspection techniques such as code walk-throughs. For example, consider the case of a quality attribute scenario that describes a performance response time of 15 milliseconds. This quality attribute could be tested through operational test of the system. However, there is no way that an operational system can demonstrate most facets of modifiability (unless the modifiability is runtime oriented, such as plug-and-play). Therefore, it may be necessary for the architect design team to inspect the relevant code structures to ensure that the system meets the expectations articulated in the modifiability scenarios. Constraints may also be verified using demonstration and inspection techniques as appropriate. Again, it is essential that test planners begin test planning with the architectural drivers specification. For each architectural driver, the development team should try to determine whether they can be tested through demonstration or inspection.

Other Elements of the Production Plan

There are often many other elements that will have to be considered for the schedule that are not technical in nature and cannot be found in the architecture design. Once the basic schedule has been created the managing engineer should also look at the dynamic nature of the organizations, the project, and the stakeholders and identify situations or conditions that may impact the schedule. Some situations to consider include:

- Training
- Subcontract/subcontractor management
- Nontechnical meetings
- Documentation (not mentioned thus far)
- Employee vacations
- Travel

The intent here is not to present a comprehensive list of items to consider for the schedule, but rather provide a few common examples to stimulate thought. Most of these items can be accommodated for by building buffer into the schedule. There is no rule of thumb for how much buffer is appropriate for all organizations, for all projects. Each organization, each project forms a different context that will have to be assessed. Historical data is probably available within your organization and should be mined and used to guide the estimation of schedule buffer.

Updating the Master Design Plan

At the conclusion of production planning, the managing engineer should update the estimated time spent in the architecture design familiarization meeting, and estimation, scheduling, and planning activities with actual performance.

Summary

Stage 7 is where production activities are planned for stage 8 production:

- Stage 7 planning: Stage 5 begins with the managing engineer estimating the duration and resources required for the architecture familiarization meetings, element estimation, and creating and documenting the production schedule.
- Architecture familiarization: The first step after planning stage 7 is to familiarize the production engineers with the architecture design. This is especially important if they were not part of the architecture design team or if they were not really involved in the design of the architecture.

- Production estimation and scheduling: Each element is assigned a responsible engineer who will act as a shepherd for the estimation of the effort required to produce an element. Estimation for each element should involve at least three engineers. ACDM uses a tailored version of Wideband Delphi estimation called Element-wise Wideband Delphi. The effort required to produce each element is estimated, and the individual efforts are used to create the overall production schedule.

Chapter 15

ACDM Stage 8: Production

Purpose

In stage 8, the elements of the system are produced, tested, and integrated into a system or product.

Preconditions

The production planning activities of stage 7 are completed and a production schedule is ready for the production engineers.

General Activities
Techniques, Templates, and Guidance

This consists of guidance for product plan tracking and oversight.

Primary Artifacts

- Detailed designs
- Units of implementation (software, hardware)

Postconditions

The system or product is ready for deployment in whole or in part.

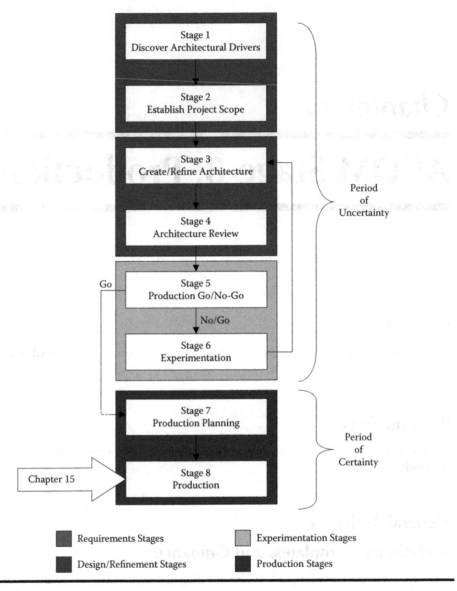

Figure 15.1 Stage 8.

Description of Stage 8

In the production stage, the development team will essentially perform the detailed element design, produce and test the elements, assemble the elements into a system or product, and test the integrated system or product. Production may be of the entire system, or may be carried out in increments. ACDM may seem to be waterfall in nature, but ACDM can be used to iteratively develop the system or product. In addition to the technical activities associated with producing the system or product, another essential activity of this stage is tracking and oversight of the production activities. The managing engineer will work with general project management to ensure that the team is adhering to the production plan, detecting deviations, and taking corrective action as necessary.

Table 15.1   Stage 8 Activities, Outputs, and Responsibilities

General activities	Implement, test, and integrate the system/product elements. Test the integrated system or product.
General outputs	Detailed design and implementation artifacts, such as code modules, hardware, and so forth.

Role	Stage 8 Recommended Responsibilities
Managing engineer	The managing engineer is responsible for working to help general project management in coordinating and tracking the development of the system.
Chief architect	The chief architect will assist detailed designers and implementers through the production process by helping engineers to understand the architecture design and resolve issues between the design and the detailed design and implementation. The chief architect will work to ensure that the implementation adheres to the architecture design.
Chief scientist	The chief scientist will assist detailed designers and implementers in resolving technical issues associated with production of the system/product. The chief scientist is responsible for conducting/assisting in integrated system/product test.
Requirements engineer	The requirements engineer is responsible for conducting/assisting in integrated system/product test.
Quality process engineer	The quality process engineer is responsible for leading integrated system/product test and ensuring that defects found during this test are recorded and addressed.
Support engineer	The support engineer will continue to support production engineers and the architecture design team with any tools required for detailed design, implementation, or testing.
Production engineers	Production engineers are responsible for detailed design and implementation of the system/product elements, unit test of the elements, and assisting in product/system test.

Stage 8 Planning

The element construction activities of stage 8 were planned in stage 7. In stage 8 the plan devised in stage 7 is carried out. Note that the master design plan, which guided the design activities up to stage 8, is now essentially a recorded history of the design activities for the system. At this point it is a good idea to ensure that the master design plan is current, and it should be archived. The information in the master design plan can be used on subsequent projects implementing ACDM for planning, estimation, management, and oversight. Over time, the body of data collected in the master design plans can be archived and used to tailor and refine the organization's design process. In Section 3, guidelines for instantiating and tailoring ACDM will be presented and discussed.

Design Consistency

Developing an architecture design for a software-intensive system does not preclude the need for detailed design of the elements. Once the elements of the architecture are defined and the architecture has reached a point of stability, the elements will have to be designed by production engineers in greater detail so that they can be implemented. However, it is critical that the detailed element designs match the architecture designs. If the transformation from architecture design to detailed design is not consistent, then the implementation will not match the architecture, and it will not likely possess the properties designed into the architecture. This is especially problematic with the detailed software designs of the elements. ACDM does not prescribe how to do detailed software element design. The production engineers may use object-oriented software design methods, structured software design methods, and so forth. ACDM can and does work with any of these design methodologies because architectural design concerns are inherently different from those of detailed design and implementation concerns. These different concerns are illustrated in Table 15.2.

To ensure that detailed designs match the architecture design, it is wise to review designs to ensure that they conform to the architecture design prior to producing the elements. This can be an informal activity or a formal milestone in the production of the elements. This kind of oversight is similar to a building architect reviewing construction progress at the site of a building that he or she designed. If there are problems at the building site, ambiguities, or problems with the design, then the architect will be consulted to rectify these issues. The architect of a software-intensive system should have a similar relationship with those producing the elements and integrating them into a system. If detailed designers, implementers, and integrators find problems that have architectural impact, then they must be able to communicate these to the architect. The architect must resolve these issues and communicate the fixes back to the designers, implementers, or integrators, as the case may be. The chief scientist should also be available to assist the production engineers with technical issues that may arise during production. The chief scientist can be likened to a structural engineer who may be consulted from time to time during the construction of a building to assist the architect and technicians. Certainly the chief architect must also be a consummate technologist, but often he or she is preoccupied with the big-picture design details. The chief scientist certainly has an important role in the architecture design, but his or her focus is on the technical details of the design and implementation. This is a powerful combination of roles, especially in larger system development projects.

Just as detailed designs must conform to the architecture design, implementations must conform to the detailed designs as well. Again, this seems to be most problematic with software design

Table 15.2 Design Concerns

General Architecture Design Concerns	General Detailed Design and Implementation Concerns
System/product stakeholders	Detailed requirements elicitation and analysis
Business processes and operational models	
Identification of system context	User interface design
Architecture drivers elicitation	Language features
Defining infrastructure	Algorithmic efficiencies
Gross partitioning of system into elements	Data structure design
Systemic production and integration	Software application testing
Systemic testing	Implementation of functionality

and production. For small projects, code reviews can be used to ensure that software implementations adhere to the detailed designs. Depending upon the scale and scope of the system and development effort, reviewing every line of code to ensure that it remains faithful to the design from whence it came may be a bit too ambitious for a single chief architect or even an architecture design team. Code reviews or inspections are nothing new, and there are many ways to do code inspections—the grandfather of all code inspections is described by Fagan (1976). Code reviews are a powerful technique for ensuring high-quality code, but they can be expensive. The decision to conduct or not conduct code reviews should be something that project management decides depending upon cost/benefit analysis. If an organization is building a control system for an airplane, then perhaps code reviews are a good idea and will pay for themselves many times over. However, if an organization must meet a target market window and is willing to compromise some quality to make that window, then it may decide to not use code reviews. If code reviews are utilized, then part of the review should include examining the code to ensure that it conforms to the detailed designs. Code reviews need not be an all-or-nothing proposition. Selected, critical elements can be identified vis-à-vis the architecture, and the code associated with these elements can be inspected. Again, when inspecting the code associated with these elements, check to ensure that it adheres to the detailed designs. Although this is not a total design conformance check, it is better than no check at all.

Element Integration

The architecture can serve as a harness or scaffolding for element integration. It can be useful to have a team responsible for creating the architecture infrastructure—this can greatly ease integration for complex systems.

As elements are completed, production engineers are responsible for testing or qualifying each element per the element production plans they created. In addition to element test, the system or product will be tested after the elements are integrated into a complete system or product. Many different strategies can be used to perform element test and integrated system test. Testing should be coordinated by the quality process engineer working with the requirements engineer and the chief scientist per the integrated test plan created in stage 7.

Production Effort Tracking

Often when sitting in project status meetings it is common to hear engineers say, "I am about 50 percent complete with that task." This is especially true when the task is software development. The problem with these assessments of progress is that they are nearly always made based on the engineer's "gut-feel" for how done he or she is. Objective assessment of progress made on the construction of physical things is a little easier than it is with software. With physical things it is often possible to objectively measure how much has been built and how much has to be built. Objective progress measures are harder with software because we cannot see it, touch it, or examine it in its totality (e.g., it is perceived differently from different perspectives). Although totally objective assessments of software completion are currently impossible, we can do a better job of tracking progress than by relying on gut-feel and instinct. ACDM prescribes tracking progress using earned value. Earned value is an objective measurement of effort expended, and how much work has been accomplished on a project over time. Earned value, performance measurement, management by objectives, and cost schedule control systems are similar concepts, utilizing similar techniques. The essence of earned value is that each project task is assigned a weighted, relative value. The total "doneness" of the project is measured by the sum total of the task values. As each task is completed, the development team is credited with the value of each task, but only when the task is completed in its entirety. This is an important concept—no partial credit can be awarded. If partial credit is awarded, then this will degenerate into gut-feel progress measures. Using the earned value measurement, management has deeper insight into how much work has actually been completed against the amount of work planned to be accomplished. Earned value can help to avoid the situation where the last 10 percent of a project takes 150 percent of the schedule and budget. Earned value is a natural fit for ACDM because all estimation, planning, and scheduling emanate from the architecture design. ACDM uses the schedule derived in stage 7 from the architecture design elements to track the progress of the production stage. This approach works if the entire system is being built in a waterfall fashion or incrementally. The process for using earned value on projects utilizing ACDM as their design process is described in the following paragraphs.

Once the individual element production estimates have been made, the total project construction time can be calculated from the element estimate as described in stage 7. To use earned value tracking, an earned value has to be established and assigned for each architecture design element. Element granularity is important. If the granularity of what is being tracked is too coarse, then the project will go from zero earned value to done in a few discrete jumps. This does not provide much insight into progress, and it may cause a bit of consternation because the project may be at zero earned value for a long time, then jump to 50 percent earned value, then to done in the blink of an eye. If the elements in the architecture are few and relatively small, then each element might be the right granularity for tracking progress in a meaningful way. However, if the elements are large and complex, it may make sense to reduce a single element to subtasks for earned value tracking. In this case, the earned value for a single element would be the sum total of the earned value of each subtask. Management will have to decide what level of granularity is appropriate.

Earned value is derived from the total estimated production time and the estimated element production estimates. For example, assume that we have a project whose rolled up estimate is 1,000 engineering hours in duration. Next, assume that we have a task that is 15 hours in duration. The 15-hour task represents 1.5 percent of the 1,000-hour total project duration; therefore, the earned value for this task is 1.5 (Humphrey, 1989; Pressman, 2005). The total project duration (Dt) and the earned value for any given task (EvT) is calculated as:

$$Dt = \Sigma \text{ (task duration}_T) \text{ for all tasks}$$

$$Ev T = \text{(task duration}_T)/(Dt)$$

When a task is completed, it contributes its earned value to the project's total earned value. The earned value then can be used to objectively measure the production effort. Using earned value we can measure:

■ The percentage of production completeness
■ How well the team is performing with respect to the production schedule
■ Deviation from the production schedule

Total production completeness at some schedule time (Ct) is measured in terms of earned value:

$$Ct = (\Sigma \text{ earned value at time } t)/Dt$$

Schedule performance can be measured by calculating the *performance index*. This is a measure of how well the team is performing with respect to the production schedule. A value of 1 indicates exact schedule compliance. A value of greater than 1 indicates schedule slippage. A value of less than 1 indicates that production is ahead of schedule. The performance index (Pi) is calculated as follows:

$$Pi = (\text{total planned earned value at time } t)/(\text{actual earned value at time } t)$$

Schedule variance is the difference between the actual earned value at time t and the planned earned value at time t. Ideally, the difference should be zero, indicating that the team is not deviating from the planned schedule. A negative value indicates that the team is behind schedule. The more negative the value, the more behind schedule the team is. A positive value indicates that the team is ahead of schedule. The more positive the value, the more ahead of schedule the team is. Schedule variance is calculated as follows:

$$\text{Schedule variance} = (\text{actual earned value at time } t) - (\text{planned earned value at time } t)$$

Tracking production progress is the responsibility of the managing engineer. However, ACDM is a design process framework, not a total software development process, and the managing engineer's role is to manage the design process. However, the managing engineer may also be responsible for the entire development project. In fact, in field trials of ACDM this was nearly always the case—it is convenient and provides continuity from design to production. In any case, the production plan, production oversight, and tracking methods described in stage 8 should be utilized by those managers responsible for production. The production schedule, production tracking, and oversight methods are derived from the product/system architecture. The architecture is designed and refined in a rigorous way, and the production schedule and project tracking tends to be more objective and accurate than gut-feel tracking. Note that the exact development processes used by production engineers are not specified by ACDM. Because ACDM is a design process, these details are intentionally omitted. However, ACDM can be used with a number of existing process frameworks. Chapter 18 is dedicated to integrating ACDM with existing process frameworks, specifically:

- Traditional waterfall models
- Extreme Programming (XP)
- Scrum
- Team Software Process (TSP)
- Rational Unified Process (RUP)
- Agile Unified Process (AUP)
- Capability Maturity Model Integrated (CMMI)

These are popular development methodologies today; however, most give very little guidance on design. The ability to weave together ACDM with existing process frameworks is a key strength of ACDM. This enables organizations to continue to utilize a specific development process framework, or adopt a specific process framework, but complements existing development processes with a more robust design process.

Summary

During stage 8 the elements of the architecture design are produced. The element estimation forms are miniplans that will guide the production work of the engineers producing the elements. Once the architectural elements are produced, they will be integrated into an ensemble and tested. Throughout production, the effort is tracked using the production schedule and earned value tracking.

SECTION

Chapter 16

Transitioning Design Practices, Processes, and Methods

It is not necessary to change. Survival is not mandatory.

W. Edwards Deming (1948–)

Thus far the mechanics of ACDM has been presented in something of an idealist way, focusing on initial (green field) product or system development situations. However, this is rarely the situation that engineers and organizations find themselves in. Various process frameworks and design methods are usually defined and explained in ideal situations and contexts, just as ACDM has been described thus far. However, this leaves the practitioner to figure out how to use the method or framework in an industrial organizational setting. This is often a very difficult and problematic proposition because frameworks, methods, processes, technologies, and so forth must be tailored to meet the exact business, organizational, and technical context that the system or product is being built in. Adopting new ways of designing and building software-intensive systems is problematic in two dimensions. First, the required tailoring is not trivial and necessitates a great deal of experience with the frameworks, methods, and processes, as well as the business, organizational, and technical domains. Second, introducing and transitioning frameworks, methods, technologies, and processes in an organization is a difficult proposition because people are often resistant to change. What is needed by practitioners and organizations are hints and guidelines for tailoring and transitioning frameworks, methods, and techniques into practice. To these ends, this section of the text provides guidelines for tailoring, instantiating, transitioning, and successfully adopting ACDM in various project contexts, organizations, and domains. Hopefully this will help practitioners overcome the difficulties associated with introducing and transitioning ACDM into their organization and projects. Much of the information provided here is based on experience in using ACDM on real projects in various business, organizational, and technological contexts.

General Transitioning Strategies

The term *transitioning* here refers to introducing ACDM or other design practices, processes, and methods into projects, or more broadly into the overall organization building software-intensive products and systems. There is no simple recipe for transitioning ACDM because organizations, business contexts, requirements, and so forth are different. Whether an organization decides to use ACDM or not, the design process should be established deliberately. Roles, responsibilities, artifacts, deliverables, milestones, and so forth should be determined as part of defining the design process. ACDM is essentially a design process framework, and if it is used, it will have to be instantiated to fit an organization. No method, process, or framework is a turnkey silver bullet, one-size-fits-all proposition. ACDM is no exception to this rule. The existing development processes will be affected when instantiating ACDM within a project or organization. As ACDM is inserted into an organization, the organization must stay in business. There are a number of big-picture concerns that will dictate how to sensibly introduce and transition ACDM within the context of an organization and a project. Some of the key concerns will be discussed in the sections that follow.

Change Agents

Change agents is a term used to refer to individuals who promote change within an organization to improve the way that systems and products are built in an organization, to reduce cost, improve quality, and reduce time to market. Ironically, change agents do not need to be architecture experts or ACDM experts, but they must understand the following:

■ Costs and benefits of adopting architectural practices and ACDM
■ Impact to organizational structure and processes
■ Impediments to adopting architectural practices

Change advocates do not need to be managers, but they must have access to appropriate levels of management support to institutional change. Change advocates must keep in mind the territorial nature of human beings, whose tendencies are to protect organizational boundaries they are comfortable with. Successful change advocates are able to penetrate organizational boundaries, gain trust, and acquire support to build broad coalitions within organizations. Management support is required to obtain the authority and budget required to institute change. Changing the hearts and minds of engineers involves:

■ Appealing to emotion: Engineers are often dedicated to their organizations and take pride in contributing to the corporate mission. Awarding top performers, those who provide the best suggestions, those who do the best job, often helps use this dedication to advance change agendas.
■ Appealing to reason: Engineers are creatures of logic and reason. Using cost/benefit data can help change the hearts, minds, and eventually the behavior of engineers. Most managers are particularly interested in hard data that shows clear cost/benefit comparisons.
■ Coercion: The use of bonuses and reprimands, or the "carrot and stick" method, has been a popular way to modify the behavior of employees. This does not usually work well with a highly educated workforce—the best engineers will leave rather than be coerced to do anything.

To successfully utilize any of these approaches to change behavior, ultimately management support will be required. Indirectly, this means that management support is required before any meaningful change can take place. While changing the hearts and minds of engineers using these techniques may seem straightforward enough, how do you change the hearts and minds of managers? This is usually more challenging than the former, and without changing managers' hearts and minds, the rest of the technology introduction and transition is probably a moot point. Managers must first be made aware of the method, tool, technique, framework, and so forth through executive seminars, conferences, and so on. To sell senior management on new approaches for designing and building systems and products, change advocates will need to appeal to their reason. The best way to convince management to adopt new ways of designing and building systems and products is build an economic case for how much money and other resources will be saved, or how much faster the system or product can be built. The simple fact is that managers understand their corporate world through the economics. Case studies illustrating cost and benefits from similar organizations can be helpful in obtaining management buy-in. The change advocate's job is to describe how much the organization will have to invest, how much return can be expected for a given investment, and how long it can take to realize the return on that investment. Management must understand that adopting architecture design practices is not a one-time, quick fix, but rather an investment. Lasting change and continuous improvement require lifestyle changes, not quick fixes. For example, people who adapt short-term fad diets may lose weight quickly, but data shows that most of these kinds of dieters will regain the weight they lost and more within a relatively short period. However, those who focus on lifestyle changes, including exercise and eating better food, tend to lose weight slowly but permanently.

Getting an organization to adopt sound architecture design processes and practices is like any other technology insertion or process improvement problem. Organizations generally take two approaches: top-down or bottom-up. In the top-down approach, a manager will decree that the organization will use processes, tools, techniques, methods, and so forth that he or she specifies. Although decreed by management, it is hard to change the real behavior of engineers in the trenches. In the bottom-up approach, engineers in the trenches see value in new architecture design practices and try to institute change from their position in the organization. Unfortunately, managers may be reluctant to spend money on anything that does not translate into functionality. Both top-down and bottom-up approaches can work, but in practice absolute approaches such as these have unpredictable results. Successfully adopting new architecture design processes and practices really requires three important ingredients to improve the chances of success:

- A champion who thoroughly understands architecture design, its role in product/system development, and the impact it has on an organization. The champion must be the change advocate who "leads the charge."
- A talented architect who understands architecture design principles, and is a good leader and communicator.
- Management support and endurance throughout the introduction and adoption.

Introduction, adoption, and transition efforts need to be carefully thought through and planned to help ensure success. When planning these efforts, company history, company culture, organizational structure, available resources, human resources, current state, desired state, and opportunities for improvement all affect the planning. However, the most important first step in planning a transition effort is to understand the current state of an organization. Promoting change without a current understanding of state is usually more harmful than a well-understood chaotic environment! The current state that must be understood before planning change includes the current organizational structures, the available talent, and what current design processes and practices are being used. Changing organizational structures, the way engineers design and build systems, or the tools that they use, without a current understanding of what they do and how they do, is a recipe for disaster. It can also sour the organization on future change efforts. A plan for change is essential, but devising the plan is impossible without understanding the current organizational state. The following age-old quotes sum this up nicely:

> If you don't know where you are going, any road will do.
>
> **Chinese proverb**

> If you don't know where you are, a map won't help.
>
> **Watts Humphrey's proverb**

A Strategy for Change

Although there is no single recipe for change, there is an enormous body of experience throughout industry for organizations building software-intensive systems and products. What is provided here is a strategic framework to guide change advocates in planning the introduction, adoption, and transition of architecture design practices and ACDM in general. The transition framework includes five key elements: sponsorship, baseline, plan, execute, and reflect.

Sponsorship

The importance of top management support and leadership cannot be overstressed as key elements in successful implementation of organizational change. Management support is required for the resources and authority they wield, and the credibility and leadership they provide to the change effort. Laying the groundwork for a successful improvement effort begins with management. It should not be surprising then that the first step in the transition framework is to establish and secure management sponsorship for the change effort. The benefits and vision for the change have to be transferred from the change advocate to the managers who will ultimately sponsor and lead the change effort. The manager must be able to articulate the need, set the vision, and define the basic purpose and goals of the change efforts, and parameters or requirements for adopting new practices. He or she will get this information from the change advocate. Management needs to take a long-term perspective when considering technology adoption or process change. The vision for how the change can be instituted has to be planned by the change advocate. Once the techniques and methods have been selected and the plan has been made, the rest amounts to selling the idea. This first "sale" is critically important because management must be convinced to the level that they will compel others to stick with the change plan during early stages, when resistance and obstacles may seem insurmountable. It is best if the manager's leadership style is a participative one—where he or she evangelizes the change himself or herself. The more engaged management is, the easier it can be to establish an organizational culture that is amenable to change. Many changes in architecture design practices and design processes involve organizational transformations that can include operating in new ways, developing a new organizational culture, and adapting new processes and tools. Some approaches for securing sponsorship have been alluded to, but a concise list is provided here:

- Motivation for change: The change advocate must describe to management the opportunity for change or organizational improvement. This usually includes a description of how products or systems can be designed and built more predictably, in a timely manner, with higher quality, with few resources, at a lower cost, and so forth. Often this means diplomatically pointing out shortfalls in the current practices; concrete data should be used to illustrate problems and issues. However, the change advocate must present this information in a politically correct way so as to not indict individuals, projects, or organizations. Show data without referencing products, projects, or individuals.
- Best practices: The change advocate must describe those best practices that he or she believes would improve the current organizational practices. Again, data speaks volumes. Industry data and case studies from similar kinds of organizations can help convince management that there really is a better way.
- Cost of change: Change is not free. The change advocate must try to estimate the resources required to introduce and adopt the new practices. These costs may include (but are not limited to) training, tooling, short-term productivity losses (due to adopting new methods, processes, and tools), training personnel, and so forth.
- Potential returns: Describe the potential return on investment for the cost expenditure and successfully adopting the new practices. In many cases the return on investment will be difficult to determine and will have to be estimated. Consider using industrial case studies from similar kinds of organizations, projects, or domains. These are often available in publications or at conferences.

Change advocates should have these elements ready before they approach managers with their ideas. It may take many hours and many interactions with managers before their sponsorship has been secured. Be prepared, be patient, be persistent.

Baseline

In planning to transition to more disciplined architectural design processes, the change advocate must understand and acknowledge the existing organizational culture, business and market context, and current design processes. If these are ignored, the change advocate will be viewed as naive and arrogant, and this will only increase resistance to change. Failing to baseline the organization's current state is a sure recipe for disaster. Although ACDM may seem like a good idea as written, in practice it will need to be tailored to fit an organization. As previously mentioned, tailoring any method, process, framework, and so forth is not as easy as following a recipe—this is because every organizational context is different. What guides this tailoring is the current state of the organization. Baselining current design practices will help reveal opportunities for improvement, but will also uncover practices that can be reused. Reusing sound practices gives credit to the organization and the engineers who developed the practices. It is always easier for organizations and engineers to embrace "homegrown" best practices than it is to have an outsider say, "No, what you are doing is wrong and I know what is best." No one in his or her right mind would actually say this outright, but this is the message that is sent when current practices are summarily shunned and new practices are mandated (sometimes by outsiders) with muscle from management. Any new design practices and processes need to be aligned with current organizational needs, and business and personnel processes that may be in place. This can include financial systems and processes, merit and promotion systems, job titles, marketing processes, training processes, and so forth. Understanding these processes is critical because often they are constraining factors for the kinds of new design practices that can be adopted by an organization. For example, the process by which marketing interacts with potential customers may dictate how the organization is able to conduct architecture drivers elicitation workshops. In many organizations it may be impossible to change these practices. In this case, the established marketing processes become constraining factors for adopting ACDM, and the associated ACMD processes and techniques will have to be tailored to work in this context. This is not good or bad—it is just reality. Determining what to change and how to change is highly dependent upon understanding these factors.

Changing processes, adopting new methods, or inserting new technology under these dynamic conditions can be challenging for an organization. This is no different for an organization adopting ACDM. It is important to restate that ACDM is not a development process; it is a design process. ACDM was designed to be less disruptive to the overall organizational development processes and for easy use with existing development processes. There are natural insertion and departure points built into ACDM to make it easier to adopt and merge with existing development processes. Some of the specific ways that ACMD can be merged into existing frameworks will be discussed later. Baselining current practices can be thought of as taking an inventory of what the organization currently does. While ACDM focuses on the design process, it might be best to inventory the organization's total product development process before making changes to the organization's design process. This will provide better insight for what design practices to target, their effect on the total product/system development process, and what can and should be improved in current practices. In many organizations, it is often the case that the problem is not a lack of design processes and practices, but rather there are multiple, inconsistent approaches for designing systems and products. In these cases, different practices should be cataloged for analysis and comparison. Table 16.1 is a template that can be used to catalog this information for later analysis and comparison.

The Plan

Once the organizational design practices, processes, methods, and so forth have been baselined, opportunities for improvement can then be identified and a strategy for improvement devised. These opportunities are usually revealed as gaps between actual performance/results using the current design practices and the desired performance/results. Change advocates must devise a strategy for what they plan to change; why they plan to change the specified practices, processes, methods, and so forth; what the gain or advantage will be in the change; and how they will transition to the new practice. This must be aligned with the business context, but also support new and emerging business goals that are motivating the need for change. The plan is a critical communication tool for managers who will fund and support the change and for the engineers who will most likely have to change the way they design and build systems. The plan should be as specific and detailed as possible. In addition to a detailed description of the plan, provide an executive summary that gives an overview for management. In the executive summary, summarize:

- What will change
- Why the particular practices are targeted for change

Table 16.1   Template for Cataloging Practices, Processes, and Methods

Name	Provide a name or reference for this practice, process, or method.
Purpose	Describe what this practice, process, or method is used for.
Applicable organization/ team	Describe the organizations, teams, and so forth that use the method.
Basic description and procedures	Describe the essential practice, process, or method used. Describe essential roles that carry out the practice, process, or method; who does what; when they do it; how they do it; and so forth.
Preconditions	What must happen, what must be produced (artifacts), and what must be done before this practice, process, or method is utilized or carried out?
Postconditions	What happens or what is produced as a result of carrying out this practice, process, or method?
Context	What is the context for this practice, process, or method? Are there particular conditions when it must be used? Are there other conditions when it does not work or is not recommended for use?
Scale/scope	Describe the scale and scope of applicable projects, teams, and organizations that use this practice, process, or method.
Supporting tools	Describe any supporting tools required to carry out this practice, process, or method, and how and why they are used.

- How the change will be instituted
- The cost and impact for the change
- How long it will take to institute the change
- The expected results and return on investment

In the plan, it is essential that key measures are identified to measure the effect of the change. Focus on measuring return on investment as early as possible. Some measures may include some or all of the following:

- Product cost and schedule
- Product metrics such as size, complexity, and quality
- Stakeholder satisfaction (product, product development services)
- Design and development process
- Quality/defects

Measurement is continuous—try to identify interim as well as long-term measurements. Assume that we want to measure system quality. This is good, but it may take months or years to get a single data point. Interim measures should be selected that measure other aspects of the newly instituted or changed methods, processes, and practices. Consider measuring defects, quality of interim artifacts, satisfaction, cost/schedule, and so forth. It is impossible to manage what is not measured. It is also impossible to measure the effectiveness of change—or to justify the need for change in the first place.

When adopting and transitioning new design practices, it is important to try to limit the disruptive nature that change is likely to cause. It is strongly advised that change advocates target easy things to change first. This approach is often referred to as "picking the low-hanging fruit." The low-hanging fruit are those things that are relatively easy to change or improve and will yield immediate positive results. This is a low-risk approach that will provide early success, build confidence, and help to build or continue sponsorship. Early failures in change or process improvement efforts are greatly magnified and can undermine future efforts to improve the design process. If there are early successes, more ambitious changes can be planned later. If there are failures or marginal successes in more ambitious change efforts, they are more likely to be tolerated if there are early successes. When changing design practices, processes, and methods, it is wise to initially target small teams and projects as test beds. The target teams should be comprised of the more talented engineers who understand the proposed changes and who are more open to changing the way they design and build systems. This will increase the likelihood of initial success and allow the bugs to be worked out of the new practice, process, or method. Limiting the scope of the changes to a single test project will allow more data to be collected to verify the new approaches, and if the new/changed practices, processes, or methods do not work, the impact of failure will be minimized and controlled. Again, total reinvention of processes is usually not the best approach, but often the best practices exist locally. We may find the necessary best practices among the existing processes, and sometimes it is a matter of tweaking existing practices. Totally new design practices, processes, and methods are hard to adopt and transition into because they are unfamiliar to the engineers, support staff, and management. For this reason, adopting totally new processes can be a bit more disruptive and riskier. However, in some situations total and wholesale reinvention is warranted. As changes to design practices, processes, and methods or new ones are being considered, the change advocate should involve practicing engineers. They will do the work, they have done the work, and they will most directly be affected by the plan. If the practicing engineers understand the problems, the reasons for the change, and help define the change, they are most likely to support and embrace the new practices, processes, and methods. This gives credit to internal engineering excellence and increases the chances of successfully adopting new design practices. This builds ownership for the change plan, and the practicing engineers will often evangelize the change effort themselves. This can significantly reduce the burden on the change advocate, who must champion and sell the new approaches to management, engineers, and the organization at large. Plan for short awareness seminars and status meetings for management to keep them abreast of the progress of change and to keep them engaged in the effort. The plan should also include initial training and continuous training as necessary for engineers as well as management. Asking engineers to use or implement new practices, processes, or methods they are not familiar with is unfair and will lead to frustration. Failing to equip the engineers will frustrate them with the change and could compromise the change effort. However, training engineers in new practices, processes, or methods can be an incentive for them to try new things. Training represents a significant cost that is often overlooked when an organization is planning to change how it designs and builds systems and products. If an organization is unwilling to fund training, then it is unreasonable to expect to have high expectations from the change effort. Many change and improvement efforts include the adoption of new tools. Tools are important, but tools are not a replacement for sound processes, practices, and methods. Once practices, processes, and methods are sound, then tools can be selected to support them. Tools should complement the design process, not define them as they so often do in practice.

Execute

Once the plan is in place and approved by management sponsors, it must be faithfully, but not blindly, executed. It is essential that the engineers affected by and responsible for implementing the change are briefed on the strategy. This is best done through a presentation to the practicing engineers, affected support staff, and their most immediate management. Often, practitioners are kept in the dark about such changes. Again, this can result in alienation and will undermine the changes. It is best to engage those most affected by the changes to help with planning them. If the practicing engineers were not involved in the planning process, then it is essential that they are briefed before attempting to execute the plan. As new design practices, processes, and methods are adopted by the organization, it is essential that their effects be measured and assessed honestly. It is important to ensure that the newly adopted practices, processes, and methods are actually used, that they are being used properly, and that the progress and effect of their adoption and use are being monitored and measured. Often organizations adopt new practices, process, or methods in word but not in deed. For example, engineers may go through the motions of adopting good architecture design practices and create an architecture design because they are forced to do so. Once the design is done, they have completed their obligation and the architecture design goes on the shelf and the "real work" of grinding out code begins—in other words, the design is not used by anyone for anything. This serves no one. Designing the architecture is a waste of time and energy other than it meets some process obligation. It is critical during the initial adoption and transition that the change advocate ensures that the new practices, processes, and methods are actually used and their effectiveness measured. If they are not being used, then measurement is meaningless. If they are being used, but not measured, then we do not know if they are effective. Change advocates should continually analyze measurement data and address shortcomings quickly, candidly, and honestly. Do not try to put lipstick on a pig—it will ruin trust and confidence in the change effort. It can be instinctive to hide problems, but eventually broken practices, processes, and methods will be discovered. Unfortunately, the change advocate must take the brunt of the responsibility for failures, but he or she must also analyze them to discover root causes and avoid similar problems in the future. If there are too many failures, the change effort will have no future. This is why initial changes should be relatively easy and yield the greatest return for the time and resources invested. New processes should be tested on smaller, lower-risk, isolated projects. The organization must also be somewhat tolerant when adopting new design practices, processes, and methods. There are often difficulties when engineers design and build systems and products in a new way. Often it will take longer to do some things using unfamiliar design practices, processes, and methods. These start-up difficulties should be considered when planning projects that will also be the target of a change program. If there are issues that occur in adopting and using new design practices, processes, and methods, they should be noted and fixed if possible. Any spot changes and modifications made to fix operational problems should be noted and incorporated into the practice, process, or method.

Reflect

One of the most common problems when changing how an organization designs and builds software-intensive systems is that after new practices, procedures, and methods are introduced, their effectiveness and the effectiveness of the change effort are not objectively evaluated. The reflection step is an opportunity for the organization to evaluate the effectiveness of the changes made to existing practices, procedures, and methods or any new ones introduced and adopted. Once the planned adoption of new design practices, processes, or methods has stabilized and their use has normalized, the change advocate should arrange a meeting or series of meetings with the practicing engineers to reflect upon the change effort and its results thus far. Note that *stabilized* does not necessarily mean that the new or changed processes, practices, or methods are optimal or even successful. *Stabilized* means that the methods are understood and being used, and there is some organizational experience with the processes, practices, or methods, for better or worse. The purpose of the reflection meeting is to gather and analyze the data collected on the implemented changes and identify areas for further improvement. The organization should consider the following:

- Have the new design practices, processes, or methods met the expectations, and are they an improvement over the design practices, processes, or methods they replaced?
- Are the selected measures adequate for determining the effectiveness of the new design practices, processes, or methods? Is it possible to define how effective the methods are?
- Describe anything that may have made changing existing design practices, processes, or methods, or adopting the new design practices, processes, or methods, particularly problematic or difficult. Describe anything that may have eased the change of existing design practices, processes, or methods, or eased the adoption of new design practices, processes, or methods.
- Is there any evidence that the new design practices, processes, or methods result in increased overall time and resources required to produce systems and products?
- Have the new design practices, processes, and methods affected the overall quality of the final product or system? Describe how. In what ways has the quality improved or decreased?
- How can the newly implemented design practices, processes, or methods be enhanced to be more effective?
- What other opportunities exist for improving design practices within the organization?

Reflecting is a necessary step for determining how effective the current changes are, but also in identifying new opportunities for improving how an organization designs and builds products and systems. The reflection meeting should include as many of the engineers involved in introducing, transitioning, adopting, changing, and using the design practices, processes, and methods as possible. Again, this fosters ownership for the change and improvement effort, but from a practical standpoint this is where the real problems occur. Engineers forced to implement the changes or adopt the new design practices, processes, and methods are often in the best position to suggest improvements.

After the first iteration through these fives steps, new opportunities for improving the design process can be identified, planned, and evaluated. If at any point management sponsorship is lost, the change advocate must return to the first step and establish sponsorship. This illustrates why data collection is so important to the change/improvement effort. If sponsorship is lost once the change/improvement effort is under way, the data collected can be used to justify the effort and reestablish the sponsorship. If no data was collected, or if there are no objective measures, then it can be difficult to justify the change/improvement effort and reestablish sponsorship.

Practical Ideas for Transition and Adoption

There is no one-size-fits-all design process. However, in any organization, regardless of the size and scope of projects, there are numerous opportunities to improve existing design practices. ACDM has undergone considerable use in industry. A key part of field testing ACDM involved transitioning ACDM into an organizational context. Through these experiences, a number of themes continually emerged. Keeping these themes in mind proved to be helpful to organizations trying to adopt more disciplined methods for designing software-intensive systems. Much of this experience and guidance is described here. If it is impossible to institute a complete design process like ACDM, various practices, processes, and methods can be implemented that will improve the design work and quality of designs. This is low-hanging fruit that can provide a relatively high return for little investment. These key themes are described below.

Apply Common Sense Liberally

Frameworks are great starting positions, but they should never be followed blindly. They are necessarily abstractions and are incomplete. They need to be instantiated or tailored for an organization's particular circumstances and business context. ACDM focuses on the design process, and this differentiates it from other software development process frameworks. However, ACDM is no different from other software process improvement frameworks in that it attempts to generalize and codify a set of best practices and techniques. With this in mind, organizations must keep common sense front and center at all times. This advice applies to those leading the change: senior management, the change advocate, the architect, and the engineers of the organization. There is a temptation in organizations to follow the precepts of a framework like a cake recipe, even if it leads the organization off a cliff. It is critical that the spirit and intent of a framework and any related practices, processes, or methods are understood and adhered to, not the letter of the law—especially when the letter of the law violates common sense! There must be continual, unbiased analysis of the design process and the practices and methods that are part of it. When analysis stops, or when analysis is used to further political agendas, then common sense will be lost. When common sense is lost, organizations institute rules. When rules are followed blindly, processes become ritual. Rituals become nothing more than action without understanding the reason for what we do. A state of ritualization like this is often comfortable, but it is a dangerous state for an organization to be in. When an organization is in this state, if the conditions that established the ritual in the first place change, people are often unable to depart from the ritual. If changes are detected, it is often difficult for ritualized organizations to change and adapt due to the inertia imposed by ritual. Organizations with high ritualization find it difficult to innovate or be responsive to new and changing market forces. History is replete with examples of companies that have failed because they were incapable of adapting to evolving technologies, business models, markets, and so forth. At all times an organization should:

- Understand its economic, marketing, and business context—all design practices, processes, and methods should emanate from this
- Know why the current design practices, processes, and methods are being used
- Create an environment where the current way of doing business can be respectfully challenged without fear of reprisal

- Maintain a process for proposing, analyzing, addressing, and implementing suggested changes
- Be ready and willing to invest in tailoring standard frameworks, processes, methods, techniques, and so on to best meet the needs of the organization
- Measure and analyze the design process and look for inefficiencies and opportunities for improvement

An organizational culture that embraces these key points is more able to adapt good design processes and continually evaluate, improve, and change them as the business context evolves.

Introduce Templates

Common templates for design, documentation, and other work can be derived from an organization's existing body of materials. The best organizational examples can be selected and tailored as templates for general use. If there are no organizational examples, steal from the best (textbooks, case studies, conferences, etc.) and use them as starting positions and tailor as necessary to meet the needs of the organization. ACDM provides numerous templates that adopters can utilize as starting points, but plan on tailoring them to suit the business needs of the organization. Templates generalize and codify best practices. The use of templates is a simple way to get engineers to create artifacts they would not otherwise create, and to consider and address various aspects of the design they might otherwise overlook. Templates promote consistency. Templates can also be an implicit way to introduce design processes.

Create a Technical Career Track

Many organizations today lament the fact that they have no architectural design expertise, and in general lack senior technical expertise. It is common for organizations to train engineers in the use of various technologies; however, this training often lacks focus and is not correlated with long-term career or organizational competence goals. Often training is identified in accordance with an organization's immediate technical needs on a present project. Few organizations have technical career tracks that allow them to grow architects that possess the technical expertise, domain experience, and organizational savvy that provides long-term competitive advantage. Many high-caliber technical experts drift from company to company like hired guns looking for a place where they can ply their talents and do what they really like to do—design and build complex software-intensive systems. Too many organizations today do not make permanent homes for these talented engineers. A long-term investment that an organization can make is to establish a technical track where the very best engineers the organization has are groomed for senior technical positions, such as architect. To define technical career tracks, senior technical positions (such as architect) must be defined. The senior technical positions should be a highly selective career track, and the best should be compensated on par with management at similar organizational positions. The training and experience required to reach a particular technical position should be clearly defined. Engineers selected to be groomed for these senior technical positions should receive formal training, but they should also be mentored by senior architects within the organization. In addition to technical training, those being groomed for senior technical positions (such as architect) should receive training in leadership, communications, and even business and marketing. Training and mentoring should be preconditions for promotion and continuation in the technical career track.

The performance of the engineers selected for these tracks should be monitored, and it should be possible for them to "wash out" of the career track. The training and mentoring that is part of the technical career track can be used to identify those engineers who might not be suitable in senior technical positions. It can be helpful if an organization establishes formal training programs for architects.

Establish an Architecture Design Team

A great way to begin a program to adopt and improve architecture design practices is to establish an architecture design team or some similar body that can provide design guidance to the organization. Nothing speaks louder than action, and establishing an architecture design team sends the message that management is serious about design. This team will do more than draw pictures, but should also help decide what practices, processes, and methods might best fit the needs of the organization. They may actually design or assist engineers with design, help document designs, evaluate designs, or provide some combination of these services. Design teams can be established for a project, department, division, or corporately. There are many ways that architecture design teams can be structured within an organization, and the implementation should be left to the organization. The roles defined in ACDM can help organizations structure design teams, and the stages described by ACDM can serve as a starting point for defining what architecture design teams can do for an organization. Architecture design teams can serve as a liaison between the technical construction, design, and management teams at all levels. The roles and responsibilities of the architecture design team should be defined, as well as its relationship to management on a project. The architecture design team must have technical authority for the systems and products that are built. A key role that the architecture design team plays is to inform management of the impact of design decisions on the organization's business context, and informing engineers why various architectural drivers are in place. Besides the technical work, the architecture design team serves a valuable role as arbitrator between the managerial/marketing community and the technical community.

Institute Architecture Evaluations

Instituting architecture design evaluations for all projects, critical projects, or projects over a certain amount of money is a great way to introduce, transition, and establish disciplined design practices. The author has worked with several organizations to help institute mandated architecture design evaluation for all projects. These organizations implemented the architecture design evaluations in a very similar way, which will be explained here. The first step is to train an internal team of evaluators. While consultants can be used to help train evaluators and help with initial evaluations, it is better if the organization does not rely solely on external consultants for the long term. The evaluation should be a seamless part of the organization's development process. The evaluation team could use ATAM, a tailored version of ACDM's evaluation techniques, or some equivalent method, or even a homespun method. Whatever method is used, it is critical that the method be thorough, repeatable, predictable, and produce consistent results. The method should be applied fairly on all projects in the same way. The method should be as cost-effective, short in duration, and nonintrusive as possible. Those being evaluated should not feel threatened by the process. These points cannot be overemphasized. Failure on any one of these points may result in the failure in the adoption of evaluations and any other design improvements.

Instituting evaluations requires a policy change from management that establishes that architecture designs must be evaluated at some project milestone. The evaluation team should report to management in charge of the development projects. The evaluation team must have sufficient authority and expertise to evaluate architecture designs for all organizational projects. It is best if the architecture design evaluation is a milestone on every project's schedule. The evaluation policy should state that to move forward with construction, projects must complete an architecture design evaluation at a predefined schedule milestone. The evaluation should be done by the central architecture evaluation team, and a summary of the key findings of the evaluation should be sent to project management. This part of the process must be done in a way that is not threatening to the team whose architecture is being evaluated. The results should not indict anyone on the develop team, but the evaluation results should focus on technical issues uncovered during the evaluation. As part of the evaluation follow-up activities, the project team should describe how they plan to address the issues uncovered during the evaluation. This plan should be similar to the issue deposition described in stage 5 of ACDM, and the plan should be part of what senior management receives after the evaluation. This processes is illustrated in Figure 16.1.

This example uses a waterfall model, but there is no reason why a similar evaluation team could not be used at strategic points in an iterative development strategy. Instituting centralized evaluations like this is simple and elegant, and has a far-reaching impact on the quality of product and system designs. The intrusion at the project level is minimal. Project teams can remain autonomous, and the organizational structure is only minimally impacted by the addition of the central architecture evaluation team. Implementation of the centralized evaluation is relatively inexpensive. The major cost is in training the personnel that make up the central architecture evaluation team.

Managers have a limited amount of time, and have a hard time knowing what details they should be paying attention to. Architectural design evaluations implemented in this way give management insight into issues uncovered during the evaluation, without having to worry about all the technical details. In some processes, the design is a process hurtle—just create the design and move on with the real work of construction. Evaluations implemented this way force project teams to pay closer attention to design. It is more than a mere process hoop to jump through because the design will be evaluated by architecture experts. Initially the architecture evaluation group will be called upon for evaluation services—in some cases even grudgingly. However, as the project teams gain experience with architecture through evaluation, the value of design often becomes apparent to the projects. At this point the central architecture evaluation team can provide broader architecture services and assistance with designing, documentation, and so forth. The centralized architecture evaluation team can start with small, easy things like providing templates and checklists for documentation, design representations, architecture drivers, and others, as needed by the project teams.

Barriers to Adoption: Common Anti-Practices

Some organizations have a difficult time adopting new processes, especially when it comes to design processes. The reasons for the difficulties are varied, but there are trends and behaviors worth noting that are common barriers to adopting sound design practices. These barriers are called anti-practices, and a few common ones are described below.

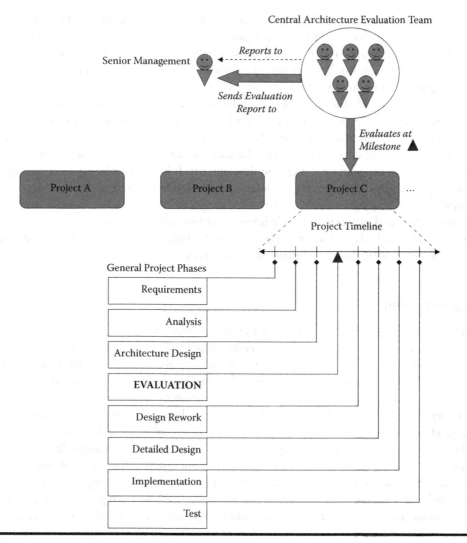

Figure 16.1   Instituting an organizational evaluation process.

Business Context Mismatch

It may be impossible to adopt appropriate practices, processes, or methods if the business context is not well understood. It does not matter if the organization is a raging capitalist retailer, bleeding-heart nonprofit, or gigantic military organization, all have a business context. If the business context is not understood, then it is impossible to select the appropriate design practices, processes, and methods and optimally tailor them. The author had the dubious experience of training a group of engineers in architectural design in an organization that did not develop software-intensive systems, but rather procured them. Much of the time, energy, and expense of training the organization's procurement staff in architectural design were largely wasted. Clearly this is an example of mismatch among the training, expectations, and business context. In this organization, there was a training budget and a senior manager who thought he knew something about architecture design. In his zeal to do the right thing, the organization threw money at the problem by training procurement specialists and managers in architecture design. This led to a great deal of frustration for the attendees, who felt that the training was not helpful. What they needed was training that would help the organization specify and procure the right systems in a cost-effective way. This frustrated the instructor, who had to train people who were not interested in architectural design, would never design a software-intensive system, and just did not "get it." As anticipated, the training went largely unused by this organization, which went on procuring systems as it always had. The real problems and issues they faced were never addressed.

In other cases, design strategies are adopted that are counterproductive to the organization's business goals and mission. Again, this frustrates the practitioner who must use the practices, processes, and methods that do not work. The staff is often faced with devising convoluted work-arounds to do the real work of design and development. It is the front-line project managers who are left trying to find the best way to adhere to and use less than optimal practices, processes, and methods. Senior management is frustrated when the practices, processes, and methods do not help the bottom line, and may even adversely impact cost and schedule. Architectural design practices, processes, and methods that are misaligned with the business needs will make it very hard or impossible to amortize the cost of adoption and transition.

Abandonment

In some cases change advocates will do all the right things: they get management support; understand the business case; select complementary design practices, processes, and methods; and devise a good transition strategy. They start the transition, and after a while the effort seems to fizzle. This can be very frustrating for the change advocate—get over it! Organizations will return to their natural state of equilibrium until the changes are internalized and create a new equilibrium in the organization, that is, the new practices are internalized by the practitioners. Until then, the change effort will require constant energy from the change advocate and management. Adopting and transitioning to a new way of designing and building systems is no cakewalk—if it were easy, all organizations would build systems in the most optimal way. There are many reasons for this. The most fundamental issue contributing to the difficulty of changing organizational behavior is that people are fundamentally resistant to change. Initial costs for changing, adopting, and transitioning to any new practices or technologies can be high and are often a risky undertaking. While an organization changes how it designs systems and products, it must continue to produce systems and products. It can be difficult to implement or transition architecture design technologies while sustaining the business. When new practices, processes, and methods are adopted by organizations, it may fall behind as its employees struggle to learn the new ways. As mentioned earlier, this is part of the cost of improvement. Unfortunately, this is intolerable by organizations that are short-sighted or select projects with immediate needs. Projects such as this should be avoided as targets for trying new processes. In such situations, organizations will abandon the new stuff and return to the old ways of doing business—often at the first sign of trouble. These situations should be avoided at all costs because they will eventually lead to an abandonment of the overall change effort. Unfortunately, organizations tend to focus on the return and not the investment part of the phrase "return on investment." The word *investment* obviously means money, but it also means schedule time and working through difficult transition periods as new design practices, processes, and methods are learned and operational problems with them are worked out. Unfortunately, the cost of abandoning the new practices and reverting to old ways is very high. All the money spent instituting the new practices is lost. The investment in the stalled project using the new practices is lost upon abandonment, and there will be high costs associated with restarting the project again.

What cannot be easily measured is the demoralization to the engineers that occurs in these situations; this almost makes it impossible to attempt change in the future.

Change advocates should go slow and pick easy things that provide high return first—this quickly builds confidence and provides value. As mentioned previously, it is strongly recommended that a small group or project serve as the test bed for implementing new practices, processes, and methods. This limits cost and the organization's exposure to risk until the changes, and the value they provide, are better understood. To counter the visceral reaction to abandon the change effort at the first sign of trouble, change advocates should manage the expectations of leaders throughout the organization early and often. Change advocates should try to anticipate potential problems and estimate the total cost of adopting new ways of designing and buildings systems and products. This should be presented to management as the investments and risks inherent with changing and improving the practice. The organization must be prepared to endure the inevitable costs and risks of overcoming inertia when changing organizational behavior, and focus on endurance and long-term goals, objectives, and payoffs.

Lip Service

Lip service is an expression used to describe a situation where one party agrees to do something but their verbal agreement is not supported by their action—they simply do not do what they said they would do. Sometimes within organizations engineers, managers, marketers, and other personnel are quick to pay lip service to improving design practices. In many cases it is the politically correct thing to do, especially in situations where an organization has had trouble with recent projects and there is an obvious need to "fix the problem." The expedient thing to do is embrace the new or changed practices, processes, and methods and continue on as before. This was a common occurrence in the Total Quality Management (TQM) movement in the 1980s. The problem was not with TQM, but rather with organizations that paid lip service to TQM-oriented improvement efforts. In these organizations, they would do the initial kickoff meetings, and after the initial fanfare of the TQM introduction, people forgot about TQM, and it became just another passing fad. This same situation can happen when adopting new architecture design practices, processes, and methods—ACDM is no different. What an organization says it is doing is not important. What it actually does is important—talk is cheap, whiskey costs money. If the engineers doing the design work do not use the practices, processes, and methods prescribed by ACDM (or any other framework), then they cannot expect to change or improve their results. When evaluating whether or not an organization is actually using the practices, processes, and methods it professes to be using, look for evidence in the artifacts and data. If there is no change or improvement long after there should be, then it might be the case that the change effort is a victim of lip service.

Software Is Easy

The key message of the text has been that software-intensive systems have to be designed holistically. Systems have physical elements, infrastructure, and software. Unfortunately, many organizations treat software as a second-class citizen; this is especially true in organizations that were historically hardware companies. In one case the author was addressing a group of software engineers from a company that built aircraft braking systems. He asked the group what business they were in, and the group emphatically replied that they were in the business of building braking systems for airplanes. The author then asked the group, "Can someone tell me how to build a braking system for an airplane?" The room fell completely silent until one engineer raised her hand and said, "We don't really build braking systems, we write the software." This was not done to humiliate these software engineers but rather to make a point. The first point is that the software for the system is a very crucial part or element of the system. Without the software, the braking system does not work—the hardware is a pile of worthless junk. The software, then, is a real and first-class part of the system, just like the brake pads, nuts, bolts, hoses, and cables. The second point is that while this organization does not admit it, it is also in the software business because without software, it does not have a product! Overcoming the bias that software is easy can be hard to do. Many organizations do not realize that software is problematic and costly because they do not measure anything related to software. This seems to be especially prevalent in organizations that historically focused on hardware, but were forced to use and write software for their products. In some organizational cultures around the world, software engineering is not viewed to be real engineering, and computer science is not real science. Software development is viewed as work for a technician or as something else that real engineers (mechanical, electrical, etc.) or real scientists (physics, chemists, etc.) do. Those who write software are often not compensated on par with real engineers and scientists. Without fail, this disregard for the importance of software shows in the cost, timelines, and quality of the systems and products built. In some cases these organizations design and build very complex systems and products controlled by millions of lines of software. Such is the case with modern aircraft and automobiles, which are flying, rolling computer systems and networks. However, this is the case with more and more everyday consumer products. Sooner or later, these organizations have serious problems with software and are unable to produce quality systems and products in a timely, cost-effective way because software is not given first-class engineering attention.

In another case, the author was asked to help an organization with its software problems associated with building a consumer electronics product with a great deal of embedded software. Upon closer analysis, it was discovered that the organization would first design the electrical and mechanical hardware to near completion, in isolation from software design. When the hardware development was almost complete, some of the engineers who were involved in building the system electronics were selected to begin writing the system software. The first software written was patches to repair hardware deficiencies. If there were delays in the development of the electrical or mechanical parts of the system, this caused the software development to start late. Because of this late start, software was often blamed for schedule overruns. The software was not systematically designed and was hastily written and defect laden.

The result for one product that the organization built was that it did not fare well in the marketplace due to a poor user interface and less than optimal functionality that should have been delivered by the software. Clearly the problem was that the organization was designing products the same way it did when its products had no software. Software was an afterthought, and it was not designed or given first-class engineering attention. It is obvious to most engineers that poorly designed hardware translates into poorly designed systems. But for some reason, it is hard for some organizations to grasp that poorly designed software also translates into poorly designed systems. This organization lost significant market share because of these problems with the software embedded deep within their products, and it took the organization several years to recover technically and regain a reputation of quality. In these organizational cultures it can be difficult to introduce, adopt, and transition disciplined practices, processes, and methods for designing and building software-intensive systems. Unfortunately, it often takes a dramatic failure or loss due to poorly designed software to get the organization's collective attention to change its hearts, minds, and behaviors.

Delegation by Dumping

Change advocates and managers do not have enough time to do everything by themselves, so they hire others to help. Once on board, they are assigned work, and in its most basic form this is delegation. However, while ordering someone to do something is delegation, it is not effective delegation. If the individual does not have the resources to do the job, or if he or she does not understand the purpose and goals of what he or she is being asked to do, it is unlikely that he or she will succeed. This is delegation by dumping. If this is done, the employee stuck with the work can be resentful, especially if there are inadequate resources to do the job, and the goals, success, and completion criteria are not clear. Sometimes the task is impossible. This results in a great deal of frustration, resentment, anger, and feelings of helplessness and hopelessness on the part of employees. Unfortunately, this is exactly how change programs are implemented. Management may support the change program, but once the plans are written, the plan is thrown "over the fence" to the engineers in the trenches for implementation. If engineers are handed a plan describing a list of changes to their design processes with the order to "just do it," this will usually result in resentment, anger, and poor morale in the engineering community. The best engineers will leave the project or the organization.

There is a significant difference between thoughtful delegation and delegation by dumping. Serious damage to morale and performance is a natural by-product of poor delegation practices. Good, healthy delegation can help build enthusiasm for change efforts. The change advocate should work closely with teams to carefully introduce change plans in a cooperative way, inviting feedback and criticism from the engineers. This builds ownership for the new practices. Consider the following points for transitioning and implementing the change plans:

- Be clear about the changes and specific in the description of the changes. Think through the design task based upon what is currently done, what the current results are. Describe the desired results and the changes in behaviors necessary to realize the desired state. Describe the timeline for adoption and transition. Describe feedback, measurement, and monitoring processes and instruments. Describe any flexibility there is in the new practices, processes, and methods as well as any inflexibility there may be.
- Be sure that the staff that is charged with implementing the changes have the time and resources to successfully do so. Some efforts will be hard; be up front with the team and ask for the extra effort. The team should be encouraged and reminded that they can do it, but also the task is reasonable. This is a huge distinction between delegation and dumping.
- Actively monitor the progress of the effort to be sure that the new design practices, processes, and methods are really being performed. Measure and collect data. Do not wait until the project is over to see how well the new practices worked. Be friendly and helpful as you monitor—listen to the engineers, and encourage candid feedback and criticism. Tailor practices, processes, and methods that are obviously broken, but make sure that you give them a chance. Change frequently gives teams a feeling of instability and confusion, and it is difficult to obtain reliable performance measures. Provide feedback to let the team know whether they are properly using the new design practices, processes, and methods. Provide assistance to the teams as needed to implement, use, or fix problematic practices. Praise and reward performance publicly—do not miss an opportunity to give praise or recognition.
- Share information openly. As data becomes available, present the results of the new practices to the team. Present the data/results to the team first, and invite their critique of the data/

results and of the new design practices, processes, and methods they implemented. Formally reward the group for their effort with awards.

■ Delegate with style and grace. It is easier to move mountains or change the course of a river than it is to change human behavior, especially if you alienate those whose behavior you hope to change. Be humble and pleasant in your dealings with the employees that will implement your change plans. The success or failure of the plan will ultimately depend upon them.

My Food Bowl ... Grrr!

"Grrr!" This is often the reaction that projects, teams, and organizations have when a change advocate comes in from the outside and proposes changing the fundamental ways that engineers do their most intimate design work. One of the greatest sources of job dissatisfaction, and a fear that most employees share at one level or another, is loss of autonomy. A change advocate must understand that much of the resistance to change generalized earlier comes from a fear of loss of autonomy. Products built in silos or stovepiped organizations that get their own funding have their own resources, engineers, and so forth. In some organizations, these organizations even compete with one another. Think of a soccer team where each team member is more concerned about personally scoring a goal than about the team winning the game. This is exactly what happens in some organizations where product teams compete against one another. The design practices, processes, and methods in each of these teams may be different—and perhaps for good reason. When baselineing organizational practices, competing practices should be evaluated across the silos and best practices should be identified and publicized. This is often the first source of resistance that a change advocate will run into. These organizations are often reluctant to allow visibility into what they do because they fear that scrutiny will uncover problems. The key fear is that uncovered problems could result in loss of autonomy, and the organization will instinctively protect itself from this. Once the organizational practices are baselined and a set of changes are planned and a target organization or project selected, there can still be reluctance to change. Often this is due to a feeling of loss of autonomy. This is exacerbated if the changes were dumped on the organization without guidance, explanation, or resources to implement them. In these extreme cases, the project or organization could feel that it is being punished for something because it has lost its autonomy and now has to do things in a new way. This feeling of loss of control is compounded if the work of the project or organization is closely monitored and measured. Loss of autonomy is scary, and it is scarier in some cultures where there is a higher degree of liberty than in those where the collective is emphasized. Change advocates must recognize this as a real and potentially serious impediment to introducing new design practices. It is best if they address it directly and assure organizations, teams, and individuals that they will not lose autonomy. Set clear goals for the changes, explain how they will be instituted, and emphasize the benefits of adopting the new practices, processes, and methods. Allow individuals to voice their concerns regarding autonomy, and address each concern. Ignoring this very real organizational fear can cause suspicion to grow that can lead to resistance. This is a chronic problem in organizations with poor communication channels, and a situation that should be remedied before any serious change effort is undertaken.

Lack of Focused Talent

Before you think, "Wow, that is an arrogant section title," be advised that not all talent is equal, and that modern software-intensive systems and products are built by teams with diverse, focused talent. While organizations may be full of talented engineers and scientists, they can still create systems and products with very poor designs. In many organizations that the author has helped to improve designs and design processes, there was an abundance of talent. In fact, there was no shortage of engineers who understood design. However, the abundance of talent is both a blessing and a curse, and is often part of the problem when attempting to change organizational behavior. Talented engineers and scientists are reluctant to listen to other engineers and tend to believe that their approaches to designing and building software-intensive systems are superior to others'. This can be a hard statement to swallow, but it is true in organizations with highly educated and experienced engineers and scientists. Often leading an organization like this is more like herding cats than leading human engineers in the construction of a system or product. In these cases there can be a lack of talent focused on the design process—everyone designs and builds his or her part of the system in isolation. Integration is often a nightmare in organizations like this. It should be no surprise, then, that changing and improving the state of the design process in these organizations will be met with skepticism and strong resistance. In these situations, it is extremely important that the most talented engineers and scientists are at the vanguard of the change effort. In these organizations, sheer technical and scientific prowess is most often what is respected more than any organizational authority. If the most talented engineers and scientists can be convinced to adopt new design practices, processes, and methods, then the change effort stands a chance of succeeding.

Marketing and Engineering Disconnect

One of the more chronic problems in organizations building software-intensive systems is a disconnect between the marketing and sales personnel who bid for the projects and the engineering community that must design, build, deliver, and maintain the system. Often the marketing and sales teams do not have technical backgrounds, or they possess insufficient breadth of experience to bid on projects to build software-intensive systems and products. In many cases the project bids include cost, schedule, and requirements that are unrealistic. Promises are made that violate physics, chemistry, and mathematics. When the deal is sealed by the marketing and sales teams, their job is done. It is the engineers that must deliver on the promises made by marketing and sales. If the engineers cannot deliver on those promises, they will be blamed, yet they had no input on the bidding process or the promises made. This can be a frustrating and demoralizing situation for the engineers. In this situation, new design practices or methods are not going to help—this is a broken business process. New design practices or methods that are adopted and instituted in this case will eventually be overcome by unrealistic schedules, cost estimates, or unachievable architectural drivers. This process can be easily fixed by including the chief architect, management, and sales/marketing in the project bidding process. The architect should be a full member, not just a token presence whose voice is ignored. In fact, it should be the case that technical promises should not be made without the architect's approval—this only makes sense because he or she is the one that must deliver. Certainly architects should not be in charge of these aspects of a project or organization. However, they need to be included in this critical process before any meaningful technical design practices and methods can be adopted and have a positive impact on the products and systems the organization builds.

Training and Transition Planning

Many organizations are willing to spend significant sums of money on training engineers. However, there is rarely a plan for how to transition new knowledge and newly trained engineers into the organization. Engineers get training, return to the organization, and without a plan for transition, the engineers and organizations do what they always have done. Nothing changes, nothing improves. This is drive-by training. Two key symptoms of drive-by training include:

- Not Training the Right People: Often the wrong people are recruited into a training program. They are not qualified, or they are not in a position to put the training into practice. Often people are sent to training to fill up the course, to meet some number of mandatory annual training hours, or some other similar mindless reason. Unqualified students are often frustrated and may be put into an uncomfortable situation to explain to their supervisors why they did so poorly in a training course. This is demoralizing, wastes time and money, and does more to hurt an organization than to help it.
- No Opportunity to Use the Training: In many situations, engineers are trained on techniques which they will never have an opportunity to use. For example, consider the engineers in an organization building embedded control software that are trained on J2EE technologies. This is probably not a good match since it's unlikely that this training will be used, but this kind of thing happens all the time. Ideally engineers should have an opportunity to apply the techniques learned in the training as soon as possible after the training has concluded. This is why a transition plan is essential to a training plan.

If these symptoms are present, then there is probably no rhyme or reason to the training – it is training for the sake of training. Drive-by training makes everyone in an organization feel good (human resources, management, and engineers), but has little effect on organizational competence or the bottom-line. Technical training should be based on meeting long term and short term business goals and organizational needs, not fads, random topics, or other similar reasons. If an organization determines that training in architecture design (or any other topic for that matter) would bolster technical competence and further the organizational business goals, then a broad plan that should be developed that includes training and transitioning the technology into practice.

An example from the author's experience illustrates the right way to implement training and transitioning within an organization. The organization described here is a producer of consumer of electronics. The organization's process improvement group analyzed product development costs and quality at the direction of management, who suspected costs could be lower and quality could be better. Based on their analysis they determined that improvements in systemic software design would promote broad-based reuse and the establishment of product lines. This would dramatically reduce development costs and simultaneously improve quality. A plan was developed to address both the immediate organizational training needs and how the technology would be transitioned into practice within the organization. The plan included broad introductory training in architecture design that would be provided to the general engineering community. The best students from these initial classes were selected to go on to more advanced training. In addition to the technical training provided to the engineering community, "awareness" seminars were provided to management at all levels. While this broad-based training was underway, the process improvement group (leading the effort) developed transition plans. The short term transition plans included establishing a technical track for architects and creating an architecture community that served as a corporate pool of project design expertise. Longer term plans included implementing a product line for a set of related products and instituting broad-based architecture design reviews. At the writing of this text the organization has successfully implemented all of the short term training and transition plans and is currently in the process of undertaking the longer term plans. The organization is now developing the next steps for the organization to improve architectural competence. This is a good example of how to successfully train engineers and transition training into practice to improve how an organization builds products. Some best practices from this and other similar experiences include:

- Identify Organizational Needs First, Plan for Training Second: Organizations should identify training needs in terms of business goals rather than just do random training. Do not guess about what kind of training is needed and do not train engineers in the latest fads. Align training based on needs that emanate directly from issues associated with product quality, schedule, costs, and so forth that are impeding progress towards organizational business goals.
- Train Management: Include line, mid-level, and senior managers in the training effort. Most of this training should be short duration training designed to make managers aware of the new technologies, methods, and so forth that their engineers are learning. Training duration should be a day or two for line managers, a half to full day for mid-level managers, and 90 minute seminars for senior managers. This training is essential for building sponsorship for transitioning the lessons into practice.
- Plan the Implementation of New Practices: Now that your engineers have learned something new, it is essential that there is a plan for how the new methods, techniques, tools will be used within the organization. It is also essential that metrics be collected to measure effectiveness, as well as cost and savings (time and/or money) to show return on investment.

Summary

Clearly design is a beneficial and necessary step when designing modern, complex software-intensive systems. However, transitioning disciplined, repeatable, and effective design practices into an organization is challenging. Organizations are comprised of people who are often reluctant to change. Loss of autonomy and self-determination is a constant fear for the people of any organization. It can be difficult to show return on investment for architecture design practices because the savings are often only quantifiable in terms of cost avoidance. This is a hard case to make and a hard position to defend without data. Organizations in trouble because of their designs (or lack of them) are usually easier to change. Key points to remember when trying to change an organization's design practices, processes, and methods include the following:

- There needs to be a champion, or change advocate, who is able to lead the adoption of new design practices, processes, and methods. Change advocates must have vision, credibility, and some authority. They need management support and must have the architectural expertise or access to architects who have the expertise to establish, introduce, and transition the new design practices, processes, and methods or change the existing ones.
- When considering a change to an organization's design practices, processes, and methods, it is critical to analyze the business context. Change advocates should think in terms of how improving the current design practices, processes, and methods can improve the organi-

zation's bottom line. If new design practices are adopted without a focus on the business context, then the wrong practices may be adopted, causing failure, frustration, and distrust of any future changes.

■ When changing an organization, the following elements are critical for implementing new design practices: There must be a strategy for building sponsorship in management for the changes. The current practices must be baselined. There must be a plan of action that describes what new practices, processes, and methods will be adopted, changed, and so forth. The plan must include how the new practices will be measured. The new design practices, processes, and methods must be executed in an honest way, preferably in a small team/ project in a controlled setting. Once use of the new design practices, processes, and methods has stabilized, the organization must reflect upon the results, adjust where necessary, and look for opportunities for more improvement. Once the new practices have been proven, only then should they be transitioned into practice within the broader organization.

■ It can be difficult to change or introduce new design practices, processes, and methods while sustaining the business at hand. Change advocates should always focus on the low-hanging fruit first, that is, do the easy things that will improve the situation and provide immediate returns.

Chapter 17

Other Design Considerations: Legacy, Design by Selection, and Maintenance

The cattle cannot speak: it is hard to know what ails them when they cry: When systems that contain commercial products fail, it can be very difficult to detect the cause of the error. The source code is not available, nor are the design assumptions and constraints that guided the developers of the products.

David Carney, Software Engineering Institute, Carnegie Mellon University

The world of an architect is never perfect. ACDM has been presented in Section 2 under relatively perfect conditions, where a new product or system is being developed in totality from scratch by co-located teams of designers and implementers. Under the harsh light of reality, this is rarely the case, and system development is often a complex mix of organizations, legacy systems, and new technologies. In this chapter we will delve into these programmatic imperfections and discuss ways in which ACDM can be used in various situations. Various techniques will be presented that can be used with ACDM to help in these realistic situations. In particular, we will discuss how ACDM fits into situations where:

- New systems must interact with legacy systems/elements or "legacy-ware"
- A significant portion of the system utilizes commercial software and hardware elements
- Teams are faced with maintenance of a system after initial delivery

Architecture and the architect can play a vital role in these situations. ACDM can be tailored to help guide the efforts of the architecture design teams.

Design with Legacy-Ware

ACDM has been presented thus far in terms of "green field" development, that is, building a brand new system from the beginning. This is rarely the case in practice. Many systems and products are designed and built to utilize systems or elements that have been built previously—often with technology that may be currently obsolete. These are legacy elements or legacy systems; for simplicity, we will refer to this as legacy-ware. Legacy-ware can include legacy hardware, software, peripherals, firmware, infrastructure, and so forth that must interoperate with, or in some way be incorporated in whole or in part with, the design for a new system or product. In some cases, the legacy-ware may have been designed and built by the organization building the new system, by some third-party organization, or inherited through merger or acquisition. In many cases, the job of interoperating with legacy-ware is not as simple as trading data between the old system and the new one. This can certainly be tricky enough, but many times there are other, far more confounding factors that can complicate the interoperation and influence of the design of the new system. Obviously, data between legacy and new systems or elements can be incompatible. This can be as simple as reformatting data, or as complex as dealing with incompatible numeric representation standards. Besides data incompatibilities, there may be a need to export legacy services to new systems and new elements. A common example is making legacy COBOL applications and data available to modern systems connected to the Internet. There may be a need to coordinate run-time operations and communications. It is almost always the case that there are operating system and language differences between the new and legacy systems and elements. New systems may have quality attribute requirements never designed into the legacy-ware, and if the new systems must interoperate with legacy-ware, it may be difficult for the new system to satisfy emerging quality attribute requirements. Examples include security for highly distributed operations and servers, timing requirements that necessitate coordination between the legacy-ware and new systems, and availability requirements that depend upon the interoperation between new systems and legacy-ware.

The strategy in which the new system is introduced and the transition from the legacy-ware to the new system or the newly enhanced system can deeply affect design. In some cases, new systems must replace the functionality of the legacy systems all at once. This can be a daunting challenge that goes beyond mere design and implementation concerns. Designers and management must work together and address issues such as ensuring that the new system can do what the old system did plus any newly specified functionality and behaviors. While coordinating the conversion to the new system, organizations must continue to provide essential services, conduct business as usual, and coordinate design, construction, and installation of the new system. Sometimes it is impossible to turn off the legacy system on one day and switch to a new system on the next. In many cases, there is a long transition process where legacy elements are replaced in a piecemeal fashion with new elements that will complement and eventually replace legacy elements of the system. In this case, the new and old systems will be woven together for a time from an operational and design standpoint. The switch from legacy to new system is more of a continuum than a discrete event. This is the exact approach that is being used on the new U.S. air traffic control (ATC) system that will replace the existing systems. If started today (in 2008), the replacement of the legacy ATC system is estimated to take upwards of 20 years and over $70 billion. Incremental, phased replacement of legacy-ware deeply affects the design of the new system and its constituent elements. If the replacement system is not properly designed and the logistics of the replacement system and elements are not exactly choreographed, then the project could be placed in serious jeopardy. An earlier effort to replace the ATC in the 1980s resulted in one of the most costly system development failures in history (U.S. Government Accounting Office, 1999). The U.S. Federal Aviation Authority attempted to modernize the ATC with a massive effort that began in 1981 and ended in complete failure in 1994. The government and its contractors burned through $3.7 billion, but nothing was built or modernized. The project was finally shut down by Congress. Nothing came out of the project—not a single piece of production software or hardware was ever constructed or procured. There was a long list of process problems and technical challenges. One key reason for the failure was a lack of a central architecture and a clear migration path from the legacy system to the replacement system. When faced with the task of designing new systems that must interoperate with legacy-ware, there are four general situations that designers should consider:

- Isolated legacy interoperation: This is the situation where a new system(s) is developed and is relatively separate, distinct, and reasonably encapsulated from the legacy-ware. Essentially, the new systems will communicate and otherwise interoperate with the legacy-ware. The new system(s) essentially extends and complements the legacy-ware's functionality. Besides designing new systems to interoperate with the legacy-ware, the legacy-ware (hardware, software, infrastructure, and so forth) may have to be modified or extended to facilitate the desired interoperability.
- Complete legacy replacement: In this case, the legacy-ware is replaced with new systems. At a defined point in time, the legacy-ware (hardware, software, infrastructure, and so forth) is "turned off" and the new system is "turned on," and the legacy-ware is replaced from that time forward.
- Staged legacy migration: In this situation, new systems will eventually replace the legacy-ware, but this is not a discrete event. Legacy-ware is replaced over an extended period of time, typically with incremental delivery of new software, hardware, infrastructure, and other elements. Eventually the legacy-ware services are migrated to the new system(s) over a given time period.
- Reuse of legacy elements: In some cases, a part(s) of a legacy system must be used in new systems that are developed. These can include code elements like libraries, runtime elements like applications, and physical elements like hardware and infrastructure parts and pieces.

Each of these situations presents unique design and planning challenges for the architect. In using ACDM where any of these situations exist, there are tailoring guidelines that the architecture design team may want to consider. Projects should always begin with stage 1, to discover the raw architectural drivers for the system; after all, this is how the team discovers there are technical constraints involving legacy-ware. After stage 1, analysis of the raw architectural drivers should commence, culminating in the architecture drivers specification in stage 2. However, this is where a departure from the normal ACDM staging might be advisable when a project is constrained by having to interoperate in some extensive, nontrivial way with legacy-ware. It is necessary to have a full understanding of the legacy system's structures, elements, and behavioral and quality attribute properties before designing the new system elements. This knowledge is gained through analysis of the legacy system design artifacts and as-built structures—more details and guidance on this in a moment. However, for planning purposes, this analysis can be folded into stage 2, or a special stage can be inserted between stages 2 and 3 for analyzing and discovering the architecture of the available legacy-ware.

This activity begins with the architecture design team taking the time to review design documentation pertaining to the legacy-ware to ascertain its structure and relevance to the as-built system structures. Unfortunately, many legacy systems have design documentation that is out of date with the as-built system, or the design was never written down. In more extreme cases where there is no design documentation, the team must discover and reconstruct the underlying architecture of the legacy-ware. Architecture discovery and reconstruction amount to examining existing artifacts such as design documentation, code, requirements documentation, and any other artifacts that describe the legacy-ware's as-built structures. This effort amounts to architecture design forensics—the legacy system design is the victim, and the architecture design team plays the role of detective. Architecture design discovery and reconstruction can be part of ACDM stage 2, or a separate stage inserted between stages 2 and 3. Architecture design discovery and reconstruction should occur before designing the new system (stage 3). Certainly this effort extends the duration of stage 2—sometimes considerably—depending upon the nature of the legacy-ware, the new requirements, and the condition/existence of the design artifacts.

Legacy-Ware Forensics

Forensic analysis of legacy-ware begins as a process of analyzing legacy-ware design documentation to see if it matches the actual legacy-ware structure. It is often a frustrating and time-consuming process of following clues to discover how an operational system was structured, and why it was structured as it was, and reconstructing and documenting the design of the as-built system. The strategy for conducting legacy-ware forensic analysis depends upon the availability and condition of the design and system elements. In general, this strategy should include four steps: (1) design artifact analysis, (2) system structural analysis, (3) conformance analysis, and (4) redocumentation.

Design Artifact Analysis

The first step in legacy-ware forensics is to examine the existing design to see if it is understandable and usable. Initially, the architecture design team should gather all of the design artifacts that are available. In many cases, this is often a difficult first step because the design was never documented, or more commonly, it was documented in inconsistent ways by different engineers. Once gathered, this information is analyzed by the architecture design team using a team inspection technique. Each member of the team is given time to review one or more design artifacts. After individual reviews, the team will convene and the chief architect will lead an inspection of the document. Each section is called out by the chief architect, who paraphrases or explains the section to the rest of the architecture design team. The team will be invited to critique or comment on the material to clarify points, disagree with explanations, add information, and so forth. All of these issues will be captured. It is strongly recommended that teams limit the amount of time in the inspection to no more than 90 minutes. Much longer, and the engineers will glaze over and the effectiveness of the analysis will suffer. This process will continue until all of the design artifacts have been analyzed. This exercise is a good first step at familiarizing the architecture design team with the intended design, and providing all of the team members with a common idea of the content of the legacy-ware design artifacts. Things that are often missing from legacy design artifacts include:

■ Design rationale: Is there any information that describes why certain design decisions were made? If not, is there any evidence that might lead the team to assume that certain design decisions were made for a particular reason. This rationale can influence any number of design decisions that the team makes as they design the new system to interoperate with, replace, migrate to, or utilize legacy elements.

■ Views: Are there a complete set of views of the system from the static, dynamic, and physical perspectives? If not, the architecture design team will have to reconstruct them.

■ Consistency: Are the views consistent—is it possible to see how views are related? Does the document use consistent terminology and notation? If not, then the team may not be able to ascertain how the design structures are manifest in the system structures.

■ Clarity: Are there keys or legends on the drawings? Is the notation used understandable? Are drawings and the general design described with appropriate prose? If not, the architecture design team may not be able to understand the design or, worse, may misunderstand the design.

■ Completeness: Does the artifact(s) seem to address the design down to a sufficient level of detail? If the information is very general and abstract, then it will not be useful in understanding the legacy structures.

■ Relevance: How long ago was the document written—is it likely that the system artifacts follow the design? Has it been updated in accordance with changes made to the design?

■ Requirements: Is it clear what the legacy system's key requirements are? Are these requirements still valid? How do the legacy system's requirements relate to the new system's requirements? While we do not need all of the detailed requirements, the design artifacts should state (or reference documents that do state) what requirements the design is supposed to satisfy.

The architecture design team should keep these points in mind as they analyze the existing legacy-ware design artifacts.

Structural Analysis

Structural analysis in this context refers to the activities of examining the static, dynamic, and physical structures of the as-built system, and cataloging them and their relationships to one another. Armed with an understanding of the intended design (insomuch as it is possible to derive from the legacy design artifacts), the architecture design team can then undertake a structural analysis of the actual system artifacts, like code, data sources, processes/threads, hardware, and so forth. The purpose of structural analysis is to discover the actual, as-built structures of the system with the intended design to ensure they are the same (this is conformance analysis). Although it would be great if there were comprehensive tools to do this, unfortunately at the writing of this text there are not. Conducting this analysis will be time-consuming in the best of situations, and can be very difficult or impossible under certain circumstances. The architecture design team can approach this analysis from any one of the three perspectives. However, as Figure 17.1 illustrates, there is a natural mapping between static structures and dynamic structures, and dynamic structures and physical structures.

Using Figure 17.1 as a reference, structural analysis can begin with an analysis of the static structures of the system. This is the source code for the applications, processes, threads, and so forth that will make up the system and their relationships with one another. Alternatively, the architecture design team may decide to analyze the physical structures of the system first. These structures are the computer systems, peripherals, networks, infrastructure, and other hardware elements of the legacy system, and their relationships to one another. This part of the reconstruc-

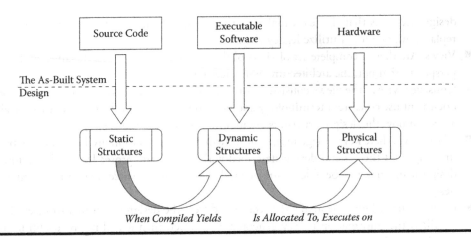

Figure 17.1   Architectural design discovery and reconstruction.

tion can be relatively easy because the physical elements of the system are often plainly visible and can be inventoried. Of course, the operative term here is "relatively easy." Some systems have physical elements distributed and interconnected globally. Other systems are complex, closely coupled elements and systems of systems, such as those found on airplanes, cruise ships, automobiles, and similar embedded systems. A simple inventory of these systems' physical elements can be challenging. If it can be determined that there is little or no dependence between the static structures and the physical structures (usually there is not), then both can be analyzed simultaneously. In general, the dynamic structures will be analyzed last because they are derived from the static structures and generally map to physical structures once built. Dynamic structures are the applications, processes, threads, and so forth that are part of the legacy system and their relationships with one another. In addition to these structures, it can be helpful if key functionality is articulated as functional use cases, and quality attribute scenarios are created to capture the as-built quality attribute properties the system possesses. Again, this is general guidance for the situation where there is source code for the system. This is clear-box analysis and essentially means that the designers can examine and directly analyze the source code. Legacy system code elements such as classes, functions, methods, and other static structures will have to be identified and cataloged, as well as their relationships with one another. From this, dynamic structures can be derived and mapped to physical elements, essentially completing the structural analysis. This is an oversimplification to illustrate the clear-box structural analysis, and in practice the architecture design team will have to devise a strategy appropriate for their situation.

Where the static structures are available, the design team will work from the code to the processes, threads, and finally to the physical elements. Once identified, these primordial structures will have to be aggregated into architectural elements. Aggregation in this context means that related code-level structures are logically associated, and their relationships are identified, to form the static structures of the architecture. The classes, functions, and so forth are grouped as larger architectural elements. As part of aggregation, the access points (interfaces) to the data and services provided by the static architectural elements must be identified and cataloged. Finally, the relationships among the static architectural elements are identified and cataloged, completing the static structural analysis of the system. The goal is to identify the responsibilities of the elements and relationships among them as described earlier, when initially designing and documenting the architecture design. This can be a difficult process in cases where the implementers did not follow the architecture design, there was no architecture design in the first place, or the system has been modified over time. Imagine a system with a million-plus lines of code where there was no architecture design to guide the initial implementation. There could be thousands or tens of thousands of classes (or more) in medium- and large-scale systems. This can result in a great number of spaghetti dependencies and relationships that are not well understood, or are not defined, or restricted in a predictable way. This is like spaghetti code, but on a larger scale—it is really spaghetti design. In the worst case, there will be no elements, just a jumbled mass of monolithic structures. Besides being difficult to understand, the quality attribute properties in legacy systems like this are difficult to ascertain, and any changes to them or interoperation with the legacy system will likewise be unpredictable.

Once the static structures have been identified, they can be compiled, and the resulting dynamic structures will emerge. At this point, the resulting dynamic elements and the relationships can be identified and cataloged relatively easily because the source code is available. The final piece of the structural analysis puzzle is mapping the dynamic structures to the physical elements of the system. Again, this can be an undertaking that ranges from trivial to extraordinarily complex, usually depending upon the scale of the system. Throughout this process, the architecture design team will need to document their findings as they analyze legacy elements.

In other cases, source code for legacy-ware may not be available. In these situations, ground-up reconstruction of legacy-ware designs from static structures (mainly source code) is impossible. Some systems may be so old that the source code has been lost; the source versions and the executable versions no longer match; executable code was provided by a third party that is no longer in business, or source code was never provided; or any number of other similar situations. The bottom line is that all that remains are the dynamic structures. In these cases, the architecture design team is left with analyzing the dynamic structures in what is called black-box analysis. Black-box analysis amounts to identifying and cataloging the applications, threads, processes, and so forth. The first step in black-box analysis is to identify the legacy dynamic structures and map them to the physical structures on which they execute. The picture of the system that will emerge is that of a set of interrelated dynamic structures (processes, applications, threads), their relationships to one another (how they communicate, pass information, control, and so forth), and how they relate to the physical elements of the system. Unfortunately, when the static structures for the legacy system are no longer available, it is impossible to modify the dynamic structures, and the architect will be completely constrained by the as-built legacy code. This can make the chore of interoperating with the legacy system extremely difficult, or in some cases impossible.

Conformance Analysis

It is important to ensure that the documented architecture design matches the as-built structures as the team moves forward with the new design. Comparing the as-built structures with the design artifacts to identify missing or incorrect information is called conformance analysis. This exercise will inform the team of the legacy-ware structures and will ensure that any interoperation with the legacy-ware and transition to the new system are less problematic. Once the structural analysis is complete, the team must determine if the documented architecture matches the as-built structures. Conformance analysis is impossible if there is no architecture design. In these situations, the architecture design team will have the daunting task of documenting the legacy system design as well as the new design. If design artifacts do exist, the architecture design team should reinspect the intended design artifacts in light of the structural analysis to determine if the intended, documented design matches the implementation. Discrepancies and missing information should be recorded. The team should also consider identifying operational use cases that the system currently satisfied, and step through the documented architecture design to check if the intended design matches the implementation. A similar analysis can be undertaken with respect to quality attribute analysis using quality attribute scenarios that describe the current quality attribute properties of the system.

Redocumentation

After conformance analysis, the architecture design team should refine the existing legacy design documentation (if it exists) based on the conformance inspection findings in an exercise called redocumentation. This can be as simple as freshening up the existing legacy documentation, or may involve documenting designs that were never designed. Many times total system redocumentation can be impractical due to schedule or cost constraints. In these situations, the architecture design team should at least focus on documenting the legacy elements, interfaces, and so forth that will play a role in the interoperability, and which will influence the design of the new system. The documentation can even be a short companion document to the existing legacy design artifacts to complement the design information that already exists. The documentation artifacts created as a result of the redocumentation effort will serve as a benchmark for the architecture design team as they move forward to design the new system. The team should ensure that they have thoroughly documented the relevant dynamic behavior, such as data flow, events, messages, modal behavior, and so forth, as well as any relevant quality attribute responses of the legacy system that may affect the interoperation between the legacy system and new system.

Other Design Considerations

Throughout the forensic design analysis, the architecture design team has to be diligent in identifying other architecturally significant issues regarding the interoperation with legacy-ware and the impact it may have on the design of the new system. While there are many facets of legacy systems that can affect the design of new systems that must interoperate legacy-ware, the architecture design team should consider the following issues at a minimum:

- Hardware and infrastructure elements: Legacy computer hardware, peripherals, networks, sensors, and so forth can present a challenge for engineers building new systems that must interoperate with legacy systems and elements. The extent and role that legacy hardware plays in the interoperation with new systems should be identified as early as possible in the design process. Potential incompatibilities must be identified, reconciliation mechanisms and strategies devised, and long-term interoperability needs identified and addressed in the architectural design. If the legacy systems continue to interoperate with the new systems for an extended period of time, replacement parts could be an issue, especially if there are a limited number available. If migration from the legacy systems is the ultimate strategy, the target platforms will need to be identified and the interface/interoperability concerned designed into the new system's architecture.
- Operating systems: It is possible that the legacy systems and new systems will not have operating systems that are compatible. In some cases the incompatibilities are a trivial nuisance,

but in other cases the incompatibilities between different operating systems can be total "show stoppers," depending upon the nature of the interaction between the new and legacy systems. Operating systems and hardware platforms can be inextricably woven together, making platform and operating systems' portability and compatibility requirements difficult or impossible to satisfy. In legacy operating systems the specific version of the operating system that the legacy hardware is running and the hardware it can run on should be identified. This can be a significant constraint for new systems that must interoperate with the legacy system. Consider the simple example of a legacy Intel computer built in 2003 running Windows OS. It is probably safe to say that the same platform could not run the version of Windows available in 2008 (Vista). Certainly there will be incompatibilities between these two operating systems, and no matter how minor, they must be identified as early as possible because they can deeply impact the architecture design. This is a relatively benign example. In large systems development, it is often the case that there are many different types and versions of operating systems used across legacy systems. Again, this can present difficult design challenges. It is a good idea to begin by baselining all of the legacy operating systems and advancing each type of operating system to a common version. In some cases, this may require updating the legacy software to operate on updated operating systems, or vice versa. Although this simplifies the design of new systems to interoperate with legacy systems, it can also be more time-consuming than it is worth. The final judgment has to be made by the architecture design team, but it should be a decision that is part of the design process.

■ Compilers and languages: A key issue facing architects that must design and build systems that interoperate with legacy-ware are the languages utilized to create the legacy system's applications. Some languages are dated and are not supported by modern hardware and operating systems. It can also be difficult to design and develop interoperable systems if the original compilers used for the legacy system are no longer available. If compilers are not available for a "dead language" and platform, then modifying the code on the legacy system to interoperate with the new system is nearly impossible. In some cases, legacy computer languages have to be used to build applications on the new systems to facilitate interoperation between the new system and the legacy elements. In these cases, the new hardware/software operating systems must support the legacy language, compilers, and so forth. Again, finding compilers for the new systems that support the legacy languages can be an issue. In addition to these potential problems, it can be difficult to find engineers that know the legacy languages to modify the legacy software to interoperate with new systems. For example, the original control systems for the B-2 Stealth Bomber were written in a language called JOVIAL. This was a popular language for avionics system development before the broad acceptance of the Ada language. However, how many hot-shot young programmers graduating from university today know JOVIAL? For that matter, how many of them know Ada?

■ Legacy data: It may be the case that the best way for new and legacy systems to interoperate is indirectly, through data repositories. However, accessing legacy data can be extremely challenging. In the simplest cases, the legacy data formats are unknown, so they must be rediscovered through a process of analysis, trial, and error. In some cases this can literally be impossible if there is no clue to the structure and format of the data files. In other cases, new systems may have to interact with legacy data services and databases. Again, this can be challenging if these services and databases are no longer supported on the new systems. Often, this situation will require that new applications be built for the legacy systems to accept queries from the new systems to retrieve the data and export the data to the new systems. Again, this can often be an extremely challenging project by itself. Another issue that can be extremely painful is if the numeric storage format on the legacy system is different from the new system's format. Differences may include big versus little endian, word size, floating point representation, and others. These differences can pose significant challenges to overcome and can have dramatic influence on the design of the new system.

■ Tools: Legacy configuration management tools, archival tools, design tools, and other similar support tools can present a significant challenge to the architecture discovery and reconstruction chore. Again, as a system stabilizes over time—that is, there are fewer and fewer changes made to it—the tools used for configuration management, compiling source code, rendering design artifacts, and so forth are not kept current and, in some cases, lost in time. Tools are critical to the architecture discovery because they are often the only access to source code and design artifacts.

■ Business processes: Legacy systems are built around business models. This may include user interaction models, work processes, business models, and so forth that were valid assumptions when the legacy system was built, but these original assumptions may be evolving and no longer valid. Legacy business processes can be the source of business and technical constraints on new systems that must interoperate with legacy systems. These constraints can be severe impositions on new systems development. As part of the architecture design discovery and reconstruction, the legacy business processes and assumptions that gave rise to them must be considered in light of different assumptions, new and improved ways of doing business, as well as the availability of new technology. This can help architects mesh together legacy business processes with new and emerging business processes to more effectively address the needs of the organization.

Architecture design discovery and reconstruction is tough work, and there are many ways that the team can work together to analyze artifacts to recreate the system design. In large systems, a division of labor is necessary, where each team member is responsible for analyzing part of the legacy system. Because this division of labor depends upon so many factors, specific guidance is not provided here, but the strategy for this analysis should be part of the stage 2 planning process.

Design by Selection

It is common today for organizations to use commercial elements or commercial-off-the-shelf (COTS) software in the products and systems they build. Using commercial elements as part of a system is a lot like using legacy-ware in that the capabilities and properties of the commercial elements must be fully understood before designing a system to most effectively use them. Of course, it is possible that legacy commercial elements must be used, but this was discussed as part of legacy-ware in the preceding sections. However, commercial elements selected are state of the art, offer cutting-edge features and capabilities, and typically have organizations or communities providing support for the commercial elements. Unfortunately, these "shoulds" are not often the case, and today's commercial elements can quickly become tomorrow's black-box legacy-ware. It is nearly impossible to build an entirely new system from scratch these days. At a minimum, operating systems and device drivers from third parties will be used. In larger, more complex systems, it can be more cost-effective and timely to buy elements that fill the requirements of a system rather than design and build them from scratch. This has been true for four decades in the computer hardware and peripheral markets, where no one would think of building anything from scratch other than very specialized hardware. Building a system's hardware elements or infrastructure is often a matter of selecting compatible elements and connecting them together. This is becoming more common in the software domain as well with the availability of critical system elements such as operating systems, databases, mathematics libraries, tools, and so forth. Commercial elements were designed and developed without a single specific application in mind, but rather for a broad range of applications and stakeholders. Today building systems that utilize a lot of commercial elements are more like design by selection rather than traditional design. In design by selection, the system is still designed. However, the design is constrained by the availability of commercial elements. Specific commercial software or hardware elements are selected based on being close enough to satisfying a particular requirement or set of requirements. Often the first question facing designers is whether to buy an element or build it. Certainly the list of reasons to buy versus build is compelling, and these will be discussed. Sometimes the choice is obvious. For example, it is hard to imagine that many organizations want to build operating systems, relational databases, or device drivers unless they absolutely have to. However, using commercial elements comes at a price that goes beyond the obvious cost of buying the element—this is only part of the total cost of ownership. The total cost of ownership for commercial elements must be fully understood before it can be possible to accurately make a case for buying an element. Total cost of ownership considerations may include:

- Product support costs: Commercial elements or legacy support costs include infrastructure establishment, tools, training, and other consulting and support costs.
- Qualification costs: Commercial element qualification costs include the time and resources required to ensure that the elements are able to meet the anticipated needs of the design elements for which they are designed.
- Incompatibility repair costs: These are the costs of repairing incompatibilities between commercial elements and other elements of the system.
- Distribution and licensing fees: If there are licensing fees associated with the use of a commercial element, then these costs must be factored into the total cost of the product or system. Distribution costs never go away and may be incurred every time the product is sold or distributed.
- Upgrade and renewal fees: In addition to purchase costs, there are often annual renewals, maintenance, and upgrade fees that must be paid. Again, these costs must be factored into the total cost.

The potential savings of using commercial elements may include reduced operational, maintenance, and construction costs (time and resources). The business case for the commercial elements should be revisited whenever:

- Elements are patched or upgraded
- Key stakeholders change
- Key technologies change or technological paradigms shift
- Internal or external business models or markets change

Short-term benefits from using commercial elements can quickly deteriorate into long-term headaches if designers are not careful in their design and selection of commercial elements.

Each commercial element selected by the designer becomes a kind of self-imposed design constraint because it weds a design to a particular product or standard now and well into the future. Of course, these issues can be mitigated by design choices. In some cases, very complex systems can be almost totally composed of commercial elements of one kind or another. As an extreme example, consider the typical n-tiered business application that uses an application framework and middleware like JBoss, back-end Oracle software, BEA Weblogic Security Framework, browsers, various operating systems, and so on. This kind of system development becomes a huge integration effort where developers find themselves "gluing" together (often incompatible) parts. The glue is often innocuous software that takes on an extraordinary importance, yet is often not well designed. It should be obvious that the overall system partitioning, to a large extent, is determined by the commercial elements available in the marketplace. The system design is a collection of commercial element ensembles woven together in most cases by glue. If not designed with great care, these systems will quickly possess all of the convoluted complexity and unpredictability of any other poorly designed system.

It is tempting to assume that development time will be reduced as the amount of commercial elements used increases, because buying elements is much faster than designing, developing, and testing homegrown elements—not to mention the reduced costs due to labor savings. This is partially true because designing and building software-intensive systems is a labor-intensive, manual process that requires a very expensive labor pool. Today the body of computer science and software engineering knowledge is huge, and as a result, the software engineering community has become specialized. Software engineers often have niche specializations in domains and computer science disciplines such as databases, graphical user interfaces, transaction processing, real-time embedded applications, security, and so forth. Each of these specializations requires unique skill sets, experience, and domain knowledge. Besides this, other engineering expertise is often required in electronics, aerodynamics, mechanics, chemistry, and other scientific and engineering disciplines. In addition to engineering and computer science expertise, domain experts in fields such as business, finance, flying, manufacturing, air traffic control, and so forth who know nothing about engineering are required to build large and complex systems. Because labor represents the largest cost by far in the development of software-intensive systems, any savings in the high cost of engineering labor and domain expertise can translate into significant cost savings for product and system development. Using commercial elements can reduce or eliminate the need for hiring and retaining specialized expertise required to design and build the product or system. Using commercial elements rather than developing elements from scratch allows an organization to leverage this expertise in the products and systems it designs and builds. Commercial elements can enable organizations to meet market windows more efficiently in terms of cost and schedule, and enable new technologies to be packaged into their systems and products. When an organization opts to buy commercial elements rather than design and build them from scratch, there is an immediate increase in productivity. Using commercial elements allows an organization to concentrate on the application and domain areas in which it is expert, rather than having to invest in developing organic expertise in engineering disciplines or application domains in which it does not have expertise. Because successful commercial elements have broad communities of stakeholders using the products, defects are often discovered quickly, and fixes are propagated across the entire community. This can translate into more reliable and capable systems that use commercial elements. Another advantage of using commercial elements is that products can often exploit existing commercial element standards, resulting in systems and products that are more extensible and interoperable.

Although commercial elements can save money and time, if used in an undisciplined fashion, they can cause as much trouble as any other poorly designed system. The broad consensus of the IT community in the early 1990s was that the more commercial elements a product or system incorporated into its design, the cheaper it would be to manufacture, distribute, and maintain.

This optimism has since been tempered with repeatedly harsh doses of reality. When designing systems that utilize a lot of commercial elements, the design process becomes a process of selection, best fit, and integration. Rather than custom machining software parts that are precisely designed to fit and operate together, designers select ensembles of commercial elements that work together to provide the specified services. In addition to satisfying the functional needs of a system or product, the commercial elements (and resulting ensembles) must also meet the specified quality attribute needs. Architects using a predominance of commercial elements need to focus on identifying candidate elements, and designing ensembles to satisfy the system requirements. However, commercial elements can constrain the architect in dramatic ways.

To illustrate these points, consider the following project case study, in this example a control system needed to precisely monitor and control a distillation process. The system required complex interactive displays that would allow operators to monitor the distillation process and change control parameters in real-time. A key quality attribute was safety, which in this context meant that if certain unsafe conditions (primarily temperature and pressure) arose during distillation, the process would automatically be shut down. The hardware and infrastructure of the system included a set of 60 sensors that monitored such things as temperature, pressure, chemical composition, Ph, and other similar information. The sensors were fixed to a large distillation vat and had to be sampled once every millisecond. Displays had to plot the time series data for all of the sensors in real-time for the operators, and allow the operators to interact to change certain parameters of the distillation process as needed. All of the data collected from the sensors for a particular distillation batch had to be stored for later retrieval and analysis by chemical engineers after the distillation was complete. Engineers needed remote access to data from any distillation batch. Engineers needed immediate access to distillation data once the process concluded from any corporate location in the world. The computer hardware and infrastructure were left to the judgment of the developing organization. Once the developing organization could demonstrate that the system worked for one distillation vat, all of the existing vats in the client organization would be transitioned to the new automated distillation control system.

The author found himself contracted to assist the developing organization with the project when the system failed to meet the expectations of the stakeholders. This particular organization had built smaller control systems to monitor chemical processes, but this project was more complex and considerably larger than anything these engineers had built before. While they had expertise with a family of microcontrollers, they had no expertise in connecting microcontrollers to other general-purpose computer systems. They also had little networking and database design experience. To mitigate these risks, the organization adopted a philosophy of buying as many commercial elements as possible to satisfy as many requirements as it could. This may seem like a reasonable approach, but the key reason for the demise of this system was poorly selected commercial elements and failure to adequately consider the impact the commercial elements would have on the design of the system. Given the designers' background and experience, the engineers took their traditional approach of focusing on the instrumentation and microcontroller hardware. In interviews, the engineers admitted that the intuition of the team was that the "other stuff," like networking, data storage, and displays, was easy to do and well understood, and could be accommodated by commercial elements. Their strategy was that when the microcontrollers were designed and built, this other stuff would fall into place, and it would be a matter of just hooking up some commercial components to the microcontroller. The system was not designed, so what was actually deferred to commercial elements was not decided in an explicit way. The problem was not in deferring functionality to commercial elements. The problem was doing so without first designing the entire system, deciding explicitly what responsibilities would be assigned to commercial elements, and then strategically selecting the appropriate commercial elements. The microcontroller design and construction was relatively problem-free, but after this the team began to experience a number of difficult problems. Connectivity between the microcontroller and the outside world proved to be the first problem. The original idea was to use simple RS232 to communicate between the microcontroller and the system that would display the data and allow the operator to monitor the distillation process and change its parameters. This was a problem because it was discovered that the operators could not be located near the distillation process—it was a safety issue. This was based on an assumption from other similar control systems that they had built. Because of the long distances between the microcontroller and the operations monitoring and control station, RS232 could not be used. The team then decided to add a "relay processor" to act as a system that would connect to the RS232 and the microcontroller, and then convert the data into a form that could be sent out to an operations monitoring and control system station. The designers decided to use a relay processor because it could allow several vats to be connected and would help scale the system up. The next problem was that the RS232 could not keep up with the microcontroller and the quantities of data being generated from the sensors. Finally, the microcontroller was modified to send data to the relay process using a parallel port, but this resulted in much more complexity in the newly added relay computer. The next problem emerged in the relay processor, which added to the delay of displaying real-time information and made it impossible to provide real-time, deterministic control over the process. The original intent was to provide as much totally automated control over the distillation process as possible, but especially for the emergency shutdown requirements—this feature was not to depend upon the operator. With a host of performance problems now emerging, the developers would have to totally redesign the controller hardware, and especially the communication between the microcontroller and the monitoring and operation stations. At this point they were out of time and money. Like a pilot who is out of altitude, airspeed, and ideas, they took a drastic approach. Because the system could not be deterministically controlled, the automated shutdown requirements would not be implemented. Operators would have to monitor the process and shut it down when certain parameters exceeded safe values. To allow immediate shutdown of the distillation process, a hardwired deadman switch was added to the system that would effectively cut power to the entire system, stopping the process. This would be a stop-gap measure until the next delivery of the system.

So far in this story, it should be obvious that many of these problems emerged because the system architecture was not designed. However, at this point poor decisions with respect to commercial elements not designed into the system began to greatly amplify these problems. The displays presented a great deal of concern for the engineers. Having little expertise in creating sophisticated real-time graphical displays, the team's strategy was to buy commercial elements that would sample instrumentation and plot the data. The selection of commercial elements was deferred to a small team of engineers who were charged to find the right software, buy it, and figure out how to make it work. A key issue facing the engineers was the amount of data and the sample rate of the acquired data. Well aware of this and armed with some preliminary data, the engineers bought a software package based on a spec sheet that they got at a trade show. The display software was purchased at a hefty price, and despite the performance promises, the software lagged real-time by 15 to 20 seconds. This was an unacceptable and dangerous lag that rendered the manual shutdown solution impossible. The use of a relay processor proved to be the problem again, because the commercial acquisition and display software was designed to be used on a system connected in relatively close proximity to the sensors. The commercial acquisition and display software was purchased based on assumptions that were simply not valid. After significant additional support and consulting costs from the provider of the acquisition and display software, it was deemed that the product would simply not work. Now, many months later, the design team went back to the drawing board and redesigned the microcontroller to use telemetry to send data from the microcontroller to the process monitoring and control station. This too presented unique challenges in terms of bandwidth and technical learning curves. The team had to renegotiate the number of sensors and the sample rates to reduce the bandwidth to meet the constraints imposed by the commercial hardware now used to telemeter data from the controller to the process monitoring and control station. The original acquisition and display software was replaced with new software from a different provider.

With a functioning controller, the team focused on the problem of data storage and retrieval; again, none of this was designed until well after the control system was built and functioning. The team waited until the very end of the project to handle this issue, thinking that it would be a trivial matter to "hook up" a database to the system. The team selected Microsoft's Access as an inexpensive commercial database to store collected sensor data at the process monitoring and control station. In their haste to finish the system, they used direct calls to write data to the database on the data acquisition and display systems. Ultimately their customer planned on installing the system on 100+ vats. With no centralized data repository designed into the system, this solution left their client with distillation data scattered on 100+ machines and made it extremely difficult for them to consolidate and manage the data. Furthermore, their client was reluctant to connect the monitoring and control stations to an external network for security reasons. The developers thought that it would be a simple matter for their client to upload data from the data acquisition and display system to a central server already in their client's inventory. Besides not designing a centralized storage system, no business process or strategy for storing, managing, and accessing hundreds of thousands of Access database files was ever discussed or conceived until the data arrived. While Access is not a bad product, it was a poor choice because it did not scale for this application. Because the developers used direct calls to write data, it was very difficult to migrate away from Access to a different commercial database product. The development team installed a server using a centralized Oracle database and connected it, as well as the process monitoring and control stations, to an internal network. The idea was to use the central data server as a gateway to the data. The plan was to modify the monitoring and control stations to directly write the acquisition data to the centralized data server. This resulted in numerous problems in performance, and in several cases connectivity was lost with the central data server. This resulted in lost real-time acquisition data. The team reverted to the use of local Access databases at the monitoring and control stations, but had to write an unplanned and somewhat significant application that would send the data to the central server after the distillation was complete. This seemed easy at first, but turned out to be challenging for the team given their lack of experience with these types of applications. At this point the developers were totally out of their realm of expertise.

Finally, with a single-vat process monitoring and control system with a central data server fully operational, the team turned their attention to scaling their system up to function with the 100+ distillation vats in their customer's inventory. At this point a new problem emerged. The team realized that when installing their system to monitor the more than 100 vats, the customer would have to acquire and maintain licenses for the dozen or so commercial products that were now woven into their system—for each vat installation. The cost of buying the commercial elements for the remaining vats was high, but predicted. Unfortunately, the annual maintenance and licensing costs were not anticipated. The cost of these licenses for the 100 vats exceeded $100,000 annually. This was a reoccurring cost for the customer that it did not anticipate—no one did because the system was not designed and the architecture was not understood until after the system was built.

In this case study, the lack of architecture design was greatly magnified by the cavalier selection and use of commercial elements. The system was a continuous source of frustration throughout its entire life cycle. As the commercial elements were upgraded and evolved over time, features that used to work incrementally broke and had to be repaired. Incompatibilities emerged between commercial elements that affected their communication and interoperation. As the commercial elements evolved, the system's performance was impacted. Tuning the system was an ongoing and problematic chore. This project experienced a 125 percent schedule slippage for a two-year project. However, the cost overruns were not linear with the schedule delays, but significantly higher than a linear increase. This was because of the various commercial elements that were purchased and discarded, licensing fees, and so forth. The real cost overruns were never revealed to the author, but they were well in excess of 200 percent. The data storage and retrieval part of the system never worked to the satisfaction of the client and was not used because of myriad technical problems. This was a medium-sized project with some challenging technical problems, but the challenges quickly became problems instead of opportunities because of the team's failure to design the system and plan for the use commercial elements.

Common Mistakes

There are a number of key mistakes that are often made when using commercial elements, most of which were illustrated in the previous case study. One important point the reader should have taken from this case study is that even if a system is composed predominantly of commercial elements, the system still must be designed. Responsibilities should be explicitly assigned to all of the elements—even if they are commercial elements.

Another key mistake that is commonly made is in the identification of candidate commercial products. If you ask any group of engineers how they find out what commercial products might satisfy their needs, most will answer "Google." Most designers looking for commercial elements and products will begin and end their entire commercial element identification, selection, and qualification with Web-based searches. Critical products and elements are identified and selected based on informal searches with information available on Web pages or in glossy marketing pamphlets. These are used as the only source of product information and are accepted as facts without further research checking. Too often in practice there is no deliberate process or criteria for selecting commercial elements.

Once candidate commercial elements are identified, the process of qualifying or certifying that they will best fit the needs of the system design is too informal. A common qualification criterion includes some or all of the following:

- "It should be cheap or free."
- "Use X because we have always used it."
- "Use X because it's my favorite."

Often, engineers download demos of commercial elements and will "play with them" until they are satisfied with the product and decide to buy it for use in the system. Informal qualification like this is fraught with problems. The roles and responsibilities of the commercial elements are often ill-defined, and therefore there are no clear qualification criteria or guidelines for evaluating them. Commercial product developers make assumptions about the general needs of stakeholders to meet a broad marketplace. Functionality is usually the focus of most commercial element specifications, but designers also make assumptions regarding structure, and therefore quality attribute requirements. Engineers designing systems tend to focus on what functionality commercial elements will provide, and often overlook quality attribute properties, side effects, and trade-offs. It is impossible to know for sure if a commercial element will meet all of the specific requirements until it is tested in the lab. However, the question is: What do you try out in the lab? How do you test drive the commercial elements in the lab? Experiments have to be designed, and component qualification can become an expensive proposition. The ever-present risk with using commercial elements is the potential for architectural incompatibilities or mismatch. The purpose of qualifying commercial elements is to avoid mismatch. Architectural mismatch occurs when system designers make assumptions that are different from those made by commercial element designers. Functional mismatch may be obvious, but other kinds of mismatch may be more subtle. The qualification process should include evaluating relevant quality attribute properties. For example, how secure is the element? How reliable? How does the element perform? Will it scale? These assumptions must be fully understood and qualified before designing the architecture as discussed in stages 1 and 2 of ACDM. If systems had one commercial element, the risk of getting it wrong would be small. It is usually the case that systems are composed of complex ensembles of commercial elements. The behavior of ensembles utilizing commercial elements can be highly unpredictable and difficult to test. In real systems, a single commercial element is not usually the problem in a system, but rather the interactions between commercial elements. In these cases, subtle incompatibilities and undesirable quality attribute side effects emerge once the system is assembled. Even more insidious is a system that appears to work in the lab but fails (functionally or with respect to quality attributes) when deployed in real operational conditions and loads.

Other business-oriented concerns associated with the total cost of ownership and use of commercial elements are rarely ever included as part of the evaluation and qualification process. In most cases evaluation and qualification of commercial elements only occurs once during initial design and construction of the system. Releases and patches to commercial elements are also changes to your system that uses the commercial elements; this could mean that your system will have to be tested again through no fault of your own. If a system utilizes a variety of commercial elements, all of which are changing over time, the combinatorial effects of these changes can result in chaos for a system. Too often, new releases or changes in commercial elements are not reevaluated, and incompatibles emerge long after the initial system delivery. Unfortunately, evolution of the commercial elements is usually out of your control, and the product evolution might be undesirable for your product, organization, market, and client base. If a system was not designed to allow commercial elements to be exchanged, then it may not be cost-effective or possible to migrate to a different commercial element. Often the effects of evolution are more subtle and affect quality attribute properties, and are usually more difficult to detect until the system is put into operation. In more extreme cases, vendors might stop supporting a particular product, and vendors can go out of business.

To avoid these mistakes, once the system is designed (and as part of the system design activities) architects need to survey the available commercial elements that could be utilized. Specific qualification criteria for the candidate products need to be established in concert with systemic design. Qualification criteria are usually more complex than a single discrete measure. Candidate products will possess strengths and weaknesses. Usually there is no perfect fit; there is only a best fit when utilizing commercial elements, especially when composing ensembles of commercial elements into a larger system. If there is no criterion for what is needed in the design, then it is impossible to intelligently evaluate commercial elements.

Commercial Element Qualification with ACDM

In building systems that will utilize a preponderance of commercial elements, the standard ACDM staging should be tailored to select the most suitable commercial elements and certify that they will fulfill their designated role in the architecture. Stages 1 and 2 will remain largely unchanged. These stages will be used to get the architectural drivers and establish the architecture drivers specification. However, the design stage (stage 3) will be modified to identify commercial products/elements, identify appropriate candidates, and certify that those selected are suitable for the purpose. Because commercial elements are not always a perfect fit, the architecture design team will have to adjust the design as various elements are selected to compensate for architectural mismatches as they emerge. Again, designing systems that use commercial elements is design by selection and integration. Stage 3 begins with the architecture design team identifying responsibilities from the architecture drivers specification that could be satisfied through the use of commercial elements. Usually the functional requirements are the first responsibilities addressed, but the team must not forget that as commercial elements are identified, they must also meet the various quality attribute expectations. The notional architecture should be designed with placeholders for potential commercial elements.

At this point in stage 3 the team will begin the commercial element identification and qualification process. This process will help the architecture design team select the appropriate commercial elements for the design. As the qualification process unfolds, candidate commercial elements will be evaluated. Some of the candidates will be found to be fit for purpose, and others will be abandoned. This is not unlike the process of putting together a jigsaw puzzle. To a large extent, the commercial elements available, and how they interoperate with other commercial elements, will determine how the system is partitioned. On one hand, this sounds a bit like a "chicken or egg" problem—there must be a notional architecture to identify candidate commercial elements that will form the architecture design. A useful analogy is to think of the artist who is creating an oil painting. The artist will typically start with a pencil drawing that outlines a rough approximate form of the picture. In our world, the notional architecture serves as this initial form. The artist will continue to refine the pencil rendering until he or she feels confident to commit to using the oil paint, at which point it will become difficult to undo any unwanted work. For our systems using commercial elements, we will iteratively evaluate candidate commercial elements, adjust the architecture, and when confident in the architecture design, commit to the commercial elements and the ensemble and build the system. So partitioning and designing the system becomes an iterative process of identifying candidate commercial elements, evaluating them, selecting the appropriate elements, evaluating the ensemble, and adjusting the design to ensure the fitness of the system. There are various qualification processes that the architect can consider using. The process explained here is designed to be used in conjunction with stage 3 of ACDM. It is assumed that a notional architecture has been designed, and elements that could be satisfied by commercial elements have been identified. Each step of the ACDM qualification process is outlined below.

Step 1: Identifying Candidate Elements and Products

As the architecture design team designs the notional architecture they will identify commercial elements that may be used in the system. As mentioned throughout the text, responsibilities should be explicitly assigned to the elements and relationships of the design—even if these are commercial elements. For each element in the architecture that is targeted to be satisfied through the use of commercial elements, various alternative candidate products must be identified unless alternatives are not available. The element responsibilities assigned in the notional architecture form the basis of how the team will identify candidate elements and quantitatively evaluate them. Again, it is worth mentioning that commercial elements may include software libraries, applications, application frameworks, hardware, firmware, and so forth. Even operating systems and computer languages can be evaluated using the qualification process described here. This means that any notional design must be representative of the various perspectives as well. The identification step is the first step in the qualification process and amounts to a canvassing of the marketplace to identify candidate commercial elements that might fill the need. Various venues can be used to find the candidate commercial elements, including trade shows, technical publications, and the Web.

Step 2: Establishing Comparison Criteria

The result of the market search is to identify candidate elements. As illustrated in Figures 17.2 and 17.3, each product is a candidate because of its potential to satisfy a set of responsibilities associated with an element in the architecture design. In this simple example, a partial client/server system architecture is shown to illustrate the candidate commercial elements. The client application provides specialized data analysis capability over a local area network. In this example, the system must authenticate users to ensure that they are permitted to access the data in the database. It is important to note the role that perspective plays in the identification of commercial elements in this simple example. In the static perspective, code-oriented structures are identified (code libraries); in the dynamic perspective, runtime structures are identified (applications and database); and in the physical perspective, physical elements are identified (computer platforms and operating systems). Note that languages would certainly be an important consideration here, but are dependent upon, and will in part be bound by, the final products selected. Again, this is an incomplete design, and maybe other commercial elements would be considered in reality. If there is only one commercial element available in the marketplace for a particular element, then the choice comes down to using the commercial element or not, and this becomes an issue of buy versus build. This can be a risky position. Once the various candidate elements have been identified, the architecture design team will have to compare each set of candidates to select one to fulfill the responsibilities of each element. An explicit assignment of functional and quality attribute responsibilities to elements and partitioning is not shown in Figures 17.2 and 17.3 for the sake of brevity. However, this assignment must be made as part of the notional architecture design prior to the initial selection of candidate elements. The comparison criteria should be a concise list of features and quality attributes that are desired for the element, not the features and qualities inherent in the candidate elements. The features and qualities needed in the design element will be used to compare each of the candidate elements.

Step 3: Creating the Comparison Matrix

In this step, the team will create a matrix that will be used to methodically compare each of the candidate elements. An element comparison matrix template is provided in Table 17.1 to illustrate how to construct such a matrix to compare a set of candidate elements.

The element comparison matrix will help the architecture design team evaluate how well each element stacks up against one another to satisfy the specified responsibilities, and how well each of the responsibilities is satisfied by the set of candidates. An explanation how to build the matrix follows.

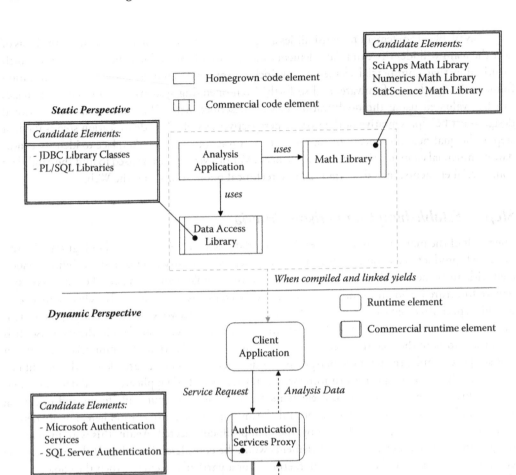

Figure 17.2   Commercial element candidates.

Across the top of the matrix is the title bar labeled "Candidate Elements for Design Element X." Again, each matrix is used to compare two or more products that will fulfill the responsibilities of a design element. The architecture design team starts building the matrix by listing the functional and quality attribute responsibilities from the responsibilities assigned to the architectural element and used to establish the set of candidate elements. Note that the element comparison matrix also lists cells for business consideration below the quality attribute responsibilities in the same column. The team should list any relevant business-oriented concerns that should also be considered as part of the product evaluation. A few common business considerations are listed in Table 17.1, for example:

■ Cost: The total cost of ownership, including initial cost, renewal fees, and licensing fees. If relevant, these can be listed and evaluated as separate items.

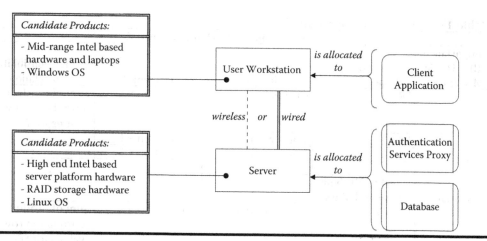

Figure 17.3 Dynamic elements mapped to physical perspective showing physical commercial element candidates.

- Learning curve: The relative difficulty and complexity of installing, using, and maintaining the product. The learning curve of any given product may depend upon the expertise of the engineers in the organization.
- Support: The level of support services available and supplied by the provider of the candidate element.
- Provider reputation: The industry reputation of the element provider, including financial stability, market position, service quality, recommendations from other customers, and so forth.
- Volatility: The technical stability of the product. Emerging commercial product domains are evolving, and the products are upgraded, patched, and replaced frequently. This is a sign of product volatility. This can be a source of risk that should be considered when evaluating commercial elements.

These are a few common business considerations, and not all of these may be applicable. It is also probable that the reader can think of other issues that may be relevant to his or her system and project context. In many cases, the business considerations interact and may be dependent on one another. For example, the level of support may affect the cost of a product and the learning curve. Sometimes support includes training and consultation, thereby easing the learning curve. However, the total cost of commercial element ownership usually goes up as more support is required. Note that the left-most column, labeled "Importance," is for establishing the relative importance of each responsibility. Any weighting can be used; the author prefers a simple ternary weighting of high, medium, and low. In this example, high importance is worth a value of 3; medium, a value of 2; and low, a value of 1. In this example, a high importance means that this responsibility is absolutely essential to the overall system's fitness for purpose. A medium importance means that the responsibility is strongly desired, and without it various features and qualities may not be fulfilled in the system. A low importance means that the responsibility is a "nice to have" and will make the overall system more appealing to the stakeholders. The business consideration should also be weighted in importance in a fashion similar to that of the functional and quality attribute responsibilities. This rating will help determine how well a commercial element correlates to the important responsibilities. The importance weighting is subjective and should be determined

Table 17.1 Element Comparison Matrix

Importance (I) = H = 3; M = 2; L = 1	Functional Responsibilities	Element A	Element B	Responsibility Correlation ↓
	FR – 1	Correlation × I_{FR-1}	Correlation × I_{FR-1}	Sum of product correlation row values for FR – 1
I_{FR-2}	FR – 2	Correlation × I_{FR-2}	Correlation × I_{FR-2}	:
I_{FR-3}	FR – 3	Correlation × I_{FR-3}	Correlation × I_{FR-3}	:
:	:	:	:	:
Importance	**Quality Attribute Responsibilities**			
I_{QA-1}	QA – 1	Correlation × I_{QA-1}	Correlation × I_{QA-1}	Sum of product correlation row values for FR-1
I_{QA-2}	QA – 2	Correlation × I_{QA-2}	Correlation × I_{QA-2}	:
I_{QA-3}	QA – 3	Correlation × I_{QA-3}	Correlation × I_{QA-3}	:
:	:	:	:	:
Importance	**Business Considerations**			
I_1	Cost	Low: 3 Mid: 2 } × I_1 High: 1	Low: 3 Mid: 2 } × I_1 High: 1	Sum of product correlation row values for FR – 1
I_2	Learning curve	Low: 3 Mid: 2 } × I_2 High: 1	Low: 3 Mid: 2 } × I_2 High: 1	:
I_3	Support	Good: 3 Mid: 2 } × I_3 Weak: 1	Good: 3 Mid: 2 } × I_3 Weak: 1	:
I_4	Provider reputation	Good: 3 OK: 2 } × I_4 Poor: 1	Good: 3 OK: 2 } × I_4 Poor: 1	:
I_5	Volatility	Stable: 3 Variable: 2 } × I_5 Unstable: 1	Stable: 3 Variable: 2 } × I_5 Unstable: 1	:
Product Correlation →		**Sum of Element A Values**	**Sum of Element B Values**	

by the team using a voting method such as those described earlier in the text for establishing importance.

In the next step in completing the matrix, the architecture design team will list the commercial elements that are part of the evaluation across the top of the matrix. In the template shown in Table 17.1, they are labeled element A and element B. There must be at least two products for the evaluation, but there could be many more. Once the products are listed, the comparison can begin. For each product column the team will have to determine how well it meets the functional and quality attribute responsibilities and the business considerations listed in the matrix. This is called the product correlation factor. The product correlation factor is a weighted rating based on any available information about the product. This can come from product specifications, interviews with producers or users, marketing brochures, trade organizations, publications, testimonials, case studies, and other similar sources. The rating the author prefers is a three-level one, as follows:

- High correlation: The product fully meets and exceeds the stated responsibility.
- Good correlation: The product partially meets the stated responsibility (for example, with respect to performance, the product may only perform good enough to meet minimal expectations).
- Poor correlation: The product does not meet the responsibility.

Note that the correlation rating for the business considerations is a little different, and often has to be tailored a bit depending upon the type of considerations relevant to the project and the system context. In general, the more positive factors of a business consideration are given higher values. This concept is explained using the example of business consideration correlation ratings shown in Table 17.1:

- Cost: In most cases, the less that a product costs, the more attractive it is. Therefore, relatively low costs are given higher correlation ratings (low cost = 3), and higher costs are given lower correlation ratings (high cost = 1).
- Learning curve: The easier it is to learn how to use, configure, install, and maintain a product, the more attractive it is. Therefore, low or shallow learning curves are given higher correlation ratings (low curve = 3), and steeper learning curves are given lower correlation ratings (high curve = 1).
- Support: Better support is more attractive and is therefore given higher correlation ratings (good support = 3), and weaker support is given lower correlation ratings (weak support = 1).
- Provider reputation: The more solid the provider reputation, the higher the correlation ratings (good reputation = 3, poor reputation = 1).
- Volatility: A highly stable product with a long track record in the marketplace is given higher correlation ratings (stable = 3) than an emerging product (unstable = 1).

Note that the responsibility rating includes a zero rating. This is because it is possible that a given commercial element will not address a particular responsibility at all. However, with respect to the business concerns (at least those listed here), every product will correlate with this in some way, even though it may be weak. If you find that you have business concerns that can have zero correlation, then by all means include a zero rating. However, it is unlikely. In the category of support, we often say that a product has no support, but even in the worst cases there are usually some manuals or minimal help-line support. Regardless how abysmal it is, technically this is support, so it is hard to give it a zero correlation, even if we want to. The correlation values can be determined and assigned in a number of ways. One of the more effective ways is to assign a small team of engineers (two or three) to complete an element comparison matrix for each set of competing candidates. Each engineer on the team should do his or her own correlation research for the product candidates. The teams should then share their findings and review their correlation ratings. There may be some negotiation among the teams on a final assignment of correlation ratings and selecting the final commercial element. This is not an onerous process, and the resulting correlation values are much more thoughtfully assigned. A key benefit of using this process is that it brings together diverse engineers by defining common criteria for evaluating commercial elements.

Once the correlation values are established, it is time to take out your calculator. For each cell in the matrix, the responsibility correlation rating is multiplied by the importance rating. This yields the Importance weighted correlation. Once the importance weighted correlations are calculated, the values of the cells in each row are added up. This sum is placed in the cell at the right-most column of the matrix corresponding to the row. In the matrix template shown in Figure 17.1, this right-most column is called the responsibility correlation. This value indicates how well each responsibility is satisfied by the set of products. Alternatively, to determine how well the products correlate individually with the high-, medium-, and low-priority responsibilities, the table can be constructed to separate and group the responsibilities by priority. This can provide insight into how well the candidates correlate to responsibilities, and their relative priorities. Low values for a particular responsibility indicate that no matter what product is selected, the responsibility may not be well served. If there is low correlation with the group of high-priority features, this may be a more significant problem than if there is low correlation with the medium- or low-priority features. Low responsibility correlation may mean that other commercial elements have to be considered that better satisfy that responsibility. If other products cannot be found, or they correlate no better, then this can be an indication that the architecture design may have to be repartitioned, responsibilities reassigned, or perhaps the planned use of commercial elements may not be a good idea. This is valuable buy-versus-build information.

After calculating the responsibility correlation values, the importance weighted correlation for each column is added for each candidate element. This is the product correlation value placed in the row labeled "Product Correlation" at the bottom of the columns in the template shown in Table 17.1. This value indicates how well products meet the overall responsibilities of the design element relative to one another. This value by itself is not an indication of which product should be selected, but coupled with the responsibility correlation values can provide a good indication of whether or not the right commercial elements were considered. For example, using Table 17.1 as an example, imagine that element B had a higher product correlation than element A, but the responsibility correlation for some high importance responsibilities was relatively low. This is not an indication to select element B. This may mean that the designers need to consider evaluating other products for the design element. It may be the case that software "glue" may have to be designed and developed to repair architectural mismatches—this should be factored into the evaluation of the commercial elements. If there are no other commercial elements available, the architecture design team may have to reconsider design and the fundamental partitioning of the system. This is fundamentally redesign of the system to address shortcomings in correlation scores. The point is that both the responsibility correlation and the product correlation values provide a more complete picture of how well the commercial elements satisfy the responsibilities assigned to the design elements. This process of evaluation is repeated for each set of candidates for each design element. To demonstrate how the element correlation matrix is used, Table 17.2 shows a matrix completed for two commercial elements.

In this small contrived example, there are two candidate products in the set, there are seven key functional requirements, three quality attributes, and five business concerns. Each of the functional requirements, quality attributes, and business concerns is prioritized as described above (high = 3, medium = 2, low = 1). Note that each set is organized by priority to ease the analysis, which will become apparent as the example unfolds. As described above, the architecture design team compares and evaluates the element producer's claims with respect to the functional requirements, quality attributes, and business concerns. Based on their findings, the team will assign values that rate how well the product correlates (or satisfies) the functional requirement, quality attribute, or business concern for each row. Again, the rating described above was used: 2 = well correlated, 1 = minimally correlated, 0 = no correlation. At each cell intersection between the product on the column and rows, the team will multiply the correlation with the importance weighting of the functional requirement, quality attribute, or business concerns represented by the row. This is the element product correlation rating. At the right-most column, the total of each element product correlation rating is added together. In the example in Table 17.2, the total row sum is shown with the total possible as follows: sum/total possible. Again, this is to help analysis by quickly exposing those requirements, quality attributes, or business concerns that are not served very well by any of the candidate elements. In this example (Table 17.2) the reader should see that the high-priority functional requirements and quality attributes seem to have reasonably good correlation at 67 percent. Note that FR – 4 has no correlation. This column can help inform the architecture design team about what they need to conduct further analysis to help determine whether commercial elements will fulfill the needs of the design element. Again, low correlation can be a sign that there are design problems, or that a weak set of candidate elements were selected.

Step 4: Verification of Candidate Features and Properties

The evaluation process described in step 3 is for the purpose of narrowing down the list of commercial elements to those most likely to work best for the design. However, once the commercial elements have been selected, their functional and quality attribute properties still must be verified. The purpose of verification is more than just playing with each element in isolation, in an ad hoc way. The architecture design team must ensure that each commercial element functions as advertised and possesses the necessary quality attribute properties. In addition, the architecture design team must ensure that the ensemble of commercial elements functions as designed and has no adverse side effects on the anticipated systemic quality attribute properties. Unfortunately, we can never really be sure until we completely build the system and deploy it in an operational environment. But this type of verification goes a long way to identify risks and problems with individual commercial elements and, more importantly, with commercial element ensembles.

This verification step is also an opportunity for the architecture design team and development teams to overcome learning curves associated with using the commercial elements. The verification process begins by validating that the commercial element function is as promised and possesses the necessary quality attribute properties. Recall that the responsibilities are the provides and requires assumptions assigned by the designer. The provides assumptions are the data and services provided by the element, and the requires assumptions are the data and services required by the element. Verification should be planned to test the specific responsibilities assigned to the design element to ensure complete and thorough coverage. Verification will take time and resources, and this cost must be factored into the total cost of element ownership. Engineers will be required to plan the verification activities, set up the test environments, conduct the specific verification

Table 17.2 Example of Element Comparison Matrix

Importance (I) = H = 3; M = 2; L = 1	Functional Responsibilities	Element A	Element B	Responsibility Correlation ↓
		Candidate Elements for Design Element X		
3	FR – 1	$1 \times 3 = 3$	$2 \times 3 = 6$	$\Sigma = 9/12$
3	FR – 2	$2 \times 3 = 6$	$1 \times 3 = 3$	$\Sigma = 9/12$
3	FR – 3	$1 \times 3 = 3$	$1 \times 3 = 3$	$\Sigma = 6/12$
2	FR – 4	$0 \times 2 = 0$	$0 \times 2 = 0$	$\Sigma = 0/8$
2	FR – 5	$1 \times 2 = 2$	$0 \times 2 = 0$	$\Sigma = 2/8$
1	FR – 6	$2 \times 1 = 2$	$1 \times 1 = 1$	$\Sigma = 3/4$
1	FR – 7	$2 \times 1 = 2$	$2 \times 1 = 2$	$\Sigma = 4/4$
		FRΣ = 17 High = 30	FRΣ = 15 High = 30	
	Quality Attribute Responsibilities			
3	QA – 1	$2 \times 3 = 6$	$2 \times 3 = 6$	$\Sigma = 12/12$
3	QA – 2	$1 \times 3 = 3$	$2 \times 3 = 6$	$\Sigma = 9/12$
2	QA – 3	$0 \times 2 = 0$	$1 \times 2 = 2$	$\Sigma = 2/8$
		QAΣ = 9 High = 16	QAΣ = 14 High = 16	
	Business Considerations			
3	Cost	(High) $1 \times 3 = 3$	(Med) $2 \times 3 = 6$	$\Sigma = 6/18$
3	Provider reputation	(Good) $3 \times 3 = 9$	(OK) $2 \times 3 = 6$	$\Sigma = 15/18$
3	Volatility	(Stable) $3 \times 3 = 9$	(Vari) $2 \times 3 = 6$	$\Sigma = 15/18$
2	Learning curve	(High) $1 \times 2 = 2$	(Mid) $2 \times 2 = 4$	$\Sigma = 6/12$
2	Support	(Good) $3 \times 2 = 6$	(Weak) $1 \times 2 = 2$	$\Sigma = 8/12$
		BCΣ = 29 High = 39	BCΣ = 24 High = 39	
Total Product Correlation		$\Sigma = 55/85$	$\Sigma = 53/85$	

activities, and document the results. Besides keeping a record of the qualification, this information can be used to train other engineers on the use of the commercial elements based on what they learned testing it. In addition to engineering hours, specialized tools, environments, computing hardware, and consulting expertise may be required to facilitate the verification. All of this adds to the cost of adopting the commercial elements and should be considered in terms of the total cost of ownership. During the verification process, the actual capabilities of the commercial elements may not meet the advertised functional and quality attribute properties. These should be carefully recorded and their impact on the design analyzed. If the deviation is significant enough, the architect may have to reconsider the use of that commercial element, or alter the design to compensate for the deviation. If it is determined that the element is not fit for purpose, the architecture design team still has a few choices:

1. Revisit the element comparison matrix to see if another product can be used.
2. Try to find other commercial elements that can be considered.
3. Develop "glue" software or hardware that will compensate for shortcomings in commercial elements.
4. Abandon the use of commercial elements for the design element and develop the element from scratch.

Assuming that the selected elements pass the individual element verification, interactions between the selected elements should be checked to ensure that the ensemble of commercial elements meets the expected functional and quality attribute needs expressed in the architectural drivers. Most often, systemic quality attribute properties are affected by combinations of commercial elements that were never anticipated by the element providers, or the architect who designed the system using the commercial elements. Element interactions can be anywhere in the system where two or more commercial elements send or receive data, use one another's services, are physically connected to one another, or any other similar interactions. A good way to quickly identify interelement interactions is to create an element interaction matrix as shown in Table 17.3.

The rows and columns list each commercial element selected as part of the system ensemble, and qualified in isolation. The architect starts with the first element in the first row, moves across the row to the first column, and determines if there is an interaction between the elements at the row/column intersection cell. Each cell should be marked in one of three ways:

1. Interaction: This indicates that there is an interaction between two commercial elements at the intersection at this cell. The cell should contain an annotation indicating that there is an interaction (I) and may contain a reference to a note that further explains the interaction.
2. No interaction: This indicates that there is no interaction between the two elements at the intersection at this cell. The cell should contain an annotation indicating that there is no interaction (NA).
3. Unknown: In some cases, it may not be clear if there will be any interactions between the elements required. Further investigation will be required.

This continues for each column and each row. The reader may question the wisdom of having to consider the diagonal cells that identify element interactions between the same elements. However, this can be an issue to consider if there are different instances of the same commercial product. The element interaction matrix can also show trends. This is illustrated in the example element interaction matrix, where we can see that element D is particularly sensitive in the system because all of the elements interact with it. This can highlight particularly sensitive areas of the system that may be risky and need special design attention.

Strategies for Addressing Architectural Incompatibilities

Architectural incompatibility has received little systematic attention and is often treated as a second-class citizen in industry and academic communities. Many writers indicate that architectural incompatibility should be avoided at all cost. Ideally, we would always opt to avoid architectural mismatches anytime they occur. In fact, this is the reason for the qualification process described in the previous section, but of course it is not always possible to avoid mismatch in practice. There are many commonsense ways to avoid architectural incompatibilities. Adhering to well-established standards can go a long way to help avoid architectural incompatibilities. However, standards are

Table 17.3 Element Interaction Matrix

	Element A	Element B	Element C	Element D
Element A	NA	U	NA	I
Element B		NA	I	I
Element C			NA	I
Element D				NA

Note: NA = not applicable, no interactions between X and Y; I = interaction between X and Y; U = unknown if there are interactions between X and Y.

often silent on various quality attribute properties the element may or may not possess. Standards may not help if you must integrate legacy elements that do not adhere to the standard. Another good idea is to develop contingency plans that include the use of alternate products and fallback positions in the event that the selected commercial elements are no longer available, or if incompatibilities emerge. Fallback positions should include alternative elements, alternative ensembles, or developing new elements from scratch. Mismatches can be more than just technical in nature; they can be economic or business model oriented.

But despite these best efforts, architectural incompatibles are a fact of life. Mismatch can be resolved by designing and building "glue-ware," which can be software or even hardware to resolve incompatibilities between elements. In practice, detecting and resolving architectural mismatch is often seen as a job for the interns and junior programmers. Subtle incompatibilities or side effects are often found in quality attributes such as performance and security, among others, after commercial elements are procured and integration or testing has begun. A system is an ensemble of elements, and the system is only as fit as its weakest element—so an ad hoc approach using less experienced engineers to construct some glue-ware may not be the best way to address architectural incompatibilities. The quality of incompatibility repair may mean the difference between achieving and failing to meet systemic behavioral and quality attribute requirements. Two elements being incompatible does not automatically preclude their use in a system. However, mismatch resolution mechanisms need to be designed in a deliberate and disciplined way, just as any other part of the system—they are as critical as any other element of the system. The obvious way to repair the incompatibility is to change the code of the offending element(s). One big reason for this approach being rejected is that the organization may have no desire or ability to modify the source code or the hardware of the elements. It is often impractical to modify source code because the documentation of the elements may be weak or nonexistent. The source code or tools required to modify the elements may no longer be available. An alternative to modifying element source code is to reconcile interactions in a way that resolves the incompatibilities. Architectural mismatches can occur between commercial, legacy, and homegrown elements. Architectural incompatibilities should be identified as early as possible in analysis and addressed during design (stages 2 and 3). Certainly if considerable legacy-ware and commercial elements are used in a design, it is wise to take this into consideration during the evaluation in stage 4. Besides the obvious incompatibilities that may exist because of technical constraints before design begins, incompatibilities may emerge over the life cycle of a system. A system may be comprised of completely compatible elements on the day it is delivered. However, over time, as patches, updates, and upgrades gradually replace the original elements—especially commercial elements—incompatibilities can emerge. An alternative to modifying element source code is to reconcile interactions in a way that resolves the incompatibilities. There are some architectural approaches for managing architectural incompatibilities.

Software Wrappers

Wrappers are software mechanisms that are used to encapsulate one or more elements that may be architecturally incompatible, or may be affected by other changes in the system. Wrappers encapsulate the software elements and make their services and data available, but hide the underlying interface details. Wrappers are a tactic that is applied to static structures. Therefore, to utilize wrappers, the static structures of the commercial or legacy elements that we wish to encapsulate must be available to the architects and implementers. Because wrappers hide the underlying details of the interfaces of the encapsulated elements, changes to elements inside the wrapper and outside the wrapper can be isolated by the wrapper. Wrappers help resolve architectural mismatches by resolving parameter type differences, providing default parameter values, and resolving incompatible parameter-passing mechanisms (pass by reference versus pass by value). Wrapping can be thought of as interface translation where the underlying element is preserved without change, and the wrapper resolves the incompatibility. Wrapper mechanisms can also be used like layers to hide underlying hardware elements, low-level software drivers, and operating system details. Wrappers of this type effectively isolate software elements from other elements of the system and the underlying implementation detail—and the incompatibilities. Once compiled, the wrapper and the underlying element collapse into a process, object, thread, or other similar runtime element. From the dynamic perspective, the operational capability (services and data) is encapsulated and is accessed through the wrapper's interface. Wrappers can be used whenever the static structures of the commercial elements are accessible. Wrappers can be employed as a tactic whenever there are architectural incompatibilities in the initial design, or where elements may change and those changes ripple to other elements of the system. The wrapper concept is illustrated in Figure 17.4.

Software elements with incompatible interfaces.

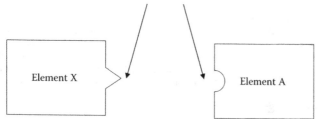

Note that the elements here are code oriented structures – the perspective is static. In this example there is one incompatible interface, but in practice there could be many incompatibilities. Below the wrapper is shown encapsulating Element A – presumably Element A is a commercial element or legacy code element.

Wrapper

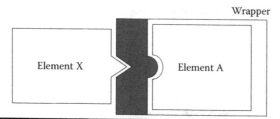

Figure 17.4   Software wrappers.

Intermediaries

Intermediaries are runtime mechanisms that resolve the differences between architecturally incompatible elements. Intermediaries are processes or threads that facilitate interelement operation and effectively hide the services and data from the architecturally incompatible elements. An intermediary could also be a physical piece of hardware that acts as a kind of adapter between incompatible elements. The intermediary is designed to act as a kind of glue or proxy between incompatible elements by reforming data, repackaging service and data requests, coordinating interelement operations, hiding service and data access details, and providing other similar kinds of reconciliation. Because intermediaries are runtime mechanisms, the underlying static structures of the incompatible elements are not necessary. Intermediaries can be complex. The intermediary concept is illustrated in Figure 17.5.

Scaling up ACMD

One constant theme of this book so far is that size and scope dramatically influence the design process. In smaller projects where the design team and production teams are closely coupled or are one and the same, a single team can use ACMD as described in Section 2, with little tailoring, to design the system or product architecture. However, as system size and scope increase, more levels of abstraction are required—both architecturally and organizationally. More architects may be required—perhaps multiple design teams, each designing major parts of the system. In this case, coordinating the interaction among the architects and organizations can become complex, time-consuming, and expensive. In large-scale system/product development, it is essential that the overall design context be established by a small core team of architects, and it must be adhered

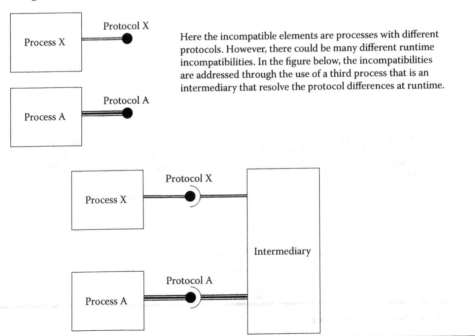

Here the incompatible elements are processes with different protocols. However, there could be many different runtime incompatibilities. In the figure below, the incompatibilities are addressed through the use of a third process that is an intermediary that resolve the protocol differences at runtime.

Figure 17.5   The intermediary.

to by the downstream organizations designing and building the various parts of the system. It is quite possible that in large system development, an element is a system in and of itself. In these situations multiple architectural teams can use ACDM to coordinate the various levels of decomposition. This assumes that all of the teams building the various elements can be directed to use a design process similar to ACDM. This is shown conceptually in Figure 17.6.

The diagram shows a core architectural design team that is responsible for designing the overall system design. This team will elicit the initial architectural drivers and establish scope (stages 1 and 2). The team will then design the architecture, review it, and then refine it until it is ready for production (stages 3 through 6). After the coarse-grained architecture design is baselined (a go decision is made in stage 5), the team can plan the effort based on the architecture (stage 7). It is important that the core architectural design team work with the subordinate teams to

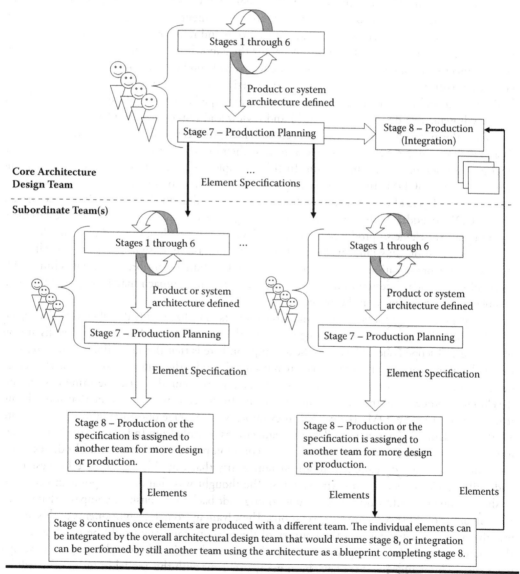

Figure 17.6   Large-scale development with multiple teams using ACDM.

negotiate schedules and budgets and plan the effort. The elements of the architecture at the core architectural design team's level of decomposition will be very coarse grained. The elements of their architectural design could be systems, or other significantly large-scale elements. The architectural design documentation that this team produces must include element specifications for the subordinate teams that will design the elements and undertake the next level of decomposition or implementation.

Once the subordinate teams receive the element specifications, they will use the core architectural design team's design as a framework for the detailed design of the elements they are responsible for. Again, the design elements at this scale and scope may be entire systems. From the core architectural design team's vantage point, the subordinate teams will be carrying out stage 8 activities. However, from the perspective of the subordinate teams, they will begin ACMD anew with stage 1. Again, this is assuming that the elements that the subordinate teams will design and build are sufficiently large enough to require more requirements gathering and analysis (stages 1, 2), design and evaluation (stages 3, 4), experimentation and refinement (stages 5, 6, 3), and eventual production (stages 7, 8). The stakeholders for the subordinate architecture teams will be the core architecture design team. The subordinate teams will conduct the stage 1 architecture drivers elicitation workshops with the core architecture design team, and the subsequent stage 2 work leading to the architecture drivers specification. After scope has been established, the subordinate teams will iteratively design the element(s) and review and refine the design(s) (stages 3 through 6). When the architecture design(s) has been baselined, the team will plan the production (stage 7) and then produce the elements (stage 8) or pass their designs to the next downstream team for finer-grained design or implementation. In this example the assumption is made that all of the teams are using ACDM. In extraordinarily large systems development, it is possible that there could be a few layers of design teams, each using ACDM as described here. This is like recursively using ACDM to address different hierarchies of design. Eventually the top-level core design team will integrate the elements produced by the lower-level teams who designed and built the elements. This is the situation illustrated in Figure 17.6. If the lower-level design teams are not all using ACDM, or the organization is comprised of a highly distributed workforce, where it is impossible to establish a standard design framework, a slightly different approach may be required that will complement such a context and workforce.

Today it is common for both small and large projects to utilize highly distributed or decoupled workforces. At first glance the reader might assume that this is identical to the previous discussion of the size and scope issues. However, the assumption here is that the subordinate teams are self-directed, autonomous organizations that are not directly under the control of the core architecture design team. As such, these organizations are not directly bound to use the same design and development processes of the core architecture team. In this case, we will assume that subordinate teams are not using ACDM. The canonical example is the average outsourcing model of the late 1990s in the United States, where offshore organizations (mainly from India) were utilized by U.S. (onshore) companies to write software. It was a common practice at this time to blindly delegate the chore of software development to an offshore entity that would be responsible for designing and building elements or even entire systems. The thought was that at some point in time, the offshore company would send perfectly functioning code back to the onshore company that would meet all of the onshore company's expectations. The advantage touted by proponents of this model was that the local labor rates in the country of the offshore company would be much less than those rates in the onshore company's country, thereby resulting in substantial savings in development costs. Unfortunately, there have been many problems with this model in terms of schedule, quality, integration, and the real cost of designing and building products and systems this way.

One of the primary problems was that onshore organizations did not design the systems, and as a result, they subcontracted the software development in an ad hoc fashion. It was a common practice to dump raw requirements into the lap of multiple offshore companies and wait for them to write and deliver the code. If organizations using offshore labor do not develop a well-defined architectural design, it is impossible to specify the elements for the offshore company to design and build, and it is impossible to evaluate or measure compliance with the overall system architectural design. Many of the problems are not discovered until significant commitments have been made. This approach to developing systems and products using a highly decoupled workforce is more like delegation by dumping.

Today we have more experience in using highly distributed workforces to develop large, complex software-intensive systems. Just as an architect must understand the design hierarchy he or she will work within (described in Chapter 1), an organization must first understand and define the nature of the relationships it has with the distributed organizations it will work with. Will the local organization be participating in system construction as the designer or integrator, developing some of the elements, maintaining the system after delivery, or some combination of these? Will the local organization outsource the whole system construction? In the latter case the design will be outsourced as well, and this becomes a contractor/subcontractor relationship. This can work, but if the local organization needs any insight into the design of the system or product for maintenance, enhancement, or integration, then it may be disappointed unless it is more engaged with the teams designing and producing the elements. These relationships should be deliberately determined before the teams are established or contracts are written because they will deeply influence how the system will be designed and built. The most important aspects of creating a highly effective and productive distributed workforce are establishing a core team of architects at the onshore company, empowering them to establish the architectural design, and using the architecture design as a contract between the distributed teams designing and producing the elements (Sangwan et al., 2006). The architecture must be designed for distributed teams to design and produce the elements. It is highly recommended that the onshore organization form a core architecture design team that is responsible for the system design. They should:

- Specify and describe for nonlocal organizations the elements that are to be created and what is expected from the elements in terms of functionality and quality attribute properties
- Inspect remotely produced designs for elements to ensure they comply with the element specification
- Test the elements
- Integrate, or closely guide the integration of, the elements, and test the overall system once implemented
- Have oversight and insight into what the subordinate organizations are doing, measure their progress, and influence how they design and develop elements

In these situations, the core architecture design team plays a vital role in the project, and the distributed nature of the workforce will deeply influence the architectural design. When teams are distributed and autonomous, it is essential that the elements of the design are partitioned in such a way that the elements can be assigned to teams to work on in near total isolation. This necessitates a highly decoupled design that will in turn impact other quality attributes of the system, such as performance, security, and others. To achieve this, element interfaces must be well designed, specified in detail, and enforced by the central architectural team. These interfaces will become the connective tissue of the architecture and the organizations, and will serve as a contract between the teams. It is always a good idea to have well-defined interfaces as a work product of architecture design, but it is essential when using a highly distributed workforce. A team working on a single system element will necessarily have a relatively high level of communication needs within the team. If the team members are not co-located, the communication between the members of the team will become a huge overhead and an impediment to designing and building the element. If a system is designed without considering the distributed workforce as a key business constraint, this situation can easily happen. It is critical that the people and teams working on the same elements are co-located to facilitate the high volume of communications. This will be a prime business constraint influencing the architect and the overall systemic architecture design.

ACDM can be used by highly distributed workforces much in the same way as described earlier for larger organizations and depicted in Figure 17.6. However, the main difference between these situations is that the central architectural design team may not have direct authority to dictate that the remote teams utilize ACDM or any design processes, notations, and so forth. This can make it more difficult to establish the compatible design processes, notation, and so forth between teams. This can impede communication. One approach is for the core architecture design team to use ACDM exactly as described. The design they produce must include detailed element interface specifications; again, these will be the contract between the various distributed teams designing and building the system or product. The central design team will refine the architecture until it is ready for production (stage 7). Once completed, the central architecture design team can use the architecture design to negotiate the element design and construction work with the remote teams to establish schedules and deliverables for stage 8 production. Although the remote teams may not be aware of the fact that they are part of stage 8, the core architecture design team can use the artifacts created in stage 7 to monitor and track the progress of element construction. In these situations, it may not be necessary to share the overall system architecture design with the remote teams, but rather deliberately restrict their visibility to the element and interface specifications for which they are responsible. This is a grand-scale application of the principle of information hiding. Restricting remote teams' visibility of the overall systemic design can prevent them from bypassing established interfaces, semantics, or otherwise violating the architectural design conventions and principles because they have no visibility into anything other than the elements and interfaces they are responsible for. Stage 8 will actually be carried out by the remote teams with oversight from the core architecture team. It is highly recommended that integration of the final product or system be done by the core architecture design team after the elements are thoroughly certified. If elements that are received by any remote element providers violate the established, agreed-to element contracts, they should be returned as any defective product would be. If overall design and final integration is not done locally by the core architecture design team, it is strongly recommended that system/product procurement models be considered, rather than a design process like ACDM.

ACDM in Maintenance

Unfortunately, many organizations are under the impression that the architect and the architectural design are only useful until the product ships or the system is deployed. In other words, there is no place for architectural design after implementation and test. This is an unfortunate misconception. Architecture design can provide a great deal of insight after the product is shipped or the system is deployed by helping with maintenance that is often an inevitable part of the life cycle. The nature of the postdelivery work varies greatly, depending upon the domain and business context. For example, consider the IT domain and the systems that support the banking, insurance, or similar kinds of IT-oriented industry applications. These systems are long-lived and are upgraded, extended, and changed constantly over their operational life cycle. However, consider the case of an embedded automotive engine control application. Once this system is loaded on the engine control processor hardware, it is rarely upgraded, extended, or changed unless there is a serious problem with it. The general nature of the postdelivery work in each of these domains is quite different. First and foremost, architecture designs can only help with postdelivery maintenance if the architecture design representations are kept current. Unfortunately, there always seems to be enough time to change systems, but not enough time to document the changes to the design artifacts. If changes are made to the system but they are not reflected in the design artifacts, then the as-built structures and the artifacts that describe them become out of sync. If the design artifacts are out of sync with the as-built structures and are used to analyze the system and make judgments about the effects of changes to the system, then the analysis and resulting conclusions may be flawed. In terms of systemic maintenance, architecture designs can be used to guide engineers' efforts to find and isolate defects, tune the system, and manage change throughout the life cycle.

The first way that the architecture design can be used is to help find the general location of defects, trace their effects, and isolate and repair them in the system. If a system or product is large, complex, or highly distributed, it can be a time-consuming and costly chore to find a defect—and many times the exact nature of a defect is never fully understood. The architecture design can help engineers isolate defects by comparing defect symptoms with the various element responsibilities. This can help architects isolate the defect to a set of likely elements that should be tested or inspected. This can speed system repairs and limit the potential side effects of repairs. Similarly, a system often needs to be "tuned" after deployment to improve performance, security, and availability, and address other shortfalls in systemic quality attribute properties. Again, the architecture design can help engineers identify bottlenecks (performance), risky exposure points (security), single points of failure (availability), and other similar issues that are systemic in nature. Of course, these should be discovered throughout the design, but often changes in operational environments, business and marketing contexts, stakeholders' expectations, and so forth drive changes that may cause quality attribute issues to arise that necessitate postdelivery tuning. The architecture design representations are the first place that engineers will go to study the system structures and look for opportunities to tune the system to better meet emerging needs. Finally, the architecture design artifacts are extremely useful in analyzing the impact of systemic changes in response to changing requirements. Again, requirements change is only the symptom. The real causes of change are:

- Internal/external business models
- Key stakeholders
- Marketing
- Technologies

Changes in these may eventually result in changes in the requirements that will impact the design of the system. If the architecture design artifacts match the as-built structures, engineers can study the designs to determine if the effects of the changes are internal, external, or systemic.

- Internal effects: In these cases, the proposed changes to the system are confined to the internals of one or more elements; the changes will be less onerous than other kinds of changes with broader impact. In these cases, the changes are isolated by the walls and interfaces of the elements. If we can anticipate changes to a system during initial design, we can design the system so that the effects of changes are isolated to the internals of elements.

■ External effects: In these cases, the proposed changes to the system will ripple outside of element boundaries and affect the interactions between the elements, the interfaces of the elements, or possibly cause the introduction of new elements. However, the same general system structure and patterns are intact. These kinds of changes are relatively more onerous that those isolated to the internals of the elements, with no impact to interfaces or the resultant need to add elements. If we can anticipate changes to a system, this kind of response is usually not the most desirable. However, the damaging effects of ripple can be controlled and limited if the change was anticipated in the design. Unfortunately, these situations usually arise when changes are unanticipated and were not well accommodated for in the design.

■ Systemic effects: In these cases, the proposed changes result in systemic changes that impact the overall topology of the design, invalidate the fundamental design approaches and structure, change the fundamental communication and interaction mechanisms, undermine the system partitioning, and so forth. These kinds of changes were not anticipated and usually result in system redesign or replacement. Although every system eventually faces this situation, we would like to delay its arrival at least until the investment in the system has been recouped.

It should be obvious that there are increasing costs associated with each of these kinds of system changes, with internal effects being somewhat less expensive (resources and time), and external effects being more expensive than internal effects but less expensive than systemic effects. Systemic effects would obviously be the most expensive kinds of changes to a system. Having a current set of architecture design artifacts can help an organization determine if changes are minimal or extensive, and if it is time to upgrade or replace the system. Without a current architecture design, this kind of simple analysis is impossible. The architecture design artifacts can help an organization plan a migration strategy from the old system to a new one by prioritizing upgrades and planning how old services will be phased out and new ones phased in. All of these essential maintenance activities depend heavily on current architecture design artifacts.

ACDM can also play a role in the maintenance of a system throughout its life cycle. As changes, repairs, and so forth are requested, the architecture design team will treat them as they would raw requirements in stage 1. These repairs, upgrades, and so forth should be sorted into their respective architecture drivers categories (functional, quality attribute, business or technical constraint) in stage 2. To establish the scope in stage 2, the effects and impact of the repairs and upgrades on the existing design should be analyzed in terms of their internal, external, or systemic effects. At this point the team is prepared to negotiate and prioritize the work. Once the scope of the work is agreed to, the architecture design team will change the design to reflect the changes to the system in stage 3. Once the design is changed, the team should undertake a review of the changes in stage 4. In stage 5, any issues raised in the stage 4 architecture evaluation must be addressed in stage 5, and experiments planned as appropriate in stage 6. Experiments with ACDM indicated that the review is usually relatively short (in comparison to initial design evaluations), and there were rarely any issues that required extensive experimentation to resolve. Once the changes are agreed to, and the design altered and evaluated, the team will plan and implement the changes (stages 7 and 8). When using ACDM to maintain a system, the nature of the process itself forces the architecture design team to evaluate the changes against the existing structures, and modify and evaluate the design, before changing the as-built structures. This goes a long way to ensuring that the architecture design artifacts match the actual system implementation.

Summary

In this chapter we discussed ways in which ACDM can be used to design systems that must interoperate with legacy systems and elements, or utilize a significant amount of commercial software and hardware. We also introduced how to use ACDM in the maintenance of a system. In each of these situations the ACDM was tailored to fit the circumstances. As stated throughout the second section of this text, ACDM has to be tailored in practice to meet the exact needs of the organization, stakeholders, and architecture design team. Legacy-ware, commercial elements, and maintenance are stark realities that face all projects and organizations building software-intensive systems. Architecture still plays a significant role in cases where legacy and commercial elements are key parts of the system—the architecture design can and should play a critical role in designing these systems. ACDM can be used in these situations as a design process, and to manage changes in systems through their designs. However, ACDM should be tailored to meet the realities of the situation. The best guidance that the author can provide in tailoring ACDM or any other framework is to apply good engineering common sense. Illustrated in this chapter are specific examples of ACDM tailoring based on best practices to fit these likely situations and business contexts.

Summary

Chapter 18

Using ACDM with Software Development Frameworks

A puritan is a person who pours righteous indignation into the wrong things.

Gilbert K. Chesterton (1874–1936)

The puritan approach of using a method, framework, process, and so forth without tailoring it to fit the specific organization's business, technical, and marketing context is naive at best. Like commercial software, software development and process frameworks, and methods were created with a relatively general audience in mind. This is true for ACDM as well. Tailoring the method has been a continual theme throughout the text. ACDM is a design process framework with numerous techniques, templates, checklists, and guidance to help practitioners adopt and tune the method for practical use in a variety of situations. Although ACDM is first and foremost a design process, it provides guidance for planning the production phases. However, ACDM lacks specific prescription for how to conduct the production phases. This has been omitted intentionally. Since the mid-1980s a tremendous amount of work has been done in the area of defining software development processes, measuring process effectiveness, and improving development processes. Numerous software development process frameworks have emerged over the years as a result of this work. The argument could be made that we do not need another one—which is why ACDM does not attempt to define the detailed software development process. Architectural design has been identified in numerous reports and studies as a key success factor in developing software-intensive systems. However, it interesting to note that in general, modern software process frameworks do not address the specific details of the design process. ACDM tries to address this gap that is left by most process frameworks.

One of the goals of creating ACDM was to allow it to be used with a variety of existing development frameworks. However, this leaves the organization using ACDM to figure out how to plan and coordinate the detailed design construction phases. In field trials of ACDM, organizations and teams building small- to medium-sized products and systems simply extended ACMD to be a full software process framework. However, many of these organizations did not have any processes, so adopting ACDM was relatively easy to do. These organizations also tended to have a decidedly technical focus and ACDM, being a design framework with a technical focus, was appealing to these organizations. The problem is that many organizations have a considerable investment in various software development process frameworks. These investments are cultural, monetary, and in terms of training and expertise, infrastructure, tooling, and organizational structure. Again, this was considered when ACDM was being designed, and changing these structures was well out of the realm of the author's intent and interest. However, it would be nice if an organization's existing software development processes could be complemented with predictable and disciplined design processes.

Terminology

The first question in the reader's mind might be: What is a software development process framework, and how is it different from what ACDM offers? Of course, the answer to this is "it depends." A development process is the general ritual that organizations follow to develop products. While this is generally applicable to any manufacturing domain, for the purposes of this text we can safely say that the development process is the general ritual or procedures that organizations follow to develop software-intensive systems and products. For much of the 1980s to the present, the focus of process improvement communities has been on software development processes, even though products and systems involve more than just software. Another common confusion is the term software life cycle, which is often synonymously (and often incorrectly) used to refer to software development processes. The software life cycle tends to be very abstract, describing general stages of software development projects. Software life cycle is more than system or product development; it refers to the cradle-to-grave way that requirements are gathered and analyzed, and software is developed, tested, deployed, maintained, and finally decommissioned. A similar life cycle model, called the V-Model (Forsberg et al., 1996), exists in the system engineering community. The general temporal organization of these general phases often defines the kind of software life cycle an organization uses. Organized one way, the life cycle might be a waterfall, and in another way it might be iterative or spiral. These various life cycles are depicted in Figure 18.1.

Each of these life cycles serves different business and system development contexts. A waterfall process might be used in situations where the product or system requirements and technologies are well understood. Iterative or spiral life cycles are often used in business contexts where the requirements are volatile, technologies are not well understood, or both. In theory, iteration helps to identify and control risks due to volatile requirements or challenging technology earlier than waterfall approaches do. All of these approaches are a bit naive in their purest, most abstract form. Iterative software development life cycles seem to be most favored today. However, in practice, if one were to closely examine what an organization really does when it builds software-intensive systems, a combination of iteration and waterfall life cycle is often used. ACDM is a good example of combining life cycle models in that it utilizes fast iteration early in a project to identify and resolve risky requirements and technologies during the period of uncertainty. Once the architecture design is stable, the period of uncertainty is overcome, and a more straightforward waterfall-oriented approach can be taken, or various iterations can be used to build and deploy various versions of the product or system.

Software process frameworks provide more detail than general life cycle models do, but still need to be instantiated or tailored for a specific project and organization. Software process frame-

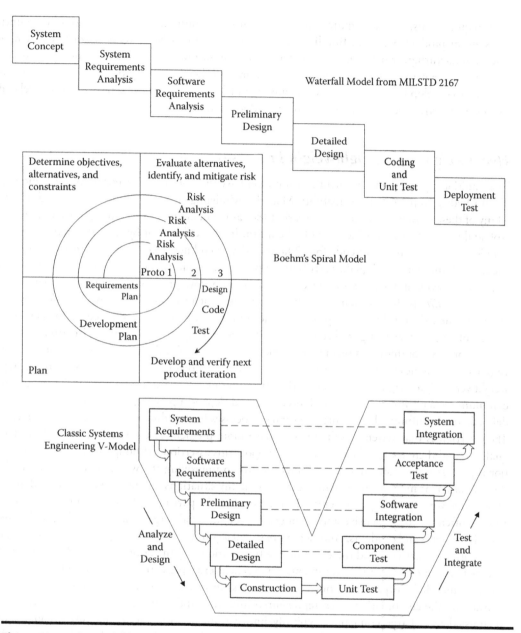

Figure 18.1   General life cycle models.

works combine a general software life cycle model(s), but prescribe specific roles, responsibilities, artifacts, procedures, methods, and so forth that should be produced when following the process framework. Organizations often start with a software process framework and tailor it to their specific software development process. Instantiated organizational software processes are far more specific process frameworks and describe specifically what is done, what is produced, and by whom. Organizational software processes may define specific roles, responsibilities, artifacts, procedures, document formats, templates, standards, and so forth. On closer examination of an organization's development process, we find that there is not a single continuum of activities that elicit requirements, analyze requirements, and document requirements, design, and so forth until a system or product pops out. Building complex software-intensive systems is not like assembly line manufacturing, which is more or less a continuum of raw ingredients entering one end of a manufacturing plant and the product rolling out on the other end. The processes used by an organization to develop software-intensive systems are much more like a set of separate but interrelated processes that are used together to develop a product or system.

Heavyweight versus Lightweight Processes

The traditional process improvement communities have their origins in waterfall life cycle models, Total Quality Improvement, Capability Maturity Modeling, ISO 9000, Six Sigma, and others. Many of these movements began in the early 1980s as the demand for software spiraled out of control, and project failure was increasingly the norm. It was self-evident by then that putting smart people in a room to hack out code for 12 hours a day would not necessarily lead to a system with the desired functional and quality attribute properties. The tradition of using process frameworks to guide the work of designers and developers, and to improve practice, goes on to this day.

Today *agility* is the hot item in software development processes. If the word *agile* does not appear in the title or subtitle of a process framework, it seems that it is snubbed by the new generation of engineers as being "old school" and "too heavyweight." Similarly, purists from the traditional process communities seem a bit suspicious of the current lightweight process movement. In practice, extremes are usually never the best answer, and this is certainly the case in the heavyweight versus lightweight process debate that rages on today. The traditional process improvement communities tend to be documentation-centric and depend upon highly structured, rigorously defined, and faithfully followed organizational processes for building software-intensive systems. The assertion is that systems built this way have more predictable costs, schedule, and product quality—and there is a good deal of data to support this assertion. Although these types of traditional process frameworks have contributed greatly to improving the way that systems are built, they are often far more onerous than necessary in many situations and business contexts. Many of these frameworks were originally created with large U.S. Department of Defense projects in mind and are often far too expensive and cumbersome for the small organizations building software-intensive systems and products. Another, more recent argument is that rigid processes tend to stifle organizational creativity, and there is evidence from various organizational case studies to suggest that there is some truth to this argument. An excellent example is the case study (Hindo, 2007) that describes 3M Corporation's outstanding success in its ability to capitalize on technological innovation. The combination of entrepreneurial invention and large corporate structure is often an unusual mix. Large companies typically find it difficult to innovate, and small companies often find it difficult to achieve predictable, cost-effective, large-scale production. However, 3M is a 100-year-old company that has enjoyed a reputation as one of the world's most innovative companies on the planet, with much of its revenue based on innovative new technologies developed within 3M. This success has been attributed to an environment that encouraged risk-taking and a certain tolerance of failure as a catalyst for discovery. Within 3M's research and development organization, extremely lightweight processes allow engineers the freedom to explore ideas without the burden or pressure of meeting statistical measures and goals or time-to-market deadlines. One 3M research engineer asserted that 5,000 ideas have to be explored to find one that will be profitable.

Despite the track record of innovation, a change in executive management resulted in fundamental changes to these lightweight research and development processes at 3M. The new CEO, a strong advocate of Total Quality Management (TQM) and Six Sigma–based process frameworks, decided to institute rigorous process controls to measure, manage, and improve 3M's innovation process. A strict phase-review process was instituted to advance only promising research. Under this process, if a research project was not deemed to result in a profitable product after a review, the project was cancelled. The goal of this kind of rigid process control was to accelerate, systematize, and transition innovation into profitable products for the marketplace. Management's goal was to make innovation more predictable and cost-effective. However, innovation and discovery are necessarily a chaotic and unpredictable process where raw statistical measure does not tell the whole story of successful innovation. For example, the Post-It Note invented at 3M is a classic example of a failed adhesive that found success in a totally unplanned application in the Post-It Note. Post-It Notes were used for a long time in the 3M labs before someone within the organization was inspired to market it as a product to the consumer. Based on the original research goal, which was to develop a new adhesive, the statistics would have showed this research program to be a failure. However, the reality is that the ingenious Post-It Note has resulted in billions of dollars in revenue for the 3M Corporation. According to engineers at 3M, under the new regime of closely monitored, controlled research, the adhesive for Post-It Note would have been cancelled long before the Post-It Note would have been invented and its commercial potential explored.

Under the new processes, research projects were cancelled that did not yield results in a timeframe consistent with the statistics and within the rigidly defined process framework. Although revenue from manufacturing existing products grew under the rigid process controls, revenue from new innovation plummeted. The application of rigorous process controls to research and development functions effectively stifled creativity. Failure was not tolerated, as it was bad statistically, and unfettered exploratory costs that the statistics showed would not lead to profitable products were eliminated. Traditionally, 3M had been a place where researchers were given broad latitude to pursue research where it led. However, many of the best researchers left 3M for greener pastures where they could pursue their research agendas in unfettered environments.

The effect of these changes was stunning. In 2004, 3M was ranked first on Boston Consulting Group's Most Innovative Companies list. It dropped to second in 2005, third in 2006, and down to seventh in 2007. Prior to the adoption of rigorous process controls, one-third of 3M's products were based on new innovation. After the adoption of rigorous process controls, this slipped to one-quarter. According to this case study, the rigid process controls seemed to serve the manufacture of established products well, but severely impacted the research and innovation organizations within 3M. For a company like 3M, failing to innovate in its market segment can be a slow death sentence. This negative trend at 3M has been more recently addressed by a new CEO, who has removed much of the rigidity in the research and development organizations within 3M and has reinstated many of the former practices. This begs the question: Why do organizations insist on extremes: lightweight or heavyweight, high control or laissez faire control? There seems to be no room for both or middle ground. This case study (and similar ones) would seem to indicate that high-control, heavyweight processes may have a place in routine production and manufacturing environments, but not in dynamic, innovation-oriented environments. Why not apply both?

A small uprising against the monolithic waterfall-oriented process frameworks began in the mid-1980s, especially in smaller dynamic organizations. But even these organizations realized that they too needed some more disciplined processes, and that ad hoc hacking could be a recipe for disaster. This led to the exploration of alternative process frameworks that could provide just enough process for smaller, dynamic organizations building software-intensive systems. Another important consideration of many researchers was to create affordable process frameworks that could be easily and cheaply adopted. It costs a great deal of money, effort, time, and resources to develop, institute, transition, measure, and maintain heavyweight, high-control process frameworks. These costs were, and still are, a major problem for smaller high-tech organizations.

A process framework emerged in the mid-1980s that changed the way that engineers thought about development process frameworks. Rapid Application Development (RAD) burst on to the techno scene in the 1980s and is the grandfather of the agile process frameworks that proliferate today (Martin, 1991). Although having only a small legion of followers and largely discredited by the mainstream process communities of the time, RAD planted a seed that is still bearing fruit today. At its core, RAD made use of a spiral life cycle model that had been theorized by Boehm in his landmark paper (Boehm, 1986). However, RAD operationalized the concept in a more concrete framework that organizations could quickly, easily, and cheaply instantiate and maintain. Throughout the late 1980s and early 1990s, models like the Software Capability Maturity Model (Paulk et al., 1995) dominated, but lightweight process frameworks slowly and steadily gained ground and more credibility. This shift from heavyweight to lightweight process frameworks can be attributed to the fact that the largest producer and consumer of software products worldwide in 1980 was the U.S. government, and in particular the U.S. Department of Defense. The mega-scale, complex, software-intensive systems were and are built by highly distributed workforces. This necessitated the use of very rigid processes to ensure product quality, predictable costs, delivery schedules, and traceability of requirements to ensure compliance with product specification. These systems typically had very high price tags, long development and deployment life cycles (8+ years of development and test, 30+ years in operation), tens of thousands of requirements, and were often pushing the technological envelope. The needs of the largest stakeholder in a given market segment tend to drive the state of the practice and the behavior of software producers, which was the case until the mid-1990s.

With the emergence of cheaper, more powerful computer hardware, networks, and especially the availability of the Internet vis-à-vis the World Wide Web, a slow shift in the marketplace began. The general global population became the largest consumers and users of software and the Internet and began to influence the market in dramatic ways, and consumers and producers of software-intensive systems and products. In addition, more embedded applications found their way into everything from toys to radios to automobiles. Few consumers are aware of embedded software-intensive systems or give them a second thought (unless they break). However, embedded software-intensive systems are growing rapidly in capability, scope, and complexity. As a result of these developments, the balance of influence has slowly shifted from the U.S. government as the driving force behind software development to the general global population of businesses and private citizens. No longer do government stakeholders exert massive influence on the IT marketplace or fuel its innovation engine—a large global market force does. By 2000, the U.S. government and all of its appendages were just another consumer in a vast global market of stakeholders. This new generation of stakeholders did (and does) not care about maturity ratings, waterfall life cycles, or whether the Ada computer language is used, but wants more capable software, and faster and cheaper applications than ever before. The pace of innovation today is dizzying to the most astute technologist. In many cases, money is made by those who show up in the marketplace first with feature-laden products. This is a whole new business model and has resulted in a major paradigm shift in how we think about building products and the process we use to design and produce software-intensive systems and products.

The mainstream process communities of the 1980s and 1990s have had to accept the fact that the traditional process frameworks may not be the best fit for today's more dynamic business context. Clearly there has been a sea change from traditional heavyweight processes to more lightweight or agile processes. Initially agile process frameworks were not looked upon favorably by the traditional process community. For example, those who did business with the U.S. federal government in the 1990s had to achieve certain process maturity ratings according to the Software Capability Maturity Model. If an appropriate maturity level was not awarded, it became difficult to get contracts in this lucrative marketplace. Furthermore, attaining and maintaining these maturity levels was very costly to the organization and impossible for all but the largest contractors. However, as the demand for software-intensive systems and products from commercial and private citizens outstripped the demand from the government communities, development organizations began to turn away from traditional process frameworks like the Capability Maturity Model to adopt agile processes that would better serve the emerging dynamic business context. Many process experts began to realize that large document-centric process frameworks might not be the best frameworks for all organizations. Early lightweight or agile process frameworks like RAD faded away and gave rise to a number of agile process frameworks like XP, Scrum, and a plethora of others, whose ranks continue to grow today. In a twist of fate as ironic as the cost of software rising above the cost of hardware in the 1980s, agile processes have overtaken the more traditional frameworks (like CMM) in number and in the breadth of industry use. Although there are many agile development processes in use today, they seem to share similar traits. Most have the spiral life cycle model at their core, and proclaim to minimize risk by developing software in short, quick iterations, typically lasting one to four weeks. In practice this varies greatly, and some organizations do away with the notion of formally defined iterations altogether. An iteration is a minisoftware project that includes some level of planning, requirements gathering/analysis, design, coding, and testing. The goal is to provide a chunk of functional code at the end of each iteration, although the functionality provided may not be something worth releasing to the customer or market. Progress in agile methods is measured in terms of functionality delivered. The primary objective of each iteration is to release some functionality without defects, although integration and systemic quality attributes are not explicitly addressed. At the conclusion of each iteration, the team reevaluates project priorities and starts the next iteration.

Agile methods emphasize face-to-face communication with customers and typically require close physical proximity to stakeholders—with an almost exclusive focus on users. Most agile methods replace extensive documentation with informal, direct personal interactions with the customers. In agile processes products and systems are "grown" in short development cycles, and product designs and requirements emerge and morph over time. If a point is reached where the product can no longer allow new features to be added, it is "refactored" or redesigned in light of what is known about the existing implementation. Of course, agile development processes have plenty of issues that we are now realizing after ten years of use in industry. The problem with many agile methods is that they do not scale very well to larger, more complex projects. They depend upon the development team being close in proximity—ideally co-located—to the stakeholders. Many of these agile processes quickly degenerate into chaos if the workforce is even a little distributed and stakeholders are not immediately available. Today it is common for software-intensive systems to be built with workforces and stakeholders scattered around the world. Agile methods tend to focus exclusively on the user stakeholder, so there tends to be an overemphasis on code and functionality required by a few of these stakeholders. Broader systemic properties (quality attribute properties) are not gathered and prioritized with other stakeholders' needs, and are often not addressed in a systemic way. Because agile methods focus on generating code and, by principle, allow structures to emerge over time in an ad hoc way, the systemic properties will also emerge in an ad hoc way. The assumption in most agile process frameworks is that if the system gets to a point where the overall quality attribute properties are not what is needed or expected, or it becomes difficult to add new functionality, or it is impossible to maintain the system, you simply redesign and reimplement it. This is a naive assumption in many business and project contexts. For example, imagine simply refactoring a system with several million lines of code. The shear volume of code makes this totally impossible. In other cases, some systems must be rigorously tested when the smallest changes in the software are made. Avionics systems must undergo rigorous testing for the smallest changes in the control system software. If such a system were totally refactored, the cost in recertifying the airplane would be cost-prohibitive. The dirty little secret about refactoring is that it is often not done until the system functionality is impacted. This is because management typically has no problem funding the development of new functionality that translates into revenue, but not in refactoring (essentially redesigning), which does not directly translate into revenue.

In the worst cases, agile processes are adopted by organizations and teams because there are few document requirements and processes. In these cases, the agile process usually degenerates into codified hacking. Today agile methods are more appealing to many developers because they can get to the job of writing code faster and avoid all the bothersome paperwork associated with product development. However, a major theme of this text is that systemic properties depend upon structure, and structures must be designed to achieve systemic properties such as security, performance, modifiability, availability, and so forth. The improper application of agile processes results in a plethora of problems long ago solved by the traditional process communities—hence, it would seem that we are coming full circle. The reader might be saying, "Just tell me which approach is better." Sorry, it is not that easy and the correct answer is "it depends." Different business and project contexts require different approaches. An organization that is building an avionics system cannot afford a single defect that results in crashing the operational flight control program. In such environments, functionality must be added in a very predictable way, with predictable impact on systemic properties. In high-risk products such as this, rigorous process and quality controls are absolutely warranted.

Some organizations have to invent totally new products and rapidly enter or create new markets, and it is more important to be first with something rather than a perfect product. In these cases some failure and defects are tolerable in return for being first in the market. In these cases, a more lightweight process that removes the burdens of high-ceremony processes is certainly called for. ACDM was created in a postagile world where the right answer is not heavyweight or lightweight, but rather "right-weight." This means that an organization must apply common sense and honestly analyze business and project needs and adopt those processes that will help the organization accomplish its goals. Often this means that right-weight is a combination of heavyweight and lightweight processes to achieve organizational goals. However, just using a heavyweight process framework does not automatically guarantee sound design practices, and using lightweight process frameworks does not preclude the use of sound design practices. Architectural design provides a critical staging point that guides the rest of development and can serve highly agile processes as well as more rigid, high-ceremony organizational processes.

ACDM and Software Development Process Frameworks

ACDM was developed through industrial trial and error over a six-year period of time as a framework for designing software-intensive systems. Although ACDM does not address detailed design and implementation, it was designed so that stages 7 and 8 could serve as a staging point for using any variety of development processes to perform detailed design and implementation. ACDM does provide guidance for using the architecture for estimating, planning, and constructing elements, and integrating the system—which can be used to complement any development processes used in conjunction with ACDM. Most process frameworks focus on construction concerns, but tend to lack guidance on the design process. During the field trials of ACDM, the method was integrated with a variety of organizational software development processes and software development process frameworks, including:

- Traditional waterfall models
- Extreme Programming (XP)
- Scrum
- Team Software Process (TSP)
- Rational Unified Process (RUP)
- Agile Unified Process (AUP)
- Capability Maturity Model Integrated (CMMI)

To these ends, this chapter is dedicated to describing approaches and experiences in integrating ACDM with these process frameworks.

ACDM and Waterfall

The waterfall development model is the oldest software development framework, emerging in the 1970s, and was codified most famously in MILSTD 2167. The waterfall model is derived from manufacturing processes that emerged in the early 20th century. The term waterfall is applied because activities cascade down a single thread of steps from requirements to delivery. Again, Figure 18.1 shows the waterfall model as it appears in MILSTD 2167, but there have been many variants of it. The waterfall model is still used today in many industries and domains. The appeal of the model is its simplicity. It is logical and predicable; the boundaries of each step are clear and unambiguous; and it is easy for management to picture where their project is in the life cycle. Because each step of the process is self-contained, it is easy to structure organizations into specialized teams to work each step of the process. This approach has an assembly line feel of standard horizontal integration found in manufacturing organizations where each activity of the life cycle is undertaken by an individual or team, and the artifacts move forward to the next step in the model for further transformation. The waterfall model is documentation-centric, where the output of each step is documentation. Despite its longevity, the waterfall model has a number of drawbacks. Because each step is totally self-contained, often copious amounts of documentation are required to facilitate communication between steps. This becomes a much greater problem as organizations become specialized and focused on each step of the model in isolation, and is further exacerbated if the teams are distributed. The creation of documentation can become a time-consuming task that can seriously slow down the construction of a system. The waterfall model depends upon teams or individuals completing each step of the model completely before moving on to the next step. Often it is impractical to completely finish a step before moving on. This can be problematic in the requirements step, especially in environments where the requirements are prone to change before the entire process can be completed. The waterfall model is highly dependent upon freezing requirements, so that complete system designs and implementations can be created. It is often impossible to specify all of the stakeholder requirements up front. This can result in costly and time-consuming rework later in the life cycle unless strict requirements freezes and baselines are enforced, but this is usually impractical. In the waterfall model, code is not generated until very late in the process. On large projects it can be a very long time before any useful functionality is delivered to the customer stakeholders. Like many process frameworks, the waterfall model pre-scribes the temporal ordering of the activities, but does not provide any specifics on how to carry out the activities.

ACDM can be used to complement the waterfall model by providing better requirements and design processes to ensure that downstream detailed design and coding better meet the needs of the stakeholders. The merger of ACDM and the waterfall model is shown in Figure 18.2.

In Figure 18.2, the system requirements analysis, software requirements analysis, and prelimi-nary design steps are replaced with ACDM stages 1 to 7. Projects start with system concept stage and then transition into ACDM. The specific techniques and artifacts of stages 1 through 6 can be applied directly. The iteration built into ACDM improves the quality of the requirements gathered and the quality of the design produced, which is critical to the later waterfall stages. ACDM stage 7 can be used to plan the construction steps of the waterfall: detailed design, coding and unit test, deployment test. These waterfall stages will essentially be ACDM stage 8.

ACDM and Extreme Programming (XP)

XP is an agile development process that possesses all of the classic agile process features described earlier. XP is iterative, depends upon close customer interaction, is highly code- and functionality-centric, and the product/system is grown over time. Beck (2000) describes XP as a lightweight method that is appropriate for small- to medium-sized teams, and for software projects whose requirements are vague and volatile. XP is lightweight in that it prescribes almost no documenta-tion artifacts be created other than code as a result of the using the process. The method is highly dependent upon having a clearly defined stakeholder community that is end-user-centric who can be communicated with in an informal way by simply walking down the hallway or popping your head over the cubbie wall. Beck asserts that the close proximity of developers and stakeholders enables high-frequency communication necessary for resolving requirements issues and providing feedback on the product as it is being built. XP is most effective with small development teams of ten or less, according to Beck. At its heart, XP is based on five key principles to guide programmers to choose best practices and strategies for developing software:

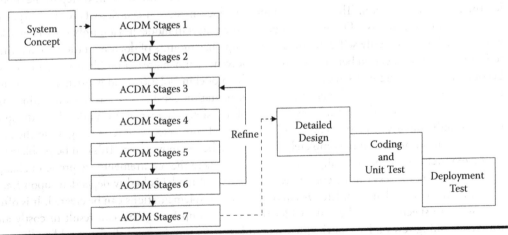

Figure 18.2   ACDM and the waterfall model.

- Rapid feedback: Programmers can learn most effectively when they can get direct, rapid feedback about the system. Beck asserts this is done best when developers write code for small tasks and apply what they learn to the next tasks. Rapid feedback can make communication easier and learning faster. A fundamental feedback mechanism is testing. Programmers and users unit test every day. Rapid customer feedback is also important. Customers describe functionality, programmers estimate the work to build the functionality, and then the customers get immediate feedback on the features by testing it out. As a result, the programmers and customers get continuous feedback about system functionality.
- Assume simplicity: Programmers focus on small simple problems and solve today's problem today and tomorrow's problem tomorrow. The granularity of problem scope is important and should be sufficiently small for XP teams to address.
- Incremental change: Programmers do not make big changes. Instead, they solve small problems and make small changes to the system. Beck asserts that if additions or changes to the system take too long, the requirements can change.
- Embracing change: Rather than resist change, XP teams are instructed to always prepare and develop systems with the assumption that change can and will happen at any time, and that it should be welcomed.
- Quality work: Beck asserts that programmers produce the highest-quality product only when they enjoy their work. XP is enjoyable for programmers because it eliminates unnecessary activities and allows them to focus on writing software.

An XP project revolves around iterations that are planned in a "just in time" fashion. A project using XP is divided into a set of iterations of one to three weeks in length. The iteration length is fixed throughout the project duration. The iterations are used to plan the work, track effort, and measure progress, although the exact nature of what will be done in each iteration is not planned at the beginning of the project. Because the details of the work, design, and so forth are not determined, the number of iterations for a project is not known and is not established at the beginning of the XP project. Each iteration begins with a planning meeting where the work that will be undertaken in the iteration is determined. The XP process framework strongly discourages planning iterations in advance to implement anything that is not functionality immediately needed by the customer. Just-in-time iteration planning is prescribed as the only way to remain nimble enough to address ever-changing user requirements. XP prescribes the use of "user stories," which serve the same purpose as use cases. User stories are written by the customers in terms of those things that the system needs to do for them. They differ from traditional use cases in that they are much more abbreviated (a few informal sentences of prose), and they are written by the customer in the customer's language, rather than in techno-speak. The collection of user stories takes the place of a traditional requirements document. The user stories are used to plan the work. A release plan, which is akin to the project plan, is developed from the user stories. Once the release plan is created, it is used to create iteration plans for the individual iterations. The essence of release planning is that members of the development team estimate each user story in terms of ideal programming weeks. XP defines an ideal week as the amount of time a developer thinks it will take to turn user stories into functional code and test the code if they had nothing else to do. Customers and the development prioritize the user stories. User stories are written on 3 × 5 index cards or Post-It Notes. Together, developers and customers arrange the cards on a table or on a whiteboard to partition and prioritize the collection of user stories. The highest-priority user stories are implemented first. The rate of progress, or "project velocity," is measured by the number of user stories that can be implemented per unit time—usually measured in terms of how many user stories are completed per iteration. This information can be used to schedule the work and time product releases. However, it can take a few iterations to collect enough data to estimate project velocity where no organization data exists. The number of iterations multiplied by the average project velocity can be used to determine how many user stories can be completed. Project scope (in terms of the total number of iterations) can be estimated by dividing the total number of user stories by the project velocity to determine how many iterations (time) will be required to complete the project.

There are two kinds of testing and test strategies within XP: unit test and acceptance test. Unit tests are written by the programmers; they control and conduct each unit test. Code developed in any given iteration must pass all unit tests before advancing to acceptance tests. The second testing strategy is acceptance testing. Acceptance tests are written by customers. User stories play an important role in the creation of acceptance tests. Acceptance tests are created to verify that a specific user story has been correctly implemented. Customers decide if the application has passed the acceptance test. Teams using XP continue iteration after iteration, as described, until the complete software product is built. The key assumptions that are the source of XP's popularity are also the very source of its weaknesses as a process framework. Some of these issues include:

■ No written requirements or requirements agreements: The project begins without any formal understanding or agreement as to what is needed by the stakeholders. XP depends upon frequent and immediate interaction with stakeholders—a situation that is often impossible to accommodate. The most troubling aspect of XP is that the development team has no idea of the project or system end state or what constitutes success on the project because no measures or expectations are established other than the simple user stories. In many situations, development organizations need a much firmer grasp on product and systems requirements to identify inherent technical risks and project costs and schedules before committing resources to the effort. In XP the requirements are solely focused on functionality, so systemic quality attribute properties emerge. In many application domains, this is simply not acceptable. XP has no notion of identifying systemic quality attributes, designing these properties into the system early, confirming that the design will promote these properties, or validating that the system or product possesses these properties.

■ No up-front design: XP espouses the notion that up-front design is not a productive use of time, and that writing functional code is the only real measure of productivity. Because code is written without a guiding systemic design, the overall system or product architectural structure morphs many times in the course of the project. Interdependencies between what is created in one iteration can (and usually does) affect what is created in other iterations. The impact is almost always felt in the systemic quality attribute properties, and it becomes difficult to manage complexity. The most immediate effect of not having a deliberate architectural design is that it becomes difficult to change the software in a predictable way. Furthermore, it is difficult to communicate the structure of the system to other engineers. This undermines the fundamental tenant of XP, that it is more cost-effective to incrementally add code and "grow" a system. To address the situation where the system structures become intractable and problematic over time, refactoring is prescribed. In sufficiently small systems, refactoring can satisfactorily address these issues. However, constant refactoring can be problematic and creates an unnecessary project overhead that can be avoided by a little up-front design. In small projects the overhead is negligible, but in marginally larger projects or complex systems and products the overhead can be all-consuming. In cases where hardware and software are tightly coupled, such as in an embedded application domain, refactoring may involve changing hardware, firmware, and software, and may simply be impossible. Design is critical in application domains where systemic properties are as essential as the functionality. In these cases the XP approach of allowing design structure to emerge, and refactoring as necessary, does not result in predictable systemic properties. Another problem with refactoring is that defects can be reintroduced into the system, and refactored systems must be completely regression tested. This can drive up the cost of system development, and in some cases it is cost-prohibitive.

■ XP quality assurance mechanisms: Unit and acceptance tests are useful in everyday coding and were around long before the advent of XP. However, XP's implementation of acceptance testing can be problematic. Because there is no agreed-to requirements or design artifacts, acceptance tests are defined by the user as the project evolves, and are subject to the evolving whims of customers. Furthermore, unit and acceptance tests do not uncover design defects, which are among the most costly of defects, until it is too late. Pair programming is a quality mechanism that addresses code-level constructs, but again, it has little impact in ensuring overall systemic design quality, or ensuring that a system possesses the necessary quality attribute properties. All of these issues result from the fact that architectural designs are not deliberately designed or scrutinized.

At first glance, it may seem that ACDM is the antithesis of the key assumptions and principles motivating XP. Under the XP paradigm, Beck indicates that systemic structures emerge and potentially change at every iteration. A key assumption of XP is that because of frequent requirements changes, early design efforts are a waste of time. XP does advocate using metaphors to describe the overall system.

A metaphor is a common vision of how the system or application works. Metaphors are overly simplistic descriptions of how the program works, such as "This program works like two tennis players volleying the ball back and forth between them" as a description for a peer-to-peer application. Metaphors are a poor replacement for first-class design. Any design in XP teams is left to coders, who will implement the functionality. XP's guiding philosophy is that better systems are built more efficiently by writing code than by designing, extensive planning, or other similar overhead. However, XP does acknowledge that system structures emerge through code development, and that the system might become messy over time. Again, if systemic structures become unwieldy, XP prescribes refactoring, which may not be cost-effective or practical. Predictable system properties such as scalability, performance, reliability, security, and others must be designed into the system from the beginning. Predictably designing these properties into the system is difficult with a strict XP approach.

While practitioners like many aspects of XP, many also recognize the need for more robust requirements work, design, and planning than XP prescribes. Despite these deep philosophical differences, ACDM can complement XP in a couple of ways. XP fundamentally addresses the process of code production, and ACDM addresses the design process—which are complementary concerns. In cases such as those where a project is large and distributed, customers are not easily accessible, systemic quality attribute properties are essential, or the system is sufficiently complex, deliberate up-front design is critically important. Once a system such as this is sufficiently partitioned through design, then it may be possible for XP teams to interact with stakeholders (who are concerned with element-level details) to refine and develop the elements of the system in relative isolation. The system's architectural design can be used to restrict visibility, and XP teams can then focus on what they are good at (interacting with stakeholders and producing functional code) without adversely affecting overall systemic structures. This works because the overall system structure is defined and constrained by the architecture design. In these situations, ACDM can essentially coexist side by side with XP. Because XP says nothing about eliciting architectural drivers, planning, or system design, ACDM stages 1 through 6 can be used until the production stages are reached. Recall that in stage 7, ACDM provides guidance for using the architecture design to plan and track the implementation. Stage 7 can be used as a staging point for determining how many XP iterations there should be and what functionality will be assigned to the iterations. The prioritization of architectural drivers is already built into the specific ACDM methods, techniques, and templates, and can be fed forward from ACDM stages into XP production cycles. Essentially, ACDM stage 8 can be comprised of a series of XP iterations where the product is built incrementally. In environments where there are a lot of volatile requirements, XP iterations can be coupled with ACDM to understand requirements and mitigate technical risks early through design, and later as the elements of the system are produced. Early systemic risks can be addressed by ACDM design iterations, and later implementation-oriented risks can be addressed by XP iterations. Because XP team visibility is restricted to the element level of detail, the effects of refactoring should be limited to the element level. XP has been successfully coupled with ACDM in stage 2 to understand requirements and define scope so that a more robust, production-oriented design could be developed. XP has also been used in stage 6 to conduct experiments, and XP is especially useful if experiments involve a great deal of coding.

ACDM and Scrum

Scrum, like other agile development frameworks, is structured around iteration and incremental product development. Scrum also emphasizes code production and deemphasizes highly structured processes and up-front design. Scrum is often misrepresented as a development process, but it is actually a management process for agile software development. Jeff Sutherland and Ken Schwaber piloted and formalized Scrum as a general management technique at Easel Corporation in 1995. They refined and extended Scrum for use in software development projects (Schwaber and Beedle, 2004). Proponents of Scrum indicate that it enables rapid software development and a high degree of flexibility in the software development process.

Scrum is structured around three fundamental principles: iteration, increment, and communication. Iterations in Scrum are called Sprints. Sprints are fast and short development cycles, similar to iterations in XP, in which shippable functionality is developed. The operative concept here is shippable functionality—the goal of every Sprint is to produce shippable code. Each Sprint of the project results in a product or system increment that delivers ever-increasing functional capability. Customer and development teams must be in close proximity to one another to facilitate high-frequency communications required for project planning, tracking, and reviewing product/ system functionality. Scrum prescribes three specific roles: the product owner, the Scrum master, and the Scrum team. The product owner is responsible for representing the stakeholders' interests, usually from the business and managerial points of view. The product owner is responsible for creating the list of requirements and prioritizing them. In an approach similar to that prescribed by XP, Scrum's product owners create "stories" that describe the functionality that they desire in the system. The Scrum master is responsible for facilitating Scrum, holding daily Scrum and review meetings, shielding the Scrum team from outside distractions and impediments, and ensuring that team members follow Scrum practices. The Scrum team is responsible for planning items, which they will develop in each iteration. If necessary, the Scrum team can be further decomposed into subteams, but it's not clear what guides this other than the intuition of the Scrum team and Scrum master. Scrum starts with a list of requirements created by the product owner, which is called the product backlog. The product owner prioritizes the project's items in the product backlog based primarily on his or her business needs. Once the backlog is prioritized, the product owner, Scrum master, and Scrum team will conduct a Sprint planning meeting. The meeting begins with the product owner presenting the prioritized product backlog to the Scrum master and Scrum team. This is an opportunity to discuss rationale and negotiate priorities (to resolve technical and logistical dependencies, for example). During the meeting the product backlog will be refined as necessary. Once established, the product backlog will be used to schedule work. The Scrum master and Scrum team will select the highest-priority functionality from the product backlog and assign it to the first (or next) Sprint for implementation. The list of functionality selected for implementation in a given Sprint is called the Sprint backlog, which includes items for shippable functionality, responsibilities for each item, and their status. Sprints are generally 30 days in duration—in which time, all of the selected items from the product backlog must be implemented, tested, and delivered. During a Sprint, the Scrum master holds daily Scrum meetings with the Scrum team. In the daily meeting, Scrum team members must answer the following questions:

- What have you done since the last daily meeting?
- What are you going to do between now and the next daily meeting?
- What is preventing you from doing your work (these are called impediments)?

Daily Scrum meetings are supposed to last 15 to 30 minutes. This meeting facilitates communications and gives members the necessary information to adjust their work based on other members' status, project status, the Sprint status, and the project schedule. This is also an opportunity to identify impediments that are slowing or preventing progress. Once the Sprint has concluded, the Scrum team and Scrum master will arrange a Sprint review meeting with the product owner to present the functionality that was developed in the Sprint and get direct feedback from the product owner. After the Sprint review meeting the Scrum master and Scrum team conduct a Sprint retrospective meeting to identify opportunities to improve their Scrum process and performance. The process is repeated until all the items in the project backlog are implemented and the product or system is developed and deployed.

Scrum does not offer any specific guidance for designing, evaluating, or using architecture designs as part of the development process framework. Often, Scrum teams have no architecture design to guide the product or system implementation. In this respect, Scrum suffers from the same kinds of issues that XP does, in that product or system structures emerge over time. Not surprisingly, Scrum does not scale up very well to larger projects. In situations where systemic quality attributes are critically important, products and systems built using Scrum may not meet the expectations of the product owners. Obviously, early deliberate architecture design can help Scrum teams overcome these kinds of issues and design-oriented defects. Again, despite obvious differences, Scrum and ACDM can be paired together. Scrum is more of a management and oversight framework than a software development framework, and offers very few specifics on software design, development, evaluation, or quality assurance mechanisms. Because ACDM does offer very specific guidance on many of these technical activities, Scrum and ACDM fit relatively well together. Many of the detailed techniques in the ACDM framework can be used to complement the more general prescriptions provided by Scrum.

Scrum relies on the product owner to gather and document requirements in terms of stories. Not much guidance is provided by Scrum on the specifics of how this is done. ACDM stages 1 and 2 provide detailed guidance for getting the architectural drivers in a relatively structured way.

The outcome of stages 1 and 2 is more prescriptive than what is prescribed by Scrum in terms of eliciting, documenting, organizing, and analyzing stories. The key mechanism of ACMD for gathering requirements and constraints is the architecture drivers elicitation workshop, which is a structured way to interact with product owners. The operational descriptions described by ACDM can be the foundation of the stories prescribed by Scrum to capture the product owner's requirements. Furthermore, ACDM provides techniques for gathering constraints and quality attribute requirements in addition to functional requirements as prescribed by Scrum. ACDM also prescribes methods for prioritization that can be used to complement the general prescriptions provided by Scrum for the product owner to prioritize the requirements. After stages 1 and 2, the Scrum team can move on to designing the architecture. For accommodating the design, evaluation, and refinement of the architecture design, the concept of a Sprint has to be altered a bit to include the concept of a Design Sprint. Design Sprints can be used to design, evaluate, and refine the architecture design. The deliverables from Design Sprints are not a functional product, but tangible design artifacts. Design Sprints are conducted before the development. The ACDM stages and Sprint activities roughly correlate, as shown in Table 18.1.

Note that this does not show multiple ACDM refinement iterations between stages 3, 4, 5, and 6. The notional architecture (stage 3), initial design evaluation (stage 4), experiment planning, and experimentation (stages 5 and 6) will map to Design Sprints. The initial design (notional architecture) and evaluation will map to Design Sprint 1. These two stages (stages 3 and 4) are grouped together because there are no equivalent Scrum activities. The next two stages (stages 5

Table 18.1   A Mapping of ACDM and Scrum Activities

Sprint Type	ACDM Activity or Stage	Scrum Activity
Pre-Sprint	Stage 1	Develop stories.
Pre-Sprint	Stage 2	Create product backlog.
Pre-Sprint	Stages 1 and 2	Prioritize the project backlog.
Design Sprint 1	Stage 3: Scrum team creates architecture design.	No equivalent Scrum activity
	Stage 4: Evaluate the architecture design with the product owner.	
Design Sprint 2	Stage 5: Plan experiments for next Design Sprint.	Sprint planning meeting
	Stage 6: Conduct experiments and review results with product owners.	Sprint review meeting
Sprint retrospective meeting		
N/A	Stage 7: Plan the construction of the system or product based on the architecture design.	Create product backlog.
Scrum Sprints	Stage 8: Production (repeated in successive Sprints)	Sprint planning meeting traditional Scrum Sprint Sprint review meeting Sprint retrospective meeting

and 6) can be roughly mapped to a Sprint planning meeting to plan the experimentation, and once the experiments are conducted, they can be reviewed with the product owner in a Sprint review meeting. This forum can be used to review and discuss the findings of the Scrum team based on the outcomes of the experiments. At this meeting go/no-go decisions can be discussed. Further product and system refinement, priorities, and product options can be negotiated based on the design. After the Sprint review meeting, a Sprint retrospective meeting should be held to evaluate the process and look for improvement opportunities. The ACDM refinement iterations can be repeated and mapped to subsequent Design Sprints until a go decision is reached. At this point, ACDM stages again map nicely to, and complement, the more general Scrum activities. Once the architecture design is deemed fit for production, ACDM stage 7 can be used to create the product backlog. At this time, ACDM architecture-based estimation techniques can help the product owner, Scrum team, and Scrum master create and prioritize the product backlog. Once the product backlog is created, ACDM stage 8 can begin which maps to standard Scrum Sprints where functional elements are produced and delivered to the product owners. Each Sprint should begin with a Sprint planning meeting to decide on and prioritize the Sprint backlog. Once planned, a traditional Scrum Sprint will ensue where elements are developed. After the Sprint concludes, a Sprint review meeting is held with the customer, and a Sprint retrospective meeting is held to evaluate the process and look for improvement opportunities. The Scrum Sprints can continue until the system is implemented and delivered to the product owners.

At this point, the astute reader is wondering where test occurs. XP has specific guidance regarding test, but Scrum does not. ACDM addresses design validation through evaluation and defers unit and integration test until stage 8, which is sparsely populated with specific implementation and test processes. Again, ACDM is a design process framework, not a development framework. ACDM does recommend that the architecture drivers specification be used as a guide for test planning and system test, but specific details are not provided. This is done to allow teams the maximum amount of flexibility in adopting a variety of implementation, deployment, and test processes. Scrum seems to imply that test is part of the Sprint review meeting where functionality developed during the Sprint is reviewed with the product owners. In actuality, neither framework addresses test planning or testing in sufficient detail. Resolving this issue and planning for test should be a key consideration for anyone who attempts to weave these methods together.

ACDM and Team Software Process (TSP)

The Team Software Process (TSP) (Humphrey, 1999) is a small-team (3 to 15 engineers) software development process framework developed at the Software Engineering Institute (SEI). TSP is one of a suite of frameworks from the SEI for improving the process of software development. Related to TSP are the Personal Software Process (PSP) (Humphrey, 1995) and the Capability Maturity Model Integrated (CMMI). PSP is targeted at measuring and improving individual software development habits. CMMI is a process improvement framework for organizational software development processes. TSP stands in the middle of these two frameworks to address the needs of small teams of engineers developing software. The TSP framework provides teams with specific roles, scripts for carrying out prescribed activities, checklists and guidance for producing various artifacts, and a well-defined framework in which activities and artifacts are structured. In reality there are two versions of TSP. TSPi is a reduced-scale version of TSP, especially tailored for smaller teams and academic environments. Standard TSP is designed for use in larger projects and organizations. Both utilize the same basic concepts and methods of TSP, so no differentiation will be made here in discussing how ACDM fits within the TSP framework. Like most modern agile methods, TSP follows an iterative development life cycle. Each cycle includes requirements, design, implementation, and test development processes. TSP departs from other agile methods in that it tends to have a more document-centric focus and is far more prescriptive and detailed in the activities associated with the framework. TSP also has highly defined measures for quality and performance that are based on traditional statistical analysis. For this reason, TSP is not viewed as a truly agile development process framework by many practitioners, but this judgment is left to the reader. In most modern agile process frameworks, productivity is measured in terms of delivered functionality, and quality control is measured in terms of the number of outstanding defects per cycle or iteration. However, this is often a shortsighted approach. Although useful in the immediate here and now, this does little for fixing long-term organizational development and systemic problems. Like it or not, TSP has the potential to address these issues better than XP, Scrum, or their derivatives, but arguably it comes at the cost of some agility.

The TSP framework is structured around cycles with specific activities defined by the framework. TSP can be structured in a more waterfall-oriented life cycle with iterations for requirements, design, code, unit test, and integration, or it can be structured into more XP-like cycles, where functional code is developed after each cycle. Like other agile process frameworks, basic functionality is developed in the initial cycle, becoming the basis for what is developed in subsequent cycles. The product emerges after successive iterations. The general TSP structure is shown in Figure 18.3 (McAndrews, 2000).

Each activity in TSP is guided by a script that lists preconditions, specific steps, postconditions, and artifacts created. TSP also includes various templates to support document creation. From Figure 18.3 it should be obvious that TSP is considerably more heavyweight than other agile team processes. A project using TSP starts with a team launch. The TSP team launch is a four-day workshop that consists of nine separate meetings designed to create a cohesive team and develop a common understanding of the project. The key outcomes of the team launch are to:

- Establish the product and business goals
- Assign team member roles and define team goals
- Produce development strategy
- Develop team plans, estimate the size of the products, identify tasks, and assign work to the cycles
- Develop the quality plan
- Create individual work plans
- Conduct risk assessment
- Prepare management overview briefing and launch report
- Conduct management review of goals, plans, and strategy

Once the team launch is complete, the team can begin the cycles. TSP is a rather large process framework, and a complete discussion of each activity, technique, document, and so forth is well beyond the scope of one section, in one chapter. Suffice it to say, even with all of TSP's prescriptions, guidance for designing the system's architecture is lacking, and much of the design guidance is weak. TSP addresses design in terms of high-level design and detailed design, but many of the prescriptions are quite dated and do not reflect today's best architectural design practices. TSP provides four design templates: the operational scenario template, the functional specification template, the state specification template, and the logic specification template. Guidance for using these in a practical way is a bit naive. TSP is also weak in terms of the processes for eliciting

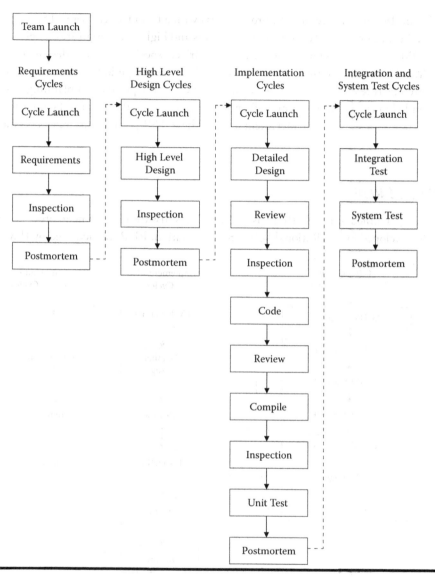

Figure 18.3   General TSP structure.

requirements from the stakeholders, and TSP focuses on functional requirements. TSP has very little guidance for how to elicit, analyze, organize, and document quality attribute requirements. There is no notion of using quality attribute scenarios or operational scenarios as ACDM prescribes. TSP makes general mention of nonfunctional requirements such as testability, usability, and reusability, but these are not addressed in any systematic way.

ACDM can be used with TSP to significantly improve these areas, with specific processes for eliciting the architectural drivers, designing, and documenting the design. TSP is a process framework that focuses on managing team activities, not architectural design, making ACDM and TSP nice complements to one another. By examining the general structure of TSP shown in Figure 18.4, we can see how ACDM might be used to complement the TSP framework with better design processes.

In Figure 18.4 we can see that the project starts with a team launch as any TSP project would. However, the traditional TSP cycles for requirements and high-level design are completely replaced with ACDM stages 1 through 6. The architecture drivers specification and design artifacts specified by ACDM can replace those prescribed by TSP. Once the period of uncertainty is traversed and the architecture design is established, the ACDM stage 7 production planning based on the design can help plan the subsequent TSP cycles. Essentially, TSP cycles can be used then to produce the code in a waterfall or incremental way. These TSP production cycles become ACMD stage 8.

ACDM and RUP

The Rational Unified Process (RUP) is an iterative software development process framework originally developed by the Rational Software Corporation. RUP was acquired by IBM in 2002.

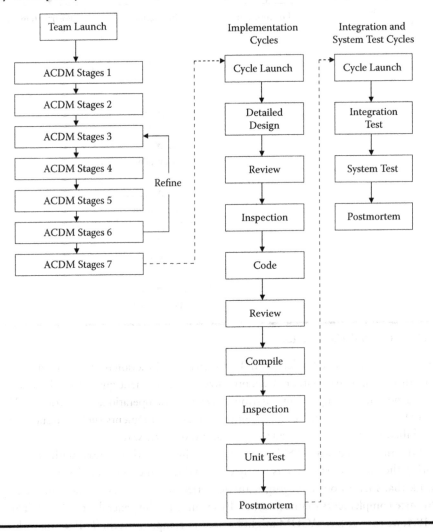

Figure 18.4 Integrating TSP and ACDM frameworks.

RUP was derived from Boehm's spiral model and emphasizes many of the collaborative, iterative themes of agile methods. However, RUP is not considered an agile method, but rather extensive in its prescriptions for activities and artifacts in comparison to Scrum- or XP-like software process frameworks. RUP has an extraordinary number of roles (20+ in total) and artifacts prescribed. A complete treatment of the RUP process framework is impossible here and has been the subject of very thick textbooks. For the sake of brevity, we will focus on RUP's general philosophy and organization, the overall life cycle approach, RUP's prescriptions for design, and how ACDM might be used to supplement architectural design using RUP's software process framework.

The RUP framework is structured around nine key primary disciplines that are process areas deemed critical to the software development process. All roles, disciplines, activities, and artifacts emanate from these process disciplines:

- Business modeling: Processes focused on modeling the business of the client organization and the general problem domain.
- Requirements: Processes for discovering the requirements, documenting use cases, and managing requirements changes.
- Analysis and design: Processes for performing analysis and design, and selecting suitable technological solutions for the system or product to satisfy the use cases.
- Implementation: Processes that address the transformation of the models into implementation and the testing of the implementation.
- Test: Processes for finding defects and validating that the system works as designed, and verifying that the requirements are satisfied.
- Deployment: Processes for the timely delivery and deployment of the system and the support of end users in the use of the operational system or product.
- Project management: Processes for planning and managing the project, including risk management, personnel management, assigning tasks, tracking progress, coordinating internal and external iterations, and ensuring that a quality product is delivered on time.
- Environment: Processes for supporting the development effort by ensuring that processes, guidance, standards, and tools are available for the team as needed.
- Configuration and change management: Processes for managing project artifacts, tracking artifact versions over time, and controlling and managing changes to them.

The overall RUP life cycle is based on Boehm's spiral model (Boehm, 1986). RUP activities are organized around six general phases that are more waterfall oriented; however, iteration occurs within the phases. RUP phases include inception, elaboration, construction, transition, production, and retirement. Each of these phases is explained in more detail below.

- Inception phase: The inception phase roughly maps to ACDM stages 1 and 2. Key objectives include defining the business case, eliciting the initial requirements, establishing system context, and determining scope. These objectives are nearly identical to those of ACDM stages 1 and 2, and specific ACDM techniques defined in these stages for gathering, documenting, and analyzing architectural drivers can be used to complement RUP. Other RUP activities in the inception phases include scheduling and work estimation. Again, ACDM templates and techniques defined in stages 1 and 2 for planning the work and documenting the plan (master design plan) can complement RUP's prescriptions.
- Elaboration phase: The elaboration phase roughly maps to ACDM stages 3 to 7. RUP's key goals for the elaboration phase include designing the architecture and developing construc-

tion plans. RUP also prescribes identifying and eliminating the high-priority risks of the project. This maps nicely to ACDM's iterative design (stage 3), evaluation (stage 4), and experimentation (stages 5 and 6). ACMD's purpose for iteratively designing, evaluating, experimenting, and refining the architecture is to identify and address technical risks before production. Construction planning in ACDM's stage 7 based on the architecture design complements RUP's prescription for creating coarse-grained project plans for the entire RUP. Element-wise Wideband Delphi based on the architecture can provide high-fidelity estimation and early insight into how long it will take and what resources might be required to build the elements and integrate the system.

■ Construction phase: The construction phase maps to ACDM stage 8. The primary goals of the construction phase include creating the detailed designs, element development, testing, and integration of the system elements. Certainly the production plan created in ACDM stage 7 and the tracking techniques presented in stage 8 can be used to track construction. ACDM does not prescribe how to do the detailed designs or execute the actual software development, but RUP provides detailed recommendations and tools for both. Again, this is a nice, complementary use of both the RUP and ACDM frameworks.

■ Transition phase: The transition phase has no mapping to ACDM. Again, ACDM is a design process framework and intentionally allows an organization to determine the best way to transition the product or system into the production environment. RUP describes the transition phase as the point when the final product baseline is created and deployed, and training materials and documentation are completed and transitioned to the customer. One could argue that these activities map to the ACDM stage 8 activities, but ACDM gives no prescriptions for these activities.

■ Production phase: The production phase is the final RUP phase. The term *production* in the RUP context corresponds to the customer using the system or product in a production environment. The primary focus of the production phase is supporting the customers as they work with the system, monitoring the system to ensure proper operation, responding to change requests and defect reports, and so forth. The production phase ends with the development of plans for how the system will be decommissioned. Again, ACDM does not specifically address these activities, although the architecture design plays a critical role in these important activities, as described in Chapters 16 and 17.

RUP also defines numerous roles. Simply fulfilling all of the required roles and clearly establishing their responsibilities and interrelationships on real projects can be a daunting task. RUP defines roles in terms of who performs a given task, the activities, and the artifacts they produce. In practice, sorting out the differences between the roles and determining if all of them are necessary can be challenging, and it often takes experience using RUP to get it right. The 20+ RUP roles will not be described in detail here. However, ACDM roles should be mapped to RUP roles and ensure full coverage of design responsibilities.

RUP prescribes that numerous artifacts be created as part of process framework. RUP describes approximately 14 different artifacts (depending upon how they are structured). In a nominal project, 20 or more may be produced, and often many more are created through the use of the RUP process framework and the associated tools. Although RUP seems daunting and heavyweight, the framework is supported by numerous tools to help create these artifacts. Again, all of the RUP artifacts will not be discussed in detail here for the sake of brevity. In general, RUP's documents fall into several general categories, as follows:

- Program management documents
- Organizational planning
- Benefits management
- Stakeholder management
- Issue and risk management
- Quality management
- Requirements management
- Technical documents

These are RUP document artifact categories prescribed by the RUP framework. Each of these categories has at least one document, but most have many documents associated with them. While there are a variety of artifacts called for in ACDM, the key artifacts are the architecture drivers specification, the architecture design, the master design plan, and the production schedule. The other artifacts created in ACDM are working artifacts to support the creation of these key documents. The mapping between ACDM and RUP artifacts is not straightforward. Because RUP requires so many artifacts, adding to this daunting list may not be the best approach to wedding the two frameworks. However, various techniques defined in ACDM can complement RUP methods for developing the comprehensive set of RUP artifacts. The architecture drivers specification, and specifically the techniques for documenting functional and quality attribute requirements, and business and technical constraints, can contribute to the RUP requirements documentation. RUP and ACDM both prescribe the use of use cases to define functional requirements, although the approach for developing them is a bit different. However, RUP does not offer similar prescriptions for defining quality attribute requirements, and this can certainly complement RUP's requirements documentation. The master design plan defined by ACDM may not be required if ACDM is used in a RUP project management context, but techniques and guidelines for producing the master design plan and the production plans can contribute to the development of RUP planning documents. Most importantly is the design documentation. Because RUP emerged from the object-oriented community, object-oriented analysis and design is the recommended approach for designing and building systems. However, a constant theme throughout this text has been that architectural design should not necessarily be biased toward a particular language paradigm because any fixed paradigm may not be suitable for all application domains. ACDM is neutral with regard to design paradigm and provides a lot of guidance for how to design, and document the design. These techniques, coupled with the iterative approach to creating design, can be applied within a RUP project context and can help create more robust architectural designs.

The RUP is a comprehensive software development process framework, and a key criticism is that it is too heavyweight for all but the largest of products and systems. There are many roles, activities, and artifacts that can complicate the instantiation and use of RUP. If the choice is made to incorporate ACDM into the RUP framework, care should be taken to not further complicate the instantiation and use of RUP. An alternative to the traditional heavyweight RUP framework is Agile RUP (Ambler, 2002). The Agile RUP, or AUP, is a far simpler framework, easy to grasp, and easy to implement in most organizations; however, it remains faithful to the RUP framework's key philosophies. It describes XP-like techniques, including test-driven design, agile change management, and refactoring to improve productivity and speed the deployment of functionality. AUP focuses on the disciplines of testing, deployment, configuration management, project management, and environment. Each of these AUP disciplines addresses the same process concerns as traditional RUP. Conspicuously absent from the AUP disciplines are the requirements, design, and analysis disciplines. This is because AUP stresses the same informal customer-developer interactions to define requirements as XP does. AUP also focuses on creating functionality, allowing design structures in an informal way to emerge as they do in XP. These techniques work together to deliver functionality to the customer faster. Other philosophies borrowed from agile methods include:

- Communication: Rather than having highly partitioned teams, activities, and strictly defined roles, as described by RUP, AUP stresses that developers, managers, and customers be co-located to enable high-frequency communication. AUP does not prescribe strict roles like RUP, but rather stresses that teams can be more flexible if everyone learns about various parts of the system. Specialization is avoided to prevent a few people from being overloaded. Rotating team members helps disseminate knowledge and helps the team to be more productive and flexible in work assignments.
- Simplicity: Unlike RUP, AUP stresses simple processes, simple documentation, and self-guided teams. A key philosophy of AUP derived from XP is that engineers are not likely to read or use detailed process documentation, but are more effective with high-level guidance. Everything from processes to technical documentation is concisely described using a handful of pages rather than hundreds of pages.
- Lightweight, high-value processes: AUP, like XP, stresses high-value activities that directly produce functionality or support the production of functionality. Activities that do not result in functionality are shunned.
- Tool independence: AUP, unlike RUP, does not prescribe a specific toolset. Any toolset can be used with AUP, and the recommendation is that tools best suited for the job be selected and utilized.
- Tailor as needed: AUP describes the four phases of inception, elaboration, construction, and transition, but comes with the recommendation that the underlying techniques used in these phases be tailored to suit the team and project.

Instead of the waterfall-like approach of RUP, AUP stresses small, fast releases, built around short iterations. Like XP, AUP teams strive to deliver functional releases at the end of each iteration. ACDM can be used in the early stages to define the architectural drivers and establish the design. Many of the artifacts prescribed by ACDM can supplement the lightweight documentation approach called for in AUP. ACDM stages 1 to 6 can be mapped to the inception and elaboration phases almost directly. ACDM stages 7 and 8 can help enhance AUP production planning and tracking artifacts. ACDM is probably a more natural fit for AUP than it is for RUP—certainly weaving the two frameworks together will be far simpler. However, in either RUP or AUP the iterative approach for designing the architecture (design, evaluation, experiment, and refine) in ACDM can help.

ACDM and CMMI

The SEI has been involved for many years in the development and transition of capability models for improving the practice of software engineering. These models are based on best practices and are structured to help organizations build high-quality systems and products in a more predictable way through the use of disciplined development processes throughout the entire life cycle. The Capability Maturity Model Integration (CMMI) is essentially a process improvement framework that organizations can use to improve the way that they build software-intensive systems. It can be used to guide process improvement across a project, a division, or an entire organization. CMMI can help in terms of establishing process improvement goals and priorities. It provides guidance for creating quality processes, and provides a point of reference for evaluating the effectiveness of existing processes and organizational process maturity. CMMI is based upon best practices from multiple disciplines and developed through a partnership of industry, government, and SEI stakeholders. CMMI is not a prescriptive development process that describes the details of how to develop systems, but it provides general guidance in specific process areas by providing goals and practices needed to meet those goals.

CMMI has separate models for systems engineering, software engineering, integrated product and process development, and supplier sourcing. These models are referred to as disciplines in the language of CMMI (CMMI Product Team, 2002) and are briefly explained in the paragraphs below.

The systems engineering discipline covers the development of systems that may or may not include software. The purpose of the systems engineering discipline is to help engineers transform customer needs, expectations, and constraints into product solutions and support them throughout the life cycle.

Software engineering discipline covers the development of software systems. The purpose of the software engineering model is to help engineers apply systematic, disciplined, and quantifiable approaches to the development, operation, and maintenance of software.

The Integrated Product and Process Development (IPPD) discipline provides a systematic approach for achieving timely collaboration of stakeholders throughout the life of the product to better satisfy customer needs, expectations, and requirements. The processes to support an IPPD approach are integrated with the other processes in the organization. The IPPD model is designed to be combined with other organizational practices used to produce products.

The supplier sourcing discipline is used to coordinate the efforts of suppliers used to build systems and products. As development efforts become more complex, projects often use suppliers to perform functions or provide elements for systems and products. In these cases, the project benefits from enhanced analysis and monitoring of supplier activities related to product design, development, and delivery. The supplier sourcing model covers acquiring products from suppliers under these circumstances.

Each of these models organizes prescribed practices into related process areas. The CMMI process areas are divided into four main categories: process management, project management, engineering, and support. CMMI is further organized into one of two representations: a continuous representation or a staged representation. In the staged representation, process capability is measured in terms of maturity level, of which there are five. Within each maturity level there are process areas that are a group of related practices. If an organization satisfactorily performs all of the process area associated with a maturity level, it is said to have achieved that level of maturity. Each level builds on processes established in the previous maturity level. For example, assume an organization achieves level 2. When striving to achieve level 3, the organization must continue to perform all of the practices of level 2 while adding the practices of level 3. In the continuous representation, the same process areas of the staged model are described. However, an organization may implement any of the process areas it chooses to. Organizations are evaluated on how well they perform the individual process areas they selected. The traditional representation is the staged representation, and this continues to be the more popular representation of CMMI.

CMMI is a massive process improvement framework that is best suited for very large organizations such as government agencies, their contractors, large corporate entities, and other similar bureaucracies. Large organizations using CMMI often have huge process improvement teams to oversee organizational process maintenance and improvement efforts. These teams also conduct CMMI process audits to evaluate compliance with CMMI and to measure the process maturity of the organization. A common criticism of CMMI is that its massive size and artifact-driven nature are costly, slow, burdensome, and stifle innovation. The cost of complying with CMMI is far more than most medium and small organizations can bear. Although CMMI is a large framework for process improvement, most ironically it describes what an organization must do to improve processes, not how to actually do any of the processes. Obviously, there are numerous details about CMMI that are omitted here simply because a moderately complete treatment of CMMI is the subject of a book. However, these details are not needed to explain how ACDM can be used with the CMMI process framework. First, we have to consider the process areas of the CMMI. These are listed in Table 18.2.

Because CMMI indicates that these process areas should be implemented but does not prescribe how to implement them, some of these process areas can be satisfied by ACMD. In this way, ACDM can help an organization comply with the CMMI without having to define these processes from scratch. From this standpoint, ACDM can be used in an organization exactly as described in Section 2 and will help the organization meet CMMI standards for several process requirements. Table 18.3 shows the process areas that could potentially be satisfied by using ACDM exactly as described in Section 2.

Of course there will be some variability in the coverage that ACDM will provide in any given CMMI process area, dependent upon how an organization instantiates ACDM. If an organization must adhere to the CMMI strictly to demonstrate a particular maturity level, ACDM can serve as a starting point for an organization in defining many of the specific processes to achieve CMMI compliance. When instantiating ACDM within an organization using the CMMI framework, the organization should carefully map the specific ACDM stages and the activities within each stage to specific CMMI process areas. This can ease later audits and CMMI-based appraisals.

Summary

There are numerous process frameworks available for an organization to structure its organizations and projects. A few have been discussed here, but there are many others and many variants of these. All have strengths and weaknesses, but in general they tend to have weaknesses in describing how to design the architecture, document it, and how to use it to help guide detailed design and construction. ACDM is a design process, and as such, it naturally complements many of these process frameworks with more robust requirements and design techniques and processes for designing. The examples here are only intended to serve as examples for how ACDM can be integrated with other process frameworks, and in what ways ACDM and other process frameworks complement one other. Organizations should carefully study candidate process frameworks, ACDM, and the organizational business goals, and carefully choose their processes and weave them together, focusing on simplicity, right-weight, and common sense.

Table 18.2   CMMI Process Areas

Process	Process Area	Corresponding Maturity Level
Requirements management engineering	Engineering	2
Project monitoring and control project management	Project management	2
Project planning project management	Project management	2
Supplier agreement management project management	Project management	2
Configuration management support	Support	2
Measurement and analysis support	Support	2
Process and product quality assurance support	Support	2
Product integration engineering	Engineering	3
Requirements development engineering	Engineering	3
Technical solution engineering	Engineering	3
Validation engineering	Engineering	3
Verification engineering	Engineering	3
Organizational process definition process management	Process management	3
Organizational process focus process management	Process management	3
Organizational training process management	Process management	3
Integrated project management project management	Project management	3
Integrated supplier management project management	Project management	3
Integrated teaming project management	Project management	3
Risk management project management	Project management	3
Decision analysis and resolution support	Support	3
Organizational environment for integration support	Support	3
Organizational process performance process management	Process management	4
Quantitative project management project management	Process management	4
Organizational innovation and deployment process management	Process management	5
Causal analysis and resolution support	Support	5

Table 18.3 CMMI Process Areas Addressed by ACDM

Process	Process Area	Corresponding Maturity Level
Requirements management engineering	Engineering	2
Project monitoring and control project Management	Project Management	2
Project planning project management	Project management	2
Product integration engineering	Engineering	3
Requirements development engineering	Engineering	3
Technical solution engineering	Engineering	3
Validation engineering	Engineering	3
Verification engineering	Engineering	3
Risk management project management	Project management	3

References

Ambler, S. 2002. *Agile modeling: Effective practices for extreme programming and the unified process*. New York: John Wiley & Sons.

Barbacci, M., Ellison, R., Lattanze, A., Stafford, J., Weinstock, C., and Wood, W. 2003. *Quality attribute workshops*. 3rd ed. CMU/SEI-2003-TR-016, Carnegie Mellon University/Software Engineering Institute, Pittsburgh, PA.

Bass, L., Clements, P., and Kazman, R. 2003. *Software architectures principles and practices*. 2nd ed. Boston: Addison-Wesley.

Beck, K. 2000. *Extreme programming explained: Embrace change*. Reading, MA: Addison-Wesley.

Boehm, B. 1981. *Software engineering economics*. Englewood Cliffs, NJ: Prentice Hall.

Boehm, B. 1986. A spiral model of software development and enhancement. *ACM SIGSOFT Software Engineering Notes* 11:14–24.

Boehm, B., and Victor, B. 2001. *Software defect reduction top 10 list*. Technical Report USC CSE 2001-510, National Science Foundation/University of Southern California, Center for Empirically Based Software Engineering.

Bowman, T., Holt, R. C., and Brewster, N. V. 1999. Linux as a case study: Its extracted software architecture. In *Proceedings of the 21st International Conference on Software Engineering*, Los Angeles, May 16–22, 1999, pp. 555–63. New York: ACM Press.

Brooks, F. 1995. *The mythical man-month: Essays on software engineering*. Reading, MA: Addison-Wesley.

Broom, G., Casey, S., and Ritchey, J. 1997. Toward a concept and theory of organization-public relationships. *Journal of Public Relations Research* 9:83–98.

Broy, M., and Denert, E., eds. 2002. *Software pioneers: Contributions to software engineering*. New York: Springer.

Buschmann, F., Meunier, R., Rohnert, H., Sommerlad, P., and Stal, M. 1996. *A system of patterns: Pattern-oriented software architecture*. New York: Wiley.

Carney, D. 1998. *Quotations from Chairman David: A little red book of truths to enlighten and guide on the long march toward the COTS revolution*. Pittsburgh, PA: Software Engineering Institute, Carnegie Mellon University.

Clements, P., Bachmann, F., Bass, L., Garlan, D., Ivers, J., Little, R., Nord, R., and Stafford, J. 2003. *Documenting software architectures: Views and beyond*. Boston: Addison-Wesley.

Clements, P., Kazman, R., and Klein, M. 2001. *Evaluating software architectures: Methods and case studies*. Boston: Addison-Wesley.

Clements, P., and Shaw, M. 2003. *The golden age of software architecture: A comprehensive survey*. CMU/SEI-2003-TR-016, CMU-ISRI-06-101, Carnegie Mellon University/Institute for Software Research, Pittsburgh, PA.

CMMI Product Team. 2002. *CMMI for systems engineering, software engineering, integrated product and process development, and supplier sourcing (CMMI-SE/SW/IPPD/SS, V1.1): Improving processes for better products: Staged representation*. CMU/SEI-2002-TR-012, ESC-TR-2002-01, Carnegie Mellon University/Institute for Software Research, Pittsburgh, PA.

Coleman, D., Lowther, B., and Oman, P. 1995. The application of software maintainability models in industrial software systems. *Journal of Systems Software* 29:3–16.

Fagan, M. E. 1976. Design and code inspections to reduce errors in program development. *IBM Systems Journal* 15:182–211.

Fagan, M. E. 1996. Advances in software inspections. *IEEE Transactions on Software Engineering* SE-12:744–51.

Forsberg, K., Mooz, H., Cotterham, H. 1996. *Visualizing project management*. New York: John Wiley.

Gamma, E., Helm, R., Johnson, R., and Vlissides, J. 1995. *Design patterns: Elements of reusable object-oriented software*. Boston: Addison-Wesley.

Garlan, D., and Shaw, M. 1996. *Software architecture: Perspectives on an emerging discipline*. Upper Saddle River, NJ: Prentice Hall.

Goodyear, M., Ryan, H., Sargent, S., Taylor, S., Boudreau, T., Arvanitis, Y., Chang, R., Kaltenmark, J., Mullen, N., Dove, S., Davis, M., Clark, J., and Mindrum, C. 2000. *Enterprise system architectures*. Boca Raton, FL: CRC Press.

Guo, G., Atlee, J., and Kazman, R. 1999. A software architecture reconstruction method. In *Proceedings of the First Working IFIP Conference on Software Architecture (WICSA1)*, San Antonio, TX, February 22–24, 1999, pp. 225–43. Norwell, MA: Kluwer Academic Publishers.

Hamlin, A. D. F. 1909. *A text-book of the history of architecture*. New York: Longmans, Green, and Co.

Harris, D. R., Reubenstein, H. B., and Yeh, A. S. 1995. Reverse engineering to the architectural level, 186–95. In *Proceedings of the 17th International Conference on Software Engineering (ICSE)*, Seattle, April 23–30, 1995. New York: ACM Press.

Hindo, B. 2007. At 3M, a struggle between efficiency and creativity: How CEO George Buckley is managing the yin and yang of discipline and imagination. *BusinessWeek*, June 11.

Hughes, T. P. 1989. *American genesis: A century of invention and technological enthusiasm*. Viking: New York.

Humphrey, W. 1995. *A discipline of software engineering*. Reading, MA: Addison-Wesley Professional.

Humphrey, W. 1989. *Managing the software development process*. Reading, MA: Addison-Wesley.

Humphrey, W. 1999. *Team software process*. Reading, MA: Addison-Wesley.

INCOSE (International Committee on System Engineering). http://www.incose.org/.

Jackson, M. A. 1983. *System development*. Englewood Cliffs, NJ: Prentice Hall.

Jacobson, I., Christenson, M., Jonsson, P., and Overgaard, G. 1992. *Object-oriented software engineering: A use case driven approach*. Reading, MA: Addison-Wesley.

Krutchen, P. 1995. The 4+1 view model of software architecture. *IEEE Software* 12:42–50.

Krutchen, P. 2004. *The rational unified process: An introduction*. 3rd ed. Reading, MA: Addison-Wesley Professional.

Maier, M., and Rechtin, E. 2000. *The art of systems architecting*. 2nd ed. Boca Raton, FL: CRC Press.

Marca, D., and McGowan, C. 1988. *SADT: Structured analysis and design technique*. New York: McGraw-Hill.

Martin, J. 1984. *An information systems manifesto*. Englewood Cliffs, NJ: Prentice Hall.

Martin, J. 1991. *Rapid application development*. New York: Macmillan Publishing.

McAndrews, D. 2000. The team software process (TSP): An overview and preliminary results of using disciplined practices. CMU/SEI-2000-TR-015, ESC-TR-2000-015, Carnegie Mellon University/Software Engineering Institute, Pittsburgh, PA.

Meason, G. L. 1828. *The landscape architecture of the great painters of Italy*. C. Hullmandel's Lithographic Establishment, London.

Oxford English Dictionary. 2004. Oxford: Oxford University Press.

Parnas, D. L. 1972. On the criteria to be used in decomposing systems into modules. *Communications of the ACM* 15:1053–58.

Paulk, M., Weber, C., Curtis, B., and Chrissis, M. 1995. *The capability maturity model: Guidelines for improving the software process*. Reading, MA: Addison-Wesley.

Pressman, R. 2005. *Software engineering: A practitioners approach*. 6th ed. Singapore: McGraw-Hill.

Rechtin, E. 1991. *Systems architecting: Creating and building complex systems*. Englewood Cliffs, NJ: Prentice Hall.

Sangwan, R., Bass, M., Mullick, N., and Paulish, D. 2006. *Global software development handbook*. New York: Auerbach Publishing.

Schwaber, K., and Beedle, M. 2004. *Agile project management with Scrum*. Redmond, WA: Microsoft Press.

Schwaber, K. 2007. *The enterprise and Scrum*. Redmond, WA: Microsoft Press.

Sowa, J. F., and Zachman, J. A. 1992. Extending and formalizing the framework for information systems architecture. *IBM Systems Journal* 31(3).

Thome, B., ed. 1993. *Systems engineering: Principle and practice of computer-based system engineering*. New York: John Wiley & Sons.

U.S. Government Accounting Office (GAO). 1999. *Observations on FAA's air traffic control modernization program*. Testimony before the Subcommittee on Aviation, Committee on Commerce, Science and Transportation, U.S. Senate, March 25.

Vitruvius. 1914. *The ten books on architecture*, trans. M. H. Morgan. Cambridge, MA: Harvard University Press.

Yourdon, E. 1989a. *Modern structured analysis*. Englewood Cliffs, NJ: Yourdon Press.

Yourdon, E. 1989b. *Structured walkthroughs*. 4th ed. Englewood Cliffs, NJ: Yourdon Press.

Zachman, J. 1987. A framework for information systems architecture. *IBM Systems Journal* 26(3).

Index

A

Analysis of systemic structures using quality scenarios, architecture design evaluation workshop, 284–288

Apathy in architecture design evaluation, avoiding, 265–266

Approval of experimentation, 325

Architect, 77–113

Architectural decomposition, 86–89

Architectural driver discovery, 161–200
  activities overview, 161
  architecture drivers elicitation workshops
    business constraints, identification of, 185–186
    conducting, 174–189
    introductions, 176–177
    operational descriptions, identification of, 177–182
    product or system overview, 177
    quality attribute requirements, identification of, 182–185
    raw data consolidation, 187–189
    summary, 186–187
    technical constraints, identification of, 186
    workshop overview, 176–177
  description of stage 1, 164–165
  fixed cost, impact of, 198–199
  guidance, 161–162
  master design plan, 165–174
    architecture drivers elicitation workshop, planning, 168–174
    creating, 189–200
    updating, 189–200
  postconditions, 163
  preconditions, 161
  preexisting specifications, ACDM requirements elicitation process, 199–200
  primary artifacts, 162–163
  purpose, 161
  schedule creation, 190–198
    assigning completion values, 194–195
    roll-up schedule, 195

tracking progress, 195–198
    work breakdown structure, 190–194
  schedule planning, impact of, 198–199
  techniques, 161–162
  templates, 161–162

Architectural drivers, 33–48
  architectural design documentation, 143
  business constraints, 47–48
  defined, 34–36
  high-level functional requirements, 36–40
  quality attribute requirements, 40–45
  technical constraints, 45–47

Architectural incompatibilities, addressing, 411–414
  intermediaries, 414
  software wrappers, 413

Architectural life cycle, 6–12
  adoption, 8
  business models, 9–10
  chaos, 8
  dissemination, 8
  harvest, 8
  marketplace, 10
  stakeholders, 9
  sunset, 8–10
  technological environment, 11

Architectural structures, 49–75
  framework application example, 68–75
    tactics, 72–75
  framework of structural reasoning, 64–68
    elements, 66
    perspective, 64–65
    quality attribute effects, 67
    relationships, 66
    semantics, 67
    structural variants, 67–68
    topology, 66–67
    usage context, 67
  patterns, 61–63
  perspective, 50–57
    dynamic perspective, 52
    physical perspective, 52–57
    static perspective, 51